MISSISSIPPI WRITERS
Reflections of Childhood and Youth

MISSISSIPPI WRITERS

Reflections of Childhood and Youth

Volume IV: DRAMA

Edited by
DOROTHY ABBOTT

UNIVERSITY PRESS OF MISSISSIPPI
Jackson and London

Center for the Study of Southern Culture Series

Copyright © 1991 by the
University Press of Mississippi
All rights reserved
Manufactured in the United States of America
94 93 92 91   4 3 2 1
The paper in this book meets the guidelines for permanence
and durability of the Committee on Production Guidelines for
Book Longevity of the Council on Library Resources.

Library of Congress Cataloging-in-Publication Data
(Revised for vol. 4)

Mississippi writers.

(Center for the Study of Southern Culture series)
Contents: v. 1. Fiction — v. 2. Nonfiction —
v. 3. Poetry — v. 4. Drama.
1. American literature—Mississippi. 2. American
literature—20th century. 3. Children—Literary
collections. 4. Youth—Literary collections.
5. Mississippi—Literary collections. 6. American
literature—Collections. 7. Mississippi—Literary
collections. I. Abbott, Dorothy, 1944–
II. Series.
PS558.M7M55 1985   813'.008'09762   84–5131
ISBN 0–87805–232–1 (pbk. : v. 1)
ISBN 0–87805–231–3 (hard : v. 1)

British Library Cataloging-in-Publication data available

CONTENTS

ACKNOWLEDGMENTS

THE EDITOR would like to express heartfelt gratitude to the University of Mississippi's Center for the Study of Southern Culture. Without the support of its director William Ferris and associate director Ann J. Abadie this anthology would not have been completed. This anthology moved from the stage of ideas and research to publication because the Phil Hardin Foundation awarded the project a challenge grant. I would especially like to thank C. Thompson Wacaster, vice-president for educational programs and research, and the board of directors of the Phil Hardin Foundation for their important contribution. CREATE, Inc. in Tupelo and many people from around the state came forward to meet the challenge by generously donating funds to match the grant. For this, I thank them all. Their names are appropriately listed in this collection. JoAnne Prichard, my editor at the University Press of Mississippi, gave much assistance, as did associate director Seetha Srinivasan, associate director and marketing manager Hunter Cole, promotions manager Beverly Ray, and managing editor Ginger Tucker. The editor also wishes to thank the following authors and publishers for permission to print the designated selections. Rights in all cases are reserved by the owner of the copyright.

Allie's Mark by Patricia Boatner was first produced at Gulfport Little Theatre, January 1988. Copyright © 1988 by Patricia Boatner. Printed by permission of the author.

Bluesman by Charlie R. Braxton. Copyright © 1991 by Charlie R. Braxton. Printed by permission of the author.

Wings by Larry Brown. Copyright © 1991 by Larry Brown. Printed by permission of the author.

Siege: The Battle of Vicksburg by Robert Canzoneri. Copyright © Robert Canzoneri. Printed by permission of the author.

Excerpt from *Requiem for a Nun* by Ruth Ford adapted from William Faulkner's novel *Requiem for a Nun* first produced at the John Golden Theatre, New York City, on January 28, 1959. Copyright © by William Faulkner and Ruth Ford. First published by Random House.

The Freedom Kick by Shelby Foote was first produced at "The Time Has Come" festival in Greenville, Mississippi, April 29, 1982. Copyright © 1982 by Shelby Foote. Printed by permission of the author.

viii   *Acknowledgments*

The Battle of Harrykin Creek by Evans Harrington was first produced during
the William Faulkner conference in Oxford, Mississippi, August 1976. It is
based on William Faulkner's story "My Grandmother Millard and General Bedford Forrest and The Battle of Harrykin Creek." Copyright © 1976 by Evans
Harrington. Printed by permission of the author.

Crimes of the Heart by Beth Henley was first produced at Actors Theatre of
Louisville in February 1979. It was given its New York premiere by the Manhat-
tan Theatre Club in 1980. Published by Viking Press and Penguin Books. Copyright © 1981, 1982 by Beth Henley. Reprinted by permission of Viking Penguin
USA.

Miss Ida B. Wells by Endesha Ida Mae Holland was first produced by University
of Buffalo department of theatre and drama, February 20, 1986. Copyright
© 1986 by Endesha Ida Mae Holland. Printed by permission of author.

Excerpt from *Shango Diaspora: An African-American Myth of Womanhood and
Love* by Angela Jackson. Copyright © 1991 by Angela Jackson. Printed by
permission of the author.

*You Can't Judge a Book by Looking at the Cover: Sayings from the Life and
Writings of Junebug Jabbo Jones* by John O'Neal and Barbara Watkins. Copyright © 1987 by John O'Neal. Printed by permission of the authors.

Two Kinds of People by Linda Peavy. Copyright © 1991 by author. Printed by
permission of the author.

For Lease or Sale by Elizabeth Spencer was first produced by Playmakers Repertory Company, Chapel Hill, North Carolina January 25, 1989, David Hammond, director. Copyright © 1989 by Elizabeth Spencer. Inquiries concerning
all rights to the play must be directed to The Lucy Kroll Agency, 390 West
End Avenue, New York, NY 10024.

The Glass Menagerie by Tennessee Williams was first produced at the Civic Thea-
tre, Chicago, Illinois, December 26, 1944 and at the Playhouse Theatre, New
York City, March 31, 1945. Copyright © 1945 by Tennessee Williams and
Edwina D. Williams; renewed 1972 by Tennessee Williams.

Excerpt from *Native Son* adapted by Richard Wright and Paul Green from the
novel *Native Son* by Richard Wright. *Native Son* was first produced on Broadway by John Houseman and Orson Welles at Mercury Theater, 1941. Copyright
© 1941 by Paul Green and Richard Wright; © 1968 by Paul Green and Ellen
Wright (in renewal); © 1980 by Paul Green and Ellen Wright (revised). Reprinted by permission of Ellen Wright and Samuel French, Inc.

Fannie Lou Hamer: This Little Light. . . by Billie Jean Young. Copyright ©
1983 by Billie Jean Young. Printed by permission of the author.

The Colonnade by Stark Young was first published by Theatre Arts Inc. Copyright
1924 by Stark Young.

INTRODUCTION

An Ineluctable Need to Tell

JERRY W. WARD, JR.

THE FINAL VOLUME of *Mississippi Writers: Reflections of Childhood and Youth* brings us fully into the presence of the ingredient that gives flavor and vitality to many literary works by Mississippians: speech and the kinds of talking accomplished in speech. How one speaks, as George Bernard Shaw illustrated wonderfully in *Pygmalion*, can either provide a great deal of information about a person's social background or conceal everything as it functions as a mask of identity. From another angle, talk is richly informed by the values, habits, and behaviors of a culture, and it is of singular importance in beginning, maintaining, or ending human relationships. In fact, some consider that our talking to one another is a kind of social glue.

Our best writers are especially attentive to the consequences of talk and to the choices of diction, turns of phrase, and delivery that vary among individuals. They seek to represent in a distilled form the dramatic potential in our ineluctable need to talk. When one tries to discover why Mississippi seems better endowed than many other states with writers, one provisional answer may be that Mississippi has a rich oral tradition and good talkers. That fact has been a godsend for the writers from Mississippi who have produced an impressive body of fiction and drama.

Southerners and Mississippians, oral tradition notwithstanding, do not have a providential monopoly on how to do things with words. The literature that reflects their experiences does reveal a strong, and rather historical, investment in exploiting the possibilities of language. Some who have made careful inquiries into the motives that have driven Southerners to develop special rhetorical skills conclude, as Fred Hobson did in *Tell About the South: The Southern Rage to Explain* (1983), that the driving forces were history and a deep conviction that there was something "to explain,

to justify, to defend, or to affirm." Such a theory is certainly valid
and useful in explaining the defensive postures Southerners have
chosen or have been forced to take. But Southerners have much
in their culture(s) to celebrate as well as defend. The works to
which we return again and again are not apologia but creative
expressions of the human experiences that occur between the ex-
tremes of tragedy and comedy. In those works the centrality of
speech in life is affirmed; there is evidence that the writers did
much more than "work at," as that phrase is humorously used in
Linda Peavy's *Two Kinds of People,* transforming the linguistic giv-
ens of their culture into literature.

As we read through the selections of drama in this volume, we
find that the writers have reshaped the everyday flow of Southern
talk, channeled its energies in purposeful ways, and heightened
its implicit dramatic qualities. Throughout our childhood and
youth we had been in the circle of verbal artistry. Yet, like the
young Frederick Douglass amidst the singers of sorrow songs, we
"neither saw nor heard as those without might see and hear." We
were certainly unaware that the content of everyday conversation
was the raw material of art, that simple and colorful language,
as it is presented in Patricia Boatner's *Allie's Mark,* could tell us
so much about human strength and dignity. What we talked about
or listened to was funny, sometimes sad or frightening or hurtful,
embroidered with jokes and downright lies, boring, full of refer-
ences to what was immediate and familiar or remote and strange,
and deadly serious in the mouths of adults. Only through the
agency of drama, the restructuring of talk into the focused dialogue
of complication, conflict, and resolution, do we gain aesthetic distance and the outside perspective on what was so common in our
lives. Fortunately one need not be a Southerner to appreciate the
essential qualities that manifest themselves in the talking that is
so significant in the dramas collected here.

How drama emerges from everyday Southern talk is illustrated
well in *You Can't Judge A Book by Looking at the Cover: Sayings
from the Life and Writings of Junebug Jabbo Jones* by John O'Neal
and Barbara Watkins. The narrator Junebug begins with the "Po
Tatum Hambone Blues," a device that necessitates his explaining
how it is, "I finally come to understand that I was supposed to

be a storyteller." As we listen to the story of Po Tatum's early life in Pike County, Mississippi, his ramblings around the country, his shady dealings and romantic exploits, his breach of decorum at his mother's funeral, and his death in Chicago, we begin to realize how very much the narrator himself is a character, a biased informant, in the tale he spins. As listeners, we begin to wonder why is Junebug telling us this tale. What is the importance of Po Tatum's life? The only action we witness is Junebug's talking, and that is just the point of the performance. Here is drama in its fundamental form—a speaker and an implied audience. We are the real audience for the telling of the life of a black man from Mississippi in time past, and our pleasure depends on just how skillfully the performer uses language and style. Akin to the Junebug drama is Shelby Foote's *The Freedom Kick*, wherein a black photographer speaks to an invisible companion about his family, Reconstruction and the cost and bittersweet satisfaction of freedom. Endesha Ida Mae Holland's *Miss Ida B. Wells* offers a privileged glimpse of Wells's examining the importance for history of making the facts of her life recoverable through autobiography.

These one-person stories show us in a small compass the use that can be made of story in creating larger, more complicated narratives, especially the narratives of family life. In Linda Peavy's *Two Kinds of People*, which focuses on a few hours of a family visit, a string of anecdotes about church members tells us a great deal about life in the town; it is more important, of course, that we recognize how the memories and the questioning and answering that occur weave a strong bond, how talking secures our links with relatives even as it imposes constrictions on our behavior. Beth Henley's Pulitzer Prize winning *Crimes of the Heart*, an exceptionally fine example of contemporary comedy, depends greatly on building perspectives by incongruity of life in a small Southern town. Those perspectives are constituted in part by stories told by the three sisters, Lenny, Meg, and Babe, and in part by our awareness of the idiosyncrasies that give the family an identity and that provide the grounds for tragicomedy. Given that the play pivots on violations of the social order and decorum still valued highly in non-urban Southern communities, Henley succeeds in blending sense of place with action that blatantly calls into question the myths Southerners live by. What prevails is the integrity of family as the ultimate source of love and understanding. It is equally possible, as we discover from Elizabeth Spencer's *For Lease or Sale*, Tennessee Williams's *The Glass Menagerie*, and Stark Young's *The Colonnade*, for family to be the privileged space for misunderstanding and recriminations that have disruptive consequences.

In Elizabeth Spencer's *For Lease or Sale*, the subject is the impact the inevitable need to sell the family home has on three generations. In the exchanges among the members of the family, memories and judgments, ideas about propriety and maintaining traditions, and the politics of place all emerge. Stark Young's *The Colonnade* uses family history as an occasion to examine the conflicts between a father and son who hold vastly different opinions about the meaning of honor. The probing into the rift also treats in a very symbolic way the problem of change in Southern life, the rigid codes of the nineteenth century being replaced by the imperatives of the New South.

The source of conflict in Tennessee Williams's *The Glass Menagerie* is not honor so much as the differing notions mother and son have about responsibility and the realities of modern life. Partly autobiographical, Williams's memory play juxtaposes the romanticism of a genteel Mississippi past with the stoicism of the urban in the 1930s. Charlie Braxton's *Bluesman* also explores the family theme against the larger backdrop of blues culture that is a quite significant feature of Mississippi life. In portraying the extent to which a bluesman must run his fingers over the jagged grain of life, the play does not fail to emphasize the strong sense of family as an agent in resolving problems of competing values or of the importance migration and return to the source has had in the lives of black Mississippians. Braxton's realistic treatment of blues ethos is complemented by Angela Jackson's *Shango Diaspora*, where the blues is raised to a mythopoetic level that connects the deeper levels of woman's blues with African mythology. In varying degrees, these plays direct us to the sustained interest Southern dramatists have in using history to inform or to give substance to their works.

Robert Canozeri's *Siege: The Battle of Vicksburg*, for example,

is actually based on the historical accounts of the civilians and soldiers who lived through this turning point of the Civil War during
the spring and summer of 1863 and shows how the past gains im-
mediacy once written documents are rendered as oral communica-
tion. Canzoneri's intention, in his own words, was "not to impose
theatrically upon actual events, but to discover in what happened
a dramatic development that illustrates history rather than violating it." On the other hand, Evans Harrington's *The Battle of
Harrykin Creek* involves a double comedic exxaggeration of history. The initial exaggeration is embodied in William Faulkner's
short story "My Grandmother Millard and General Bedford Forrest and The Battle of Harrykin Creek," which brings to the fore-
ground a number of improbabilities concerning plantation life and
romance in the midst of the Civil War. Although Harrington is
very faithful in retaining the dialogue from Faulkner's story, he
renders the story as musical comedy and increases our tolerance
for history as antic behavior found within the Sartoris family. It
is the disarming charm of Southern talk that makes us so receptive
to the liberties Faulkner and Harrington take with history.

Each of the dramatic works in this volume gives a special meaning to a remarkable passage from one of the production notes
Tennessee Williams wrote for *The Glass Menagerie*. "Truth, life,
or reality," Williams observed, "is an organic thing which the poetic imagination can represent or suggest, in essence, only through
transformation, through changing into other forms than those
which were merely present in appearance." In the case of drama
by Mississippians, we have Southern talk merely present to the
ear given back to us in engaging theatrical forms. As speech is
filtered through the imaginations of Mississippi writers, it can be
changed into dramas that give us stimulating access to the values
and verities of our heritage.

THE PHIL HARDIN FOUNDATION
AND THE
MISSISSIPPI WRITERS SERIES

IN 1964 Mr. Phil B. Hardin of Meridian, Mississippi, established an educational foundation. At the Foundation's organizational meeting, Mr. Hardin made the following statement:

> My material wealth has been principally acquired by the operation of my bakery business in the State of Mississippi and from the good people of that state. For a long time I have been considering how my estate could best be used after my death. I have finally conceived the idea of creating a charitable foundation through which the bulk of my estate can be used for furthering . . . the education of Mississippians.

Upon his death in 1972, Mr. Hardin willed a portfolio of stocks and bonds, as well as the bakeries, to the Phil Hardin Foundation. The directors of the Foundation use income from these sources to make grants intended to improve the education of Mississippians. Since the transfer of Mr. Hardin's estate to the Foundation in 1976, the Phil Hardin Foundation has distributed over 5.4 million dollars for this purpose.

In 1983 the Foundation directors authorized a challenge grant to support the publication of the series of anthologies entitled *Mississippi Writers: Reflections of Childhood and Youth.* This series recognizes the accomplishments of our state's authors. The series also introduces young Mississippians to their state's literary heritage, perhaps providing thereby a "shock of recognition" and the transmission of values revealed in that heritage: family, community, a sense of place and history, the meaning of justice and honor, the importance of enduring in the struggle for just causes, the significance as we live out our lives one with another of "courage . . . and hope and pride and compassion and pity and sacrifice." By so doing the series may help young Mississippians come to grips with the complexities of Mississippi culture and heritage and of the larger society that now more than ever impinges on this place. As importantly, the series may help forge a sense of common identity and interest.

The Phil Hardin Foundation is honored to join with other Mississippians to make possible the publication of the *Mississippi Writers* series. Mississippians can accomplish more working together than working alone.

C. Thompson Wacaster
The Phil Hardin Foundation

The Following People, Organizations, and Businesses Generously Contributed Funds to Match the Challenge Grant Awarded by the Phil Hardin Foundation

Dr. and Mrs. Joe Bailey
Mr. and Mrs. Charles G. Bell
Ms. Jane Rule Burdine
Mrs. Roberta J. Burns-Howard
Mrs. Betty W. Carter
Centennial Study Club (Oxford)
Mr. Henry Chambers
Coca-Cola Bottling Co. (Vicksburg)
Mr. and Mrs. Sam W. Crawford
CREATE, Inc.
Ms. Carole H. Currie
Mr. and Mrs. Glen H. Davidson
Mr. and Mrs. William Deas
Mr. and Mrs. Herman B. DeCell
Mrs. Keith Dockery McLean
Mr. and Mrs. Robert B. Dodge
Fortnightly Matinee Club (Tupelo)
Dr. and Mrs. Jan Goff
Dr. and Mrs. William Hilbun
Mr. and Mrs. Howard Hinds
Mrs. Mary Hohenberg
Mr. Irwin T. Holtzman
Mr. Stuart C. Irby, Jr.
Stuart Irby Construction Company
Dr. and Mrs. David Irwin
The Honorable and Mrs. Trent Lott
Mr. and Mrs. T. M. McMillan, Jr.
Miss Marjorie Milam
Mrs. Blewett Mitchell
The Honorable G. V. Montgomery
Mrs. Gaines Moore
Mrs. L. K. Morgan
R. R. Morrison and Son, Inc.
Mr. Richard A. Moss
National Association of Treasury Agents
Mr. William M. Pace
Mrs. A. E. Patterson
Dr. Max Pegram
Mr. and Mrs. Jack R. Reed
Dr. and Mrs. Pete Rhymes
Dr. Stephen L. Silberman
Mr. and Mrs. Bill Spigner
Mr. and Mrs. Landman V. Teller
Dr. and Mrs. P. K. Thomas
United Southern Bank (Clarksdale)
University Press of Mississippi
Mr. and Mrs. Harold Wilson
Mr. Sam Woodward

MISSISSIPPI WRITERS
Reflections of Childhood and Youth

Allie's Mark

PATRICIA BOATNER

CHARACTERS

ALLIE   Elderly woman (85), lined face, unruly hair, confined to wheel-chair.

NURSE   Mid-30's, prim, efficient.

JOEY   About 60, slight, slow-witted, handyman.

TIME

Present, mid-morning

PLACE

Allie's room at local nursing home

(*At Rise:* NURSE *enters pushing* ALLIE *in wheelchair from opening in curtain at UPSTAGE LEFT*)

NURSE   Here we are, Miss Allie. Back where you belong.

ALLIE   Says who?

NURSE   Now, now, dear. It's not going to be one of your bad days, is it?

ALLIE   Not if you go away and mind your own business.

NURSE   Taking care of you is my business. (*Stops wheelchair near CS*) And you know the rules at our Home, don't you?

ALLIE   I don't remember any rules. You know I can't remember anything any more. Where's my glasses?

NURSE   Right in the drawer where they always are. (*Gets glasses from nightstand drawer, hands them to* ALLIE) And frankly, Miss Allie, your memory seems to come and go whenever it's convenient for you. This is the third time this week you've slipped into Mr. Johnson's room and . . . .

3

ALLIE (*Putting on glasses*) No such thing. I didn't slip anywhere. I wheeled right down the middle of the hall. (*Slaps arm of chair*) Fact is, a body couldn't *slip* anywhere in one of these dang contraptions if she wanted to.

NURSE It is against regulations to be on the men's ward, much less in one of their rooms.

ALLIE He's got a nice new television.

NURSE Which was not even on. And am I supposed to believe that chair accidentally got wedged against the hall door? Really! And the two of you in wheelchairs. Just exactly what did Mr. Johnson think he was doing?

ALLIE I'm not sure. Don't think he was either. (*Grins*) But I was willing to give him all the help I could.

NURSE Honestly, Miss Allie, if I weren't such a patient person, I'd be very angry with you. Such behavior—and today, of all days, with us losing poor dear Elizabeth.

ALLIE (*Mimicking*) Losing poor dear Elizabeth? Ha! Guess I'm not the only one around here with a bad memory. Dear Elizabeth was a whining, cantankerous old bag of bones . . . .

NURSE Allie!

ALLIE . . . That nobody liked. I ought to know, since I'm the one got stuck with her for a roommate. And besides that, we didn't *lose* her. She just finally did what she's been threatening to do for months. She died.

NURSE That's enough, Miss Allie. Let's show some respect for the departed.

ALLIE How about some respect for the not-so-departed? First I get pushed out of my room before I even have breakfast, then when I go looking for some company to talk about it, you nearly break the door down and burn my wheels up getting me back here. Can't you make up your mind?

NURSE I'm sorry about having to move you out of the room so early, but it couldn't be helped. (*Dusts nightstand with handkerchief as she talks*) There are things that must be done after one of our residents goes. And that's no excuse for you being in Mr. Johnson's room.

ALLIE Excuse? I don't need an excuse. I'm a grown woman— grown and alive. Alive, you hear. Not gone, not lost. Not dead, like dear Elizabeth. I am alive, and if you don't believe me, just ask Mr. Johnson!

NURSE (*Taps fingers together*) We are not going to get into that again. And I don't want you to get upset. It's bad for your heart.

ALLIE   My heart's doing fine. It's the rest of me that's not working so well.

NURSE   Nevertheless, perhaps I should get you a mild sedative. I'm sure it was a shock to find your roommate . . . gone like that, the very first thing in the morning.

ALLIE   Well, actually Elizabeth *went* about midnight.

NURSE   Midnight? Are you sure of that?

ALLIE   Sure, I'm sure.

NURSE   How can you be so sure?

ALLIE   Because that's when she stopped snoring.

NURSE   That doesn't necessarily mean . . . .

ALLIE   Listen, Missy, I've been sleeping in here with that woman for a year now, and I know what I'm talking about. I've yelled at her, I've rolled her on her side and turned her on her stomach—I've even stuck a sock over her nose. Believe me when I say there's only one thing could stop her snoring. And she stopped right at midnight.

NURSE   Good heavens! (*Pause*) The doctor did say it seemed to have happened some hours earlier, but . . . . (*Looks at* ALLIE) Why did you wait so long—until almost seven o'clock before you called anyone?

ALLIE   Nothing anyone could do. I checked. Then I went back to bed and enjoyed the first night of peaceful sleep I've had since I can't remember when.

NURSE   Miss Allie, you are incorrigible!

ALLIE   When you get to be past eighty-five, you've got a right to be anything you want, now and then.

NURSE   Age is no excuse for insensitivity.

ALLIE   Neither is youth. (*Jerks thumb toward curtain US*) Are you all about done in there? A person could get claustrophobia with that curtain pulled so long.

NURSE   Yes, we're nearly finished. Just a little longer and we'll have everything all cleaned and spotless. Then we'll open it up again. By tomorrow, you'll have another roommate and forget all about Elizabeth. Life does go on, doesn't it?

ALLIE   On and on and on.

NURSE   And we must make the best of it, mustn't we? Now, I have to see that Elizabeth's things are all properly packed. But I shouldn't be long. I'll come back after lunch, and if you promise to behave, I'll take you to the day room for the sing-along. Won't that be nice?

ALLIE   No, that won't be nice. I hate sing-along. Everybody sings along in a different key on a different tune, and I get a headache.

NURSE   Now, Miss Allie . . . .

ALLIE   And stop calling me 'Miss Allie.' I'm not a Miss. I'm a Mrs. Mrs. Jess Warthrop, that's me. (*Voice rises*)   I'm not some old maid. I'm a married lady, I am, with a fine husband . . . and a baby son . . . and . . . and . . . . (*Voice fades as she looks around room, her gaze settling on pictures of husband and son*)

NURSE   Of course, you're Mrs. Warthrop. But everyone has always called you Miss Allie. You know that. No need to get upset.

ALLIE (*Vaguely*)   Jess . . . he'll be home . . . any time now . . . and I have to . . . .

NURSE   No, Allie. (*Sits on edge of bed, turns* ALLIE *to face her.* ALLIE *stares blankly*)   You must listen carefully, dear. Look at me, Miss Allie. And try to think. Think hard, now. Jess won't be coming home. He . . . went away, dear. Long ago. And your son is grown up now.

ALLIE   My . . . little Bobby?

NURSE   Bobby is a big man now.

(ALLIE'S *gaze wanders. She reaches for doll on bed, but* NURSE *moves it away and takes* ALLIE'S *hands*)

NURSE   Bobby works in Asia in the oil fields now. He writes faithfully every month. You just got a letter, remember?

ALLIE   Bobby's . . . gone away?

NURSE   Yes, dear. That's why you came to live with us after you had your stroke. There was no one else to take care of you.

ALLIE   Jess . . . .

NURSE   Your husband is gone, too. He's been gone a long time.

ALLIE   Gone?

(NURSE *nods.* ALLIE *squints, then blinks and sits up straight, jerking hand from* NURSE)

ALLIE   Malarky! Jess is not gone. He's dead! Just like old Elizabeth!

NURSE   Well, yes, I suppose you could say that.

ALLIE   I suppose you could. Jess got off balance in the hay loft and fell on his own pitchfork. Now, that's more than just gone. When you bury a body with three pitchfork holes in it, it's *dead*.

NURSE   I'm surprised you remember, but I believe that is what happened.

ALLIE   Of course, that's what happened. I know that. My husband killed himself off in a stupid freak accident . . . and my boy took off for some foreign country where I can't go. (*Looks vague a moment, then snaps head up and glares at* NURSE)   I know all that. My mind might wander now and then, but it hasn't left completely. And even when it wanders, it's seeing and hearing things—lots more than you know, Missy. Having a wandering mind doesn't make a body stupid!

NURSE No one ever said you were stupid, Miss Allie. (*Rises*) As for your wandering mind—that's of far less concern around here than your wandering body. No more trips to the men's ward, do you understand?

ALLIE What am I supposed to do, just sit and look at the walls? I need some fresh air now and again.

NURSE You are not going to find the air a bit fresher in Mr. Johnson's room.

ALLIE (*Grinning*) Want to bet?

NURSE Don't be difficult, Miss Allie. If you want to occupy yourself, there are plenty of activities to choose from. Like the sing-along.

(ALLIE *makes a face, turns away*)

NURSE Or our ceramics class.

ALLIE That stuff smells awful. And looks worse.

NURSE Or needlework . . . .

ALLIE I can't hold on to a needle with these hands.

NURSE Or afternoon bingo.

ALLIE I can't hear the numbers. And when I do hear them, that sneaky Martha Abbott steals all the good cards.

NURSE You do try a saint's patience. If I could trust you to stay where you should, I'd take you back to the rose garden.

ALLIE Rose garden? Three scraggly bushes and some wilted petunias sitting against a concrete wall right out in the broiling sun. Some garden! Two minutes and a body's seen it all. Why, if I wasn't tied to this danged chair, I'd plant a real garden. My roses took blue ribbons at every fair, you know. (*Speech slows, gaze goes to picture of farm at LS*) Why, I could sit on my front porch and look at them . . . and smell them. Yes . . . you ought to come out sometimes. I could . . . give you some cuttings. People used to come from all over . . . for my prizewinning rose cuttings.

NURSE Yes, dear, they used to. But that was a long time ago. And unfortunately, we don't have room for a large garden here at the Home. (*Looks at picture of farm*) Dear me, that picture is down again, isn't it? (*Crosses to LS, picks up picture*) The frame is really too heavy to hang on our tabs. I'll send Joey, the handyman, in. Maybe he can come up with some way to keep it on the wall. (*Puts pic down*) If he can't, I'm afraid this will just have to go.

ALLIE Go?

NURSE But don't worry about it, dear. We'll find something smaller
but just as nice to replace it. And right now, I want you to brush
your hair and try to decide what you want to do this afternoon. (*Gets
brush and mirror from nightstand drawer, puts on top of
nightstand*) There now, you fix yourself up nice and I'll be back
shortly. (*Pats* ALLIE's *head, then exits USL*)

ALLIE (*Still staring at pic*) Go? Have to go, huh? We'll see about
that. (*Wheels across room to pic, muttering*) This is my room and
nothing *goes* unless I go. And I'm not making plans to go any time
soon. (*Picks up pic, rolls toward bed, struggling to hold pic*) What
do they expect—hanging a fine big picture on a sorry little hook like
that. Stick-on picture mounts. Ha! Not enough stick-on to hold a
butterfly, much less a fine picture like this. It's bound to fall down.
You'd think they'd know that. Even *I* know that, and half the time,
I don't know anything. (*Stands pic against bed, touches it lovingly,
tracing outline of house*) Fine house, that is. Fine house. Good
place to raise a boy. Big rooms, nice big yard.

> (ALLIE *reaches for baby doll, rocks back and forth, cuddling
> doll, dreamy expression on her face*)

ALLIE Yes, that tree's got a sturdy limb for a swing. Why, we can
plant a rose garden in front and a vegetable garden in the back. Lots
of work to be done, but we can make it a showplace. Something
people'll take notice of. Something we can pass on to our boy.
Something . . . something that'll last and last. (*Raises doll to her
shoulder, pats its back*) Shhh, baby, don't you fret. Momma's here,
little Bobby. And Poppa will be home soon—real soon. (*Stops
rocking, looks around, confused*) We've got . . . lots to do . . . lots
of work around here . . . when Jess gets home. And . . . I've got
to . . . fix myself up, don't I? Why, I must look a fright. (*Plops doll
on bed*) Nap time. You sleep tight, cause I've got to . . . I've got
to . . . (*Spies brush*) I've got to brush my hair. (*Moves to nightstand,
picks up brush and mirror, peers into mirror*) Lordy! Who's that?
Lordy, Lordy, Lordy, is that me? Oh, Lordy, that's not me! (*Swipes
at hair with brush, makes face, turns mirror face down on nightstand.
Then she looks at picture of Jess*) Jess . . . that you? It is you, isn't
it? (*Pause.* ALLIE *studies pic of Jess, picks up mirror again and studies
her reflection. Then looks at Jess again*) How come you still look
young and handsome as ever, and here I am, old and ugly, and tired.
You scoundrel! You sorry old scoundrel! You always did get the best
of things, didn't you? I never could depend on you. You never were
there when I needed you—when the work was to be done or a problem

came up. No, you were always off chasing rainbows. It was me had to plant the garden and paint the porch and patch the roof, and take in sewing to pay the bills. And if that wasn't enough, when you finally did decide to come home to stay, you went right out and fell on your own pitchfork. That really topped the cake, you know that? And now, here I am . . . all by myself. Crippled up . . . (*Looks in mirror*)   Face wrinkled as an elephant's behind, not enough good teeth left to chew chicken soup, and hair like a wild rooster. (*Lowers mirror*)   And there you sit, grinning and good as ever. Dang you! Dang you, Jess, the least you could have done was stick around long enough to get old with me. (*Lowers head*)   Dang you . . . dang you.

(*KNOCK from behind curtain US as* ALLIE'S *voice fades.* ALLIE *rocks slightly, head bent. Another KNOCK, then* JOEY *enters UL*)

JOEY   Howdy, Miss Allie. Got something needs fixin'?

(*No response from* ALLIE. JOEY *shuffles to her side*)

JOEY   Miss Allie?

ALLIE (*Starts, looks up*)   Land's sake! You trying to scare a body to death, sneaking up like that?

JOEY   Didn't sneak up. Knocked twice over there before I . . . .

ALLIE   You're late. You're always late. And we've got lots to do around here. (*Puts brush and mirror on bed and picks up doll again*)   Now, you get on out to the barn and finish up that hay. I've got this baby to care for.

JOEY   Barn? We ain't got no barn.

ALLIE   No more excuses, Jess Warthrop! You get out there and toss that hay right this minute. And for Lord's sake, will you hold that pitchfork with both hands!

(ALLIE *turns attention to doll.* JOEY *looks confused, takes a few steps, stops, comes back to* ALLIE'S *side*)

JOEY   Uh, Miss Allie. Excuse me, Miss Allie.

ALLIE   Shhh!

JOEY   Yes ma'am.

ALLIE   Don't you have work to do?

JOEY   Yes ma'am.

ALLIE   Then get to it.

JOEY   Yes ma'am, I'm trying. But . . . well, Miss Allie, we ain't got no barn around here. And even if we did . . . well, I don't know if I could work in it. I got strict orders about what I can do, you know.

(ALLIE *stops rocking and stares at* JOEY)

JOEY   I got to follow orders. And the nurse . . . she said to come
in here and fix the picture. You got a picture needs fixing, Miss Allie?

(ALLIE *blinks rapidly, sits up straight*)

ALLIE   Picture?

JOEY   Yes ma'am. They told me you had a picture needs a new
hanging hook on it. Hey, this must be it, huh? (*Sees pic leaning
against bed, takes it to wall at CL*)   Must be. Let's see . . . oh,
yeah, it must hang right over here. This right, Miss Allie?

ALLIE   Right? Yes, I reckon that's right. (*Carefully puts doll on bed,
then looks at* JOEY *and the picture, frowning*)

JOEY (*Fishes in pocket, looking for hooks*)   Say, Miss Allie, you didn't
really think I was him, did you?

ALLIE   Him? Who?

JOEY   Mr. Jess. You was talking like you thought I was him, but you
didn't, did you. You was just funnin' me, wasn't you?

ALLIE   Course I was. Don't talk like a moron, Joey. Why would I
think you were Jess? You don't look anything like my Jess. He was
a great big scrapping man, not a little scrawny squirt like you.

JOEY   Well, I reckon I am kinda scrawny. (*Looks down, then flexes
arm*)   But I'm strong. Just feel that muscle, Miss Allie. Hard as a
rock. Just feel.

ALLIE   If I want to feel a man's muscle, I'll pick my own, thank you.
Now, get my picture put back up.

JOEY   O.K. But I don't know if I got one of those stick-on tab hooks
that'll hold it. (*Rummages in nail apron*)   It sure is heavy.

ALLIE   Why don't you throw away those dang tabs and hang my
picture on a nail so it'll stay?

JOEY   Aw, I can't do that. It's against the rules.

ALLIE   Against the rules? Why?

JOEY   Nails make holes in the walls.

ALLIE   Holes can be filled up, can't they? That's what putty is for.

JOEY   Yes, but . . . now, wait a minute and I'll explain.

ALLIE   You'll explain?

JOEY   Yes ma'am. They explained it all to me, cause I'm the
handyman, so I got to understand these things. The reason we can't
make holes or marks is cause it takes lots of time to fix them, that's
why. And we don't have no time.

(ALLIE *waves hand in disgust and turns wheelchair away from*
JOEY)

JOEY   It's true, Miss Allie. Why, every time somebody leaves, we got to hurry fast as we can to get everything spic and span, cause there's lots of other people out there waiting to get in this Home.

(ALLIE *looks around, mouth drawn*)

JOEY   There is, for true. Remember last month when Sarah Carpenter left?

ALLIE   Died, Joey. (*Spins chair around*)   Sarah died. Say what you mean.

JOEY   Yeah, well . . . when she . . . died. Anyway, she musta gone plumb crazy that day, cause she wrote all over her wall. I mean *all* over it. (*Leans forward, lowers voice*)   And it was dirty words, Miss Allie. Real dirty words.

ALLIE   Sure was, weren't they? (*Grins, then straightens face quickly*)   As a matter of fact, I had a visit with Sarah that afternoon just before her heart attack.

JOEY   Miss Allie, you didn't help her write them things, did you?

ALLIE   Me? Why, Joey, you know me better than that.

JOEY   Why'd she do it? How come she put all them bad words on the wall like that?

ALLIE   Maybe she just couldn't keep them inside any longer. Maybe she had to put them somewhere, and there was that wall . . . that nice white wall . . . .

JOEY   Well, let me tell you, it took me hours to get them marks off, and then I had to repaint the whole room. Took me two days, it did. And all that time, somebody else was waiting out in the cold.

ALLIE   Out in the cold?

JOEY   (*Nods*)   Just like I was before I came here. Why, lots of folks ain't so lucky as you and me.

ALLIE   You think me and you are lucky, Joey?

JOEY   Sure do. Got good food and a bed and lots of friends. Course, I got me this job, too, so maybe I'm luckier than you, huh?

ALLIE   Yes, Joey, I guess you are at that.

JOEY   Yes ma'am, this is the best home I ever had. (*Looks at pic of farm*)   Except for them days at your place. I reckon them days was the very best of my life.

ALLIE   What days?

JOEY   Sure did love that old farm of yours. (*Kneels in front of pic, begins emptying contents of nail apron on floor*)   I'd have stayed there forever, if I could'a. But that's the way it goes, huh? Hey, we gotta find something here big enough to hang that picture on. Can't leave it on the floor like this.

ALLIE   You been to my farm? (*Rolls chair closer*)

JOEY   Sure, but it was a long time ago, tho'.

ALLIE   How long?

JOEY   Way back when I was a boy. You remember, don't you, Miss Allie? We talked about it before—lots of times. Don't you remember? It was one of them times when Mr. Jess was off somewhere—I don't know where. And you was keeping kids for the county that summer. Must'a been six or seven of us. The others left when school started, but I stayed on a while, cause you was teaching me some things, and I couldn't learn much in school. I wasn't too smart, you know. But I learned some things from you, especially about gardening. You was the best gardener I ever did know.

ALLIE   You . . . lived at my house?

JOEY   Sure did. Slept in the room with Bobby. He was just a little feller then.

ALLIE   No such thing! (*Grabs* JOEY'S *arm, shakes him*)   You never were at my house. You're telling fibs again, aren't you, Joey?

JOEY   No ma'am, Miss Allie. No ma'am . . . I ain't. It's the gospel truth, I swear. I never could tell fibs to you . . . and even if I'd wanted to, I knew you'd whallop me good.

ALLIE (*Lets go of* JOEY'S *arm*)   Did I whallop you?

JOEY   Yes ma'am. Mostly cause I couldn't remember to wash my feet after I went to the outhouse. I always had to go in the middle of the night, and I was always barefooted, and I always forgot to stop on the back porch and wash my feet in that tub you kept out there. (*Scratches his chin*)   Course, what really got me in trouble was when I took the shortcut through the chicken yard. That's when I really got my whallopings.

ALLIE   And you should have! You know how bad feet smell after a trip through the chicken yard? And then to climb in bed on my clean sheets . . . .

JOEY   I knew you remembered.

ALLIE   I remember a skinny little kid . . . but that couldn't have been you. Look at yourself. You're an old man.

JOEY   I wasn't then. That was fifty years ago. Why, you was a young woman yourself then, Miss Allie.

ALLIE   Fifty years?

JOEY   Yes ma'am, right at it.

ALLIE   Fifty years. No wonder I couldn't remember. And no wonder you got to be an old man. (*Puts hands to her face*)   Lordy me, Joey, if you're old, what am I?

JOEY Aw, Miss Allie, we all get old, but you're still a mighty handsome lady.

ALLIE And you get to be a bigger fibber all the time. I know what I am—at least, most of the time. (ALLIE *looks at pic, smiles sadly*) But once in a while, I forget. I mean, I get to feeling like I could get up out of this wheelchair and move right to that porch, and rock a while, or go work in the garden, or push Bobby in the tree swing . . . or maybe . . . run out and meet Jess . . . when he comes home.

(ALLIE *and* JOEY *stare at pic a moment. Then* ALLIE *shakes herself and looks at* JOEY)

ALLIE Course, it's not likely I'll ever do any of those things again. But it's the thinking about them that keeps me from feeling old and worn out clean through. If now and then, I can feel—well, maybe not quite young, but not quite so old—don't you see, I can keep hanging on. I got to keep believing that as long as I'm alive, there just might be a *chance* I could go back there someday. Just a chance, so I can't give up. You understand that, Joey?

(JOEY *nods slowly, then cocks his head, then shakes head slowly*)

ALLIE No matter. (*Pats* JOEY'S *arm and looks at pic again*) I used to think I'd like to go back for a visit some Sunday afternoon, just to see the old place. But it probably doesn't even look the same now. Probably wouldn't even recognize it.

JOEY Heck, Miss Allie. It ain't even there any more.

ALLIE Not there? What do you mean, not there any more?

JOEY It's gone. Been gone for years.

ALLIE Good Lordy, Joey! You're as bad as the rest of them around here. A farm can't just be gone. It can't die off like people do, and it can't disappear into thin air. It can change or get run down or burn to the ground and be rebuilt, but it *cannot* just be gone!

JOEY I'm telling you it is. And I wouldn't fib to you. They put the new Interstate right smack in that spot. (*Demonstrates by waving arms and hands as he speaks*) They got four lanes all coming together there now, with them big curved roads making circles all over where the fields was, and one of them high bridge overpasses running right over where the house was, with big old tall concrete things holding it up where them trees used to stand out front. That's the busiest road I ever did see. Everybody's got to go that way now to get in or out of town. Heck, before I came to live here, I used to go out there every day about dark and watch all them cars with their lights on going up and down and round and round. Looked just like one of them rides at the carnival.

ALLIE (*Looking stunned*) At . . . my . . . farm?

JOEY That's right. Only you couldn't tell there was ever a farm on that spot now. There ain't no sign of it left. No sign at all.

ALLIE No sign? A lifetime . . . and no sign? Just like that?

JOEY No ma'am. I reckon this here picture is about all there is left of it, huh? (JOEY *stares at* ALLIE, *then looks at pic*) Well, now, that settles it. I got to find some way to hang up this picture. You just got to have it in here, and they won't let you keep it if it don't hang right. (*Picks up hooks and looks at them*) Maybe I can use a couple of these things—one on each side. What'd you think, Miss Allie?

ALLIE I tell you what I think. (*Squares shoulders*) I think you ought to use that big nail right there and put that picture up to stay.

JOEY I can't, Miss Allie. I told you, it's . . . .

ALLIE Against the rules, I know.

JOEY That's right.

ALLIE Listen to me, Joey. Whose room is this?

JOEY It's yours, but . . . .

ALLIE Who pays for it?

JOEY Well, I reckon you do.

ALLIE You bet I do. Every nickel I get every month, I pay for it. So if it's my room, and I pay for it, don't you think I ought to have a say in what goes on the walls?

JOEY I reckon so. But if it leaves marks . . . .

ALLIE One little hole. One little mark. That's not too much to ask. If a body can't leave marks on her own wall, where can she leave marks?

JOEY (*Frowning*) But if they found out . . . .

ALLIE Once the picture's hung, nobody can see behind it, can they?

JOEY Nooo . . . .

ALLIE And after I'm . . . gone, well, you can get in here quick-like and fix it, can't you?

JOEY (*Thinking hard*) Maybe . . . if I worked real fast . . . maybe I could fix one little hole before they saw it.

ALLIE Sure you could. And you better use that biggest nail so it'll stay good and firm.

JOEY Yeah, maybe . . . maybe.

(JOEY *and* ALLIE *both start when* NURSE *enters suddenly from ULS*)

NURSE   Joey, I thought I'd find you here. I have another job for you. (*Pauses at CS, looking at pic*) Dear me, are you having trouble with that picture?

ALLIE   No trouble. He's working on it.

JOEY   Yeah. (*Scrambles to feet, holding large nail in one hand behind his back*) Yeah, I'm working on it.

NURSE   I'm sure you are. But I think this is a hopeless project. Perhaps I should just take this with me now and get it out of the way. There's simply no way to hang it properly.

(NURSE *moves toward pic.* JOEY *steps in front of her*)

JOEY   Is so! I got it all figured out! I'm . . . I'm gonna use . . . wait, now, I've got it all figured. I'm gonna . . . use two of them hooks. Yeah, maybe three. Yeah, I'll use three of 'em. That'll do it.

NURSE   I doubt it. However, if you want to try. . . .

(JOEY *and* ALLIE *speak in unison*)

JOEY   I do!

ALLIE   He does!

NURSE   Very well. But please come to my office when you're finished. I have a chair that needs repairing. (*Turns toward curtain, pauses at* ALLIE's *side, smooths* ALLIE's *hair and pats her head*) And Miss Allie, I do wish you'd neaten your hair up before I come back. (NURSE *exits UL*)

ALLIE   (*Glaring after* NURSE *and rumpling her hair*) Neaten my hair up? Well, Miss Prim and Prissy, this is as neatened as it gets. And I happen to like it this way, not that you'd care what I like! (*Turns, flashes grin at* JOEY) Joey, you just might be smarter than anybody ever realized.

JOEY   I sure am. (*Holds up nail*) Maybe I'm getting smarter as I get older.

ALLIE   I expect you are. Now, are we going to hang my picture?

JOEY   Sure are.

ALLIE   Then give me that hammer.

JOEY   (*Giving* ALLIE *hammer from nail apron*) What are you. . . .

ALLIE   Hold that nail to the wall for me.

JOEY   Heck, I can hammer it in, Miss Allie. You don't have to . . . .

ALLIE   Yes, I do, Joey. Now, stop arguing and hold the nail.

JOEY   Yes ma'am. (*Holds nail to wall*) But you got to hit it straight and hard.

(ALLIE *nods, rolls chair close to wall, grips hammer awkwardly, but purposefully*)

JOEY   Yeah, I reckon this'll do it all right. And when you leave, I'll slip in here before they even tell me to, and I'll fix it good. I'll be smart, too. So smart, nobody'll ever know there was even one little old mark in this room. Nobody.

ALLIE (*Raises hammer, stretches in chair, takes aim on nail*)   Except me! I'll know! (*Strikes nail*)   I'll know! (*Strikes nail again hard*)

CURTAIN

Bluesman

CHARLIE R. BRAXTON

CHARACTERS

STUMP 'HOLE' JACKSON   Stump is a middle-aged Black man from a small rural town in Mississippi. He is a very sensitive man with a strong sense of pride. He is a determined man who has carried the burden of being a Black man in a state that has been a stronghold for white supremacy all of his life and, because of this, Stump carries some very deep psychological and emotional scars. Using the Blues as his own psycho/spiritual medicine, Stump managed to heal some of his wounds, but he soon realized that he would never be completely free of his pain until he left Mississippi altogether.

JULIA JACKSON   Although slightly younger than her husband, Julia's experiences are almost the same as Stump's. As a Black woman growing up in rural Mississippi she has experienced much of the same racial oppression that her husband has, only she has not internalized the injuries as much as her husband. Julia sees a future Mississippi that her husband can't see. She sees a Mississippi that her daughter, Freddie Mae, can truly be a part of. It is because of this vision that Julia is reluctant to leave with her husband for Chicago.

FREDDIE MAE   Freddie is a very serious blend of both her mother and her father. She agrees with her father that Mississippi has not really changed enough for her to stay and chase her dreams. But, on the other hand, she really doesn't hate Mississippi. In fact, she is rather proud of the state.

THE SCENE

A typical living room in a poor rural Mississippi Black home. Most of the furniture is either second hand or throw away from various white people that Julia has managed to work for. There are a few pictures on the wall, mostly religious stuff. There is a picture of Jesus, a picture of a preacher and a small calendar with the state flag flying in the breeze,

17

and not too far from the calendar is a needlepoint wall hanging that says, "Be it ever so humble, there's no place like home."

Prologue

(*It is dusk as the curtains open and the lights fade in. We hear sounds of Stump as he knocks on the screen door only to receive no answer. After a few knocks we hear the sound of the screen door opening and Stump's footsteps.*)

STUMP   Hey up in here . . . . . (*He enters the stage*) . . . . Where y'all at? (*He puts down his bag*) Julia . . . . . .Freddie Mae . . . . y'all here. (*He goes to the hallway exit*) Julia! Julia . . . . (*He walks over to the couch and sits down*) Well, I guess not. Wonder where she could be . . . . and at this time a' evenin'. Hope she ain' heard 'bout me coming and gone 'n flew the coop, her and Freddie Mae . . . . 'cause I'd sho' hate it if they did. (*He reaches for his harp*) Hmp, looks like the place ain't changed too much since the last time I came here. Furniture still looks the same, the house looks the same . . . . yard too. Just like Mississippi . . . . ain't nothing' changin' but the time. I suppose that's why I left it . . . . yep, that's exactly why I left it. (*He plays his harp*) You know it seems that every time I come back ta Mississippi, I git this lil' ole bitty knot in the bottom of my gut, and fo' the life of me, I just can't seem ta shake all the while I'm down here. Wonder why is that? I mean I was born and raised here just like the people on that welcome ta Mississippi sign . . . . and I can't smile with glee everytime I hear Mississippi's name called. Ya see fo' me this place ain't never been no pic-nic in the park . . . . been mo' like a fish fry with me fryin' in the pot fo' supper. (*He plays his harp*) You know somethin', almost everywhere I go and every club I play everybody seem ta love the Blues. Black folkes, white folkes rich folkes and po' folkes all of 'em just can't seem ta git enough of the Blues. And that's good 'cause if they love 'em as much as they say they do then they'll know that the Blues can teach ya a whole lot if ya know how ta read between the lines . . . . Yeah, ya just gotta know how ta read between the lines.

(STUMP *plays his harp one more time as the curtain draws to a close. He gradually fades music to a slow halt.*)

ACT I

(STUMP *is sleeping restlessly on the couch. He is tossing and turning, mumbling inaudible words in his sleep. From backstage Julia can be heard talking to Freddie Mae.*)
(*Enter* FREDDIE *and* JULIA)

FREDDIE I tell ya, mama, that was the best I've ever heard Shady Grove choir sang . . . . and yo' solo was real pretty.

(STUMP *rises from his sleep*)

STUMP (*Yawns*) Oh, me me.
FREDDIE Daddy, you back! (*She rushes over to hug* STUMP)
STUMP (*Hugs* FREDDIE) Hey now, how's my lil' sugar dumplin'?
FREDDIE Fine, daddy, I'm doin' just fine.
STUMP Well now step back and let yo' daddy take a good look at ya.

(FREDDIE *steps back and whirls around proudly*)

FREDDIE See.
STUMP Well look a'here, look a'here . . . . girl you done grown on up, ain't ya?
JULIA Well, what'd expect!? You ain't seen the girl in near 'bout three years.
FREDDIE Mama, he saw me summer before last.
JULIA Hush gal, I ain't talkin' to you.
STUMP (*Taking a step towards* JULIA) Hey there Julia.
JULIA Hey!? You been gone all this here time and that's all you got ta say?
STUMP (*Takes another step*) Now Julia, I know it's been a long time since my last visit . . . .
JULIA Oh, it sho' has been a lil' while since I last saw yo' rusty Black end, but long ain't the word for it . . . . mo' like fo'ever.
STUMP I know Julia, and I'm real sorry.
JULIA (*Puts her hands on her hips*) Sorry!? Huh, sorry don't shine my shoes, it don't keep a roof over my head, and it sho' can't keep me safe and warm at night.
STUMP Aw, Julia.
JULIA Don't you aw, Julia me, you low down dirty snaggle tooth humped back pender headed polecat, you . . . . 'cause I don't even much wanna hear it.
STUMP But baby, if ya just let me try ta explain . . . .
JULIA Explain! You wanna explain to me, lil' ole po' Julia Marie Jack-

son, why you, who s'pose ta be my husban', just upped and lef' me here with a whole heap 'a bills ta pay and young'un ta raise, all by my self.

STUMP   Julia, I didn't just up and leave you and Freddie Mae.

JULIA   Ta hell you preach!

STUMP   Julia, you know I begged you ta come with me.

JULIA   And I told you I wasn' goin'!

FREDDIE   Mama.

JULIA   Shut up gal, can't you see grown folkes is talkin'!

FREDDIE   Yeah mama, but . . . .

JULIA   I said hush up! (*Pause*)   Now take yo' tail ta bed fo' I slap the taste out yo' mouth!

FREDDIE   But mama . . . .

JULIA   I said get!

FREDDIE   Yes maam.

(*Exit* FREDDIE)

STUMP   Now look a'here Julia, I know you mad at me 'n' all, but you ain't got no call to be takin' it out on Freddie Mae. She ain' done nothin' to you; if I'm the one you mad at then I'm the one you should be dealin' with . . . . I ain't gonna stand fo' you mistreatin' my baby.

JULIA   Well, look who's talkin', Mr. High 'n Mighty hisself. Boy, you got some nerve . . . . first you leave me 'n Freddie Mae for God knows how long, and now, after all this time, here you come talkin' 'bout what you ain't gone take—I'm the one who decides what Freddie will or will not do—I'll decide what's best for her 'cause she's my daughter and I'm the one who stayed with her.

STUMP (*Holding his hands up in surrender*)   Look Julia, I didn't come here to start no fuss. I just came here to see you and Freddie Mae.

JULIA   Well you've seen us, so you might as well gone 'bout yo' bizness.

STUMP   Julia, I just got here.

JULIA   And you can just leave too.

STUMP   So this is what it's gonna be like this time around?

JULIA   It's been like this almost every time you been here and gon' always be like this too . . . . to tell the truth I really don't see why you keep comin' down here . . . . ain't nothin' down here for ya . . . . least not here.

STUMP   Now Julia, you know you don't mean a word you sayin'; you just mad 'cause you ain't seen me in a long time . . . . but after tonight, everythang'll be alright.

(STUMP *walks over to* JULIA *and tries to embrace her*)

JULIA (*pulls away*) Gitta 'way from me, negro! I done told you, I don't wanna be bothered with ya.

(*She sits in a chair facing* STUMP *with a faraway look in her eyes*)

STUMP Damn it, Julia, why you wanna do me like this!?

JULIA Why did you wanna do me the way you been doin' the last ten years?

STUMP Now Julia, I thought we've done been through all this mess befo' . . . . Be damn if it don't seem like every doggone time I come down here, we always have to go through the same ole, same ole . . . . and I'm tired of it.

JULIA And I'm tired of it too, but we gone go through this every time you bring yo' black end down here. I ain't gon' ever give up 'till you make up yo mind!

STUMP About what?

JULIA What you gonna do and where you gonna stay from now on.

STUMP You know good 'n damn well where I'm gonna stay and what I'm gonna do. I'm gonna stay in Chicago and I'm gonna play the Blues 'til the day I die.

JULIA So where does that put me and Freddie Mae?

STUMP Where ever y'all wanna be put.

JULIA Just like that!? You gonna put me 'n Freddie Mae wherever it is we wanna be put, like we some kinda sack 'a walkin' talkin' potatas? Stump we yo' family!

STUMP I know that.

JULIA Then why in hell don't you act like it and take some responsibility.

STUMP And do what!? What Julia!? I'm sendin' y'all as much money as I can every month.

JULIA That's not what I'm talkin' 'bout.

STUMP Oh, you want me ta come crawlin' back down here and beg some two bit redneck to let me work some small time penny annie back breakin' dead end job for little a' nothin' . . . . uh uh, not Stump "Hole" Jackson. I'd rather die and go straight ta hell and work for the devil himself.

JULIA And what about me and Freddie Mae? What we 'spose to do, huh? Ya want us to sit down here like two knots on a long log and wait fo' you to finally decide that right here is where you really belong? Is that what you want?

STUMP Naw, I want y'all to come with me.

JULIA And I want you to live down here with us.

STUMP Julia can't you understand that I can't crawl back down and live life on my knees.

JULIA Stump, I ain't askin' you to crawl, I tellin you to walk and be a man . . . .

STUMP Baby, you know, black as I am, I can't be no man in Mississippi.

JULIA Stump . . . . I can't see myself livin' up north . . . . and I don't think I'll ever go.

STUMP Yeah I pretty much know that.

JULIA Then why in the world do you keep on wastin' yo' wind tryin' ta talk me into it?

STUMP I keep hopin' I can change yo' mind, baby.

JULIA I sho do hate it.

STUMP Yeah, so do I.

(STUMP *takes a seat on the couch and lights his last smoke*)

JULIA I s'pose you'll be leaving first thang Sunday mornin'?

STUMP Julia, I just got here.

JULIA I know you just got here . . . . I was just wantin' ta know what time you gone be leavin' Sunday.

(JULIA *walks over to look out the window*)

STUMP Sounds ta me like you tryin' ta tell me to leave.

JULIA It sho do, don't it.

STUMP Yeah, it does.

JULIA Well, maybe I am an' then again, maybe I ain't . . . . what's it to you . . . . ain't no grits off yo' gravy. You know you gone be leaving sooner or later, anyhow. So why not gone 'n get it ova' with.

STUMP Cause I don't want to.

JULIA You might as well want to, ain't nothin' here for ya.

STUMP Julia, you still my wife.

JULIA And a long time ago, you was my husband . . . .

STUMP I'm still yo' husband . . . . we's still man and wife.

JULIA Not in my book you ain't . . . . (*She walks casually back to her seat*) . . . and we ain't either.

STUMP What you mean by that?

JULIA Just what I said.

STUMP Lawd, have mercy.

JULIA Ain't no use in callin' on the Lawd, 'cause he didn't start this mess, you did.

STUMP I know, and I'm tryin' ta straighten it all out now.

JULIA Well, yo doin' a mighty terrible job of it then . . . . Honey, I can tell ya that right now.

STUMP Well hell, Julia, give me a break . . . . cut me some slack.

JULIA   Cut you some slack! Huh! give you a rope, you mean.

STUMP   Ya see, there you go again. Damn, you just like everybody else 'round here; always tryin' to tear me down. Can't listen to what I got ta say; can't believe in me enough to believe in my dreams. Yet 'n still you want me ta be what you want me to be; damn what I feel or think . . . . I ain't shit to you but a means to an end.

(*There is a long pause, during it,* STUMP *takes a deep sigh, gets up, walks to the window*)

JULIA   Stump. (*He doesn't hear her*)
      Stump.

STUMP (*Turns around slowly*)   Yeah.

JULIA   Since you gon' be stayin' for a few days I reckon you gon' be needin' a place ta sleep.

STUMP   I guess so.

JULIA   Well, you can sleep on the couch, it's good 'n comfortable.

STUMP (*Under his breath*)   Don't I know it.

JULIA   What you say?

STUMP   Yeah, yeah, I'll sleep here . . . . for the night, then in the morning I'll find somewhere else ta stay.

JULIA   'Bout how long you gon' stay?

STUMP   Oh, about a week or two, then I'm gone go back to Chi-town.

JULIA   A week 'a two?! That's the longest you've ever stayed here since you've been gone. How come you stayin' so long this time?

STUMP   I got somethin' to do down here.

JULIA   Somethin' like what?

STUMP   I'll tell ya later. Right now I just want ta get all this out about you thinkin' I just upped and left you and Freddie Mae.

JULIA   Hell, you did.

STUMP (*Raises his voice*)   The hell, I didn't.

JULIA (*Stands up*)   Don't you go raisin' yo' voice in my house!

STUMP (*Even louder*)   I'll do what I damn well please! This is still my house too. I send you money every stankin' month to help pay for this raggedy piece 'a shit!

JULIA   I said lower yo' damn voice! Can't you see, that girl is sleep in yonder! (*Points to* FREDDIE'S *exit*)

(STUMP *puts his hand over his mouth and looks toward* FREDDIE'S *exit.* JULIA *sits back in her seat.* STUMP *walks behind the couch and puts his hand on the back of it*)

STUMP (*slightly desperate*)   Look, Julia, all I want right now is for you to give me half a chance to explain to ya why I left Mississippi.

JULIA   I already know.

STUMP   The real reason why I left had nothin' ta do with you or Freddie Mae.

JULIA   What the hell you mean it had nothin' ta do with us!?

STUMP   (*Drops his head*)   I left this place 'cause I just couldn't take it no mo'.

JULIA   What you mean you couldn' take anymo'.

STUMP   Goddamn it Julia, will you, for the first time in yo' naggin' ass life, just shut up and hear me out. (*Pause,* STUMP *sighs*)   For the umpteenth time, I'm tellin' you I didn't leave you and Freddie Mae because I didn't love y'all . . . or to go 'round chasin' other womens.

(STUMP *squats behind sofa*)

JULIA   Then why did you leave us?

STUMP   Just hold on, I'm getting' to that part.

JULIA (*With a bit of sarcasm*)   I can hardly wait.

STUMP   I left Mississippi 'cause I couldn' stand livin' here another minute.

JULIA   What did you say, Negro!?

STUMP   I mean it Julia, I don't belong down here . . . . I don't fit in around here anymo'.

JULIA   And that's all it was!? Stump you must take me fo' a complete fool! I know good 'n goddamn well you don't expect me to believe that; after all these long, hard, thankless years I don' spent layin' awake praying to the good lord to help me to understand the real reason why you lef' me years ago, to believe a stankin' bullshit story like that! I know way betta than that!

STUMP   I know it sounds crazy to you . . . .

JULIA (*Interjects*)   You damn right, it sounds crazy.

STUMP   But it's the truth, Julia, I swear fo' the Lawd Gawd, almighty.

JULIA   Now wait a minute, Negro. A few minutes ago you said somethin' 'bout playin' Blues with the devil; now you swearin' fo' the Lawd. How in the world do you 'spect somebody to ever believe a word you sayin' when ya keep changin' up sides on 'em.

STUMP   'Aw hell, Julia.

JULIA   Don't you (*Mockingly*) 'Aw hell' me, Negro . . . . Just answer my damn question.

STUMP   I'm tellin' ya the truth, Julia. What else you want me ta say, huh? You want me ta tell ya how I had been wantin' ta leave you and Freddie Mae for some real fine hi-yella gal and run up north. If that was true, I'd tell you . . . . But it ain't true. (*Pause*) Julia, I love you mo' than any other thang on this here earth . . . . mo' than life itself. I didn' leave you and Freddie cause I wanted to, I did it cause I had to.

JULIA   Why?

STUMP   It's like I said befo' I don't seem to fit into things 'round here . . . . I mean I feel like I'm totally outta place every time I come down here.

JULIA   Huh, I can remember a time when you used ta fit in real good 'round here.

STUMP   Aw, hell I was a chap back then . . . . I didn' know any better back then but this here old place.

JULIA   Well, we did have some pretty good times growin' up back then.

STUMP   Fun! Girl the only thang I'n remember 'bout back then was them hard assed times we had; and how much I hated myse'f for bein' a poor black boy from Plumnelly Mississippi.

JULIA   Well I sho' do hate that you felt that a 'way, but they ain't a damn thang I can do fo' ya . . . . 'cause Julia Marie Jackson ain't never hated herse'f.

STUMP   Oh yea, then how come you used ta git mad whenever I sang that Leadbelly song?

JULIA   What song?

STUMP (Sings)   Black gal, Black gal . . . .

JULIA   Aw hell, I hated that song 'cause I didn' like the way you used ta sang it.

STUMP   That's 'cause you didn' like me callin' you black.

JULIA   It wasn't.

STUMP   The hell it ain't. You never did like yo' pretty skin.

JULIA   That's a lie . . . . I ain't got no pretty skin.

STUMP   Naw, not now ya don't. That's 'cause you done messed it all up with them damn skin lighteners and stuff . . . . I told you in the first place, you didn't need that junk.

JULIA   Well you didn' know what it was like fo' a girl my color to grow up back then. I just wanted to be like some of them hi-yella girls in school back then.

STUMP   Why?

JULIA   'Cause they always seem ta git everythang back then . . . . includin' the good men.

STUMP   Oh, I ain't no good man, huh?

JULIA   You left me didn' ya?

STUMP   Well you can bet that I didn' leave you 'cause you wasn' lite, bright and damn near white.

JULIA   Well, go 'head 'n make fun 'a me and my se'fhatin' Mississippi ways.

STUMP   Aw, cool off baby. You ain't the only one ever done somethin' stupid to theyse'f on account o' they se'fhatin' ways. You remember that time I damn near burnt my head off tryin' to straighten my hair.

JULIA (*Chuckles*)   Boy, do I remember! Boy you ran like a po'cupine with his tail on fire. How old was you back then?

STUMP   Oh, 'bout sixteen or seventeen.

JULIA   Seems like it took them fo'ever ta catch up with you and put yo' pender head out.

STUMP   Well, I'm damn sho' glad they did, 'cause if they hadn't I'd be slap ball-headed right now.

JULIA   And you'd be one ugly sight too.

(JULIA *lets out a little laugh*)

STUMP   I'd be even uglier with it straighten.

(*Pause.* STUMP *plays a lick on his harmonica*)

JULIA   Stump.

STUMP (*Stops playing the harmonica*)   Yeah.

JULIA   Tell me how in the world did you come ta hate yo' own so.

STUMP (*Sighs*)   I s'pose that the only real reason I could give at the time was, I was black and po' and everybody else who looked like me was in the same bad fix. We all had raggedy houses with no runnin' water and a stankin' assed outhouse. We didn' have much money and had bills on top of bills on top o' bills . . . . And there wasn't nobody Black 'round here that ya could look up to 'n say that you'd wanna be like 'em, someday. That's cause didn't nobody Black have nothin' hardly . . . . and . . . . and those few who did have a lil' piece 'a som'thin' most o' them tommin' fo' Mista Charlie.

You know I swo'e ta myself that I'd never cow tow to no white man for anything . . . . and fo' a long time I kept my promise.

JULIA   That's cause you didn' ever see much 'a white people back when we was real young. It was our folkes who had ta bow and scrape so you could run 'round the house talkin' all yo' bad talk back then.

STUMP (*Not hearing her he keeps talking*)   Then I had ta grow up . . . . become a man . . . . get a job and feed my family. That's all I really wanted was to git a job . . . . any job that paid me some decent money while I kept workin' on playin' the Blues.

JULIA   In Mississippi!? Ha! Boy you was doin' real good ta have the lil' job you did have back then . . . . And as fo' this Blues mess, boy, you knew way back when you started tryin' ta play that stuff for money, wasn't nobody gonna pay you no big money for it. You the one that was bein so stupid for even tryin' it . . . . I still don't understand why you so damn determined to do somethin' like that anyway.

STUMP 'Cause it's my dream ta take the blues places where it ain't neve been.

JULIA And you catchin' pure'dee hell tryin' ta find yo' damn dream, ain't ya?

STUMP Yeah, but I'm closer up there than I ever was livin' down here.

JULIA I still don't understand, Stump.

STUMP That's the problem, you never tried.

JULIA Hell, if you were me would you?

STUMP Freddie Mae understands me.

JULIA That don't mean she forgave you fo' leavin' her . . . . for not bein' there when she needed you . . . . when I needed ya.

STUMP Naw, now, don' you go bringin' Freddie Mae into this mess, cause I had a nice long talk to her when she came to see me last summer, and she told me herse'f that she understands . . . . and that she don't hate me fo' what I did. She knows that I had to leave for my own good.

JULIA What good did it do you, ta up 'n leave yo' own wife 'n chap, huh? I s'pose next you gone tell me that doin' it was the right thang too.

STUMP For me it was.

JULIA And what 'bout me!? What 'bout was right fo' me 'n Freddie Mae? Ya could'a thought 'a us instead 'a bein' so selfish.

STUMP Julia, I asked you to come. I wanted y'all ta come up with me so bad, it hurts to think about it sometimes. Why in the world do ya think I keep tryin' to talk ya into comin' up with me? Huh? You think I like livin' up there in that cold assed place all by myse'f. You think that it's easy livin' with myself knowin' I got a wife and kid down here in Mississippi. Hell, I wanna get y'all outta here! (*Pause*) Julia, when I first asked you ta marry me, I promised myself that I was gonna be the kinda man you could always respect . . . . not some dumb ass negro who didn' know his guts from a bucket 'a spoilt chitterlings. I wanted ta be somebody you could be proud of.

JULIA You was somebody to me . . . . long time ago.

STUMP You ain't never gonna forgive me, is ya, Julia?

JULIA Naw, not no time soon.

STUMP Well, I really can't say, I blame ya. If I were in yo' shoes I'd probably feel the same way . . . . but, all I'm askin' ya to do is try 'n understand why I had ta go.

JULIA I am tryin' ta understan'. (*She gets emotional and tries to fight back her tears*)   I been tryin' ta understan' ever since the day you walked out the door . . . . and I swear, the mo' I try, the mo' harder it gits. Ever' now 'n then I think I come close ta understandin' . . . . and then . . . . sometimes I just can't . . . . it hurts Stump . . . . it just hurts too much.

STUMP (*Feeling remorse*)   Yeah, I know what ya mean, baby . . . . I know just what you mean.

JULIA   Stump . . . . why don't ya just come on back home?

STUMP   Cause this ain't my home no mo' . . . . I live in Chicago.

JULIA   Oh so that's how you feel about thangs. (*She tries even harder to restrain her sadness, wiping the few tears that fall from her eyes*)   I guess you feel the same way 'bout me 'n Freddie Mae.

STUMP   I done told you a hundred times or mo', y'all's my family and I love y'all mo'n you'd ever know.

JULIA   Well you sho' gotta funny way 'a showin' it.

STUMP   Listen Julia, I'm gettin' a lil' tired 'a you always bringin' up me leavin' you 'n Freddie Mae. How come you don't ever talk about how you didn' go ta Chicago with me when I asked ya to? Huh? What 'bout that!? Why don't cha talk about how come you, my wife, who s'pose ta love and support me, like I did you . . . . And you sho' can't say I didn', 'cause you know I did . . . . But did you—no, you didn'. I don't understand why we couldn't all just have packed up 'n headed for Chicago like I had asked ya to. Ah, but no . . . . you didn' wanna do that . . . . naw suh . . . . that was too much like right.

JULIA   So you just upped 'n lef' without me.

STUMP   You damn right, I left . . . . I had to.

JULIA   And ya didn' look back.

STUMP   That's a lie! (STUMP *gets up and paces in front of the couch. He sighs*)   Damn it Julia, you doin' it to me again.

JULIA   Negro, I ain't done nothin' to you . . . . yet.

STUMP   Ya tryin' ta make me feel guilty.

JULIA   You should feel guilty without my even tryin'.

STUMP   And what about you?

JULIA   What you mean, what about me?

STUMP   You should feel guilty some too.

JULIA   'BOUT WHAT!?

STUMP   About what! How 'bout not leavin' with me when I asked you to!

JULIA   Ha . . .

STUMP   You can 'ha' all you want to, but it don' change the fact that if you had 'a lef' with me, we'd still be as happy as two peas in a pod.

JULIA Naw we wouldn've been. I don't like livin' in no big city. I'm a country girl and that's where I belong . . . in the country.

STUMP Stay here . . . . for what!? Ain't nothin' here for us but a hard way ta go 'n a short time ta git there. You know how hard it is fo' black folkes ta make a decent livin' down here . . . . and you still wanna stay down here! I swear I don' understand . . . . I can't see why you love this place so. It sho' ain't done that much fo' you.

JULIA And it ain' don' that much to me ne'ther.

STUMP So you think.

JULIA I know it ain't . . . . and you do too.

STUMP Oh, yes it has . . . . you just don't know.

   (STUMP *sits on the arm of the couch*)

JULIA And you don' know what this place has done fo' me. I'm here ta tell ya, Mississippi's my one and only home. The only thang I've ever known. I was born and raised here. So was my Mama 'n Daddy, and they Mama 'n Daddy . . . . why we Felders go back with this lan' fo' generations 'n generations. As far back as anyone can remember, my folkes, and yo' folkes too, have been here in Mississippi . . . and don't nobody I know ever really leave. Now we might think about it . . . . we might even talk about it, but we never leave. We can't. We's kinda like these here old trees—we's rooted here. We might swing this a'way and we might swing that a'way, but baby, you can bet yo' bottom dollar we ain't goin' nowhere besides where we are.

STUMP And that's why ain't nobody in either one of our families ever got anywhere—they too crazy to get up 'n move on to bigger and better things in this world. Now, I'm different, I don't mind takin' a chance on myse'f, 'cause I think I'm worth it.

JULIA And what 'bout us? Don't you think we worth sacrificing for?

STUMP You don't call leavin' yo' wife and daughter to go live in a strange city for ten hard years a sacrifice!? Julia, I worked at the post office for ten long hard years. I played some o' the dingiest and dirtiest joints in Chicago trying to make it, so I could make a better life for you 'n Freddie Mae. I don't see why you don't still believe me. I did everything I could ta help ya. I sent ya money. I wrote you letters. And, when I didn't write I'd call—Hell I'm the one who paid for you to get the phone in the first place. Plus I came ta see you and Freddie Mae every chance I got. Now in light o' all that, you can't tell me I don't love you, baby.

JULIA You don't.

STUMP Well I'll just be damn. I give up. You win Julia . . . . you can stay here as long as you want. I don't care . . . . Just let me take Freddie back with me.

JULIA   What did you say?

STUMP   You heard me.

JULIA   Naw, I just know he didn' . . . . I just know better than that, lawd . . . . he didn' ask me ta let him take my baby up north with him . . . . I know waaaaaay better than that!

STUMP   Why not?

JULIA   I don't want Freddie Mae to grow up in Chicago. She don't belong up there.

STUMP   Take a good look around here . . . . just look at this place! Is this what you want fo' yo' daughter? Huh!? You want her to grow up in a place like this!? You want her ta go through what we went through when we were her age!?

JULIA   I don't see what's wrong with this place. We both grew up here and we seemed to be alright.

STUMP   On the outside maybe . . . . but on the inside there's a whole us sufferin' from Mississippi.

JULIA   Well, I still think that anywhere in Mississippi is bettern' Chicago.

STUMP   I think that the gal's old enough ta make up her own mind, so why don't we let her.

JULIA   Cause I done told ya I don't want her up there . . . .

STUMP   Julia, I can't leave both of y'all down here. I just can't do it.

JULIA   Well, well, sounds like you gotta problem.

STUMP   I was hoping you'd see it as our problem.

JULIA   I use' ta but not anymo' . . . . I done been figgered my problem out long time ago.

STUMP   Julia, you can't mean that.

JULIA   Oh yes I do . . . . mean it with all my heart.

STUMP   So does that mean that you don't love me no mo'?

JULIA   Now, I never said that.

STUMP   Well so far you haven't said you do.

JULIA   Do what!?

STUMP   Love me.

JULIA   I love ever'body, Stump . . . . no matter how lowdown 'n dirty they do me . . . . I'm a Christian.

STUMP   Then if you such a Christian, why can't you fo'give me for leavin' you 'n Freddie Mae?

JULIA   I never said I was good Christian . . . . ain't nobody perfect . . . 'Cept the good Lawd hisse'f.

STUMP   All the mo' reason to forgive me then.

JULIA   Stump, if you would'a come back a few years ago and said, 'Baby, I'm sorry. I didn't mean ta run off 'n leave you 'n Freddie like I did. I understand why ya can't leave Mississippi and I loves ya anyway. If you wanna stay here and live . . . . if that's what'll really make ya happy, then I'll stay here 'n work hard and try to make a livin' as best I can for us.' But, naw . . . . you just had ta leave for Chicago. Ya couldn' wait ta go, could ya? And what's so bad about it, is you didn' even much have the decency to let me know you were leavin'.

STUMP   And what would you've done if I did tell ya, huh? Go with me!? knowing you . . . . I doubt it!

JULIA   That ain' got nothin' ta do with the fact that you snuck off like a damn thief in the night.

STUMP   And stole yo' heart.

JULIA   Now . . . . you looka here, negro, I'm 'bout this far from kickin' yo' black ass out that door . . . . so, if I was you, I'd watch what I'd say ta me.

STUMP   I'm sorry.

JULIA   Naw, you ain't.

STUMP   Ya see, there ya go again! No matter how hard I try ta be good to you . . . . and Lawd knows I try . . . . you won't even try ta be understandin'.

JULIA   And what 'bout me? What 'bout you tryin' ta understand me? I'm yo' wife, ain' I!? Ain' you s'pose ta love 'n understand me like I'm s'pose ta love 'n understand you? Huh? (STUMP *remains silent*)
      Then where's my love and understandin'? Hell, I want the same thangs you want outa life . . . . I just don' want it the same way you do . . . that's all. And I feel that if you was any kind of a man, you'd be able ta understand and respect me for what I am. I'm a country girl from downhome Mississippi. And that's all I'll ever be, 'cause that's all I wanna be.
      Ya see Stump, I don't hate Mississippi like you do . . . . that's 'cause I don't hate myself like you do. Oh, now I'll admit that there may've been some time when I didn't know quite where I was goin' or what I was gonna do when I got there, but I never really hated myself; 'cause deep down inside I know I am somebody. And it don't matter what anybody in this world do or say ta me . . . . it won't hurt me. . . . 'cause I'm Julia Marie . . . . and gone be so 'til the day I die.

STUMP   It's good you feel that way Julia. But it's a whole lotta people from here who don't.

JULIA   Well, I sho' feel sorry for 'em.

(There is a pause as the tension begins to ease a little)

JULIA Stump.

STUMP Yeah baby, what is it.

JULIA *(She shakes her head with doubt)* Nothin'.

STUMP Naw . . . . now . . . . what is it?

JULIA It ain't nothin'

STUMP Now look Julia, if ya got somethin' ta say, ya might as well spit it out.

JULIA You gon' think it's crazy.

STUMP Well it can't be any mo' crazy'n this here whole conversation.

JULIA Stump, I just can't see why is it you keep 'a holdin' on ta all that hate fo' this place. You been gone a long time now, why can't you just let yo' feelin's go?

STUMP Because I just can't . . . . this place holds too many bad memories fo' me, Julia . . . . done done too much to my soul.

JULIA I still don't know what you mean.

STUMP Mississippi ain't done nothin' but held me back . . . . beat me down . . . . kept me from being what I always wanted ta be.

JULIA A bluesman.

STUMP Yeah, a bluesman . . . . a one hundred per cent pure'dee gut bucket bluesman.
   Ever'body seem ta love the doggone Blues, but very few people really know what it takes to know the Blues. *(There is a lull in the conversation as* STUMP *sits with* JULIA *on the opposite end of the couch)* Look Julia, let's drop all o' this mess 'n move on to somethin' else.

JULIA Like what!?

STUMP I don't know . . . . Let's talk 'bout the future.

JULIA What future!?

STUMP Our future.

JULIA Negro, we ain't go no future.

STUMP We could if you just give it a chance.

JULIA *(Her voice softens)* Stump.

STUMP Baby, now befo' you go blowin' up 'n all, just hear me out. I know I ain' been the best husband in the world, but I do love ya, and I know if ya just give me just a lil' bit of a chance I could make it up to ya.

JULIA Stump.

STUMP Now baby, I know just what you gon' say, and I know you right. But baby, I got some good news that's really gone change yo' mind.

JULIA Look Stump, I got somethin' ta tell ya.

STUMP Yeah baby, what is it this time.

JULIA Stump, I know by now you must really think that I jus' hate yo' guts. . . . and you really gon' think it even mo' when I tell you what I gone tell ya.

STUMP Julia, I know that you ain't stone crazy for me right now, but. . . .

JULIA (*Cutting him off*) Look Stump, jus' let me finish tellin' ya this while I still got the nerve.

STUMP Tell me what, baby.

JULIA Stump, when you was 'a tellin' me how much you needed me all the while you was up there in Chicago, how many of them Chicago girls were you dealin' with?

STUMP Now look here, baby, I don' told you that them old gals didn' mean a thang ta me.

JULIA Like I didn' mean a thang ta ya?

STUMP Now you know I never said no such a' thang . . . . you know that, Julia.

JULIA So you have had quite a few women up there, huh?

STUMP Naw . . . . I ain't had no whole lotta o' 'em . . . . mo' like two 'a three.

JULIA Two 'a three . . . you mean ta tell me that you only had two or three women during the whole time you was up there. That's two 'a three too many right there!

STUMP Now hold on Julia, it ain't what you thinkin'.

JULIA Oh it ain't, huh?

STUMP Naw.

JULIA Then what was it like?

STUMP Now you looka here woman, you know damn well I ain' no saint. I got itches ta scratch and a belly ta rub, ya know.

JULIA Oh yeah, well so do I.

STUMP What do you mean?

JULIA Jus' what I said.

STUMP I know you didn' mean what I thought you meant.

JULIA And what if I did?

STUMP (*Sighs and tries to maintain his cool*) Julia, have you been seein' another man while I was gone?

JULIA Yeah, I have.

STUMP Who is it?

JULIA Why should you even care, you don't live here anymo'.

STUMP I said who is it!

JULIA Nonna yo' damn biz'ness!

(STUMP *walks over to* JULIA *and grabs her by the shoulders and shakes her a little*)

STUMP Goddamn it, I said who was it . . . . tell me who was it!!!

JULIA Fred Nobles . . . . it's Fred Nobles!

STUMP Fred Nobles!? (*He releases her*) Of all the people in the world why'd ya have ta go pick him!?

JULIA I didn' just go out 'n pick him just like that . . . . it jus' sorta happened . . . we didn' plan it.

STUMP Oh, so you was just feelin' kinda lon'some and you decides ta invite Fred Nobles, a man known here and yonder fo' foolin' round with other folkes wifes, over for a visit. Don't ya think that's a lil' bit outta place. I mean he sho' ain' the most decent man in the world ta be alone inna house with. And ta top it all off, he's s'pose ta be my best friend.

JULIA Fool, don't you know when it comes ta yo' woman, you ain't got no best friend.

STUMP Shut up woman . . . . (*Draws back his hand to hit her*) . . . . fo' I slap the taste out yo' mouth!!

JULIA I wish you would hit me . . . . (STUMP'S *hand freezes*) . . . .go 'head . . . . so I can send you closer to the Lord than you ever been! (STUMP *lowers his hand and his head in despair*) I don't know who in the hell you think you are. You go off 'n leave me down here and I don't hear from you fo' months and months on end; and whenever I do see ya, we spend most o' the time fussin' and a' fightin'.

STUMP It ain't my fault, you the one always startin' it.

JULIA (*She continues*) We may be husband 'n wife, but we's a long way from bein' anythang close ta lovers. Hell, I can't recall us bein' close friends since the day you lef'.

STUMP It ain't 'cause I haven' tried.

JULIA (*Ignoring him still*) And I know good 'n damn well, you didn' expect me ta be sittin' down here waitin' on you ta come on home ta me! 'Cause you a fool if you did! I ain' no old maid and I sho' ain' one o' them dried up old widows sittin' up in the church, waitin' on Jesus . . . . I'm a woman . . . . and I got needs too! So, befo' you go callin' me all o' them dirty names you got rollin' 'round in yo' head; you just stop and ask yo'se'f 'bout all them bar-room hussies you done been with and then you decide who's the real tramp.

STUMP Julia, I ain't been with no bar-room hussies . . . . and I sho' ain' been with nobody's best friend!

JULIA And you really expect me ta fall fo' that!? Negro, you might as well fess up ta ya own sins 'cause you ain't no better'n me. (*There *is a long silence as each one of them stares the other down. Finally* STUMP *breathes a heavy sigh and reaches in his shirt pocket for a cigarette. He has none. He looks in his suitcase)* What're you lookin' for?

STUMP My cigarettes.

(There are no cigarettes in his suitcase so STUMP *heads out the door)*

JULIA Where you goin'?

STUMP To get me some cigarettes . . . . I'll be back later on.

JULIA What time?

STUMP I don't know.

*(*STUMP *exits as* FREDDIE MAE *enters through the hallway exit)*

FREDDIE *(Calling)* Daddy, Daddy, where're you going?

JULIA Let 'em go girl.

FREDDIE But where's he going?

JULIA He's goin' fo' a little walk, he'll be back later on.

FREDDIE Mama, did y'all have another fight, already? Daddy hasn't been here a good day yet and y'all fighting already. I thought that things were going to work out alright this time. Mama, what happened?

JULIA I ain' gone talk about it.

FREDDIE Why!?

JULIA *(Frustrated)* Cause I just don't! Now sut up 'n gone back ta bed.

FREDDIE But Mama, I can't sleep.

JULIA I don't care . . . you just get yo' butt back in the bed. Don't you know you got school in the mornin'!

FREDDIE Yeah, but . . . .

JULIA I don't wanna hear no but, I said take yo' ass ta bed!

FREDDIE Yes mam. *(Exit* FREDDIE MAE*)*

*(*JULIA *paces the floor a bit. She straightens up the pillows on the couch. Afterwards she begins to sweep in front of the couch. Slowly she works her way toward the discarded cigarette package. She sweeps it toward the telephone table. She spots the package, picks it up and looks at it with deep concentration. She looks quickly at the telephone and makes a call)*

JULIA Hello, Johnny, let me speak to yo' brother, please . . . . Hello, Fred, this is Julia . . . . uh huh. I kno' you was just about ta come over; that's why I'm callin' you, to tell ya not ta com'. Why? Cause I don' want you to. I kno' I didn' say that two weeks ago, but things are different now. What . . . . what's wrong? (*Sighs*) Fred, this little thang we been havin', it's over. Why? 'Cause it really wasn' right from the start and it's don' gon' too far. It's gotta stop and I mean right now! I'm tired of it, just plum tired!

Now, now, Fred, don't you go lyin' 'bout how much you love me, 'cause you kno' damn well you don't. All I was to you was a warm thang fo' you ta lay up on ever' now 'n then, that's all . . . . Aw, now Fred, you knew deep down inside that it was bound to come ta this one day. You knew when we started this thang a while back . . . . well now it's over.

Why? (*Sighs*) Look Fred . . . . Stump's back again . . . . and I don' come ta see that, in spite of all the things that we've don' ta one 'nother . . . . we still kinda care fo' each other. I think that maybe we might be able ta make our marriage work out . . . . who knows, maybe I'll even move ta Chicago . . . . I doubt it, but you never know.

What did you say? Does Stump know 'bout us? (*Pause*) Yeah, I told him tonight. I really don't know how he's taking it, right now. He went out ta get some ciggerettes. But don't worry 'bout it, I don't think he's gonna go out lookin' for ya or nothin' like that . . . . Yeah, I'm sure . . . . anyway, why are you so worried? I'm the one who's got ta face him fo' the rest 'a my life, not you. Okay, okay, so he's a lil' hot with you too, but, like I said, he ain't gone git ruff with you. Stump just ain't that kinda person. He'd rather leave you alone than hunt you down and shoot ya. So don't worry . . . . What you say? You worried 'bout me!? For what? You think I'm goin' back to Stump outta guilt! Listen Fred, no matter what happened b'tween you 'n me, it don't change the fact that I still love Stump Jackson. He's still my husband and the father of my daughter. All the good lovin' in the world ain't gon' change that.

Yeah, he left me and went to Chicago, and for all I kno' he might've been with a hundred different girls by now but, the fact is I know Stump still loves me and my girl, why else would he keep com'in back to see us and send us money ever' month . . . . which is way mo' than I can say for you. (*Sighs*) Listen, I gotta go . . . . Stump'll be here any minute now and the last thing I want him ta see is me talkin' ta you on the phone . . . . Oh yeah, he'll kno' it's you alright . . . . how . . . . he just will. Yeah, Fred I wish you all the luck in the world too . . . . good-bye. (*Hangs up the phone*).

(JULIA *begins to do a gospel/blues moan, moves to the sofa and sits down to wait for* STUMP.)

ACT II

(It is dark. Totally dark. In the background we hear the sound of FREDDIE MAE'S *footsteps softly making her way on stage.* FREDDIE *calls her mother very softly. There is no answer,* JULIA *is sound asleep. Light: Fade in.* FREDDIE MAE *stands at the edge of her exit's threshold looking at her mother.)*

FREDDIE *(Softly)* Mama . . . . you woke? *(There is no answer.* JULIA *turns over in her sleep).*

JULIA *(In her sleep)* Stump . . . . that you, baby . . . come on ta bed.

*(*FREDDIE MAE *tips over to her mother and looks at her with a smile.* JULIA *turns over again and mumbles inaudible gibberish.* FREDDIE *laughs silently, claps her hand over mouth and tips hurriedly to the edge of the stage. Once there she sits down.)*

FREDDIE *(In a hushed tone)* Mama's callin' Daddy's name again . . . . she does that from time to time . . . . call Daddy's name. I guess she be dreaming 'bout the good old days when her and Daddy were together. Mama think I don't remember them days, but I do.

I remember the day when Daddy first left for Chicago. I was about seven or eight 'round then. I've must've cried every night for a solid month. I never did see Mama cry, but I know she did. She cried those silent tears . . . . you know . . . . the ones that really hurt, but don't show. Those are the kind of tears Mama cry almost every night since Daddy left. Maybe that's why she acts so mean and bitter all the time. I try to talk to Mama about it, but she won't listen. She says I'm too young to understand what she's going through. But that ain't true. I might be young, but I ain't dumb. I got eyes. I can see a whole lotta things goin' on 'round here.

Like that time when we was behind on our light bill and the light man told Mama that he wouldn' turn our lights off if she would do him a little favor. Boy! Mama stepped back, put her hands on her hips, got that head ta shakin' and man did she evermo' put a cussin' on that po' man. *(Chuckles)* He was so scared he left without even turnin' off our lights. It was just the same, the money came from Daddy in the mail that same evenin'. We were lucky . . . . and I thought, that day, that my Mama was the strongest woman in the whole world. *(Pause)* That night, I heard my Mama cryin' in her room. When I went over and knocked on the bedroom door I didn' get no answer so, I tried again only this time I knocked and asked her what was

wrong, she said (*Mocking* JULIA)   Nothin' baby . . . . nothin' a' tall,
go on back ta bed.

I knew she was just sayin' that to keep me from seeing her cry,
but wasn' nothing' else I could do 'cept go back ta bed and cry with
her. I used ta say ta myse'f if he was here none 'o this kinda mess
would be happin' . . . . But Daddy wasn' here . . . . he was nine
hundred miles away and wasn' nothin' he could do from Chicago, but
send money 'n and call like he was doin'.

I don't blame Daddy anymo' . . . . I think I understand why he
left now. Chicago's a big place . . . . full of all kinds things to do
and see . . . . And a whole lotta Black folkes do seem ta be gettin'
over up there.

Daddy wants to be a big famous Bluesman. He wants ta take his
music all around the world . . . . in ever' li'l' town and all the big
cities in the world. And he says that the only way ta do that is ta
put yo' music on records. I can understand that 'cause I wanna be
a bigtime writer for one o' them famous newspapers; and, maybe, be
an editor someday. That way, I could have my stuff all over the world
just like them other folkes . . . . I'd be famous too . . . . only this
time it be our side of the story gettin' told.

Mama keep tellin' me that one day I'll be able to do just that. But
she know good 'n well, I ain't gone be able ta do it here in Mississippi.
Ain't nothin' down here for a young Black person . . . . least not like
it is elsewhere. And yeah, I'm with Mama on one thang, I really love
Mississippi to the bottom of my heart . . . . but, I ain't scared ta
leave it . . . . 'cause I know that no matter where I go, Mississippi
gone follow . . . . 'cause I am Mississippi. (*Sounds of* STUMP's *harp
can be heard faintly in the background*)   Oh, oh, here come Daddy.
I better get outta here fo' Mama wakes up and find me sittin' here!

(*Exit* FREDDIE MAE. *Suddenly we hear the sound of* STUMP's *singing from back stage.*)

STUMP (*Singing*)   Oowee baby, why ya wanna do me like a dog.
I say oowee baby, why ya wanna do me
like a dog.
don't ya know I work real hard fo' ya baby.
keep ya livin' high on the hawg.

(STUMP *enters very softly so as not to disturb* JULIA, *but* JULIA
wakes up the instant STUMP *is on stage.* JULIA *rises and sits down
on the couch.*)

JULIA   You back, huh.
STUMP   Yeah.

JULIA I been tryin' ta wait up fo' ya.

STUMP So I see.

JULIA Where ya been?

STUMP Walkin' . . . .

JULIA Walkin' . . . . where?

STUMP I don't know where all I went. I just walked and walked 'till I got tired o' walkin'; then I went over to Mama Joe's fo' a cold beer and a pack 'a ciggerettes . . . . and you'll never guess who I saw.

JULIA Fred Nobles.

STUMP Yep, that's who it was, alright.

JULIA What happened!?

STUMP Oh nothing . . . .

JULIA What you mean nothin' happened!?

STUMP Nothin' to really talk about . . . . except we had a lil' fight.

JULIA What?! Y'all got ta fightin'!! (STUMP *nods his head*) Stump, how could you do that ta Fred?

STUMP What you mean, how could I do that ta that lowdown dirty dog!? Hell, Fred's the one who started it all. The only thang I did was finished it for him. (STUMP *holds up his fist*)

JULIA He didn' hurt you none, did he?

STUMP Naw . . . . the real question is what did I do ta him.

JULIA Stump, ya didn' hurt him, did ya?

STUMP Naw I didn' hurt 'em all that bad . . . . just cold cocked 'em a lil' bit . . . . he'll be alright once he come to.

JULIA Well Stump, how did it all start?

STUMP Julia, it all happened so damned fast, I can hardly remember it all.

JULIA Then just tell me what ya remember.

STUMP OK . . . . like I told you befo', after I got tired of walkin' I went over to Mama Joe's ta drink a beer and ta cool off some . . . . 'cause I was pretty damn mad at you; not so much for what you had done, but fo' who you had done it with. Fred Nobles was s'pose ta be my best friend. I sorta trusted him ta do me right . . . . and he didn'.

JULIA Stump . . . . I'm . . . .

STUMP Look baby, ain't no need fo' you ta go apologizing ta me. I knew that after 'while you was gone start ta see somebody. Hell, I ain't no fool . . . . I know you got needs, and I know that I ain't been here ta take care o' 'em either. I mean we all gotta have it some-times—I know that! It's just that I couldn' take the fact that Fred Nobles, my so-called best friend, was messin' around with my wife. For some reason that hurt me more'n anythang, baby.

JULIA   Stump, I done told ya I didn' mean fo' it ta happen that 'a way. I was just lonesom' and he was just always there . . . . I don't love 'em.

STUMP   Yeah, I know, but it still hurts.

JULIA   Well how do you think I felt when you went runnin' off ta Chicago and leavin' me here with a child ta raise by myself.

STUMP   Well if ya wanted another man why didn' ya just git a damn divorce then!?

JULIA   'Cause I don't wanna divorce . . . .

STUMP   Then what in the hell do you want?

JULIA   I want you, Stump, I want you.

STUMP   You don't really mean that.

JULIA   Yeah, I do.

STUMP   Then why in the world are we goin' through all o' this fuss every time I come home?

JULIA   I guess it's all my fault.

STUMP   Naw, it ain't all yo' fault, some of it is mine too . . . .

JULIA   Well then who the rest belong to?

STUMP (*Playfully*)   Mississippi.

(*They both laugh. After laughing there is a pause while* STUMP *lights a cigarette.*)

JULIA   Stump, you got a comb on ya?

STUMP   Yeah. (*Reaches in his jacket pocket and gives her a comb*) Here. (*There is a real tender moment of silence as* STUMP *watches* JULIA *comb her hair*)   Know somethin', baby.

JULIA   What's that, Stump?

STUMP   After all these years, you still the prettiest thang I ever laid eyes on.

JULIA (*Blushed*)   Why thank ya . . . . you don't look too bad yo'se'f . . . . city boy. (*They both laugh*)

STUMP   Ya know baby, all my life I been dreamin' 'bout bein' a famous Bluesman and playin' my music all over the world. But all I ever heard anybody say ta me was "Boy you know damn well you ain't gonna git nowhere playin' that mess . . . . don't you know that the Blues is the devil's music." So I grew up thinkin' that there must be somethin' wrong with me 'cause I can play the Blues better'n I can do anythang else. Then I had ta put up with people always tellin' me how I wasn' ever gonna amount ta nothin' 'cause I was so damn Black 'n ugly. Well I proved them all wrong! I showed them who's nothin'. I'm Stump "Hole" Jackson and I am a stone to the bone Bluesman. (*He plays a lick on his harp*)

JULIA   Stump . . . .

STUMP (*Puts harp down*)   Yeah.

JULIA   You never did tell me how that fight got started between you and Fred.

STUMP   I didn' did I? Okay, it started like I said, I was just sittin' at the bar over at Mama Joe's, mindin' my own bizness when in walked Fred Nobles, all lit up like a Christmas tree. At first I started ta go over and whoop his ass real good, but I thought about it and figured it wasn' worth the trouble. I mean it's like you said, it ain't like you both plan ta hurt me, it just kinda happened. So, I figured, why not just try ta just git the hell out befo' I'd changed my mind and go 'n do somethin' ta hurt Fred. After all, I was still mad as hell at the both of y'all. . . . but I still didn' wanna hurt nobody . . . . not me . . . . I ain't no fightin' man . . . . but naw, that doggone Fred Nobles just had ta say somethin' smart 'bout you.

JULIA   What did that no count negro say 'bout me?

STUMP   He said that you had the prettiest titties he'd ever seen in his whole entire life, and that included his wife.

JULIA   That lowdown dirty son-ova- . . . .

STUMP   But wait, I ain't told you the rest of it. He said that if he had a quarter fo' every time you 'n him did the 'doo', he'd have enough money ta buy everybody in Mama Joe's a fish plate and a cold plate and still have money left ta buy me a one-way ticket back to Chicago. That's when I cold cocked him! (*Hits his palm with his fist*) Baby, you should've seen the look on his face when his butt hit the ground. (*Chuckles*)   He looked like a klansman who just staggled into NAACP rally. (*Chuckles some more*)

JULIA   You must'a hit him pretty hard, huh?

STUMP   Hard!? Baby, I hit that negro so hard, he flew over six chairs and three tables!

JULIA   Then what'd you do?

STUMP   I left . . . . did some walkin' . . . . and then came home.

JULIA   Listen, Stump, I'm real sorry 'bout all this . . . . I didn' mean for all o' this mess ta happen.

STUMP   Look, let's just fo'get about the whole thang . . . . and try 'n git on with our lives.

JULIA   You real serious 'bout that, ain't ya?

STUMP   As serious as I'll ever be.

JULIA   Then where do we go from here?

STUMP   I don't know. It's really all on you.

JULIA   Me!? Why's it gotta all be on me? Why can't it be on you some?

STUMP Cause, you the one that don't want ta move.

JULIA And I ain't gonna move either.

STUMP Julia, you know, you 'bout as stubborn as a mule.

JULIA And you 'bout as swift as one if you think I gone pick up and run off ta Chicago with you. I done told you I ain't goin' and that's that . . . . besides we ain't got no place ta stay 'sides that lil' matchbox Freddie told me you stayed in . . . . I don' like livin' in no apartment . . . . I don't like it!

STUMP You ain't got ta live in one . . . .

JULIA I know I ain't 'cause I ain't going.

STUMP Naw, that ain't what I mean . . . . You see I done bought us a lil' house.

JULIA What'd you say!?

STUMP I said I done got us a house.

JULIA You lyin', Stump.

STUMP I swear fo' the Lawd God almighty hisse'f . . . . (*Reaches into his inside jacket pocket*) Look, here's the deed. (*Gives the deed to* JULIA)

JULIA Well I'll be damn, you sho' wasn' lyin'.

STUMP I told you I was serious 'bout you 'n Freddie.

JULIA Then why didn' you just tell me 'bout this over the phone.

STUMP 'Cause you wouldn' believe me 'till you see it with yo' own two eyes . . . . besides, I kinda wanted ta surprize you with it.

JULIA Well you sho' did that, alright.

STUMP Does that mean you gone come?

JULIA Naw, it means that you just surprized me . . . .

STUMP Now look Julia, I done come a mighty long way to get y'all and I ain't gone sit here and let you disappoint me like this. I want a answer and I want it right now!

JULIA You already know the answer . . . .

STUMP Well, I wanna another one . . . . yes.

JULIA Can't give ya that one.

STUMP Well you better give me somthin'.

JULIA Okay, then, I'll think about it some.

STUMP Think about it!? What's there ta think about!? If I was you, I'd be itchin' ta git the hell outta here on the P.D.Q.

JULIA Well I ain't you and I sho' ain't itching ta run away on the first thang smokin! I just can't pick up and run off ta some big city like you can. I like livin' down here . . . . and I don't hate this land, like you do, Stump.

STUMP Look Julia, my leavin' Mississippi ain't got nothin' ta do with this here land. This good earth ain't never done anythang bad ta me.

Naw, I don't hate no piece 'a land, it's just some people I can't stand; and as it turns out, most of the people I can't stand the most just happen ta run this state.

JULIA   Aw, Stump, thangs like that are gonna be changin' soon . . . . there's a new day a' comin' fo' us down here in Mississippi, and I intend ta see that Freddie Mae gits a part of it.

STUMP   Well, the way I see it, that new day is a long long time comin' and neither one of us can afford ta stay 'round here and wait fo' it ta come. We gotta do what's best for us right here 'n now.

You know that this state is last in just about everythang . . . . and I do mean everythang! Education, healthcare, job opportunities . . . . you name it, chances are Mississippi is at the bottom of the list. And ya wanna know why? 'Cause all these damn rednecks and good ole boy politicians spend too much time and energy tryin' ta keep us po' Black folkes down. These ole funky white folkes are so damn blind, they can't even see that everytime they cut us down, they be bleedin' right along with us. Hell, if they would spend all o' that time, energy and money ta do what's best fo' all o' the people of this state, Mississippi would be a real promised land . . . . but as it is right now, Mississippi ain' nothin' but a livin' hell for po' Black folkes.

JULIA   But thangs are changin', Stump.

STUMP   Yeah, but not fast enough fo' me. I can't make it down here, baby . . . . not like I can up in Chicago. They just too many thangs workin' against me down here.

JULIA   It's thangs workin' against you up there too. In fact the same thangs that worked against you up there are the same thangs that were workin' against you down here. Hell, when it comes ta racist white folkes ain't no such thang as a Mason-Dixon line . . . . this is America all over.

STUMP   Yeah, well at least up north they got sense enough ta try and fool ya into thinkin' that everythang's gonna be alright. (*Pause*)   Hey, I got another surprize fo' ya. I'm gonna put out a record.

JULIA   Say what?

STUMP   I'm gonna put out a record.

JULIA   Now how you gon' do that?

STUMP   I got me a recordin' contract.

JULIA   With who?

STUMP   Work Song Records.

JULIA   Never heard o' em.

STUMP   It's one of them small independent record companies outta Chicago. You know the Blues is really a big thang in Chicago and all the big cities up north . . . . over in Europe too. A Blues musician can really make a decent livin' fo' himse'f providin' he's willin' ta work hard and stick to it. It's like once you git that good break you almost there . . . . and baby, I'm almost there.

JULIA   How do you know they ain't gone rob you blind . . . . take yo' music 'n sell it all over the world and not give you one red cent.

STUMP   'Cause I've already check them out. They seem like pretty good folkes.

JULIA   And what 'bout yo' job at the post office?

STUMP   I plan ta keep it fo' the time being. I don't know how good the record's gonna do . . . . and I can't afford ta take any chances . . . . I still gotta family ta feed. (*Pause*) Julia, I really want thangs ta work out between us . . . . baby, ya gotta believe me.

JULIA   I'm beginnin' to.

STUMP   Then why won't you come back with me?

JULIA   Well ta tell the truth, right now, I don't know if I could really trust ya after all these years.

STUMP   So that's it . . . . you still think I'm gone run out on you again.

JULIA   If you were me, wouldn' you?

STUMP   Yeah, I guess I would . . . . but I ain't gonna do that, Julia . . . . I swear I ain't.

JULIA   And I'm s'pose to believe that?

STUMP   You got to.

JULIA   Why?

STUMP   'Cause I need you, baby. I really don't see how I made it this far without you. It sho' wasn' easy . . . . and it damn sho wasn' fun. (*Pause*) Listen Julia, I know you don't trust me like ya used to; and I really don't blame ya if you don't ever want ta go anywhere with me, but ya gotta believe that I love. I really do, baby . . . . and if ya just give me one mo' chance, I swear fo' Gawd, I'm gonna spend the rest of my natural born life makin' up fo' all the hurt and pain I done caused you . . . . but ya just gotta trust me enough to take one mo' chance on me . . . . just one mo.

(FREDDIE MAE *appears on stage. She stands at her exit unnoticed by her parents*)

JULIA   Well . . . . I . . . .

FREDDIE   Go on Mama . . . . say yeah.

JULIA (*Shocked, she turns toward* FREDDIE *who walks closer to the two*)   Freddie Mae, what in the world are you doin' up at this time of night . . . . and eavesdroppin' at that!

FREDDIE   Mama, I wasn' eavesdroppin' . . . . I was just going to the bathroom and I just couldn' help but overhear y'all fussin' and fightin'. So I came out here to see what's the matter.

JULIA   You don't need ta know anythang 'bout this . . . . this is grown up's bizness . . . . you way too young ta understand any o' this.

FREDDIE   Mama, I may be young and I may not be married, but that don't mean that I can't understand what goin' on. I ain't no chap no mo' mama . . . .

JULIA   Well you sho' ain' no woman . . . . so if I was you I'd watch my mouth!

FREDDIE   Mama, I don't mean no disrespect.

JULIA   You bet' not mean any.

FREDDIE   All I'm tryin' ta say is that we suppose ta be a family, Mama . . . . and family's suppose ta stick together and work thangs out.

STUMP   That's right, baby, that's sho nuff right.

FREDDIE   Mama, I was kinda young when daddy first left for Chicago, but I wasn't too young to remember him askin' you to go with him. I remember him askin' you to come to Chicago each and every time he came back ta visit . . . . And every time you told him no. To tell you the truth, Mama, I always felt like somethin' was wrong 'bout us not going to Chicago with Daddy.

JULIA   Yo' Daddy left us!

FREDDIE   Yeah Mama, I know that, and I'm not sayin' that what he did was right, but I still think that our not supportin' him wasn' right either . . . . there's wrong on both sides Mama.

JULIA   So what ya want me ta do 'bout it?

FREDDIE   Stop tryin' to make Daddy feel so guilty for what he's done. It's over and done with. What we all need to be doing is workin' out all y'all problems so we can move on with our lives.

JULIA   Have you forgave yo' Daddy?

FREDDIE   Yeah Mama, I have forgiven him.

JULIA   So I guess you gone want ta up and leave this place too, huh?

FREDDIE   To tell the truth, I wouldn' mind it.

JULIA   Why!?

FREDDIE   Ain't no real opportunities for me down here, Mama.

STUMP   Gone girl, tell it like tis.

JULIA   But I thought you wanted ta go on ta college and write fo' one o' these newspapers down here?

FREDDIE   Oh, I still want ta go ta college and be a reporter, but not down here.

JULIA   Why?

STUMP   The girl just told ya why, Julia, there ain't nothin' here for her.

JULIA She never thought that way 'til I let her spend that summer with you in Chicago.

FREDDIE Mama, I've always felt this way . . . . even before you let me stay with Daddy.

JULIA And I s'pose you hate Mississippi too, huh?

FREDDIE No I don't Mama . . . . I can't . . . . Mississippi's too much of a part of who I am and what I aim to be. But understand Mama, that the Mississippi that I know and love is totally different from the Mississippi that they be tryin' to push to us on T.V. My Mississippi is a state full of people I know and love.

STUMP Amen, Freddie Mae, I couldn've said it any better myself.

FREDDIE Well, wait a minute Daddy, 'cause I got a few words to give to you.

STUMP Ta me!?

FREDDIE Yeah . . . . 'cause I been listenin' to you talk bad about Mississippi for as long as I can remember now. And I can understand how ya feel . . . . God knows, I've felt that way myself every once in a while . . . . but I still don't hate this place.

STUMP Now wait a minute Freddie . . . .

FREDDIE Naw, now Daddy, you done had your say for the longest of time, so just listen to me for a change, okay. (STUMP *says nothing, just nods his head*) 'Bout how long have you been playin' the Blues, Daddy—almost all yo' life right?

STUMP Yeah.

FREDDIE Daddy, have you ever stop to think that ever time you play the Blues you be praisin' the great spirit of all the people who've ever suffered through life down here so that we could take ourselves just a lil' bit further than where we were befo'.

   The Blues is our music Daddy. There ain't no way you can play it the way you do and not feel the true spirit of Mississippi . . . . I mean, I'm talkin 'bout the Blues spirit. Shoot, it ain't nothin' but the naturalness of our big beautiful boot black souls wailin'.

   Yeah Daddy, like it or not, Mississippi is still yo' home and all the runnin' in the world ain't gonna get you away from home . . . . so ya better learn ta love it now, 'cause it's gonna be with you 'til the day you die. You know what I mean?

STUMP Yeah, I think I do.

JULIA If he don't I do.

STUMP I know what she's talkin' 'bout.

JULIA Well act like it then.

STUMP I'll try if you agree to do yo' part.

JULIA What's that?

STUMP   Come back ta Chicago with me.

JULIA   Now Stump you know . . . .

STUMP   Look I know what you gonna say . . . .

JULIA   Naw you don't. . . .

STUMP   You gon' say yeah?

JULIA   Naw.

STUMP   Well then.

JULIA   But I was going to say that I will come visit ya for a few days
. . . . and . . . . if I think that thangs gon' work out I might . . . .
I say I might just think about stayin' for a while.

FREDDIE   Alright! (*She hugs* JULIA)

STUMP   That's my baby! (*Hugs* FREDDIE *and* JULIA)

FREDDIE   Looks like we gon' be a family again.

STUMP   Sho do, don't it.

FREDDIE (*Yawns*)   Well I guess I'd better go on ta bed now.

JULIA   Yeah, 'cause woke or not you gonna get up and take yo butt
on ta school.

FREDDIE   Yeah, Mama, I know. Goodnight y'all. (*Exit* FREDDIE
MAE)

STUMP   Night night, baby.

(*Afterwards there's a brief moment of silence.* STUMP *breaks the
silence by playing his harp softly.* JULIA *smiles and moves closer
to her husband. She is smiling while* STUMP *is playing.*)

JULIA   Stump, that's a real pretty song, what's the name of it?

STUMP   Guess.

JULIA   I don't know, what is it.

STUMP   Black Gal.

(*They both laugh as* JULIA *falls into* STUMP'S *arms. The laughter
subsides.*)

JULIA   Know somethin', Stump?

STUMP   What's that, baby?

JULIA   I know I gave you holy hell every time you came back down
here, but deep down inside I was always glad that you kept on comin'.

STUMP   So am I, baby . . . . so am I.

(*They kiss*)

CURTAIN

Wings

LARRY BROWN

CHARACTERS

CLARENCE, LEON, VERA, IRENE

SETTING

The story takes place in Jackson.

ACT I

(*A shabby, crowded room containing a bed and a kitchenette, cheap furniture. There is a table at center stage and two chairs flanking it. An old worn sofa has magazines piled up on it. A woman in her early sixties is preparing cereal at the table. There is a cot in the room and on the cot lies a big shapeless lump wrapped in quilts. Clothes are hung along the walls, indicating an absence of adequate closets. The room is the cheapest of government housing. There is a door in the left wall and a door in the right wall*)

IRENE Clarence? (*Turning briefly to the bed*) Come on, now. Get up. It's nine o'clock. Get up out of that bed.

(*The lump stirs beneath the quilts, but no sound comes out from under them, only a shifting, a turning and moving, as if whoever is under them is seeking a better place to rest*)

Clarence. Clarence! Get up now.

(IRENE *has the cereal in the bowl but she's waiting to pour the milk. She puts one hand on her hip and adjusts her glasses. She licks one finger and flips a page on a newspaper lying on the table, her lips moving as she reads*)

CLARENCE   Ummasheepsomomama. (*The voice under the quilts is badly muffled; it's not clear what he's saying*)

IRENE   What? (*Glancing in his direction, then back to the paper*) Come on and get up, honey. Mama's got your breakfast ready. I wish you'd look in this paper what it says about these people up in Chicago.

CLARENCE   Cartoons on?

IRENE   Nope. Today's not Saturday.

CLARENCE (*Pause*)   I want to watch cartoons.

IRENE   You can't. They're not on today. Get up.

CLARENCE   What's on?

IRENE   I don't know. You get up.

CLARENCE   Aw mama.

IRENE (*Reads some more, then looks at him*)   I'm fixin to pour this milk. (*She holds the carton of milk over the bowl*) You better get up.

CLARENCE (*In a disgusted voice*)   Aw mama don't pour it yet.

IRENE   You get out of that bed. It's nine o'clock.

CLARENCE   Aw mama. I don't want to get up.

IRENE   Well you've got to. Aunt Vera's coming over this morning and you've got to be up when she gets here.

CLARENCE   Aint Vera?

IRENE   That's right. (*She sets the milk down, goes back to reading*)

CLARENCE   What's she comin over for?

IRENE   She's just coming for a visit. Now you get up.

CLARENCE   Aw mama. Just let me sleep a little bit.

IRENE   No sir. You get up right this minute.

(*A little time passes, maybe fifteen or twenty seconds. She is reading and he is trying to go back to sleep*)

CLARENCE   What time's Let's Make a Deal come on?

(IRENE *is not paying attention; she's reading and shaking her head over some bad news in the paper*)

Mama you know what?

IRENE   What, dear? (*Distracted, not really hearing what he's saying*)

CLARENCE   Let's move.

(*She doesn't seem to hear him. He uncovers part of his head. He watches her reading. He has a blue toboggan rolled down on his head. He begins to sit up in the bed, gathering the quilts about him. He has a heavy, slow drugged-sounding voice)*

I don't like it here.

IRENE   Come on and eat your cereal, dear. Mama's got a lot to do today. (*Talking to the paper*)

CLARENCE   It ain't nothin to do around here.

(*He sits on the edge of the cot, pulling the quilts slowly up over his head. He pulls one quilt up until his head is completely covered and the rest of it hangs over him like a poncho. He rises, tottering, in a Frankenstein walk.* IRENE *is busy reading*)

Ahhhhhhhh. Arrrrrr. (*He stands erect, his arms extended stiffly before him*)

Whur's your daddy, little girl. I'm gonna eat you up. I'm gonna eat all your sheep up. (*His legs are splayed; he's walking as if he doesn't have knees, getting closer and closer to* IRENE)   I'm gonna eat all them sheep up, little girl. Then I'm gonna eat you up. (*A hollow, demented laughter comes*)   Arrrrr.

(*He grabs his mother from behind and puts his arms around her. He's still got the quilt over his head and she's trying to read the paper. He's growling now*)

IRENE   Clarence. (*Trying to shrug him off*)

CLARENCE   I done eat all them chickens in the barn up, little girl. You look like you got some good juicy meat on you, I guess I'll just eat you up too.

(*He picks her up like a toy and she starts to kick and protest. He's gnawing at her neck through the quilt, growling viciously, but then he starts laughing*)

IRENE   Clarence, you silly thing. Put me down.

CLARENCE (*He holds her in his arms, swinging his head ponderously beneath the quilt*)   Ahhhhhh.

IRENE   Clarence. Clarence! You put me down. (*He stops, but still holds her aloft*)

IRENE   Oh! Clarence! You're hurting me! You don't know how strong you are.

CLARENCE   Aw I ain't hurting you. I'm just playin.

IRENE   You play too rough for me.

CLARENCE   Arrrrrrr? (*He shakes her*)   You scared. Ain't you? Little girl.

IRENE   Ooo yes I'm just scared to death.

CLARENCE   You don't want me to eat all your Sheep up do you?

IRENE   Oh no. Oh . . . Clarence. Please. My heart . . .

CLARENCE   You gonna fix me some breakfast if I don't eat all your Sheep up?

IRENE   Oh yes sir. (*She's about to pass out*)

CLARENCE   What you gonna fix me?

IRENE   I'll fix you some frosted flakes.

CLARENCE (*He waits for a moment*)   All right, little girl.

(*He sets her down and then pulls the quilt sideways off his head and stands spraddlelegged before her in a pajama top and shorts. He is a large man of indeterminate age and simple demeanor with a happy, childlike grin. Completely uninhibited.* IRENE *limps back to the table and holds one hand over her heart. She glances down at him*)

IRENE   Where's your pajamas?

CLARENCE   I scared you didn't I mama? Boy mama I scared you that time. I bet you's bout to doodoo all over yourself. (*He starts putting the quilt on the bed, folding it*)

IRENE (*Goes to the bed*)   Where *are* your pajamas? (*She searches among the sheets and finally finds them. She holds them up to him*)
   (*Sudden rage*)   Why didn't you sleep in your pajamas? Now you tell me! What did I tell you about not sleeping in your pajamas?

CLARENCE (*His countenance changes from happiness to fear. He speaks in a pleading voice*)   Mama.

IRENE   Have you been nasty again? Have you? (*She holds the pajamas up and shakes them*)

CLARENCE (*Shakes his head dumbly*)   No mama.

IRENE   You tell me the truth! You answer me!

CLARENCE (*Backs away and turns around and looks back at her. He can't take his eyes off her face*)   I ain't done nothin mama.

IRENE   What did I tell you?

CLARENCE   I didn't do it, mama!

IRENE   Yes you did!

CLARENCE   I didn't! Mama I didn't!

(*He breaks down and starts crying. She is furious. She hurries and gets a pair of rumpled pants off a hanger on the wall, knocking down other things in her haste. She goes to him and kneels in front of him, holding the pants out for him. She shakes them impatiently*)

IRENE   Here. You put these on.

CLARENCE   Mama.

(He starts stepping into the pants and she helps him get them on. He pulls them up and fastens them with his head lowered)

I ain't done nothin mama. I ain't.

IRENE   Then why didn't you have your pajamas on?

CLARENCE *(In a pitiful, broken voice)*   I don't know mama. I get hot.

IRENE   What did I tell you would happen if you did that again? What did I tell you?

CLARENCE *(He's almost through crying and now there is a note of defiance in his voice)*   Mama I ain't *done* nothin. I ain't *done* nothin mama.

IRENE   Don't you remember what I said? What they do to little boys who are not good? Who do nasty things with themselves?

CLARENCE   Ain't done nothin nasty, mama. Just took my jamas off.

IRENE   You get over and sit down. You put your shoes on.

(CLARENCE goes to the cot and sits. IRENE is still on the floor, searching for his shoes and socks)

The idea. Where's your shoes? Where did you take them off?

CLARENCE   I don't know, mama. I forgot.

IRENE *(She comes up with one sock and hands it to him)*   Put that sock on.

CLARENCE *(He obeys)*   All riiiight.

IRENE   I talk to you and talk to you and . . . *(She looks up, horrified by something she's just thought of)*   Have you got any more of those books?

CLARENCE *(He's puzzled)*   Books? *My* books?

IRENE   No. Here's your other sock. Here's your shoes. *(She pulls a pair of tennis shoes from under the cot and starts helping him put them on, kneeling in front of him)*
(Viciously)   You know what I mean. Those dirty books. Like you had before. The ones I got so sick over.

CLARENCE   I got my animal books. I got that snake book.

IRENE   Don't you do me like that.

CLARENCE   Like what?

IRENE   You know what I'm talking about. I mean those dirty magazines, those nasty magazines. Pick up your foot. With those naked women in them. Have you brought some more of them home?

CLARENCE   Naw mama. I ain't got none of them. You said I couldn't have no more of them. Don't you remember, mama? I had one cost three dollars and you burnt it up. Don't you remember, mama?

IRENE   Hold still. I wish you'd learn how to tie your shoes. You know what the doctor said about my heart. You know any excitement is bad for my heart. Do you want me to have another stroke? What would happen to you then?

CLARENCE   I don't know.

IRENE   I better not catch you with any more of those books. You know what I'll have to do, don't you?

CLARENCE   Uh huh.

IRENE   What?

CLARENCE (*Pause*)   Whip me.

IRENE   That's right. You think mama likes to whip you? You think mama enjoys you getting a whipping?

CLARENCE (*Turns sullen*)   I don't know. Don't hurt no way.

IRENE   Well. What do you think would happen if Aunt Vera came over here and found a dirty book lying around?

CLARENCE   I don't know. Fuss. Mama? Why did Aint Vera make us move out of her house? Does she not like me?

IRENE   Of course she likes you. Aunt Vera loves you.

CLARENCE   She wants me to go back to school.

IRENE   I don't want to hear any more of that nonsense. (*She finishes tying his shoes*)   Nobody's going to send you to school. Do you think mama would let anybody send you to school?

CLARENCE   I don't know. (*Pause*)   I kinda liked school.

IRENE (*Gets up from the floor wearily*)   Well. That's all settled. Now. Come on and eat your breakfast.

CLARENCE (*Pouting now*)   I ain't hungry.

IRENE   Come on now. Mama's got your cereal all ready. Sit down at the table and eat. Be a good boy. Mama's tired. I didn't sleep good last night. My heart hurt me all night long.

CLARENCE   I don't want to eat nothin. I want to watch tv.

IRENE   You can't watch tv. Vera's coming over and we've got to talk. You've got to eat and go out and play.

CLARENCE   Ain't nobody to play with around here.

IRENE   Well then you can go down to the store. You can go talk to Mr. Clark. He might need you to help him some today. You might could make a little money helping him.

CLARENCE   I don't want to go out.

IRENE   Why not? Come on and eat. (*She pulls him up by the hand and leads him to the table*)

Come on, now. Sit down and eat. Aunt Vera'll be here in a little bit.

CLARENCE (*As he sits*) I'm afraid I'll see Leon if I go out. (*He stares at his cereal as if he doesn't know what it is*)

IRENE Oh, you won't see Leon. Leon's in jail. I told you that. I don't know what you're worried about him for anyway. You're twice as big as him.

CLARENCE (*Looks up at her where she's doing something at the stove*) Mama?

IRENE What, dear?

CLARENCE How long's Leon have to stay in jail? How long you have to stay in jail?

IRENE I don't know. It depends on what you do, I guess. If you do something real bad they keep you in jail for a long time. Like if you kill somebody or something, then they keep you in jail for a long long time.

CLARENCE Did Leon do somethin real bad?

IRENE He wrote some bad checks to Mr. Clark.

CLARENCE Is that real bad?

IRENE Well. It's not good. It's the same thing as stealing when you know a check is bad. It's the same thing as robbing Mr. Clark.

CLARENCE I like Mr. Clark.

IRENE I do too. Mr. Clark's a nice man. (*She sighs*) I don't know what we'd do if it wasn't for people like Mr. Clark. (*She goes over to the table and pours the milk on his cereal and he starts eating immediately, the spoon gripped in his fist*)

CLARENCE I hope they keep Leon in jail for a long long time. (IRENE *picks up the paper and starts reading again*)

IRENE Yes dear.

CLARENCE I don't like Leon.

IRENE Don't worry about him, dear.

CLARENCE I do. I worry about Leon all the time.

IRENE I don't know why.

CLARENCE Cause. He's mean.

IRENE (*Not looking up now. She's absorbed in the paper*) Eat your breakfast now.

CLARENCE He's real mean. (*He looks at her with a silent plea*) That's why I don't want to go out. He . . . . does bad stuff. (*He lowers his head and resumes eating*)

IRENE (*She hasn't appeared to be listening but she raises her head now and looks at him*) Has Leon done anything to you?

CLARENCE (*Shakes his head quickly and vigorously*) No ma'am.

IRENE   Are you sure?

CLARENCE   Yes ma'am. (*He busies himself eating and keeping his mouth full so he can't talk*)

IRENE   Then how do you know he's so mean?

CLARENCE   I just do. These kids told me he was mean. These kids that live down here. They told me not to mess with Leon.

IRENE (*Laughs lightly*)   Oh, those kids. Those kids'll tell you anything because they know you'll believe it. Don't you know that? Like when they told you there was a mad dog loose and you ran all the way home? Scared to death? You can't listen to one thing those kids say. (*She goes back to the paper*)

CLARENCE   Well they said Leon was mean and he is. He did that check thing to Mr. Clark and it made Mr. Clark mad.

IRENE   I guess so. It would make me mad if somebody stole some of my money.

CLARENCE (*Stops eating*)   It would?

IRENE   It certainly would. Finish eating, dear. I've got to wash your bowl. Aunt Vera will be here soon.

CLARENCE   Mama? If you lost some of your money would it make you mad? If you lost some?

IRENE   Well . . . I don't guess it'd make me mad. I'd be sorry I lost it. I might be mad at myself.

CLARENCE (*Desperately trying to tell her something with his eyes*)   I member that time I lost that money. That made you mad. You got real mad. When I lost that grocery money. You member that time?

IRENE   Yes I do.

CLARENCE   Boy you got real mad about that, mama.

IRENE   Oh, let's don't talk about that again. That's all over and done with now. That was a long time ago. When we first moved here.

CLARENCE   That was when Mr. Clark gave us some groceries cause we didn't have any money.

IRENE   No, honey. Mr. Clark gave us some groceries because you *lost* our money.

CLARENCE   I got some money.

IRENE   You do?

CLARENCE   Uh huh. I been savin it. You know what I'm gonna buy with it?

IRENE   What?

CLARENCE (*Smiling shyly*)   Gonna buy you a birthday present.

IRENE   You don't have to buy me a birthday present. (*She looks the paper up and down, licks a finger and turns a page*)   You should spend your money on yourself.

CLARENCE   I want to spend it on you. Cause I lost yours that time and made you so mad. (*He has a look of incredible guilt on his face*)
   I'm gonna make some more money this summer cuttin people's yards and stuff. I'm gonna save it all up and you know what I'm gonna do with it? I'm gonna buy our house back where we used to live so we can move back there.

IRENE   Well. I doubt if we'll ever get to move back there, honey. Aunt Vera is renting that house now. Some other people are living there now.

CLARENCE   I like to cut yards.

IRENE   There's not many yards around here, honey. When you live in an apartment you don't have a yard.

CLARENCE   We had a pretty yard.

IRENE   We sure did. We had the prettiest yard on our street. Are you through eating?

CLARENCE   Almost. I wish we still lived in our house.

IRENE   It wasn't our house, honey. It was always Aunt Vera's house.

CLARENCE   How long are them people gonna keep livin in our house?

IRENE   I don't know. It doesn't matter. The important thing is for you and me to be together.

CLARENCE (*Shakes his head slowly*)   I don't like this place. It stinks. We ain't got no yard. (*He stops eating now, and she goes over and gets the bowl*)

IRENE   Did you get enough?

CLARENCE (*Dully*)   I get tard climbin all them steps.

IRENE (*Cheerfully*)   Things could be worse, too. (*She goes to the sink and clatters things around.*)
   Count your blessings, that's what I always say. We've got a roof over our heads and something to eat.

CLARENCE   Nothin good. Old rice and stuff. I don't like them old beans and junk. (*He glowers suddenly at the table*)   That old stuff makes me want to puke.

IRENE   Now you just stop talking like that. I do the best I can. Get over there and straighten up your bed and pick up those books. You hear?

CLARENCE   Aw mama.

IRENE   Go on. You mind me.

CLARENCE   I don't want to. I want to watch tv.

IRENE   No. If you start watching that tv you'll watch it all day.

CLARENCE (*Sullen*)   I want to watch Let's Make a Deal.

IRENE   No. Get over there and make up your bed.

CLARENCE (*Sudden anger. He yells*)   I want to watch Let's Make a Deal! Shit!

I R E N E (*Jerks around from the sink*)   What did you say?

C L A R E N C E   I said I . . .

I R E N E   Before that! (*She goes to the table and stands over him*)
I mean—after that! What did you say?

C L A R E N C E (*Stands up and screams into her face*)   I SAID I WANT
TO WATCH LET'S MAKE A DEAL!

I R E N E (*Points to cot*)   You get over there and make up that bed young
man. This instant!

C L A R E N C E (*Pushes past her and heads toward the tv, a small set on
top of the counter*)   I'm gonna watch my show.

I R E N E (*Tries to hold him back*)   Clarence. Clarence, you stop! (*She
pushes against his chest. He tries to keep her hands off him as he
advances on the tv*)
You better mind me! I'm your mother!

C L A R E N C E   I want to watch Bob Barker! You hear me? I want to
watch my show!

I R E N E (*Struggling with everything she's got to hold him back. He breaks
away, pushes past her easily*)   You make up your bed! You . . . (*She
stops and sobs, once, deeply. Her voice is broken and quavering*)
You big baby! (*She rushes after him, tugging at him. He's turning
on the tv*)
You mind me! Do you hear?

C L A R E N C E (*Turns on her savagely*)   I don't want to mind you! Don't
have to mind you! You can't make me! I want to go back home!

I R E N E   You don't have a home! This is it! This is the only one you've
got!

C L A R E N C E   I do too have a home! And it's got a yard! And a swing!
I want my dog back!

I R E N E   Well I want a lot of things too! I want you to make up your
bed! Right now! (*She snaps the knob off*)

C L A R E N C E (*Snaps it back on*)   Leave it *alone* mama. (I R E N E goes
and gets a cloth belt, brings it back, starts whipping his legs weakly
while he stands there like a rock*)

I R E N E   Now you just mind me! You hear me? You just mind me right
now!

C L A R E N C E   You know what that feels like? That feels like about a
bee sting, at's what that feels like. It don't even hurt.

I R E N E   I'll make it hurt. You just watch me!

C L A R E N C E *Snatches the belt from her, throws it out across the stage*)
Now let's see you whip me.

I R E N E (*Stamps her foot*)   Quit it! You stop it! Clarence! Clarence, if
you don't mind me . . .

C L A R E N C E (*Guards the tv with his body*)   Want to watch tv, mama.

IRENE (*Her voice is wavering and without strength*) You're disobeying me. I won't put up with this defiance any more. Clarence, do you hear me? Get away from that tv! (IRENE *goes to him and tries to physically separate him from the television. He shrugs her off. She doubles her fists and hits his shoulders and neck. He ducks his head and simply endures these blows*)

Damn it! You big . . . you big bully!

CLARENCE Oww! Durn it, mama! (*She hits his ear*) Oh! You hurtin, mama!

IRENE I mean to hurt you! I mean to make you mind once and for all!

CLARENCE You better quit it, mama. Mama!

(*He shoves her back, into the cabinet. She slips and almost falls, then clutches the counter*

IRENE That's right, just push your mother! Talk ugly to her. Bring home dirty books and do dirty things . . .

CLARENCE (*Moves away from the tv and goes back to his cot, his head down, his lower lip pooched out*) You're mean, mama.

IRENE (*Follows him, still talking as he goes to the cot*) I have to be mean. I have to talk awful to you to get you to mind. Because you're just a spoiled baby! A baby!

CLARENCE (*Gets on the cot and pulls the covers up over his head*) Hush mama.

IRENE (*Stands over him with clenched fists*) I do the best I can. I try to feed you and give us a place to live and you're not happy. You think I like it here?

CLARENCE (*Jerks his head out from under the covers long enough to yell*) You moved us here! (*Jerks it back under*)

IRENE I had to! There's no place else to go! Oh, God.

(*Long pause. She hangs her head and moves listlessly to the table and pulls out a chair and drops into it. She puts her head on the table and cries into her arms.* CLARENCE *doesn't move under the quilts*)

I'm sorry. Oh honey, I'm so sorry. Why do you make me talk to you like this? Don't you know I'm doing the best I can? (*She raises her head to address him*) You used to be so good when you were little. Your father and I, we were so proud of you. (*She gets up and goes to a box of tissues on the counter and starts to dry her eyes*)

If your father had lived, maybe we'd have something and wouldn't have to depend on Vera. I don't like it here. But don't you understand?

We have to stay here. This is our home now. If you don't mind me, if I can't control you . . . Clarence? Are you listening? I'm trying to protect you. You're the only thing I've got that's mine. (*Pause*) Don't you know how easy it would be for me to lose you? (*A knock comes on the outside of the left door, three quick raps*)

VERA (*Offstage, dimly*) Irene?

IRENE (*Hurries to the bed, pulling at* CLARENCE) That's Vera! Clarence, get up. Vera's here. (*She pulls the cover off his head*)
Just a minute, Vera! Help me get this straightened up.

(CLARENCE *gets up quickly and starts picking up the books scattered at the foot of the bed.* IRENE *hurriedly folds the quilt*)

CLARENCE Where's my shirt, mama?

IRENE I don't know. Hurry. Coming, Vera. I've got to let her in. Just sit down. Put your books up.

VERA (*Knocks again*) Irene?

IRENE Coming. Oh, my hair. (*She tries to rearrange it with her fingers*)

CLARENCE Where you want me to put em, mama?

IRENE Just anywhere. I've got to let her in. (*She crosses to the door and opens it.* VERA *steps in. She is an attractive woman in her forties. She is dressed as if she holds some influential job*)
Did you think I wasn't coming?

VERA I was starting to wonder. (*She looks around*) What are you doing, rearranging the furniture? (*She hugs* IRENE) It's good to see you. (*She smiles at* CLARENCE, *then goes to him and hugs him. He doesn't know what to do, doesn't return the hug, just stands holding the books*) Hey, Clarence.

CLARENCE Hey Aint Vera.

VERA Have you been reading your books?

CLARENCE I been lookin at em, yeah.

IRENE Say yes ma'am, honey.

CLARENCE Yes ma'am.

IRENE Come on and sit down, Vera. We were just trying to clean up a little. It's so crowded we don't have room for everything. (*This line and next are said a little too cheerfully*)
I guess we're just not used to having such a small space. (*She moves back and pulls out chairs from the table*)

VERA I'll get you some more sometime, Clarence. I meant to stop by the library this morning and look for some. I was just in such a rush. You ought to get him a library card, Irene. You could ride the bus over there. Or I could take you over one day.

IRENE (*She sits*)   Oh, we don't get out much. Clarence, put the books down and put on your shirt. Then you can run down to the park while Aunt Vera and I talk. (CLARENCE *starts putting his books away*)

VERA (*Takes her coat off*)   The park? That's two blocks away. It's cold out there anyway. The halls in this place are like ice.

(*She sets her purse and coat on the bed and sits in the chair* IRENE *has drawn out for her.* CLARENCE *unbuttons his pajama top*)

IRENE   Clarence? Uh uh, honey, not in here. Don't undress in front of Aunt Vera. Take your shirt and go in the bathroom and change. Go on.

VERA (*Frowning as* CLARENCE, *chastened, gets his shirt and leaves through the door on the right wall*)   My God, Irene. He was just going to put on his shirt. You embarrassed him.

IRENE   Well. I'm the one that's got to raise him. You never had a burden like that on you.

VERA (*She gets up long enough to find her cigarettes and lighter in her purse, then brings them back to the table. She lights one and sighs, sits down*)   No. You're not ever going to let me forget it, either. Are you? You got an ashtray around this place anywhere?

IRENE   You ought to stop smoking those nasty things. I was reading in the paper just the other day about how many women in this country die from lung cancer. Ralph always smoked.

VERA   Ralph didn't die of lung cancer, either, did he? There's one. (*She gets up and gets an ashtray from the counter and sets it on the table, then sits again*)

IRENE   I bet your lungs are black as soot. I don't know why you keep smoking.

VERA   I guess I'm hooked.

IRENE   Ha. Hooked. Look at all the money you waste. You've always wasted gobs of money.

VERA   I don't know why I keep coming over here. I really don't. We can't sit down and have a decent conversation.

IRENE   I'm just trying to look out for you.

VERA   I'm grown now, remember? I have to look out for myself.

IRENE (*Crosses her arms and legs briefly, swings her leg, gets a smug look on her face*)   Oh I know that.

VERA (*Wearily*)   Okay, Irene. (*Brightening*)   How's Clarence been doing? Which of the books did he like best?

IRENE (*Thinking it over*)   He liked the one with the snakes a lot. That one and the one with the dinosaurs. He likes any kind of book about animals. Of course I have to read them to him.

VERA   No, you don't have to. Have you ever tried to help him read? Have you ever sat down with him and showed him? It's not hard, you know. Take him and show him, this is an a, this is a b?

IRENE (*Firmly, shaking her head*)   He can't understand anything like that.

VERA   How do you know? Have you ever tried?

IRENE   He has limited intelligence. You know that.

VERA   I don't think he does. I just think he's never been given a chance. I know he's a little slow but . . .

IRENE   I know. I'm his mother. I've raised him. Tried to raise him. I've done the best I could.

VERA (*Tapping the ashes off her cigarette, leaning toward* IRENE *with great sarcastic impatience*)   Horseshit.

IRENE   Well. That's your opinion.

VERA (*Points toward the door* CLARENCE *went through*)   He wouldn't be in the shape he's in today if you'd let somebody try to educate him. If he'd been given a chance . . .

IRENE   We gave him a chance.

VERA   Three weeks! You couldn't wait to get him out of that school.

IRENE   They didn't teach him anything.

VERA   They didn't have time to. They begged you to let him stay.

IRENE   He didn't like it. He wanted to come home a lot.

VERA   Didn't you?

IRENE   What in the world are you talking about?

VERA   I'm talking about starting to school for God's sake. What do you think I'm talking about?

IRENE   Huh. I remember when you started to school. You cried every day for weeks because you didn't want to go. Mother and Daddy like to have never got you to where you'd go without crying.

VERA (*Pointing again*)   That's right. And he's no different.

IRENE   Well. That's a lot of water over the bridge now anyway.

VERA   Not necessarily. He could still go. There's plenty of schools in town for special students.

IRENE   He's too old for that. He's not a child any more.

VERA   You treat him like one. I lay in my bed at night and cry when I think about him. He doesn't have to be the way he is. (*She looks down and shakes her head*)   Damn, I'm sick of this argument.

IRENE   Why don't you quit bringing it up, then?

VERA   Because he's my nephew.

IRENE (*As if she's been waiting for this*)   Didn't stop you from evicting us, though, did it?

VERA (*Stretches back in the chair as if she's tired, closes her eyes briefly*)   I knew that was coming. I knew it. I don't know why I keep coming over here and letting myself in for it. I know I don't deserve it.

IRENE   I wouldn't have done it to you.

VERA   You don't know what you would have done. I can't stand for you to say that to me. You don't know what I felt like. You can't put yourself in my shoes. (*With bitter logic*)   Death is a lot different from divorce, Irene. You didn't have any say so when Ralph . . . died.

IRENE   You can always get another husband. I can't.

VERA   Oh Irene. You think every man would have rejected you because of Clarence. You don't know. You never tried. You just gave up.

IRENE   I never turned against my family.

VERA   Neither did I! Damn it. You make me feel like shit. Do you know that? I never did one thing for you, did I? I'm tired of you putting all this guilt on me. Have I asked you for one penny of that money back? Have I?

IRENE   Well. No.

VERA   I've never asked but for one thing. For you to try to help him.

IRENE   I tried. They said he was slow. They said he would always be slow.

VERA (*Leaning over*)   But they never said he couldn't learn.

IRENE   I didn't want him in there with all those awful people. There was no telling what kind of people were in there.

VERA   What kind of people do you think are out on the streets of Jackson? It's dangerous to let him walk around by himself like that. Somebody could do something to him.

IRENE   What do you mean?

VERA (*Long pause*)   You know what I mean. Did he ever tell you the truth about that money?

IRENE (*Nodding*)   Well. I questioned him about it. Several times. I'm satisfied he lost it.

VERA   Somebody probably took it away from him and he was scared to tell you about it.

IRENE   Clarence wouldn't lie to me. He's too innocent to tell a lie. He's always told me the truth.

VERA   As far as you know. But you don't know everything.

IRENE   I know Clarence. He wouldn't lie to me.

VERA   I don't think he would on purpose, just to be lying. But I think he might get too scared to tell you the truth about some things. He knows how you are.

IRENE   Wait a minute. He's standing in the bathroom listening to us. Clarence? Are you finished in there?

CLARENCE (*Off*) Yeah mama. I mean. Yes ma'am.

IRENE Well come on out, dear. Did you use the bathroom?

CLARENCE I peepeed.

VERA My God.

IRENE Well flush the toilet and come on out. (*The toilet flushes and* CLARENCE *steps out with his shirt tucked in.* VERA *and* IRENE *look at him*)
Button your top button. (*He does so*) Now get your coat.

CLARENCE Aw mama. Gosh dang.

IRENE Go on.

VERA Don't send him out, Irene. He doesn't want to go. Let him stay here. I never even get to see him. You're always sending him out.

CLARENCE (*Accusing her suddenly*) Yeah, mama. You always send me out.

IRENE You heard me. Do you remember what happened a while ago? (VERA *stops looking at* CLARENCE *and looks at* IRENE)

CLARENCE (*Looking down*) Yes ma'am.

IRENE You remember what I told you?

CLARENCE Yes ma'am.

IRENE All right then. Get your coat. Go walk around for a while. Aunt Vera and I have to talk.

VERA (*Imploring her*) Irene. (*Reluctantly,* CLARENCE *goes to the wall over the cot and takes down his coat, a worn field jacket, and starts putting it on*)
It's kind of cold out there. I had to run my heater coming over here.

IRENE It's not going to hurt him. He's strong as a horse. Never been sick a day in his life.

CLARENCE I don't never get sick, Aint Vera.

VERA That's great, Clarence. I wish I was never sick.

CLARENCE I don't never even take a aspirin.

VERA Is that right?

CLARENCE (*Grinning hugely*) You know why?

VERA (*Smiling*) Why, honey?

CLARENCE Cause I don't never have a headache. I feel good *all* the time.

VERA I bet you do.

CLARENCE (*Happy, enthusiastic*) Boy mama has headaches all the time. She gets headaches from all the music they play around here. I like it though. I can lay here and listen to music all night sometimes. That's one thing's kinda good bout livin here, music all time.

IRENE   Finish up, now. Aunt Vera and I have to talk.

VERA   I wish you'd let him stay.

IRENE   It won't hurt him to go out for a while. He needs some fresh air anyway.

CLARENCE   How long you want me to stay gone, mama?

IRENE   I don't want you to stay gone, Clarence. I just want you to let Aunt Vera and I talk.

CLARENCE   How long?

IRENE   I don't know.

CLARENCE   Bout a hour?

VERA   Irene!

CLARENCE   I'll stay gone bout a hour. But then I'll come back. Maybe Aint Vera'll still be here when I get back.

VERA   I hope so.

CLARENCE   I like them books you got me.

VERA   I'll get you some more. Soon. (*Pause*)   I miss you.

CLARENCE   I miss you too. You know what Aint Vera?

VERA   What?

CLARENCE   I wish we still lived over there. Close to you. In that white house we used to have.

IRENE   Clarence?

VERA   I do, too. I hope maybe some day you can move back over there.

CLARENCE (*Glancing at* IRENE)   I guess I better go. Will you see Christy and Cindy when you get back home?

VERA   No. They're away at college. They'll be back this weekend.

CLARENCE   I's just gonna tell you to tell em I said hi.

VERA   I will. They said tell you hi, too. They love you.

CLARENCE (*Shyly*)   I know. I love them too. Love you too. (*He moves toward the door*)

VERA   You're not going to give me a hug before you go?

CLARENCE (*Stops, embarrassed*)   Aw. I guess. (*He bends over and almost lifts her out of the chair hugging her*)
    Bye. (*He goes out and pulls the door shut*)

VERA (*Turns to* IRENE)   I still don't think you should . . . (*The door opens and* CLARENCE *sticks his head back inside*)

CLARENCE   Mama? You sure Leon's in jail?

IRENE   Yes, dear, I'm sure.

CLARENCE   I hope I don't never have to go to jail. They don't give you nothin but bread and water in jail. (*He closes the door*)

VERA   What's he talking about? Who's Leon?

IRENE   Just some boy that lives around here. Some black boy he knows.

VERA   And he's in jail?

IRENE   That's what I understand. I think he wrote some bad checks on Mr. Clark down at the store.

VERA   And you let Clarence get around him? What is wrong with you?

IRENE   Well I can't keep him cooped up in here all day. He has to get out some.

VERA   Oh Irene. I worry about him so much. (*Pause*)   What were you crying about before I came in? I heard you yelling all the way down on the first floor.

IRENE   Nothing. I was just trying to get him to make up his bed.

VERA   I heard you. Something was going on. You were yelling something at him.

IRENE   Sometimes I have to yell at him. He's . . . headstrong.

VERA   He's strong, too.

IRENE (*Uneasily*)   Yes. He is. Very strong. (*She rubs her chest*)

VERA   Have you had any more of that . . . trouble with him?

IRENE   What do you mean?

VERA   You know what I mean. Those Playboy magazines. And. The other.

IRENE   It hasn't happened again, as far as I know. I wish you wouldn't bring it up. I don't even like to talk about it.

VERA   Why? Does it scare you?

IRENE   Of course it scared me. It's . . . unnatural.

VERA   Oh, shit, it's not unnatural. Every boy does that.

IRENE   How do you know so much about it? You haven't got any boys.

VERA   I just know. I asked Johnny about it one time. He told me.

IRENE   What did he tell you?

VERA   I thought you didn't want to talk about it.

IRENE (*Huffy*)   I don't. You're the one who brought it up.

VERA (*Laughs*)   He said all boys do that. He said it was natural.

IRENE   And you believe that?

VERA   I guess. I don't know why he'd lie about it.

IRENE   He lied about other things.

VERA   Not really. He just didn't tell me he'd had a girlfriend for two or three years.

IRENE   He didn't tell you the truth. It's the same thing. I knew he was trash the first time I saw him. He always had those shifty eyes. I don't know why you ever married him.

VERA   I married him because I loved him.

IRENE   Yes and you still do. You'd take him back right now if you could. If he came in that door right now you'd take him back in an instant.

VERA   No I wouldn't. I don't need him now.

IRENE   Why? Have you got somebody else?

VERA   Maybe.

IRENE   Are you dating anybody? Anybody in particular?

VERA   Welllll. There's one man I've been seeing. He's really nice. He's the nicest thing I've seen in a while. You know what I mean?

IRENE   Where'd you meet him?

VERA   In a bar.

IRENE   Huh. I'm surprised at you. Don't you know you're not going to meet a man worth anything in a bar? All they want is one thing. That's why they go there. To pick up women.

VERA   Irene, you're a real antique, you know that?

IRENE   Nice people don't hang around in bars.

VERA   (*Grins*) You'd be surprised. I've met some awfully nice people in bars.

IRENE   Why I'd be ashamed. How old is he?

VERA   Thirty-five.

IRENE   What?

VERA   So? What's wrong with that?

IRENE   He's younger than you! Humpf. Probably just a gigolo after your money.

VERA   He's a lawyer. Makes gobs of money. He has a practice with his partner right here in town.

IRENE   Divorced, too, I guess.

VERA   Never been married.

IRENE   You won't settle down. I don't know why you don't settle down. Find somebody nice and get married again.

VERA   That's what I'm trying to tell you. He *is* nice. I wouldn't mind settling down with him. But if I ever get married again I'll live with him first.

IRENE   Live with him? Mother would turn over in her grave if she heard you talk like that. (*Pause*) I guess you've even been to bed with him.

VERA   I wouldn't tell you if I had cause I'd never hear the end of it. But, yeah, if I ever get married again I'll live with him first. Find out what he's like in the morning. Whether he sends me Valentines and remembers my birthday.

IRENE   You know what Clarence told me a while ago? That he was saving his money to buy me something for my birthday.

VERA   That's sweet. He loves you, Irene.

IRENE   (*sighs*)   I know it. But I don't know what's going to happen to him. I'm getting too old. I'm afraid I'll have another stroke sometime. Or just one day get to where I can't take care of him.

VERA One day. That's right. (*Pause*) Listen. I had a reason for coming over here today.

IRENE I haven't been able to . . .

VERA It's not about the money.

IRENE Oh. Well you know I'm going to pay you back. Every penny.

VERA I'm not worried about it. I'm not worried about the money. I'm worried about Clarence. And you. You're in bad health, admit it. This is no place for you to live. This is the worst part of town. I wouldn't even drive through here at night. I'm not lying.

IRENE Well. We don't go out at night.

VERA I don't even like it in the daytime. You're always hearing about somebody getting raped around here. Or somebody getting robbed. I don't want Clarence walking around on these streets. He trusts everybody, Irene. He's not like other people. He doesn't have any meanness in him.

IRENE He never has. But sometimes I can't control him.

VERA Listen to me. What do you think he'll be like in ten more years? When you're ten years older?

IRENE I don't know.

VERA Have you thought about it?

IRENE I try not to. It scares me to think about it.

VERA What do you think will happen to him when you die?

IRENE I don't know.

VERA You do know.

IRENE I don't want to talk about it.

VERA We *have* to talk about it. He's your son.

IRENE Well, he's your nephew, too. Isn't that what you said a while ago?

VERA (*Gets another cigarette. She lights it. She's bracing herself for something*) I think it's about time we had a long talk with Clarence. About his future. I know what you think. You think that if you died he could come and live with me.

IRENE I never said that. Have I ever asked you for anything? (VERA *just looks at her*) Well? Where else could he go? Do you want to see the state take him?

VERA Let me tell you something, sister dear. I've put up with this for years, this . . . guilt trip, or whatever you want to call it. I've never denied you anything I could spare. I took everything you said to me when I had to rent that house out. I had to have the money.

IRENE And we needed a place to live.

VERA You lived there for ten years. Rent free! For god's sake, Irene. What do you want? Somebody to give you a place to live all your life? I can't take everything on me. I've got my own family to think about. I had two girls to raise and send to school. I had to have that money. Don't you know what it did to me? To ask you to move?

IRENE   You didn't ask us. You told us.

VERA   Oh Irene. Don't start it all over again. I let you stay as long as I could. Don't you see? I didn't have Johnny's money any more. I had to have that money just to pay my bills every month and survive. And buy my kids' clothes and food. It's two hundred and fifty dollars. That's a lot of money to me.

IRENE   I live, we live on less than that every month.

VERA   I know you do.

IRENE   You don't know what it's like to be on food stamps. The way people look at you when you go buy groceries. You know what we eat? Peanut butter and cereal. Generic food. We buy chicken when it's on sale.

VERA   I know what you eat. I know.

IRENE   No. You don't know. You don't know what it's like to spend two hours making up your grocery list.

VERA   It didn't have to be like this. If you'd put him in a school and gotten you a job . . .

IRENE   I didn't want him in a school. I didn't want him in there with all those retarded people.

VERA   They're not all retarded.

IRENE   They are! Every one of them is!

VERA (*Tries to placate her with gestures, lowering her voice*)   All right, okay. I don't want to argue. The last thing I want is to argue with you. I want you to know what's going on. (*Sighs*)   I think I may have some good news for you.

IRENE   What?

VERA   I didn't know whether to tell you or not. I didn't want you to get your hopes up for nothing. But it's like this. Cindy's boyfriend bought her an engagement ring yesterday. They're getting married.

IRENE   Oh, well. But I don't see what that's got to do with us.

VERA   And Christy graduates this year.

IRENE   She does? How long's she been in school?

VERA   Four years.

IRENE   It doesn't seem that long.

VERA   It does to me. But anyway. What I'm trying to say is. I'm not trying to lay any of my troubles on you. You've got enough of your own.

IRENE   What is it?

VERA (*Pause*)   Cindy's pregnant.

IRENE   Oh *no*, Vera.

VERA (*Sits erect, closes her eyes, shakes her head rigidly*)   Let's don't even talk about it. They're going to get married. Ronnie works on the campus, he's got a good job. She's going to quit school. But Christy's going to graduate. She's already got a job lined up in Memphis.

IRENE   Well. I hate it about Cindy. I'm sorry.

VERA   I've been knowing it for a while. We've cried and cried over it. I just hated to tell you. But I could've been the same way. I could have been pregnant when I married Johnny. It's a wonder I wasn't.

IRENE   I don't know what to say. I hate you're having . . . such troubles.

VERA   I'll get over it. Don't worry. The thing is, I won't have to pay that tuition any more. I don't need the rent on the house any more, Irene. I mean, I need it, but I can make it now without it. (*She reaches over and touches the hand of her sister again, holds it briefly*)

Do you see what I'm saying? I can tell Jerry and them I need the house now. I don't want to. They're nice people. They love the house. But I know you and Clarence need a place to stay. I'd never ask them to leave if it wasn't for y'all. I wouldn't do it for anybody else.

IRENE (*Suddenly anxious*)   You mean we could move back?

VERA   Wait a minute, wait a minute. I don't know when yet. I mean, let's don't get in a rush. I haven't even said anything to Jerry and Linda yet. I wanted to talk to you first. I wanted to get everything straight.

IRENE   Oh Vera. I can't wait to tell Clarence. He'll just be thrilled. He's always wanted to move back. We moved around so much before Ralph died, and after that he thought of that house as home. He was so happy there. Lord. I know it depresses him to stay here. I've prayed for this, Vera.

VERA   You've got to understand something.

IRENE (*All enthusiasm dies*)   What?

VERA (*Slowly, with evident great pain and caution*)   If I give up something, you've got to give up something.

IRENE   What are you saying?

VERA   All right. You and Clarence can have the house back. Sometime. I need to give them time to find a new place. They're good people. They've got three little girls. (*Sad smile*)   They call me Aunt Vera. I'm going to feel like a real shit when I go over there and tell them they can't live there any more.

IRENE   Oh I can understand that. I'm sure they've gotten attached to the house. But we lived there a lot longer than they have.

VERA   I'm not going to let you have the house unless you agree to put Clarence in some kind of school where he can learn something. How to read. How to function on his own. How to learn enough skills to where he can at least make a living. That's it. I've already made up my mind.

IRENE (*Sudden, fierce anger*)   Well just let me tell you something, miss priss. I've made up my mind too. You don't dictate the terms of our life. We don't need your charity.

VERA   You do need it. You can't survive down here.

IRENE   We've made it so far. By God it'll be a cold day in hell before we ever ask you for anything again. I think you just better get on out of here. (IRENE *rises from her chair but* VERA *doesn't*)

VERA   Would you sit down? I'm trying to help you.

IRENE   No you're not. You're trying to run my life.

VERA   Well somebody needs to run it. You're so damn hardheaded. You won't let anybody tell you anything. You're so scared somebody's going to take him away from you for five minutes.

IRENE   That's right. He's all I've got. I've got to hold onto him.

VERA   But you're hurting him! Can't you see that? Part of the way he is is because of you.

IRENE   He was born like he is! He was in the womb too long!

VERA   Would you please sit down? I'm trying to talk to you.

IRENE   I don't want you to talk to me. I won't live by your rules. I don't have to knuckle under to you. I may have to live in a project and buy my groceries with food stamps but I don't have to listen to you. He's not going to any school!

VERA   Why? You want me to tell you? (*She stands*)   I know why. I've always known why. It's so you can control him. You don't want him to learn anything. You want him to depend on you for the rest of your life. He could have his own life, Irene! His own life. He could read. Don't you think he'd like to sit down and read a story by himself? He could get a job and be somebody.

IRENE   He can't.

VERA   You want him to stay the way he is.

IRENE   He'll always be the way he is.

VERA   Not if we help him!

IRENE (*Really vicious now*)   Oh you're so goody goody. Yes. You've always been so concerned about him. You didn't want him around your daughters, though, did you? You were afraid, weren't you?

VERA   You don't have any right to talk to me like that. You don't . . . you shouldn't talk about him like that.

IRENE   You just go on and leave us alone. We don't need you.

VERA   Clarence does!

IRENE   I'm all he needs.

VERA   You don't even know where he is. You send him out on the street like a goddamn dog!

IRENE   You get out of here. You get out of my house.

VERA   Just let him go back to a school for a while. Let him see if he likes it. What would it hurt? I'm offering you the house. What more do you want?

IRENE   I don't want anything from you.

VERA   He wants to go back. He said he did. You know he does. And if you'd put him back in school he'd learn something. He's not dumb. He's not like you think he is.

IRENE   I don't think we have much else to talk about, Vera. Clarence will be back in a little while. I don't want to get him upset.

VERA   You had him upset when I got over here. What were you saying to him?

IRENE   That was between me and him. We just had a disagreement. But I handled it.

VERA   I don't see how you could handle him. He's a lot stronger than you. Don't you want the house? You could still get your food stamps. And I could help you out some. The school won't cost anything. You'll be better off than you are here. Just think about it. Please. Look around you. Look at what you're living in.

IRENE   I know what I'm living in. Poverty.

VERA   It doesn't have to be like this. You don't have to live on handouts. Let's sit back down, okay? Talk this over like two grown people?

IRENE *(Wearily)*   I don't know what good it's going to do to talk. (*They sit down again*)

VERA   You owe it to Clarence to let him at least try to make something out of his life. My kids are already grown and in college. Clarence is still where he was when they used to play together. It's not his fault.

IRENE   But it's mine. That's what you're saying.

VERA   Don't get mad again. I'm just saying it's not too late to correct it. I know he could get a job somewhere if he had a little education.

IRENE   Doing what? Making brooms? Billfolds?

VERA   There are organizations that help people like him. They can help him get a job.

IRENE   Sweeping a floor somewhere.

VERA   So what? He'd be bringing home a paycheck every week. You wouldn't be living in a housing project. Don't you know he'd be proud of that? Of himself?

IRENE   I suppose.

VERA   You know he would. He could have friends, Irene. Who does he know besides you and me and the girls? He doesn't know anything but loneliness.

IRENE   I guess you're right about that. When he was little it was no problem. We always lived around a bunch of kids. But all these children are scared of him. (*Pause*)   Or they make fun of him.

VERA   Maybe that's why he doesn't like to go out.

IRENE   I just don't know about this school thing. I'm afraid he wouldn't like it. He might not be happy.

VERA   You might be surprised.

IRENE   I'd miss him so bad.

VERA (*Silence*)

IRENE   It might be the best thing for him, though.

VERA   It *is* the best thing. Listen, I'm just trying to help. Would you at least think about it? Don't say anything to him yet. About moving back, I mean. This is something for you to decide. On your own. But I don't see anything else you can do. You've got to get away from here.

IRENE   When could we move back?

VERA   I don't know. Maybe in a month or so.

IRENE   All right. What if we move back, and he starts in one of these schools. Then what if he doesn't like it, or he can't learn anything? Are you going to let us stay in the house?

VERA   I'll put it like this. If you move back in my house, he's going to stay in a school. Even if I have to carry him every morning myself. He's going to have a chance this time.

IRENE   Well. Since you put it like that, I don't know.

VERA   You don't know.

IRENE   That's right. I'll just have to think about it. I've got my doubts.

VERA   All right, then. You think about it. (*She checks her watch*)   I've got to get to work. I'm late as it is. (*She gets up and gets her purse and coat, starts putting on the coat*)   If you want me to, I'll carry both of you over to that new school one day and let you look it over. You might like it if you took a look at it.

IRENE   I doubt it. All those things look alike.

VERA   This one has good people working in it. They care about people like Clarence. I have a friend who works there. I know what I'm talking about. (*She opens her purse and takes out some folded money*)   Here.

IRENE   What's that?

VERA   Take it. Go on. It's not much. Twenty dollars.

IRENE   I don't want to take any more money from you. I've borrowed so much already.

VERA   Oh hush. Go down to the store and buy him some fruit. Or a steak. Something he likes.

IRENE (*Gets up and takes the money*)   Well. I'll take it for him. I thank you. We both do. I'll pay you back one of these days.

VERA   Tell Clarence I had to get on to work. And tell him I'll bring him some more books next time. Now I've got to run. Call me sometime. You never call me. (*She hugs* IRENE *tightly*)   Just think about what I said. Think about him.

IRENE   I'll think about it. But I can't promise anything.

VERA   Well. I guess that'll have to do for now. I've got to go. I'll see you.

(VERA *goes out, closing the door behind her.* IRENE *looks at the money for a moment, then starts counting it, licking her finger as she flips through the bills*)

CURTAIN

ACT II

(A *bleak, shaded area with benches in a deserted playground. There are dead leaves littered on the stage, a ragged wall behind with dirty words or slogans spraypainted on it.* CLARENCE *is sitting on a bench alone, facing the audience at center stage, looking down at a grocery store checkout rag he has found. He is absorbed in what he's doing and does not see* LEON *approaching from behind, obliquely from stage right.* LEON *is a small black in his late teens or early twenties.* LEON *is stepping quietly with the grace of a hunting cat. His manner is threatening, sadistic. A mean little smile flickers across his face as he sneaks up on* CLARENCE. *There is total silence on the stage.* CLARENCE *has his head down as* LEON *gets closer. Finally* LEON *is standing directly behind* CLARENCE, *grinning.* LEON *leans over, until his mouth is almost touching the ear of* CLARENCE)

LEON (*Screams*)   What's up Clarence!

CLARENCE (*Leaps up and trips in wild fear, topples down.* LEON *is laughing at him, slapping his thigh and the bench, staggering around.* CLARENCE *looks up at him in shock*)   Leon. I thought you . . .

LEON   Hoo hoo. Woooeee! What you doin on the ground, Clarence? You takin a nap?

CLARENCE   I. You. Scared me. Thought you's . . .

LEON (*Something like humor is on his face, but it's not humor. He walks around the bench*)   Let me hep you up, Clarence. You gonna get you clothes dirty down there on the ground. (*He extends a hand*)

CLARENCE   I can. (*Grunts*)   Get up. (*He gets up on his knees and struggles up clumsily*)

LEON (*He's half drunk, weaving a little. He gets out a pack of Kool cigarettes and opens the pack by biting a hole in one bottom corner.* CLARENCE *watches his every move.* LEON *grins and shakes his head. He spits out whatever he bit off. He lights a cigarette with a match brought from a box in his pocket. He shakes the match out and thumps it at* CLARENCE)   Boo!

CLARENCE (*Jerks back*)   Oh. Don't Leon. You might burn me.

LEON (*Exaggerated patience*)   Aw Clarence. I wouldn't burn you like that. (*He puts one foot on the bench, rests an arm on a thigh, leans toward* CLARENCE)   If I wanted to burn you I'd set you on fire.

CLARENCE   Don't.

LEON   C'mere, Clarence. (*He sits on the bench, the cigarette in his mouth, both hands in his pockets*)   Come on. Ain't seen you in a while. Come on over here and tell me what's been happenin.

CLARENCE   I don't want to.

LEON   Come here. (*He takes one hand out and points with a finger straight down at the bench. He takes the cigarette in the other hand*)

CLARENCE   I got to go home. My mama's waiting for me.

LEON   Aw yo mama ain't waitin on nothin. Waitin for Days of Our Lives to come on. Git over and sit. Down. Now.

CLARENCE (*In a pouty voice*)   Well I can't stay but a little bit. (*He sits down as far away from* LEON *as he can*)

LEON (*Imitates* CLARENCE's *tone exactly*)   Well I cain't stay but a little bit. I got to go home and git me some titty milk from my mama. (*Changes back to normal voice*)   Ain't that right?

CLARENCE (*Looks down*)   No.

LEON (*Sees the papers on the ground*)   What you readin there, Clarence? One a them grocery store magazines?

CLARENCE   I don't know. Somethin I found.

LEON   Let me see it.

CLARENCE   Huh?

LEON   I said let me see it. You deaf? Go get it.

CLARENCE (*He gets up and picks the paper up, hands it to* LEON.

LEON *starts looking through it*)   It ain't mine. Somebody left it. It's got a pitcher of some dogs in there.

LEON (*In a disgusted voice*)   Yeah, I know. Probably got some damn woman in here had fourteen puppies or somethin. Man this stuff'll eat up what little brains you got. (*He stops and looks up*)   Oh. Oh ho ho. I see now what you lookin at. Yeah. You checkin these women out, ain't you, Clarence? (*He turns the pages around to show* CLARENCE)   Look at this one here. Um um. Ain't she somethin fine? What could you do with that, Clarence? Huh?

CLARENCE (*Looks once and then quickly looks away*)   Nothin.

LEON   Now don't tell me that, Clarence. (*He leans back and stretches his legs out, letting the pages fall in his lap*)   I know what you can do. Yes sir. I done seen you in action.

CLARENCE   I ain't gone. Do nothin like that. Ever.

LEON (*In mock astonishment*)   Clarence. Claaarence. You wouldn't do nothin wit no woman? You? The Stroker Kid?

CLARENCE (*Clasps his hands between his knees and shakes his head once, hard, looking down*)   Uh uh.

LEON   Never?

CLARENCE   Never. Not ever.

LEON (*Folds the paper and tosses it aside*)   Not till the next time you get a chance, you mean. I know you, Clarence. You sly devil. You the strong silent type. Ain't you?

CLARENCE   I don't know. I got to go in a little bit, Leon.

LEON   Aw man. Loosen up. Live a little. I come all the way down here to see you and you just dry. Don't want to talk. Yon't a drank? I got a little nip here.

CLARENCE   No. I don't want none of that stuff.

LEON   It's Crown, man. Fo fifteen a half pint. (*He pulls the bottle out and shows him. He shakes it at him*)

LEON   Go on. Get you some.

CLARENCE   I don't want none of that stuff, Leon.

LEON   Hell, man. I ain't took but one drank out of it. Go on. I don't mind lettin a white man drank after me.

CLARENCE   Uh uh.

LEON   Sheeit fire. My old buddy won't even take a drink with me. I guess I'll just have to drink yose too. (*He takes the cap off and takes a sip. He offers it to* CLARENCE *again*)   Come on, man. It'll warm you up.

CLARENCE (*Shakes his head and looks away*)   No.

LEON (*Gets another drink and caps the bottle, puts it away*)   So what's been happenin while I been gone? You holdin down the neighborhood?

CLARENCE My mama sent me down here for a while. Her and Aint Vera's talkin.

LEON That the nice lookin white lady I seen comin outa yo buildin? Drives that white Riv?

CLARENCE (*Looks at him*) What?

LEON That eighty-two, man. Is that her car?

CLARENCE She's got a white car. I don't know what kind it is. It's long.

LEON That yo aint, huh?

CLARENCE That's Aint Vera. She don't live around here.

LEON I can see that. She loaded or somethin? She got a nice set of wheels.

CLARENCE I don't know.

LEON I bet she got a sugar daddy keepin her up. That right?

CLARENCE I don't know. (*Pause*) She gets me books.

LEON (*Astonished laugh, wide-eyed disbelief*) Books? What you want wit books? You cain't read, dummy. Man you cain't even halfway talk.

CLARENCE (*Shrugs*) I look at the pitchers. I got one about snakes. I'm gonna look at it when I get home. What time is it?

LEON What? You takin medicine?

CLARENCE Naw. I just need to know when a hour is. I'm sposed to be back in a hour.

LEON How long you been gone?

CLARENCE I don't know.

LEON Well how in the hell you supposed to know when to be back? Man you need somebody to lead you around on a leash. (*He shakes his head and pulls the bottle back out and gets another snort*)

CLARENCE You gonna get drunk. If you drink that stuff.

LEON Huh. I better. I'll take it back and get a refund if I don't. What you think this shit is? Tea?

CLARENCE It looks like tea.

LEON Man. You eat up with the dumbass. What'd you do? Fall on yo head when you was little? Man you act like a car run over yo head.

CLARENCE Did they put you in jail?

LEON (*Sharply*) Who told you that?

CLARENCE Nobody.

LEON Yeah. Somebody. Yo mama tell you that?

CLARENCE I knew it.

LEON You mama told you.

CLARENCE I knew it. You shouldn't rob Mr. Clark, Leon.

LEON (*Turns surly*) I ain't robbed that old fool. He gone wish he hadn't seen me. I got somethin laid up for him. (*He hunches down on the bench, shaking his head*)   Imon teach him to mess wit me. Somebody always got to be messin wit me.

CLARENCE   You don't know what time it is?

LEON   It ain't time for you to go yet.

CLARENCE   It's not?

LEON   Naw, man, you got all kinds of time. I'll tell you when it's time. (*He gets another drink*)

CLARENCE   She didn't say I had to come home. I just told her I'd come home. In a hour.

LEON   Well it ain't a hour yet. I'll tell you when to go. Want to talk to you. (*Pause*)   Yeah, man, them suckers put me in that jail. I been in there for a *week*! Buncha humble, man. I tell you. It's a humble. Talk to you like dirt in there, man. Always say do this and do that.

CLARENCE   Boy I wouldn't want to go to jail.

LEON   Aw man it ain't nothin to it. It ain't nothing to it. Buncha small-time cops is all. Think they big men walkin round cause they got all the keys. Keep you out in a pen like a cow, man. Make you clean up and stuff. I ain't got no time for that shit. I told em off.

CLARENCE   You did?

LEON   Sho I did! What you think I am, a wimp? Man I told em I was *thew* playing they nickel ass games. (*He points his finger down at the bench a few times*)   I told em I wanted to see my lawyer. Buncha hicks. They didn't have nothin on me no way. They wadn't nothin wrong with that check, man. That was my uncle's check, man. It was good. It was a good check. That old tightwad just wouldn't pay it.

CLARENCE (*Amazed*)   Your uncle? Wouldn't give you any money?

LEON   Naw, man. He a old fool. He's tight as Dick's hatband. Man he so tight he squeak. I wrote a little twenty dolla check on him man and he gits me thowed in jail. Had me in that old rat hole for a week sweepin up and stuff. Moppin a old flo. Him and old man Clark just alike. Both of em got old moldy money laid back probly got a fungus on it cause it ain't been out of they pockets in so long. Tight, man, tight. Too tight.

CLARENCE   I used to have an uncle. Uncle Johnny. My Aint Vera lets us borry money. All the time.

LEON   Say she do?

CLARENCE   Sometimes.

LEON   She got plenty a money?

CLARENCE   I guess.

LEON   What's she do?

CLARENCE   I don't know.

LEON (*Disgusted*) Man you don't know nothin. You know that? You so dumb it's pitiful.

CLARENCE I know it.

LEON You do, huh? (*Pause*) Well, listen here, man. Yo mama sendin you to the grocery store today?

CLARENCE Uh uh. She don't let me go buy groceries no more.

LEON She don't huh?

CLARENCE No. Not since I told her I lost that money.

LEON She still think you lost that money?

CLARENCE Yes. I didn't tell her. I didn't.

LEON What'd you tell her?

CLARENCE (*Pause, looks away*) You know.

LEON Yeah, I know. I want to know if you know. I want to know if you remember.

CLARENCE (*Looks back and down*) I remember.

LEON Well. Just don't you forget it.

CLARENCE I won't.

LEON You better not. Cause you know what I told you. I told you what they'd do if you told. What'd I tell you?

CLARENCE Said they'd put me in jail.

LEON That's right. (*He gets another drink*) Only they won't put you in the jail I's in. They'd put you in the bad jail. The one they got downtown. You know what's in the bad jail?

CLARENCE Don't tell me. I don't want to know.

LEON In the bad jail's where they put people does things like you did wit Lawanda. Old big fat Lawanda? Remember Lawanda? (*He holds his hands out and cups mammoth imaginary breasts briefly*)

CLARENCE (*This is hurting him badly*) Don't. I got to go. (*He starts up but* LEON *catches his arm and holds onto him*)

LEON You better sit down.

CLARENCE I got to go home! (*He's trying to jerk away and* LEON *can't hold him*)

LEON You better sit down! You better sit down if you don't want me to tell your mama!

CLARENCE (*Walks woodenly back to the bench, sits, doubles over*) I'm sick. I want to go home. My mama wants me to come back home.

LEON Aw yo mama don't want you back home. I ain't finished tellin you about the bad jail.

CLARENCE I don't want to go to the bad jail.

LEON Yeah, they got old bugs crawlin around in the bad jail. Biggest bugs you ever seen. Old cockroaches and rats. Old big gray rats. Come in there at night and gnaw your face off if you ain't got a stick to beat em off. And you know what they do to you in the bad jail if they catch you with a stick?

CLARENCE What?

LEON Take it away from you.

CLARENCE Oh. My stomach hurts. I'm sick.

LEON You ain't sick. You just a big old crybaby. (*He stops, changes his tone, grins*) Say you ain't seen Lawanda?

CLARENCE No. I don't want to see her.

LEON Well. I didn't know. I thought maybe you and Lawanda'd been partyin some. You know. Thought maybe you'd been up there to see her while I's in jail.

CLARENCE No. I ain't.

LEON Come on, now. You been slippin up there seein Lawanda? Beatin my time? I bet you took a sixpack up there and kicked back. Watched old Johnny Carson or somethin.

CLARENCE No.

LEON Come on, man. You can tell me. You sweet on Lawanda, ain't you? You like them old big gals, don't you?

CLARENCE I don't like Lawanda. She's mean.

LEON Aw man you just don't know how to handle her.

CLARENCE I'm gonna have to go home now, Leon. My mama told me to come on home. I better go.

LEON You want me to tell you what you can do with yo mama?

CLARENCE No.

LEON All right, then. You set there. I ain't through talkin to you yet. Man you a drag. You the biggest drag I know. (*He gets another drink*) I tell you what, though. (*He looks around, runs his tongue over his lower lip as he thinks about what he's about to tell* CLARENCE) I'm fitna go up here and see Lawanda a minute. (*He waits for a reaction.* CLARENCE *doesn't say anything*) You want to go? Won't cost you but ten dollars. Member Lawanda? Hoo! I remember you! (*He sobers and changes his tone of voice*) You know Lawanda been askin me about you.

CLARENCE (*Looks dumbfounded*) She has?

LEON Sho. Sho she has. She was askin me other day when I seen Clarence. She say (*High falsetto*) 'Clarence such a sweet boy. I wish he'd come back and see me again.' (*Earnest, normal voice*) That's what she said.

CLARENCE She did?

LEON Yeah. She did. That wadn't all she told me neither. Naw. She sweet on you, man. Man she tellin everybody you her boyfriend.

CLARENCE She *is*?

LEON Yeah, man. She proud a you. But, uh, say, man. It gone cost you ten dollars to go back and see her. You got ten dollars?

CLARENCE (*Looks out over the stage briefly and grips the bench with both hands*) Uh uh. I ain't got no money.

LEON Come on, man. You got some money. You always got some money. Old moneybags Clarence. Got a roll choke a goat. Ain't that right?

CLARENCE I don't know.

LEON How much of that old spendola you luggin around with you today Clarence?

CLARENCE I ain't got much. I'm savin it.

LEON Savin it? Man that's a waste. What you savin it for?

CLARENCE I'm just savin it. I got to buy somethin.

LEON What you got to buy?

CLARENCE I got to buy my mama a birthday present. I'm gonna buy her somethin nice. This time.

LEON Aw, man. How much money you gonna spend on yo mama?

CLARENCE I'm gonna spend four dollars on her.

LEON Looka here. Last of the big spenders. Man I bet you gonna buy her a punchbowl or somethin, huh?

CLARENCE I might. I don't know.

LEON Man. You don't even know how far out of it you are. Wow, man. Imon tell you what, Clarence.

CLARENCE What?

LEON I need to borrow about fo dollars. You got fo dollars, ain't you?

CLARENCE I'm savin it.

LEON I know you savin it. But looka here. If you let *me* have that fo dollars, at's just like puttin money in the bank. You know why?

CLARENCE Why?

LEON Cause. See, I'm gone pay you back five. That's a twenty-five per cent return on your investment, man. You can't beat that with a stick.

CLARENCE I don't want to. I have to save it.

LEON I need to get me a sixpack, man. Listen. I got to go see somebody this evenin. You know what I mean?

CLARENCE No.

LEON I got to go see my lady, man, when she gets in from work. Now see, she gone be all uptight and shit cause I been in jail, I got to deal with that, but I get her some Miller and everything'll smoove over. Then me and her can get down to what we needs to be doin.

Dig? So you just let me have that four dollars, then when I pay you back, you'll have five. Man that's makin money.

CLARENCE I better keep it.

LEON (*Impatient*) Look, man, you gonna be makin a dollar. I'm gonna pay you back five.

CLARENCE I don't want to.

LEON Hey man, I don't care *what* you want. I been in jail a week. I'm ready to party. And I got to have some Miller to take to my lady. Now you let me have that four dollars.

CLARENCE I don't want to, Leon.

LEON I done told you . . .

CLARENCE I'm savin it! I got to buy my mama a present!

LEON Listen. You better give me that four dollars.

CLARENCE No.

(LEON *appears astonished, then amused. He shakes his head at the futility of* CLARENCE'S *refusal*)

LEON (*Wearily*) All right, then. I guess I'll have to just go on over and tell yo mama about you and Lawanda.

CLARENCE No, Leon. Don't! (*He turns to* LEON *and grabs the sleeve of his coat.* LEON *looks down at the hand*)

LEON Man you better git yo hands off me. (CLARENCE *takes his hands off*) What you mean grabbin me? You want me to knock a knot on yo head? Huh? Man I'll hit you so hard . . .

CLARENCE You better not.

LEON Say what? What you gonna do about it? Huh? You gonna whup me? (*He gives* CLARENCE *a shove*)

CLARENCE No . . .

LEON Damn right you ain't. You better keep your hands to yourself.

CLARENCE I'm fixin to have to go home. It's time for me to go.

LEON Fine. (*He holds his hand out*) You give me that money first.

CLARENCE I can't. (*He shakes his head and won't look at* LEON) That's all the money I got.

LEON Now fool! What did I just finish tellin you? Huh? About Lawanda? About yo mama? About what you and Lawanda done over there in that buildin? Now you want yo mama to know all about that? You want to get yo mama all upset like that time you took all them old dirty books home? Make her have another stroke? Huh?

CLARENCE (*He's terrified, shifting around on the bench*) No. She . . . she'd get sick again. She'd get real sick.

LEON (*In a loud voice*)   Then give me the money!

CLARENCE   Leon. You'll get me in trouble.

LEON   *Get* you in trouble? Man you already in trouble.

CLARENCE   No I ain't.

LEON   Man you gone be in trouble when they find out what you been doin wit Lawanda. What you think they gonna do when they find out about that?

CLARENCE (*Shakes his head wildly*)   I don't know.

LEON   I know. They gone take you over there and put you in that old bad jail.

CLARENCE   Leon, don't.

LEON   Them old rat's be comin in there at night, man, trying to eat yo face off. Old bugs'll be crawlin all over you. Crawl up on yo head and yo ears, git in you food. You gone wish you'd give me that four dollars then, ain't you?

CLARENCE   That's the only money I got. I'm savin it.

LEON   Ain't gone do you no good in that jail.

CLARENCE   I'm gonna tell on you, Leon.

LEON   Who you gonna tell?

CLARENCE   You *made* me do it!

LEON   I ain't made you do nothin.

CLARENCE (*He stands up and shouts at* LEON)   You took my money! Told me to tell my mama I lost it! It's your fault! You did it! I'm goin home!

LEON   You come here. (*He grabs* CLARENCE *and turns him around*) You better just keep yo big mouth shut, you hear me? Ain't nobody gonna believe you anyway.

CLARENCE (*Tries to pull away*)   My mama will! You let me go! I got to go home! She's waitin on me!

LEON   Ain't nobody gonna believe a big dummy like you.

CLARENCE   My mama will. You let me go.

LEON   She ain't gonna believe you. Ain't nobody gonna believe you. You ain't gonna tell em nothing about me, you hear? You better keep yo mouth shut about me.

CLARENCE (*Pushes against him with both hands*)   Let me go! I'm gonna tell!

LEON   You ain't. You ain't tellin nothing. (*He grabs* CLARENCE *by the shirt collar, jerking him while he's yelling at him*) You hear me? (*He gets up in* CLARENCE'S *face with a crazy gleam in his eyes, a vicious, twisted joy*) If you tell on me I'm gonna tell on you. Bout you and Lawanda on that mattress. Bout what you did!

CLARENCE   Quit it, Leon. I'm gonna hit you!

LEON You go on and hit me. Come on. Let's see you hit me. You won't hit nobody else. You scared to hit me. You ain't nothin but a big old baby anyway.

CLARENCE I ain't no baby. (*He grabs* LEON's *hand with both of his, trying to free himself*) You're just mean to me. You're always mean to me!

LEON You fixin to cry? You always cry. Old crybaby. Come on and cry. You gone cry when they put you in that jail.

CLARENCE They ain't puttin me in no jail!

LEON They gone come over to yo house and get you. Put the handcuffs on you.

CLARENCE (*Shoves him hard. Shoves him down*) Shut up!

LEON (*Glowers up at him from the stage floor*) You done messed up now. You don't do that to me.

CLARENCE I didn't mean to.

LEON Now I know they gonna put you in jail. Cause I'm fixin to go tell em.

CLARENCE No you're not.

LEON Yes I am.

CLARENCE (*Advances on him before he can get up*) You better not. I'll hit you. I will! (*He stands over him with his fists clenched*)

LEON You get out of my way. I'm fixin to whip yo ass. (LEON *starts up but* CLARENCE *shoves him back*)

CLARENCE I don't want to fight, Leon!

LEON That's too damn bad. (*He starts up again but* CLARENCE *pushes him, hard*)

CLARENCE Leave me alone, Leon! I don't want to fight! Not supposed to fight!

LEON You a fool, man. I'm fixin to hurt you. (*He gets up on one knee and* CLARENCE *bends over him, forcing him back*)

CLARENCE No you're not! (*He straddles him quickly, pinning him down*)

LEON (*Straining wildly*) Get off me! Get yo ass off me!

CLARENCE You gonna tell!

LEON I'm fitna knock the . . . (*Draws his fist back*)

CLARENCE No! (*He grabs the arm. They grapple.* CLARENCE *has his back to the audience and he hits him*) Now stop it, Leon!

(*He stands up and away from* LEON, *frightened now of what he has done.* LEON's *eyes burn with a cold fury as he raises up on one elbow and rubs at the blood on his mouth*)

Leon? I didn't mean it.

LEON   You dumb son of a *bitch*.

(LEON *rises in one fluid movement with his hand going into his pocket.* CLARENCE *takes a step back.* LEON'S *eyes are locked on him and the hand comes out of his pocket holding something. The hand moves up in front of him, directly between them, and* CLARENCE *watches in silent horror as a switchblade springs open, the steel bright and terrible, in the hushed silence an audible CLICK)*

CLARENCE   No, Leon. Please.

(*He tries to step back but* LEON *circles him quickly, the knife low and straight out now.* LEON *backs* CLARENCE *toward the bench, jabbing, grinning, playing with him.* CLARENCE *has his hands out in front, trying to ward him off)*

LEON   That what you want me to cut first? Huh? Want me to cut them hands? (*He slashes out quickly and back in as* CLARENCE *jerks back reflexively, terror on his face)*   Huh? You better move them hands.

CLARENCE   No. Please. Don't. (*His face crumples. The first tears come)*   Don't cut my hands Leon.

LEON   Now we gonna see that crybaby cry.

CLARENCE   I'm scared, Leon. You scarin me.

LEON   You think I'm you mama, titty baby? You think that cryin shit gonna do you any good now?

CLARENCE (*He sobs now, shaking his head, badly off balance as* LEON *continues to feint and jab)*   No.

LEON   You gimme that damn money.

CLARENCE   Okay. *Okay*.

LEON   Hand it over here. Hit me in the damn mouth. Cut yo ass off for you.

CLARENCE   No. Don't, Leon. Now. Now. I'll give you my money and I won't tell my mama.

LEON   You got that right. You ain't tellin nobody, fool.

CLARENCE   Cause my mama's been real sick. We have to save our money, Leon. We ain't *got* much money. My daddy's dead, Leon. And we ain't got no place to live but here. (*He pulls the wadded money from his pocket and holds it out)*

LEON (*He holds his other hand out, beckons with his fingers, and smiles)*   You put that money right here. In my hand,

CLARENCE (*Snatches it back)*   No! You might cut my hand.

LEON   That depends on how fast you are, titty baby. You fast enough, I won't cut you.

CLARENCE   I ain't fast.

LEON   You better get fast.

CLARENCE   I can't. Just take it. I'll get some more.

LEON   Get fast now.

CLARENCE (*Pleading*)   Listen, Leon. I'll go home and get some more. I know where there's some more *hid at*, Leon.

LEON   You lyin. Lyin like a dog.

CLARENCE (*Shakes his head wildly*)   No. Uh uh. I promise, Leon. I got some more money at home. I'll go home and get it.

LEON   Call the po-lice you mean. Have me back in that jail, them suckers tellin me what to do. Back in that damn cage. Naw. You'll tell.

CLARENCE   Oh no. I wouldn't call the police.

LEON   Shit you wouldn't. Fool. I ain't no fool like you.

(*He steps in front of* CLARENCE, *so that his back is facing the audience, and slashes once. The money falls on the stage floor (There must be some blood introduced here some hidden way) and* CLARENCE *draws his hand back and grasps it and wails in pain*)

Man. You slow as shit. Dumb as dirt. Yeah. You'd tell.

(LEON *goes in on* CLARENCE. CLARENCE *catches the knife hand and the other hand.* LEON *tries to pull free, but* CLARENCE *has his tongue between his teeth and his face horribly contorted. Their gasps are the only sounds. They struggle perhaps ten seconds, and there is a sudden, violent motion toward* LEON, *who bows backward from the blow, centerpunched. He slumps toward* CLARENCE, *his head almost nuzzling into* CLARENCE'S *chest. He puts his arms gently around* CLARENCE, *who, stunned, watches the head gradually fall back, the eyes roll up, the arms, limp and outspread like broken wings coming together behind his back, relax in death.* CLARENCE *catches* LEON *before he can fall*)

CURTAIN

ACT III

(*The apartment again,* IRENE *is sitting at the table, reading a magazine. She has a cup of coffee. She sips the coffee and flips slowly through the magazine, quite content alone. Suddenly,* CLARENCE *bursts into the room, slamming the door and going to sit on his bed. His hand is in his coat pocket)*

IRENE (*Looks up*)   Goodness. What's wrong with you?

CLARENCE (*He sits on the bed, not looking up*)   Nothin.

IRENE   What's the matter with you?

CLARENCE   I'm cold. It's cold outside.

IRENE   Why you're shaking.

CLARENCE   I'm gonna go to bed. (*He picks up the quilt and unfolds it, pulls it up over him and lies down on his back)*

IRENE (*Gets up and goes to him*)   Clarence? Are you coming down with something? Are you getting the flu?

CLARENCE   I don't know. I just want to lay down for a while. I'm cold.

IRENE   Maybe I'd better take your temperature. You're just shivering. (*She puts her hand on his forehead*)   Have you got a fever?

CLARENCE   I don't know.

IRENE   Well what are you shaking about?

CLARENCE   I don't . . . know.

IRENE (*Puts one hand on her hip*)   Have those kids been tellin you things again?

CLARENCE   Ma'am?

IRENE   Have those kid told you some story again? You know they're just pulling your leg.

CLARENCE   I don't know.

IRENE   I don't think you've got fever. Have you got a chill? Clarence? Are you having a rigor?

CLARENCE   I'm just cold. Mama? Would you sit down and hold me? I'm scared.

IRENE (*Sits down beside him*)   Why Clarence. A big old boy like you? What in the world are you scared of?

CLARENCE   I just want you to hold me. Mama? Hold me, Please?

IRENE (*Bends over and puts her arms around him briefly, adjusts the covers tighter about him*)   I didn't know it was so cold outside, honey. I'm sorry. You want me to fix you some hot chocolate?

CLARENCE   I don't know. I think I'm sick. I don't want no hot chocolate. I just want to lay down a while.

IRENE   Well don't you want to take your coat off? Take your shoes off.

CLARENCE   I'm all right. I'm just . . . cold. Hold me, please.

IRENE   You're just about too big to hold. You're grown now. (*She waits a moment*)   Guess what?

CLARENCE   What?

IRENE   Vera let me borrow some money a while ago.

CLARENCE   She did.

IRENE   She sure did. And you know what else?

CLARENCE   What.

IRENE   I've got a surprise for you. A good surprise.

CLARENCE   You do.

IRENE   I sure do. It's the best surprise you've had in a long time. Can you guess?

CLARENCE   Naw. I mean . . .

IRENE   Well just think of the best thing you can think of. What would make you happier than anything. Right this minute.

CLARENCE (*A long pause*)   I don't know, mama.

IRENE   Oh, come on, now. Guess. It's a good surprise. It's something you've been wanting. For a long time. Guess the best thing you can guess.

CLARENCE (*Turns and puts the side of his face flat on the bed, toward the edge, so that he is facing the audience but seeing nothing*)   The best thing?

IRENE   The very best thing.

CLARENCE (*A very long pause*)   I don't know.

IRENE   Oh, Clarence. You're not even trying. Now come on, guess. What would you like to have if you could have anything in the world?

CLARENCE   Anything in the world?

IRENE   Anything. Anything you wanted.

CLARENCE   Well, I wish . . .

IRENE   What?

CLARENCE   Sometimes I wish I was little again. Sometimes I wish you and me lived by ourselves. All by ourselves. You know what I'd have? If we lived by ourselves and I could have whatever I wanted?

IRENE   A dog.

CLARENCE   Uh uh. A treehouse.

IRENE   A treehouse?

CLARENCE   Uh huh. With a rope.

IRENE   Oh, Clarence. Wish for something good. Something big. Something big and white.

CLARENCE   That's what I'd want. I'd live in the treehouse. And I wouldn't let anybody mean in there. Cause I'd be the boss.

IRENE   Would you be happy then?

CLARENCE   Yes. Yes ma'am.

IRENE   Are you not happy?

CLARENCE   I don't know. I guess.

IRENE   What's wrong? Is there something wrong?

CLARENCE   I'm scared. I'm scared of the bad jail.

IRENE   Oh, honey. Nobody's going to put you in jail.

CLARENCE   I hope not.

IRENE   Well. We'll talk some other time. We don't have to talk right
now. If you don't feel good. But I do have a surprise. We're going
down to the store after while and get something you like. Would you
like that?

CLARENCE   I don't want to go back out. I want to stay here.

IRENE (*Touches his forehead again*)   Clarence, you are in a cold sweat!
What is wrong with you? Have you hurt yourself?

CLARENCE   I . . . think so. My hand hurts.

IRENE   Your hand hurts?

CLARENCE   Uh huh.

IRENE   Well let me see it. What did you do to it?

CLARENCE   No. I don't want you to see it. I want to go to sleep.
(*He turns in the quilts and rolls away from her*)

IRENE   Now, Clarence. Turn back over here. Look at mama. Clarence?

CLARENCE   I don't want to, mama. I just want to go to sleep.

IRENE   Let me see your hand.

CLARENCE   No mama.

IRENE   Let me see it. What are you afraid of? (*She draws it out from
under the covers and looks at it*)   Clarence.

CLARENCE (*There is blood all over it*)   I hurt it.

IRENE   Why honey it's cut! (*She looks at him fearfully*)   Clarence!
Turn around. Clarence.

CLARENCE (*Turns over suddenly and sits up in the bed*)   Mama if
you tell somebody somethin and they don't tell it. I mean. If you
do somethin and somebody sees you and they tell you they're gonna
tell on you. Does that. Mama? Can they put somebody in jail for being
mean to you?

IRENE   What are you talking about? What's happened to your hand?

CLARENCE   Mama I'm in trouble.

IRENE   Why honey you're not in any trouble.

CLARENCE   I am, mama. I . . . mama, Leon said he was gonna
tell on me and I told him not to cause he was gonna tell about me
and Lawanda.

IRENE   Who? Clarence, what are you talking about?

CLARENCE   He said he's gonna tell on me, mama. He said he's gonna
tell you and they'd put me in jail.

IRENE   Jail?

CLARENCE   That's what he said. (*He starts crying*)   He said . . . he told me about the bad jail. He said it had rats in it. Mama I don't know what to do.

IRENE Leon?

CLARENCE He said he's gonna *tell* you, mama. I told him I's savin my money and he said I was a baby and he said he's gonna hurt me. And I told him to quit and he wouldn't quit. I hit him mama. He tried to stab me. He's dead, mama, Leon's dead.

IRENE (*She gets up*) Oh. My dear God. Clarence.

CLARENCE I don't want to go to the bad jail. He said it's got rats. Oh mama I'm scared, I'm scared they gonna put me in there. Will you hide me, mama?

IRENE Clarence, honey. Leon's not dead. He can't be dead.

CLARENCE He *is*, mama. If they find Leon they'll come get me. I know they will. (*He grabs her and holds onto her with his head on her shoulder*) He made me tell you I lost that money that time.

IRENE (*A dazed look begins to come onto her face*) Money?

CLARENCE That money, mama. He made me tell you I lost it. He said he'd tell if I didn't.

IRENE (*She pries his hands off her with a great effort and pushes him back*) Clarence. Clarence! Oh, let me get something to wrap up your hand. Just sit still. (*She goes and finds a towel and comes back and sits down beside him again*) Let me wrap this up. Now you . . . you just start at the first . . . and tell mama everything that happened. Oh, my God, Clarence. (*She's doing all she can to keep from breaking down in front of him, but she begins to cry silently as he talks*)

CLARENCE (*He gives an immense sob*) I don't know, mama. It happened so fast. He said Lawanda had some books and he took me over there. But she didn't have no books. I told you I didn't want to go, mama. I told you I was scared. You said Leon was in jail. That's what you said. But he wasn't!

IRENE Clarence, you . . . you're not making any sense. I don't understand what you're talking about. Just. Please. Slow down.

IRENE I told you he was mean! I told you he was mean and you didn't believe me. You said those kids said that. Mama if Leon's mean why don't they keep him in jail? Why did they let him out? You won't let em take me, will you? You'll hide me, won't you?

IRENE Hush now. Just hush. Let me think. We've got to decide what to do.

CLARENCE Let's go over to Aint Vera's, mama. I can hide over there. They won't find me over there. Let's go. Let's go right now.

IRENE Did Leon make you do anything with that girl?

CLARENCE Don't, mama. Don't.

IRENE   You tell me. You tell me the truth.

CLARENCE   He always did something to me. He took that twenty dollars away from me when we first got here. He showed me some pitchers of some women. He took me to see Lawanda and he said he'd tell you if I didn't give him my money.

IRENE   Did you do anything with that girl? Answer me, Clarence. You answer me! A black girl?

CLARENCE   You got sick over them pitchers! I couldn't tell you about that! You'da got sick again. I didn't want to get put in jail. I had four dollars I was savin. I never was mean to him or nothin. He always teased me and stuff. Called me names. He took my money every time. He always snuck up on me.

IRENE (*Her hands slowly come together in the center of her chest*)   Oh, no. Please, God, no. Not now.

CLARENCE (*He's not looking at her and doesn't realize what is happening*)   I told him I didn't want to fight. He said he was gonna tell. I hit him. He pulled that knife out. He . . . cut my hand. And blood come out of it. I told him I wouldn't tell on him. But I was tired of him doing stuff to me. I *hated* him! I got ahold of his hand. And he couldn't get loose. I had to make him stop. I was scared he'd come back.

IRENE   Honey. Honey. You killed him? You killed Leon?

CLARENCE   I had to, mama. He had that knife.

IRENE (*She is suddenly in terrible pain with it centering in her chest. She holds it in both hands, gathering the material of her dress between her fingers. She moans and rocks back and forth*)   Clarence. You've got to do something right now. Before I pass out. Go over to the telephone. Right now. (*He stands up and stares at her with witless fright*) Dial nine. Go over. Clarence I . . . I can't get my breath. Dial nine. One. Hurry.

CLARENCE   What, mama? Mama? What?

IRENE   It's nine one one. Nine eleven. Just tell them. Tell them your mother's sick. (*She folds over slowly onto the bed*)

CLARENCE (*He goes to her and tries to rouse her. He can't*)   Mama? Nine what? Nine what, mama? Nine what? Mama!

CURTAIN

ACT IV

(*A simple but tastefully furnished room with a table and chairs, shelves of books, a sofa.* CLARENCE *is sitting at the table reading, dressed in slacks, soft shoes, a white shirt. He turns the pages slowly, intently. A knock is heard at the door to the room. He looks up)*

V E R A (*Offstage*)   Clarence? You almost ready?

C L A R E N C E   Yes ma'am. Almost.

V E R A   Can I come in?

C L A R E N C E (*Looks back down at his book*)   Yes ma'am. (V E R A *enters, dressed for work, putting on her watch*)

C L A R E N C E   I'm just going over my words. Good morning.

V E R A   Wonderful morning. You've been reading that same book for a week. Aren't you tired of it?

C L A R E N C E   I like this book. It's good.

V E R A (*Looks at her watch*)   Well, we've got a few minutes yet. You want me to go over your words with you?

C L A R E N C E   Aw. I don't guess. I think I know em.

V E R A   I'll be glad to.

C L A R E N C E   I know. I know em though.

V E R A   You're getting to where you won't let me help you with anything. You're so independent.

C L A R E N C E   I guess. What's that?

V E R A   Well. (*She draws out a chair and sits*)   It means like on your own. You know. Like this. Having your own house. Doing things by yourself. You get that from your mother.

C L A R E N C E   I do?

V E R A   Sure you do. She was very independent. You're a lot like her.

C L A R E N C E   I am?

V E R A   Of course. I can see her every time I look at you.

C L A R E N C E   Are you like her?

V E R A   Oh, I don't know. A little, I guess. I'm stubborn like her.

C L A R E N C E   You're getting gray hair like hers was.

V E R A   Lord, don't remind me. Is it that bad?

C L A R E N C E   Nah. It's not that bad.

V E R A   Oh you're just saying that. So. You get a new book today, don't you?

C L A R E N C E   If I pass my test.

V E R A   You'll pass it. You've passed every one. Did you eat breakfast?

C L A R E N C E   I fixed me some eggs. I don't usually eat but four but I was hungry so I ate five. And three pieces of toast. I think I need some milk.

V E R A   We're going by the store this afternoon. We've got to decide what you want to cook on the grill tonight. What do you want?

C L A R E N C E   I don't know. I like ribs.

V E R A   Okay.

CLARENCE But I sorta like chicken, too.

VERA It's up to you.

CLARENCE But I sorta like steaks, too. What you want me to cook?

VERA I don't care. We'll eat whatever you fix.

CLARENCE What time's Jack coming over? What does he want?

VERA I don't know. I haven't asked him.

CLARENCE Well be sure to ask him. I need to know.

VERA I'll call him when I get to work.

CLARENCE Uh. I might drink me a beer tonight.

VERA You might not, too.

CLARENCE Aw come on.

VERA I don't know.

CLARENCE Aw. (*Grins*) Come on come on come on.

VERA Well. Maybe just one.

CLARENCE One big one.

VERA One little one. And no hitting the cooler before Jack gets here. (*Pause*) You want to get a movie?

CLARENCE Oo yeah! Let's get that kookoo's nest again.

VERA Now we've seen that thing three weekends in a row. Let's get a love story this time.

CLARENCE Aw I don't want to see no old love story. I want to see that big Indian pull that sink out of the floor again and throw it through the window. That's my favorite part.

VERA I like a good love story.

CLARENCE I don't know what you want to watch an old love story for. All you do is cry when it's over with.

VERA I don't always cry. Only if it's sad.

CLARENCE Let's get two movies and you can watch one and then me and Jack can watch one. He likes the same kind of movies I like.

VERA I know it. Ya'll don't ever want to watch what I want to watch.

CLARENCE That's cause you're a woman. We're men. Can we get two?

VERA We'll see.

CLARENCE We better go, now. I don't want to be late. I got a lot to do today.

VERA We've got time. I'm not in any hurry.

CLARENCE We might be late, though.

VERA You won't be late. I'll get you there on time. Have I ever let you be late before?

CLARENCE Well, naw. I mean no ma'am.

VERA You already got your house cleaned up?

CLARENCE I cleaned it up last night before I went to bed.

VERA   You wash your dishes?

CLARENCE   Washed em quick as I got through with breakfast.

VERA   Oh. Well. What about your clothes?

CLARENCE   They're all clean. Everything's okay, Aunt Vera.

VERA   Yeah. I guess so. (*Pause*)   I wish Irene could see you now.

CLARENCE   You think she'd be happy?

VERA   I know she would.

CLARENCE   I can read. I read this whole book. (*He holds up a child's reader*)   All by myself.

VERA   You're getting better all the time.

CLARENCE   I am. I can do lots of things by myself now.

VERA   You can come stay with me any time you want to. You know that. You don't have to stay out here by yourself all the time.

CLARENCE   I know. I just . . .

VERA   You like having your own place to live.

CLARENCE   Well. Yeah.

VERA   You like taking care of yourself.

CLARENCE   I guess so.

VERA   One of these days you'll be able to do everything by yourself. Then you won't even need me.

CLARENCE   Yes I will. I always will.

VERA   You might not.

CLARENCE   Now you sound like mama.

VERA   I do, huh?

CLARENCE   Just like her.

VERA   I just worry about you. I'm always afraid something's going to happen. I always look over here at night before I go to sleep to see if your light's on. After everything that's happened. After all that stuff in court . . . I just like to keep my eye on you. I can't help it. I guess you think I treat you like a baby sometimes.

CLARENCE   I'm glad they gave me to you.

VERA (*Pause*)   I know you still miss her. We both do. But she'd be glad for you, Clarence. It'll get better. It just takes time.

CLARENCE   I'm all right now. Most of the time. You know when I think about her the most? At night. (*Smiles shyly, shakes his head gently*)   We'd always watch tv at night. We'd turn the lights off. We did that every night.

VERA   Do you still do that? Watch tv with all the lights off?

CLARENCE   Yeah. That's when I think about her. I say my words first. Then I think about mama. And. Other stuff.

VERA   What other stuff?

CLARENCE   Just stuff.

VERA   Leon?

CLARENCE   Yeah. A little. You know what? Leon was smart. He was a lot smarter than me.

VERA   If he was smart he'd have left you alone. If he was smart he'd have run from you.

CLARENCE   He couldn't run.

VERA   Honey. You've got to put all that behind you. It's done now. You can't spend the rest of your life regretting it. You'll get over it. Believe me. You're stronger than you think you are.

CLARENCE   You think so?

VERA   I know so. You get stronger all the time. Every day.

CLARENCE   Can we go now? I don't want to be late.

VERA   You're never late. You're always the first one there.

CLARENCE   We better hurry anyway, though. I get my new book today. (*He gets up and moves toward the door*)

VERA (*Gets up*)   Well wait on me.

CLARENCE (*Stops at the door*)   I'm ready to go. Come on.

VERA   Oh, Clarence. (CLARENCE *goes out and* VERA *stops at the door and starts to pull it shut*)   We've got plenty of time. (*She shuts the door and the lights gradually go down*)

CURTAIN

Siege: The Battle of Vicksburg

ROBERT CANZONERI

FOR BILL BARNETT

CHARACTERS

WOMEN

Mary Burson, white Vicksburg woman, about 30
Dora Scott, white Vicksburg woman, about 20
Mrs. Luke, white Vicksburg woman, about 60
Martha, Dora's servant, black, about 45
Mrs. Grimm, Northern Sanitary Commission woman

CIVILIAN MEN

George, Mary's servant, black, about 20
Abraham, Mrs. Luke's servant, black, about 70
Doctor Foster
Gentlemen
Charles Dana

CONFEDERATE SOLDIERS

Colonel Hall
Major Robinette
Lieutenant
Private Marks, about 17
Shanghai, a sergeant, about 25
Private Williams, about 60
Corporal Holmes

Starving Soldier
First Confederate Soldier
Second Confederate Soldier
Deserter
General Pemberton
General Bowen
Others

Author's Note: The play has been drawn from accounts and letters written by people who lived through the siege of Vicksburg, either as civilians in the town or as soldiers defending or attacking it. In translating into a coherent evening's experience events that transpired on the river, in the town, and through the battlelines over a period of weeks, it has been necessary to compress time and space down to the limits of the stage, to combine, in some cases, more than one real person into a single character, and, of course, to render written into spoken language. The attempt, nevertheless, has been to present a true account—not to impose theatricality upon actual events, but to discover in what happened a dramatic development that illuminates history without violating it.

UNION SOLDIERS
Sergeant Wells
Private Watts
Corporal Steitelmeyer
Private Holmes
Captain
Cook
First Union Soldier
Second Union Soldier

Third Union Soldier
Color Sergeant
First Relief Soldier
Second Relief Soldier
General Grant
General Sherman
Others

SETTING

The city of Vicksburg, Mississippi, from May 18 to July 4, 1863. The downtown area of the Town is visible as a silhouette, dominated by the courthouse with Confederate flag atop, far up stage right; downstage from it are Sky Parlor Hill and, farther downstage, a Cave Area in which people have already been living for some time. Toward center stage from Sky Parlor Hill, on a hill of its own, is MRS. LUKE's house. From near center stage on left are the battle lines: first the Confederate lines, stretching from near upstage to near downstage; facing them, farther left, are the Union lines—the first of these rather far left, the later ones closer in. Beyond them, far upstage, is a tree, where GRANT and PEMBERTON will meet, and a Redan above a battle area. Far left, from upstage to downstage, there are: a Union Hospital Tent, a Mess Tent, and finally a log on which SHERMAN and ROBINETTE will sit. Downstage is free for movement across the stage.

ACT I

Scene 1 (May 18)

(*Dark. Silence. Daylight comes up on the entrance to* DORA's *cave, down right. There is a chair beside the opening, shaded by a sheet on poles. Beside it stands a table with a pitcher and a bowl, covered with a napkin.* DORA *comes out of the cave, shades her eyes, looks off right, fanning in the heat. There is the dull report of a mortar from up right, beyond the Town, which is now visible.* DORA *becomes very still, listening. The mortar shell can be heard, approaching.* DORA *becomes agitated.*)
DORA (*Shouts off right*) Martha! Martha! (*Rushes back into the*

cave. The sound of the mortar shell in flight ends in an explosion just off right. As the sound dies out, DORA *rushes out of the cave.*) Martha!

MARTHA (*Appears from right, carrying a bucket of water*) Here I am, Miss Dora.

DORA Oh, thank God. I heard it coming, and I couldn't see you.

MARTHA It didn't get me, but there ain't nothing but a hole where Mr. Turner's garden used to be. (*Pours water from the bucket into the pitcher*) Here. (*Pours water from the pitcher into the bowl; wets a handkerchief and hands it to* DORA) Wipe your face. You'll feel better.

DORA (*Presses the handkerchief to her forehead*) Was it close to you?

MARTHA Close enough. I got under that little fig tree right by the path. It sounded like hail on the leaves.

DORA You could have been killed! (*She sits*)

MARTHA (*Covers the pitcher and bowl with napkin again*) Little shoots of corn Lucas had up about knee high, all over the place. Won't be no roasting ears out of that garden.

(*The mortar fire on the right is from the river. Now faint cannon fire begins from far left, the landward side of the city; at first* DORA *doesn't notice where it is from, but almost at once she is alarmed; this is something new. The cannon fire repeats at intervals throughout the scene*)

DORA I thought they towed those mortar barges out of range. I declare, it's got to where you can't believe anything you hear. (*Cannon fire again from far left, faintly;* DORA *pauses, listening*) What's that?

MARTHA (*Has started into the cave, but comes back*) What's what, Miss Dora?

DORA Shhh! Listen. (*Waits through a moment of silence until there is the dull sound of cannon again*) There. Hear that?

MARTHA Don't sound like thunder, to me.

DORA But that's to the east. They said General Pemberton was holding the Yankees at the Big Black River. (*Agitated*) That's too far to hear cannon from, isn't it?

MARTHA (*Holds up hand for silence; they listen again; cannon sounds again*) Wherever it is ain't too far.

(*Now there is the faint sound of rifle fire from far left.* MARTHA *and* DORA *hear it and freeze. The light dims on them and the Cave Area, comes up down center on* MARY *and* COLONEL HALL, *caught as they rush downstage from below* MRS. LUKE'S *house.*

*Sounds of cannon and rifle fire from left gradually increase during
the scene; daylight gradually dies out until there is a red sunset
glow beyond the Town.* MARY *and* COLONEL HALL *stand facing
left, listening a moment; finally* MARY *speaks.*)

MARY   What was I saying, Colonel? (*Wryly*)   I think it was 'I hope
it will never come to . . .' this.

HALL (*Listens intently to the gunfire: nods to himself*)   Parrott gun.
Once they're in range. . . . (*Turns to* MARY)   You won't be safe
in your house. (*Wry humor*)   I hope you have a hole to crawl into.

MARY (*Same wry humor*)   I'm afraid we're all caught like rats in a hole.
(*Shivers*)   Yes. My husband saw to that before he was sent to Virginia.
But I don't want to go into that cave until I have to. (*Impatiently*)
Can't we hold them off on our own ground? You'd think they carry
more supplies on their backs than we have stored up on our own land.
We let them have Port Gibson, then Raymond. . . .

HALL   Well. . . , *let* them have. . .?

MARY (*Continues enumerating without withdrawing 'let'*)   . . . Jackson,
Clinton, Sid Champion's farm—and what now? Did they grow wings
and fly across the Big Black?

HALL   I understood that Johnston was going to follow in through Jackson and hit them from the rear. (*Short laugh*)   Maybe he's chasing
them over to us. (*Sighs*)   Well, I'd better get to my reserves.

MARY   How many do we have?

HALL   Here? Maybe five thousand. And from the sound of things, we'll
soon have whatever's left of Pemberton's. And Bowen's. And Loring's.

(*From the left,* PRIVATE MARKS *enters, trying to run, exhausted,
dazed, sweaty, grimy.* MARY *rushes to him and grasps his arm.
He tries to focus on her; his mouth forms the word "Retreat."* MRS.
LUKE *rushes in from her house, center stage.*)

MARY (*To* PRIVATE MARKS)   Are you hurt?

MRS. LUKE   Here! What are you doing? Where are you going? (PRI-
VATE MARKS *begins to fold;* HALL *helps hold him up.*)

MARY (*Calls back toward her house*)   George! George! Bring some
water!

GEORGE (*Off*)   Yes ma'am.

MARKS (*Dully, as if it is a cry he has been repeating through the long
rout*) Retreat!

MARY   Retreat?

MRS. LUKE   Shame on you. Shame!

HALL   What happened?

MARY Turn and fight, man!

HALL Were you with Pemberton?

(*In the faint light to left there is movement, gradually increasing, of soldiers retreating into the city*)

MARKS (*Licks his dry lips, tries to pull himself together*) Retreat.

(GEORGE *arrives with a dipper of water.* MARY *holds it for* MARKS. *He drinks.*)

MARY Where's your canteen? Where's your rifle?

COLONEL HALL Speak up, man. Who were you with?

MARKS (*Looks at his hands for the rifle that isn't there*) It. . . . I must have lost it. (*Puts his head down in his hands and sobs*)

HALL (*Shakes* MARKS) Were you with Pemberton?

MARKS (*Nods*)

(*Other Confederate troops begin to trickle past.* MRS. LUKE *and* MARY *shout at them in exasperation.*)

MRS. LUKE Be ashamed! Be ashamed!

MARY Turn and fight! Turn and fight! Are you going to let them take the city?

(*The soldiers drag on, fall one by one in exhaustion, the last near* DORA'S *cave, down right, dimly lighted. As the scene continues, we see* DORA *become aware of them and send* MARTHA *with bucket and dipper to give them water.*)

HALL (*To* MARKS) Did everybody run? Were you all routed like this?

MARKS (*Nods; begins to get hold of himself*) Yes sir. I think so, sir. We burned the bridge, but they came on anyway. (*Looks at his hands as if holding rifle*) Right into our fire. (*Pauses*) We were there in the brush, shooting while they came screaming and firing up through the clearing, and all of a sudden we were running. And we were screaming too: Retreat! Retreat! (*Puts his head down in his hands again*)

(*The rifle and cannon fire are closer. An old man,* PRIVATE WILLIAMS, *has sunk down exhausted nearby.*)

MARY Broke and ran!

MRS. LUKE Aren't you ashamed?

MARKS (*Looks up at her*) I don't know, ma'am. I don't know. I guess it'll come whether I am or not.

MRS. LUKE Well, you *ought* to be ashamed. All of you! Is this the way you protect your women?

WILLIAMS   Well, ma'am, we woulda fought real good, but General Pemberton come up and says, 'Stand your ground, boys. Your general is with you.' And then, bless you, lady, the next thing we seen of him, he was sitting on his horse behind a house—*close* behind. (*Shrugs*) Well, when we seen that. . . . (*Shakes his head ruefully*)

(MARY *laughs;* MRS. LUKE *joins in.* HALL *laughs too, but his laughter becomes jubilant, a rallying cry.*)

HALL   George, run down to General Lee's headquarters and tell him we'll need to open the arsenal. These men will have to be armed.
GEORGE   Yes sir.
HALL (*To* MARKS)   Private, we're going to make a stand. Report back to the trenches.
MARKS   The trenches?
HALL (*Fiercely, pointing off left*)   You'll probably recognize them. They're dug in the ground. (*Turns to* WILLIAMS)   You too, private. (MARKS *and* WILLIAMS *drag themselves off left as* HALL *continues, to* MARY)   Mrs. Burson, when George comes back, have him gather up as many shovels as he can find and bring them to the trenches. They're pretty much washed out, and we'll need to dig in as fast as possible.
MARY (*Gives in for a moment*)   It won't do any good, Colonel, don't you see? We're beaten. We're beaten.
HALL   Nonsense. (*Laughs*)   I don't know why, but, my God, this is exhilarating! (*Calls out*)   Men! To the trenches! (*Shakes a fallen man by the shoulder, rouses him; others begin to rise*)   Rally to the trenches! We'll hold the sons of bitches there!

(HALL *leads the reviving soldiers off left. Cannon, closer still, fires. We hear the Parrott shell approaching, striking, exploding at a distance, left. Rifle fire is very near. The sun is setting beyond the Town.* DORA *and* MARTHA *stand in the dim light looking after the soldiers who have been drawn left by* HALL'S *shouting;* MRS. LUKE *and* MARY, *too, look after* HALL *and the soldiers.*)

MARY   I can't believe they just ran away.
MRS. LUKE   Nothing *to* the young folks nowadays. It's the way they was brought up.
MARY (*Amused; looks at spot where* MARKS *had been; shakes her head*)   Well, retreat must have been heard of in the past. That boy didn't make up the word.
MRS. LUKE   Pshaw! How you talk! (*Flings her hands into the air*)   Biscuits for supper!
MARY   What?

MRS. LUKE (*Hurrying back up center toward her house*) Burning for sure! I left that Abraham to watch them, but every time he sits down he goes to sleep.

(MRS. LUKE *exits from the lighted area.* MARY *climbs a hill toward the left, gazes outward, rubs her eyes.* GEORGE *returns, sees her, climbs up beside her. She points.*)

MARY Am I seeing things, or is that field blue? (*Laughs*) Like the field of bluebonnets we saw that time in Texas. Remember?

GEORGE Yes'm. (*Laughs too*) Only these bluebonnets have got guns.

MARY (*Sighs; gathers herself*) Colonel Hall wants you to round up all the shovels you can find and take them to the trenches.

GEORGE Yes ma'am.

MARY Mrs. Luke should have one or two, and Mr. Turner. Oh, you know. See if you can get Abraham to help you.

GEORGE Yes ma'am. I reckon digging in's all that's left to do.

MARY *and* GORGE *continue looking out to the left. The light dims rapidly. At the Confederate trenches, left center, campfires begin to come up. Farther out in the distance, far left, the Union campfires begin to glow.*)

MARY You'll take care of me, won't you, George?

GEORGE Yes'm. (*Turns and waits for her to follow*) I'd better see you back to the house and go get those shovels.

(MARY *and* GEORGE *start down the hill, to the right. Light dims on them, comes up dimly overall. The gunfire has died out for the night. In the dimming light, we see a panorama, from left to right, of distant Union campfires; Confederate campfires along the trenches;* HALL *at tent behind the lines and* SHANGHAI, WILLIAMS *and other soldiers working in the trenches, including* MARKS, *who is whittling a board into a makeshift shovel;* MRS. LUKE *scolding* ABRAHAM *at her house up center;* MARY *and* GEORGE *walking right a bit, downstage;* DORA *and* MARTHA *lighting a fire to prepare supper; other people bustling near more distant caves; the Town up right in faint light. Far up left, light comes up on* GRANT *and* SHERMAN *on horseback, looking over the defenses. As lights dim further overall,* GRANT *points to Redan up left.* SHERMAN *nods. We hear a bugle call from the Confederate lines, echoes from the Union lines. A harmonica begins "Lorena" from the Confederate lines, finishes as lights go down on* GRANT *and* SHERMAN. *The song is picked up from distant Union lines for a moment, then dies out.*)

Scene 2 (May 22)

(*Morning. Bugle call from Union lines, picked up by Confederate lines. We see light coming up gradually on the Town, up right; on the Cave Area, with* MARTHA *beginning breakfast and others stirring farther right; on* MARY *with guitar and* GEORGE *loaded with stuff walking from center stage to the cave left of* DORA'S; *on soldiers in trenches coming awake, pickets returning to trenches,* HALL *approaching the trenches from near center stage. On her front porch,* MRS. LUKE *settles into a rocking chair and begins shelling peas, humming a hymn tune and singing a snatch of it now and then.* ABRAHAM *is taking food to the Confederate trenches.* MARKS *is setting up a barricade to make it possible to get above a very low crouch in their shallow trench.* SHANGHAI *and* WILLIAMS *man rifles, looking left toward Union lines. Union soldiers are going through similar preparations for the day. Beyond Union lines, a* COOK *is serving food to a few Union soldiers. Lights stay dim, although we can see the activity elsewhere, then brighten somewhat at Union Mess Tent.*)

FIRST SOLDIER (*As* COOK *serves him*)   What kind of slop have you got for us this morning?

COOK   Hell, boy, this here is the best. Rebel dainties for Yankee bellies.

FIRST SOLDIER (*Sniffing meat*) That does smell like pretty good pork.

COOK   Pretty good! That pig is mighty nigh kin to the President of the Confederate States.

SECOND SOLDIER (*As he is served*)   This Jeff Davis's great aunt? (*Eyes piece of pork*)   Looks tough enough.

COOK   Nephew, more likely, considering the way it was hung and where we got it. Joe Davis's farm, back up the road. Jeff's brother.

THIRD SOLDIER (*Being served*)   I'm sure you purchased this hog directly from the gentleman himself—with genuine Confederate currency, likely, complete with a mighty familiar portrait.

COOK   Well, I think the boy was a little shy of cash at the time. Gave him a promissory note.

FIRST SOLDIER   Promised they'd hang brother Jeff before the year was out, I reckon.

COOK   Promised they'd come back and chase down his chickens, next. Said they'd practiced up by chasing the brave defenders of his beloved Southland.

FIRST SOLDIER (*Laughs; looks suddenly awkward; hauls out watch and chain and looks aside as he hands it to* COOK)   I figure I'll be too busy today to look at a timepiece. Think you could hold this for me?

COOK (*Takes it*) You can pick it up at suppertime.

FIRST SOLDIER And this picture. (*Hands picture to* COOK) Uh, my folks' address is on the back.

COOK (*Turns picture over, nods, then looks at picture*) Bound to be your sister. No young lady this elegant would give you her picture unless she was unavoidably kin.

FIRST SOLDIER You might write a few words. Say I was thinking of them. And her.

COOK (*Looks at him seriously*) Sherman's given the order?

FIRST SOLDIER (*Nods; looks toward Redan, up left*) We'll be right up front.

(*Light comes up on Redan. Cannon is ready to defend it; Confederate soldiers move about within.* COOK *and* SOLDIERS *look toward the Redan.*)

COOK I thought they tried that—and got hell beat out of 'em.

SECOND SOLDIER Yeah, but they went up through those ravines. Like trying to climb up out of a well, even if the Rebs hadn't clogged 'em up by cutting trees. (*Gives* COOK *a leather pouch*) We're going right down the road at 'em.

COOK (*Sarcastically*) Hell yes. Just run up and ram your fist down the mouth of a cannon. You can do it. (*Takes items handed him by* THIRD SOLDIER) Sherman would do it himself, if he didn't have to be at dinner tonight with General Grant.

THIRD SOLDIER It ain't just Sherman this time. I hear that McPherson and Quinby and McClernand and everybody's set to attack all down the line.

(*As light dims on mess tent,* FIRST SOLDIER, SECOND SOLDIER, *and* THIRD SOLDIER *move upstage behind Union lines, get rifles, and fall into formation with other armed Union soldiers. Light comes up on Redan, with Confederate soldiers working on the barricades, cannon at ready and rifles stacked at the ready. At the cry of "Charge!" the Union soldiers rush toward the Redan firing rifles; Confederate soldiers leap to man cannon and rifles, begin firing; firing comes from far left also, and from the far left of the audience, but the visible battle is at the Redan up left. Union soldiers fire on the run; some are hit and fall, including* FIRST SOLDIER. *Light dims as they are momentarily held, but firing continues through rest of scene. Lights come up on Cave Area, down right.* MARY) *and* GEORGE *are busying about her cave, just toward center stage from* DORA'S. MAJOR ROBINETTE *enters with a tent fly, which he sets up over the cave entrance, with* GEORGE'S *help, during the scene. At his arrival,* MARY *is in the cave; she comes out as he is setting down the poles and unrolling the fly. Throughout, battle sounds are heard from the Redan area, etc., as well as occasional mortars far right.*)

MARY   Oh, Major Robinette. Back so soon.

ROBINETTE   Yes, ma'am. We'll have you comfortable before you know it.

MARY   I suppose James Bowen was wise to insist that I leave the house. (*Looks wryly at cave; on the verge of sarcasm*)   Do thank him for me.

ROBINETTE   The general asked that you remember him to your husband when you write him next.

MARY   I will, of course. (*Short laugh*)   I suppose wives are to obey their husbands' friends, in their husbands' absence. Is that Biblical, Major.

ROBINETTE   (*A bit uncomfortable*)   General Bowen's a good man, ma'am. A great soldier.

MARY   Well, in the circumstances. . . , I guess he's right.

ROBINETTE   He sends regrets that he can't help you in person, as he is . . . pretty well occupied.

(*The battle sounds from the Redan intensify.* MARY, ROBINETTE, *and* GEORGE *pause and listen.*)

MARY   Are we really surrounded?

ROBINETTE   Well, ma'am, they're all around us, but don't you worry. Our men are dug in. And General Loring's joined forces with Johnston. They ought to strike from the rear any day now.

MARY   (*Motions toward battle sounds up left*)   But this is an attack, isn't it? Aren't they charging the trenches?

ROBINETTE   (*Shrugs*)   Those Mississippi troops held the Stockade Redan Tuesday, didn't they?

MARY   (*Laughs*)   You're partial to your own, Major. Those Louisiana troops held too. (*Looks around her;* MARTHA *comes out of* DORA'S *cave and begins setting up to cook dinner*)   Holding them out just means starving us out, anyway.

ROBINETTE   If General Grant thought so, why would he be charging?

MARY   Maybe he doesn't know how many of us are down to cornbread and bacon. In fact, Major, I doubt that *you* realize that we've been under fire for the past year, and short of food longer than that. (*Tries to shrug off her impatience*)   But, why am I complaining. We're alive. Most of us.

ROBINETTE (*Laughs*)   Last night I was walking behind two elderly ladies when here came a mortar shell, right for us. I dived under a wagon just as the shell exploded, and when my ears quit ringing I heard a little voice from across the street, saying, 'Oh, sister, are you killed?' And then from my side, "No, sister,' and then, absolutely serious, 'Are you?'

GEORGE (*Laughs, puts hand over mouth, repeats the line sotto voce*)   'No, sister. Are you?'

MARY (*Laughs too; realizes that* ROBINETTE *is trying to get her mind off the situation*)   I'll be fine. The cot you brought just fits in the little chamber, (*Indicates the cave behind her*)   and beside it there's a cut-out deep enough for me to stand upright.

ROBINETTE   That's good, ma'am. If the men in the ditches (*Nods toward Confederate trenches, left center*)   stand upright even for an instant. . . . (*Breaks off; turns to* GEORGE)   It must have been quite a job to dig the cave.

GEORGE   Yes sir. Only, Master Burson hire it dug.

MARY   Cave digging is big business here, with its own experts. And of course the price goes up with every shell that drops in the city—just like everything else. (*Turns to* GEORGE)   George, I guess you'd better start cooking some of that bacon before it gets so valuable we'll be afraid to eat it. (*To* ROBINETTE)   Will you dine with us, Major? You're truly most welcome to what we have.

ROBINETTE   Thank you, ma'am, but if you'll excuse me . . .

MARY   Please don't misunderstand. We *are* down to cornbread and bacon, but we have plenty of that.

ROBINETTE (*Light begins to dim on Cave Area*)   I quite understand, and it would be a real pleasure, but . . . (*The guns at the Redan grow more fierce*)   duty, you know. Will you let me pay a visit when I can get away?

(*Light dims out on Cave Area as we see* GEORGE *building a fire,* ROBINETTE *taking his leave, going left across the front of the stage. Light comes up on* MRS. LUKE *and* ABRAHAM *in* MRS. LUKE'S *kitchen.*)

MRS. LUKE   Here, you, Abraham, take this mess of peas down to Mrs. Simmons. Tell her I said not to waste any of the juice. These here's the last we're likely to see.

ABRAHAM   Yes, ma'am.

MRS. LUKE   And tell her I hope she's feeling better, though the Lord knows, how could she with them head pains and these shells loud enough to split your skull. Hold on.

ABRAHAM (*Has started off; stops*)   Yes'm?

MRS. LUKE   Tell her if her sister needs to get away, send word and I'll come sit with her.

ABRAHAM   Yes, ma'am.

MRS. LUKE   Run along. And hurry back, or your share of the peas'll be cold.

(*We hear a Parrot shell approaching from the left.* MRS. LUKE *and* ABRAHAM *stand very still, listening. It passes over them and explodes nearby.* ABRAHAM *winces.* MRS. LUKE *merely checks cornbread in iron skillet on stove.*)

ABRAHAM   After dinner, can we go find us a cave to get in, please ma'am?

MRS. LUKE   Pshaw! How you talk! If the Lord means to take us, He'll take us in a cave as easy as here. Run along, now. Shake a leg.

ABRAHAM (*Resigned*)   Yes'm. I reckon He would if He wanted to. But I hope He don't.

(*Light dims on* MRS. LUKE *and departing* ABRAHAM, *comes up on the Redan, up left, as a second wave of Union soldiers charges over dead and wounded into fire from Redan. We watch the attack for a moment before light dims there and comes up near trenches, left, on* HALL *watching attack off to the side, behind a parapet. The noise of the Redan attack becomes background. We see* SHANGHAI, WILLIAMS, *and* MARKS *left of* HALL *in trenches, occupied with their own continuing battle with Union troops* [unseen], *in their trenches; we hear their rifle fire and the whir of Minié balls. A* LIEUTENANT *dashes up, exposed to fire, excited.*)

LIEUTENANT   Colonel! I have a message from. . . .

HALL   Down, man! Get down!

LIEUTENANT (*Wide eyed, looking at "distant" battle*)   But, sir. . . .

HALL   You'll be killed! Down!

LIEUTENANT (*Being brave*)   Do you order me down, sir?

HALL   Damn it to hell, yes. I order you down.

LIEUTENANT   Then I'll get down, sir. (*Crouches beside* HALL) General Bowen, sir, wants you to send all the men you can to spare up to the Stockade Redan.

HALL   And you made it here exposed like that? The Lord protects drunks and fools, they say. (*Eases down to* SHANGHAI) Sergeant, report to Stockade Redan with. . . , well, as you go, take every third man.

SHANGHAI   Yes, Colonel.

HALL   Keep under cover. And come back as soon as the attack is over.

SHANGHAI   We'll make it, Colonel. (*Creeps off toward up left;* WILLIAMS *and* MARKS *are alert with rifles, crouched behind breastworks*)

HALL (*To* LIEUTENANT)   Now, you keep down. I'm going back to a higher position and try to scout the attack.

(HALL *keeps low, goes up a ravine toward center, gets on a higher place. As he is looking with glasses toward Redan, we hear a Minie ball coming from left;* HALL *staggers and falls, clutching his leg.* LIEUTENANT *glances back, sees* HALL *down, runs toward him; stops, turns back and signals* MARKS *to come with him. They go up the ravine, keeping low, and take* HALL *by shoulders and legs, haul him out of lighted area as Minié balls whir around them, hitting trees with a thunk. Light dims on them and the trenches and Redan, comes up on the Cave area, where* MARY *and* DORA *are outside at tables, finishing their dinners.*)

MARY (*Looking into coffee cup*)   I think it's coffee I miss the most. Real coffee.

DORA   What kind is that?

MARY   Made from sweet potatoes.

DORA   Well, I've been able to get milk, so far. I can stand the food better than I can stand. . . . Well, I wish I'd stayed home.

MARY   Where is home?

DORA   It was New Orleans, until I got married, but I moved with my husband up to Holly Springs. That was quite a change, I can tell you, but we had a pretty little house with wisteria shading the porch. He was just getting his law practice started. . . . (*Shakes herself out of the beginnings of reverie*)   Of course, when he sent me here, Charles thought this was going to be the safest place in the South.

MARY   It may be.

DORA   But since then, they've been coming at us from every direction, and shooting those big old shells. I stay in the cave when they're close, but I tell you, one of these days I'm going crazy in there. You'll hear me trying to dig my way out, straight up. With my fingernails. And even out here. . . . Do you know how long I've seen nothing but that tree, that hillside, that . . . that . . . (*Points to the ground*)   that rock? I must have stared at that rock a hundred times. (*Gets up, picks up rock, throws it as far as she can*)   There. Why didn't I do that a long time ago?

MARY (*Laughs*) You see? It's not so hard to get a change of scenery. Listen, while the mortars are pretty quiet, let's go up to Sky Parlor Hill.

DORA Do you think it's safe?

MARY No.

DORA (*Sits looking at* MARY *a moment, then leaps up*) Let's go!

MARY I'll take my husband's glass.

> (*Light dims on Cave Area as she rushes into her cave, and Dora stands looking about, excited but apprehensive. Light comes up on* MRS. LUKE'*s place, up center;* LIEUTENANT *and* MARKS *are approaching with* HALL *on a stretcher.* MRS. LUKE *is in rocking chair on front porch, reading a newspaper. She speaks to herself as they come closer.*)

MRS. LUKE Pshaw! Just listen to that! (*Shakes out newspaper in disgust*)

LIEUTENANT Mrs. Luke?

MRS. LUKE (*Peers over newspaper at* LIEUTENANT) Yes? What is it?

LIEUTENANT It's Colonel Hall, ma'am. He's been shot in the leg, and the doctor says can you take him in.

MRS. LUKE (*Stands*) Why of course. Here, now. Bring him on in.

> (*As they start past her with the stretcher,* MRS. LUKE *moves toward the screen door to open it.*)

HALL (*Salutes* MRS. LUKE, *cries out*) Hurray for Vicksburg and the Southern Confederacy!

MRS. LUKE (*Unintentionally blocking the doorway*) Hush. Hush, now. You've got no call to be shouting, in your condition. (*Lifts newspaper, finds place*) Just listen to this! (*Reads*) '. . . the government had full control of the railroad and steamboat transportation all last summer and fall, but little provision was made for a siege, and many of the articles that were brought here remained exposed to the rain until they were unfit for use.'

HALL Begging your pardon, Mrs. Luke, but that isn't exactly news, is it?

MRS. LUKE News? When's the last time we got any news? Rumors, is all. Not fit to print.

HALL That's Marmaduke Shannon, in the *Whig*—and subject to question, if you ask me. What's the date on that paper?

MRS. LUKE March the fifth.

HALL You see?

MRS. LUKE See what?

HALL And this is the twenty-second day of May? That's six weeks old.

MRS. LUKE Pshaw! It's just as true today.

HALL If you'd look into the *Citizen*. . . .

MRS. LUKE How you talk! That fire-eating editor—Swords is just the right name for him!

HALL I'm afraid we're all swords now, ma'am. And eating fire.

MRS. LUKE And blame it all on J.M. Swords, I say. Here! Here! Don't just stand there! (*Moves aside*) Take him inside and put him to bed. Make haste!

(*Lights dim on* MRS. LUKE'S *house, come up on* MARY *and* DORA *on Sky Parlor Hill, right.*)

MARY Isn't it beautiful? This has been a favorite place of mine since I was a little girl.

DORA (*Very uneasy*) Yes, but, look. That clump of trees. (*Points toward far left*).

MARY So that's where the Yankee cannons are. Watch for a puff of smoke and let's see how long it takes to hear the shot. (*Pauses, watching*) There! Now listen. (*Listens intently for a moment before we hear the boom of the cannon*) Look! Did you see that? Just as the boom reached us, there was another puff. Now, listen. . . .

(*We hear a mortar shell approaching from up right.* MARY *and* DORA *whirl to see where it is going.* MARY *points, down toward the base of the hill. Before the mortar shell strikes, the cannons off left take up a heavy barrage again; the mortar shell explodes, below* MARY *and* DORA, *right.*).

DORA Oh! We'd better get back to our caves! We'll be killed!

MARY The cannons are aimed at the fortifications. And we can always dodge the mortars. Look. (*Points off right, toward the river*) There's a gunboat.

DORA Where?

MARY Over there on the Louisiana side. (*Firing continues from left, now we hear a single shot from town, up right, a Confederate cannon*) We're firing on it! See? See? There's the splash of the shell! (*Shakes head, disappointed*) It's just out of range.

DORA (*Points*) What's that?

MARY (*Looks through telescope;* ROBINETTE *approaches from left*) I don't know. It looks like a couple of boats, with other boats tied to them, full of men.

ROBINETTE Ladies. Allow me. (*Takes telescope, focuses*) Those were our prisoners, ma'am. They're being ferried across the river to a Federal camp.

MARY   We're giving them back?

ROBINETTE   (*Nods*)   If we keep them, we have to feed them. We drove eight or nine hundred mules out of town today, for the same reason.

MARY   Oh. (*Thoughtfully*)   Then we do expect a long. . . . We may as well prepare for real suffering.

ROBINETTE   Forgive my intrusion, Mrs. Burson, but I found your cave deserted and thought you might have come for the view. (*Seems ill at ease*)

MARY   (*Realizes that she has not introduced* DORA)   Forgive *me*. I was so taken with the scene. Mrs. Scott, Major Robinette; General Bowen has kindly assigned him to look after my welfare. Mrs. Scott is my next-door neighbor, Major. But as much as I enjoy her company, I don't want to be a cave dweller a minute longer than I have to. (*Takes telescope and watches Federal prisoners crossing the river*)   We do expect a long siege, don't we, Major? They're landing. See? (*Hands telescope to* DORA, *turns to* ROBINETTE *for response*)

ROBINETTE   Well, ma'am. . . . Do you want us to surrender?

MARY   (*Thinks a moment; the sounds of attack are strong from up left. Another cannon shot is fired from Town, up right. A mortar shell comes in as though above Town, flutters to a stop a distance upstage from them, explodes*)   I don't know what I want. We didn't want to secede from the beginning, most of us. But what did that matter? The men we sent to Jackson to vote against it couldn't make themselves go against the rest of the state. So we became part of the uprising—and the infection has come to a head here. (*Pauses*)   This is a boil that has to be lanced, and I'm afraid we'll suffer until it is. But, Major, (*Looks toward the sounds of firing from left*)   I flinch from the surgeon's knife.

DORA   (*Has been looking through telescope toward prisoners*)   They're walking away, down the river bank. (*To* MARY)   You make it sound so awful!

MARY   Worse that it is?

ROBINETTE   (*Lightly*)   Yes, worse than it is. We don't know, ma'am, how long it may take, but we're going to keep Grant out of Vicksburg. And, even if you ladies have no business up here, (*Points all around*)   what a view! Where else in the world can you see so magnificent a river, such rugged hills, pleasant fields . . . , and at the same time what promises to be a classic battle? I'd rather be in the thick of things, myself, ma'am, than to live so that the best I could say for my life was that I got through it without being much disturbed. Why, do you realize they call this the Gibraltar of the Confederacy? And they say our whole noble cause will stand or fall by what we do here?

MARY (*Wryly*) I'm afraid it's just such rhetoric that has put us under fire. But, it may be only high-sounding phrases that will rally us to whatever salvation we find. (*Turns to* DORA, *determined to shake off her seriousness*) What are you seeing?

DORA I've been watching a little tug, steaming down to the gunboat over there, and then over to those other boats near the canal.

ROBINETTE Those are transports.

DORA And now it's running very fast up the river, there.

MARY (*Trying to see*) Up the mouth of the Yazoo?

DORA I guess so. I can't tell. (*Lowers telescope;* MARY *takes it from her hand*)) It was like a little water spider, scooting around like that. (*Mortars have begun falling closer to them; shivers*).

MARY (*Looking toward the trenches, left*) I can see our troops working at their guns. (*Scans distance*) I suppose the Yankees are too well hidden. I can't see them.

(*Firing has come up harshly again, up left.*)

DORA I'm scared.

ROBINETTE Come along. I'd better see you ladies to safety. (*Offers arm to* DORA; *they start down hill*)

MARY (*Takes a last look left through telescope; to herself*) Here's an officer—coming from the lines, I guess—all bandaged and bloody. His head. . . . And ambulances, one . . . , two . . . , three. . . . (*Lowers telescope*) Our boys.

> MARY *follows* DORA *and* ROBINETTE *off right as lights dim on them and come up on* MRS. LUKE *seated beside* HALL'S *cot, trying to feed him soup. He is wan and feverish, but as bent on arguing as she is.*)

HALL But, ma'am, I distinctly remember that *you* were the one shaming out boys for retreating.

MRS. LUKE Of course I was. They ought to be ashamed, running away like that.

HALL And you keep telling me that you read nothing but the *Whig* because it's the only paper that prints the truth?

MRS. LUKE Yes sirree!

HALL (*Shakes his head*) Which paper turned out to be right? Maybe you don't remember, but it was 'fire-eating' editor Swords of the *Citizen* who wrote about secession. Your *Whig* editor Shannon said we should stay in the Union—is that what happened? Why, ma'am, endorsing Shannon is like endorsing the priests of Baal over Elijah, when they, like the *Whig*, couldn't conjure up so much as a spark, but Elijah, like Swords and the *Citizen*, called down fire from heaven to consume wood, bullock, stone, water and all.

MRS. LUKE Here now. Hold on. Swallow this. (*Forces spoonful of soup into his mouth*) Pshaw. J. M. Swords didn't prophesy secession; he brought it about. If Elijah had been like Swords, he would have poured oil over the altar, instead of water—and struck a sulphur match to it. (HALL *raises up on one elbow to argue;* MRS. LUKE *pushes him back down*) Lie down, there. You're in no shape to be sitting up. Here, drink this.

HALL (*Takes spoonful of soup; laughs*) I declare, you're a puzzle to me, Mrs. Luke. Shaming the troops when they don't fight for a cause you don't believe in.

MRS. LUKE Nonsense. The house is on fire, no matter who set it; you think I want the bucket brigade to quit and let it burn? (*Pokes spoon into his mouth again*) Swallow.

(*Lights go down somewhat on* HALL *and* MRS. LUKE, *come up on panorama so that we see* MARY, DORA, MARTHA *and* GEORGE *at dinner in Cave Area, Town in the background,* WILLIAMS *and* MARKS *as sharpshooters in trenches, and Redan with Union soldiers crouched at the foot, battered colors reached as far up the side as possible, bodies strewn behind them. Confederate soldiers in Redan roll handmade "grenade" down among the Union troops. One snatches it up and throws it back; it explodes overhead. Another grenade rolls down and explodes among the Union troops. Lights dim out over all; camp fires begin to appear along the lines. As darkness comes on, we hear the order, at Redan, to withdraw; bugles sound retreat and Union soldiers take the colors and retreat under rifle fire. Slowly, light comes up more fully on* WILLIAMS *and* MARKS *crouched at ready in the trenches.* ABRAHAM *approaches from right, bringing hardtack and bacon.* SHANGHAI *returns to join them from up left. Across from them, to their left, we can now make out the trench and barricade of the Union lines; gradually light will come up on it as the scene progresses.*)

SHANGHAI Well, they didn't get through that time.
MARKS Y'all held them? How close did they get?
SHANGHAI They was coming up the side of that Redan like monkeys. If you'da stood up, they'da dug their fingernails into your ribs and climbed right over your head.

MARKS God awmighty.

SHANGHAI If I'da had a chaw of tobacco, I could of blinded three or four of them with one spit, they was packed in so close.

MARKS I wish I'da been there! I'da. . . . (*Hesitates, remembering retreat, bites a hardtack* ABRAHAM *has brought*) These here things are worse'n iron.

WILLIAMS Keeps your jaws in shape for telling all the lies you'll be expected to tell after the war's over. I recollect the time up at Bull Run when most of us had sort of sauntered back a ways to get a better view, you know, and some of the other boys had taken refuge behind a big old sycamore, to avoid the cannon balls that was flying so thick. First one man had got himself behind the tree, and then another got behind him, and another behind him until there must have been two dozen of 'em, all in a line, hanging onto each other as tight as they could. Pretty soon, the Yankees begun firing around on one side of the tree, and the line would swing over the other way, so they'd fire on *that* side, and the line would swing back the other way, and they kept it up till it looked just exactly like an old hound's tail wagging. Well, sir, we all fell down and rolled on the ground, we was laughing so hard, and when we'd got ourselves together again, by God we charged the Yankee lines like it was nothing.

MARKS (*Laughs, then thinks a second*) I didn't know you were at Bull Run. How did you get from up there all the way down here?

WILLIAMS The long way, son. The long way.

(*From the distant Yankee lines the faint voice of* SERGEANT WELLS *calls out*)

WELLS Hey, Reb! Johnny, over there!

SHANGHAI Whatcha got to say, Yank?

WELLS Want a little coffee?

SHANGHAI These here roasted acorns'll do.

WELLS Why'nt you come over for a spell? We'll let you go back.

SHANGHAI On my own two legs?

WELLS Sure. Guaranteed. Come on over. (*Calls down the line*) Hold your fire, boys. This here's a visitor.

SHANGHAI All right. Here I come.

MARKS (*Takes him by the arm*) You aren't really going, are you?

SHANGHAI Hell yeah. They ain't going to hurt me. Might give me a drink of whiskey, even. (*Holds his hands out so they can be seen*) Here I come.

(*As* SHANGHAI *makes his way between lines, lights come up on* MRS. LUKE, *seated by* HALL'S *cot,* ABRAHAM *standing nearby, hat in hand*).

MRS. LUKE   We've had a devotional every night since I married Mr. Luke forty-two years ago, rest his soul. (*Mortar explodes near Town*) Isn't that true, Abraham?

ABRAHAM   Every single night, yes ma'am. (*Afterthought*)   Praise the Lord.

(*Mortar shell is heard approaching the Cave Area; dim light there; we see* GEORGE *in mime showing where it will fall; people run into caves ahead of the explosion;* MARY *steps into the mouth of her cave;* GEORGE *steps in behind her just as the shell explodes*).

MRS. LUKE   Do you have a favorite passage you'd like to read, Colonel Hall?

HALL (*more feverish than before*)   No, ma'am. Whatever your custom is.

MRS. LUKE   Well, our custom is to let a guest choose. (*Mortar shell is heard approaching;* HALL *raises up in some alarm;* ABRAHAM *draws his head down between his shoulders, waiting;* MRS. LUKE *glances toward the sound as if mildly curious; shell strikes to the right and explodes*)   But I was reminded today of a passage in the second Book of Kings, the tenth chapter, where Jehu got all the worshippers of Baal in one house. . . .

(*Mortar shell approaches Cave Area;* GEORGE *has stepped outside, points out its destination, steps back into cave at the last moment as the shell explodes*).

ABRAHAM   Please, Miz Luke, couldn't you just read 'The Lord is my shepherd'?

MRS. LUKE (*Ignores both the mortar and* ABRAHAM)   And put his own troops outside, and told them. . . . Here, listen to this.

ABRAHAM   The part where it says He prepareth a table before me in the presence of mine enemies.

MRS. LUKE (*Reads*)   'Jehu said to the guard and to the captains, Go in and slay them: Let none come forth. And they smote them with the edge of the sword.'

HALL (*Raises himself up on one elbow; quite feverish*)   Tell me, ma'am. Why did you pick *that* out to read?

MRS. LUKE   Maybe your talk about the priests of Baal put it in mind. (*Closes the Bible with a sense of satisfaction*)   It's all here, every bit of it. Right in the Good Book, if you know where to find it.

HALL All what, ma'am? Are you saying we're worshippers of Baal? That we will be put to the sword?

MRS. LUKE (*Can't resist the dig; pats the Bible*) Well, surely you know what the Book says about them that lives by the Swordses of this world.

HALL (*Laughs*) Oh, that's mean, Mrs. Luke. But it's Jehu that lives by the sword and the worshippers of Baal that die by it. What does that signify in our situation?

MRS. LUKE Pshaw. It's plain as the nose on your face.

HALL (*The exertion has been too much*) I'm afraid . . . , Mrs. Luke . . . , the nose on my face isn't very plain to me . . . right now.

MRS. LUKE Here, you, Abraham. Fetch that little bit of brandy from the pantry. (*Feels HALL's forehead*) And then go tell Dr. Foster we need him, whenever he can come.

(*Lights dim on MRS. LUKE and HALL as she settles beside his cot to keep watch; ABRAHAM goes off. Lights come up on the Cave Area with MARY and DORA outside their respective caves, MARTHA alongside DORA, GEORGE farther out, watching the sky. Far left, light begins to come up on SHANGHAI stumbling in the dark toward the Union lines where WELLS, WATTS, and STEITEL-MEYER await him in makeshift trenches and barricades.*)

MARY They seem to have found our range.

DORA Why would they aim at us? We're no threat to them.

MARY (*Laughs*) Maybe they're upset because their attack failed. George says some people in town are celebrating.

GEORGE Yes'm. I heard old Mr. Farnsworth say he wisht we had some fireworks. (*Laughs*).

MARY You know, if the mortar shells weren't so dangerous, they'd be beautiful to watch. . . .

(*A mortar shell is fluttering a distance off, back toward Town.*)

GEORGE (*Pointing toward it*) Over yonder, Miss Mary.

(*The mortar rises above the Town, fuse burning, sparks trailing behind. It reaches a rather high point and begins coming downward. MARY, GEORGE, DORA and MARTHA are ready to run inside, but hold a moment longer, watching. The mortar shell explodes, still high in the air.*)

MARY Beautiful!

(Another shell is fluttering toward them already, from a bit farther right than the first.)

GEORGE   Over there. Here it comes!

(MARY, DORA, GEORGE and MARTHA scramble into the caves. Lights dim on caves. A trail of sparks comes through the trees to the ground nearby. There is a huge explosion. Throughout the following scene, we hear mortar shells in the air and exploding in the Cave Area, as from a distance. Light is focused now on Union lines as SHANGHAI reaches them.).

WELLS   That you, Reb?

SHANGHAI *(Falsetto)*   No, it's Molly Bunch herself, come to give you boys a little . . . pleasure.

WELLS *(Gives SHANGHAI a hand over the barricade)*   And mighty welcome. I'm Wells. This here's Bugger Watts, and Herman Steitelmeyer. Molly Bunch, is it?

SHANGHAI   Masterson, from Missouri. They call me Shanghai.

WATTS   Here. Sit down. *(All sit or hunch down behind barricade)* How come they call you Shanghai?

SHANGHAI *(Shrugs)*   They never saw fit to let me know. Where y'all from?

WELLS   Illinois. This here's an Illinois regiment.

SHANGHAI   Wattses and Wellses I've heard of, but Steitelmeyer— that's got to be Yankee, all right.

STEITELMEYER *(Wryly)*   Yep. They have names like that up there. But who the hell is Molly Bunch? I have to admit, female names get my interest quicker than yours and mine.

WELLS   Give him a pull on that bottle, first.

(WATTS hands SHANGHAI a bottle.)

SHANGHAI   Much obliged. *(Drinks)*

WELLS   Now. Molly Bunch.

SHANGHAI   Unfortunately, I've never met the lady. Seems she runs a famous house here, with a large female population. Got a lot of brass, too. A while back she threw a big party in the middle of town and sent special invitations to all the ladies and the preachers.

WATTS *(Laughs)*   Did any of them show up?

SHANGHAI   Well, I guess what they did was send representatives, cause at the height of the ball, as they say, some righteous citizens come rushing in with the local fire equipment and hosed down Molly and all her girls.

STEITELMEYER   All those wet girls! Oh, Lord. I used to go down and watch the baptizings when I was a boy, just to see 'em come up out of the creek with their clothes all plastered to their. . . . (*trails off dreamily*).

SHANGHAI   Y'all have duckings, too? I though they just sprinkled, up in cold territory.

STEITELMEYER   What do you mean, up in cold territory? Hell, I bet I live farther south than you do. Right out of Cairo.

SHANGHAI   (*Laughs*)   Pretty near. Matter of fact, we got names like that where I live, too. But I figure if you're going to be a Southern patriot, you might as well talk like one.

(*The bottle has been to* WATTS *and* STEITELMEYER; *now* WELLS *holds it up for a toast.*)

WELLS   No offense, Reb. It's just that I never drink without saying, the Union, now and forever. (*Drinks; hands bottle to* SHANGHAI)

SHANGHAI   Thank God I don't have to say that before drinking, or I'd have to turn teetotaler. (*Holds bottle up*)   The Confederate States of America. (*Drinks; hands bottle on to* WATTS; *laughs*)   There's a funny kind of fellow in our outfit always says,

> All you Lincolns, Hallecks, Grants,
> Go to thunder in your pants.

(WATTS *is drinking, chokes; they pound him on the back.*)

WELLS   You Johnny Rebs got some sense of humor.

SHANGHAI   Well, I didn't think it was much, either, but Watts here nearly died laughing.

WATTS   Hell, I wasn't laughing. I just swallowed wrong.

WELLS   (*Winks at* SHANGHAI)   Not used to the strong stuff, huh Bugger?

WATTS   I can drink you under any day of the week.

SHANGHAI   (*Placative*)   I'd love to have a go at that myself. Even losing would be a real pleasure.

(PRIVATE HOLMES *has come into view up the Union trenches, crouching along behind the barricades; he comes hesitantly toward the group*)

PRIVATE HOLMES   Uh. I hear you got a . . . a Confederate over here.

SHANGHAI   (*Looks around at the others*)   Since I don't see nothing but blue, I must be it. (*Holds out his hand*)   Masterson, of Missouri.

PRIVATE HOLMES   Holmes. Missouri too.

SHANGHAI (*Looks at him closely*) Cape Girardeau?

PRIVATE HOLMES Yeah! That where you're from too?

SHANGHAI Nope, but I'd bet my last dollar you got a brother by the name of Chadwick.

PRIVATE HOLMES Chad! You . . . know him?

SHANGHAI (*Points across to Confederate lines, right*) He's right about over yonder, this minute. Probably sound asleep already.

PRIVATE HOLMES That's him. Went to sleep before the chickens, my mother used to say. But come the first crack of light, and Chad would be out of bed. 'Get up, Billy, it's day,' he'd tell me. He's . . . doing all right, I reckon.

SHANGHAI Fit. Got all his parts. (*Half rises*) Well, boys, I better get on back, I reckon. I thank you for the hospitality. (*To* PRIVATE HOLMES) You got any . . . (*Sees that* PRIVATE HOLMES *is not able to talk at the moment*) I'll tell him. (*Shouts right*) It's me, boys! Don't get carried away. (*Cautiously rises to get over barricade, turns back to his hosts and says as a final salute*) Keep your heads down.

WELLS (*Giving him a hand over the barricade*) Hell, I can tell a Mississippi rifle when I hear one. You couldn't hit a barn at ten paces with one of those things.

SHANGHAI Well, be careful anyway. We might throw one at you.

(*Lights dim out on Union soldiers and* SHANGHAI *as he starts to his own lines, right. Lights come up somewhat, briefly, on* MRS. LUKE, *sponging the forehead of the sleeping* HALL, *then up on Cave Area. There is the flicker of flames in Town, up right.* MARY *and* GEORGE *are outside their cave;* MARY *retreats inside as a mortar shell approaches;* GEORGE *points it out before following her inside. The shell strikes nearby, explodes.* GEORGE *comes out of cave, followed by* MARY. *A* GENTLEMAN *rushes past, pointing toward Town.*)

GENTLEMAN Incendiaries! They've infiltrated the city!

GEORGE (*Ignores him; watches sky for other mortar shells*) Seem like they know just where we are.

MARY (*Has trouble getting her breath*) Do you think we'll live through the night, George? What if one hits directly on the cave?

GEORGE It ain't hardly going to do that, Miss Mary. Now, you go on and get some sleep. These here shells is bound to move on pretty soon. (*Takes pistol from belt*) And I got the pistol all ready. I'll be lying down across the front of the cave, here, and anybody want to get in got to deal with me.

MARY (*Rubbing her temples*) I can't think, George. I feel like they've

been blowing up inside my head. (*Looks toward* DORA'S *cave*)   I
guess Dora's asleep. . . . Trying to sleep.

GEORGE   Yes'm. You go too. I'll watch out for you.

MARY (*Looks fearfully upward*)   Oh, Please, God, make them stop.
You're right, George. I may as well lie down. What's the little song
Dora says she thinks of, the one her grandmother taught her when
she was little? I want to remember it. (*Closes her eyes tightly*).

> Lord keep us safe this night,
> Secure from . . . from all our . . . fears
> May angels guard us while we sleep,
> Till morning light appears.

(*Starts into cave*)   I'll have to learn the tune.

> (MARY *enters her cave.* GEORGE *takes a look around, lies down
> in cave entrance. Mortar shell flutters over, explodes nearby.*)

Scene 3 (*May 25*)

(*Lights come up on all areas dimly. At Caves,* MARY *is sewing,* DORA
*reading. We hear an occasional mortar shell, but well off to the
right; they listen, but go on with they are doing. Throughout the
scene, until the truce, we hear constant cannon and rifle fire. On
the Confederate lines, we see* SHANGHAI *and* MARKS *crouched
in place,* WILLIAMS *in place but asleep. In Union trenches,*
WELLS, WATTS, *and* STEITELMEYER *are in place. Lights come
up on* MRS. LUKE'S *house; she is in rocking chair on the porch;*
DR. FOSTER *comes out door with black bag.*)

DR. FOSTER   He's no better, that's a fact.

MRS. LUKE   Did y'all decide what to do? It's been a week, him laying
there out of his mind and me run out of rising for biscuits. I don't
know how long he can last on a little cornmeal gruel every day.

DR. FOSTER   Three days is what it's been, Mrs. Luke. And it's not
an easy decision. Dr. Ray wasn't sure either.

MRS. LUKE   Seems pretty cut and dried to me. Either you leave it
on or you chop it off.

DR. FOSTER (*Sits on steps; very fatigued*)   If gangrene sets in, he's
a dead man.

MRS. LUKE   If thy leg offend thee, cut it off. It's in the Bible, Dr.
Foster. The Lord knew what he was talking about. Pshaw, better to

have one leg than nothing. Why, old man One-legged Smith had four-teen children. Lived to be ninety-something years old. Amputate, Dr. Foster, and be quick about it.

DR. FOSTER (*Shakes his head unsurely*)   At least we've still got a little chloroform, so they don't feel it the way they do in the field . . . , until they wake up.

MRS. LUKE   Then use the knife, I say.

DR. FOSTER (*With some irritation*)   Perhaps you'd like to watch? Come down any time—one of us will be at it. You slice all the way around the leg, lay back a flap of skin and muscle, make a quick cut to the bone, stroke through with the saw, then toss the leg onto a pile of other legs—and arms, hands, fingers. Tie off the artery. Stitch the flap down over the stump, and . . . on to the next one. (*As if to himself*)   Most times all you've done is bury part of them a few days before the rest. (*Looks up at* MRS. LUKE)   I have nightmares, ma'am, about that tangled mass of human parts rising on Judgment Day.

MRS. LUKE (*Shifts uncomfortably*)   Well, like I say, it's a medical deci-sion, and you've no business asking the likes of me.

DR. FOSTER (*Slaps his thigh, rises*)   I'm going to try to save the leg. I hope you don't mind if I do a little surgery here this afternoon. I don't want to move him.

MRS. LUKE   Pshaw, how you talk. Of course you can, if you need to. (*As* DR. FOSTER *half salutes her and moves away*)   Just try not to mess up the bedsheets.

(*Lights dim on* MRS. LUKE's *porch, come up on* MARY *and* DORA *outside their caves. Mortars continue off right, but are not a threat.*)

MARY   I keep thinking I might go back to the house. Mrs. Luke has survived all right so far, and she's just up the hill. (*Laughs*)   While you were over at Mrs. Barlow's this morning, I went over to the rectory. Do you know Mrs. Lord? And the Rector? (DORA *shakes her head*) Well, they've spent the last couple of nights in one of the big caves— room after room with long corridors, they said, and as many as two hundred people.

DORA (*Slight shudder*)   I don't think I could stand that. (*Looks off right*)   I left Martha to help Mrs. Barlow out for a while. She ought to be back. (*Settles back; returns to the subject*)   I like some privacy, myself.

MARY   Me too. But anyway, they said that when the mortars were so thick and fast the other night a man ducked in and stayed till morning, and when the shelling stopped he gathered himself up to leave and said, (*Rather pompously*) 'You know, don't you, that all that dirt over your heads wouldn't amount to a thing if a mortar made a direct hit.' So Mrs. Lord said, 'I suppose that's why you kept us company last night . . . , to demonstrate your courage.'

(MARTHA *has approached from right, carrying a pan; she waits, aside, until* DORA *addresses her.*)

DORA   Did you bring the milk, Martha?

MARTHA   (*Comes toward her*) No'm. Ain't going to be no more milk. But Miz Barlow sent part of the cow. (*Holds out the pan*)

DORA   Oh! Killed by a shell?

MARTHA   Yes'm. You want me to cook this for dinner?

DORA   I guess so. It will be good to have fresh meat, but . . , what am I going to do without my milk?

MARY   George dug me some sassafrass roots for tea. You're welcome to some of that.

DORA   I thought I could make it as long as I had milk and bread, but the yeast is gone, and now the cow. Anyway, I guess Mrs. Barlow won't have so much trouble.

MARY   Trouble? What do you mean?

DORA   Some of the soldiers tried to make her give them some milk yesterday. Pushed their way right into the house.

MARY   *Our* soldiers?

DORA   (*Nods*) They were rude and awful, called her "old woman," and everything. If Mr. Barlow had been there, they wouldn't have dared.

MARY   Our own boys. I know they're hungry, but I do wish they'd act better.

DORA   Oh, but that's nothing compared to the Yankees. Mrs. Barlow's niece is caught in the lines outside the city, and she wrote the most (*Shudders violently*) horrible things about them.

MARY   A letter? How did she get it in?

DORA   By a courier that got through with messages from General Johnston. They say he's coming, from Clinton. Oh, I hope it's true!

MARY   (*Wryly*) They say. Oh, there goes that thread, breaking again. It's gone plumb rotten. (*Tying thread*) What was it Ida had to say?

DORA   Ida?

MARY   Mrs. Barlow's niece. I'm sure it's the one. We used to swing on the grapevines together, down behind their pasture, when she'd come to town for a visit.

DORA   Well, she says there was a planter nearby who was supposed to be very cruel to his slaves, and all the slaves went over to the Yankees and told about him, so some soldiers came to his house and put a candle in a gun and shot his wife with it, and they pinned one of the children to the wall with a bayonet, and cut off both the man's arms and both legs.

MARY   Surely not!

DORA   That's what her letter said. She said another little girl had hidden under the house, and after they left she found her father and took him to a neighbor's house, him just rolling along with no arms or legs— and only lived a short time.

MARY   (*Shakes her head in horror, then suddenly giggles*)   Oh, I shouldn't laugh. But . . . , rolling along? (*Can't keep from laughing;* DORA *laughs tentatively with her*)   You know that can't be true. Can it?

DORA   I . . . I don't know.

(GEORGE *has come up from left and stood waiting to speak; sees opening now.*)

GEORGE   Please, ma'am, I went up to the pasture and got the mule like you told me. . . .

(*A mortar approaches, closer than the others.* GEORGE *watches where its path seems to be. It falls and explodes to the right, upstage from them. There are screams, then cries of anguish.* GEORGE *rushes off right as* MARY *and* DORA *rise in alarm.* MARTHA *has been preparing to cook the meat; she stops, stands waiting.*)

MARY   (*In some confusion*)   What on earth . . . ? Who do you suppose . . . ?

(DORA *has dropped her book. She stands dazed a moment, then picks up the book and looks at it without opening it, as if she doesn't quite know what it is.* GEORGE *rushes back on.*)

GEORGE   It's Nate, ma'am. He's been buried in a cave.

MARY   Oh! Were his wife and children with him?

GEORGE   No'm. They were outside. (*Starts to leave, hesitates, looking at* MARY)

MARY   Yes, go help, George. See if you can.

(GEORGE *rushes off right.*)

DORA   Nate?

MARY   He's a freedman. A carpenter. (*Dazed*)   He was in his cave. (*Listens to sounds of grief*)   Oh! It breaks my heart. Say a prayer, Dora. Say a prayer. (*Looks at her cave*)   Will we all be buried? (*Rises; decisively*)   I'm going back to my house.

MARTHA   Miss Mary, that ain't likely to be safe neither. They say up
at Miz Barlow's that Mr. Tucker been trying to get Miz Tucker up
out of her invalid bed to go to the cave he fixed up for her, and she
wouldn't budge. (*Interrupted by renewed wailing; hesitates; continues*)
So last night he taken her hand and said, 'Come on. You got to.'
And she finally got up, and he hadn't no more than help her out of
the house when a shell come right through the roof into the bed she
just got out of.

MARY   Exploded?

MARTHA   Yes'm. There ain't no more bed, or floor, or nothing.

MARY   (*Sits again*) You're right, Martha. No place is really safe.
(GEORGE *returns, dispirited*)   Did you find him, George?

> (GEORGE *nods slowly and turns away. Throughout the scene we
> hear occasional rifle fire and cannon from left, mortars from up
> right and right, exploding off a distance. From the left,* ROBINETTE
> *approaches, sees that they are all strongly affected, holds back a
> moment, finally speaks*)

ROBINETTE   Pardon me, Mrs. Burson. Mrs. Scott. I just wanted to
let you know, there'll be a ceasefire beginning at two o'clock.

MARY   Ceasefire? What . . . What does that mean?

ROBINETTE   Nothing, ma'am, except three hours of quiet. It's to bury
the dead caught between the lines.

GEORGE   (*Pulls himself together*)   Maybe if them guns gonna stop I
can get that mule to go, like you ask me to.

MARY   (*To* ROBINETTE)   I wanted him to ride down to the lines toward
Warrentown and try to locate a cousin of my husband, but. . . . What
happened, George?

GEORGE   Well, Miss Mary, I caught the mule and got on him, all
right, and we was going along down past Mr. Turner's store, and come
out on that rise there, you know? And all of a sudden shells start
swooping at us like jay birds at a cat, boom over here, boom over
there, and bullets whizzing around like bees. So I whup on the mule
to get out of there, but he stops dead still in his tracks, won't move
for nothing. (*Laughs*)   Them shells and bullets keep coming, and that
mule stand there like a rock. You couldn't budge him with a crowbar.
I tol' him, I say, 'I ruther be a *moving* target,' but he don't pay no
mind. I beat him and kick him, and that don't make no difference
either, so I got so mad I got off'n him and hit him in the head with
my fist. It hurt *me*, but he don't bat an eye. So I told him, 'All right,
you just stand here and get killed. I'm going home.' I run back down
off the rise, and he just stand there. But I kept looking back, and

I can see his eye cock around, watching me, and time I was back down by the store he kind of droop his head and follow me back up to the pasture like a whipped puppy. (*Starts toward center stage*)   I better go catch him now for when the guns quit.

MARY   Be sure to stop by Mrs. Luke's and ask about Colonel Hall.

(GEORGE *exits from lighted cave area.*)

ROBINETTE   Pardon my asking, ma'am. Was there bad news? You all seemed . . . upset, when I came up.

MARY (*More sarcastically than she intends*)   And there's nothing going on to be upset about, is there Major? (*Takes a deep breath*)   I'm sorry. (*Bitterly*)   Just another of us killed. One less mouth to try to feed, I suppose. (*Begins to pull herself with an effort back to a semblance of brightness*)   Of course, there's one more mouth to feed, too. Born this morning, in the back of the big cave the Lords were in. (*To* DORA)   You'd never guess what they named him. William . . . *Siege.*

DORA   Poor child.

MARY   William Siege Green.

ROBINETTE   It has a certain. . . . (*Half laugh, shrug*)   I have to get back to the lines, Ladies. Enjoy the truce. I'll spend it trying to get a look at the Yankee fortifications. (*Starts left, turns back*)   I know a man born the day Andrew Jackson took office, and his mother named him Old Hickory. (*Waves and moves left toward the lines*)

(*Lights dim on Cave Area as* DORA *finds her place and resumes reading,* MARY *her sewing. Half light comes upon* MRS. LUKE *on her porch, rocking, looking anxiously around toward the front door. Separate spot comes up a bit on* DR. FOSTER *and an* AIDE *working over* HALL, *beyond door.* GEORGE *stops by, from right, sits on step, mimes conversation with* MRS. LUKE. *Light comes up on Confederate lines.* SHANGHAI *is sighting his rifle over the barricade.* MARKS *is alert to do so if necessary.* WILLIAMS *is still asleep.*)

SHANGHAI   If that damfool shows himself again, by God I won't miss.

MARKS   Is he crazy, making you shoot at him this way?

SHANGHAI   Hell, they know these Mississippi rifles couldn't hit. . . .

(*Lights comes up quickly on Union lines, on* WATTS, *who stands into full view, thumbs nose, drops out of sight.* SHANGHAI *fires, misses, pulls rifle in, attempts to stomp it; his hat rises slightly above the barricade; there is a shot from Union lines;* SHANGHAI'S *hat flies off.* WILLIAMS *comes awake, starts to get up.*)

MARKS Keep down!

SHANGHAI Might as well throw rocks as shoot one of these damn things. By God, I can stand to starve, I can stand the heat, I can stand the stink of all them rotting Yankees, but I can't stand shooting and not hitting! Hell, with my old rifle I could knock squirrels out of trees at this distance. Put it through the head so as not to spoil the pelt.

(Lights begin to come up on the area between the lines, strewn near Union lines with dead Union soldiers.)

MARKS Ain't it about time for that truce? Maybe you can stand the stink, but it's hard enough to keep that spoiled bacon down without that. . . . *(Gags; points across to one of the bodies)* That poor son of a bitch has been lying there for two days, twitching his legs every now and then. If these here Mississippi rifles are so bad, how come they don't just come on out and get him?

WILLIAMS *(Yawns)* Aw, give us that good a chance and we could hit 'em, and they know it. You'll notice they don't stand still and give us a target. Where's that canteen? *(MARKS hands him the canteen; he takes a swallow, shivers)* God bless us. Once that river water gets warm, it's rotten. *(Begins to have the shakes)* I can feel that stuff going through me like a dose of calomel.

(From down the lines we hear the order "Ceasefire!" being passed. SHANGHAI passes it along, ties handkerchief to his bayonet and sets rifle up atop the barricade. The last cannon boom sounds, and a final rifle shot or two. Silence. Lights come up over the whole panorama: MARY, DORA, and MARTHA by their caves, and MRS. LUKE on her porch, sit still, listening to the silence. WELLS, on Union lines, puts up a flag on the barricade, holds his hands high, rises above the barricade.)

WELLS Hey, Reb! Shanghai!

SHANGHAI *(Stands and points)* That one over yonder, Wells. He's been kicking for two days.

WELLS Yeah. I know. *(WELLS and STEITELMEYER climb over barricade and check the wounded soldier; WELLS calls over to SHANGHAI:)* Too late.

(SHANGHAI shakes his head. MARKS stands and rubs his cramped back. WILLIAMS tries to pull himself up, but sits back hard. MARKS helps him to his feet. WATTS has come from behind Union barricade and helps with bodies; he, WELLS and STEITELMEYER drag the dead toward their lines, heads averted from the stench.)

WATTS (*Yells over to* SHANGHAI *et al*) Why don't you give us a hand?

SHANGHAI They ain't none of ours. What I want *you* to give *me* is about four square inches to shoot at, next time.

WATTS Hell. What you need is half an acre.

(*Lights dim somewhat on* SHANGHAI, WELLS, *et. al, and come up on* ROBINETTE, *down left, making his way curiously between the lines. Across the Union lines, a bit upstage, lights come up on* GENERAL SHERMAN *and his* AIDE. SHERMAN *gestures for* AIDE *to bring* ROBINETTE *to log down left, and proceeds there himself; when* ROBINETTE *joins* SHERMAN *at log, the spot is on them.*)

SHERMAN Major. (*They shake hands*) I have a few letters here for some of your officers and men. (*Hands him packet*) Their Northern friends will appreciate my delivering them before they get too old.

ROBINETTE Yes, General, they would be *very* old if you waited to bring them into Vicksburg yourself.

SHERMAN So you think mine a rather inefficient mail route?

ROBINETTE (*Keeps trying to see the Union fortifications without being too obvious*) Well, you do have to travel by parallels and zigzags.

SHERMAN Yes, it's a slow way of getting into a place, but it's a very sure way, and I will deliver the next batch sooner or later. (*Motions to the log; they sit*) You do have an admirable position for defense here, and you've taken excellent advantage of these hills and ravines.

ROBINETTE Thank you, General. We intend to add all the ingenuity of man to what the Lord was so generous as to provide.

(*Lights dim on* SHERMAN *and* ROBINETTE, *come up on* MRS. LUKE *in rocking chair as* DR. FOSTER *comes out of house onto the porch, exhausted.* MRS. LUKE *gets up, motions him to chair.*)

MRS. LUKE Here. Sit down. How is he, Doctor? Will he be all right?

DR. FOSTER (*Sits*) I hope so, ma'am. We can pray. (*Listens; becomes aware of silence for the first time*) What is it?

MRS. LUKE What's what?

DR. FOSTER It's quiet. There's no shooting. (*Stands and looks about a bit wildly*) Is it over? Have we quit?

MRS. LUKE It's only a truce, Doctor. To bury the dead. (DR. FOSTER *collapses back in the chair, head in hands*) Here, now. (*Reaches out as if to touch his shoulder, draws back*) I got enough coffee hid back to make one pot. I reckon this is the time to use it. Hold on, now. Just sit tight.

(Lights dim on MRS. LUKE *and* DR. FOSTER *as she goes into the house; they come up on the Cave Area.* MARY *is pacing about;* DORA *is seated, with her book, finger holding her place.)*

MARY   Oh, I can't stand it. It hurts my ears.

DORA   *Hurts* your ears?

MARY   *(Laughs)*   It's a good hurt. Let's go somewhere. *(Stops)*   Listen. *(A mockingbird is singing)*

DORA   To what?

MARY   That mockingbird.

DORA   He sings all the time, even when the guns are at their worst.

MARY   But *listen.* It's different. You can really hear him. Let's go somewhere. Get up! *(Pulls* DORA *to her feet, swings her around)*

DORA   *(Laughing)*   Where to? Town? Sky Parlor Hill?

MARY   Just around. Where there are trees and flowers. Smell that? The Cape Jessamine's in bloom. There are plums turning on that tree. I want to. . . . We've got three hours. Come on!

*(*MARY *and* DORA *start off right; lights dim on them, come up on trenches and between lines.* SHANGHAI, WELLS, *et al, are miming conversation. Downstage from them,* PRIVATE HOLMES *is talking to his brother, Confederate* CORPORAL HOLMES.)*

PRIVATE HOLMES   Here's some jam Ma sent. I guess what she sent you didn't get through.

CORPORAL HOLMES   Last thing I got was some of her ginger cakes, and they wasn't anything but crumbs. I ate 'em, though. That was half a year ago, I reckon. Got a letter since then, but I've forgotten just when that was.

PRIVATE HOLMES   Last I heard, she and Pa were fine. Getting the plowing done, she said. Sis had her a beau.

CORPORAL HOLMES   A beau! Why, she ain't old enough for that!

PRIVATE HOLMES   She's going on ten. *(Laughs)*   Naw. It was just a joke. They tease her about Herbie Waters.

CORPORAL HOLMES   That runny-nosed little. . . .? Tell Ma if he starts coming around, sic the dogs on him. Plowing. I remember trying every dodge in the business to get out of it.

PRIVATE HOLMES   Yeah. *(They sit in silence a moment, relishing the thought of back home)*   Well, y'all better give up soon, Chad, so we can get back and help Pa.

CORPORAL HOLMES   Give up hell. Don't you damyankees know when you've stepped into a den of wildcats? *(Looks around;* SHANGHAI, WELLS, *et al., are separating, going back to their own lines)*   I guess we better get back before she starts up again. Thanks for the stuff, Billy. And the news from home.

PRIVATE HOLMES   Sure, Chad. (*They shake hands and start away*) Keep your head down. I'm bound to shoot it if I can see it.

CORPORAL HOLMES   You too, Billy. I think I've got a bead on where you're located.

(*Lights come up over all as troops set up again.* ROBINETTE *is crossing from down left toward center, laughing to himself as he gestures that he had come up empty handed as far as seeing fortifications is concerned.* MRS. LUKE *is handing* DR. FOSTER *a cup of coffee.* MARY *and* DORA *are returning from off right to their caves, with* MARTHA *and* GEORGE *approaching from behind caves, around their left. The soldiers in the trenches take down flags and get down behind barricades. Suddenly cannons boom, a mortar shell lifts over Town, explodes. Rifle fire comes up strong. Civilians are caught in a listening air as lights dim on panorama, focus strong spot on* SHANGHAI, MARKS, *and* WILLIAMS. MARKS *turns to say something to* SHANGHAI, *rises slightly above the barricade; there is a rifle shot from Union lines.* MARKS *jerks erect and falls twisted between* SHANGHAI *and* WILLIAMS.)

ACT II

Scene 1 (May 27)

(*Lights come up slowly over the entire panorama; we see the activity of preparing breakfast at the Caves; in both the Confederate and Union lines, soldiers are digging farther in and setting up for sharpshooting; at Redan, Union soldiers are digging under, to undermine it. Both mortars and cannons are heard throughout the scene. The lights focus on* MRS. LUKE, *center, at the cotside of* HALL. *She holds a pail.*)

MRS. LUKE   Well, it's a pity it couldn't be winter. (*Examines the bandaged leg*) That thing is hot as blazes. . . . The Lord forgive me.

HALL (*Still feverish, but alert*)   Forgive you for what, Mrs. Luke?

MRS. LUKE   For saying 'blazes,' of course.

HALL   Why people say it all the time, ma'am. The fire blazes on the hearth. The woodman blazes a trail.

MRS. LUKE   Be ashamed! You know I was using it as another name for . . . the bad place. No worse to say it outright. (*Suddenly cries out*) You, Abraham! (*Normal voice*) Somebody told me that up North they can cut two feet and more of ice off a pond in the winter and save it all summer in the root cellar. (*Laughs at the idea*)

HALL   Yes ma'am. That's a fact.

MRS. LUKE   Pshaw! How you talk! Did you ever see them do it?

HALL   No ma'am, but it's a well known fact. . . .

MRS. LUKE   But you didn't see it, and neither did anybody else. (*Shouts off again*) Abraham! (*Checks bandage again*) Wouldn't it be nice if it was true! Or if it would hail the way it used to. The old folks used to tell how it stormed every July with hailstones big as the goiter on Aunt Bessie's neck—which they said was bigger than your fist—and they'd gather them in washtubs and have cold lemonade for a week. (ABRAHAM *has entered, stands waiting; she gives him the pail*) Here, now. Take this buttermilk down to General Lee. Make haste.

(*A shell lands close by*)

ABRAHAM   Yes'm.

HALL   (*Picking at her*) It'll be spoiled before it gets there. General Lee's in Virginia.

MRS. LUKE   (*Not to be outdone; speaks to* ABRAHAM, *but keeps eyes on* HALL) And you might mention to him that there's a Colonel Hall here who thinks we have only one General Lee.

HALL   (*Laughs*) While you're down at the lines, Abraham, make your way across to General Grant and ask him not to shell so close to the house; tell him Mrs. Luke is afraid he'll break one of her flowerpots.

ABRAHAM   Yes suh. (*Starts left, turns back*) You want me to ask him could he come over for a feast of cornbread and salt meat?

HALL   Certainly. That's sure to tempt his palate.

MRS. LUKE   Now hold on here! You'll do nothing of the kind.

HALL   Well, maybe you should just ask him over for a cup of burnt acorn coffee.

ABRAHAM   Yes suh. I spect he don't get much of that, either.

MRS. LUKE   Get along with you. Shake a leg. And don't you go near that General Grant, you hear me?

ABRAHAM   (*Starts left again, holding in laughter*) Yes'm. If you say so.

MRS. LUKE   And when you come back, bring me that bucket from the well house. I've got to cool this leg off some way.

ABRAHAM   (*Continues left*) Yes'm.

HALL   Are you going to set the bucket out and hope it fills up with hailstones?

MRS. LUKE   Lie still there. You've got no business carrying on. I know what I'm about.

> (*Lights go down on* MRS. LUKE *and* HALL, *come up on Cave Area;* MARY *and* DORA *are seated;* MARTHA *and* GEORGE *clear away after breakfast.*)

DORA   I wished for you yesterday, while you were off visiting. You would have thought I was crazy, sitting out here by myself laughing aloud. It's this book. Here, (*Rises and starts toward her cave*)   I've got to read it to you. (*Sees that* MARY *seems distracted*)   It's short. It won't take a minute. (*Pauses, turns to* MARY)   You won't mind?

MARY   Oh. No. Of course not.

DORA   (*Uncertainly*)   It's *Nicholas Nickleby.* By Dickens. You know how I love the things he writes.

MARY   (*A trifle impatient*)   Yes, yes. Do bring it and read it to me.

> (DORA *hesitates a second, then goes into her cave.*)

GEORGE   (*Clearing away remnants of breakfast*)   You not feeling good, Miss Mary?

MARY   Oh, I'm all right, George.

GEORGE   You ain't eating enough to keep a bird alive.

MARY   Well. . . . Save what I left, George. We shouldn't waste anything.

GEORGE   Yes'm. But waste ain't what I got on my mind right now. Maybe you need me to go get Dr. Foster.

MARY   No, I'll be fine. I'm just. . . .

GEORGE   Not happy.

MARY   (*Nods*)   Not happy.

GEORGE   Well, maybe something good will happen to perk you up.

DORA   (*Hurries from her cave with the book, finger in place*)   Here it is. (*Loses place as she opens book*)   Oh, bless me, I've lost the place again. (*Searching*)   Here it is. No, this is where. . . . (*Searches again; can't find it; sits abruptly in frustration*)   Well, anyway, it's where this old man throws a cucumber over the fence, where Mrs. Nickelby is, and turnips and radishes, and all kinds of vegetables, and they just come sailing over the fence and bouncing around, you know? (*Looks at* MARY, *who is not responding*)   I thought it was the funniest . . . (*Sits back*)   You're not listening.

MARY   (*Gets up abruptly*)   I'm sorry. I guess I'm not.

DORA   Anyway, it turns out that he's just getting her attention so he can propose marriage.

(*A mortar shell comes closer than the others; they all listen until it strikes and explodes.*)

GEORGE (*Taking breakfast things to cave*) You reckon that's how come them Yankees throwing all that stuff in here? (*Exits into cave*)

DORA What is it, Mary. You've seemed strange all morning.

MARY It's just . . . something I saw yesterday, on the way to Emma's house. (*Agitated*) I'd do better just to stay here in my cave, much as I hate it.

DORA Well, *I* think you ought to tell about it instead of brooding—and being such poor company.

MARY (*Trying to shake it off*) It was just a horse.

DORA Just a horse?

MARY A big horse, what my father would have called a Noble Black. He was tied to a tree in a ravine, and I noticed that he was struggling . . . .

DORA Was he hurt?

MARY A soldier said he'd been hit in the flank by a Minié ball. It was terrible. The poor thing would reach up into the tree as far as he could and clamp down on leaves and branches with his mouth, and his whole body would quiver.

DORA (*Shudders*) Didn't anybody do anything?

MARY The soldier got his halter off; then he leaned against a tree and moaned and shivered, and he would turn and look as if . . . asking for . . . something.

DORA They didn't just let him suffer!

MARY They found his master, but he wouldn't let them shoot him. He said maybe he would get better. You could tell he had already been starving, and now. . . . Finally he staggered down to a little stream and fell in, with his head out on the bank, and those eyes. . . . I kept wanting to leave, but I couldn't—until I saw that one of the soldiers had gotten an axe, and. . . . When I looked back they were dragging. . . .

DORA Oh!

MARY (*Pushes on*) And I thought, there he goes. And tomorrow there will be other sufferings, and the next day more, and his suffering will be forgotten. Isn't it awful to wait for tomorrow's suffering, hoping it will drown out what we suffered yesterday?

(*There is a sudden increase of both mortar and cannon fire from up right. They look up, wondering.* GEORGE *comes out of the cave.*)

DORA What is it?

MARY   It's from the river. Sounds like their mortars, and . . . those are our shore batteries, aren't they, George?

GEORGE   Yes'm. Sound like maybe a gunboat trying to make a run past.

MARY   Let's go watch it! Come on!

DORA *(Flustered)*   Where . . . ?

MARY   Sky Parlor Hill. Let's go.

GEORGE   Miss Mary, that ain't safe. You know they say for you not to go up there.

MARY   Well, I'm going. I want to see this. You, Dora?

(DORA *gets up a bit uncertainly.*)

GEORGE   If y'all bound to go, I better go watch out for you.

MARY *(Pulling DORA with her)*   Bring the glass, George. Hurry! We don't want to miss it.

(MARY *and* DORA *run off toward Sky Parlor Hill;* GEORGE *ducks into the cave. Lights dim on Cave Area and come up on* SHANGHAI *and* WILLIAMS *in the trenches. The* LIEUTENANT *comes creeping toward them with two rifles. We can make out* WELLS, WATTS, *and* STEITELMEYER *on Union lines, keeping an eye on the Confederates, but talking with* CHARLES DANA, *the reporter.*)

WILLIAMS   Well, we crept up behind a little hummock of pasture, keeping low, so's the owner wouldn't risk the life of his prize rooster trying to save him from the pot, and we wasn't three feet from him, and him raring up to crow like he done every morning just at that time, and I'll be double damned if an old hound dog didn't jump out from the brush and . . . 'Squawk!' All that was left was a couple of feathers floating back down through the air. Now would you believe that old dog had up and planned his attack for the very minute me and Charlie did?

SHANGHAI   I don't see why not. I kind of calculated that you and another one like you might add up to the mental capacity of an old hound. But now that story about the goat. Why don't you tell that again and see if it's any more convincing the tenth time around?

(*Across in the Union lines,* WATTS *leaps up, thumbs his nose, and drops immediately out of sight. While he's up,* SHANGHAI *squeezes off a shot, but we see it puff into the dirt beneath the barricade.*)

SHANGHAI   Goddamn him. One of these days. . . .

LIEUTENANT *(Has reached the trench with the rifles)*   New delivery, boys. Somebody floated these things through the gunboats on logs. (*Laughs*) Just give a look. (*Hands a rifle to* SHANGHAI *and one to* WILLIAMS)

SHANGHAI Enfields. Well, I'll be a boar hog. (*Laughs*) By God, Bugger Watts, just wait till the next little ass-showing you take it into your head to do. (*To* LIEUTENANT) You got cartridges?

LIEUTENANT (*Points back along trenches*) They're on their way. We're going to have them all down the line. (*Starts to creep back along the trenches*) Keep your heads down.

WILLIAMS (*Mimicking* LIEUTENANT *as soon as he is out of hearing*) Keep your heads down. Hell, kid, I was planning to lift mine just slightly and let 'em save me the trouble of parting my hair.

> (*Light dims on trenches and comes up on Sky Parlor Hill, where* MARY, DORA, *and* GEORGE *are looking down right.* GEORGE *has the telescope. Throughout the scene there is firing from batteries and boats.*)

DORA (*Points, counting*) One, two, three, four, five. Five of them coming up the river.

GEORGE Yankee gunboats, ma'am. I reckon they figure they try that many, some of 'em may get past the city. But, listen. We shooting at 'em. Hear that big gun? They call it Whistling Dick.

MARY (*Pointing up right*) Look! Up river! What *is* that? That is the biggest monster I've ever seen.

GEORGE Another kind of gunboat, I reckon. Leastways it's shooting like one.

DORA It's ugly! (*Shouts as though to the shore batteries*) Hit it! Sink it!

MARY It's trying to come down river, and the other ones are going up. Does that many any sense? (*Points down right*) See that one? It's coming right up under the shore guns.

GEORGE I spect what they doing, they trying to get that big one past, and these other ones down here trying to draw the fire.

MARY (*Still following the gunboat under the shore guns*) No. Now it's turning back.

GEORGE (*It confirms his theory*) Yes'm. Now, you see, that other one coming up. He taking the fire now. They swaps off.

DORA (*Pointing up river*) What's happened to that big ugly one? Look! It's just kind of wallowing there.

MARY Here, George, give me the glass. (*Looks up right through telescope*) Look. The men are all scurrying around.

DORA Let me look.

MARY (*Hands* DORA *the glass, then points down right*)   Now two of the gunboats are pulling up into range.

GEORGE   Yes'm. (*Points up right*)   See that tug? He coming down to help the big boat.

DORA (*Sweeping the telescope up and down right*)   Where? Where is it?

MARY (*Laughs*)   Find it without the glass first, Dora. Then you'll know where to aim.

DORA (*Looks up right, then raises glass*)   Oh. I see it now. See the chug-chug-chug? Seems so close you ought to hear it.

MARY   Here, let me look again. (*Takes glass*)   That tug is pulling alongside. The men are getting off the big boat. Can you see that?

GEORGE (*Wistfully*)   No'm. I can't tell too much.

MARY (*Hands him the glass*)   Here. Now, I want it back if anything happens.

GEORGE (*Focusses glass up right*)   Yes'm. They getting off, all right.

MARY   They're right under our guns. Look. You can see the shells splash around them.

DORA   Kill them! Kill them!

MARY (*A bit uncomfortable with that*)   I don't care if the men get off, but, oh, I do hope they sink that ugly monster. Wouldn't that be fun!

GEORGE   They done all off. (*Hands glass to* MARY)   See? That tug pulling away, now.

MARY (*Looking up right through glass*)   Nobody left that you can see. Do you suppose some of them were killed when it was hit? Or wounded, maybe, and still inside? Look! Could you see that?

DORA   What?

MARY   We hit it again. Right at the waterline. Look! It's sinking! We did it!

DORA (*Takes the glass*)   Let me see.

MARY   It's going down so fast you don't need the glass to see it.

GEORGE (*Laughs*)   No'm, you sho don't. It's going to go plumb under.

(MARY *and* DORA *wave handkerchiefs and cheer.*)

GEORGE (*Points down right*)   Them little gunboats done pulled back down the river, too. (*Scans river to far up right; points*)   But looky yonder. Up past where our guns can reach it, up by them transports.

MARY (*Takes glass, looks where he is pointing*)   Oh. Now, that is strange. It's big, too. What do you reckon it is? (*Hands glass to* GEORGE)

GEORGE   I don't know, Miss Mary. I guess it might be a man o' war, from what I've heard people say down on the river. (*Swings glass down to sinking boat)* Look at them smokestacks, still smoking. Just them and the horn still showing.

DORA Let me see. (*Takes glass, focusses*) Why doesn't it go on and sink?

MARY (*Takes glass from her, looks*) Must be sitting on the bottom. But, we got it. (*Looks at* DORA, *they laugh*) Is that a good sign? Are we going to hold out?

DORA We're going to hold out!

> (*Lights dim on Sky Parlor Hill, come up on* MRS. LUKE *and* ABRAHAM, *outside her house, center.* ABRAHAM *is hammering on a kind of rack, bucket sitting nearby.*)

MRS. LUKE Never you mind what it's for. Just build it the way I told you. I know what I'm about. Did General Lee taste the buttermilk while you were there?

ABRAHAM No'm. He say thank you kindly, but he put it in his tent.

MRS. LUKE Saving it for dinner, I reckon. He didn't mention whether the last I sent was good or not, I suppose?

ABRAHAM No'm. He just say thank you kindly.

MRS. LUKE I keep thinking I get the taste of bitterweeds, myself. Ain't there a better place to keep the cow, so the milk won't taste?

ABRAHAM No'm. Not where it ain't going to get kilt by one of them shells.

MRS. LUKE I'd hate to be sending him bitter milk. I'd just hate that. What would he think? Here, now. Be ashamed. You're getting that all crooked.

ABRAHAM (*Mutters half to himself*) Maybe if I knew what I was making. . . .

> (*Lights dim out center, come up on Union lines, left, with* WELLS, WATTS, STEITELMEYER, *and* DANA *talking, as before. In dim light, we see a soldier come down the Confederate lines with cartridges for* SHANGHAI *and* WILLIAMS; *we see them loading the Enfields as the scene progresses.*)

WELLS I'd hate to tell you what a damn fool I think you are to get in the middle of this just to write about it.

DANA Well, my *official* business is to send reports to the Secretary of War. I don't mind running up and down these trenches. (*Laughs*) The other day, though, when I was on a hill looking at the courthouse 'way off, I kept swatting at insects whizzing this way and that way past my ears, and had started in cussing because I couldn't see what they were when it dawned on me. . . .

WELLS (*Snort of a laugh*) Civilians!

DANA (*Good naturedly*) My first thought, of course, was to get on the ground, but I thought, Now, which way? If I lie straight down, the bullets from the right and left are going to get me, but if I lie down crossways, then I'll get it from the front.

WELLS See? If you'd been trained as a soldier, you'da learned that the last thing you want to do is think.

DANA Well, it didn't take too long to figure that since it didn't make any difference, I'd better lie any way I fell.

STEITELMEYER Yep. It's a pretty good bet that flat down's safer than straight up.

WATTS Unless they got them Mississippi rifles, and then it wouldn't matter if you stood on your head and waved Old Glory with your feet.

DANA Well, I didn't try that. I just lay as still as I could until the whizzing stopped and crawled on my belly back to the trenches.

WELLS (*Pointedly to* WATTS) Matter of fact, it's pretty stupid to expose yourself to fire *any* time.

WATTS Aw, ain't nothing going to happen. . . .

(GRANT, *in a private's uniform, has come up on the rise left of them, stands looking over them toward the Confederate lines.* STEITELMEYER *spots him, yells.*)

STEITELMEYER Hey, you old bastard! Get your ass down if you don't want extra holes in it!

(*All turn and look at* GRANT, *who stands there a moment longer.*)

DANA Good Lord, man, that's General Grant!

(STEITELMEYER *gawks a second, then crouches and creeps through trenches toward upstage.* GRANT *casually disappears over the rise.* SHANGHAI *and* WILLIAMS *have loaded their Enfields and are on the alert.* WELLS, WATTS, *and* DANA *laugh over the* GRANT *incident, then* WATTS *get his urge to expose himself, stands suddenly, thumbs his nose.* SHANGHAI *fires.* WATTS CRUMPLES. WELLS *gets a shot off immediately, then turns with* DANA *to* WATTS.)

WELLS Goddamn them English! Just goddamn them. Sent them Enfields, the bloody bastards. Just goddamn them.

(*Lights dim over whole area, not completely down, and come up on Cave Area, where* MARY *and* ROBINETTE *are seated outside her cave.*)

ROBINETTE I'm delighted to see your spirits high, ma'am. There's never any reason to give up hope.

MARY Well, I must say, seeing that monster of a boat sunk by our guns did give me a lift.

ROBINETTE That was the *Cincinnati*, one of their finest ironclads. We've picked up a trunk from it that belonged to a doctor. (*Takes letter from pocket, unfolds it*) Dr. Richard Hall. This is a letter he didn't get to mail. I'm taking it to General Bowen.

MARY Oh. To his family?

ROBINETTE (*Nods*) In Fairfield, Indiana. (*Shows letter to* MARY; *she takes it gingerly*)

MARY (*Reads*) 'Dear Anna and Mother: Again I write for the satisfaction of my loved ones at home, and. . . .' (*Can't read on; hands letter back to* ROBINETTE)

ROBINETTE Well, ma'am. . . . You might be interested, though, in the part about the *Cincinnati*. What it was like to be on board? (*No response from* MARY; *he reads on, trying to get her mind off the idea of the family*) 'It is so warm and suffocating in my room on the gundeck that I have been compelled to sleep in the turret over the pilot house. Sleeping on the hard floor has made me sore all over.' And, listen to this: 'Today we are ordered to run down to Vicksburg and take a 200-pound English Parrott that has been a great bar to our progress. It goes by the name of 'Whistling Dick,' a soubriquet given it by our boys from the peculiar noise its balls make as they hurtle through the air.'

MARY But, that's *our* name for it!

ROBINETTE Yes ma'am. Word passes between us, you know. Listen to this: 'We have also to destroy a masked battery that holds General Sherman in check.' (*Waves in the direction of Redan, up left*) That's Stockade Redan, you know, ma'am. 'This battery has destroyed a great number of his brave boys; they have made two charges and both times been repulsed. He says that if the *Cincinnati* will take the battery and shell the pits that he and his men will go into Vicksburg. Well, we will do it for him and give him a chance.' (*Laughs*) Didn't quite turn out that way, did it?

MARY I *am* thankful for that.

ROBINETTE (*Reads again*) 'The battle still rages at all points with unstinted fury. I am thinking there will be no stop until Vicksburg is taken or we are all worse than whipped.' (*Folds letter and puts it back in pocket; with satisfaction*) Worse than whipped is what they're getting.

MARY (*Tentatively*) Is he . . . dead?

ROBINETTE That we don't know, ma'am.

*(From far up right, over the river beyond the Town, calcium flares
rise and give a peculiar glow to the night.)*

MARY What a strange light!

ROBINETTE Calcium flares. Just got them. They light up the whole
river so the Yankee gunboats won't try at night what they can't do
in the daytime.

MARY *(Sudden decision, reaches out her hand)* Let me see it.

ROBINETTE *(Uncertainly)* The letter?

MARY Yes. Please.

ROBINETTE *(Reluctantly; remembering her first reaction)* Well,
ma'am. . . . *(Takes letter from pocket, hands it to MARY)*

MARY *(Unfolds letter, skims down to end, reads out)* 'Dear ones, we
are now under way, where to I am unable to say.'

*(Holds letter a moment, then hands it to ROBINETTE; a second
calcium flare silhouettes the Town; MARY sits musing, thinking as
much of her own plight as that of the letter writer)*

It rhymes out, doesn't it? 'We are now under way . . . , where to
I am unable to say.'

*(Lights dim through last speech, leaving the light from the calcium
flare as the only illumination; it slowly dies.)*

Scene 2 *(June 20)*

*(Lights come up over whole panorama, most strongly on the Confed-
erate trenches. Firing of the various guns is background noise. On
the Union lines, WELLS and STEITELMEYER are relieved; they
go back to cook tent, left, where COOK dishes up what is obviously
a full meal. ABRAHAM is taking a small plate covered with a cloth
to SHANGHAI and WILLIAMS. HALL is propped up in his cot
at MRS. LUKE's house, center, reading a book; the wooden frame
ABRAHAM was building earlier holds a bucket from which water
drips on his bandaged leg. MARTHA is outside Caves, down right,
putting cornbread on the fire. GEORGE is cooking a piece of meat.
Left center, ABRAHAM arrives at Confederate lines, gives food to
SHANGHAI and WILLIAMS.)*

ABRAHAM Here's supper, but don't blame me.

SHANGHAI Hell, we been down to quarter rations for weeks. (*Lifts back cloth and stares*) But . . . , what do you call this?

ABRAHAM It ain't none of my doing, but the cookman call it pea bread. And that there with it is a little bit of bacon—I guess it still is.

WILLIAMS (*Takes a piece of pea bread, tries to bite it, but can't; tries to cut it with his knife, but that won't work*) What's this here pea bread made with, pea gravel?

ABRAHAM Just ground up peas, suh, and water. Like corn pone. (*Hides a smile*) Only it don't cook up like no corn pone.

SHANGHAI (*Examining a piece*) They ought to try molding it into cartridges. It's sure as hell heavier than lead. And harder.

WILLIAMS (*Has been mounting bayonet on rifle, now sets piece of pea bread on wooden base of barricade, stabs it with bayonet*) Ah, that got it. (*Holds up pea bread and breaks it on open*) I just wonder what sagacious and prolific genius come up with this. Like rock on the outside and still mush on the inside. I swear to God, it's burnt, but that there in the middle is still raw.

ABRAHAM They give it to some of the sick ones, first. (*Starts off, right*) Course, the ones that got it down couldn't hold it down.

WILLIAMS This here's all we need. We been laying in the ditches under sun and rain for a full month, stiff and sore, covered with dirt, populated by our own colonies of bodyguards, (*Scratches himself wildly*) and now they feed us the world's most powerful and certain emetic, so we can lie in our own vomit and there won't be no degradation left to anticipate.

SHANGHAI (*Quietly*) They'll keeping hoping for a few days that our bellies will accept this here stuff, then they'll ruin what little corn we got left trying to piece it out with this here pea meal, and when we're finally laying here without strength enough to pull a trigger, well, they'll give up and go back to cooking the peas straight, which God knows is bad enough. (*Throws a chunk of pea bread back toward where* ABRAHAM *arrived from, toward center*) If there's an honest commissary in the entire Confederate Army, I'll eat what's left of my shoe. If there's one with brains, I'll eat . . . , hell, I'll even eat a piece of one of them goddamn pea biscuits!

WILLIAMS You heard what some of them Louisiana boys did to a Mississippi commissary the other night, didn't you?

SHANGHAI I believe last time you told it, it was a Tennessee commisary. (*Settles in for the long story he knows is coming*)

WILLIAMS Oh, no. Mississippi. Well, sir, they happened upon him hid behind his tent, cooking his own supper. Bacon, by God, that wasn't even spoiled, and slap-jacks made out of real flour, and with molasses to pour over 'em, too. Well, that there's enough to drive the men wild, but they held theirselves and watched from the brush till he had a bellyful and put the rest away and they seen where he'd hid his whole store of goods. O' course as soon as he had laid down on his humble couch, as they say, to seek his repose, his stores beat a hasty but silent retreat. Next morning he had to smell them mouth-watering aromas wafting up from the next camp and didn't dare say a word about what had been stole from him, or his own men might have got as much as they could of what he'd stole from them by slitting open his overfed belly.

(Lights dim out on trenches as WILLIAMS *ends his story, come up center on* HALL, *still reading, and* MRS LUKE, *who brings him a cup of tea.)*

MRS. LUKE   Here. You'll wear your eyes out, reading that stuff. Drink this tea.

HALL *(Lays book aside, takes tea)*   Thank you ma'am. I'm sure it's mighty welcome.

MRS. LUKE   Well, I've tried blackberry leaves and raspberry leaves on you, but I believe this here's the best I've come up with.

HALL   What's this made of?

MRS. LUKE   Two parts raspberry to one part blackberry, but it's the little bit of sassafras that makes the difference, to me.

HALL *(Sips tea)*   It . . . tastes just fine.

MRS. LUKE   Mrs. Baker showed a receipt for corn beer I might try. Said it was superior to any cider or beer, and innocent even for a child, if taken as soon as the gas forms and not left to sour.

HALL   It would be a change, I suspect.

MRS. LUKE   Well, now, I don't hold with strong drink except when needed, but the receipt does say 'Innocent for a child.' The very words.

HALL   I must admit, ma'am, that for me there's been many a night recently that some strong liquor would have been mighty welcome.

MRS. LUKE *(Nods)*   It's all I'd expect from a body that reads the *Citizen* and books like . . . that.

HALL *(Amused)*   This? Why this is Edgar Allen Poe, the South's greatest genius.

MRS. LUKE   Genius, you say! Madman and lunatic. Died in the gutter drunk as a hoot owl.

HALL   I'm surprised, ma'am, that you have the books of such a man in your house.

MRS. LUKE They were my husband's. It was his only vice, reading such stuff. And reciting it. (*Quotes disgustedly:*) 'Quoth the raven!' (*Pauses*) That, and snoring.

HALL (*Shifting his bandaged leg*) Well, I must admit, this contraption looks like some device of torture Mr. Poe might have dreamed up, but it has proven a real instrument of mercy.

(*Lights dim on* HALL *and* MRS. LUKE, *come up on Cave Area,* MARTHA *cooking cornbread,* GEORGE *cooking meat.*)

MARTHA You sure that come from a mule? It don't smell too bad.

GEORGE They say it's pretty good, if you forget what it is. It's better'n what was hanging in the shop along with it. Ugh.

MARTHA What's that?

GEORGE Skinned rats.

MARTHA (*Shudders*) People eat 'em?

GEORGE Man buying one says he try to catch 'em in a trap, he hate to spend money on them so. Say he ain't got nothing else to eat, and when you starving they make a pretty good squirrel stew. Better'n dog, he say, and almost as good as cat.

MARTHA That man trying to make a fool out of you.

GEORGE I don't know. He bought that rat.

(*A young Confederate soldier is dragging listlessly by from right, hollow cheeked, perhaps feverish. He smells the cornbread and approaches* MARTHA.)

STARVING SOLDIER Is there. . . . Could I just lick the bowl?

(DORA *comes out of her cave, yawning. Stops, looks at* STARVING SOLDIER.)

DORA What is it?

STARVING SOLDIER Just the bowl, ma'am. Would you mind if I licked the bowl?

DORA Why, of course not. (*To* MARTHA) Give him the mixing bowl, Martha. Do have some more meal?

MARTHA Some, ma'am. I was wondering if you want me to make him some of that gruel.

DORA Yes. Get the sugar and milk. I'll get my nutmeg.

STARVING SOLDIER (*Has been scraping bowl with fingers, licking them*) That would be so good of you, ma'am. (*Sits dizzily on the ground*) I've had nothing that would stay on my stomach for. . . . I don't know how long. (*Looks down at his dirty ragged uniform*) I've lost track of. . . . (*Brushes at uniform*) Please, ma'am, excuse my. . . .

DORA   It's all right. It's all right. Here, Martha, is that about ready?

MARTHA   Yes'm. You want to grate some nutmeg on it?

DORA   Pour it up, first. There. (*Grates nutmeg*)   Who would believe that I still have a nutmeg? It does give a little flavor to things. Here. (*Hands bowl of gruel to* STARVING SOLDIER)

STARVING SOLDIER   (*Drinks gruel with great relish*)   Nothing in the world ever tasted that good! I'll be better, ma'am. (*Gets up and goes off left*)   Thank you, ma'am. I'll be better.

DORA   I'm glad you found another place to get milk, Martha. Maybe we'll all be better.

(MARY *comes out of her cave, straightening her hair. She sniffs, looks doubtful.*)

MARY   Is that beef, George?

GEORGE   Well, sort of.

MARY   Did you get some rest? I fell asleep and dreamed. . . . My husband. . . . We were on a riverboat, gliding along. there was dancing, music. My little girl. . . . (*Shakes her head to clear it; to* GEORGE) Sort of?

GEORGE   Yes'm. The only kind they had.

MARY   (*Steps over and looks at meat*)   It looks a little dark. (*Suspiciously*)   George, is that mule?

GEORGE   Yes'm, and I spect you better not think about it.

MARY   Think about it! (*Sits*)

DORA   I wish I'd never *heard* about it. (*Sits*).

GEORGE   Well, it ain't going to taste as bad as starving does.

MARY   (*Sighs*)   You're right, George, I know. But . . .

(ROBINETTE *has come up from left, now makes his presence known.*)

ROBINETTE   Good evening, Mrs. Burson. Mrs. Scott. I see you are about to have supper. I'll only stay a moment. I just wondered if everything is all right. Is there anything I can do for you?

MARY   Good evening, Major. You might try to work a miracle. Turn that creek water into wine, and that hunk of mule into . . . something edible.

DORA   Mary! That's getting close to sacrilege!

MARY   I don't mean it that way. (*Rubs her temples*)   If I didn't believe we go to a better place, I don't think I could. . . . Major, what do you think the menu will be in heaven?

ROBINETTE   Well, ma'am, I was in Vicksburg only once before the war, and the dining room at the Washington Hotel sounds like heaven to me now. The maitre d'hotel would stand there among the tables wiping moisture from his face and swatting at flies, and as the servants brought out platters he'd bawl out, 'Now, then, here is a splendid goose! Ladies and gentlemen, don't neglect the goose and applesauce!'

MARY (*Laughs*) Who could neglect the goose and applesauce?

DORA Goose and applesauce!

ROBINETTE (*acting maitre d' still*) 'Here's a piece of beef that I can recommend. Upon my honor, you will never regret taking a slice of the beef.'

MARY *Never* regret it, not as long as I live.

ROBINETTE (*Takes out handkerchief, mops forehead*) 'Oyster pie! Oyster pie! Never was better oyster pie seen in Vicksburg!'

DORA Nor anywhere in the world! Just smell it!

ROBINETTE 'Ladies and Gentlemen, just look at that turkey! Who's for turkey!'

MARY (*Leaps up*) Turkey! All for turkey, dance in a circle! (*Grabs* DORA's *hand; each of them takes a hand of* ROBINETTE; *they dance about as* MARY *sings to the tune of 'Eating Goober Peas'*) Eating oyster pie, eating turkey too. Goodness how delicious, eating (*Trails off*) goose and . . . whatever else you said. (*They stand laughing a moment;* MARY *turns to* ROBINETTE) All right. You may report to General Bowen that his charge is content. She will eat whatever her faithful servant prepares for her . . . and be thankful.

ROBINETTE Excellent. You know, ma'am, we intercepted a message from Admiral Porter to General Grant, and he said it looks as if the inhabitants of Vicksburg are taking on the quality of the food they eat, since they seem to be stubborn as mules.

(*Two* CONFEDERATE SOLDIERS *have come up, ragged, but not as bad off as the one* DORA *has fed. They act as if they have heard there may be food to be had here, and smell the cooking, but they are shy about approaching with* ROBINETTE *there. As they pass, left to right, they go into the following dialogue, partly out of envy and partly to be funny:*)

FIRST CONFEDERATE SOLDIER (*Sniffing the aroma of cooking meat*) Fido! (*To* SECOND CONFEDERATE SOLDIER) I wonder what's happened to Fido.

SECOND CONFEDERATE SOLDIER Last I saw of him, he was chasing a cat in this direction.

FIRST CONFEDERATE SOLDIER (*Calling out again*) Fido! Oh, Fido!

(Lights dim on Cave Area as SOLDIERS *exit right. Lights come up on Union Cook Tent area;* WELLS, STEITELMEYER, *other* UNION SOLDIERS *sit about picking their teeth, smoking pipes, etc.)*

WELLS   Hell, let's don't just sit around here all afternoon. Let's get a move on.

STEITELMEYER   You that eager to get back in the trenches?

WELLS   Trenches be damned. What I'm eager to do is make a little excursion up to Chicksaw Bayou. Friend of mine up there catches the biggest crawdads you ever saw. Makes a gumbo out of 'em.

STEITELMEYER   Aren't you ever satisfied? A plateful of new potatoes, pickled cabbage, fresh ham. . . . Hell, you must have put away half a dozen biscuits with that good butter. *(Turns toward Cook Tent)*   I could use some more of that, myself. Hey, Cook!

(The scene is interrupted by the arrival of MRS. GRIMM *and a* CAPTAIN. WELLS, STEITELMEYER, *and the* OTHER SOLDIERS *look at each other as if to say, Caught!)*

CAPTAIN   Men, I am honored to present to you Mrs. Harriet Folsom Grimm, of the Sanitary Commission, a fine and noble lady from our home state of Illinois. She was present when our regiment left for the war, and she is now among us on the battlefield, bravely administering to our needs. Mrs. Grimm.

MRS. GRIMM   Before you left Chicago, we ladies presented your regiment with a flag, and your colonel when he received that flag pledged himself that it should ever be defended and sustained with honor. What has become of that flag? I desire to see how well you have kept that promise.

*(*COLOR SERGEANT *rises from the rear of the group and brings forward the rather tattered flag. The men look at each other, not particularly fond of* MRS. GRIMM's *rhetoric.)*

MRS. GRIMM   When we gave you this flag, it was bright and new. Why are there holes in it now? Have you been negligent in caring for your colors?

(The men look at each other now in thorough disgust; does she think they aren't in battle? Does she think they are kindergarten children?)

CAPTAIN   Well, Color Sergeant?

COLOR SERGEANT   Well, you know, sir. . . . *(The* CAPTAIN *signs with a motion of his head that the response is to* MRS. GRIMM*)*   Well, ma'am, the flag has been in battle, you know, and marked with bullets and fragments of shell. The two men who carried it before me fell with it in their hands, and both are dead, now . . . , ma'am.

MRS. GRIMM Enough. You have redeemed your pledge, and I will tell the women of Chicago who presented the flag to you, when I go back, how nobly your pledge has been redeemed. (*Takes the flag in her arms*) And now, before I go, let us sing The Battle Hymn of the Republic.

(*The soldiers have been scornful of the 'show,' but stand and gradually join in as* MRS. GRIMM *sings the first few bars.* WELLS *chokes and turns aside, wipes at his eyes, begins to sing again. Lights dim on the scene; the sound of their singing dies to a distant whisper, then silence. Lights are down over all; as moon rises, lights come up over all, most strongly on* MARY *outside her cave. Campfires come up on lines, some lights in the Town. We have been hearing the sounds of battle through the last scene, but now there is only an occasional distant mortar.* MARY *walks from cave entrance down right toward bushes, pauses as if smelling honeysuckle, looks around in the moonlight, stretches her arms wide. In the distance, a whippoorwill calls.* MARY *stands very still, listening. In a moment we hear an answering call, closer at hand.* MARY *stands listening as the light gradually dies; the whippoorwills continue to cry into the darkness as the lights dim to blackout*).

Scene 3 (July 1)

(*Lights come up over all; we see* DORA *and* MARTHA *going off right on a visit,* MARY *and* GEORGE *working on the outside area of the cave,* MRS. LUKE *helping* HALL *sit up in bed,* SHANGHAI *shaking* WILLIAMS *awake in their cramped positions in the trench,* WELLS *and* STEITELMEYER *coming from Cook Tent to relieve their relief soldiers on the line. Light focusses on* MRS. GRIMM, *farther up left, at a Hospital Tent. She comes out into the open, sits in a chair against a tree, fans herself with her hand.* CAPTAIN *walks up.*)

CAPTAIN Good morning, Mrs. Grimm. I see you're spending your spare time taking care of the sick.

MRS. GRIMM   As well as I can. Those tents are stifling. It's a wonder those poor feverish boys can breathe.

CAPTAIN   I know. We'd put the tents on higher ground, to get whatever breeze there is, but they'd be even more exposed to fire.

MRS. GRIMM   One boy, right in there, just woke up as I came by. His lips were dry and parched, and his cheeks were so red with fever they might have been painted. and he told me that he'd actually slept a little, and he dreamed he was back at the old spring at home, but just as he was about to take a good cold drink, he woke up. (*Sighs*)   All I could do was make a little warm lemonade. (*Points to barrel nearby*) That river water is terrible after it's stood in the sun all day. Can't we get them some cooler water? Or at least cleaner?

CAPTAIN   There are a few springs, and a well or two, but they're a distance from here.

MRS. GRIMM   Whoever hauls this stuff from the river can haul from a spring just as well, can't he?

CAPTAIN   Yes. Of course. But the men near the fresh water are mighty jealous of it.

MRS. GRIMM   Sneak it. Steal it. Take it by force, Captain. These boys need it.

CAPTAIN (*Uncomfortable*)   Yes, ma'am. I'll send a foraging detail.

MRS. GRIMM (*Settles back in her chair, notices a stirring in the weeds just ahead of her*)   What's that? It looks like partridges running through those weeds. See? They keep shaking, but I don't see any birds. (*Remembers something*)   While I think of it, I want the men called together again this evening for my temperance lecture.

CAPTAIN   Well, Mrs. Grimm. . . . If you think it's the proper time.

MRS. GRIMM   The sooner the better, Captain. The devil doesn't stop his evil work while we tarry. (*Leans forward toward weeds*)   What *is* that? I don't see a thing in those weeds to make them shake like that.

CAPTAIN (*Can't help taking some pleasure in the effect*)   Why, those are bullets, Mrs. Grimm.

MRS. GRIMM   Bullets? (*Stands in some alarm*)   Bullets don't come as near as that?

CAPTAIN   Oh, yes. They're flying around here quite thick.

MRS. GRIMM (*Looks about, uncertain*)   They're awfully close. Where would we be safe?

CAPTAIN   We consider it safe right here, ma'am. (*Points toward the weeds*)   That seems to be the end of their range. They fall a little short, you see. (*Gives a slight salute, starts off; some weariness in the tone*)   Well. Till this evening.

(MRS. GRIMM *watches the weeds for a short moment, then goes to tent. Just as she leans to go in through the flap, we hear a Minie ball whizz into the tree she has been sitting in front of. She turns, startled, sees where it hit, points dramatically to the spot—right where her head had been—and glowers accusingly after the* CAPTAIN. *Light goes down on her. Union cannons begin a barrage from left. Light follows across from left to right as if following a shell. We get a glimpse of* MRS. LUKE *and* HALL *set as though listening to the shell as it passes over, then lights come up on Cave Area, where* MARY *and* GEORGE *retreat into her cave. Shell explodes just right of them, and we hear a series of explosions on a curve up to the Town, up right. Now a barrage begins from behind the audience and there are explosions from far right to center, near* MRS. LUKE's *house. A* GENTLEMAN *hurries along near caves, frightened, darting here and there for shelter. He sees* MARY'S *cave, shouts in.*)

GENTLEMAN   Please! May I come in? (*Leaps inside as shell explodes nearby*).

MARY (*Voice from inside cave*)   You're welcome, sir. Here, stand in the little alcove, opposite me.

GENTLEMAN   Thank you, ma'am. I was just on my way. . . .

(*A shell lands at entrance of cave, bounces inside. We can see the smoke from its fuse coming from cave entrance. The* GENTLEMAN *gasps, gives a little cry*)

MARY (*Voice from inside cave*)   Here, sir! Take this.

(GEORGE *dashes from cave, clutching hot shell, dumps it far down right, retreats and falls flat. Silence. The shell does not explode. The barrage has ceased.*)

GEORGE (*Stands up slowly, watching the spent shell; finally gives a little laugh*)   It ain't going to go off, Miss Mary.

MARY (*Cautiously comes out of the cave, followed by* GENTLEMAN, *who holds a blanket in front of him to shield off any fragments*)   Are you all right, George? That was close!

GEORGE   Yes'm. I guess it figured to scare us to death, since it couldn't blow us to pieces.

GENTLEMAN (*Looks at blanket in surprise*)   Oh. My. I seem to . . . have your blanket.

MARY (*Tries not to laugh*)   You looked so. . . . I just handed you the first thing I could find. I'm afraid it wouldn't have been much protec-

tion. (*To* GEORGE)   You were very brave, George. Thank you. No
one could have known that shell wouldn't explode.

GEORGE   Well, Miss Mary, I figure it might as well go off in my hand
as under my feet.

GENTLEMAN (*Murmurs*)   I'm grateful. Grateful, ma'am. (*Does not
look at* GEORGE; *wanders off*).

MARY (*Looking after him*)   I don't think I ever saw anybody so petrified
with fear. (*To* GEORGE)   But you weren't, and don't think *I'm* not
grateful to you, even if *he* . . . (*Looks beyond audience, where barrage
came from*)   I get so furious! I want to fight them myself. You give
me courage, George. I feel it in my bones, now: We're going to hold
out. We will never surrender.

> (DORA *and* MARTHA *rush on right, returning from their visit,*
> DORA *quite agitated.*)

DORA   Mary! Are you all right? I could see the shells landing right
over here!

MARY   Yes, we're all right. Thanks to George.

DORA (*Still agitated; to* MARTHA)   What we can take, Martha. Just
what we can take in our hands. Hurry!

> (MARTHA *goes into their cave.*)

MARY   What? What are you doing?

DORA   I'm leaving. I've got to get out.

MARY   But . . . , how will you do that? Did something happen?

DORA   I don't know. (*Sits; tries to calm herself*)   I guess I've known
all along that we could be killed at any moment, but. . . . When
we stopped by the Porters', they told us that their young daughter-in-
law had her thighbone crushed. They may have to take the leg. And
then we went to get the milk at Walkers', and the black girl there
. . . . A shell . . . sheared her arm off, clean, at the shoulder. Mutilated.
For life. (*Puts her head in her hands*)   I couldn't stand that. (*Shudders*)
Part of you gone! I'd rather die. (*Looks up at* MARY)   Don't think
harshly of me. I've got to get out. I've lost my nerve. (*Shouts toward
her cave*)   Hurry, Martha, for God's sake!

MARY   But, how will you get through the lines?

DORA   I don't know. I've heard that they let some women through down
south of the Jackson road. I'll try there. Maybe they'll give me a pass.
(*Toward cave again*)   Martha!

MARTHA (*Comes from cave with two carpetbags*)   Yes ma'am. This
here is all I can carry.

DORA (*Looks at carpetbags a second, then jumps up*)   I don't care.

Let's go. Every minute I stay it's worse. (*Hugs* MARY *quickly*)   Pray for me.

> (DORA *and* MARTHA *exit through audience, angling toward left behind them.*)

MARY (*Stands looking after them, stunned, for a moment before she can speak; futile gesture:*)   Goodbye, Dora. Goodbye, Martha. We'll . . . miss you.

GEORGE (*Musingly*)   'All we can carry in our hands.'

MARY   What's that, George.

GEORGE   Nothing, Miss Mary. Onliest thing is, one pair of hands going empty.

> (*Lights dim on Cave Area, come up on* MRS. LUKE *at cotside of* HALL. *She has a newspaper; he is sitting up.*)

HALL   Now that's not fair, ma'am. Just because one officer pulls a trick like that, doesn't mean we're all that way.

MRS. LUKE   Trick! Trick, you call it! Get the date all set and the wedding right upon us, and then run out when he finds his wife and children are on their way to be with him? I don't call that a trick. No sir. I call that a . . . a dastardly act, toward an innocent Vicksburg girl.

HALL   His wife and children coming *here*? If you'd just let me see the date on that paper! Do you have a complete set of the *Whig* from the first issue till the last?

MRS. LUKE (*Moves paper to keep him from seeing date*)   I didn't finish. Now, don't interrupt again. (*Reads*) 'He hastily departed,' as any coward would, 'leaving the girl. . . .'

HALL   Now, you're adding in things, and you know it.

MRS. LUKE   Hush.' . . . leaving the girl to breathe:
> Oh that a dream so sweet, so short enjoyed,
> Should be thus sadly, cruelly destroyed.'

And how much better off she'll never know.

HALL (*innocently*)   What poem is that? It has a familiar ring. (*Reaches for paper*)   Let me see it.

> (MRS. LUKE *starts to show him the poem, realizes he's tricked her, jerks the paper back, but* HALL *has seen the date.*)

HALL   Aha! April fourth. April fourth! 'Six weeks before the troops got backed up into here! Couldn't you find any older gossip than that?

MRS. LUKE (*Unfazed; has finger on another item*)   Listen to this.

HALL   Oh, no, I won't. (*Puts fingers in ears*)   Not another word.

(MRS. LUKE *begins reading anyway, but we cannot understand her;* HALL *is quoting 'The Raven' loudly to drown her out. Their garbled duet dies out as lights dim on them, come up on* SHANGHAI *and* WILLIAMS *in trenches, both exhausted, just hanging on. Faintly we can see the Union lines, which have moved closer to Confederate lines now.*)

SHANGHAI (*Weakly*)   Them bastards digging again?

WILLIAMS (*Has to drag his attention to the question*)   I don't know. You hear anything?

SHANGHAI   Naw. Just looks kind of suspicious. They get any closer, maybe we can snatch a handful of that chicken I been smelling. (*Goes suddenly rigid as we see an arm swing over the Union barricade, throwing something toward them which lands with a thud behind* SHANGHAI; *he turns to grab up the grenade, but picks up instead a piece of hardtack.*)   Hardtack, by God. Look. It's got writing on it. (*Makes it out:*) 'Starvation.'

WILLIAMS   Somebody knows me by name.

SHANGHAI   Crawl up there and get a pen from the Lieutenant. You need the stretch anyway.

(WILLIAMS *creeps along trenches upstage, out of sight.* SHANGHAI *keeps his rifle at ready. From Union lines comes a shout.*)

STEITELMEYER   Hey, Reb. Did you get the message?

SHANGHAI   Just hold your horses. You'll get yours.

STEITELMEYER   You hold your *mule*, Reb. If you can keep it down.

(*There is laughter from the Union lines.* SHANGHAI *does not reply.* WILLIAMS *returns with the pen.* SHANGHAI *writes on the other side of the hardtack, very carefully keeping down, lobs the hardtack back to Union lines. Lights dim on* SHANGHAI *and* WILLIAMS, *come up on Union lines,* STEITELMEYER *and* WELLS.)

WELLS   Did you get it?

STEITELMEYER   Yeah. (*Reads from hardtack*)   'Forty days rations.' (*Laughs*)   Forty days *behind* on rations, he ought to say.

WELLS (*Muses*)   Hell, if I was starving, I'd have eaten the damn thing, not thrown it back.

(*Lights dim on them, come up at Tent behind Union lines, where the* CAPTAIN *stands as* UNION SOLDIER *approaches with very ragged and gaunt Confederate* DESERTER, *who drags his rifle with a piece of more or less white cloth tied to the bayonet.*)

CAPTAIN   So this is our latest deserter.

UNION SOLDIER   Yes sir. He says he's hungry.

CAPTAIN   I see no reason to doubt his word.

DESERTER   I ain't et in two-three days, sir. Nothing attall. And before that, it was pea meal I throwed up. I'd mightily appreciate a bite of real food, if it's handy.

CAPTAIN   There may be. But, tell me. How are things in Vicksburg now?

DESERTER   Starving, sir. Everybody. They just about give up. No spirit left.

CAPTAIN   Well, General Grant thinks that there's still a strong will to survive. What do you say to that.

DESERTER   Yessir. The General's got it exactly. Pretty near starving, but a strong will to survive.

CAPTAIN   How are the troops?

DESERTER   Sick, sir. That's how come the lines is so thin. And what's there so weak, you could walk right in most any place.

CAPTAIN   What about the fortification on the Jackson Road? We breached it by mining under it yesterday, but when we charged, the Rebels held.

DESERTER   (*Looks about a bit desperately*)   Like you say, sir. Held, but just barely. One more little push and. . . . (*Sees what he considers a way out; confidentially*)   I tell you one thing not generally known, sir, but it's a fact as I'm standing here. You know who's caught in the city there? Jefferson Davis himself. Seen him with my own eyes.

CAPTAIN   Here, now, this is the baldest lie yet. Jeff Davis in Vicksburg?

DESERTER   It's a fact, sir. I swear it. Why, you can hold me prisoner till you take the city and hang me by the neck till I'm dead if you don't find him there.

CAPTAIN   (*Turns away*)   If this one don't take the cake! (*To* UNION SOLDIER)   Take him down to the mess tent and stuff his miserable craw. Then send him packing.

DESERTER   Yes sir. Thank you, sir. You won't regret it.

(UNION SOLDIER *marches* DESERTER *off left as lights dim, then come up on Cave Area, where* MARY *is talking with* ROBINETTE.)

MARY   I'm so worried about her. She's frantic. They won't let her through the lines, will they?

ROBINETTE   Well, I doubt that they will. Grant seems to want to keep us all bottled in now—so we'll run out of food sooner, I suppose.

MARY   Well, you tell General Bowen that I for one don't want us to surrender, ever.

ROBINETTE   That's the spirit! We've lasted this long, and we can keep it up.

MARY   Of course we can. I don't want to give them the satisfaction. Oh, here. Let me show you. (*Goes to chair by tent fly, picks up some needlework*)   I'm embroidering wreaths on the General's collar.

ROBINETTE   Why, you do beautiful work with the needle, ma'am. He'll be mighty proud of that.

MARY   (*Sits, takes up needle*)   It's nearly done. Perhaps I can finish, and you can deliver it for me.

ROBINETTE   Fine. It will be a pleasure to watch you at . . . , such a domestic task. (*Sits opposite her*)   There hasn't been much to remind us of home, lately. (*Sits watching* MARY *engrossed in her work for a moment, then begins singing softly to himself, to the tune of 'Listen to the Mockingbird'*)

> 'Twas at the siege of Vicksburg,
> Of Vicksburg, of Vicksburg—
> 'Twas at the siege of Vicksburg. . . .

MARY   (*Looks up at him*)   What's that you're singing?

ROBINETTE   (*Laughs*)   Oh, just a version of 'Listen to the Mockingbird,' the way some of the boys sing it in the ditches.

MARY   Well, sing it so I can hear it.

ROBINETTE   (*Sings*)

> 'Twas at the siege of Vicksburg,
> Of Vicksburg, of Vicksburg—
> 'Twas at the siege of Vicksburg. . . .
> When the Parrott shells were whistling through the air.
> Listen to the Parrott shells,
> Listen to the Parrott shells,
> The Parrott shells are whistling through the air.

MARY   (*Laughs*)   Wait. Is there more? I wonder if my guitar will still play. (*Runs into cave; voice from cave:*)   It's been so long since I've heard music. (*Comes out with guitar, sits, starts to tune it*)   It may be out of tune forever.

ROBINETTE   You play the guitar, too? You *are* an accomplished woman.

MARY   I used to play. Oh, I have other talents too. I once balanced a broom on my chin for nearly half an hour, but I had to give that up. My mother said it was *very* unladylike.

ROBINETTE   I'm sure it was charming.

MARY   Not a bit. It was fun, though, except my neck was stiff for days.

Here. I think it's about as near tuned as I can get it. Is there another verse?

ROBINETTE (*Nods; sings as* MARY *plays*)
> Oh! well we will remember,
> Remember, remember,
> Wishing it was cold December,
> And the Minié balls that whistled through the air.
> Listen to the Minié balls,
> Listen to the Minié balls,
> The Minié balls are singing in the air.

MARY (*As they both laugh*) I'll have to get my fingers limbered up. And we'll have a party. Wouldn't that be fun? And sing and sing. And maybe they'll hear us, and know that we'll never give up.

ROBINETTE I think it's a grand idea. I'll bring my banjo.

MARY Yes! Please do. (*Taking up sewing again, singing to herself,* ROBINETTE *humming along:*)
> Listen to the Minié balls,
> Listen to the Minié balls—
> The Minié balls are singing in the air.

(*Lights dim on Cave Area, come up on* WELLS *and* STEITEL-MEYER *as their relief approaches through the Union trenches.*)

FIRST RELIEF SOLDIER All right, Wells. You stand relieved. (*Starts to settle in*) Chicken for supper.

WELLS (*Makes a face*) Chicken again? Lord! Not for me, thanks. (*Waves him back*) You can go back and eat my share. They must have appropriated every single chicken from every single chickenhouse in the county.

FIRST RELIEF SOLDIER You mean, you'll stay on and I can go back?

WELLS Just what I said.

FIRST RELIEF SOLDIER Suits me, Wells. I ain't screaming for duty in this hole. (*Starts back up the line*)

SECOND RELIEF SOLDIER (*Disgustedly*) All right. Steitelmeyer. You're relieved. Just my goddamn luck to draw a chicken lover.

STEITELMEYER Better luck than you think, boy. I ain't about to leave here for no greasy barnyard fowl. Go on back with your friend.

SECOND RELIEF SOLDIER Wahoo! I had a string of luck going, and look at this here! I better hurry back to the game while it's still hot! (*Crawls after* FIRST RELIEF SOLDIER)

WELLS (*Watches them out of earshot*) Just like I figured. Been so tied up in a card game it ain't registered yet. (*Laughs*) He don't have any idea how dead his luck is.

STEITELMEYER (*Laughs too*) Break out one of those jars of 'fruit' you got from home the other day. I reckon that'll sustain us.

WELLS (*Uncovers jar, unscrews cap, takes a drink*) Oh, my. That's got power. (*Hands jar to* STEITELMEYER) If that Grimm woman could have seen through the label on that box, she'da died.

STEITELMEYER And if those poor boys we just suckered knew we was sitting here with the devil's brew while they're fixing to be herded in dry as a bone to hear her sermon on the subject, well, they'd do to us what Johnny Reb hasn't so far managed.

WELLS (*Takes another drink, laughs*) Chicken my ass. It was that old hen I couldn't stomach.

(*Lights dim on them, come up on Cave Area as* MARY *rises and hands collar to* ROBINETTE. *He bows, starts to depart, but* DORA *and* MARTHA *enter from left, dusty and exhausted.*)

MARY Dora! You're back!

DORA Yes. (*Looks about rather wildly*) We'll have to wait till tomorrow to try the river, I guess. It's nearly dark.

MARY The river?

DORA They say some people have had permission to cross. (*Breaks down*) Oh, it was terrible. The officers sent our request to the Union lines, under a flag of truce, and they sent word back that if the lady hadn't wanted to seal her fate with Vicksburg, she shouldn't have stayed six weeks before realizing it. And . . . , here we are.

(*A mortar shell strikes, not close, but* DORA *draws in her breath, frightened.*)

ROBINETTE Can I be of help, ma'am?

DORA Oh, thank you. I don't know. I'll try the river in the morning. I've got to get out!

(DORA *wanders as though distracted into her cave.* MARTHA *has set down carpetbags, shakes her head in commiseration.*)

MARTHA She sho in a state. Ain't nothing I can do with her.

MARY Maybe a night's sleep. . . .

MARTHA (*Doubtful*) Maybe.

(MARTHA, MARY, *and* ROBINETTE *stand looking helplessly at each other as lights dim on them, come up on* MRS. LUKE *and* HALL, *the latter standing, albeit gingerly.*)

MRS. LUKE Pshaw! What do you mean? You can't go down to the lines tomorrow!

HALL I believe I can. I think I can make it.

MRS. LUKE You'll fall on your face before you get down the hill. Why, there ain't enough strength in that leg to hold up a man half your size.

HALL (*Laughs*) By the Great I Am, it's nearly normal. I will get back to my troops.

MRS. LUKE Don't blaspheme in this house, sir. The Lord will strike you dead before the Yankees get a chance to cripple you again.

HALL I meant no sacrilege, ma'am. That was an exclamation of . . . thanksgiving.

MRS. LUKE Pshaw. It's just that you're dying to get away from here. I know. I know.

HALL No. No . . .

MRS. LUKE Go along with you, then, and when they bring you back more dead than alive, I suppose you think I'll have to take you in again, just like that.

HALL I would certainly hope so, ma'am. No one ever had better care than I've had here.

MRS. LUKE (*Hides her feelings with a shout*) Abraham! (*To* HALL) If you're bound and determined, I want to be sure he'll be here to help you when you leave in the morning. Abraham! Here now! Shake a leg!

> (*Lights dim on* MRS. LUKE *and* HALL, *come up on* MRS. GRIMM *behind Union lines, giving her lecture to a small restless group, including* FIRST *and* SECOND RELIEF SOLDIERS. *We can see, in fainter light,* WELLS *and* STEITELMEYER *in the trenches, drinking from the jar.*)

MRS. GRIMM And do you know what they found in the grain bins? Rats. Giant rats, running around in the grain that sinful men put by the gallon into their bellies. Oh, the Devil takes care of his own, all right. He lures them with the false pleasures of the flesh and wags that forked tail in evil glee as he watches them guzzle the leavings of long, slimy, slick-tailed alley rats. . . .

> (*Lights dim on* MRS. GRIMM *and Union trenches, come up on* MARY *and* GEORGE *in front of their cave.* MARY *is seated, holding her guitar.*)

MARY Remember the song I used to play so much, George? The one my husband used to sing to me?

GEORGE Yes'm. I know the one you talking about. Why don't you sing it?

MARY I can't even bring myself to name it. I know I couldn't sing it, but . . . (*Sits a moment with guitar in playing position, then begins to play 'Beautiful Dreamer'; after a few bars, she seems to gain strength, begins to sing softly:*)

> Starlight and Dewdrops are waiting for thee.
> Sounds of the rude world, heard in the day.
> Lulled by the moonbeams have all passed away.
> Beautiful dreamer, queen of my. . . .

(*Voice falters, but she keeps playing, and in a bar or two hums the melody out to the end.*)

(*Lights dim slowly so that we go to total blackout at the end of the last imagined vibrations of the song.*)

Scene 4 (July 2)

(*Lights come up over all,* MARY *and* GEORGE *busying about at the cave,* SHANGHAI *and* WILLIAMS *in Confederate trenches,* WILLIAMS *still weaker than before,* WELLS *and* STEITELMEYER *in Union trenches, pretty much at ease, but watchful; focus on* HALL, MRS. LUKE, *and* ABRAHAM, *at cotside, center.*)

MRS. LUKE You didn't make it off the porch this morning, and if you make it that far now, you won't make it down the street. Pshaw. Not a lick of sense. What difference is it going to make if you wait another day?

HALL Maybe none, maybe a lot. Nobody knows. But I've got to get back to the ditches, ma'am. My men have been there for six weeks without relief, while I've been lying up here in the lap of luxury.

MRS. LUKE Lap of luxury! Hssst! Hssst! Don't use language like that. . . . What would people think?

HALL (*Laughs*) It's just a common phrase, Mrs. Luke.

MRS. LUKE Common is the word for it, all right.

HALL I mean to say, I've been fed and tended to—and I'm mighty grateful—while the boys have been suffering from hunger, and exposure, and lice . . . not to mention the danger of having their heads shot off.

MRS. LUKE Well, if you want to say that you've been treated with Christian charity, it would certainly have a better sound to it—and if I do say so as oughtn't, it's true.

HALL Absolutely true! And I'll phrase it that way, ma'am, as you suggest. Now, if you can spare Abraham.

MRS. LUKE Well, if you won't listen to reason, I wash my hands of it. Here, you, Abraham, help the colonel.

HALL Just come along with me, Abraham. I think I'll be able to walk on my own.

(HALL *limps out of spot, left,* ABRAHAM *following.* MRS. LUKE *stands shaking her head after them; as lights dim she is saying:*)

MRS. LUKE Pshaw! Not a lick of sense. It's what comes of reading old Swords in the *Citizen* instead of Marmaduke Shannon in the *Whig*. Scrambles the brains. That's why we're holed up here being shot at, instead of . . . doing whatever we were doing. (*Tries to think for a moment, then gives a brief laugh*) Been so long, I can't remember what that was.

(*Lights out on* MRS. LUKE, *up on* SHANGHAI *and* WILLIAMS *in the trenches.* WILLIAMS *is obviously not well.*)

SHANGHAI I been telling you, man, you better report to the hospital. Hell, there ain't no sense dying on your own when you could have help from the Yankees on one side and the doctors on the other.

WILLIAMS I'll make it.

SHANGHAI Make what? The sick list is all you ought to be making right now.

WILLIAMS (*Rouses somewhat*) I don't know. I reckon I've been in this one position so long I've kind of growed to it. It's like if I was to leave, the whole line would give in, you know? And all this . . . time . . . would be wasted.

SHANGHAI Hell, Williams, ain't a one of us we can't get along without for a spell.

WILLIAMS I tell myself that, Shanghai. I tell myself that, but . . . , goddamnit, when I've gone seems like a hundred years past what I could stand, I ain't about to quit now. (*Tries to seem his old self*) It's like that ole hound, maybe I told you about.

SHANGHAI Not more than thirty-forty times. Look. Ain't that the edge of a Yankee hat sticking up over the barricade? Just to keep your hand in, why don't you make him mess his britches?

(WILLIAMS *eases up to rifle slot in barricade, aims, fires. Hat flies off. We hear* STEITELMEYER'S *voice, though light stays dim on Union lines, and* WELL'S *laughter at him:*)

STEITELMEYER   Great jumping toads! Just my hat. I thought he had me.

WILLIAMS   (*Drops back, exhausted*)   See? I ain't lost my eye, yet. And it don't take much effort.

SHANGHAI   Oh, it don't? Then how come you fell back down like a stuck hawg?

(*Lights fade out on Confederate lines, come up on Cave Area. We see* DORA *coming in from right, followed by* ROBINETTE *and* MARTHA, *each with a carpetbag.* MARY, *at her cave, goes to* DORA'S *cave entrance to meet them.*)

MARY   They didn't let you across? Oh, I'm sorry.

(DORA *is too fatigued to be distraught. She drops into her chair.*)

ROBINETTE   We thought we had clearance from the Yankees, but as soon as the boat got out into the river, they started firing.

MARY   No one was hurt!

ROBINETTE   No, ma'am. I think they must have seen it was a lady, and were just warning her to turn back.

DORA   Well, I've tried everything I know. I guess I'm here to stay. (*Sits up; to* MARY)   It's not that I'm afraid to die. I could stand that. But to go through life without an arm. . . . I don't know. I've always been afraid. . . . When I was little, cutting sugar cane with a knife, I sliced my finger. It wasn't much, really, but when I saw the blood, I just knew I had cut off my finger, and. . . . There is something horrible to me about mutilation. (*Sits back*)   But, I guess if it's God's will, it's God's will.

MARY   He has taken care of us this far. He'll take care of us to the end.

DORA   (*Not maliciously; as if off in her own thoughts*)   Will He? He took your little girl.

MARY   To a better place. If I didn't believe that, I. . . .

DORA   Oh, Mary! I'm sorry. It's just that. . . . I keep thinking that maybe the way they say scorpions do, we should sting ourselves to death.

MARY   (*Shudders*)   No. We won't give in. And you . . . you have no right to be weak. Now, you get a nap, and I expect you out here in an hour or two, whether they're shelling us or not, reading me that . . . that funny thing you wanted to read me before. And, Major, you're to bring your banjo, as you promised.

ROBINETTE I regret to say it, ma'am, but there are rumors. . . . Well, General Bowen is to join General Pemberton and meet with Grant tomorrow. There'll be a ceasefire.

MARY Surrender? Surely they're not talking surrender!

ROBINETTE I don't know, ma'am. They haven't confided in me. Some say they will, but others say it's to arrange another truce to bury the dead.

MARY If I thought Jim Bowen would wear my sewing to talk surrender, I'd tear out every thread.

(*Lights dim on them, rise on* HALL *and* ABRAHAM *at the Confederate lines.*)

HALL (*Pulling himself along, but resolute*) Right on down here, Abraham. Now keep low.

ABRAHAM Yessuh. I know. I come down here every day.

HALL (*Approaching* SHANGHAI *and* WILLIAMS) It was right up there that I was hit. There's my sergeant, just as I left him. Shanghai!

SHANGHAI (*Turns to* HALL; *he is, of course, gaunt and worn, not as* HALL *left him*) Colonel! You're back! By God, that's a good sign.

(WILLIAMS *tries to rise.*)

HALL Stay down. Stay down. It's good to see you boys. I regret being laid up so long.

SHANGHAI This here calls for a drink. I just wish we had the wherewithal.

HALL Abraham, go up to General Bowen's headquarters and tell him I've returned. And ask him if there's a tad of brandy left for a small celebration.

ABRAHAM Yessuh. I'm on my way.

(ABRAHAM *goes off up the lines as* HALL *settles himself gingerly behind the barricade with* SHANGHAI *and* WILLIAMS; *he peers through the barricade.*)

HALL By God, they're right in our noses, aren't they?

WILLIAMS The other night one of them yelled over here and woke me from a dream of home. Said how the hell could he get any rest with me snoring so.

(*They laugh. At this moment, farther upstage where* ABRAHAM *would be, there is an explosion. Dirt flies. Light comes up beyond Union lines, near* WELLS *and* STEITELMEYER, *as body of* ABRAHAM *lands there.* WELLS *crawls toward him as lights dim overall to blackout*)

Scene 5 (July 3)

(*Lights come up over all. There is no firing on the lines, but mortars continue to fall near the Town every couple of minutes.* MARY, GEORGE, DORA, *and* MARTHA *stand near caves as if listening, waiting.* MARTHA *is fearful of surrender,* DORA *uncertain,* MARTHA *and* GEORGE *noncommittal.* MRS. LUKE *is rocking on her porch, reading the Bible.* HALL *is about where he was hit earlier, looking out over the lines.* SHANGHAI *and* WILLIAMS *are standing, bent and stiff, looking across at* WELLS *and* STEITELMEYER, *who are looking back at them, waiting. At Tent behind the Union lines, the* CAPTAIN *is talking with* ABRAHAM. *Far up left,* GRANT *and* PEMBERTON *are seated beneath a tree talking in pantomime, with* BOWEN *and other officers behind them; light is stronger here than elsewhere, next strongest on* ABRAHAM *and* CAPTAIN, *whose dialogue is all we hear.*)

CAPTAIN You seem to be all right, now. Just knocked you unconscious. To tell you the truth, I don't see how the hell you got blown over here.

ABRAHAM Nawsuh. I don't neither. It wasn't my intention, suh.

CAPTAIN Well, what happened. Do you remember?

ABRAHAM I'uz just walking along, and then I was up in the air.

CAPTAIN How high up did you get?

ABRAHAM (*Thinks a minute; gets a sly look*) Oh, 'bout three mile.

CAPTAIN (*Begins to think he's dealing with a childlike mind*) Oh. About three miles. What did you see up there?

ABRAHAM (*Playing him*) I saw the Lawd, suh. Yassuh, sitting there in glory.

CAPTAIN Did He . . . speak to you?

ABRAHAM Yassuh. He didn't have time for much talk, but He did say a couple of words.

CAPTAIN Let's see if I can guess. He said, 'You're free.'

ABRAHAM   Nawsuh. He say, 'Fried chicken.'

CAPTAIN (*Not sure whether his leg is being pulled or not*)   Uh, well, all right. We'll see if we can round you up some, Rastus, since it seems to be the Lord's will.

ABRAHAM   Abraham, suh.

(*Lights dim out on them, come up on* MRS. LUKE, *rocking and reading the Bible, as we see* GRANT *and* PEMBERTON *rise, shake hands, and separate toward their officers, at the end of the dialogue below, when lights dim out on them and on* MRS. LUKE.)

MRS. LUKE   Just listen to this. (*Looks up as if thinking someone is there; reads anyway*)   'Joshua said unto the people, "Shout: for the Lord hath given you the city."' (*Nods wisely to herself*)   Verse the seventeenth: 'And the city shall be accursed, even it, and all that are therein, to the Lord. Only Rahab the harlot . . . (*Shocked by this unexpected bit; goes on in a daze*)   shall live, she and all that are in her house, because. . . .' (*Closes Bible abruptly*)   Pshaw! How you talk! Why that has nothing in the world to do with Vicksburg! (*Muses*)   Molly Bunch, do you reckon? And all those . . . girls? No, no. I know better. (*Opens Bible again, toward the beginning*)   I set out to read about Abraham, anyway. Poor thing. Poor thing. I reckon he has gone to be with the Lord.

(*Lights are down on her and* PEMBERTON *and* GRANT. *In dim light,* WELLS, STEITELMEYER, SHANGHAI, WILLIAMS, *and* HALL *ease down into battle position again. Suddenly cannons begin firing, rifle fire takes up; mortars continue to explode. Lights come up on Cave Area, where* MARY, DORA, GEORGE, *and* MARTHA *are gathered.* MARY *goes into a dance.*)

MARY   You hear? You hear? We haven't surrendered! We haven't!

(DORA *sits, still uncertain as to her feelings.* MARTHA *takes up work again, as does* GEORGE. ROBINETTE *rushes up, carrying his banjo.*)

ROBINETTE   Mrs. Burson! We didn't surrender!

MARY   I hear. I hear. I never thought those guns would be like music to me. (*Laughs*)   And you've brought your banjo.

ROBINETTE   They won't say what the meeting was about, but obviously they didn't come to terms.

MARY   Oh, George. Run get my guitar. Let's celebrate. Dora, get up, now, and be happy.

(MARY *pulls* DORA *to her feet, tries to make her dance around;* DORA *is reluctant, but gives in. The* GENTLEMAN *who was frightened in* MARY'S *cave is passing from left to right, giving them wide berth, but* MARY *sees him, runs to him and pulls him over to the group.* GEORGE *has gone into cave, returns with guitar.*)

MARY   You have to sing too, sir. No excuses.

(GEORGE *hands her the guitar;* MARY *quickly tunes it.*)

MARY   All right, now, you know what we're going to sing!

(*She strikes up 'Dixie';* ROBINETTE *joins in with the banjo.* DORA *begins to sing, then* GEORGE *and the* GENTLEMAN. MARTHA *goes silently about her work. From around Cave Area, other voices join in, then from center state, and on across to the lines, where we hear the Confederate soldiers joining in. As song ends, the lights go to blackout.*)

Scene 6 (July 4)

(*It seems to be just another day of the siege, firing is as usual.* ABRAHAM *is working around Tent behind Union lines.* WELLS *and* STEITELMEYER *are in Union trenches, as are* SHANGHAI *and* WILLIAMS *on the Confederate lines.* HALL *is at Tent behind Confederate lines.* MRS. LUKE *is rocking on her porch as she reads old copy of the Whig.* MARTHA *and* GEORGE *are working outside the caves.* MARY *is busying about, helping* GEORGE. DORA *comes from her cave, unseen by* MARY, *paces nervously a step or two, returns into her cave. The mockingbird sings;* MARY *stops to listen.* ROBINETTE *is crossing downstage, left to right, toward Cave Area. Suddenly, firing ceases. There is silence except for the mockingbird, which keeps singing. Everyone becomes very still, listening.* HALL *limps toward Confederate lines, despondent;* WELLS, STEITELMEYER, SHANGHAI, *and* WILLIAMS *all stand at the same time.* HALL *grasps* SHANGHAI *by the hand, then* WILLIAMS. *With rifles,* WELLS *and* STEITELMEYER *approach, shake hands with* SHANGHAI *and* WILLIAMS, *salute* HALL. *Troops are moving from left to right, first very ragged Confederate soldiers, who come in toward center and stack their rifles; some are weeping, others look relieved, still others too dazed and far gone to register.* WILLIAMS *turns away and breaks down;* SHANGHAI *puts an arm around his shoulder and helps him toward center where they add their rifles to the stack.* DORA *comes back out of her cave, listens, sobs, collapses into her chair.* MARY *stands very still, unbelieving. As* ROBINETTE *approaches, he shakes his head, unable to speak.* MARY *just stares without moving.* MARTHA *keeps working;* GEORGE *stops for a moment, begins again. Now Union troops are coming from left toward center; they shake hands, sometimes hand out food, as they come. We can hear the sound of troops far upstage moving in from left toward Town.* MARY *turns, goes rigid, fists tight at her side; then she turns and looks at* GEORGE *as if to ask if he is still with her.* GEORGE *picks up some of the cooking equipment,* MARY *takes her guitar, and they start toward center, back to her house.* MARTHA *moves toward center and Union troops a step or two, then stops; we see her caught undecided between staying with* DORA *and leaving.* MRS. LUKE *keeps rocking, but, only once, wipes at her eyes. The Union* CAPTAIN *approaches* ROBINETTE, *salutes, stands at attention as* ROBINETTE *unbuckles his sword and hands it to him. We have a broad panoramic view, with lights gradually dimming until focussed in a spot on the courthouse in town, where the Confederate flag is lowered and the Union flag is raised. Light grows stronger as the flag nears the top of the staff, so that the scene closes with the sharp spot on the flag in the silent dark.)*

THE END

Requiem for a Nun

WILLIAM FAULKNER AND RUTH FORD

This play was written not to be a play, but as what seemed to me the best way to tell the story in a novel. It became a play, to me, only after Ruth Ford saw it as a play and believed that only she could do it right. When in English, it is her play. What she adds to it, to make it a better play, is Ruth Ford.

WILLIAM FAULKNER

CHARACTERS

NANCY MANNIGOE, TEMPLE, GOWAN STEVENS, GAVIN STEVENS, GOVERNOR, PETE, MR. TUBBS

SETTING

The action of the play takes place in the present time in the town of Jefferson, Yoknapatawpha County, Mississippi—before and after the trial of one Nancy Mannigoe for murder.

There are three acts.

ACT I

Scene 1

Courtroom, 5:30 p.m. November thirteenth.
  A bell begins to toll. The curtain rises, symbolizing the rising of the prisoner in the dock. The bottom of the stage is in darkness, so that the visible scene is not only spotlighted but elevated slightly—

the symbolism of the elevated tribunal of justice of which this, a
county court, is only the intermediate, not the highest stage.

   The defense lawyer is GAVIN STEVENS, *about fifty. He looks*
more like a poet than a lawyer and actually is: a bachelor, descendant
of one of the pioneer Yoknapatawpha County families, Harvard and
Heidelberg educated, champion not so much of truth as of justice,
or of justice as he sees it, constantly involving himself, often for
no pay, in affairs of equity and passion and even crime too among
his people, white and Negro both, sometimes directly contrary to
his office of County Attorney which he has held for years, as is
the present business.

   The prisoner is standing. She is a Negress, quite black, about
thirty—that is, she could be almost anything between twenty and
forty—with a calm impenetrable almost bemused face, not looking
at anything, but looking out and up as though at some distant corner
of the room, as though she were alone in it. She is—or was until
recently, five months ago to be exact—a domestic servant, nurse
to two white children, the second of whom, an infant, she smothered
in its cradle five months ago, for which act she is now on trial for
her life. But she has probably done many things else, chopped cot-
ton, cooked for working gangs—any sort of manual labor within
her capacities, or rather, limitations in time and availability, since
her principal reputation in the little Mississippi town where she was
born is that of a tramp—a drunkard, a casual prostitute, being
beaten by some man or cutting or being cut by his wife or his other
sweetheart. She has probably been married, at least once. Her
name—or so she calls it and would probably spell it if she could
spell—is NANCY MANNIGOE.

   There is a dead silence in the room while everybody watches her.

JUDGE (*Offstage, speaks through a microphone*) Have you anything
to say before the sentence of the court is pronounced upon you?
(NANCY *neither answers nor moves; she doesn't even seem to be
listening*) That you, Nancy Mannigoe, did on the thirteenth day of
June, willfully and with malice aforethought kill and murder the infant
child of Mr. and Mrs. Gowan Stevens in the town of Jefferson and
the County of Yoknapatawpha . . . It is the sentence of this court that
you be taken from hence back to the county jail of Yoknapatawpha
County and there on the thirteenth day of March be hanged by the
neck until you are dead. And may God have mercy on your soul.
NANCY (*Quite loud in the silence, to no one, quite calm, not moving*)
Yes, Lord. Thank you, Lord.

(There is a gasp, a sound, from the invisible spectators in the room, of shock at this unheard-of violation of procedure: the beginning of something which might be consternation and even uproar, in the midst of, or rather above which, NANCY *herself does not move. From somewhere among the unseen spectators there comes the sound of a woman's voice—a moan, wail, sob perhaps. The bell tolls. The curtain descends rapidly, the lights go out. A moment of darkness. Then the curtain rises.)*

Scene 2

GOWAN STEVENS' *living room. 6:00 P.M. November thirteenth.*
    The double doors in the center of the room stand open on an elevated foyer. Three steps down take you into the living room. There is a fireplace, left, with gas logs. The atmosphere of the room is smart, modern, up to date, yet the room itself has the air of another time—the high ceiling, the cornices, some of the furniture. It is all in tones of gray, with a solid red carpet.
    Sound of feet, then the lights come on as if someone about to enter had pressed a wall switch, then the door opens and TEMPLE *enters, followed by* GOWAN *and* GAVIN. *She is wearing a black dress, black coat, black fur, and carries a black hat and black bag in her hands.* TEMPLE'S *air is brittle and tense, yet controlled. Her face shows nothing as she crosses to the center table and stops.* GOWAN *and* STEVENS *wear dark gray suits and overcoats, and are carrying their hats.* STEVENS *stops just inside the room.* GOWAN *drops his hat on to the chair in passing and goes on to where* TEMPLE *stands at the table, stripping off one of her gloves.*

TEMPLE *(Mimics the prisoner; her voice, harsh, reveals for the first time repressed, controlled hysteria)* Yes, God. Guilty, God. Thank you, God. If that's your attitude toward being hung, what else can you expect from a judge and jury except to accommodate you?

GOWAN Stop it, Boots. Hush now. Soon as I light the fire, I'll buy a drink. *(To* STEVENS) Or maybe Gavin will do the fire while I do the butler.

TEMPLE I'll do the fire. You get the drinks. Then Uncle Gavin won't have to stay. After all, all he wants to do is say good-bye. He can almost do that in two words, if he tries hard. Then he can go home.

(She crosses to the hearth, kneels, and turns the gas valve, and lights the fire)

GOWAN (*Anxiously*)   Now, Boots.

TEMPLE   Will you for God's sake please get me a drink?

GOWAN   Sure, honey. (*He turns; to* STEVENS)   Drop your coat anywhere.

> (*He exits into the dining room.* STEVENS *does not move, watching*
> TEMPLE *as the log takes fire*)

TEMPLE (*Still kneeling, her back to* STEVENS)   If you're going to stay,
why don't you sit down? Or vice versa. If you're not sitting down,
why don't you go? Let me be bereaved and vindicated, but at least
let me do it in privacy.

> (STEVENS *watches her. Then he crosses to her, taking the handker-
> chief from his breast pocket, stops behind her and extends the hand-
> kerchief down where she can see it. She looks at it, then up at him.
> Her face is quite calm*)

TEMPLE   What's that for?

STEVENS   It's all right. It's dry too. (*Still extending the handkerchief*)
For tomorrow, then.

TEMPLE (*Rises quickly*)   Oh, for cinders. On the train. We're going
by air; hadn't Gowan told you? We leave from the Memphis airport
at midnight; we're driving up after supper. Then California tomorrow
morning; maybe we'll even go on to Hawaii in the spring. No; wrong
season; Canada, maybe. Lake Louise in May and June—(*She stops,
listens a moment toward the dining-room doors*)   So why the handkerchief? Not a threat, because you don't have anything to threaten me
with, do you? And if you don't have anything to threaten me with,
I must not have anything you want, so it can't be a bribe either, can
it? (*They both hear the sound from beyond the dining-room doors
which indicates that* GOWAN *is approaching.* TEMPLE *lowers her
voice again, rapidly*)   Put it this way, then. I don't know what you
want, because I don't care. Because whatever it is, you won't get it
from me. (*The sound is near now—footsteps, clink of glass*)   Now he'll
offer you a drink, and then he'll ask you too what you want, why you
followed us home. I've already answered you. No. If what you came
for is to see me weep, I doubt if you'll even get that. But you certainly
won't get anything else. Not from me. Do you understand that?

STEVENS   I hear you.

TEMPLE   Meaning, you don't believe it. (*Quicker, tenser*)   I refuse
to answer your question; now I'll ask you one: How much do you—(*As*
GOWAN *enters, she changes what she was saying so smoothly in mid-
sentence that anyone entering would not even realize that the pitch*

of her voice had altered)—are her lawyer, she must have talked to you; even a dope fiend that murders a little baby must have what she calls some excuse for it, even a—

GOWAN   I said stop it, Boots. (*He carries a tray containing a pitcher of water, a bowl of ice, three empty tumblers and three whiskey glasses already filled. The bottle itself protrudes from his topcoat pocket. He approaches* TEMPLE *and offers the tray*) That's right. I'm going to have one myself. For a change. After all these years. Why not?

TEMPLE   Why not?

(*She takes one of the filled glasses.* GOWAN *offers the tray to* STEVENS, *who takes the second one. Then he sets the tray on the table and takes up the third glass*)

GOWAN   Nary a drink since we've been married. So maybe this will be a good time to start again. At least, it won't be too soon. (*To* STEVENS)   Drink up. A little water behind it? (*As though not aware that he had done so, he sets his untasted glass back on the tray, splashes water from the pitcher into a tumbler, and hands the tumbler to* STEVENS *as* STEVENS *empties his glass and lowers it, taking the tumbler.* TEMPLE *has not touched hers either*)   Now maybe Defense Attorney Stevens will tell us what he wants here.

STEVENS   Your wife has already told you. To say good-bye.

GOWAN   Then say it. One more for the road, and where's your hat, huh?

(*He takes the tumbler from* STEVENS *and turns back to the table*)

TEMPLE (*She sets her untasted glass back on the tray*)   And put ice in it this time, and maybe even a little water. But first, take Uncle Gavin's coat.

GOWAN (*Takes bottle from his pocket and makes a highball for* STEVENS *in the tumbler*)   That won't be necessary. If he could raise his arm in a white courtroom to defend a murdering nigger, he can certainly bend it in nothing but a wool overcoat—at least to take a drink with the victim's mother.

TEMPLE (*She is watching, not* GOWAN *but* STEVENS, *who watches her in return, grave and soberly*)   Don't forget the father too, dear.

GOWAN (*Mixing the drink*)   Why should I, dear? How could I, dear? Except that the child's father is unfortunately just a man. In the eyes of the law, men are not supposed to suffer. The law is tender only of women and children—particularly of women, particularly particular of nigger dope fiend whores who murder white children. (*Hands the highball to* STEVENS, *who takes it*)   So why should we expect Defense Attorney Stevens to be tender of a man or a woman who just happened to be the parents of the child that got murdered?

TEMPLE (*Harshly*) Will you for God's sake please get through? Then will you for God's sake please hush?

GOWAN (*Quickly*) Sorry. (*He turns toward her, sees her hand empty, then sees her full glass beside his own on the tray*) No drink?

TEMPLE I don't want it. I want some milk.

GOWAN Right. Hot, of course.

TEMPLE Please.

GOWAN (*Turning*) Right. I thought of that too. I put a pan on to heat while I was getting the drinks. (*Crossing toward dining-room exit*) Don't let Uncle Gavin get away until I get back. Lock the door, if you have to.

(*He exits. They don't move until the slap of the pantry door sounds*)

TEMPLE (*Rapid, hard*) How much do you know? (*Rapidly*) Don't lie to me; don't you see there's not time?

STEVENS Not time for what? Before your plane leaves tonight? Nancy has a little time yet—four months, until March, the thirteenth of March—

TEMPLE You know what I mean—her lawyer—seeing her every day— just a nigger, and you a white man—even if you needed anything to frighten her with—you could just buy it from her with a dose of cocaine or a pint of . . . (*She stops, stares at him, in a sort of amazement, despair; her voice is almost quiet*) Oh, God, oh, God. I talk about no time . . . and it's playing me button, button. She hasn't told you anything. It's me; I'm the one that's—don't you see? It's that I cannot believe—will not believe—impossible—

STEVENS Impossible to believe that all human beings really don't— stink? No, she has told me nothing more.

TEMPLE (*Prompts*) Even if there was anything more.

STEVENS Even if there was.

TEMPLE Then what is it you think you know? Never mind where you got it; just tell me what you think it is.

STEVENS There was a man here that night.

TEMPLE (*Quick, harsh*) So I was right. Did you frighten her, or just buy it? (*She stops; it is as if she had heard a sound presaging GOWAN's return, or perhaps simply knew by instinct or from knowledge of her own house that he had had time to heat a cup of milk. Then continues, rapid and quiet*) There was no man here. You see? I told you, warned you, that you would get nothing from me. Oh, I know; you could have put me on the stand at any time, under oath; of course, your jury wouldn't have liked it—that wanton crucifixion of a bereaved mamma, but what's that in the balance with justice? I don't know why you didn't. Or maybe you still intend to—provided you can catch us before we cross the Tennessee line tonight. (*Quick, tense, hard*) All right. I'm sorry. I know better. So maybe it's just my own stinking after all that I find impossible to doubt. (*The pantry door slaps again; they both hear it*) Because I'm not even going to take Gowan with me when I say good night—And who knows what you might tell each other.

(*She stops.* GOWAN *enters, carrying a small tray bearing glass of milk and a napkin, and comes to the table*)

GOWAN   What are you talking about now?
TEMPLE   Nothing. I was telling Uncle Gavin that he had something of Virginia or some sort of gentleman in him too that he must have inherited from you through your grandfather, and that I'm going to give Bucky his bath and supper. (*She touches the glass for heat, then takes it up to* GOWAN) Thank you, dear.
GOWAN   Right, dear. (*To* STEVENS) You see? Not just a napkin; the right napkin. That's how I'm trained. (*He stops suddenly, noticing* TEMPLE, *who has done nothing apparently; just standing there holding the milk. But he seems to know what is going on; to her*) What's this for?
TEMPLE   I don't know. (*He moves; they kiss, not long but not a peck either; definitely a kiss between a man and a woman. Then, carrying the milk,* TEMPLE *crosses toward the hall door. To* STEVENS) Good-bye then until next June. Bucky will send you and Maggie a postcard from Lake Louise.
STEVENS   Where will you go then?
TEMPLE   (*She goes on to the door, pauses and looks back at* STEVENS) I may even be wrong about Temple Drake's odor too; if you should happen to hear something you haven't heard yet and it's true, I may even ratify it. Maybe you can even believe that—if you can believe you are going to hear anything that you haven't heard yet.
STEVENS   Do you?
TEMPLE   (*After a moment*) Not from me, Uncle Gavin. If someone wants to go to heaven, who am I to stop them? Good night. Good-bye.

(*She exits, closes the door.* STEVENS, *very grave, turns back and sets his highball down on the tray*)

GOWAN   Drink up. After all, I've got to eat supper and do some packing too. How about it?

STEVENS   About what? The packing, or the drink? What about you? I thought you were going to have one.

GOWAN   Oh, sure. Sure. (*Takes up the small filled glass*)   Maybe you had better go on and leave us to our revenge.

STEVENS   I wish it could comfort you.

GOWAN   I wish to God it could. I wish to God that what I wanted was only revenge. An eye for an eye—were ever words emptier? Only, you have got to have lost the eye to know it.

STEVENS   Yet she still has to die.

GOWAN   Why not? Even if she would be any loss—a nigger whore, a drunkard, a dope fiend—

STEVENS   A vagabond, a tramp, hopeless until one day Mr. and Mrs. Gowan Stevens out of simple pity and humanity picked her up out of the gutter to give her one more chance— (GOWAN *stands motionless, his hand tightening slowly about the glass.* STEVENS *watches him*) And then in return for it—

GOWAN   Look, Uncle Gavin. Why don't you go for God's sake home? Or to hell, or anywhere out of here?

STEVENS   I am, in a minute. Is that why you think—why you would still say she has to die?

GOWAN   I don't. I had nothing to do with it. I wasn't even the plaintiff. I didn't even instigate the suit. My only connection with it was, I happened by chance to be the father of the child she—Who in hell ever called that a drink?

(*He dashes the whiskey, glass and all, into the ice bowl, quickly catches up one of the empty tumblers in one hand and, at the same time, tilts the whiskey bottle over it, pouring. At first he makes no sound, but at once it is obvious that he is laughing; laughter which begins normally enough, but he still pours whiskey into the glass, which in a moment now will overflow, except that STEVENS reaches his hand and grasps the bottle and stops it*)

STEVENS   Stop it, now. Here.

(*He takes the bottle from* GOWAN, *sets it down, takes the tumbler and tilts part of its contents into the other empty one, leaving at least a reasonable, a believable, drink, and hands it to* GOWAN. GOWAN *takes it, stopping the crazy laughter, gets hold of himself again*)

GOWAN   (*Holding the glass untasted*)   All those years on the wagon— and this is what I got for it: my child murdered—You see? All these years without the drink, and so I got whatever it was I was buying by not drinking, and now I've got whatever it was I was paying for and it's paid for and so I can drink again. And now I don't want the drink. So I have a laugh coming. That's triumph. Because I got a bargain even in what I didn't want. Half price: a child, and a dope fiend nigger whore on a public gallows: that's all I had to pay for immunity.

STEVENS   There's no such thing.

GOWAN   From the past. From my folly. My drunkenness. My cowardice, if you like—

STEVENS   There's no such thing as past either.

GOWAN   That is a laugh, that one, Only, not so loud, huh? to disturb the ladies—disturb Miss Drake—Miss Temple Drake. Now, Mrs. Gowan Stevens—Sure, why not cowardice. Only call it simple over-training. You know? Gowan Stevens, trained at Virginia to drink like a gentleman, gets drunk as ten gentlemen, takes a college girl, who knows? maybe even a virgin, cross-country by car to another college ball game, gets drunker than twenty gentlemen, gets lost, gets still drunker than forty gentlemen, wrecks the car, passes eighty gentlemen now, passes completely out while the virgin is being kidnapped into a Memphis whorehouse—(*He mumbles*)—and loved it.

STEVENS   What?

GOWAN   Sure. Call it cowardice.

STEVENS   Not the marrying her afterward, at least. What did you—

GOWAN   Sure. Marrying her was purest Old Virginia. That was indeed the hundred and sixty gentlemen.

STEVENS   The prisoner in the whorehouse; I didn't quite hear—

GOWAN   (*Quickly: reaching for it*)   Where's your glass? Dump that slop—here—

STEVENS   (*Holds glass*)   This will do. What was that you said about held prisoner in the whorehouse?

GOWAN   (*Harshly*)   That's all. You heard it.

STEVENS   You said "and loved it." (*They stare at each other*)   Is that what you can never forgive her for?—for having created that moment in your life which you can never forget nor condone nor even stop thinking about, because she herself didn't even suffer, but, on the contrary, even liked it—That you had to lose not only your bachelor freedom, but your man's self-respect, to pay for something your wife didn't even regret? Is that why this poor lost doomed crazy Negro woman must die?

GOWAN   (*Tensely*)   Get out of here. Go on.

STEVENS   In a minute. What else happened during that month, that time while that madman held her prisoner there in the Memphis whorehouse, that nobody but you and she know about, maybe not even you know about?

(Still staring at STEVENS, *slowly and deliberately* GOWAN *sets the glass of whiskey back on the tray and takes up the bottle and swings it bottom up back over his head. The stopper is out and at once the whiskey begins to pour out of it, down his arm and sleeve and onto the floor. He does not seem to be aware of it even. His voice is tense, barely articulate*)

GOWAN   So help me, Christ . . . So help me, Christ.

(*A moment, then* STEVENS *moves, without haste, taking his hat as he passes, and goes on to the door and exits.* GOWAN *stands a moment longer with the poised bottle, now empty. Then he draws a long shuddering breath, seems to rouse, wake, sets the empty bottle back on the tray, notices his untasted whiskey glass, takes it up, a moment; then turns and throws the glass crashing into the fireplace, against the burning gas logs, and stands, his back to the audience, and draws another long shuddering breath and then draws both hands hard down his face. Then turns, looking at his wet sleeve, takes out his handkerchief and dabs at his sleeve as he comes back to the table, puts the handkerchief back in his pocket and takes the folded napkin from the small tray and wipes his sleeve with it, sees he is doing no good, tosses the crumpled napkin back on to the whiskey tray; and now, outwardly quite calm again, as though nothing had happened, he gathers the glasses back on to the tray, puts the small tray and the napkins on to it too, and takes up the tray and walks quietly toward the dining-room door as the lights begin to go down*)

CURTAIN

Scene 3

Living room. 10 p.m. March eleventh.
    TEMPLE *enters from nursery, downstage right, closes door, on second thought opens it. She is wearing a long Chinese black brocade satin housecoat—the long loose pointed sleeves lined with red.* STEVENS *enters wearing a dark gray suit, a different one, and this time carries the topcoat and the hat, too. Apparently* TEMPLE *has already warned him to be quiet; his air, anyway, shows it.*

STEVENS   Well, here I am.

TEMPLE   Shhh. Close the nursery door.

   (STEVENS *crosses to the nursery door and looks inside*)

STEVENS   You're letting Bucky sleep in the room his sister was murdered in. So this is a plant.

TEMPLE   Why not. Don't the philosophers tell us that women will strike back with any weapon, even their children?

STEVENS   Including the sleeping pill you told me on the phone you gave Gowan? You came all the way back from California, almost without notice.

TEMPLE   I came all the way back from California, but I still can't seem to quit. Do you believe in coincidence?

STEVENS   I can. Yes.

TEMPLE   (*At table, takes up a folded yellow telegraph form, opens it, reads*)   Dated Jefferson, March sixth. "You have a week yet until the thirteenth. But where will you go then?" Signed Gavin.

   (*She folds the paper back into its old creases, folds it still again.* STEVENS *watches her*)

STEVENS   Well? This is the eleventh. Is that the coincidence?

TEMPLE   No. This is. (*Sits in front of the fire—clutching the folded paper*)   It was that very afternoon—the sixth. We were on the beach, Bucky and I. I was reading, and he was—oh, talking mostly, you know—"Is California far from Jefferson, Mamma?" and I say, "Yes, darling"—you know: still reading or trying to, and he says "How long will we stay in California, Mama?" and I say, "Until we get tired of it," and he says "Will we stay here until they hang Nancy, Mamma?" I say, "Yes, darling," and then he drops it right in my lap, right out of the mouths of babes and sucklings. "Where will we go then, Mamma?" So I went back to the hotel and got reservations and here we are and I got Gowan—I hope—safely in bed with a barbital, and telephoned you. Well?

STEVENS   Well what?

TEMPLE   All right. Let's for God's sake stop. (*Goes to a chair*)   Now that I'm here, no matter who's responsible for it, what do you want? A drink? Will you drink? At least, put your coat and hat down. (STEVENS *lays his hat and coat on a chair.* TEMPLE *sits down.* STEVENS *takes a chair opposite*)   So Nancy must be saved. Apparently I know something I haven't told yet, or maybe you know something I haven't told yet. What do you think you know? (*Quickly; he says nothing*)   All right. What do you know?

STEVENS   Nothing. I don't want to know it. All I—

TEMPLE   All right. Why do you think there is something I haven't told yet?

STEVENS   You came back. All the way from California.

TEMPLE   Not enough. Try again.

STEVENS   You were there. (*With her face averted,* TEMPLE *reaches her hand to the table, fumbles until she finds the cigarette box, takes a cigarette*)   At the trial. Every day. All day, from the time court opened—

TEMPLE   (*Still not looking at him, supremely casual*)   The bereaved mother—

STEVENS   Yes, the breaved mother—

TEMPLE   —herself watching the accomplishment of her revenge; the tigress over the body of her slain cub—

STEVENS   —who should have been too immersed in grief to have thought of revenge—to have borne the very sight of her child's murderer . . .

TEMPLE   (*Not looking at him*)   Methinks she doth protest too much?

(STEVENS *doesn't answer. He snaps the lighter on, lights her cigarette, puts the lighter back on the table. Leaning,* STEVENS *pushes the ash tray along the table until she can reach it. Now she looks at him*)

TEMPLE   Thanks. Now let grandmamma teach you how to suck an egg. It doesn't matter what I know, what you think I know, what might have happened. Because we won't even need it. All we need is an affidavit. That she is crazy. Has been for years.

STEVENS   I thought of that too. Only it's too late. That should have been done about five months ago. She has been convicted and sentenced. In the eyes of the law, she is already dead. In the eyes of the law, Nancy Mannigoe doesn't even exist.

TEMPLE   (*Smoking*)   Yes? (*She sits back in the chair, smoking rapidly, looking at* STEVENS. *Her voice is gentle, patient, only a little too rapid, like the smoking*)   Now try to listen. Really try. I am the affidavit; what else are we doing here at ten o'clock at night barely a day from her execution? What else did I come all the way back from California for? All we need now is to decide just how much of what to put in the affidavit. Do try; maybe you had better have a drink after all.

STEVENS   Later, maybe. I'm dizzy enough right now with just perjury and contempt of court.

TEMPLE   What perjury?

STEVENS   After my client is not only convicted but sentenced, I turn

up with the prosecution's chief witness offering evidence to set the
whole trial aside—

TEMPLE   Tell them I forgot this. Or tell them I changed my mind.
Tell them the district attorney bribed me to keep my mouth shut—

STEVENS   (*Peremptory yet quiet*)   Temple.

(*She puffs rapidly at the cigarette, removes it from her mouth*)

TEMPLE   Or better still—a woman whose child was smothered in its
crib, wanting vengeance, capable of anything to get the vengeance;
then when she has it, realizing she can't go through with it, can't sacrifice a human life for it, even a nigger whore's?

STEVENS   Stop it. One at a time. At least, let's talk about the same
thing. Then you really don't want her to die.

TEMPLE   Oh, for God's sake, didn't I just say so?

STEVENS   Then Temple Drake will have to save her.

TEMPLE   Mrs. Gowan Stevens will.

STEVENS   Temple Drake. (*She stares at him, smoking, deliberately
now. Deliberately she removes the cigarette and, still watching him,
reaches and snubs it out in the ash tray*)   All right. We produce a
sworn affidavit that Nancy was crazy when she committed the crime.
Based on what?

TEMPLE   —What?

STEVENS   Based on what proof?

(*She stares at him*)

TEMPLE   Proof?

STEVENS   What will be in the affidavit? What are we going to affirm
now that for some reason we didn't see fit to bring up or anyway didn't
bring up until after she—

TEMPLE   How do I know? You're the lawyer. What do such affidavits
need to have in them, to make them work, make them sure to work?
(*Her voices ceases. She stares at him, while he continues to look steadily
back at her, saying nothing, just looking at her, until at last she draws
a loud harsh breath; her voice is harsh too*)   What do you want then?
What more do you want?

STEVENS   Temple Drake.

TEMPLE   (*Quick, harsh, immediate*)   No. Mrs. Gowan Stevens.

STEVENS   (*Implacable and calm*)   Temple Drake. The truth.

TEMPLE   Truth? We're trying to save a condemned murderess whose
lawyer has already admitted that he has failed. What has truth got
to do with that? (*Rapid, harsh*)   Can't you get it through your head
that I will do anything, *anything*?

STEVENS   Except one. Which is all, everything. We're not concerned with death. That's nothing. What we are trying to deal with now is injustice. Only truth can cope with that. Or love.

TEMPLE *(Harshly)*   Love. Oh, God. Love.

STEVENS   Call it pity then. Or courage. Or honesty, or a simple desire for the right to sleep at night.

TEMPLE   You prate of sleep, to me, who learned years ago how not even to realize any more that I didn't mind not sleeping at night? If her dying is nothing, what in God's name do you want?

STEVENS   I told you. Truth.

TEMPLE   And I told you that truth has nothing to do with this. When you go before the supreme court what you will need will be facts, sworn documents.

STEVENS   We're not going to the supreme court. *(She stares at him)* We're going to the Governor. Tonight.

TEMPLE   The Governor?

STEVENS   Perhaps he won't save her either. He probably won't.

TEMPLE   Then why ask him? Why?

STEVENS   I've told you. Truth.

TEMPLE *(In quiet amazement)*   For no more than that. For no better reason than that. Just to get it told, breathed aloud, into words, sound. Just to be heard by someone, anyone, any stranger none of whose business it is, simply because he is capable of hearing it, comprehending it. Why blink your own rhetoric? Why don't you go on and tell me it's for the good of my soul—if I have one?

STEVENS   I did. I said, so you can sleep at night.

TEMPLE   And I told you I forgot years ago even what it was to miss the sleep. *(She stares at him. He doesn't answer, looking at her. She turns her head and looks toward the nursery door)* So it was a plant, after all; I just didn't seem to know for who. I threw my remaining child at you. Now you threw him back.

STEVENS   But I didn't wake him.

TEMPLE   Then I've got you, lawyer. What would be better for his peace and sleep than to hang his sister's murderer?

STEVENS   No matter by what means, in what lie?

TEMPLE   Nor whose.

STEVENS   Yet you came back.

TEMPLE   Mrs. Gowan Stevens did.

STEVENS   Temple Drake did. Mrs. Gowan Stevens is not even fighting in this class. This is Temple Drake's.

TEMPLE   Temple Drake is dead.

STEVENS   The past is never dead. It's not even past.

TEMPLE   Listen. How much do you know?

STEVENS   Nothing.

TEMPLE   Swear.

STEVENS   Would you believe me?

TEMPLE   No. But swear anyway.

STEVENS   All right. I swear.

TEMPLE   All right. How much do you *think* you know?

STEVENS   There was a man here that night.

TEMPLE (*Quickly*)   Gowan.

STEVENS   Let's agree that this is for your life too. So nobody but a fool would expect you to fight by Queensberry rules. But only a fool would believe you foolish enough to mistake a straw for a cudgel. Gowan wasn't here then. He and Bucky left at six o'clock that morning for New Orleans to go fishing. It was Gowan himself who gave you away—something he said to me without knowing he was doing it, which showed who planned that trip, to get not only Gowan, but Bucky too out of this house. I'm surprised you didn't send Nancy away too— (*He stops, obviously reacts to something he sees in* TEMPLE'S *face*) Why, you did. You did try, and she refused. Yes. There was a man here that night.

TEMPLE   Prove it.

STEVENS   I can't. Don't I keep on saying that Nancy has refused to tell me anything about that night?

TEMPLE   Now listen to me. (*She stands, tense, rigid, facing him, staring at him*)   Listen carefully, because I don't intend to say this again. Temple Drake is dead. Temple Drake will have been dead years longer than Nancy Mannigoe will ever be. If there is anything—anything at all—that Mrs. Gowan Stevens can sign or swear to or lie to, to save Nancy Mannigoe, I will do it. But if all Nancy Mannigoe has left to save her is Temple Drake, then God help Nancy Mannigoe. Now get out of here. (*She stares at him; another moment. Then he rises, still watching her; she stares steadily and implacably back. Then he moves*) Good night.

STEVENS   Good night.

> (*He goes back to the chair, takes up his coat and hat, then goes on to the hall door, and exits.* STEVENS *stands watching the door. When* STEVENS *is gone,* GOWAN *appears quietly in the door, in his shirt sleeves, tieless, his collar open. He watches* TEMPLE *and she stands a moment longer. Then she makes a gesture something like* GOWAN'S *in Scene 2, except that she merely presses her hands hard against her cheeks, stands a moment, then drops her hands*)

and crosses purposefully to the telephone, GOWAN *still watching her, and lifts receiver)*

TEMPLE (*Into the phone*) Three-two-nine, please. (*She does not see* GOWAN *yet. He approaches her, carrying something in his closed hand. He is right behind her when the phone answers)* Hello. Maggie? This is Temple. When Uncle Gavin—

(GOWAN *reaches roughly past her, grasps her hand holding the receiver and claps the receiver back on the stand, cutting off the connection; at the same time he flips the capsule from his other hand onto the table)*

GOWAN There's your pill too. Why don't you tell me about the man that Gavin says was here that night? Come on. You won't even have to think hard. Just tell me he was an uncle of Bucky's that you just forgot to tell me about.

TEMPLE Would you believe me if I said there wasn't one?

GOWAN Sure I would. Anything you say. I always have. That's what has sunk us. I even believed right up until tonight that it was me that planned that fishing trip. Everybody but me knew better, but that was all right, nobody needed to be fooled but me and I was already on my back when I came in. Thanks though. But I can still see, even if I don't know until years afterward what I was looking at. But try the truth maybe; there surely must be something you can tell me that I won't believe. Maybe Gavin was right and his business wasn't with my wife, but with Temple Drake. Maybe it was Bucky's papa, huh, just dropped in on the way through town—

TEMPLE Gowan, hush. (*He stops talking, looking at her*) Why can't you just hush? (*She indicates the sleeping child*)

GOWAN Don't worry, you were the one who seems to worry about waking him. I'm not going to make that much noise. I'm not going to hit you. I never hit a woman in my life, not even a whore, not even a Memphis whore, an ex-Memphis whore—Jesus, they say there are two women every man is entitled to hit once; his wife, and his whore. And just look at me; I can hit both of mine at one time, with one swing, one lick—Do you want a drink?

TEMPLE No. I don't want one.

GOWAN Come on. I'll fix you one.

TEMPLE I don't want one.

GOWAN (*Produces pack of cigarettes from his trouser pocket and offers one*) Then have a cigarette, then. For Christ's sake, do something. Don't just stand there. (TEMPLE *takes the cigarette. He produces a lighter from the same pocket and snaps it on*) Here. (*She accepts the light. He puts the lighter back into his pocket, drops the pack of cigarettes on to the table*) Okay, I've stopped. Now we can start even. If we just could, of course. But with all these big-wheel international truths knocking around here tonight, it's no wonder you and I can't get together on a little petty fact like how a man's wife just treating herself to a little extracurricular poontang should cause the murder of their child—

TEMPLE That's right. Go ahead. Then maybe we can stop.

GOWAN Because you really do believe it, don't you? That there really is some price, some point where you can stop paying, some last nickel you've got in the world that they won't ask of you, that you won't have to pay for just one mistake—mistake—mistake? Jesus, let's laugh. Come on, laugh. Don't just stand there—

TEMPLE (*Sharply*) Gowan! Stop it!

GOWAN That's right. Slap me, try that. Hit me. Then maybe I will hit you back and then you can start forgiving me for a change. You know, for the whole thing; getting drunk that day, not because I wanted to get drunk, but because I was afraid, afraid that I, the big wheel, Joe College himself, president of his frat at Charlottesville, who could even call the madams of New York City cathouses by their first names, couldn't handle a little Mississippi country girl who had never been away from home until she entered the freshman class at the State University—had to get drunk to have enough courage to persuade you to slip out of that damned baseball excursion train.

TEMPLE Did you twist my arm?

GOWAN What?

TEMPLE You didn't have to persuade—All you had to do was suggest.

GOWAN Will you shut up? Will you? Let me have a good whine while I'm at it. Tell me what you probably think I've been telling myself all these years: how, if it hadn't been for you, I might have married a good girl—a decent girl that never heard of hot pants until her husband taught her—(*He stops, drags his hands down his face again as in Scene 2*) God, we must have loved each other once. We must have. Can't you remember.

TEMPLE Yes.

GOWAN Yes what?

TEMPLE Loved one another once. We must have.

GOWAN Can't you remember! Can't you? (*She doesn't answer*) Come here.

TEMPLE (*Not moving*) No.

GOWAN   All right. If you want it this way, you can have it. You're not going to use that telephone. There was a man here that night—

TEMPLE   No.

GOWAN   (*Pays no attention*)   —since Uncle Gavin knows it, I suppose everybody else in Jefferson does too—except me of course. Though I still don't see how that brought about the murder of a six-months-old baby. Maybe Nancy caught you laying him, and killed Dee Dee in spite or excitement or something. Or maybe the excitement wasn't Nancy's; that in your hurry you forgot to move Dee Dee out of the bed, and in the general thrashing around—You see? You see what I am capable of? I don't even have to half try . . .

TEMPLE   No.

GOWAN   No what? Go on. Say it. There was no man here. (TEMPLE *says nothing*)   Go on. Can't you say it? (TEMPLE *says nothing*)   All right then. At least you didn't tell Gavin what happened here that night. So I don't want to know what happened. And so nobody else shall. Not ever. You're not going to call Uncle Gavin and agree to go tell the Governor or anybody else anything. You said it yourself: if all Nancy Mannigoe's got to save her is Temple Drake, then God help Nancy Mannigoe. Okay?

TEMPLE   No.

GOWAN   Oh yes. You see. I've even giving you one more chance. If there is any reason for grief and suffering, it's so that you will learn at least not to make the same mistake again, and to have consideration for the mistakes that other people make, and to believe that they are going to try not to make the same ones any more. But I still believe that there is some drop of blood you won't have to pay for what you did and can't recall. So you are not going to touch that telephone. Because if you go, I'm gone. (*Quickly*)   Wait. You could have quit at any time. You still can. But if you pick up that telephone and call Uncle Gavin, it will be too late. It will be me that's gone. Okay? (*She doesn't answer*)   Say yes, Temple.

TEMPLE   I can't.

GOWAN   Say yes, Temple. We loved each other once. Didn't we?

TEMPLE   We must have.

GOWAN   Then say it. You said it once.

TEMPLE   We loved each other once.

GOWAN   Then prove it. If she must die, let her. If something happened here that night that would save her and she won't tell it, then who are you—

TEMPLE   I can't.

GOWAN   Temple—(*They watch each other for a moment. Then* TEM-
PLE *turns toward the telephone.* GOWAN *moves faster, reaches it first,
and puts his hand on the receiver*)   Remember.
TEMPLE   Please move your hand, Gowan. (*They watch each other.
Then he removes his hand.* TEMPLE *takes the receiver. Into the phone*)
Three-two-nine, please . . .

CURTAIN

The Freedom Kick

SHELBY FOOTE

(Lights come up on a rather chubby, middleaged Negro who stands on an open platform beside an old-fashioned, hooded camera on a tripod. The time is 1910. He wears a well-cut suit and a high hard collar, a flowing bow-tie, and button shoes. His air is one of congenial well-being, and he gives the impression of being as much at ease under stress as he is now, with time on his hands and nothing pressing. He checks his camera, then speaks as if in answer to a question from an invisible companion. This companion is the audience)

You ask about that old time. It aint nothing I cant tell you. Kluxers, smut ballots, whipping-bees, all that: I'm in a position to know and I remember, mainly on account of my mama. That woman loved freedom like nothin ever was. She was the daughter of a free man, a barber, and when she married my daddy it like to killed him—the barber I mean. A barber had a position in those days; the shop was kind of a gathering place where the white men would sit around and talk, so he knew all the business deals and the scandal, who-all was messing with who-all's wives, and so forth. When he got the news his only child had up and married, he butted his head against the wall, kicked the baseboard so hard he lamed himself in the foot for week, and threw two of his best porcelain shaving mugs clean across the shop. My daddy, you see, was a slave from the beginning, and he had looked a good deal higher for her than that. I'm still talking about the barber, but the fact was I didn't know him. He died of a sudden seizure around the time I was born, five months after the wedding. He just thought she'd been putting on weight, when all the time it was me.

He should have known better how to handle her. Ever since she was a little girl, if you wanted her to have something, even medicine, no matter how bitter-tasting it might be, all you had to do was act like you were going to keep it from her. I know, for Ive got children of my own, including one marriageable daughter, and I wouldnt cross her for the world. Then too, he had a lot of blood-pride—claimed we had African chiefs somewhere in the background. But I dont know; I never put much stock in all that talk. You used to hear lots of such claims among the colored. If it wasn't chiefs it was French blood. Maybe we caught it from the white folks. Anyhow, he certainly didnt want the son-in-law he got.

You see, my daddy was a kind of artist, high-strung and determined. He belonged at one time to a rich lady, a widow; she gave him his freedom in her will when she died. Maybe she sort of spoiled him. Anyhow he always wore a black silk tie under a soft collar and kept his hands smooth. He was a photographer, like me; had his tent right down by the levee, the same as me, at the foot of Marshall Avenue, and country people theyd get their picture taken every time they came to town with twenty cents. Whatever else Mamma's daddy wanted, he certainly didnt want any twenty-cent artist.

But that was what he got, all right, and he butted his head and took it. What else could he do? That was during the war; I was born the day after Vicksburg fell on the Fourth. I dont remember the war, howsomever, though sometimes I think I do. The first I remember, really, was afterwards—what I'm telling now. Reconstruction, some called it. . . . The surrender was some time back and I was maybe six or seven. My daddy didnt come home one night. Then next morning here he came, with a lump beside one eye. "Where you been?" Mamma asked him, hands on hips, eyes blazing. She was worried and angry too. But he just stood there in the doorway, kind of weavy on his feet. So she got the camphor bottle off the shelf and some cotton and began to swab at the lump. The camphor fumes helped to clear his head, and while she swabbed he told her.

"I'll tell you the plain truth, Esmy," he said. Mamma's full name was Esmeralda; Daddy called her Esmy. "I was standing on the corner Third and Bird, minding my business. I wasnt even late. This man comes up, big, so tall, with a derby and a cigar, a mouth full of gold. Say, 'What you doing, boy?' I aint no boy. I look back at him, eye to eye. Then I look away, across to where the Pastime Pool Hall was. Say, 'Answer up!'—like he had every right. Did I say he was wearing a brass watch chain? Well, he was, and every breath he took it made a little line of fire run cross his vest. I said, 'Whats it to you what I'm doing?' Thats what I told him." (This is still my daddy talking.) "He was already solemn but now he got more-so. He clouded up: say, 'Dont jaw back at me, I ask you something. Come along.' Then it happen; I see what he was wearing. He let his coat kind of slide ajar and there it was. A badge. I turn to run and Blip! all I saw was stars and colored lights; the Pastime Pool Hall run round in a circle. He done hit me slap up side the head with one them billy things, birdshot wrapped in leather. Next thing I

knew it was the jailhouse and a white man looking at me through the
bars. I said, 'Captain, what was that?' 'Was what?'—the white man talking; he run his hand through the front of his hair where he had his hat
tipped back. 'That man, Captain,' I ask him, 'was that a colored *police-
man?*'"

He stopped talking. Mamma went on swabbing the lump. I was sitting
there watching, smelling the camphor. She was so mad her face just swole
up with it. I could see what was coming next, and here it came.

"Sue," she says.

"Sue who?" my daddy says; as if he didnt know, the same as me that
was going on seven or eight.

"The town of Bristol," Mamma says. "The Law. Who else? They can't
knock you round for sport and then just turn you loose like nothing happened."

"Can't?" my daddy says. He sat there for a minute, saying nothing.
He was a high-strung man; God knows he was. But not that high-strung.
So he told her: "You sue," he says, "but not in my name. I already got
one knot up side my head."

. . .(It was the times, thats what it was, the carpetbaggers coming
to town with cotton receipts already signed and the number of bales
left blank to be filled in later; the fine-dressed man selling bundles of
four painted sticks for you to use to stake off your forty acres come Eman-
cipation Day again; the nightriders pounding the roads in their bedsheets
with the pointy hoods and the hoofs like somebody beating a drum along
the turnpike. They burnt crosses every night all round us—and a man
who'll burn what he prays to, he'll burn anything. It was the times,
the whole air swirling full of freedom and danger; it was catching, you
see, and Mamma already had it bad in the first place.) . . .

What happened next I didnt see, for she didnt take me with her. She
left, walked out the door with that swole-up look still bulging in her
face, and was gone a good long time, till afternoon. Then here she came,
back again, looking a good deal worse than Daddy did. He just had him
a lump on the head but she had that and more. I broke out crying.

She went there looking for damages: "For what you done to my husband," she told them, right there in the town jail with the prisoners
watching through the bars. At first the constable and this other man
thought it was some kind of joke or something; they couldnt believe it.
But then she got angry and started to yell in a loud voice about freedom
and justice, right in their faces, and of course they couldnt stand for
that, right there in their own jail house with the prisoners looking on.
So they hit her, knocked her down. They almost had to, to get her to
stop. But she wouldnt. She was still hollering in a high voice about free-

dom and justice and the vote, lying there on the floor where they had knocked her, she wouldnt quit. And then one of the men did something I cant justify, even considering all the disruption she was making. He kicked her full in the mouth, twice; cut both her lips and knocked several of her teeth right down her throat. That stopped her, for the time being at least, and then he kicked her once more, to make certain. They didnt arrest her—which they could have done. When she came to, she picked herself up, holding her mouth, and came on home. . . . I took one look at her and burst out crying; I was high-strung like my daddy in those days. But she wouldnt tell us anything. She went to bed without even the camphor bottle, and pulled the quilt up over her face and lay there.

Next day she had a nervous diarrhea, passed three of the teeth, and she picked them out of the slopjar, rinsed them off, and put them on the mantel to remember freedom by. That might sound like an ugly thing to you; I can see how it might. But to me it always seemed real fine, since it showed how much her love of freedom meant to her even after all it got her was three hard kicks in the mouth. . . . (It was the time, I say again; all that new, untested liberty and equality coming so sudden before we had a chance to get used to them. But it worked both ways, I can tell you. You think we didn't laugh at all those white men cutting head-holes in their wives' best sheets and eye-holes in the pillow-cases? We did indeed. It was a two-sided thing.) . . .

For a while then—most of her teeth being missing on one side, I mean—she didnt much look like herself. She'd always been such a fine-looking woman; her barber daddy had kept her dressed in style. But we got used to it in time, and Mamma was downright proud. It was like she'd sued and won. She held her head high, showing the missing teeth and the sunk-in check. You couldnt down her.

(A pause; not sad—more wistful. Then he goes on)

She didnt live long, though. She had some kind of stomach ailment; it went into a tumor and she died. I was nine or ten. The night she died she put her arms around me and her tears fell onto the back of my head. "Youll be free, Emanuel," she told me; her last words. "Youll have freedom and the vote and youll be free."

But I dont know. It was true: I got them, but it seems like they dont mean so much as they did back then with the Kluxers riding the roads to take them from you. Thats how it is with most things, even freedom. You do most of your honing before you get it. Then it pales.

My daddy he outlived her many years. He had two more wives in fact, including the one that outlived him. I inherited all his clothes—and wore them, too, till I started putting on all this weight. Now all I can wear is these ties, a whole drawerful of silky bow ones. I got the business too, this box and all; I'm a artist like my daddy, with a wife and four grown children, one on Beale, one in Detroit, one in New Orleans, and one to help my wife keep house. You want me take your picture?

(*Lights down. End of play*)

The Battle of Harrykin Creek

EVANS HARRINGTON

With Music by Andrew Fox

CHARACTERS

COLONEL JOHN SARTORIS father of Bayard, uncle-by-marriage of Melisandre, officer in General Forrest's cavalry; of average size, proud and erect in bearing.

MELISANDRE granddaughter of Rosa Millard, niece of Col. Sartoris; a beautiful, romantic-minded Southern belle, about 18.

BAYARD SARTORIS son of Col. Sartoris, about 12 years old, bright and sensitive.

RINGO African-American boy, son of Lucius and Philadelphia, the same age as and constant companion of Bayard; somewhat older-looking than Bayard, and brighter.

LOUVINIA cook for the Sartorises, wife of Joby, mother of Lucius.

GRANNY (MRS. ROSA MILLARD) Col. Sartoris' mother-in-law, grandmother of Bayard and Melisandre, mistress of Sartoris plantation; a small, erect woman of iron will.

JOBY aging slave, husband of Louvinia, father of Lucius.

LUCIUS mid-thirties, slave, son of Joby and Louvinia, husband of Philadelphia, father of Ringo.

AB SNOPES poor white man, mid-forties, thin, slovenly, unscrupulous, father of the whole clan of infamous Snopeses in Yoknapatawpha County.

PHILIP ST.-JUST BACKHOUSE about 18, handsome young Confederate officer of distinguished family; slender, brave, romantic-minded.

PHILADELPHIA mid-thirties, slave woman, maid in the Sartoris house, wife of Lucius, mother of Ringo.

GENERAL NATHAN BEDFORD FORREST Confederate officer, 41, big man with a blue-black beard, vigorous, semi-literate.

FIRST CONFEDERATE OFFICER, SECOND CONFEDERATE OFFICER, CHAPLAIN, LIEUTENANT HORATIO BENBOW

*Based on William Faulkner's story "My Grandmother Millard and General Bedford Forrest and the Battle of Harrykin Creek"

188

CHORUS PARTS
  Eight Snopeses
  Four Southern Girls: Amy Lou, Latitia, Savannah, Stephanie
  Six Confederate Soldiers
  Six Union Soldiers
  Yankee Corporal

SETTING

The plantation home of Colonel John Sartoris, near Jefferson, Mississippi,
a large Southern antebellum country house which extends from center
to left stage. It is July, 1863.

ACT I

Scene 1

(*Curtain opens on family, just after they have finished dinner.* COL.
SARTORIS *is still at the head of table, stage right.* MELISANDRE
is at his left, facing audience. BAYARD *is next to her.* RINGO *lounges
against the sideboard behind them.* LOUVINIA *offers coffee to* COL.
SARTORIS)

COL. SARTORIS   Yes, thank you, Louvinia. I believe I will. It's been
  a long time since I've had your fine coffee.
LOUVINIA   It sho has, Colonel, and I reckon you'll be leaving it again
  pretty soon to go with Genrul Forrest.
COL. SARTORIS   I'll try to arrange it this time so I won't be so far
  away, Louvinia. General Forrest keeps his cavalry close to home.
LOUVINIA (*laughs*)   I hopes so. I sho hopes so. (*She goes out*)

(*During the last two speeches,* RINGO *has been making his way
along the sideboard and around behind* BAYARD *toward the front
entrance. At his first movement,* BAYARD *begins to watch him
uneasily, ease back from the table and look at* COL. SARTORIS,
trying to get his attention to ask to be excused. The minute
LOUVINIA *speaks her last word,* BAYARD *murmurs*)

BAYARD   May I be excused, Father?

(BAYARD *slips out of his chair and darts after* RINGO. RINGO *breaks into a run for the front entrance and the drum, which with drumsticks on it, sits on the front steps.* RINGO *beats* BAYARD *to it, slips the straps over his shoulders and assumes a vastly swaggering pose, starting a tattoo to herald his march.* BAYARD *reaches* RINGO *and grabs at the drum*)

BAYARD It's mine! He brought it to me!

RINGO It's ourn! You heard him say "to y'all. I brought it to y'all." First come, first served.

BAYARD He's my father. He captured it single-handed, and he's my —

RINGO Nemmine bout no father. He's my Colonel Sartoris, and I known him longer'n you. I known him fore you was borned!

BAYARD Ten days! You known him ten days fore I was borned. You couldn't even see him, even if he was around.

RINGO Ten days is ten days. I known him longer'n you, and I got it first anyway. Leggo!

BAYARD (*Shifting tactics*) You might as well put it down, anyway. We ain't gonna have time for marching. Granny's gonna call us any minute.

RINGO (*Looking back toward the house*) Maybe she'll forget it tonight, with Colonel here. Maybe—

BAYARD Hah! You ever known Granny to forget anything? Especially something to make people hop around. (*He assumes a pose, neck bowed to look over imaginary glasses, hands raised before him about eight inches apart*) She'll get that damn clock on the dining table, and—

RINGO (*Suddenly bowing, covering his head as though something were hurtling down on him from behind*) Whooie! Boy, you watch your mouth. Granny'll done have lye soap down both our th'oats, you talkin like that.

BAYARD She can't hear me. She's way upstairs. She went up to put away the pictures she was showing Father.

RINGO I don't keer *where* she at. Granny don't have to be close. She don't even have to be listening. I done had my mouth washed out with soap when she was clear the other side of Harrykin Creek. That woman know when you even *think* a bad word. (*He has turned to look at the house as he speaks. He has forgotten the drum and is holding the drumsticks loosely in his right hand*) She do that ever time Colonel come home.

BAYARD (*Easing toward* RINGO) You know how she is about pictures. She pretends she's showing how much Melisandre looks like her mother used to, but she brings Grandpa Millard's picture, too, and my mama's.

RINGO   I know it. Why she do that?

BAYARD   Father told me once Granny is real lonesome, though you'd never know it. She was a real young woman when Grandpa Millard and Melisandre's mother died in Memphis.

RINGO   They had the yellow fever, didn't they?

BAYARD   Yeah, and then when my mother died having me, she didn't have any family left except Melisandre and us. (*He has at last got into position and he snatches the drumsticks with one hand and skims the drum harness over* RINGO's *head with the other*)   Ho! There now!

RINGO   (*Catching after the drum, missing it*)   What? You sneaking Yankee. Gimme back my drum!

BAYARD   (*Skipping away and donning the drum*)   All's fair in love and war.

RINGO   (*Pursuing him ominously*)   We ain't in love, but we sho bout to have us a war.

BAYARD   Good! I'll be the drummer. (*Beats the drum loudly and swaggers in a march step*)

(RINGO *lunges for* BAYARD, *who skips aside, beating a fierce tattoo, crying derisively*)

BAYARD   Yay!

(RINGO *twice more makes a dive for* BAYARD, *crying out, too*)

RINGO   Boy! Gimme my drum!

(BAYARD *evades him, beating the drum and cheering mockingly*)

GRANNY   (*Comes to front door and silences them with one powerful call*)   Bayard! Ringo! Stop that fuss this minute. We can't hear ourselves think!

And now that we're all interrupted we might as well show John Sartoris our plan. Go call Joby and Lucius. Now!

(*Her words are like a starting signal for everyone.* BAYARD *takes off around the stage right side of the house.* RINGO *goes after him, shouting.*)

RINGO   It's my turn. I got it first.

(LOUVINIA *and* OTHERS *rush about with a fierce purposefulness.* COL. SARTORIS *watches, amazed at first but with growing amusement which he conceals from* GRANNY *and the* OTHERS *but not from the audience.* LOUVINIA *comes in with unwashed silver in a dishpan under one arm and the kitchen clock in her other hand. She sets the dishpan and clock on the table.* JOBY, LUCIUS *and* PHILADELPHIA *enter.* LUCIUS *carries a lighted lantern.* BAYARD *and* RINGO *bring in a big trunk.* LOUVINIA *takes from her apron pocket a pair of Granny's rolled-up stockings and hands them to* GRANNY, *who unrolls the stockings and takes from the toe of one of them a wadded rag. She opens the rag and takes out the key to the trunk, unpins her watch from her bosom and folds it into the rag, puts the rag back into the stocking, rolls the stocking back into a ball and puts the ball in the trunk. Then, with* EVERYBODY *watching,* GRANNY *stands facing the clock, her hands raised and about eight inches apart and her neck bowed so she can watch the clockface over her spectacles. Then, as the clock reaches the hour mark (seven o'clock),* GRANNY *pops her hands together sharply, and* EVERYBODY *breaks into frantic motion again.*

    BAYARD *goes up to Granny's room and gets her gold hatpin, silver-headed umbrella and plumed Sunday hat, also Col. Sartoris' silver-backed brushes.* MELISANDRE *goes to her room and gets her gold-backed mirror and comb, also grabs a bunch of her dresses.* RINGO *disappears through the dining room and returns with Granny's dulcimer and the silver candlesticks, a medallion of Col. Sartoris' mother, and a gold spittoon.* LOUVINIA *and* LUCIUS *all this time are taking silver dining ware from the sideboard behind the dining room table.* MELISANDRE *tries to put her dresses in the trunk, but* GRANNY *stops her)*

GRANNY   No, child. Pshaw!

(LOUVINIA *and* LUCIUS *finish packing the silver.* GRANNY *pops her hands again.* BAYARD *and* RINGO *run through the hall, bumping together.* JOBY *and* LUCIUS *close and lock the trunk and give the key to* GRANNY; *they take up the trunk and* LOUVINIA *takes up the lantern.* EVERYONE *follows them out the hall and into the yard and over to the tree stage right.* BAYARD *and* RINGO *are already there, with shovels. They pull away limbs which cover the pit and the pile of dirt which will fill it over the trunk.* GRANNY *is carrying the kitchen clock, looking at it noticeably from time to time.* JOBY *and* LUCIUS *put the trunk in the pit, throw dirt on it, smooth the dirt level and lay the brush back over it. Immediately* GRANNY *speaks)*

GRANNY   Dig it up.

(JOBY *and* LUCIUS *start fiercely uncovering the pit and digging out the dirt. and, as in a film run backward,* EVERYONE *undoes everything he has done.* COL. SARTORIS *walks away toward right when he sees what is happening. He's grinning broadly.* GRANNY *notices him and follows, still carrying the clock*)

GRANNY Well? What are you grinning at?

COL. SARTORIS (*Stifling a laugh*) Miss Rosa, I've said it all along: we need your talents at headquarters.

GRANNY (*Snorts*) That's pretty apparent, I'd say. So what do you find so funny?

COL. SARTORIS (*The laugh breaking out*) But, Miss Rosa (*Laughter overcoming him briefly*), Miss Rosa, what if the Yankees won't wait? (*He then goes into convulsive laughter*)

(GRANNY *watches, still holding clock, bristles, then bristles more. But when* COL. SARTORIS *can't stop laughing, keeps pointing at her and back at the hustling children and slaves as they return everything to its place,* GRANNY *picks up her skirts and sails up the porch steps, disappearing into the hall*)

Scene 2

(*The family is seated at dining table as before, except that* COL. SARTORIS *is missing*)

GRANNY (*Wipes her mouth and lays her napkin on the table*) Go call Joby and Lucius.

BAYARD But, Granny! Father said—

GRANNY Your father's not here.

BAYARD But Father laughed at us. He said—

GRANNY If your father didn't have such a fine sense of humor, maybe we wouldn't have to do it at all. Go call Joby and Lucius.

BAYARD But Father said what if the Yankees wouldn't wait.

GRANNY (*An ultimatum*) Bother the Yankees! We're burying the family silver!

(*The minute* GRANNY *speaks, the* WHOLE CAST, *except for her, leaps alert—*JOBY *and* LUCIUS *back at the barn, each cast member in an appropriate place, and all shout*)

ALL Bother the Yankees! Bother the Yankees!

(*Then* EVERYONE *breaks into a choreographed, much stylized repetition of the preceding action, various people coming forward with items and bits of business and leading in the singing and dancing. The song takes up after the shout*)

We're Burying the Family Silver!

We're burying the family silver,
And a few other odds and ends,
Granny's hat with plume
Father's gold spittoon—
We're burying the family silver!

We're burying the family silver,
And adding a thing or two.
Here's a dulcimer
And a coat of fur—
And maybe Melisandre! (*This is to go
  with her having dumbly offered
  a number of wrong items and constantly
  getting in the way*)

We're burying the family silver;
Granny is seeing to that.
Yankees will foray,
Skulking night and day,
So we're burying the family silver!

Bother the Yankees! Bother the Yankees!
We're burying the family silver!

We're burying the family silver,
As all worthy ancestors do;
Scions years from now
Will be telling how
We buried the family silver.

We're burying the family silver;
It gives us something to do.
And we think of you,
Our descendants too,
As we bury the family silver!

We're burying the family silver,
And we may never dig it up.
All the U.D.C.

Will lament proudly
How we buried the family silver!

Bother the Yankees! Bother the Yankees!
We're burying the family silver!
We're burying the family silver,
Again and again and again.
Father says that he
Thinks it pure folly,
But we're burying the family silver!

We're burying the family silver,
And our backs are aching and sore.
Lucius says that he
Hankers to be free,
But he's burying our family silver!

We're burying the family silver.
Granny has never been wrong.
But if it's our fate
That the Yankees won't wait,
We're still burying the family silver!

Bother the Yankees! Bother the Yankees!
We're burying the family silver!

Scene 3

(*A morning at the house.* MELISANDRE *is reading a novel in her room.* BAYARD *in the side yard is sporadically marching, using the drum as a cadence maker*)

GRANNY (*Comes from right side into dining room, raises her voice and calls*) Louvinia, it's eleven o'clock. Is dinner coming along? (*Distant popping of muskets is heard, like small firecrackers.* GRANNY *stiffens, listening*)

LOUVINIA Yessum, Miss Rosa. It's doing just fine.

(*The firing grows louder, more frequent.* BAYARD *and* MELISANDRE *stop to listen, too.* RINGO, *offstage left, is heard shouting*)

RINGO Granny! Granny!

GRANNY (*Rushes out to front porch, looking to stage left toward sound of firing and* RINGO'S *voice*) You, Ringo! What is it?

RINGO (*Bursts onto stage from left and runs up to her*) They heah, Granny! God-a-mighty, it's the Yank—(*He stops and cups his mouth guiltily*)

GRANNY (*Glowering at him*) I'll scour your filthy mouth when I have time. Now go back and get the trunk. Bayard! Lucius! Joby!

(BAYARD *and* RINGO *race into the house and out the entrance, bumping together there as usual.* LOUVINIA *comes out in a minute with the dishpan and the clock*)

GRANNY No, Louvinia! Who has time for clocks! The sideboard. The sideboard!

(MELISANDRE *runs around in circles, finally grabs her mirror and comb and starts downstairs.* BAYARD *and* RINGO *come back in with the trunk, followed closely by* JOBY, LUCIUS, *and* PHILADELPHIA. ALL *dump things into it.* BAYARD *and* RINGO *go get their things and run back and dump them. The firing is growing louder and* MEN'S VOICES *are heard shouting.* GRANNY *and* EVERYONE *else in the house are shouting exhortations to hurry.* AB SNOPES *runs in*)

AB SNOPES Miz Millard! Miz Millard! I got six Yankee hosses in your barn!

GRANNY Six Yankee horses, Ab Snopes?

AB SNOPES Yessum. They almost caught me with em, but I got em in your barn.

GRANNY That's a great help right now, Ab Snopes. Move out of the way. We're trying to bury the silver. (AB *moves aside and watches. She goes to the sideboard and helps* LOUVINIA *and* LUCIUS *put the last pieces of silver in the trunk*) Now, quick!

(JOBY *and* LUCIUS *grab the trunk and go out the door.* EVERYONE *else follows. They start toward the tree, but* GRANNY *stops them. The crescendo of firing and shouting off to the left is tremendous*)

GRANNY No, not out there. There isn't time. We'll have to do what Mrs. Compson did. The backhouse! The backhouse!

AB SNOPES Hellfire, Miz Millard! All north Mississippi's done heard —(*Like* RINGO, *he covers his mouth guiltily*)

GRANNY I'll wash out your mouth, too, Ab Snopes, but when I have time. All north Mississippi has done what?

AB SNOPES S'cuse me, Miz Millard, but all north Mississippi has done heard abut Miz Compson settin on the silver in her backhouse. There ain't a white lady between here and Memphis that ain't settin in the backhouse on a grip full of silver right this minute.

GRANNY Then we're already late. Hurry! (*This last to* JOBY *and* LUCIUS, *who have been swinging the trunk between her and* AB SNOPES)

AB SNOPES Wait! Wait! Even them Yankees have done caught onto that by now.

GRANNY Then let's hope these are different Yankees. That's all there's time for. (*To* JOBY *and* LUCIUS, *who are far ahead of her, catching up with* MELISANDRE *and* LOUVINIA, *who have run on to the privy*) Hurry!

RINGO (*Who has run back around to the front porch*) Heah they come! Heah they come!

(GRANNY *stops and turns to look where he's pointing.* JOBY *and* LUCIUS *thrust the trunk into the privy while* LOUVINIA *is calling to* GRANNY)

LOUVINIA Miss Rosa! Miss Rosa! Now! Now!

MELISANDRE Granny! Come on!

LOUVINIA (*Suddenly taking charge, pushes* MELISANDRE *into the privy*) There ain't time, Miss Melisandre. It'll have to be you.

MELISANDRE (*Trying to hold back*) Me? Me? Sitting in this place? No!

LOUVINIA (*Shoving her in masterfully*) There ain't time, child. It's got to be you.

GRANNY (*To* RINGO *at left, watching the Yankees*) Come on, child!

(LOUVINIA *gets* MELISANDRE *onto the trunk and shuts the door, just as a* YANKEE CORPORAL *comes around the front porch at left stage. He takes one look at the place and turns to signal*)

YANKEE CORPORAL All right, bring in the long pole, fellows. It's the backhouse bit again.

GRANNY (*As* SIX YANKEE SOLDIERS, *carrying a big sapling between them, run around the porch after the corporal*) What! What are you doing with that thing? Well, I never! A lady cannot have her privacy! Expect a Yankee to do such a thing.

(*All the while she is beating with her bonnet, first at the* CORPORAL, *who wards her off with elbows and leads the charge ahead, then at successive* SOLDIERS *on her side of the sapling, as they pass her, shielding themselves with forearms*)

(There is general bedlam. BAYARD, RINGO *and* ALL *the others are shouting, but the* YANKEES *with the pole run steadily on. Just before they hit the privy, a bugle blows charge at back stage and* PHILIP *with* SIX OTHER CONFEDERATE SOLDIERS *races around the back of the house, almost on the* YANKEES. *The* YANKEES *hit the privy with the pole and it literally explodes, with* MELISANDRE *sitting on the trunk screaming among the debris. The* YANKEES *immediately see* PHILIP *and the* OTHER CON-FEDERATES, *who with drawn swords are better armed, and the* YANKEES *drop the pole and run off stage right.* MELISANDRE *sits screaming on the trunk, and* PHILIP *stares at her, love-struck)*

MELISANDRE   In the backhouse! In the backhouse! Me! In the backhouse!

Scene 4

(PHILIP *is by the tree down right.* BAYARD *is with him.* PHILIP'S *sabre and belt are lying on a garden bench. He has his coat off and is wiping it with his handkerchief, but very absently. He stares at the house with an expression of helpless, ludicrous love.* MELISANDRE *is sitting in her bedroom brushing her hair and, though the front porch of the house should be lighted, she should be only faintly lighted for the audience, supposedly not visible to Philip at all)*

PHILIP (*Slowly, dreamily, not really looking at* BAYARD *at all*)   That beautiful girl. Fetch me a comb.

BAYARD   They're waiting for you in the house. Granny wants to know what's the matter.

PHILIP (*Undisturbed in his daydreaminess, as though continuing his statement about that beautiful girl*)   Your sister. And a hand mirror, too.

BAYARD   No, sir. She's just my cousin. From Memphis. (*He is nervous about getting Granny's order obeyed*)   Granny says what's the matter. She wants to get dinner started.

PHILIP (*Still undisturbed*)   That beautiful, tender girl. And send a servant with a basin of water and a towel. (BAYARD *moves slowly away, looking back at him, reluctant*)   And a clothes brush.

(BAYARD *moves to front porch.* GRANNY *emerges, followed by* LOUVINIA)

GRANNY Is the dinner ruined, Louvinia?

LOUVINIA No'm. The Yankees never bothered it none. It just kept cooking. It got mighty done, though.

GRANNY (*To* BAYARD, *who has arrived at the porch*) Well? *Now* what's the matter?

BAYARD He wants a comb and a hand mirror and some water and a towel and a clothes brush.

GRANNY Does the man think we are giving a ball here in the middle of the day? Tell him I said to come on in and wash on the back gallery like we do. Louvinia's putting dinner on, and we're already late.

BAYARD (*Very uncomfortable*) Yessum, but I don't think he'll hear me. I told him that already.

GRANNY And what did he say?

BAYARD He didn't say anything. Just (*imitating* PHILIP, *exaggeratedly*) "that beautiful girl."

RINGO (*Who has appeared behind* BAYARD) That's all he said to me, too. 'Sides the soap and water. Jest (*imitating* PHILIP *again, very broadly*) "that beautiful girl."

BAYARD Was he looking at you either when he said it?

RINGO Naw. I just thought for a minute he was.

GRANNY Hah! I sometimes think that bullets and sabres are the least fatal things that fly, especially in war. All right. Take him his soap and water. But hurry!

> (GRANNY *continues talking to* LOUVINIA *as* BAYARD *and* RINGO *go into the house and come back quickly with comb, mirror, soap and water*)

GRANNY You'd better go in and put the food back on the stove to keep it warm, Louvinia. No telling when that idiot will be ready.

LOUVINIA That food been put on and took off so many times already, it don't know which meal it is. If I don't get it out of my kitchen soon, I won't have room to start supper.

GRANNY Well, we'll just have to wait. Where's Melisandre? Is she all right?

LOUVINIA Philadelphy got charge of her. She givin her blackberry wine like you said. She seem like she bout as level-headed as she ever be, what little that is.

> (BAYARD *and* RINGO *have now taken the washing utensils to* PHILIP, *who is rubbing his coat with his handkerchief and staring at the house exactly as before*)

PHILIP (*As they set the things before him*) That beautiful girl. That

lovely, tender girl. (*He hands his coat to* RINGO) Brush it good.
(*Turning toward* BAYARD)   Your sister, I heard you say.

BAYARD   No, you didn't.

PHILIP   No matter. (*Sings "That Beautiful Girl"*)

> That beautiful girl
> Has walked
> This earth
> For years
> All unknown to me.
>
> The air should be softer;
> The sun should be brighter;
> All sound should be gentler here.
>
> That beautiful girl
> Has slept
> And walked
> And lived
> All quite naturally.
>
> Alone among strangers,
> No one to restrain her,
> What fabulous dangers
> Near.
>
> To think she was actual,
> Breathing and factual,
> Talking and smiling
> With them.
> Not private to my dream,
> Glimmering and pristine,
> Except for me all
> Unseen.
>
> And yet it's the same girl,
> The self-same girl.
> I'd know her, I've known her
> These long, long years.
> I'm going to take her away from here,
> To guard and protect her
> And understand.
>
> Because it's true that
> That beautiful girl

Has walked
My heart
For years
All quite privately.

The lips have the same curve,
The cheeks have the same flush,
The eyes have the same tender
Sheen.

I swear, I swear it that
That beautiful girl
Was mine
For years
Before
She appeared to me.

And now she'll embrace me,
Her presence will grace me,
Herself all quite palpably.

I've dreamed, I've known,
At last I've seen her,
That beautiful girl.

(GRANNY *sends* LOUVINIA *upstairs to bring* MELISANDRE *down and both go into dining room*)

PHILIP (*To* BAYARD, *who with* RINGO *has been discreetly listening and helping where he can to get* PHILIP *cleaned up*) I want a nosegay. To carry in my hand.

BAYARD Those flowers are Granny's.

PHILIP (*Rolling up his sleeves and beginning to wash*) No matter. A small nosegay. About a dozen blooms. Get something pink.

(BAYARD, *with uneasy glances at the house, goes to some of the flower beds which the* YANKEES *have trampled and picks a nosegay.* PHILIP *continues grooming himself and talking to* RINGO, *who is holding the mirror while* PHILIP *combs his hair, etc.*)

PHILIP Isn't she truly the loveliest girl you ever saw?

RINGO I don't know. I don't pay girls much mind.

PHILIP (*Oblivious*) Truly the loveliest. And you say she's the sister of that boy there?

RINGO Ain't nobody said that. She his cousin. From Memphis.

PHILIP No matter. And what is her name, did he say?

RINGO   I don't know what he say. Her name Melisandre.

PHILIP   Ah, yes. Melisandre.

(BAYARD *returns with the nosegay and hands it to* PHILIP, *fully groomed now*)

BAYARD   Here's some sweet Williams.

PHILIP (*Taking the flowers*)   That will do nicely. And now, how do I look? (*The three move toward the front porch*)

BAYARD (*Nervous, trying to hurry him*)   You look fine. Let's get on in there.

PHILIP   But will your sister approve of me? (*Stops, shocked*)   Does she already have a beau?

BAYARD (*Pulling at him*)   She ain't my sister, and she ain't seen any boys but me and Ringo for more than a year. Let's get on in there 'fore Granny decides to turn us away from the table.

PHILIP (*As they enter the parlor,* PHILIP *stops again*)   Announce me. It should be the butler. but no matter.

BAYARD (*Embarrassed*)   Go on in. They're waiting for you. They had already been waiting for you even before you wanted that nosegay.

PHILIP   No, announce me. Full name and title, just like I told you.

(BAYARD *reluctantly leads the way.* PHILIP *follows and stands with him in the double doors,* MELISANDRE *and* GRANNY *staring at them from the table.* RINGO *has followed* BAYARD *and* PHILIP *into the house*)

BAYARD (*Loud and formal*)   From Tennessee. Savage's Battalion, Forrest's Command, Provisional Army, Department of the West, Lieutenant Philip St.-Just Backhouse!

(*There is a long, complete silence. Then* MELISANDRE *screams. She sits bolt upright on the chair, as she had sat on the trunk in the privy, with her legs shut, screaming several times. Then she cries out, very clearly and in anguish*)

MELISANDRE   Backhouse! Backhouse!

PHILIP (*Advancing toward her, extending the nosegay*)   If Miss . . .ah. . .if the lady will permit—

MELISANDRE (*Leaping up, overturning her chair*)   Oh! Don't speak to me! (*As she runs out*)   Backhouse! Backhouse! Backhouse! (PHILIP, BAYARD *and* RINGO *stand looking after her in amazement.* GRANNY *follows her*)

Scene 5

(*Dinner is over.* GRANNY, AB, BAYARD, *and* PHILIP *are coming out onto the portico.* RINGO *on the steps.* MELISANDRE *is in the dark in her bed upstairs with* PHILADELPHIA *from time to time putting cold cloths on her forehead, all in silhouette. A time or two during the initial silence of this scene, and occasionally throughout the scene, we hear* MELISANDRE *crying out softly*)

MELISANDRE   Backhouse! It's all right—all I want is to be left in peace, to forget I ever was so humiliated.

PHILIP   Backhouse! Backhouse! Of all the names I might have been born to.

AB SNOPES (*Snorts*)   You're mighty lucky. You might have woke up to find folks callin you "Snopes."

RINGO   Or "Ringo." At least you got three whole names. I ain't got but one.

PHILIP   Backhouse! Backhouse! Oh, that it had been any other kind of house!

AB SNOPES   Aw, don't git upset, Son. As the feller says, a backhouse by any other name would smell as sweet.

(*The* BOYS *giggle.* GRANNY *smiles reluctantly.* AB *guffaws and slaps his leg*)

BAYARD   Why don't you change your name?

AB SNOPES   To what? Outhouse?

RINGO   There are lots of kinds of houses.

BAYARD   Sure. There's the greenhouse.

RINGO (*Mocking* BAYARD'S *announcement of* PHILIP)   Lieutenant Philip St.-Just Greenhouse! (*Looks around to see effect*)

BAYARD   No. That seems too viny and wriggly, somehow. Like snakes.

RINGO (*Tentatively*)   Well house? (BAYARD *shakes his head*) Carriage house? (BAYARD *shakes his head again*)

AB SNOPES   Smokehouse. Lieutenant Philip St.-Just Smokehouse! (*Slaps his knee.* BOYS *laugh with him and start to sing and dance*)

The House Song

(BAYARD *and* RINGO *start singing together and are joined soon by* AB SNOPES, *then, one at a time,* ALL THE OTHERS, *including* PHILIP *and* JOBY *and* LUCIUS)

BAYARD AND RINGO
Oh, there are wash houses, mill houses, cook houses,
summer houses, dog houses—(*music stops*)
AB SNOPES   Ha! That's the one! Lt. Philip St.-Just Doghouse! (*Heavy on "dawg"*)
BAYARD AND RINGO
(*Sing*)   Cat houses—

(*A silence,* BAYARD *and* RINGO *look quickly from* AB *to* GRANNY; GRANNY *glowers at* AB *who puts his hand to his mouth*)

BAYARD AND RINGO
(*Sing*)—bird houses, chicken houses.
Oh, there are tall houses, short houses, small houses,
squat houses,
Brick houses, frame houses, glass houses— (*Music stops*)
BAYARD   Lieutenant Philip St.-Just Glasshouse!
RINGO   But then he couldn't throw rocks.
ALL
(*Singing*) Oh, there are stone houses, mud houses,
marble houses—(*Music stops*)
PHILIP   Not marble nor the gilded monuments of sluttish time—
ALL (*Jeering*)   Oh, you're so hard to please; you're too picky, Philip;
Mr. Turn-up-your nose!
AB SNOPES
(*Singing*)   Oh, there are farm houses, shotgun houses,
log houses, sod houses,
But also manor houses, castle houses, palace houses,
mansion houses—(*Music stops*)
GRANNY   Build Ab more stately mansions, O his soul!
BAYARD
(*Singing*)   Oh, there are tree houses, cliff houses, club
houses, lodge houses—
RINGO (*Singing, taking second verse*)   Teepee houses, wigwam
houses, igloo houses, slave houses—(*Music stops*)

(*Brief, complete silence*)

BAYARD (*Mock-serious*)   Ringo, ain't you happy in your bondage? I
thought we had a symbiotic relationship; you served me and I protected
you.
RINGO (*Broad minstrel burlesque*)   I'se sho happy in mah bondage,
Marse Bayard. But bout dat symbiosis, we better look at hit agin.
Would you all like me to step and fetch it?

ALL
> (*Singing*) Oh, there are . . .

AB SNOPES
> Warehouses,

BAYARD
> Lighthouses,

RINGO
> Cotton houses,

GRANNY
> Teahouses—(*Music stops*)

PHILADEPHIA Lieutenant Philip St.-Just Teahouse! Tee hee!

ALL
> (*Singing*) And there are . . .

AB SNOPES
> Courthouses,

BAYARD
> Pilot houses,

GRANNY
> Halfway houses,

PHILIP
> And houses about whose repute
> There is always a certain dispute. (*Music stops*)

GRANNY Hah! Lieutenant Philip St.-Just Bawdyhouse!

ALL
> (*Singing*) There are stables and paddocks and pigpens and cotes,
> Kennels and warrens and aviaries and hives;
> There are chalets and chateaux and haciendas,
> Villas and alcazars, *ruses in urbe*—(*Music stops*)

GRANNY (*Vaguely*) In Parma there was a charterhouse, or is it in Charter there was a Parmahouse?

BAYARD AND RINGO
> (*Singly fiercely*) Haunted houses, death houses,
> charnel houses—(*Music stops*)

GRANNY Boys!

RINGO (*Hopefully to* PHILIP) Slaughterhouse? Lt. Philip—

PHILIP (*Suddenly through with it*) No! No! Stop it, I say. I can't change my name, I tell you.

> (*He laughs painfully, as though at the outrage of the whole situation, but speaks in that high-solemn, dreamy fashion with which he has said "that beautiful girl."*)

My grandfather was at King's Mountain, with Marion all through Carolina. My uncle was defeated for Governor of Tennessee by a corrupt and traitorous cabal of tavernkeepers and Republican Abolitionists, and my father died at Chapultepec. After that, the name they bore is not mine to change. (*Even more high-solemn*) Even my life is not mine so long as my country lies bleeding and ravished beneath an invaders's iron heel.

> (AB SNOPES *snickers, thinking he has to be joking, but* PHILIP *ignores him. Instead, he seems to have gotten a fascinating new idea from what he has said. His face slowly becomes rapt and beatific. He moves to steps and sits*)

PHILIP (*Slowly and softly but very distinctly*)   Unless I lose it in battle! *Unless I lose it in battle!*

GRANNY (*After a moment, impatient*)   Well, you can't very well do that sitting here.

PHILIP (*As though he hasn't really heard her*)   No. (*Stands*)   Yes. (*With that beatific expression*)   Will you excuse me please? (*He moves right, turns and looks back at them vaguely*)   Yes. (*He turns and stands looking up at, not Melisandre's room—where she is silhouetted —but Granny's. Strains of "That Beautiful Girl" song. He goes off stage left*)

AB SNOPES   Well, Miz Millard, I figger you'll be safe all right from now on, with Bed Forrest and his boys right there in Jefferson. But till things quiet down a mite more, I'll just leave the hosses in your lot for a day or two.

GRANNY (*Watching him carefully, speaking slowly*)   What horses?

AB SNOPES (*Crafty*)   Them fresh-captured hosses from this morning.

GRANNY   What horses?

AB SNOPES (*Long pause*)   *My* hosses.

GRANNY (*Pause; mildly*)   Why are they your horses, Ab Snopes?

AB SNOPES (*Starts with fine logic, immediately trips himself up*)   I'm the only grown man here. I seen em first. They were chasing me before —(*nervously*)   Spoils of war, Miz Millard! I brought em here! I tolled em in here: a military and-bush! And as the only and ranking Confedrit military soldier present—

GRANNY   You ain't a soldier, Ab Snopes. You stipulated that to Colonel Sartoris yourself while I was listening, to get out of fighting in his unit. You told him yourself you would be his independent horse-captain (*Scornfully*)   but nothing more.

AB SNOPES   And ain't that jest exactly what I'm trying to be? Didn't

I bring all six of them hosses in here in my own possession, same as if I was leading em on a rope?

GRANNY Ha! A spoil of war or any kind of spoil don't belong to a man or a woman either until they can take it *home* with them and put it down and turn their back on it. You never had time to get home with even the one you were riding. You ran in the first open gate you came to, no matter whose gate it was.

AB SNOPES (*Whining*) Now, Miz Millard—

GRANNY The first gate you came to, no matter whose it was!

AB SNOPES Yessum. And it was sho the wrong gate. I can sho see that. Well, I reckon I got to even walk back to town. The woman that would chea—(*He pauses; they glare at each other*)

GRANNY Don't you dare say it!

AB SNOPES No'm. That would ch—(*They glare at each other*) a man of seven hosses ain't likely to lend him a mule.

GRANNY There's a horse tied up at the lot gate for you now.

AB SNOPES You done been out to them hosses? You done been looking em over?

GRANNY There's a horse tied up for you, waiting.

AB SNOPES Well, I have to say thank you. I guess I'll be goin. It ain't gittin any earlier. (*Starts toward back of house; suddenly stops short*) Wait! (*Slowly, suspiciously*) Which hoss is it, Miz Millard?

GRANNY I told you. It's the one tied up to the gate.

AB SNOPES Yessum. But which one is tied up to the gate? It wouldn't be that bay with the blazed face, would it?

GRANNY It *might* have a blazed face. I didn't look closely at its face.

AB SNOPES Hellfire, Miz Millard—(*Instinctively puts hand to his mouth*) Yessum. Well, Miz Millard, I guess you didn't look close at its face; you was too busy lookin at its leg, I reckon.

GRANNY (*Innocently*) Its leg? What leg?

AB SNOPES Its right hind leg, Miz Millard. That one that's so bad splayed.

GRANNY Now that you mention it, I did think that leg was sprung a little.

AB SNOPES Yessum. It's sprung a little. It's sprung enough so that horse tries to throw its foot away ever time it takes a step with it. Well, it ain't gittin any earlier, like I say. (*Starts toward back of house*)
I just hope for the sake of the Confedericy that Bed Forrest don't never tangle with you, with all the hosses he's got. Or you'll damn sho leave him just one more passel of *infantry* fore he can spit twice.

(GRANNY *starts toward him, face blazing; he covers his mouth and darts toward tree.* GRANNY *goes into house.* AB *at right of tree glowers back meanly at the big house*)

AB SNOPES   Highfalutin Sartorises. They think they can git away with anythang, thank we'll be treated any way. Well, they don't know Ab Snopes. (*Sings*)

My Name's Ab Snopes

My name's Ab Snopes—Ab Snopes.
I was born hanging hard on the ropes.
I want to make it clear that I'm only here
To get mine from the rest of you folks.

If you're born Ab Snopes—Ab Snopes,
Enter here and abandon all hopes.
In this rich man's war and this poor man's fight
Folks like me have to play it just right.

I make the best of bein Ab Snopes.
Let them take us all for poor dopes.
Horse brands can be turned, hay barns can be burned;
They will know I'm Ab Snopes when they're ruined (*Pronounced rurned*).

Listen clearly and hear Ab Snopes.
I do not deal in trifles or jokes.

(CHORUS OF SNOPESES *dressed like and looking like* AB, *begin to emerge sinisterly from all quarters of the stage, Snopeses coming out of the woodwork, four at first, followed by two, then two more. As each appears he joins the song*)

AB AND FIRST SNOPES
Let them all beware,
AB AND SECOND SNOPES
Snopes are everywhere.
AB AND THIRD SNOPES
Foul or fair,
AB AND FOURTH SNOPES
We will soon get our share.
AB SNOPES
Oh, they put me down as Ab Snopes,
ALL SNOPESES
All the country round sneers at Snopes.
We're not gentlemen so we can't come in
To those clans that began before Snopes.

Let us clue you in on the Snopes.
Gentlemen are baffled by Snopes.
Faulkner's theories of the verities
Must be strained to obtain with a Snopes. (*Music stops*)
(*Piously, holding their hats to their hearts, chanting*)
Honor and courage and pity and pride and sacrifice!

(TWO MORE SNOPESES *appear and join in song*)

All the South will soon teem with Snopes.
Banks and mansions will be owned by Snopes.
I've a son named Flem and I count on him
To avenge all his kind in the end

Washington will soon hear of Snopes.
Southern rimsters descend from the Snopes.
At a point in time we will reach our prime:
Watergate has a date with the Snopes.

AB SNOPES
So I'm resigned to repine as a Snopes,
Martyred and maligned as a Snopes.

FIRST SNOPES (*Good contrasting voice, alone*)
Oh, the media has it in for us.
There ain't no equal time for a Snopes.

AB SNOPES
So just put me down as Ab Snopes,
Father of men who know all the ropes.

ALL SNOPES
When the coast is clear, we will still be here
And we will persevere, all us Snopes. (*Music stops*)
(*Chanting*)   We believe that Snopeses will not merely
Endure; they will prevail.

Scene 6

(*Later that afternoon.* GRANNY *is in parlor, seated in a rocker, holding the pictures she had shown* COL. SARTORIS. *Upstairs,* MELISANDRE *in subdued light is running her hands dreamily through her hair.* PHILADELPHIA *appears at parlor door and waits*)

GRANNY (*Looks up, resignedly*)   Well, what is it?

PHILADELPHIA   She want the banjo.

GRANNY   She wants the what?

PHILADELPHIA   That banjo thang. Whut we put in the trunk. She say she want to play it.

GRANNY   My dulcimer? She doesn't know how to play it. And she can't sing either. She's been reading in those novels about how young girls behave when they have a lover off at war. Those Walter Scott novels. You would think the Creator could have spared us that. Young fools in love are bad enough without Walter Scott. Tell her to forget it. Tell her to go lie down and be quiet. It's mid-afternoon, when ladies take their rest.

PHILADELPHIA   Yes'm. I'll try. (*She leaves, is seen entering* MELISANDRE'S *room. They pantomine* PHILADELPHIA'S *report and* MELISANDRE'S *sullen resentment*)

GRANNY (*Pensively, looking at pictures*)   Mid-afternoon, when ladies take their rest. How odd that sounds. Yet scarcely two years ago, it would have seemed to me a commonplace. Ladies. Rest. I took ladies for granted then, and rest, too. (*Sings, thoughtfully*)

Mid-Afternoon, When Ladies Take Their Rest

Mid-afternoon, when ladies take their rest,
They clear their thoughts and know themselves the best,
The lady whom I recall from years ago
Is startled at this woman I now know.

Mid-afternoon in Memphis in those days
The steamboats bellowed in the harbor's haze;
Street vendors cried of melon and fresh corn.
We never thought to question plenty's horn.

The silence of my rest these afternoons
Is not the kindly silence I once knew.
I hear a voice cry why are you here still—
A withered woman with a voice gone shrill.

Mid-afternoon, when ladies live too long,
They find themselves immersed in things long gone.
They feel they've learned more than they need to know;
Or if they need it, don't know why it's so.

But if the lady I once was seems doomed
To have no real rest here these afternoons,

The will's as stubborn as it is confused
And vows to see its bitter knowledge used.

Mid-afternoon, when ladies take their rest,
They clear their thoughts and know themselves the best.
The lady whom I recall from years ago
Is startled at this woman I now know.

(*She takes a deep, decisive breath, takes pictures toward upstairs
room*)

LIGHTS DOWN

Scene 7

(FOUR SOUTHERN GIRLS *are standing in the yard and on the
front steps, calling excitedly and breathlessly exchanging gossip*)

AMY LOU   Melisandre! Miss Rosa!

LETITIA   They say he was six feet tall and very blond.

SAVANNAH   I hear he kissed Melisandre right there in the backhouse!

STEPHANIE   And didn't she slap him? Mama said Louvinia said
Melisandre slapped him.

ALL GIRLS   Melisandre! Miss Rosa!

GRANNY (*Appears at entrance, welcomes them ironically*) Well,
Stephanie, and Amy Lou. Savannah, and Letitia. Come in, girls. What
brings you over so late in the day?

AMY LOU   Oh, Miss Rosa, we were so worried about y'all. We just
heard about that awful Yankee raid, and—

LETITIA   Yes! Mama said if you need anything, Miss Rosa, any help
or anything—

SAVANNAH   Oh, we've just all felt so awful. That terrible thing that
happened to Melisandre!

STEPHANIE   Yes, those horribly rude Yankees. Where is Melisandre,
Miss Rosa? (*They have all turned toward the portico*)

MELISANDRE (*Wailing from her room upstairs*)   Phil-lip!

GIRLS (*Variously*)   Oh! Mercy! Gracious! My goodness!

(GIRLS *grow quiet,* PHILADELPHIA *enters. During dialogue and
into Granny's song,* GIRLS *"oh" and "ah" in response*)

PHILADELPHIA   Miss Rosa, she still want that banjo thang.

GRANNY   I tell you she can't even play it. She can't have it, and you can just tell her so.

PHILADELPHIA (*Pause*)   Could I ax Mammy to come help me with her?

GRANNY   No, Louvinia's resting. She's had about as much of this as I want her to stand. Go back upstairs. Give that idiot some more blackberry wine if you can't think of anything else. (PHILADELPHIA *disappears*)

(*Light up on* MELISANDRE, *who rises and sweeps dreamily to the window*)

MELISANDRE (*Loudly, slowly, relishing each syllable*)   Phil-ip! Philip Saint-Just! No, it was surely Saint-Just (*French oo sound*) Philip Saint-Just (*Emotes lovingly, then registers horror and cries in anguish*) Backhouse?

(*She bursts into long, hair-raising wail, which makes* GRANNY *wince and brings* BAYARD *and* RINGO *from right of house to center, covering their ears*)

(*In a wail*)   I must express it. Give vent to my grief. If I could soothe myself with music. Music hath charms to soothe the savage breast.

GRANNY   She can quote Congreve, but that's still Walter Scott.

MELISANDRE   Oh, Philip! Philip! Philip Saint-Just (*Henceforth, she gives* Just *the French sound*)

GRANNY (*Sings*)

It's Not Love She's Got; It's Walter Scott

It's not love she's got; it's Walter Scott.
Sir Walter has taught them all that rot.
Knighthood here is still in flower,
Lovers tryst in every bower,
High romance has not gone sour
In the South!

It's not love she's got; it's Walter Scott.
Sir Walter's to blame for quite a lot:
Honor on the field of battle,
Knights erect in every saddle,
Noble pates forever addled
In the South.

It's not love they've got; it's Walter Scott.
It's not facts they see; it's what is not.

Ask Mark Twain and Mr. Cash if
They would ever act so rash if
Ivanhoe and all that trash had
Not come out!

GIRLS, BAYARD, RINGO, GRANNY

(*Chanting*)   Waverly and Kenilworth,
Ravenswood and Lammermoor,
Woodstock and Montrose, Halidon Hill,
Rokeby and Abbotsford—and Rowan Oak still?

Latimer and Richard Coeur,
Rob Roy and the "butcher boy,"
Harold the Dauntless,
Sir Roger Wildrake,
Nigel and Everard,
Quentin Durwood.

Diana loves Francis, Mathilda loves Redmond.
Flora loves Edward, and Edward loves Rose.
Rowena loves Wilfred and Rachel does, too,
But Brian loves Rachel—and so on it goes.

(GIRLS *dance, all winding up in* MELISANDRE'S *room*)

GRANNY

Pshaw! It's not love they've got; it's Walter Scott.
I won't have my house put in this spot.
With these constant interruptions,
Next we'll have a dark abduction.
Who can guess what crazy ructions
They're about!

But how deal with love and Walter Scott.
I've seen it in all those silly plots.
It's a little like religion,
Those that do not have the vision
Are ignored with calm decision
and left out!

(*While* GRANNY *is singing,* PHILADEPHIA *comes back into parlor.
She stands before* GRANNY *now with her hand extended, a key
in it.* GRANNY *sees her and understands what she wants before
starting last verse*)

I guess compromise must be my lot.
To think I would truck with Walter Scott.
But it's the greatest part of valor
In this realm so high and hallowed.
And, lest I grow pale and sallow,
I. . .must. . .stop!

(*To* PHILADELPHIA, *still holding key*) So you've got the key to the trunk? She still wants my dulcimer? But she can't play it, I tell you, or sing either.

PHILADELPHIA   Her mind's sot on it.

GRANNY (*Despairing*)   All right. Go call Joby and Lucius.

(PHILADELPHIA *hurries out, returning immediately with* JOBY *and* LUCIUS. *They start digging up the trunk*)

Scene 8

(MELISANDRE *is seated at her window with the dulcimer, singing soulfully and awfully, accompanying herself with ill-timed and dissonant strokes on the dulcimer, "Drink to Me Only with Thine Eyes."* PHILADELPHIA *sits in a straight chair, wincing, occasionally putting her apron over her head and sliding down miserably.* GRANNY, *in her room trying to sleep, keeps being startled out of recumbency. She gets up decisively and goes down into the parlor*)

GRANNY   Bayard! Ringo! (*They answer offstage, appear quickly*) Ringo, go get Lucius. Bayard, bring me the pen and ink and a sheet of paper.

(RINGO *disappears around the house.* BAYARD *goes and returns with the writing implements.* GRANNY *goes to sideboard and writes, standing up.* LUCIUS *and* RINGO *come in*)

GRANNY (*To* LUCIUS)   Ab Snopes said that Mr. Forrest is in Jefferson. Find him. Tell him I will expect him here for breakfast in the morning.

BAYARD   But Granny. General Forrest! You can't send for him like—

GRANNY   Bother "General" Forrest. I knew him when he was setting himself up in the slave business. He traded at Papa's supply house. Used to follow Papa home to get a free meal every chance he got. (*To* LUCIUS)   Tell him I'll expect him for breakfast in the morning, and to bring that boy. You can tell him, too, that I have six captured horses for him.

LUCIUS (*Reluctantly takes note*) Yessum. (*Stands reluctantly*)

GRANNY What's the matter with you? Go find him.

LUCIUS Yessum. But, Miss Rosa, them Yankees—

GRANNY Bother the Yankees! Didn't I hear you wanted to be free, that you were looking foward to being free? Maybe the Yankees will free you if they can stop tearing down folks' backhouses long enough.

LUCIUS (*Goes slowly, pauses in side yard and looks back*) This ain't no time to be free. No place to be free. Mammy and Pappy and Philadelphy scared of it. Big Miss and Colonel mad about it, not hardly trustin me no more. Yankees plumb wild, just fillin they bellies and pockets. Black folks runnin loose, starvin. I been there. I been over to Gen'l Smith's army. I seen that pack of crazy black folks followin in his dust. "Gonna cross Jordan," they says, "Mr. Lincoln our Moses. Gonna lead us outa Egypt." Free? Ain't seen no Mr. Lincoln. Ain't seen no river Jordan. Seen lots of black folks starvin. Free? What's that? (*Pause while a change comes over him, a savoring of the new, strange reality*)

But it has *happened*. I heard that Yankee soldier over to Jefferson read off of that paper, whut they call the proclamation. And the Colonel know it, and Big Miss—that's why they mad. (*Pause, relishing it though incredulous and frightened*) Free! Ain't that somp'in now. My own man. John Satoris nor nobody else don't own no part of me, of me and mine! When the time come, when this war is over and everthang settle down, and the Colonel he tell me to go plow the back forty, I gonna say, "Colonel, I druther not. It mighty hot this mawnin. I druther sit here with you on the front gallery. Maybe we have Ringo bring us a mint julep, cool us off." (*Pause, discards his daydream*)

Sho! Catch me talkin to the Colonel that way, even if I was still here. And ain't gonna be here. Gonna git me some land of my own. Gonna take Philadelphy and Ringo and git me my own farm. Have a house on it with a big, wide gallery, settin up on a hill. Have a long drive curvin up to it with cedar trees on bofe sides. Have a creek in the bottom for waterin the stock and for fishin when the corn is laid by. (*Pause, sobering again*)

Sho! And where all that hill and creek comin from? I guess Mr. Lincoln gonna lead me to that, too. Or maybe John Sartoris gonna *give* it to me. Sho! He gonna say, "Lucius, my man, I'm sorry bout ownin you like a animal all this time. "Say," I didn't mean to be treatin you like a hoss all yore life." Say, "Heah, take the back forty over across the bottom. I got more land than I can shake a stick at already, and I'd be mighty pleased if you'd take some off my hands." (*Pause*) Sho! Gonna starve, that's what we gonna do.

Still, it *has* happened. Free! It sho has a purty sound, though I cain't somehow seem to git the feel of it. (*Sings, tentative, frightened at first, but building confidence, even assertion and defiance, as he goes along*)

Free

Free.
Who ever thought this thing would come to me?
Who first thought up that purty word of "free?"
I wonder what they really mean by "free."

Free.
The mockin bird that flies and sings says, "Free."
The fish that jumps out in the lake jumps free.
But Lucius ain't a bird or fish born free.

Still . . . free!
It takes some time to feel this thing called "free."
It starts down in your chest and swells up free.
It tingles out your arms and legs all free.

Yes! free!
Like waters in the rivers and the sea;
Like sap that pushes leaves out in a tree;
Like seeds in darkness that bore even me!

Yes! Free!
I think I've *always* felt this thing called "free."
Ain't just a new right now they've give to me.
The slave behind old marster's back is free.

Yes! Yes! Free!
All things in God's creation start out free!
The horse that spits the bit remembers "free!"
The dog let off the leash runs bayin, "Free!"

Free! By God! I'm free!
They cain't scare me with black folks starvin free!
The fish swim up the river to die free.
I'll bide my time here, but I'm long gone free!

(*Goes off stage right*)

Scene 9

(GRANNY *and* MELISANDRE *are in beds asleep, the sun just coming up.* LUCIUS *comes from stage right and enters house, calls up the stairs, whispering loudly*)

LUCIUS Miss Rosa! Miss Rosa!

GRANNY (*Rises immediately, slips into robe and comes downstairs*) Well?

LUCIUS Gen'l Forrest say he respectful compliments and he cain't come to breakfast this mawnin 'cause he gonter be whuppin Gen'l Smith at Tallahatchie Crossin bout that time. But providin he ain't too fur away in the wrong direction when him and Gen'l Smith git done, he be proud to accept yore invitation next time he in the neighborhood. And he say, "Whut boy?"

GRANNY (*Long count*) What?

LUCIUS He say, "Whut boy?"

GRANNY (*Longer count*) Did you wipe the mule down?

LUCIUS Yessum.

GRANNY Did you turn her back into the pasture?

LUCIUS Yessum.

GRANNY Then go on to bed—

(*As she speaks, there is the sound of a platoon of horses offstage to right.* PHILIP *emerges beside tree and comes to stand, looking up at* GRANNY'S *room, thinking it is* MELISANDRE'S. MELISANDRE *does not wake up. Soft strains of "That Beautiful Girl" begin when* PHILIP *appears and continue as he stares at window, then fade away.* GRANNY *and* LUCIUS *stand at parlor window;* PHILIP *ignores them*)

PHILIP (*To* GRANNY'S *upstairs window*) Goodbye, Sweet Vision. Goodbye. May someone else protect you. Alas, it was not my fate to have that privilege. But I can at least divest myself of that name which so much offends you. That I can offer on the altar of my love. Goodbye. Goodbye. (*Beatific look on his face, he strides toward tree and off stage right*)

GRANNY Backhouse! You idiot, Backhouse! (*Sound of horses galloping away*) Backhouse! You, Backhouse!

MELISANDRE (*Suddenly waking and wailing*) Backhouse? Backhouse? Oh, Philip, my love. My Philip St.-Just—(*Has come to her window*) Where? Oh, where is my Philip?

(GRANNY *and* LUCIUS *cover their ears at first wail, wince during her speech*)

GRANNY   He just rode away. Go back to sleep!

MELISANDRE   But where was he? Where was he standing? I want to know just where—

GRANNY   Right square in my verbena bed. You can find the very spot. The one spot the Yankees didn't trample yesterday. Oh, he has a weakness for flowers, does Backhouse.

MELISANDRE (*Wailing*)   Backhouse!

GRANNY   And I've got a weakness for talking when I should be seeing to breakfast. Go get some sleep. Lucius. But wake Joby and Louvinia. Tell Joby to saddle the mule again.

(LUCIUS *goes out.* MELISANDRE *has retreated to her bed and taken up the dulcimer. She starts caterwauling "Drink to Me Only with Thine Eyes"*)

GRANNY (*Starts upstairs*)   You, Melisandre! No singing before breakfast, Miss! Stop it this minute!

MELISANDRE   I would think you could allow me at least that, Granny, at least to give vent to feelings which I cannot control, feelings, I remind you, which I did not bring on myself in any way—

GRANNY   Yes, yes. I've heard all that.

MELISANDRE   I remind you that, though I have forgiven you all, I did not place myself in the backhouse, did not contrive this awful fate for myself, did not of my own volition recklessly, heedlessly, irrevocably foil the only love I can ever experience for the only man I can never face—

GRANNY   Enough! I'd rather hear you sing, Melisandre. Yes! Sing!

JOBY (*Coming in on last word, looks anxious, stops and stares at* GRANNY)   Sing, Miss Rosa? Me?

GRANNY   No, you ninny, not you. You go find Bedford Forrest. Go to Tallahatchie Crossing. Sit there and wait for him if necessary. And bring him here.

JOBY   S'pose they done already started the battle?

GRANNY   Suppose they have? What business is that of yours or mine either? You find Bedford Forrest. Tell him this is important; it won't take long. But don't you show your face here again without him.

JOBY   Yessum! (*Leaves hastily*)

CURTAIN

ACT II

Scene 1

(BAYARD *and* RINGO *in the yard at right of house.* BAYARD *has the regimental drum,* RINGO *a drum of his own, clumsily made but bigger and louder than* BAYARD'S. RINGO *struts smugly.* BAYARD *half-heartedly follows him, yearning for the different drum*)

BAYARD   Ringo, don't you want to beat this one? I don't want to hog the best drum all the time.

RINGO   Nemmine. It's yores. I don't want to worry you none about it.

BAYARD   You wouldn't worry me. I'd be glad to let you beat it.

RINGO   Nemmine. It's yores. Like you said, Colonel Sartoris yore "father." (*Mocking* BAYARD'S *term*) That make it yore drum. My father made this here'n. That make it mine.

BAYARD   But we can swap em round. Father didn't say we couldn't take turn about. And Lucius didn't neither.

GRANNY (*At front door*)   Bayard. Ringo. Have you seen anything of Joby?

BAYARD AND RINGO   No'm. Sho ain't.

GRANNY   My stars. What can be keeping him? He's been gone two whole days.

BAYARD   Maybe the Yankees captured him.

RINGO   Maybe Gen'l Forrest kep him. Maybe they need a extry hand with the fightin or wuk.

LOUVINIA (*Appearing behind Granny on portico*)   An maybe neither one of them thangs is keepin him. (*To* GRANNY *with sarcasm and an air of injury*)   Maybe he drapped by the Compson place to visit a friend.

GRANNY   Now, Louvinia, for shame. It's been years since Joby has seen Elmira, far as you or I know. Every time he leaves the place you get the green eye. Ain't you ever going to let him forget he once sparked Elmira?

LOUVINIA   I let him forgit, he lible to slip up and start hit agin. Anyway, where is he? You the one axin the question.

GRANNY   You heard Lucius say Bedford Forrest was engaging Whiskey

Smith. They may have been fighting all this time. Joby may have had no chance to get to him.

LOUVINIA   Chanct! Chanct! And just maybe he's had him a chanct to get to somebody else. I'll chanct him, he gits back here.

GRANNY   Bayard, Ringo, keep a sharp eye out for Joby. Let me know the minute you see him. (*Goes inside*)

LOUVINIA   (*Walks downstage muttering*)   Gone from here two days, right in the middle of a war. Yankees swarmin all over us, and him out lookin for a chanct! (*Sings:*)

Give a Man a Chanct

Give a man a chanct, he will take it.
Give him half a chanct, he'll still make it.
Be he black or white, be he wrong or right,
Give a man just a chanct, he will take it.

Give a man an inch, he'll take a mile.
Give a man a look, he wants a smile.
Be he young or old, he was born too bold.
Best to meet any man with a scowl.

Trust a man to do right, if you care to.
Let him get out of sight, if you dare to.
Send him to the mill, he's not down the hill
Fore he's found him a frill to be rare to.

Give a man two heels, and he will kick em.
Put him with females, and he will trick em.
Be he slave or free, harken well to me,
Man of woman born is a slick un.

Give a man one leg, he will shake it.
Make that leg a peg, he'll likely break it.
Be he halt or lame, he will find some dame
If the chanct ain't to hand, he will make it.

Give a man one eye, he will wink it.
Punch him in that eye, he'll still blink it.
Be he blind and dumb, and cain't even hum,
If he cain't commit no mischief, he will think it.

But a woman cain't live without man.
There are times when we must have our man.
So take my fair warnin, to stay out of mournin,
Trust the devil before any man. (*Goes into house*)

BAYARD   What they talking about—Joby and Mrs. Compson's Elmira? Joby's too old to be interested in women, ain't he? He's your grandpa. And even if he wasn't too old, Elmira's too old to be interested in. She's oldern Louvinia, I bet. She can't hardly walk.

RINGO   I don't know nothin bout it. All I know, Mammy Louvinia say some folks never too old for some thangs.

BAYARD   (*Touches* RINGO's *drum*)   That ain't no drum atall. (*Offers his*)   You want to beat a real drum?

RINGO   (*Very smug*)   This here'n 'll do. (*Turns, beats a tattoo, begins to march proudly*)   I'se U.S. Grant and you's Pemberton. Yonder's Vicksburg over by the tree. If you ain't there by the time me and my army reaches it, Vicksburg's sho long gone.

BAYARD   (*Running ahead*)   But Vicksburg's done fell. Lucius told us Vicksburg's already gone. Remember?

RINGO   Nemmine fallin. You got a better town to defend?

BAYARD   How bout Corinth? Lucius said the Yankees going to try to take it, too.

RINGO   (*Marching in place, accompanying himself*)   Nemmine no Corinth. Corinth jest a lit'l bitty ole place right cross the hills from here. I'm gonna take me a Vicksburg. (*Moves forward*)

BAYARD   (*Runs to bench beside tree*)   No, you ain't. No Grant's gonna ever conquer Vicksburg. Not with Pemberton here.

(BAYARD *marches in place at "Vicksburg" until* RINGO *reaches him, each surges his drum into the other's, beating fiercely with shouts of battle*)

RINGO   (*Looking back over his shoulder*)   Army, retreat! We not gonna take Vicksburg today. We gonna take pity on em. We gonna give em one more chanct to surrender.

BAYARD   (*Bumping* RINGO's *drum, backing him across the yard*)   Ya-ay! You Yankees gonna give us one more chanct. We gonna run y'all right in the Big River. Hope Yankees can swim big as they can talk. Yay, Pemberton!

(BAYARD *bumps* RINGO *toward the steps, stops suddenly, stares stage left, then darts past* RINGO, *running to the house.* RINGO *turns to see what* BAYARD *was looking at, does a double-take and runs after* BAYARD)

BAYARD AND RINGO   Granny! Granny!

(They stop in front of GRANNY, *coming onto the portico.* JOBY, *dusty and tired, comes from stage left and goes to portico*)

BAYARD AND RINGO It's Joby, Granny!

BAYARD I saw him first.

RINGO I seen him at the same time.

GRANNY Well, where is he, for heaven's sake. We've waited long enough.

JOBY I'se here, Miss Rosa. Jes come in.

GRANNY Well? You have been gone two whole days.

LOUVINIA (*Coming out onto portico*) You most sholy have.

GRANNY Did you find him?

JOBY Miss Rosa, are you shore he is real?

LOUVINIA Hah! No, but I know who is real.

JOBY Miss Rosa, are you shore he ain't jes somebody who y'all tell the Yankees he's been there after they don't know whut hit em?

GRANNY Pshaw, Joby. Talk sense. Where have you been?

JOBY That's one of the main thangs I don't know, Miss Rosa. I been lots and lots of places but I don't know where none of em was, 'cept "up ahead." That's whut everybody kept telling me: He up ahead. I fin'ly 'cided "up ahead" was like Gen'l Forrest, just somep'n people tole people to keep em—

GRANNY Pshaw, Joby! Did you see the battle? Do you know who won it?

JOBY See it, Miss Rosa! I never even heard it! If wars always moves that fur and that fas, I don't see how they ever git time to fight.

(*Horses sound off stage right; everybody stops to listen.* FORREST *enters from right*)

FORREST Evenin, boys.

BAYARD (*Awed*) Evening, Sir. Are you . . .?

FORREST (*Sings*)

I Am Nathan Bedford Forrest

I Am Nathan Bedford Forrest.
In the forest I've been farthest—and I'm tired!
Bein fustest with the mostest,
Makin good the wildest boastes—makes you tired!

Oh, they talk of Forrest's Critters
And it really makes them bitter
'Cause them critters do not fritter—'way their time.

But being boss of all those critters,
Tendin to their spawn and litter,
Military baby-sitter—makes you tired!

Oh, I once had the life,
Agrarian kind of life.
Ask Andrew Lytle if you'd know.
Helped Ma to raise a fam'ly
In a farmhouse small and shambly.
The soil made my noble impulses grow.
Killed panthers single-handed,
Sold slaves to fancy dandies,
Oh, what abundant life nature bestowed.

Confound those men from the North,
Corrupt, industrial North,
Cold cash is all they ever knew.
They never would understand.
Oh no, they cannot understand.
You must be born here to see it true.
We tried our best to explain.
To spare everyone all this pain.
We really are humane through and through.

But they wouldn't listen to us,
Heaped on insults contemptuous,
Wouldn't show common acumen,
Harped on slaves as being human—so we fired!

Now I'm boss of Forrest's Critters,
Tendin to their spawn and litter,
A military baby-sitter—and I'm tired!

(*Finishes at front steps before* GRANNY) Well, Miss Rosie.
GRANNY Don't call me Rosie. Come in. Ask your gentlemen to alight and come in, too.
FORREST They'll wait there. We are a little rushed. My plans have—
(GRANNY *goes into the parlor and sits; he has to follow her.* BAYARD *and* RINGO *follow him in*) Well, Miss Rosie, I—
GRANNY Don't call me Rosie. Can't you even say Rosa?
FORREST Yessum, Miss Rosie. Well, I reckon we both have had about enough of this. That boy you sent me a message about—
GRANNY Hah! Just night before last you were saying, "What boy?" Where is he? I sent you word to bring him with you.
FORREST He's under arrest. (*With controlled exasperation*) I spent four days gittin Smith jest where I wanted him. After that, *this* boy (*Indicates* BAYARD) could have fit the battle. I won't bother you with details. Backhouse didn't know them either. All he had to do was ex-

actly what I told him. I done everythang but draw a diagram on his coattail of exactly what he was to do, no mo' and no less, which was to make contact and then fall back. I give him jest exactly the right number of men so that he couldn't do nothin else but that. I told him exactly how far to fall back and how much racket to make a'doin it and even how to make the racket. But what do you thank he done?

GRANNY I can tell you. He stood in my verbena bed at five o'clock yesterday morning, with my whole yard full of men behind him, yelling goodbye at my window.

FORREST He divided his men and sent half of em into the bushes to make a noise and took the other half, who were the nearest to complete fools, and led a sabre charge on that outpost. He didn't fire a shot. He druv it clean back with *sabres* into Smith's main body and scared Smith so bad that he threw out all his cavalry and pulled out behind it and now I don't know whether I'm about to ketch him or he's about to ketch me.

GRANNY And what about Backhouse?

FORREST My provost finally caught him last night. He had come back and got the other thirty men of his comp'ny and was twenty miles ahead agin, tryin to find somethin to lead another charge at.

GRANNY He really is determined, isn't he.

FORREST "Do you want to be killed?" I told him. He said, "Not especially. That is, I don't especially care one way or the other." I said, "Then neither do I. But you risked a whole comp'ny of my men." And he said, "Ain't that what they enlisted for?"

GRANNY Goodness, how impertinent.

FORREST I told him, "They enlisted into a military establishment the purpose of which is to expend each man only at a profit. Or maybe you don't consider me a shrewd enough trader in human meat?"

GRANNY (*Ironic*) Mercy! And what did he say to that?

FORREST He said, "I can't say. Since day before yesterday I ain't thought very much about how you or anybody else runs this war." I said, "And just what were you doin' day before yesterday that changed your ideas and habits?" He said, "Fightin some of yore war. Dispersin the enemy." I said, "Where?" He said, "At a lady's house a few miles from Jefferson. One of the servants called her Granny like the white boy did. The others called her Miss Rosie." (*Stops for breath*)

GRANNY Go on.

FORREST I told him, "I'm tryin to win battles—even if since day before yesterday you ain't. I'll send you down to Johnston at Jackson," I said. "He'll put you inside Vicksburg, where you can lead private charges day and night too if you want." He said, "Like hell you will," and I said—excuse me— "Like hell I won't."

(BAYARD *and* RINGO *look at* GRANNY *and put their hands over their mouths. She ignores them*)

GRANNY And did you?

FORREST I can't. He knows it. You can't punish a man for routin an enemy four times his weight. What would I say back there in Tennessee, where we both live, let alone with that uncle of his, the one they licked for Governor six years ago, on Bragg's personal staff now, with his face over Bragg's shoulder ever time Bragg opens a dispatch or picks up a pen. And I'm still tryin to win battles. (*Sings to tune of "I Am Nathan Bedford Forrest"*)

Taking Command

> I am Nathan Bedford Forrest;
> In the forest I've been farthest—and I'm stumped!
> I am tryin to win battles,
> To make Whiskey Smith's bones rattle,
> Be effective in the saddle—but I'm stumped!

GRANNY (*To tune of "It's Not Love They've Got"*)
> Don't tell me your woes, I've got my own.
> I'm reaping from seeds I haven't sown.
> While you men behave so bravely
> I am left with boys and slaves and
> With this moonstruck, squalling maiden
> All alone!

FORREST (*His tune*)
> Oh, I once had a life,
> Agrarian kind of life—

GRANNY (*Concluding his stanza*)
> I know—and the soil made you superb.

FORREST (*Eyeing her doubtfully*)
> But now because of a girl,
> One lone, single, young female girl—

GRANNY
> You find all your fierce machismo curbed.

FORREST
> He saved her from Yankee advances.
> Why can't she forgit circumstances—

GRANNY
> Yes, her attitude is quite absurd.

FORREST
> So take the girl firmly in hand now.

Tell her what to do and just how.
You're her Grandma and she must bow—to your will.

GRANNY (*Her tune*)
Oh, it's really as simple as all that?
Just call her and issue a fiat.
And if she ignores my saying it.
Send a soldier with a bayonet.
To convince her that I'm laying it
Down as law!

FORREST (*Modestly helpful, preening, in his tune*)
And if she gets up her dander
Maybe as her boy's commander—

GRANNY (*His tune*)
And a man than whom none's grander.
You can certainly demand her—great respect.

FORREST
Oh, I think I can say
I usually can find a way—

GRANNY
Why, yes! As I say, you are quite superb!

FORREST (*Oblivious to her mockery*)
I guess (GRANNY *joins him*) men were born to command.
Women (GRANNY *joins him*) just don't understand.

FORREST (*alone*)
The need to be firm and quite unperturbed. (*Music stops*)

GRANNY Umm—firm.

FORREST Yessum.

GRANNY Unperturbed.

FORREST Yessum.

GRANNY (*Supressing her amusement*) Wait here, Mr. Forrest. I'll be right back.

(GRANNY *smiles at him, then sweeps out of parlor, coming back with* MELISANDRE *in an elaborate, hoop-skirted Southern belle fashion.*)

GRANNY Here she is. Say it. (*To* MESLISANDRE) Melisandre, this is Mr. Bedford Forrest. (*To* FORREST) Go ahead, Mr. Forrest, say it. It's just a matter of common sense, as you've already put it so well.

(*But the moment* GRANNY *calls his name,* MELISANDRE *goes into her Walter Scott high-idyllic manner, her face taking on a noble, sweet artificiality. She takes two steps back and curtsies, spreading her hoops back, and stands up*)

MELISANDRE General Forrest. (*To* GRANNY) I am acquainted with an associate of his. Will the General please give him the sincerest wishes for triumph in war and success in love, from one who will never see him again? (*Curtsies again, spreading hoops backward, straightens, takes two steps backward, turns and sweeps out*)

GRANNY Well, Mr. Forrest?

(FORREST *begins to cough. He lifts his coattail with one hand and reaches the other into his hip pocket as if to pull out at least a musket, gets his dirty handkerchief and coughs into it a while. Puts handkerchief back and takes a deep breath*)

FORREST Can I reach the Holly Branch road without havin to go through Jefferson?

GRANNY No, Mr. Forrest. Just a moment. Get the pen and ink and some paper, Bayard. (BAYARD *goes*)

FORREST Pen and paper, Miss Rosie?

GRANNY I believe you said the purpose of your military establishment was to expend men only at a profit.

(BAYARD *returns, places writing implements on sideboard in the dining room.* GRANNY *follows him, writes rapidly, standing up.* FORREST *looks over her shoulder, reading aloud slowly*)

FORREST Lieutenant, P.S. Backhouse, Comp'ny D., Tennessee Cavalry, was this day raised to the honorary rank of Brevet Major General and killed while engagin the enemy. In place of whom Philip St.-Just Backus is hereby appointed Lieutenant, Comp'ny D., Tennessee Calvary. But, confound it, Miss Rosie, what's the difference in Backus, U-S, and Backhouse, H-O-U-S-E? Won't Backus remind her just the same as Backhouse?

GRANNY You still miss the point, Mr. Forrest. It ain't logic you're dealing with, or even facts. It's how it would read in a book. But you don't read books, do you? So I'll just remind you of those curtsies you saw and that speech you heard. If you had time, I'd let you hear her sing and play the dulcimer.

FORREST No ma'am, if you don't mind. (*Picks up* GRANNY'S *note and folds it*) But now I've got to have a battle. (*To* BAYARD) Another sheet, son. (BAYARD *lays out another sheet*)

GRANNY A battle?

FORREST To give to Johnston. Confound it, Miss Rosie, can't you understand either that I'm just a fallible mortal man tryin to run a military command accordin to certain fixed rules, no matter how foolish the bizness looks to superior outside folk?

GRANNY All right, you had a battle. I was looking at it.

FORREST   So I did. Hah! The Battle of Sartoris.

GRANNY   No. Not at my house.

BAYARD   They did all the shootin down at the creek.

FORREST   What creek?

GRANNY   Hurricane Creek.

FORREST (*Perplexed*)   Hurry-cain Creek? I never heard of it.

BAYARD   Everybody but Granny calls it Harrykin.

FORREST   Oh! Harrykin Creek. Why didn't you say so to start with. (GRANNY *looks at both of them, contemptuously.* FORREST *writes, saying the words slowly as he writes*)   A unit of my command on detached duty engaged a body of the enemy and druv him from the field and dispersed him this day, 28th July 1863, at Harrykin Creek. With loss of one man. (*Picks up sheet, waves it to dry it, starts to hall, folding it*)

GRANNY   Wait! Lay out another sheet, Bayard. (*To* FORREST)   Come back here, Mr. Forrest.

(*A commotion occurs off stage left.* AB SNOPES *is heard yelling*)

AB SNOPES   Lemme go! I'm a friend of Bedford Forrest, I tell you. I've done bizness with him. He'll have you in the guardhouse for this.

(FORREST *and* GRANNY *have moved to front steps.* TWO CONFEDERATE OFFICERS *drag* AB SNOPES *in from stage left*)

FIRST OFFICER   General, while we were at the summer house, this man was trying to lead off our horses. One of the servants came and told us. He says he knows you, says he was taking the horses to the creek to water them.

FORREST   I never saw him before.

AB SNOPES (*Whining*)   Now, Genrul, you know I sold you four hosses at Holly Branch not two months ago. I'm a hoss captin for Col. Sartoris. Miz Millard there can tell you that.

FORREST (*Looks closely at him*)   Oh, yes, now I do remember you.

AB SNOPES (*To* SOLDIERS, *who release him*)   There. See whut I tell you?

FORREST   In fact, I was hopin to meet you agin. You're a very good horse trader.

AB SNOPES   Well, Genrul, I try to do my best.

FORREST   Yessir, you're one of the few men livin who ever beat Bedford Forrest in a trade.

AB SNOPES   Well, a feller jest keeps his eyes peeled, and—whut, Genrul? You say I—

FORREST   Yessir, I got in a hurry and didn't ride any of them horses, and it turned out one of em wouldn't jump a ditch and two others was bellowsed.

AB SNOPES   Genrul, I swear I never had no idea. You sure you ain't mixing me up with Pat Stamper? Now there's a trader you got to watch. And, after all, you didn't even know me at first.

FORREST   I remember the horses, though. And they put me in mind of you. Four of the sorriest animals I ever saw. And you shouldn't be so modest. Not only to take me in a trade, but to put your country's defenders on untrustworthy mounts—probably no one else in the country can claim such a distinction.

(AB *terrified, cowers, silent*)

FIRST OFFICER   What shall we do with him, General?

FORREST   He was stealing our horses? You're sure?

FIRST OFFICER   No doubt about it, Sir.

SECOND OFFICER   None at all, Sir.

FORREST   And what do we do with horse thieves and traitors?

FIRST OFFICER   Yessir. I just wanted your word on it, General. (*Seizing* AB) Come on, you.

AB SNOPES   Wait! Genrul! You ain't gonna hang me? Not Col. Sartoris' hoss captin? You ask Miz Millard there about me, bout how I holp her steal Yankee hosses, them six hosses right out there in her pasture now, what we been keeping for you.

FORREST   Is there any truth to what he's sayin, Miss Rosie?

GRANNY (*Pause*)   What truth there is in it wouldn't feed a hungry gnat.

AB SNOPES   Now, Miz Millard. Tell him bout them hosses. Tell him how you taken em slam away from me.

FORREST   We don't have to waste any more time with this, I reckon. With yore permission, Miss Rosie—and my apologies for bringin this vermin into yore presence—I'll jest have my men—

AB SNOPES   Miz Millard, please! Don't let him—

GRANNY   Mr. Forrest. (*Pause*) Though not much of one, Ab Snopes is a father and husband. And it is true that on occasion he has seemed to work in our behalf.

FORREST   Well, I'll leave it up to you, Miss Rosie. Should I let him off?

(GRANNY *hestitates, then nods reluctantly*)

AB SNOPES   Spoken like a true lady, Miz Millard. God bless you—

GRANNY (*Offended by his hypocrisy*)   With the clear understanding that if he ever meddles with Confederate horses again, he is to get whatever punishment you deem fitting to a thief and traitor!

FORREST   Done, Miss Rosie. (*To* OFFICERS)   All right, take him out
of my sight and turn him loose. I'll remember you well if I see you
again, Snopes. Don't let it happen.

AB SNOPES (OFFICERS *drag him off*)   I was just takin them hosses
to the creek. A injustice is bein done here. (*Voice fades away*)

FORREST   Well, I'll be headin for Holly Branch—

GRANNY   No, not yet. Bring that other sheet of paper, Bayard.

FORREST (*Stopping, turning*)   Another one?

GRANNY   Yes! A furlough, pass—whatever you busy military
establishments call them! So John Sartoris can come home long enough
to—(*Stops and looks at* BAYARD *and* RINGO *and takes a deep breath*)
—so John Sartoris can come back home and give away that damn
bride!

Scene 2

(GRANNY *is striding exasperatedly back and forth in the parlor
before* MELISANDRE, *who leans theatrically against the sideboard*)

MELISANDRE   But, Granny, surely you understand that I can't have
myself thrown at the man's head like a, like a—

GRANNY   Strumpet is probably what you're fumbling for, Melisandre.
Isn't that the way they put it in your novels?

MELISANDRE   All right, yes. Like a strumpet. Or a pawn in a chess
game.

GRANNY   Yes, yes. Pull out all the stops, Melisandre!

MELISANDRE   Or, to speak in your own terms, Granny, like a horse,
like some poor mare you might trade off to Ab Snopes.

GRANNY   Hah! You surprise me! You may develop some gumption yet.
Now and then I have reason to suspect you may be my granddaughter
after all.

MELISANDRE   Then you don't think it unreasonable that I should
want a proper courtship, want at least to see the man, have him see
me, outside the odor of a wrecked backhouse?

GRANNY   I think it is idiotic. Where do you think we are, girl? In
London or Paris? This is Mississippi. We're in the middle of a war.
That boy has no time—

MELISANDRE   Oh, the war! My Philip in that war! He is so
headstrong, heedless, courageous! Don't you think I live every moment
in mortal dread? Don't you think I watch the road each day fearing

that it will bring me a messenger of doom, a fatal note bearing the news of my bereavement—

GRANNY Don't I think it? I'm positive you do—and relish every minute of it. And if Bedford Forrest didn't need need men so badly, I'd be tempted to try to arrange for your gratification. But enough of this foolishness now. I've sent for John Sartoris, and Bedford Forrest is going to have that boy and the chaplain here tomorrow at four o'clock.

MELISANDRE Then you'll have to bring me bodily down for *your wedding*, Granny. That is, if I don't manage to run away before that. It is positively medieval, you and General Forrest *arranging* my marriage this way. After all, I haven't even met this Lieutenant Backus. Why, he hasn't even asked for my hand in marriage!

GRANNY You haven't what? He hasn't what? You're even going to quibble over that, Melisandre? (*Stares at* MELISANDRE, *who turns to flounce away.* GRANNY *heaves a sigh*) All right, fetch me a pen and some paper. (*Raising her voice*) Louvinia, tell Joby to come in here.

LOUVINIA (*Coming to parlor door*) Now you ain't gonna send Joby off to find Genrul Forrest agin. You gonna do that to me?

GRANNY Nonsense, Louvinia. He had a perfectly good excuse last time—and you know it.

(MELISANDRE *returns with pen and paper;* GRANNY *writes at sideboard*)

LOUVINIA Excuse ain't whut I want him to have. I want him not to need no excuse.

JOBY (*Coming in past* LOUVINIA) Excuse for what? Who is it don't need no excuse?

LOUVINIA Not you, I'll vow! You need a excuse for bein born!

GRANNY (*Folding note*) Joby, I want you to take this note to General Forrest. He's at his—

JOBY Oh, I know right where he at. He up ahead. I done been there before. Up ahead. (*Shuffles off mumbling*)

LIGHTS DOWN

Scene 3

(*Light comes up on* GENERAL FORREST *and* PHILIP *before the curtain.* FORREST *is striding back and forth exasperatedly in front of* PHILIP, *like* GRANNY *did before* MELISANDRE. *He wheels and glares at* PHILIP)

FORREST　Whut? You won't be a party to a subter—whut?

PHILIP (*Firmly, chin-up haughtily*)　A subterfuge. S-u-b-t-e-r—

FORREST　All right, all right! I don't give a damn how you spell it. Whut's so subterfuge-y about it? You wanted to lose your name in battle, didn't you? Ain't that why you've been chasin Whiskey Smith all over Yoknapatawpha County, trying to stop a bullet or split yoreself down the middle on a sabre? And now we've figured out a perfectly sane way to have it happen—and much cleaner and more painless, I might add—and you call it a subter-fuge. Do you read those confounded novels, too?

PHILIP　My family assumes that literacy and a degree of cultural attainment are part of the equipment of a gentleman.

FORREST　Does your family assume anything about common sense and self-preservation?

PHILIP　It assumes, I believe, that there are a great many people whose sense is all too common and whose preservation is all they can understand.

FORREST　Well, around here we assume somethin about insubordination, too, and about young whelps too wet behind the ears to be called out for a duel. I suggest you not push your luck too far, Lieutenant.

PHILIP　If I have been insubordinate, I apologize. I'm afraid I have been worse. I've been *rude*. And for that I apologize, too. But I submit to you, General, that you are asking me to masquerade under false colors, to acquiesce to a military report which not only falsifies my death but—

FORREST　And I submit to you, Lieutenant, that unless you take a furlough and court Melisandre De Spain as Philip Backus, you ain't never gonna have that gal as yore bride. And she's a right purty gal, too, if I do say so myself.

PHILIP (*With beatific look*)　A beautiful girl, Sir. A beautiful, tender girl. (*Orchestra plays strains of "That Beautiful Girl"*)

LIGHTS DOWN

Scene 4

(PHILIP *is seated in the Sartoris' parlor,* GRANNY *standing by the stairway.* MELISANDRE *is preening at her dressing table upstairs.*

BAYARD *and* RINGO *are peeping in from a side window,* LOUVINIA *and* PHILADELPHIA *from the dining room door)*

GRANNY *(Calling upstairs with exaggerated politeness)*   Melisandre. Oh, Melisandre. Would you come down, dear. There's someone I'd like you to meet. (MELISANDRE *fluffs her hair, rises with exaggerated courtliness and sweeps down stairs)*   Ah, there are you are, dear. How pretty you look. May I present Lieutenant Philip St.-Just Backus of General Forrest's cavalry. You met General Forrest the other day, remember? Lieutenant Backus, this is Melisandre De Spain, my granddaughter.

MELISANDRE   Oh, it is a great honor to meet someone from General Forrest's command. How do you do, Lieutenant Backus? *(Curtsies elaborately)*

PHILIP *(Rose when she entered, now bows elaborately)*   It is my pleasure to meet you, Miss De Spain, I assure you. I have—ah— heard of you. Your beauty—ah—is famous, and I have longed for the opportunity to make your acquaintance.

GRANNY   Lieutenant Backus is on furlough, Melisandre, and has done us the honor of paying us a visit. Isn't that nice of him?

MELISANDRE   We are indeed honored, Lieutenant Backus. We have —ah—heard of you, too. Your courage in battle is well known and widely admired.

PHILIP   If Miss.De Spain would honor me by calling me Philip, I would deem it a great courtesy.

MELISANDRE   With pleasure, and if Lieutenant Backus would call me Melisandre, I would be most happy.

GRANNY   And if Miss De Spain and Lieutenant Backus will excuse me, I would deem it a great kindness. *(Curtsies elaborately)*   I must be seeing to refreshments. *(Goes toward kitchen, routing* LOUVINIA *and* PHILADELPHIA *out of doorway,then turns to make a face and shake her hands at the whole scene)*   Great Scott!

LIGHTS DOWN

Scene 5

(GRANNY, LOUVINIA, *and* PHILADELPHIA *are in the parlor.* PHILADELPHIA *looking out the window toward the tree and bench)*

GRANNY   Do you see them, Philadelphia?

PHILADELPHIA   They down to the summer house. They startin up this way.

LOUVINIA   They been down to the summer house four days now. Don't you reckon she consider this enough courtin?

GRANNY   That girl will never get enough courting. But I told her to get done with it today. That's why I had John Sartoris ride in this afternoon.

LOUVINIA   Well, I sho hope this is the day. Cookin for that boy is like cookin for a whole army. He must not a had a decent meal since he lef home.

GRANNY   It will be the day. She'd better heed what I told her. All this romantic tomfoolery with the world falling in on us from all sides. I still say we have Walter Scott to thank for most of this.

(PHILIP *and* MELISANDRE *come from stage right, holding hands, and pass the tree and bench on their way to the house*)

PHILADELPHIA   Heah they come

GRANNY   Let's clear the way for her. (*They exit*)

MELISANDRE (*Laughing*)   Oh, Philip, you do say the drollest things. (*Pauses on porch, looks at him with sudden, shy seriousness*)   Well, shall I call Uncle John? Now?

PHILIP (*Very nervous, takes deep breath*)   Yes, call him.

MELISANDRE (*Goes to stairs while* PHILIP *walks nervously about in the parlor*)   Uncle John! Would you come into the parlor, please? (*Turns to* PHILIP *and whispers*)   Don't worry. I'm sure he'll approve.

COL. SARTORIS (*Coming from under stairway*)   Yes, Melisandre? Oh, hello, Lieutenant. I'm John Sartoris. I've been hearing a lot about you.

MELISANDRE   Lieutenant Philip Backus, Uncle John. He . . . wants to talk to you.

COL. SARTORIS   And I want to talk to him. I certainly do. (*Extends hand to* PHILIP)   Won't you sit down, Lieutenant? Make yourself comfortable. (*They sit.* PHILIP *fidgets.* MELISANDRE *wrings her hands abstractedly*)   Well, Melisandre, are you going to join us, too, or is this to be a private conversation?

MELISANDRE   Oh! Oh no, Uncle John. I mean, oh yes, it's to be private. He—uh—will y'all excuse me, please? (*Rushes away*)

COL. SARTORIS (*Looks expectantly at* PHILIP. *Long silence.* COL. SARTORIS *clears his throat and* PHILIP *jumps.*   Well, young man, you want to talk to me?

PHILIP   Yes, Sir. You see, Sir. It—it's about your niece. I—we—

Scene 6

(LUCIUS, LOUVINIA, PHILADELPHIA *and* JOBY *appear in front of the curtain.* LOUVINIA *and* PHILADELPHIA *are crying silently, wiping their eyes with their aprons.* JOBY, *throughout, shakes his head with foreboding*)

LOUVINIA   Look like you could wait till after the weddin, Lucius. Not spoil that for Big Miss.

LUCIUS   I done waited too long already. Don't want to see no weddin. Don't want to see no passel of rebel soldiers orderin me round.

JOBY (*Looking behind apprehensively*)   You hush that, boy. Don't you let Big Miss hear you saying "rebel" round here. She have all our hides.

LUCIUS   Big Miss got a lot to learn, bout rebels and yankees and black folks, too.

LOUVINIA (*Slight pause;* ALL *look reluctant*)   If you feelin like that, I reckon you better go on. You jest get in trouble here. But whut you gonna do?

PHILADELPHIA   He gonna leave his wife and chile. That whut he gonna do. Jest turn em over to them rebels he talk so hard bout and run off hisself to see the big world.

LUCIUS (*Pulling her to him with gruff tenderness*)   You talkin foolish and you know it. You and Ringo be fine here, and ain't no place for y'all with the yankee army. I ain't runnin off. I gonna be fightin to end this war and end this slavery. And it ain't gonna be long neither. Then I come back to git y'all as a United States vetrun! We get us a farm. Send Ringo to school to learn to read and write. Yankees gonna set up free schools. It gonna be different. Like nothin we ever known. Ain't I been tellin y'all? We free right now. Been free since New Year's. Don't y'all feel that? Don't y'all feel that?

(*He embraces all three of them, goes off right. They stand, tentative, unconvinced smiles on their faces.* LOUVINIA *sings softly and ruefully, "Give a man a chanct, he will take it." Light fades on* JOBY *and* LOUVINIA *shaking their heads,* PHILADELPHIA *crying into her apron*)

Scene 7

(*The wedding ceremony is just being concluded in the parlor. The house is resplendent with flowers, silver candlesticks, etc. It's late afternoon.* PHILIP *and* MELISANDRE *are radiant before the* CHAPLAIN, COL. SARTORIS *and* GRANNY *on one side;* FOUR OFFICERS, *friends of* PHILIP, *are on the other side.* FOUR SOUTHERN GIRLS, *friends of* MELISANDRE, *are scattered through the group.* BAYARD, RINGO, PHILADELPHIA, LOUVINIA *and* JOBY *stand around the edges, in doorways)*

CHAPLAIN   Then I now pronounce you man and wife. What God hath joined together, let no man put asunder.

(Bustle of activity: COL. SARTORIS *and* OTHERS *kissing the bride as most move to the portico. Wine is served to toast the newlyweds.* BAYARD *and* RINGO *have run out to the front yard. Subdued laughter and talk continue in background)*

RINGO   Whoo! It sho hot in there.

BAYARD   Yeah.

RINGO   So Gen'l Forrest didn't even come.

BAYARD   Yeah. I thought he might need to come to guard Cousin Philip.

RINGO   Naw. I knew he wouldn't need to do that, whut with Col. Sartoris comin anyway. *(Wistfully)*   I thought maybe he'd have the Colonel handcuff Cousin Philip to him though, and maybe send that soldier with the bayonet along.

BAYARD *(Snorts)*   Father wouldn't need no soldier with a bayonet. *(Seeing it, though, excited)*   If I was him I would have just handcuffed Cousin Philip to me and then when they were married, unlock him and turn him over to Cousin Melisandre.

RINGO   Yeah, that would have been good.

BAYARD *(Picks up Ringo's drum, starts beating light tattoo and singing, imitating Forrest:)*
"I am Nathan Bedford Forrest
In the forest I've been farthest—and I'm tired!"

RINGO *(Picks up Bayard's drum and, accompanying himself on it, joins in:)*
"Being fustest with the mostest,
Making good the wildest boastes—makes you tired!"
(Pause, wistfully)   I wish Gen'l Forrest had of come, though.

(The sound of a single horse is heard off-stage right. A CONFEDERATE OFFICER *strides briskly to the front porch.* GRANNY *comes out to the steps)*

O F F I C E R   Do I have the honor of addressing Miss Rosie Millard?

G R A N N Y   I am Rosa Millard.

O F F I C E R (*Saluting sharply*)   Lieutenant Horatio Benbow, your servant, ma'am. I bring you General Forrest's compliments. He wishes to apologize for not attending your granddaughter's wedding, but he was unexpectedly detained. On the way over here, he stopped to take a bath in Harrykin Creek, and some sneaking horse thief made off with his horse—and all his aides' horses, too. The General walked back to Jefferson, and he's—if I may say so—he's not in any frame of mind for a wedding. He wishes the bride and groom all happiness, and he says he hopes he never sees nor hears of Harrykin Creek again. (*Salutes again, turns sharply, and walks off stage right*)

(*Amid laughter and talk the* FOUR OFFICERS *come out and take positions on the steps with drawn sabres raised and touching, for* PHILIP *and* MELISANDRE *to walk under.* BAYARD *and* RINGO *move down to right center to be out of the way but see everything*)

R I N G O   Whut they want to go into Jefferson to a hotel for?

B A Y A R D (*Shrugs*)   Granny says people always go somewhere; they call it a honeymoon. Jefferson's just as far as anybody can get right now.

(PHILIP *and* MELISANDRE *run under the swords, rice being thrown at them. They slow up and begin to dance.* OFFICERS *peel off one by one with the* GIRLS. COL. SARTORIS *and* GRANNY *join in. At the end of the dance,* ALL *except* PHILIP *and* MELISANDRE *reassemble on the portico and steps.* PHILIP *and* MELISANDRE *walk languidly to center stage, holding hands, blissfully staring into each other's faces, and* PHILIP *sings*)

P H I L I P

This beautiful girl
Will walk
This earth
Henceforth
With me alone.
the air now is softer.
The sun now is brighter.
All sounds now are gentler
Here.

(*Beaming at him,* MELISANDRE, *in her most discordant voice starts singing to same tune*)

MELISANDRE

> This beautiful boy
> Will walk
> This earth
> Henceforth
> With me alone.

(*At her first words,* PHILIP *starts violently and stares in disbelief;
she is oblivious and sings on. At "this earth" he glances back
embarrassedly at the people around the porch.* GRANNY *smiles
broadly at him and waves elaborately.* MELISANDRE *continues in
splendid, loud discord, and he joins her, trying to drown her out.*
ALL WEDDING PARTY *joins in singing the last verses with* PHILIP
and MELISANDRE *as the couple leaves the stage*)

> And now she'll embrace him,
> Her presence will grace him,
> Herself all quite palpably.

> He's dreamed, he's known,
> At last he's seen her,
> That beautiful girl!

CURTAIN

Crimes of the Heart

BETH HENLEY

CHARACTERS

LENNY MAGRATH   thirty, the oldest sister
CHICK BOYLE   twenty-nine, the sister's first cousin
DOC PORTER   thirty, Meg's old boyfriend
MEG MAGRATH   twenty-seven, the middle sister
BABE BOTRELLE   twenty-four, the youngest sister
BARNETTE LLOYD   twenty-six, Babe's lawyer

SETTING

The setting of the entire play is the kitchen in the MaGrath sisters' house in Hazlehurst, Mississippi, a small Southern town. The old-fashioned kitchen is unusually spacious, but there is a lived-in, cluttered look about it. There are four different entrances and exits to the kitchen: the back door, the door leading to the dining room and the front of the house, a door leading to the downstairs bedroom, and a staircase leading to the upstairs room. There is a table near the center of the room, and a cot has been set up in one of the corners.

TIME

In the fall, five years after Hurricane Camille.

ACT I

(The lights go up on the empty kitchen. It is late afternoon. Lenny MaGrath, a thirty-year-old woman with a round figure and face, enters from the back door carrying a white suitcase, a saxophone case, and a brown paper sack. She sets the suitcase and the sax case down and takes the brown sack to the kitchen table. After glancing quickly at the door, she gets the cookie jar from the kitchen counter, a box of matches from the stove, and then brings both objects back to the kitchen table. Excitedly, she reaches into the brown sack and pulls out a package of birthday candles. She quickly opens

239

the package and removes a candle. She tries to stick the candle onto a cookie—it falls off. She sticks the candle in again, but the cookie is too hard and it crumbles. Frantically, she gets a second cookie from the jar. She strikes a match, lights the candle, and begins dripping wax onto the cookie. Just as she is beginning to smile we hear Chick's voice from offstage)

CHICK'S VOICE Lenny! Oh, Lenny!

(LENNY *quickly blows out the candle and stuffs the cookie and candle into her dress pocket.* CHICK, *twenty-nine, enters from the back door. She is a brightly dressed matron with yellow hair and shiny red lips)*

CHICK Hi! I saw your car pull up.

LENNY Hi.

CHICK Well, did you see today's paper?

(LENNY *nods)*

CHICK It's just too awful! It's just way too awful! How I'm gonna continue holding my head up high in this community, I do not know. Did you remember to pick up those pantyhose for me?

LENNY They're in the sack.

CHICK Well, thank goodness, at least I'm not gonna have to go into town wearing holes in my stockings.

(*She gets the package, tears it open, and proceeds to take off one pair of stockings and put on another throughout the following scene. There should be something slightly grotesque about this woman changing her stockings in the kitchen)*

LENNY Did Uncle Watson call?

CHICK Yes, Daddy has called me twice already. He said Babe's ready to come home. We've got to get right over and pick her up before they change their simple minds.

LENNY (*Hesitantly)* Oh, I know, of course, it's just—

CHICK What?

LENNY Well, I was hoping Meg would call.

CHICK Meg?

LENNY Yes, I sent her a telegram: about Babe, and—

CHICK A telegram?! Couldn't you just phone her up?

LENNY Well, no, 'cause her phone's . . . out of order.

CHICK Out of order?

LENNY   Disconnected. I don't know what.

CHICK   Well, that sounds like Meg. My, these are snug. Are you sure you bought my right size?

LENNY (*Looking at the box*)   Size extra-petite.

CHICK   Well, they're skimping on the nylon material. (*Struggling to pull up the stockings*)   That's all there is to it. Skimping on the nylon. (*She finished one leg and starts the other*)   Now, just what all did you say in this telegram to Meg?

LENNY   I don't recall exactly. I, well, I just told her to come on home.

CHICK   To come on home! Why, Lenora Josephine, have you lost your only brain, or what?

LENNY (*Nervously, as she begins to pick up the mess of dirty stockings and plastic wrappings*)   But Babe wants Meg home. She asked me to call her.

CHICK   I'm not talking about what Babe wants.

LENNY   Well, what then?

CHICK   Listen, Lenora. I think it's pretty accurate to assume that after this morning's paper, Babe's gonna be incurring some mighty negative publicity around this town. And Meg's appearance isn't gonna help out a bit.

LENNY   What's wrong with Meg?

CHICK   She had a loose reputation in high school.

LENNY (*Weakly*)   She was popular.

CHICK   She was known all over Copiah County as cheap Christmas trash, and that was the least of it. There was that whole sordid affair with Doc Porter, leaving him a cripple.

LENNY   A cripple—he's got a limp. Just kind of, barely a limp.

CHICK   Well, his mother was going to keep *me* out of the Ladies' Social League because of it.

LENNY   What?

CHICK   That's right. I never told you, but I had to go plead with that mean old woman and convince her that I was just as appalled with what Meg had done as she was, and that I was only a first cousin anyway and I could hardly be blamed for all the skeletons in the MaGrath's closet. It was humiliating. I tell you, she even brought up your mother's death. And that poor cat.

LENNY   Oh! Oh! Oh, please, Chick! I'm sorry. But you're in the Ladies' League now.

CHICK   Yes. That's true, I am. But frankly, if Mrs. Porter hadn't developed that tumor in her bladder, I wouldn't be in the club today, much less a committee head. (*As she brushes her hair*)   Anyway, you be a sweet potato and wait right here for Meg to call, so's you can convince her not to come back home. It would make things a whole lot easier on everybody. Don't you think it really would?

LENNY Probably.

CHICK Good, then suit yourself. How's my hair?

LENNY Fine.

CHICK Not pooching out in the back, is it?

LENNY No.

CHICK (*Cleaning the hair from her brush*) All right then, I'm on my way. I've got Annie May over there keeping an eye on Peekay and Buck Jr., but I don't trust her with them for long periods of time. (*Dropping the ball of hair onto the floor*) Her mind is like a loose sieve. Honestly it is. (*As she puts the brush back into her purse*) Oh! Oh! Oh! I almost forgot. Here's a present for you. Happy birthday to Lenny, from the Buck Boyles! (*She takes a wrapped package from her bag and hands it to* LENNY)

LENNY Why, thank you, Chick. It's so nice to have you remember my birthday every year like you do.

CHICK (*Modestly*) Oh, well, now, that's just the way I am, I suppose. That's just the way I was brought up to be. Well, why don't you go on and open the present?

LENNY All right. (*She starts to unwrap the gift*)

CHICK It's a box of candy—assorted crèmes.

LENNY Candy—that's always a nice gift.

CHICK And you have a sweet tooth, don't you?

LENNY I guess.

CHICK Well, I'm glad you like it.

LENNY I do.

CHICK Oh, speaking of which, remember that little polka-dot dress you got Peekay for her fifth birthday last month?

LENNY The red-and-white one?

CHICK Yes; well, the first time I put it in the washing machine, I mean the very first time, it fell all to pieces. Those little polka dots just dropped right off in the water.

LENNY (*Crushed*) Oh, no. Well, I'll get something else for her, then —a little toy.

CHICK Oh, no, no, no, no, no! We wouldn't hear of it! I just wanted to let you know so you wouldn't go and waste any more of your hard-earned money on that make of dress. Those inexpensive brands just don't hold up. I'm sorry, but not in these modern washing machines.

DOC PORTER'S VOICE Hello! Hello, Lenny!

CHICK (*Taking over*)   Oh, look, it's Doc Porter! Come on in Doc! Please come right on in!

(DOC PORTER *enters through the back door. He is carrying a large sack of pecans. Doc is an attractively worn man with a slight limp that adds rather than detracts from his quiet seductive quality. He is thirty years old, but appears slightly older*)

CHICK   Well, how are you doing? How in the world are you doing?
DOC   Just fine, Chick.
CHICK   And how are you liking it now that you're back in Hazlehurst?
DOC   Oh, I'm finding it somewhat enjoyable.
CHICK   Somewhat! Only somewhat! Will you listen to him! What a silly, silly, silly man! Well, I'm on my way. I've got some people waiting on me. (*Whispering to* DOC)   It's Babe. I'm on my way to pick her up.
DOC   Oh.
CHICK   Well, goodbye! Farewell and goodbye!
LENNY   'Bye.

(CHICK *exits*)

DOC   Hello.
LENNY   Hi. I guess you heard about the thing with Babe.
DOC   Yeah.
LENNY   It was in the newspaper.
DOC   Uh huh.
LENNY   What a mess.
DOC   Yeah.
LENNY   Well, come on and sit down. I'll heat us up some coffee.
DOC   That's okay. I can only stay a minute. I have to pick up Scott; he's at the dentist.
LENNY   Oh; well, I'll heat some up for myself. I'm kinda thirsty for a cup of hot coffee. (*She puts the coffee pot on the burner*)
DOC   Lenny—
LENNY   What?
DOC   (*Not able to go on*)   Ah . . .
LENNY   Yes?
DOC   Here, some pecans for you. (*He hands her the sack*)
LENNY   Why, thank you, Doc. I love pecans.
DOC   My wife and Scott picked them up around the yard.
LENNY   Well, I can use them to make a pie. A pecan pie.
DOC   Yeah. Look, Lenny, I've got some bad news for you.
LENNY   What?

DOC   Well, you know, you've been keeping Billy Boy out on our farm; he's been grazing out there.

LENNY   Yes—

DOC   Well, last night, Billy Boy died.

LENNY   He died?

DOC   Yeah. I'm sorry to tell you when you've got all this on you, but I thought you'd want to know.

LENNY   Well, yeah I do. He died?

DOC   Uh huh. He was struck by lightning.

LENNY   Struck by lightning? In that storm yesterday?

DOC   That's what we think.

LENNY   Gosh, struck by lightning. I've had Billy Boy so long. You know. Ever since I was ten years old.

DOC   Yeah. He was a mighty old horse.

LENNY (*Stung*)   Mighty old.

DOC   Almost twenty years old.

LENNY   That's right, twenty years. 'Cause; ah, I'm thirty years old today. Did you know that?

DOC   No, Lenny, I didn't know. Happy birthday.

LENNY   Thanks. (*She begins to cry*)

DOC   Oh, come on now, Lenny. Come on. Hey, hey, now. You know I can't stand it when you MaGrath women start to cry. You know it just gets me.

LENNY   Oh ho! Sure! You mean when Meg cries! Meg's the one you could never stand to watch cry! Not me! I could fill up a pig's trough!

DOC   Now, Lenny . . . stop it. Come on. Jesus!

LENNY   Okay! Okay! I don't know what's wrong with me. I don't mean to make a scene. I've been on this crying jag. (*She blows her nose*)   All this stuff with Babe, and Old Granddaddy's gotten worse in the hospital, and I can't get in touch with Meg.

DOC   You tried calling Meggy?

LENNY   Yes.

DOC   Is she coming home?

LENNY   Who knows. She hasn't called me. That's what I'm waiting here for—hoping she'll call.

DOC   She still living in California?

LENNY   Yes; in Hollywood.

DOC   Well, give me a call if she gets in. I'd like to see her.

LENNY   Oh, you would, huh?

DOC   Yeah, Lenny, sad to say, but I would.

LENNY   It is sad. It's very sad indeed.

(They stare at each other, then look away. There is a moment of tense silence)

DOC Hey, Jell-O Face, your coffee's boiling.

LENNY *(Going to check)* Oh, it is? Thanks. *(After she checks the pot)* Look, you'd better go on and pick Scott up. You don't want him to have to wait for you.

DOC Yeah, you're right. Poor kid. It's his first time at the dentist.

LENNY Poor thing.

DOC Well, 'bye. I'm sorry to have to tell you about your horse.

LENNY Oh, I know. Tell Joan thanks for picking up the pecans.

DOC I will. *(He starts to leave)*

LENNY Oh, how's the baby?

DOC She's fine. Real pretty. She, ah, holds your finger in her hand; like this.

LENNY Oh, that's cute.

DOC Yeah. 'Bye, Lenny.

LENNY 'Bye.

(DOC exits. LENNY stares after him for a moment, then goes and sits back down at the kitchen table. She reaches into her pocket and pulls out a somewhat crumbled cookie and a wax candle. She lights the candle again, lets the wax drip onto the cookie, then sticks the candle on top of the cookie. She beings to sing the "Happy Birthday" song to herself. At the end of the song she pauses, silently makes a wish, and blows out the candle. She waits a moment, then relights the candle, and repeats her actions, only this time making a different wish at the end of the song. She starts to repeat the procedure for the third time, as the phone rings. She goes to answer it)

LENNY Hello . . . oh, hello, Lucille, how's Zackery? . . . Oh, no! . . . Oh, I'm so sorry. Of course, it must be grueling for you . . . Yes, I understand. Your only brother . . . No, she's not here yet. Chick just went to pick her up . . . Oh, now, Lucille, she's still his wife, I'm sure she'll be interested . . . Well, you can just tell me the information and I'll relate it all to her . . . Uh hum, his liver's saved. Oh, that's good news! . . . Well, of course, when you look at it like that . . . Breathing stabilized . . . Damage to the spinal column, not yet determined . . . Okay . . . Yes, Lucille, I've got it all down . . . Uh huh, I'll give her that message. 'Bye, 'bye.

(LENNY drops the pencil and paper. She sighs deeply, wipes her cheeks with the back of her hand, and goes to the stove to pour

herself a cup of coffee. After a few moments, the front door is heard slamming. LENNY *starts. A whistle is heard, then* MEG'S *voice*)

MEG'S VOICE   I'm home! (*She whistles the family whistle*)   Anybody home?

LENNY   Meg? Meg?

(MEG, *twenty-seven, enters from the dining room. She has sad, magic eyes and wears a hat. She carries a worn-out suitcase*)

MEG (*Dropping her suitcase, running to hug* LENNY)   Lenny—

LENNY   Well, Meg! Why, Meg! Oh, Meggy! Why didn't you call? Did you fly in? You didn't take a cab, did you? Why didn't you give us a call?

MEG (*Overlapping*)   Oh, Lenny! Why, Lenny! Dear Lenny! (*Then she looks at* LENNY's *face*)   My God, we're getting so old! Oh, I called, for heaven's sake. Of course, I called!

LENNY   Well, I never talked to you—

MEG   Well, I know! I let the phone ring right off the hook!

LENNY   Well, as a matter of fact, I was out most of the morning seeing to Babe—

MEG   Now, just what's all this business about Babe? How could you send me such a telegram about Babe? And Zackery! You say somebody's shot Zackery?

LENNY   Yes, they have.

MEG   Well, good Lord! Is he dead?

LENNY   No, but he's in the hospital. He was shot in the stomach.

MEG   In his stomach! How awful! Do they know who shot him? (LENNY *nods.*)   Well, who? Who was it? Who? Who?

LENNY   Babe! They're all saying Babe shot him! They took her to jail! And they're saying she shot him! They're all saying it! It's horrible! It's awful!

MEG (*Overlapping*)   Jail! Good Lord, jail! Well, who? Who's saying it? Who?

LENNY   Everyone! The policemen, the sheriff, Zackery, even Babe's saying it! Even Babe herself!

MEG   Well, for God's sake. For God's sake.

LENNY (*Overlapping as she falls apart*)   It's horrible! It's horrible! It's just horrible!

MEG   Now calm down, Lenny. Just calm down. Would you like a Coke? Here, I'll get you some Coke. (*She gets a Coke from the refrigerator. She opens it and downs a large swig*)   Why? Why would she shoot him? Why? (*She hands the Coke bottle to* LENNY)

LENNY I talked to her this morning, and I asked her that very question. I said, Babe, why would you shoot Zackery? He was your own husband. Why would you shoot him? And do you know what she said? (MEG *shakes her head*) She said, " 'Cause I didn't like his looks. I just didn't like his looks."

MEG (*After a pause*) Well, I don't like his looks.

LENNY But you didn't shoot him! You wouldn't shoot a person 'cause you didn't like their looks! You wouldn't do that! Oh, I hate to say this—I do hate to say this—but I believe Babe is ill. I mean in-her-head ill.

MEG Oh, now, Lenny, don't you say that! There're plenty of good sane reasons to shoot another person, and I'm sure that Babe had one. Now, what we've got to do is get the best lawyer in town. Do you have any ideas on who's the best lawyer in town?

LENNY Well, Zackery, is, of course; but he's been shot!

MEG Well, count him out! Just count him and his whole firm out!

LENNY Anyway, you don't have to worry, she's already got her lawyer.

MEG She does? Who?

LENNY Barnette Lloyd. Annie Lloyd's boy. He just opened his office here in town. And Uncle Watson said we'd be doing Annie a favor by hiring him up.

MEG Doing Annie a favor? Doing Annie a favor? Well, what about Babe? Have you thought about Babe? Do we want to do her a favor of thirty or forty years in jail? Have you thought about that?

LENNY Now, don't snap at me! Just don't snap at me! I try to do what's right! All this responsibility keeps falling on my shoulders, and I try to do what's right!

MEG Well, boo hoo, hoo, hoo! And how in the hell could you send me such a telegram about Babe!

LENNY Well, if you had a phone, or if you didn't live way out there in Hollywood and not even come home for Christmas, maybe I wouldn't have to pay all that money to send you a telegram!

MEG (*Overlapping*) BABE'S IN TERRIBLE TROUBLE—STOP! ZACKERY'S BEEN SHOT—STOP! COME HOME IMMEDIATELY —STOP! STOP! STOP!

LENNY And what was that you said about how old we're getting? When you looked at my face, you said, My God, we're getting so old! But you didn't mean we—you meant me! Didn't you? I'm thirty years old today and my face is getting pinched up and my hair is falling out in the comb.

MEG Why, Lenny! It's your birthday, October 23. How could I forget. Happy birthday!

LENNY   Well, it's not. I'm thirty years old and Billy Boy died last night. He was struck by lightning. He was struck dead.

MEG (*Reaching for a cigarette*)   Struck dead. Oh, what a mess. What a mess. Are you really thirty? Then I must be twenty-seven and Babe is twenty-four. My God, we're getting so old.

(*They are silent for several moments as* MEG *drags off her cigarette and* LENNY *drinks her coke*)

MEG   What's the cot doing in the kitchen?

LENNY   Well, I rolled it out when Old Granddaddy got sick. So I could be close and hear him at night if he needed something.

MEG (*Glancing toward the door leading to the downstairs bedroom*)   Is Old Granddaddy here?

LENNY   Why, no. Old Granddaddy's at the hospital.

MEG   Again?

LENNY   Meg!

MEG   What?

LENNY   I wrote you all about it. He's been in the hospital over three months straight.

MEG   He has?

LENNY   Don't you remember? I wrote you about all those blood vessels popping in his brain?

MEG   Popping—

LENNY   And how he was so anxious to hear from you and to find out about your singing career. I wrote it all to you. How they have to feed him through those tubes now. Didn't you get my letters?

MEG   Oh, I don't know, Lenny. I guess I did. To tell you the truth, sometimes I kinda don't read your letters.

LENNY   What?

MEG   I'm sorry. I used to read them. It's just, since Christmas reading them gives me slicing pains right here in my chest.

LENNY   I see. I see. Is that why you didn't use that money Old Grand-daddy sent you to come home Christmas; because you hate us so much? We never did all that much to make you hate us. We didn't!

MEG   Oh, Lenny! Do you think I'd be getting slicing pains in my chest if I didn't care about you? If I hated you? Honestly, now, do you think I would?

LENNY   No.

MEG   Okay, then. Let's drop it. I'm sorry I didn't read your letters, Okay?

LENNY   Okay.

MEG   Anyway, we've got this whole thing with Babe to deal with. The first thing is to get her a good lawyer and get her out of jail.

LENNY   Well, she's out of jail.

MEG   She is?

LENNY   That young lawyer, he's gotten her out.

MEG   Oh, he has?

LENNY   Yes, on bail. Uncle Watson's put it up. Chick's bringing her back right now—she's driving her home.

MEG   Oh; well, that's a relief.

LENNY   Yes, and they're due home any minute now; so we can just wait right here for 'em.

MEG   Well, good. That's good. (As she leans against the counter)   So, Babe shot Zackery Botrelle, the richest and most powerful man in all of Hazlehurst, slap in the gut. It's hard to believe.

LENNY   It certainly is. Little Babe—shooting off a gun.

MEG   Little Babe.

LENNY   She was always the prettiest and most perfect of the three of us. Old Granddaddy used to call her his Dancing Sugar Plum. Why, remember how proud and happy he was the day she married Zackery.

MEG   Yes, I remember. It was his finest hour.

LENNY   He remarked how Babe was gonna skyrocket right to the heights of Hazlehurst society. And how Zackery was just the right man for her whether she knew it or not.

MEG   Oh, Lordy, Lordy. And what does Old Granddaddy say now?

LENNY   Well, I haven't had the courage to tell him all about this as yet. I thought maybe tonight we could go to visit him at the hospital, and you could talk to him and . . .

MEG   Yeah; well, we'll see. We'll see. Do we have anything to drink around here—to the tune of straight bourbon?

LENNY   No. There's no liquor.

MEG   Hell. (She gets a Coke from the refrigerator and opens it)

LENNY   Then you will go with me to see Old Granddaddy at the hospital tonight?

MEG   Of course. (She goes to her purse and gets out a bottle of Empirin. She takes out a tablet and puts it on her tongue)   Brother, I know he's gonna go on about my singing career. Just like he always does.

LENNY   Well, how is your career going?

MEG   It's not.

LENNY   Why, aren't you still singing at that club down on Malibu beach?

MEG   No, not since Christmas.

LENNY   Well, then, are you singing someplace new?

MEG   No, I'm not singing. I'm not singing at all.

LENNY   Oh. Well, what do you do then?

MEG   What I do is I pay cold-storage bills for a dog-food company. That's what I do.

LENNY (*Trying to be helpful*)   Gosh, don't you think it'd be a good idea to stay in the show business field?

MEG   Oh, maybe.

LENNY   Like Old Granddaddy says, "With your talent, all you need is exposure. Then you can make your own breaks!" Did you hear his suggestion about getting your foot put in one of those blocks of cement they've got out there? He thinks that's real important.

MEG   Yeah. I think I've heard that. And I'll probably hear it again when I go to visit him at the hospital tonight; so let's just drop it. Okay? (*She notices the sack of pecans*)   What's this? Pecans? Great, I love pecans! (*She takes out two pecans and tries to open them by cracking them together*)   Come on . . . Crack, you demons! Crack!

LENNY   We have a nutcracker!

MEG (*Trying with her teeth*)   Ah, where's the sport in a nutcracker? What's the challenge?

LENNY (*Getting the nutcracker*)   It's over here in the utensil drawer.

(*As* LENNY *gets the nutcracker,* MEG *opens the pecan by stepping on it with her shoe*)

MEG   There! Open! (*She picks the crumbled pecan and eats it*)   Mmmm, delicious, Delicious, Where'd you get the fresh pecans?

LENNY   Oh . . . I don't know.

MEG   They sure are tasty.

LENNY   Doc Porter brought them over.

MEG   Doc. What's Doc doing here in town?

LENNY   Well, his father died a couple of months ago. Now he's back home seeing to his property.

MEG   Gosh, the last I heard of Doc, he was up in the East painting the walls of houses to earn a living. (*Amused*)   Heard he was living with some Yankee woman who made clay pots.

LENNY   Joan.

MEG   What?

LENNY   Her name's Joan. She came down here with him. That's one of her pots. Doc's married to her.

MEG   Married—

LENNY   Uh huh.

MEG   Doc married a Yankee?

LENNY   That's right; and they've got two kids.

MEG   Kids—

LENNY   A boy and a girl.

MEG   God. Then his kids must be half Yankee.

LENNY   I suppose.

MEG   God. That really gets me. I don't know why, but somehow that really gets me.

LENNY   I don't know why it should.

MEG   And what a stupid-looking pot! Who'd buy it, anyway?

LENNY   Wait—I think that's them. Yeah, that's Chick's car! Oh, there's Babe! Hello, Babe! They're home, Meg! They're home.

(MEG *hides*)

BABE'S VOICE   Lenny! I'm home! I'm free!

(BABE, *twenty-four, enters exuberantly. She has an angelic face and fierce, volatile eyes. She carries a pink pocketbook*)

BABE   I'm home!

(MEG *jumps out of hiding*)

BABE   Oh, Meg—Look, it's Meg! (*Running to hug her*)   Meg! When did you get home?

MEG   Just now!

BABE   Well, it's so good to see you! I'm so glad you're home! I'm so relieved.

(CHICK *enters*)

MEG   Why, Chick; hello.

CHICK   Hello, cousin Margaret. What brings you back to Hazlehurst?

MEG   Oh, I came on home . . . (*Turning to* BABE)   I came on home to see about Babe.

BABE (*Running to hug* MEG)   Oh, Meg—

MEG   How are things with you, Babe?

CHICK   Well, they are dismal, if you want my opinion. She is refusing to cooperate with her lawyer, that nice-looking young Lloyd boy. She won't tell any of us why she committed this heinous crime, except to say that she didn't like Zackery's looks—

BABE   Oh, look, Lenny brought my suitcase from home! And my saxophone! Thank you! (*She runs over to the cot and gets out her saxophone*)

CHICK   Now, that young lawyer is coming over here this afternoon, and when he gets here he expects to get some concrete answers! That's what he expects! No more of this nonsense and stubbornness from you, Rebecca MaGrath, or they'll put you in jail and throw away the key!

B A B E (*Overlapping to* M E G) Meg, come look at my new saxophone. I went to Jackson and bought it used. Feel it. It's so heavy.

M E G (*Overlapping* C H I C K) It's beautiful.

(*The room goes silent*)

C H I C K Isn't that right, won't they throw away the key?

L E N N Y Well, honestly, I don' know about that—

C H I C K They will! And leave you there to rot. So, Rebecca, what are you going to tell Mr. Lloyd about shooting Zackery when he gets here? What are your reasons going to be?

B A B E (*Glaring*) That I didn't like his looks! I just didn't like his stinking looks! And I don't like yours much, either, Chick the Stick! So just leave me alone! I mean it! Leave me alone! Ooooh! (*She exits up the stairs*)

(*There is a long moment of silence*)

C H I C K Well, I was only trying to warn her that she's going to have to help herself. It's just that she doesn't understand how serious the situation is. Does she? She doesn't have the vaguest idea. Does she, now?

L E N N Y Well, it's true, she does seem a little confused.

C H I C K And that's putting it mildly, Lenny honey. That's putting it mighty mild. So, Margaret, how's your singing career going? We keep looking for your picture in the movie magazines.

(M E G *moves to light a cigarette*)

C H I C K You know, you shouldn't smoke. It causes cancer. Cancer of the lungs. They say each cigarette is just a little stick of cancer. A little death stick.

M E G That's what I like about it, Chick—taking a drag off of death. (*She takes a long, deep drag*) Mmmm! Gives me a sense of controlling my own destiny. What power! What exhilaration! Want a drag?

L E N N Y (*Trying to break the tension*) Ah, Zackery's liver's been saved! His sister called up and said his liver was saved. Isn't that good news?

M E G Well, yes, that's fine news. Mighty fine news. Why, I've been told that the liver's a powerful important bodily organ. I believe it's used to absorb all of our excess bile.

L E N N Y Yes—well—it's been saved.

(*The phone rings.* L E N N Y *gets it*)

MEG So! Did you hear all that good news about the liver, Little Chicken?

CHICK I heard it. And don't you call me Chicken! (MEG *clucks like a chicken*) I've told you a hundred times if I've told you once not to call me Chicken. You cannot call me Chicken.

LENNY . . . Oh, no! . . . Of course, we'll be right over! 'Bye! (*She hangs up the phone*) That was Annie May—Peekay and Buck Jr. have eaten paint!

CHICK Oh, no! Are they all right? They're not sick? They're not sick, are they?

LENNY I don't know. I don't know. Come on. We've got to run on next door.

CHICK (*Overlapping*) Oh, God! Oh, please! Please let them be all right! Don't let them die! Please, don't let them die!

(CHICK *runs off howling, with* LENNY *following after.* MEG *sits alone, finishing her cigarette. After a moment,* BABE'S *voice is heard*)

BABE'S VOICE Pst—Psst!

(MEG *looks around.* BABE *comes tiptoeing down the stairs*)

BABE Has she gone?

MEG She's gone. Peekay and Buck Jr. just ate their paints.

BABE What idiots.

MEG Yeah.

BABE You know, Chick's hated us ever since we had to move here from Vicksburg to live with Old Grandmama and Old Granddaddy.

MEG She's an idiot.

BABE Yeah. Do you know what she told me this morning while I was still behind bars and couldn't get away?

MEG What?

BABE She told me how embarrassing it was for her all those years ago, you know, when Mama—

MEG Yeah, down in the cellar.

BABE She said our mama had shamed the entire family, and we were known notoriously all through Hazlehurst. (*About to cry*) Then she went on to say how I would now be getting just as much bad publicity, and humiliating her and the family all over again.

MEG Ah, forget it, Babe. Just forget it.

BABE I told her, "Mama got national coverage! National!" And if Zackery wasn't a senator from Copiah County, I probably wouldn't even be getting statewide.

MEG   Of course you wouldn't.

BABE (*After a pause*)   Gosh, sometimes I wonder . . .

MEG   What?

BABE   Why she did it. Why Mama hung herself.

MEG   I don't know. She had a bad day. A real bad day. You know how it feels on a real bad day.

BABE   And that old yellow cat. It was sad about that old cat.

MEG   Yeah.

BABE   I bet if Daddy hadn't of left us, they'd still be alive.

MEG   Oh, I don't know.

BABE   'Cause it was after he left that she started spending whole days just sitting there and smoking on the back porch steps. She'd sling her ashes down onto the different bugs and ants that'd be passing by.

MEG   Yeah. Well, I'm glad he left.

BABE   That old yellow cat'd stay back there with her. I thought if she felt something for anyone it woulda been that old cat. Guess I musta been mistaken.

MEG   God, he was a bastard. Really, with his white teeth. Daddy was such a bastard.

BABE   Was he? I don't remember.

(MEG *blows a mouthful of smoke*)

BABE (*After a moment, uneasily*)   I think I'm gonna make some lemonade. You want some?

MEG   Sure.

(BABE *cuts lemons, dumps sugar, stirs ice cubes, etc., throughout the following exchange*)

MEG   Babe. Why won't you talk? Why won't you tell anyone about shooting Zackery?

BABE   Oooh—

MEG   Why not? You must have had a good reason. Didn't you?

BABE   I guess I did.

MEG   Well, what was it?

BABE   I . . . I can't say.

MEG   Why not? (*Pause*)   Babe, why not? You can tell me.

BABE   'Cause . . . I'm sort of . . . protecting someone.

MEG   Protecting someone? Oh, Babe, then you really didn't shoot him! I knew you couldn't have done it! I knew it!

BABE   No, I shot him. I shot him all right. I meant to kill him. I was aiming for his heart, but I guess my hands were shaking and I—just got him in the stomach.

MEG (*Collapsing*) I see.

BABE (*Stirring the lemonade*) So I'm guilty. And I'm just gonna have to take my punishment and go to jail.

MEG Oh, Babe—

BABE Don't worry, Meg, jail's gonna be a relief to me. I can learn to play my new saxophone. I won't have to live with Zackery anymore. And I won't have his snoopy old sister, Lucille, coming over and pushing me around. Jail will be a relief. Here's your lemonade.

MEG Thanks.

BABE It taste okay?

MEG Perfect.

BABE I like a lot of sugar in mine. I'm gonna add some more sugar.

(BABE *goes to add more sugar to her lemonade as* LENNY *bursts through the back door in a state of excitement and confusion*)

LENNY Well, it looks like the paint is primarily on their arms and faces, but Chick wants me to drive them all over to Dr. Winn's just to make sure. (*She grabs her car keys from the counter, and as she does so, she notices the mess of lemons and sugar*) Oh, now, Babe, try not to make a mess here; and be careful with this sharp knife. Honestly, all that sugar's gonna get you sick. Well, 'bye, 'bye. I'll be back as soon as I can.

MEG 'Bye, Lenny.

BABE 'Bye.

(LENNY *exits*)

BABE Boy, I don't know what's happening to Lenny.

MEG What do you mean?

BABE "Don't make a mess; don't make yourself sick; don't cut yourself with that sharp knife." She's turning into Old Grandmama.

MEG You think so?

BABE More and more. Do you know she's taken to wearing Old Grandmama's torn sunhat and her green garden gloves?

MEG Those old lime-green ones?

BABE Yeah; she works out in the garden wearing the lime-green gloves of a dead woman. Imagine wearing those gloves on your hands.

MEG Poor Lenny. She needs some love in her life. All she does is work out at that brick yard and take care of Old Granddaddy.

BABE Yeah, but she's so shy with men.

MEG (*Biting into an apple*) Probably because of that *shrunken* ovary she has.

BABE (*Slinging ice cubes*) Yeah, that *deformed* ovary.

MEG Old Granddaddy's the one who's made her feel self-conscious about it. It's his fault. The old fool.

BABE It's so sad.

MEG God—you know what?

BABE What?

MEG I bet Lenny's never even slept with a man. Just think, thirty years old and never even had it once.

BABE (*Slyly*) Oh, I don't know. Maybe she's . . . had it once.

MEG She has?

BABE Maybe. I think so.

MEG When? When?

BABE Well . . . maybe I shouldn't say—

MEG Babe!

BABE (*Rapidly telling the story*) All right, then. It was after Old Granddaddy went back to the hospital this second time. Lenny was really in a state of deep depression, I could tell that she was. Then one day she calls me up and asks me to come over and to bring along my Polaroid camera. Well, when I arrive she's waiting for me out there in the sun parlor wearing her powder-blue Sunday dress and this old curled-up wig. She confided that she was gonna try sending in her picture to one of those lonely-hearts clubs.

MEG Oh, my God.

BABE Lonely Hearts of the South. She'd seen their ad in a magazine.

MEG Jesus.

BABE Anyway, I take some snapshots and she sends them on in to the club, and about two weeks later she receives in the mail this whole load of pictures of available men, most of 'em fairly odd-looking. But of course she doesn't call any of 'em up 'cause she's real shy. But one of 'em, this Charlie Hill from Memphis, Tennessee, he calls her.

MEG He does?

BABE Yeah. And time goes on and she says he's real funny on the phone, so they decide to get together to meet.

MEG Yeah?

BABE Well, he drives down here to Hazlehurst 'bout three or four different times and has supper with her; then one weekend she goes up to Memphis to visit him, and I think that is where it happened.

MEG What makes you think so?

BABE Well, when I went to pick her up from the bus depot, she ran off the bus and threw her arms around me and started crying and sobbing as though she'd like to never stop. I asked her, I said "Lenny, what's the matter?" And she, "I've done it, Babe! Honey, I have done it!"

MEG (*Whispering*)   And you think she meant that she'd done *it*?
BABE (*Whispering back, slyly*)   I think so.
MEG   Well, goddamn!

(*They laugh*)

BABE   But she didn't say anything else about it. She just went on to tell me about the boot factory where Charlie worked and what a nice city Memphis was.
MEG   So, what happened to this Charlie?
BABE   Well, he came to Hazlehurst just one more time. Lenny took him over to meet Old Granddaddy at the hospital, and after that they broke it off.
MEG   'Cause of Old Granddaddy?
MEG   Well, she said it was on account of her missing ovary. That Charlie didn't want to marry her on account of it.
MEG   Ah, how mean. How hateful.
BABE   Oh, it was. He seemed like such a nice man, too—kinda chubby, with red hair and freckles, always telling these funny jokes.
MEG   Hmmm, that just doesn't seem right. Something about that doesn't seem exactly right. (*She paces about the kitchen and comes across the box of candy* LENNY *got for her birthday*)   Oh, God. "Happy Birthday to Lenny, from the Buck Boyles."
BABE   Oh, no! Today's Lenny's birthday!
MEG   That's right.
BABE   I forgot all about it!
MEG   I know. I did too.
BABE   Gosh, we'll have to order up a big cake for her. She always loves to make those wishes on her birthday cake.
MEG   Yeah, let's get her a big cake! A huge one! (*Suddenly noticing the plastic wrapper on the candy box*)   Oh, God, that Chick's so cheap!
BABE   What do you mean?
MEG   This plastic has poinsettias on it!
BABE (*Running to see*)   Oh, let me see—(*She looks at the package with disgust*)   Boy, oh boy! I'm calling that bakery and ordering the very largest size cake they have! That jumbo deluxe!
MEG   Good!
BABE   Why, I imagine they can make one up to be about—*this* big. (*She demonstrates*)
MEG   Oh, at least; at least that big. Why, maybe it'll even be *this* big. (*She makes a very, very, very large-size cake*)
BABE   You think it could be *that* big?
MEG   Sure!

BABE (*After a moment, getting the idea*) Or, or what if it were *this* big! (*She maps out a cake that covers the room.*) What if we get the cake and it's *this* big? (*She gulps down a fistful of cake*) Gulp! Gulp! Gulp! Tasty treat!

MEG Hmmm—I'll have me some more! Give me some more of that birthday cake.

(*Suddenly there is a loud knock at the door*)

BARNETTE'S VOICE Hello . . . Hello! May I come in?

BABE (*To* MEG, *in a whisper, as she takes cover*) Who's that?

MEG I don't know.

BARNETTE (*He is still knocking*) Hello! Hello, Mrs. Botrelle!

BABE Oh, shoot! It's that lawyer. I don't want to see him.

MEG Oh, Babe, come on. You've got to see him sometime.

BABE No, I don't. (*She starts up the stairs*) Just tell him I died. I'm going upstairs.

MEG Oh, Babe! Will you come back here!

BABE (*As she exits*) You talk to him, please, Meg. Please! I just don't want to see him—

MEG Babe—Babe! Oh, shit . . . Ah, come on in! Door's open!

(BARNETTE LLOYD, *twenty-six, enters carrying a briefcase. He is a slender, intelligent young man with an almost fanatical intensity that he subdues by sheer will*)

BARNETTE How do you do. I'm Barnette Lloyd.

MEG Pleased to meet you. I'm Meg MaGrath, Babe's older sister.

BABE Yes, I know. You're the singer.

MEG Well, yes . . .

BARNETTE I came to hear you five different times when you were singing at that club in Biloxi. Greeny's I believe was the name of it.

MEG Yes, Greeny's.

BARNETTE You were very good. There was something sad and moving about how you sang those songs. It was like you had some sort of vision. Some special sort of vision.

MEG Well, thank you. You're very kind. Now . . . about Babe's case—

BARNETTE Yes?

MEG We've just got to win it.

BARNETTE I intend to.

MEG Of course. But, ah . . . (*She looks at him*) Ah, you know, you're very young.

BARNETTE Yes. I am. I'm young.

MEG   It's just, I'm concerned, Mr. Lloyd—

BARNETTE   Barnette. Please.

MEG   Barnette; that, ah, just maybe we need someone with, well, with more experience. Someone totally familiar with all the ins and outs and the this and thats of the legal dealings and such. As that.

BARNETTE   Ah, you have reservations.

MEG (*Relieved*)   Reservations. Yes, I have . . . reservations.

BARNETTE   Well, possibly it would help you to know that I graduated first in my class from Ole Miss Law School. I also spent three different summers taking advanced courses in criminal law at Harvard Law School. I made A's in all the given courses. I was fascinated!

MEG   I'm sure.

BARNETTE   And even now, I've just completed one year working with Jackson's top criminal law firm, Manchester and Wayne. I was invaluable to them. Indispensable. They offered to double my percentage if I'd stay on; but I refused. I wanted to return to Hazlehurst and open my own office. The reason being, and this is a key point, that I have a personal vendetta to settle with one Zackery F. Botrelle.

MEG   A personal vendetta?

BARNETTE   Yes, ma'am. You are correct. Indeed, I do.

MEG   Hmmm. A personal vendetta . . . I think I like that. So you have some sort of a personal vendetta to settle with Zackery?

BARNETTE   Precisely. Just between the two of us, I not only intend to keep that sorry s.o.b. from ever being reelected to the state senate by exposing his shady, criminal dealings; but I also intend to decimate his personal credibility by exposing him as a bully, a brute, and a red-neck thug!

MEG   Well; I can see that you're—fanatical about this.

BARNETTE   Yes, I am. I'm sorry if I seem outspoken. but for some reason I feel I can talk to you . . . those songs you sang. Excuse me; I feel like a jackass.

MEG   It's all right. Relax. Relax, Barnette. Let me think this out a minute. (*She takes out a cigarette. He lights it for her*)   Now just exactly how do you intend to get Babe off? You know, keep her out of jail.

BARNETTE   It seems to me that we can get her off with a plea of self-defense, or possibly we could go with innocent by reason of temporary insanity. But basically I intend to prove that Zackery Botrelle brutalized and tormented this poor woman to such an extent that she had no recourse but to defend herself in the only way she knew how!

MEG   I like that!

BARNETTE   Then, of course, I'm hoping this will break the ice and we'll be able to go on to prove that the man's a total criminal, as well as an abusive bully and contemptible slob!

MEG   That sounds good! To me that sounds very good!

BARNETTE   It's just our basic game plan.

MEG   But now, how are you going to prove all this about Babe being brutalized? We don't want anyone perjured. I mean to commit perjury.

BARNETTE   Perjury? According to my sources, there'll be no need for perjury.

MEG   You mean it's the truth?

BARNETTE   This is a small town, Miss MaGrath. The word gets out.

MEG   It's really the truth?

BARNETTE (*Opening his briefcase*)   Just look at this. It's a photostatic copy of Mrs. Botrelle's medical chart over the past four years. Take a good look at it, if you want your blood to boil!

MEG (*Looking over the chart*)   What! What! This is maddening. This is madness! Did he do this to her! I'll kill him; I will—I'll fry his blood! Did he do this?

BARNETTE (*Alarmed*)   To tell you the truth, I can't say for certain what was accidental and what was not. That's why I need to talk with Mrs. Botrelle. That's why it's very important that I see her!

MEG (*Her eyes are wild, as she shoves him toward the door*)   Well, look, I've got to see her first. I've got to talk to her first. What I'll do is I'll give you a call. Maybe you can come back over later on—

BARNETTE   Well, then, here's my card—

MEG   Okay. Goodbye.

BARNETTE   'Bye!

MEG   Oh, wait! There's one problem with you.

BARNETTE   What?

MEG   What if you get so fanatically obsessed with this vendetta thing that you forget about Babe? You forget about her and sell her down the river just to get at Zackery. What about that?

BARNETTE   I—wouldn't do that.

MEG   You wouldn't?

BARNETTE   No.

MEG   Why not?

BARNETTE   Because I'm—I'm fond of her.

MEG   What do you mean you're fond of her?

BARNETTE   Well, she . . . she sold me a pound cake at a bazaar once. And I'm fond of her.

MEG   All right; I believe you. Goodbye.

BARNETTE   Goodbye. (*He exits*)

MEG   Babe! Babe, come down here! Babe!

(BABE *comes hurrying down the stairs*)

BABE What? What is it? I called about the cake—

MEG What did Zackery do to you?

BABE They can't have it for today.

MEG Did he hurt you? Did he? Did he do that?

BABE Oh, Meg, please—

MEG Did he? Goddamnit, Babe—

BABE Yes he did.

MEG Why? Why?

BABE I don't know! He started hating me, 'cause I couldn't laugh at his jokes. I just started finding it impossible to laugh at his jokes the way I used to. And then the sound of his voice got to where it tired me out awful bad to hear it. I'd fall asleep just listening to him at the dinner table. He'd say, "Hand me some of that gravy!" Or, "This roast beef is too damn bloody." And suddenly, I'd be out cold like a light.

MEG Oh, Babe. Babe, this is very important. I want you to sit down here and tell me what happened right before you shot Zackery. That's right, just sit down and tell me.

BABE (*After a pause*) I told you, I can't tell you on account of I'm protecting someone.

MEG But, Babe, you've just got to talk to someone about all this. You just do.

BABE Why?

MEG Because it's a human need. To talk about our lives. It's an important human need.

BABE Oh. Well, I do feel like I want to talk to someone. I do.

MEG Then talk to me; please.

BABE (*Making a decision*) All right. (*After thinking a minute*) I don't know where to start.

MEG Just start at the beginning. Just there at the beginning.

BABE (*After a moment*) Well, do you remember Willie Jay? (MEG *shakes her head*) Cora's youngest boy?

MEG Oh, yeah, that little kid we used to pay a nickel to, to run down to the drugstore and bring us back a cherry Coke.

BABE Right. Well, Cora irons at my place on Wednesdays now, and she just happened to mention that Willie Jay'd picked up this old stray dog and that he'd gotten real fond of him. But now they couldn't afford to feed him anymore. So she was gonna have to tell Willie Jay to set him loose in the woods.

MEG (*Trying to be patient*) Uh huh.

BABE Well, I said I liked dogs, and if he wanted to bring the dog over here, I'd take care of him. You see, I was alone by myself most of the time 'cause the senate was in session and Zackery was up in Jackson.

MEG Uh huh. (*She reaches for* LENNY's *box of birthday candy. She takes little nibbles out of each piece throughout the rest of the scene*)

BABE So the next day, Willie Jay brings over this skinny old dog with these little crossed eyes. Well, I asked Willie Jay what his name was, and he said they called him Dog. Well, I liked the name, so I thought I'd keep it.

MEG (*Getting up*) Uh huh. I'm listening. I'm just gonna get me a glass of cold water. Do you want some?

BABE Okay.

MEG So you kept the name—Dog.

BABE Yeah. Anyway, when Willie Jay was leaving he gave Dog a hug and said, "Goodbye, Dog. You're a fine ole dog." Well, I felt something for him, so I told Willie Jay he could come back and visit with Dog any time he wanted, and his face just kinda lit right up.

MEG (*Offering the candy*) Candy—

BABE No, thanks. Anyhow, time goes on and Willie Jay keeps coming over and over. And we talk about Dog and how fat he's getting, and then, well, you know, things start up.

MEG No, I don't know. What things start up?

BABE Well, things start up. Like sex. Like that.

MEG Babe, wait a minute—Willie Jay's a boy. A small boy, about this tall. He's about this tall!

BABE No! Oh, no! He's taller now! He's fifteen now. When you knew him he was only about seven or eight.

MEG But even so—fifteen. And he's a black boy; a colored boy; a Negro.

BABE (*Flustered*) Well, I realize that, Meg. Why do you think I'm so worried about his getting public exposure? I don't want to ruin his reputation!

MEG I'm amazed, Babe. I'm really completely amazed. I didn't even know you were a liberal.

BABE Well, I'm not! I'm not a liberal! I'm a democratic! I was just lonely! I was so lonely. And he was good. Oh, he was so, so good. I'd never had it that good. We'd always go out into the garage and—

MEG It's okay. I've got the picture; I've got the picture! Now, let's just get back to the story. To yesterday, when you shot Zackery.

BABE All right, then. Let's see . . . Willie Jay was over. And it was after we'd—

MEG   Yeah! Yeah.

BABE   And we were just standing around on the back porch playing with Dog. Well, suddenly Zackery comes from around the side of the house. And he startled me 'cause he's supposed to be away at the office, and there he is coming from round the side of the house. Anyway, he says to Willie Jay, "Hey, boy, what are you doing back here?" And I say, "He's not doing anything. You just go on home, Willie Jay! You just run right on home." Well, before he can move, Zackery comes up and knocks him once right across the face and then shoves him down the porch steps, causing him to skin up his elbow real bad on that hard concrete. Then he says, "Don't you ever come around here again, or I'll have them cut out your gizzard!" Well, Willie Jay starts crying—these tears come streaming down his face—then he gets up real quick and runs away, with Dog following off after him. After that, I don't remember much too clearly; let's see . . . I went on into the living room, and I went right up to the davenport and opened the drawer where we keep the burglar gun . . . I took it out. Then I —I brought it up to my ear. That's right. I put it right inside my ear. Why, I was gonna shoot off my own head! That's what I was gonna do. Then I heard the back door slamming and suddenly, for some reason, I thought about Mama . . . how she'd hung herself. And here I was about ready to shoot myself. Then I realized—that's right, I realized how I didn't want to kill myself! And she—she probably didn't want to kill herself. She wanted to kill him, and I wanted to kill him, too. I wanted to kill Zackery, not myself. 'Cause I—I wanted to live! So I waited for him to come on into the living room. Then I held out the gun, and I pulled the trigger, aiming for his heart but getting him in the stomach. (*After a pause*)   It's funny that I really did that.

MEG   It's a good thing that you did. It's a damn good thing that you did.

BABE   It was.

MEG   Please, Babe, talk to Barnette Lloyd. Just talk to him and see if he can help.

BABE   But how about Willie Jay?

MEG   (*Starting toward the phone*)   Oh, he'll be all right. You just talk to that lawyer like you did to me. (*Looking at the number on the card, she begins dialing*)   See, 'cause he's gonna be on your side.

BABE   No! Stop, Meg, stop! Don't call him up! Please don't call him up! Please don't call him up! You can't! It's too awful. (*She runs over and jerks the bottom half of the phone away from* MEG)

(MEG *stands, holding the receiver*)

MEG   Babe!

(MEG *slams her half of the phone into the refrigerator*)

BABE   I just can't tell some stranger all about my personal life. I just can't.

MEG   Well, hell, Babe; you're the one who said you wanted to live.

BABE   That's right. I did. (*She takes the phone out of the refrigerator and hands it to* MEG)   Here's the other part of the phone. (*She moves to sit at the kitchen table*)

(MEG *takes the phone back to the counter.*

BABE (*As she fishes a piece of lemon out of her glass and begins sucking on it*)   Meg.

MEG   What?

BABE   I called the bakery. They're gonna have Lenny's cake ready first thing tomorrow morning. That's the earliest they can get it.

MEG   All right.

BABE   I told them to write on it, *Happy Birthday, Lenny—A Day Late.* That sound okay?

MEG (*At the phone*)   It sounds nice.

BABE   I ordered up the very largest size cake they have. I told them chocolate cake with white icing and red trim. Think she'll like that?

MEG (*Dialing the phone*)   Yeah, I'm sure she will. She'll like it.

BABE   I'm hoping.

ACT II

(*The lights go up on the kitchen. It is evening of the same day.* MEG'S *suitcase has been moved upstairs.* BABE'S *saxophone has been taken out of the case and put together.* BABE *and* BARNETTE *are sitting at the kitchen table.* BARNETTE *is writing and rechecking notes with explosive intensity.* BABE, *who has changed into a casual shift, sits eating a bowl of oatmeal, slowly*)

BARNETTE (*To himself*)   Mmmm huh! Yes! I see, I see! Well, we can work on that! And of course, this is mere conjecture! Difficult, if not impossible, to prove. Ha! Yes. Yes, indeed. Indeed—

BABE   Sure you don't want any oatmeal?

BARNETTE   What? Oh, no. No, thank you. Let's see; ah, where were we?

BABE   I just shot Zackery.

BARNETTE (*Looking at his notes*) Right. Correct. You've just pulled the trigger.

BABE Tell me, do you think Willie Jay can stay out of all this?

BARNETTE Believe me, it is in our interest to keep him as far out of this as possible.

BABE Good.

BARNETTE (*Throughout the following,* BARNETTE *stays glued to* BABE's *every word*) All right, you've just shot one Zackery Botrelle, as a result of his continual physical and mental abuse—what happens now?

BABE Well, after I shot him, I put the gun down on the piano bench, and then I went out into the kitchen and made up a pitcher of lemonade.

BARNETTE Lemonade?

BABE Yes, I was dying of thirst. My mouth was just as dry as a bone.

BARNETTE So in order to quench this raging thirst that was choking you dry and preventing any possibility of you uttering intelligible sounds or phrases, you went out to the kitchen and made up a pitcher of lemonade?

BABE Right. I made it just the way I like it, with lots of sugar and lots of lemon—and ten lemons in all. Then I added two trays of ice and stirred it up with my wooden stirring spoon.

BARNETTE Then what?

BABE Then I drank three glasses, one right after the other. They were large glasses—about this tall. Then suddenly my stomach kind of swole all up. I guess what caused it was all that sour lemon.

BARNETTE Could be.

BABE Then what I did was . . . I wiped my mouth off with the back of my hand, like this . . . (*She demonstrates*)

BARNETTE Hmmm.

BABE I did it to clear all those little beads of water that had settled there.

BARNETTE I see.

BABE Then I called out to Zackery. I said, "Zackery, I've made some lemonade. Can you use a glass?"

BARNETTE Did he answer? Did you hear an answer?

BABE No. He didn't answer.

BARNETTE So what'd you do?

BABE I poured him a glass anyway and took it out to him.

BARNETTE You took it out to the living room?

BABE I did. And there he was, lying on the rug. He was looking up at me trying to speak words. I said, "What? . . . Lemonade? . . .

You don't want it? Would you like a Coke instead?" Then I got the idea—he was telling me to call on the phone for medical help. So I got on the phone and called up the hospital. I gave my name and address, and I told them my husband was shot and he was lying on the rug and there was plenty of blood. (*She pauses a minute, as* BARNETTE *works frantically on his notes*)   I guess that's gonna look kinda bad.

BARNETTE   What?

BABE   Me fixing that lemonade before I called the hospital.

BARNETTE   Well, not . . . necessarily.

BABE   I tell you, I think the reason I made up the lemonade, I mean beside the fact that my mouth was bone dry, was that I was afraid to call the authorities. I was afraid. I—I really think I was afraid they would see that I had tried to shoot Zackery, in fact, that I *had* shot him, and they would accuse me of possible murder and send me away to jail.

BARNETTE   Well, that's understandable.

BABE   I think so. I mean, in fact, that's what did happen. That's what is happening—'cause here I am just about ready to go right off to the Parchment Prison Farm. Yes here I am just practically on the brink of utter doom. Why, I feel so all alone.

BARNETTE   Now, now, look—Why, there's no reason for you to get yourself so all upset and worried. Please don't. Please.

(*They look at each other for a moment*)

BARNETTE   You just keep filling in as much detailed information as you can about those incidents on the medical reports. That's all you need to think about. Don't you worry, Mrs. Botrelle, we're going to have a solid defense.

BABE   Please don't call me Mrs. Botrelle.

BARNETTE   All right.

BABE   My name's Becky. People in the family call me Babe, but my real name's Becky.

BARNETTE   All right, Becky.

(BARNETTE *and* BABE *stare at each other for a long moment*)

BABE   Are you sure you didn't go to Hazlehurst High?

BARNETTE   No, I went away to a boarding school.

BABE   Gosh, you sure do look familiar. You sure do.

BARNETTE   Well, I—I doubt you'll remember, but I did meet you once.

BABE   You did? When?

BARNETTE   At the Christmas bazaar, year before last. You were selling cakes and cookies and . . . candy.

BABE   Oh, yes! You bought the orange pound cake!

BARNETTE   Right.

BABE   Of course, and then we talked for a while. We talked about the
Christmas angel.

BARNETTE   You do remember.

BABE   I remember it very well. You were even thinner then than you
are now.

BARNETTE   Well, I'm surprised. I'm certainly . . . surprised.

(*The phone rings*)

BABE (*As she goes to answer the phone*)   This is quite a coincidence!
Don't you think it is? Why, it's almost a fluke. (*She answers the phone*)
Hello . . . Oh, hello, Lucille . . . Oh, he is? . . . Oh, he does? . . .
Okay. Oh, Lucille, wait! Has Dog come back to the house? . . . Oh,
I see . . . Okay. Okay. (*After a brief pause*)   Hello, Zackery? How
are you doing? . . . Uh huh . . . uh huh . . . Oh, I'm sorry . . .
Please don't scream . . . Uh huh . . . uh huh . . . You want what?
. . . No, I can't come up there now . . . Well, for one thing, I don't
even have the car. Lenny and Meg are up at the hospital right now,
visiting with Old Granddaddy . . . What? . . . Oh, really? . . . Oh,
really? . . . Well, I've got me a lawyer that's over here right now,
and he's building me up a solid defense! . . . Wait just a minute,
I'll see. (*To* BARNETTE)   He wants to talk to you. He says he's got
some blackening evidence that's gonna convict me of attempting to
murder him in the first degree!

BARNETTE (*Disgustedly*)   Oh, bluff! He's bluffing! Here, hand me the
phone. (*He takes the phone and becomes suddenly cool and suave*)
Hello, this is Mr. Barnette Lloyd speaking. I'm Mrs. . . . ah, Becky's
attorney . . . Why, certainly, Mr. Botrelle, I'd be more than glad to
check out any pertinent information that you may have . . . Fine,
then I'll be right on over. Goodbye. (*He hangs up the phone*)

BABE   What did he say?

BARNETTE   He wants me to come see him at the hospital this evening. Says he's got some sort of evidence. Sounds highly suspect to
me.

BABE   Oooh! Didn't you just hate his voice? Doesn't he have the most
awful voice? I just hate—I can't bear to hear it!

BARNETTE   Well, now—now, wait. Wait just a minute.

BABE   What?

BARNETTE   I have a solution. From now on, I'll handle all communications between you two. You can simply refuse to speak with him.

BABE   All right—I will. I'll do that.

BARNETTE (*Starting to pack his briefcase*)   Well, I'd better get over there and see just what he's got up his sleeve.

BABE (*After a pause*)   Barnette.

BARNETTE   Yes?

BABE   What's the personal vendetta about? You know, the one you have to settle with Zackery.

BARNETTE   Oh, it's—it's complicated. It's a very complicated matter.

BABE   I see.

BARNETTE   The major thing he did was to ruin my father's life. He took away his job, his home, his health, his respectability. I don't like to talk about it.

BABE   I'm sorry. I just wanted to say—I hope you win it. I hope you win your vendetta.

BARNETTE   Thank you

BABE   I think its an important thing that a person could win a lifelong vendetta.

BARNETTE   Yes. Well, I'd better be going.

BABE   All right. Let me know what happens.

BARNETTE   I will. I'll get back to you right away.

BABE   Thanks.

BARNETTE   Goodbye, Becky.

BABE   Goodbye, Barnette.

(BARNETTE *exits.* BABE *looks around the room for a moment, then goes over to her white suitcase and opens it up. She takes out her pink hair curlers and a brush. She begins brushing her hair*)

BABE   Goodbye, Becky. Goodbye, Barnette. Goodbye, Becky. Oooh.

(LENNY *enters. She is fuming.* BABE *is rolling her hair throughout most of the following scene*)

BABE   Lenny, hi!

LENNY   Hi.

BABE   Where's Meg?

LENNY   Oh, she had to go by the store and pick some things up. I don't know what.

BABE   Well, how's Old Granddaddy?

LENNY (*As she picks up* BABE'S *bowl of oatmeal*)   He's fine. Wonderful! Never been better!

BABE   Lenny, what's wrong? What's the matter?

LENNY   It's Meg! I could just wring her neck! I could just wring it!

BABE Why? What did she do?

BABE She lied! She sat in that hospital room and shamelessly lied to Old Granddaddy. She went on and on telling such untrue stories and lies.

BABE Well, what? What did she say?

LENNY Well, for one thing, she said she was gonna have an RCA record coming out with her picture on the cover, eating pineapples under a palm tree.

BABE Well, gosh, Lenny, maybe she is! Don't you think she really is?

LENNY Babe, she sat here this very afternoon and told me how all that she's done this whole year is work as a clerk for a dog-food company.

BABE Oh, shoot. I'm disappointed.

LENNY And then she goes on to say that she'll be appearing on the Johnny Carson show in two weeks' time. Two weeks' time! Why, Old Granddaddy's got a TV set right in his room. Imagine what a letdown it's gonna be.

BABE Why, mercy me.

LENNY (*Slamming the coffeepot on*) Oh, and she told him the reason she didn't use the money he sent her to come home Christmas was that she was right in the middle of making a huge multimillion-dollar motion picture and was just under too much pressure.

BABE My word!

LENNY The movie's coming out this spring. It's called *Singing in a Shoe Factory*. But she only has a small leading role—not a large leading role.

BABE (*Laughing*) For heaven's sake—

LENNY I'm sizzling. Oh, I just can't help it! I'm sizzling!

BABE Sometimes Meg does such strange things.

LENNY (*Slowly, as she picks up the opened box of birthday candy*) Who ate this candy?

BABE (*Hesitantly*) Meg.

LENNY My one birthday present, and look what she does! Why, she's taken one little bite out of each piece and then just put it back in! Ooh! That's just like her! That is just like her!

BABE Lenny, please—

LENNY I can't help it! It gets me mad! It gets me upset! Why, Meg's always run wild—she started smoking and drinking when she was fourteen years old; she never made good grades—never made her own bed! But somehow she always seemed to get what she wanted. She's the one who got singing and dancing lessons, and a store-bought dress to wear to her senior prom. Why, do you remember how Meg always got to wear twelve jingle bells on her petticoats, while we were only allowed to wear three apiece? Why?! Why should Old Grandmama let her sew twelve golden jingle bells on her petticoats and us only three!

BABE (*Who has heard all this before*)   I don't know! Maybe she didn't jingle them as much!

LENNY   I can't help it! It gets me mad! I resent it. I do.

BABE   Oh, don't resent Meg. Things have been hard for Meg. After all, she was the one who found Mama.

LENNY   Oh, I know; she's the one who found Mama. But that's always been the excuse.

BABE   But I tell you, Lenny, after it happened, Meg started doing all sorts of these strange things.

LENNY   She did? Like what?

BABE   Like things I never even wanted to tell you about.

LENNY   What sort of things?

BABE   Well, for instance, back when we used to go over to the library, Meg would spend all her time reading and looking through this old black book called *Diseases of the Skin*. It was full of the most sickening pictures you've ever seen. Things like rotting-away noses and eyeballs drooping off down the sides of people's faces, and scabs and sores and eaten-away sides of people's bodies.

LENNY (*Trying to pour her coffee*)   Babe, please! That's enough.

BABE   Anyway, she'd spend hours and hours just forcing herself to look through this book. Why, it was the same way she'd force herself to look at the poster of crippled children stuck up in the window at Dixie- land Drugs. You know, that one where they want you to give a dime. Meg would stand there and stare at their eyes and look at the braces on their little crippled-up legs—then she'd purposely go and spend her dime on a double-scoop ice cream cone and eat it all down. She'd say to me, "See, I can stand it. I can stand it. Just look how I'm gonna be able to stand it."

LENNY   That's awful.

BABE   She said she was afraid of being a weak person. I guess 'cause she cried in bed every night for such a long time.

LENNY   Goodness mercy. (*After a pause*)   Well, I suppose you'd have to be a pretty hard person to be able to do what she did to Doc Porter.

BABE (*Exasperated*)   Oh, shoot! It wasn't Meg's fault that hurricane wiped Biloxi away. I never understood why people were blaming all that on Meg—just because that roof fell in and crunched Doc's leg. It wasn't her fault.

LENNY   Well, it was Meg who refused to evacuate. Jim Craig and some of Doc's other friends were all down there, and they kept trying to get everyone to evacuate. But Meg refused. She wanted to stay on because she thought a hurricane would be—oh, I don't know—a lot of fun. Then everyone says she baited Doc into staying there with her. She said she'd marry him if he'd stay.

BABE (*Taken aback by this new information*)   Well, he has a mind of his own. He could have gone.

LENNY   But he didn't. 'Cause . . . 'cause he loved her. And then, after the roof caved in and they got Doc to the high school gym, Meg just left. She just left him there to leave for California—'cause of her career, she says. I think it was a shameful thing to do. It took almost a year for his leg to heal, and after that he gave up his medical career altogether. He said he was tired of hospitals. It's such a sad thing. Everyone always knew he was gonna be a doctor. We've called him Doc for years.

BABE   I don't know. I guess I don't have any room to talk; 'cause I just don't know. (*Pause*)   Gosh, you look so tired.

LENNY   I feel tired.

BABE   They say women need a lot of iron . . . so they won't feel tired.

LENNY   What's got iron in it? Liver?

BABE   Yeah, liver's got it. And vitamin pills.

> (*After a moment,* MEG *enters. She carries a bottle of bourbon that is already minus a few slugs, and a newspaper. She is wearing black boots, a dark dress, and a hat. The room goes silent*)

MEG   Hello.

BABE (*Fooling with her hair*)   Hi, Meg.

> (LENNY *quietly sips her coffee*)

MEG (Handing the newspaper to BABE)   Here's your paper.

BABE   Thanks. (*She opens it*)   Oh, Here it is, right on the front page.

> (MEG *lights a cigarette*)

BABE   Where's the scissors, Lenny?

LENNY   Look in there in the ribbon drawer.

BABE   Okay. (*She gets the scissors and glue out of the drawer and slowly begins cutting out the newspaper article*)

MEG (*After a few moments, filled only with the snipping of scissors*)   All right—I lied! I lied! I couldn't help it . . . these stories just came pouring out of my mouth! When I saw how tired and sick Old Granddaddy'd gotten—they just flew out! All I wanted was to see him smiling and happy. I just wasn't going to sit there and look at him all miserable and sick and sad! I just wasn't!

BABE   Oh, Meg, he is sick, isn't he—

MEG   Why, he's gotten all white and milky—he's almost evaporated!

LENNY   (*Gasping and turning to* MEG)   But still you shouldn't have lied! It just was wrong for you to tell such lies—

MEG   Well, I know that! Don't you think I know that? I hate myself when I lie for that old man. I do. I feel so weak. And then I have to go and do at least three or four things that I know he'd despise just to get even with that miserable, old, bossy man!

LENNY   Oh, Meg, please don't talk so about Old Granddaddy! It sounds so ungrateful. Why, he went out of his way to make a home for us, to treat us like we were his very own children. All he ever wanted was the best for us. That's all he ever wanted.

MEG   Well, I guess it was; but sometimes I wonder what we wanted.

BABE   (*Taking the newspaper article and glue over to her suitcase*)   Well, one thing I wanted was a team of white horses to ride Mama's coffin to her grave. That's one thing I wanted.

(LENNY *and* MEG *exchange looks*)

BABE   Lenny, did you remember to pack my photo album?

LENNY   It's down there at the bottom, under all that night stuff.

BABE   Oh, I found it.

LENNY   Really, Babe, I don't understand why you have to put in the articles that are about the unhappy things in your life. Why would you want to remember them?

BABE   (*Pasting the article in*)   I don't know. I just like to keep an accurate record, I suppose. There. (*She begins flipping through the book*) Look, here's a picture of me when I got married.

MEG   Let's see.

(*They all look at the photo album*)

LENNY   My word, you look about twelve years old.

BABE   I was just eighteen.

MEG   You're smiling, Babe. Were you happy then?

BABE (*Laughing*)   Well, I was drunk on champagne punch. I remember that!

(*They turn the page*)

LENNY   Oh, there's Meg singing at Greeny's!

BABE   Oooh, I wish you were still singing at Greeny's! I wish you were!

LENNY   You're so beautiful!

B A B E   Yes, you are. You're beautiful.

M E G   Oh, stop! I'm not—

L E N N Y   Look, Meg's starting to cry.

B A B E   Oh, Meg—

M E G   I'm not—

B A B E   Quick, better turn the page; we don't want Meg crying—(*She flips the pages*)

L E N N Y   Why, it's Daddy.

M E G   Where'd you get that picture, Babe? I thought she burned them all.

B A B E   Ah, I just found it around.

L E N N Y   What does it say here? What's that inscription?

B A B E   It says "Jimmy—clowning at the beach—1952."

L E N N Y   Well, will you look at that smile.

M E G   Jesus, those white teeth—turn the page, will you; we can't do any worse than this!

(*They turn the page. The room goes silent*)

B A B E   It's Mama and the cat.

L E N N Y   Oh, turn the page—

B A B E   That old yellow cat. You know, bet if she hadn't hung that old cat along with her, she wouldn't have gotten all that national coverage.

M E G (*After a moment, hopelessly*)   Why are we talking about this?

L E N N Y   Meg's right. It was so sad. It was awfully sad. I remember how we all three just sat up on that bed the day of the service all dressed up in our black velveteen suits crying the whole morning long.

B A B E   We used up one whole big box of Kleenexes.

M E G   And then Old Granddaddy came in and said he was gonna take us out to breakfast. Remember, he told us not to cry anymore 'cause he was gonna take us out to get banana splits for breakfast.

B A B E   That's right—banana splits for breakfast!

M E G   Why, Lenny was fourteen years old, and he thought that would make it all better—

B A B E   Oh, I remember he said for us to eat all we wanted. I think I ate about five! He kept shoving them down us!

M E G   God, we were so sick!

L E N N Y   Oh, we were!

M E G (*Laughing*)   Lenny's face turned green—

L E N N Y   I was just as sick as a dog!

B A B E   Old Grandmama was furious!

L E N N Y   Oh, she was!

M E G   The thing about Old Granddaddy is, he keeps trying to make us happy, and we end up getting stomach aches and turning green and throwing up in the flower arrangements.

BABE   Oh, that was me! I threw up in the flowers! Oh, no! How embarrassing!

LENNY (*Laughing*)   Oh, Babe—

BABE (*Hugging her sisters*)   Oh, Lenny! Oh, Meg!

MEG   Oh, Babe! Oh, Lenny! It's so good to be home!

LENNY   Hey, I have an idea—

BABE   What?

LENNY   Let's play cards!!

BABE   Oh, let's do!

MEG   All right!

LENNY   Oh, good! It'll be just like when we used to sit around the table playing hearts all night long.

BABE (*Getting up*)   I'll fix us some popcorn and hot chocolate—

MEG (*Getting up*)   Here, let me get out that old black popcorn pot.

LENNY (*Getting up*)   Oh, yes! Now, let's see, I think I have a deck of cards around here somewhere.

BABE   Gosh, I hope I remember all the rules—Are hearts good or bad?

MEG   Bad, I think. Aren't they, Lenny?

LENNY   That's right. Hearts are bad, but the Black Sister is the worst of all—

MEG   Oh, that's right! And the Black Sister is the Queen of Spades.

BABE (*Figuring it out*)   And spades are the black cards that aren't the puppy dog feet?

MEG (*Thinking a moment*)   Right. And she counts a lot of points.

BABE   And points are bad?

MEG   Right. Here. I'll get some paper so we can keep score.

(*The phone rings*)

LENNY   Oh, here they are!

MEG   I'll get it—

LENNY   Why, look at these cards! They're years old!

BABE   Oh, let me see!

MEG   Hello . . . No, this is Meg MaGrath . . . Doc. How are you? . . . Well, good . . . You're where? . . . Well, sure. Come on over . . . Sure I'm sure . . . Yeah, come right on over . . . All right. 'Bye. (*She hangs up*)   That was Doc Porter. He's down the street at Al's Grill. He's gonna come on over.

LENNY   He is?

MEG   He said he wanted to come see me.

LENNY   Oh. (*After a pause*)   Well, do you still want to play?

MEG   No, I don't think so.

LENNY   All right. (*She starts to shuffle the cards, as* MEG *brushes her hair*) You know, it's really not much fun playing hearts with only two people.

MEG   I'm sorry; maybe after Doc leaves I'll join you.

LENNY   I know; maybe Doc'll want to play. Then we can have a game of bridge.

MEG   I don't think so. Doc never liked cards. Maybe we'll just go out somewhere.

LENNY (*Putting down the cards.* BABE *picks them up*)   Meg—

MEG   What?

LENNY   Well, Doc's married now.

MEG   I know. You told me.

LENNY   Oh. Well, as long as you know that. (*Pause*)   As long as you know that.

MEG (*Still primping*)   Yes, I know. She made the pot.

BABE   How many cards do I deal out?

LENNY (*Leaving the table*)   Excuse me.

BABE   All of 'em, or what?

LENNY   Ah, Meg, could I—could I ask you something?

(BABE *proceeds to deal out all the cards*)

MEG   What?

LENNY   I just wanted to ask you—

MEG   What?

(*Unable to go on with what she really wants to say,* LENNY *runs and picks up the box of candy*)

LENNY   Well, just why did you take one little bite out of each piece of candy in this box and then just put it back in?

MEG   Oh. Well, I was looking for the ones with nuts.

LENNY   The ones with nuts.

MEG   Yeah.

LENNY   But there are none with nuts. It's a box of assorted crème —all it has in it are crèmes!

MEG   Oh.

LENNY   Why couldn't you just read on the box? It says right here, *Assorted Crèmes*, not nuts! Besides, this was a birthday present to me! My one and only birthday present; my only one!

MEG   I'm sorry. I'll get you another box.

LENNY   I don't want another box. That's not the point!

MEG   What is the point?

LENNY   I don't know; it's—it's—You have no respect for other people's property! You just take whatever you want. You just take it! Why, remember how you had layers and layers of jingle bells sewed onto your petticoats while Babe and I only had three apiece?!

MEG   Oh, God! She's starting up about those stupid jingle bells!

LENNY   Well, it's an example! A specific example of how you always got what you wanted!

MEG   Oh, come on, Lenny, you're just upset because Doc called.

LENNY   Who said anything about Doc? Do you think I'm upset about Doc? Why, I've long since given up worrying about you and all your men.

MEG (*Turning in anger*)   Look, I know I've had too many men. Believe me, I've had way too many men. But it's not my fault you haven't had any—or maybe just that one from Memphis.

LENNY (*Stopping*)   What one from Memphis?

MEG (*Slowly*)   The one Babe told me about. From the—club.

LENNY   Babe!

BABE   Meg!

LENNY   How could you! I asked you not to tell anyone! I'm so ashamed! How could you? Who else have you told? Did you tell anyone else?

BABE (*Overlapping, to* MEG)   Why'd you have to open your big mouth?

MEG (*Overlapping*)   How am I supposed to know? You never said not to tell.

BABE   Can't you use your head just for once? (*To* LENNY)   No, I never told anyone else. Somehow it just slipped out to Meg. Really, it just flew out of my mouth—

LENNY   What do you two have—wings on your tongues?

BABE   I'm sorry, Lenny. Really sorry.

LENNY   I'll just never, never, never be able to trust you again—

MEG (*Furiously coming to* BABE'S *defense*)   Oh, for heaven's sake, Lenny, we were just worried about you! We wanted to find a way to make you happy!

LENNY   Happy! Happy! I'll never be happy!

MEG   Well, not if you keep living your life as Old Granddaddy's nurse-maid—

BABE   Meg, shut up!

MEG   I can't help it! I just know that the reason you stopped seeing this man from Memphis was because of Old Granddaddy.

LENNY   What—Babe didn't tell you the rest of the story—

MEG   Oh, she said it was something about your shrunken ovary.

BABE   Meg!

LENNY   Babe!

BABE   I just mentioned it!

MEG   But I don't believe a word of that story!

LENNY   Oh, I don't care what you believe! It's so easy for you—you always have men falling in love with you! But I have this underdeveloped ovary and I can't have children and my hair is falling out in the comb—so what man can love me! What man's gonna love me?

MEG   A lot of men!

BABE   Yeah, a lot! A whole lot!

MEG   Old Granddaddy's the only one who seems to think otherwise.

LENNY   'Cause he doesn't want to see me hurt! He doesn't want to see me rejected and humiliated.

MEG   Oh, come on now, Lenny, don't be so pathetic! God, you make me angry when you just stand there looking so pathetic! Just tell me, did you really ask the man from Memphis? Did you actually ask that man from Memphis all about it?

LENNY   (*Breaking apart*)   No, I didn't. I didn't. Because I just didn't want him not to want me—

MEG   Lenny—

LENNY   (*Furious*)   Don't talk to me anymore! Don't talk to me! I think I'm gonna vomit—I just hope all this doesn't cause me to vomit! (*She exits up the stairs sobbing*)

MEG   See! See! She didn't even ask him about her stupid ovary! She just broke it all off 'cause of Old Granddaddy! What a jackass fool!

BABE   Oh, Meg, shut up! Why do you have to make Lenny cry? I just hate it when you make Lenny cry! (*She runs up the stairs*)   Lenny! Oh, Lenny—

(MEG *gives a long sigh and goes to get a cigarette and a drink*)

MEG   I feel like hell. (*She sits in despair, smoking and drinking bourbon. There is a knock on the back door. She starts. She brushes her hair out of her face and goes to answer the door. It is* DOC)

DOC   Hello, Meggy.

MEG   Well, Doc. Well, it's Doc.

DOC   (*After a pause*)   You're home, Meggy.

MEG   Yeah, I've come home. I've come on home to see about Babe.

DOC   And how's Babe?

MEG   Oh, fine. Well, fair. She's fair.

(DOC *nods*)

MEG   Hey, do you want a drink?

DOC   Whatcha got?

MEG   Bourbon.

DOC   Oh, don't tell me Lenny's stocking bourbon.

MEG   Well, no. I've been to the store. (*She gets him a glass and pours them each a drink. They click glasses*)

MEG   So, how's your wife?

DOC   She's fine.

MEG   I hear ya got two kids.

DOC   Yeah, I got two kids.

MEG   A boy and a girl.

DOC   That's right, Meggy, a boy and a girl.

MEG   That's what you always said you wanted, wasn't it? A boy and a girl.

DOC   Is that what I said?

MEG   I don't know. I thought it's what you said.

(*They finish their drinks in silence*)

DOC   Whose cot?

MEG   Lenny's. She taken to sleeping in the kitchen.

DOC   Ah. Where is Lenny?

MEG   She's in the upstairs room. I made her cry. Babe's up there seeing to her.

DOC   How'd you make her cry?

MEG   I don't know. Eating her birthday candy; talking on about her boyfriend from Memphis. I don't know. I'm upset about it. She's got a lot on her. Why can't I keep my mouth shut?

DOC   I don't know, Meggy. Maybe it's because you don't want to.

MEG   Maybe.

(*They smile at each other.* MEG *pours each of them another drink*)

DOC   Well, it's been a long time.

MEG   It has been a long time.

DOC   Let's see—when was the last time we saw each other?

MEG   I can't quite recall.

DOC   Wasn't it in Biloxi?

MEG   Ah, Biloxi. I believe so.

DOC   And wasn't there a—a hurricane going on at the time?

MEG   Was there?

DOC   Yes, there was; one hell of a hurricane. Camille, I believe they called it. Hurricane Camille.

MEG   Yes, now I remember. It was a beautiful hurricane.

DOC   We had a time down there. We had quite a time. Drinking vodka, eating oysters on the half shell, dancing all night long. And the wind was blowing.

MEG   Oh, God, was it blowing.

DOC   Goddamn, was it blowing.

MEG   There never has been such a wind blowing.

DOC   Oh, God, Meggy. Oh, God.

MEG   I know, Doc. It was my fault to leave you. I was crazy. I thought I was choking. I felt choked!

DOC   I felt like a fool.

MEG   No.

DOC   I just kept on wondering why.

MEG   I don't know why . . . 'Cause I didn't want to care. I don't know. I did care, though. I did.

DOC   (*After a pause*)   Ah, hell—(*He pours them both another drink*) Are you still singing those sad songs?

MEG   No.

DOC   Why not?

MEG   I don't know, Doc. Things got worse for me. After a while, I just couldn't sing anymore. I tell you, I had one hell of a time over Christmas.

DOC   What do you mean?

MEG   I went nuts. I went insane. Ended up in L.A. County Hospital, Psychiatric ward.

DOC   Hell. Ah, hell, Meggy. What happened?

MEG   I don't really know. I couldn't sing anymore, so I lost my job. And I had a bad toothache. I had this incredibly painful toothache. For days I had it, but I wouldn't do anything about it. I just stayed inside my apartment. All I could do was sit around in chairs, chewing on my fingers. Then one afternoon I ran screaming out of the apartment with all my money and jewelry and valuables, and tried to stuff it all into one of those March of Dimes collection boxes. That was when they nabbed me. Sad story. Meg goes mad.

(DOC *stares at her for a long moment. He pours them both another drink*)

DOC (*After quite a pause*)   There's a moon out.

BABE   Is there?

DOC   Wanna go take a ride in my truck and look out at the moon?

MEG   I don't know, Doc. I don't wanna start up. It'll be too hard if we start up.

DOC   Who says we're gonna start up? We're just gonna look at the moon. For one night just you and me are gonna go for a ride in the country and look out at the moon.

MEG   One night?

DOC   Right.

MEG   Look out at the moon?

DOC   You got it.

MEG   Well . . . all right. (*She gets up*)

DOC   Better take your coat. (*He helps her into her coat*)   And the bottle—
(*He takes the bottle.* MEG *picks up the glasses*)   Forget the glasses—

MEG (*Laughing*)   Yeah—forget the glasses. Forget the goddamn glasses.

> (MEG *shuts off the kitchen lights, leaving the kitchen with only a dim light over the kitchen sink.* MEG *and* DOC *leave. After a moment,* BABE *comes down the stairs in her slip*)

BABE   Meg—Meg? (*She stands for a moment in the moonlight wearing only a slip. She sees her saxophone, then moves to pick it up. She plays a few shrieking notes. There is a loud knock on the back door*)

BARNETTE'S VOICE   Becky! Becky! Is that you?

> (BABE *puts down the saxophone*)

BABE   Just a minute. I'm coming. (*She puts a raincoat on over her slip and goes to answer the door*)   Hello, Barnette. Come on in.

> (BARNETTE *comes in. He is troubled but is making a great effort to hide the fact*)

BARNETTE   Thank you.

BABE   What is it?

BARNETTE   I've, ah, I've just come from seeing Zackery at the hospital.

BABE   Oh?

BARNETTE   It seems . . . Well, it seems his sister, Lucille, was somewhat suspicious.

BABE   Suspicious?

BARNETTE   About you?

BABE   Me?

BARNETTE   She hired a private detective: he took these pictures.

> (*He hands* BABE *a small envelope containing several photographs.* BABE *opens the envelope and begins looking at the pictures in stunned silence*)

BARNETTE   They were taken about two weeks ago. It seems she wasn't going to show them to Botrelle straightaway. She, ah, wanted to wait till the time was right.

> (*The phone rings one and a half times.* BARNETTE *glances uneasily toward the phone*)

BARNETTE Becky?

(*The phone stops ringing*)

BABE (*Looking up at* BARNETTE, *slowly*) These are pictures of Willie Jay and me . . . out in the garage.

BARNETTE (*Looking away*) I know.

BABE You looked at these pictures?

BARNETTE Yes—I—well . . . professionally, I looked at them.

BABE Oh, mercy. Oh, mercy! We can burn them, can't we? Quick, we can burn them—

BARNETTE It won't do any good. They have the negatives.

BABE (*Holding the pictures, as she bangs herself hopelessly into the stove, table, cabinets, etc.*) Oh, no; oh, no; oh, no! Oh, no—

BARNETTE There—there, now—there—

LENNY'S VOICE Babe? Are you all right? Babe—

BABE (*Hiding the pictures*) What? I'm all right. Go on back to bed.

(BABE *hides the pictures as* LENNY *comes down the stairs. She is wearing a coat and wiping white night cream off of her face with a washrag*)

LENNY What's the matter? What's going on down here?

BABE Nothing! (*Then as she begins dancing ballet style around the room*) We're—we're just dancing. We were just dancing around down here. (*Signaling to* BARNETTE *to dance*)

LENNY Well, you'd better get your shoes on, 'cause we've got—

BABE All right, I will! That's a good idea! (*She goes to get her shoes*) Now, you go on back to bed. It's pretty late and—

LENNY Babe, will you listen a minute—

BABE (*Holding up her shoes*) I'm putting 'em on—

LENNY That was the hospital that just called. We've got to get over there. Old Granddaddy's had himself another stroke.

BABE Oh. All right. My shoes are on. (*She stands*)

(*They all look at each other as the lights black out*)

ACT III

(*The lights go up on the empty kitchen. It is the following morning. After a few moments,* BABE *enters from the back door. She is carrying her hair curlers in her hands. She lies down on the cot. A few moments later,* LENNY *enters. She is tired and weary.* CHICK'S *voice is heard)*

CHICK'S VOICE   Lenny! Oh, Lenny!

(LENNY *turns to the door.* CHICK *enters energetically)*

CHICK   Well . . . how is he?

LENNY   He's stabilized; they say for now his functions are all stabilized.

CHICK   Well, is he still in the coma?

LENNY   Uh huh.

CHICK   Hmmm. So do they think he's gonna be . . . passing on?

LENNY   He may be. He doesn't look so good. They said they'd phone us if there were any sudden changes.

CHICK   Well, it seems to me we'd better get busy phoning on the phone ourselves. (*Removing a list from her pocket*) Now, I've made out this list of all the people we need to notify about Old Granddaddy's predicament. I'll phone half, if you'll phone half.

LENNY   But—what would we say?

CHICK   Just tell them the facts: that Old Granddaddy's got himself in a coma, and it could be he doesn't have long for this world.

LENNY   I—I don't know. I don't feel like phoning.

CHICK   Why, Lenora, I'm surprised; how can you be this way? I went to all the trouble of making up the list. And I offered to phone half of the people on it, even though I'm only one-fourth of the granddaughters. I mean, I just get tired of doing more than my fair share, when people like Meg can suddenly just disappear to where they can't even be reached in case of emergency!

LENNY   All right; give me the list. I'll phone half.

CHICK   Well, don't do it just to suit me.

LENNY (*Wearily tearing the list in half*) I'll phone these here.

CHICK (*Taking her half of the list*) Fine then. Suit yourself. Oh, wait —let me call Sally Bell. I need to talk to her, anyway.

LENNY   All right.

CHICK   So you add Great-uncle Spark Dude to your list.

LENNY   Okay.

CHICK   Fine. Well, I've got to get on back home and see to the kids. It is gonna be an uphill struggle till I can find someone to replace that good-for-nothing Annie May Jenkins. Well, you let me know if you hear any more.

LENNY   All right.

CHICK   Goodbye, Rebecca. I said goodbye. (BABE *blows her sax.* CHICK *starts to exit in a flurry, then pauses to add:*) And you really ought to try to get that phoning done before twelve noon. (*She exits*)

LENNY (*After a long pause*)   Babe, I feel bad. I feel real bad.

BABE   Why, Lenny?

LENNY   Because yesterday I—I wished it.

BABE   You wished what?

LENNY   I wished Old Granddaddy would be put out of his pain. I wished it on one of my birthday candles. I did. And now he's in this coma, and they say he's feeling no pain.

BABE   Well, when did you have a cake yesterday? I don't remember you having any cake.

LENNY   Well, I didn't . . . have a cake. But I just blew out the candles anyway.

BABE   Oh. Well, those birthday wishes don't count, unless you have a cake.

LENNY   They don't?

BABE   No. A lot of times they don't even count when you do have a cake. It just depends.

LENNY   Depends on what?

BABE   On how deep your wish is, I suppose.

LENNY   Still, I just wish I hadn't of wished it. Gosh, I wonder when Meg's coming home.

BABE   Should be soon.

LENNY   I just wish we wouldn't fight all the time. I don't like it when we do.

BABE   Me, neither.

LENNY   I guess it hurts my feelings, a little, the way Old Granddaddy's always put so much stock in Meg and all her singing talent. I think I've been, well, envious of her 'cause I can't seem to do too much.

BABE   Why, sure you can.

LENNY   I can?

BABE   Sure. You just have to put your mind to it, that's all. It's like how I went out and bought that saxophone, just hoping I'd be able to attend music school and start up my own career. I just went out and did it. Just on hope. Of course, now it looks like . . . Well, it just doesn't look like things are gonna work out for me. But I know they would for you.

LENNY   Well, they'll work out for you, too.

BABE   I doubt it.

LENNY   Listen, I heard up at the hospital that Zackery's already in fair condition. They say soon he'll probably be able to walk and everything.

BABE   Yeah. And life sure can be miserable.

LENNY   Well, I know, 'cause—day before yesterday, Billy Boy was struck down by lightning.

BABE   He was?

LENNY (*Nearing sobs*)   Yeah. He was struck dead.

BABE (*Crushed*)   Life sure can be miserable.

(*They sit together for several moments in morbid silence.* MEG *is heard singing a loud happy song. She suddenly enters through the dining room door. She is exuberant! Her hair is a mess, and the heel of one shoe has broken off. She is laughing radiantly and limping as she sings into the broken heel*)

MEG (*Spotting her sisters*)   Good morning! Good morning! Oh, it's a wonderful morning! I tell you, I am surprised I feel this good. I should feel like hell. By all accounts, I should feel like utter hell! (*She is looking for the glue*)   Where's that glue? This damn heel has broken off my shoe. La, la, la, la, la! Ah, here it is! Now, let me just get these shoes off. Zip, zip, zip, zip, zip! Well, what's wrong with you two? My God, you look like doom!

(BABE *and* LENNY *stare helplessly at* MEG)

MEG   Oh, I know, you're mad at me 'cause I stayed out all night long. Well, I did.

LENNY   No, we're—we're not mad at you. We're just . . . depressed. (*She starts to sob*)

MEG   Oh, Lenny, listen to me, now; everything's all right with Doc. I mean, nothing happened. Well, actually a lot did happen, but it didn't come to anything. Not because of me, I'm afraid. (*Smearing glue on her heel*)   I mean, I was out there thinking, What will I say when he begs me to run away with him? Will I have pity on his wife and those two half-Yankee children? I mean, can I sacrifice their happiness for mine? Yes! Oh, yes! Yes, I can! But . . . he didn't ask me. He didn't even want to ask me. I could tell by this certain look in his eyes that he didn't even want to ask me. Why aren't I miserable! Why aren't I morbid? I should be humiliated! Devastated! Maybe these feelings are coming—I don't know. But for now it was . . . just such fun. I'm happy. I realized I could care about someone. I could want someone. And I sang! I sang all night long! I sang right up into the trees! But not for Old Granddaddy. None of it was to please Old Granddaddy!

(LENNY *and* BABE *look at each other*)

BABE   Ah, Meg—

MEG   What—

BABE   Well, it's just—It's . . .

LENNY It's about Old Granddaddy—

MEG Oh, I know; I know. I told him all those stupid lies. Well, I'm gonna go right over there this morning and tell him the truth. I mean every horrible thing. I don't care if he wants to hear it or not. He's just gonna have to take me like I am. And if he can't take it, if it sends him into a coma, that's just too damn bad!

(LENNY *and* BABE *look at each other.* BABE *cracks a smile.* LENNY *cracks a smile*)

BABE You're too late—Ha, ha, ha!

(*They both break up laughing*)

LENNY Oh, stop! Please! Ha, ha, ha!

MEG What is it? What's so funny?

BABE (*Still laughing*) It's not—It's not funny!

LENNY (*Still laughing*) No, it's not! It's not a bit funny!

MEG Well, what is it, then? What?

BABE (*Trying to calm down*) Well, it's just—it's just—

MEG What?

BABE Well, Old Granddaddy—he—he's in a coma!

(BABE *and* LENNY *break up again*)

MEG He's what?

BABE (*Shrieking*) In a coma!

MEG My God! That's not funny!

BABE (*Calming down*) I know. I know. For some reason, it just struck us as funny.

LENNY I'm sorry. It's—it's not funny. It's sad. It's very sad. We've been up all night long.

BABE We're really tired.

MEG Well, my God. How is he? Is he gonna live?

(BABE *and* LENNY *look at each other*)

BABE They don't think so!

(*They both break up again*)

LENNY Oh, I don't know why we're laughing like this. We're just sick! We're just awful!

BABE We are—we're awful!

LENNY (*As she collects herself*) Oh, good; now I feel bad. Now I feel like crying. I do; I feel like crying.

BABE Me, too. Me, too.

M E G Well, you've gotten me depressed!

L E N N Y I'm sorry. I'm sorry. It, ah, happened last night. He had another stroke.

(*They laugh again*)

M E G I see.

L E N N Y But he's stabilized now. (*She chokes up once more*)

M E G That's good. You two okay?

(B A B E *and* L E N N Y *nod*)

M E G You look like you need some rest.

(B A B E *and* L E N N Y *nod again*)

M E G (*Going on, about her heel*) I hope that'll stay. (*She puts the top back on the glue. A realization:*) Oh, of course, now I won't be able to tell him the truth about all those lies I told. I mean, finally I get my wits about me, and he conks out. It's just like him. Babe, can I wear your slippers till this glue dries?

B A B E Sure.

L E N N Y (*After a pause*) Things sure are gonna be different around here . . . when Old Granddaddy dies. Well, not for you two really, but for me.

M E G It'll work out.

B A B E (*Depressed*) Yeah. It'll work out.

L E N N Y I hope so. I'm just afraid of being here all by myself. All alone.

M E G Well, you don't have to be alone. Maybe Babe'll move back in here.

(L E N N Y *looks at* B A B E *hopefully*)

B A B E No, I don't think I'll be living here.

M E G (*Realizing her mistake*) Well, anyway, you're your own woman. Invite some people over. Have some parties. Go out with strange men.

L E N N Y I don't know any strange men.

M E G Well . . . you know that Charlie.

L E N N Y (*Shaking her head*) Not anymore.

M E G Why not?

L E N N Y (*Breaking down*) I told him we should never see each other again.

M E G Well, if you told him, you can just untell him.

L E N N Y Oh, no, I couldn't. I'd feel like a fool.

M E G Oh, that's not a good enough reason! All people in love feel like fools. Don't they, Babe?

B A B E Sure.

MEG   Look, why don't you give him a call right now? See how things stand.

LENNY   Oh, no! I'd be too scared—

MEG   But what harm could it possibly do? I mean, it's not gonna make things any worse than this never seeing him again, at all, forever.

LENNY   I suppose that's true—

MEG   Of course it is; so call him up! Take a chance, will you? Just take some sort of chance!

LENNY   You think I should?

MEG   Of course! You've got to try—You do!

(LENNY *looks over at* BABE)

BABE   You do, Lenny—I think you do.

LENNY   Really? Really, really?

MEG   Yes! Yes!

BABE   You should!

LENNY   All right. I will! I will!

MEG   Oh, good!

BABE   Good!

LENNY   I'll call him right now, while I've got my confidence up!

MEG   Have you got the number?

LENNY   Uh huh. But, ah, I think I wanna call him upstairs. It'll be more private.

MEG   Ah, good idea.

LENNY   I'm just gonna go on and call him up and see what happens —(*She has started up the stairs*)   Wish me good luck!

MEG   Good luck!

BABE   Good luck, Lenny!

LENNY   Thanks.

(LENNY *gets almost out of sight when the phone rings. She stops;* MEG *picks up the phone*)

MEG   Hello? (*Then, in a whisper*)   Oh, thank you very much . . . Yes, I will. 'Bye, 'bye.

LENNY   Who was it?

MEG   Wrong number. They wanted Weed's Body Shop.

LENNY   Oh. Well, I'll be right back down in a minute. (*She exits*)

MEG (*After a moment, whispering to* BABE)   That was the bakery; Lenny's cake is ready!

BABE (*Who has become increasingly depressed*)   Oh.

MEG   I think I'll sneak on down to the corner and pick it up. (*She starts to leave*)

BABE   Meg—
MEG   What?
BABE   Nothing.
MEG   You okay?

(BABE *shakes her head*)

MEG   What is it?
BABE   It's just—
MEG   What?

(BABE *gets the envelope containing the photographs*)

BABE   Here. Take a look.
MEG (*Taking the envelope*)   What is it?
BABE   It's some evidence Zackery's collected against me. Looks like my goose is cooked.

(MEG *opens the envelope and looks at the photographs*)

MEG   My God, it's—it's you and . . . is *that* Willie Jay?
BABE   Yeah.
MEG   Well, he certainly *has* grown. You were right about that. My, oh, my.
BABE   Please don't tell Lenny. She'd hate me.
MEG   I won't. I won't tell Lenny. (*Putting the pictures back into the envelope*)   What are you gonna do?
BABE   What can I do?

(*There is a knock on the door.* BABE *grabs the envelope and hides it*)

MEG   Who is it?
BARNETTE   It's Barnette Lloyd.
MEG   Oh, come on in, Barnette.

(BARNETTE *enters. His eyes are ablaze with excitement*)

BARNETTE (*As he paces around the room*)   Well, good morning! (*Shaking* MEG'S *hand*)   Good morning, Miss MaGrath. (*Touching* BABE *on the shoulder*)   Becky. (*Moving away*)   What I meant to say is, How are you doing this morning?
MEG   Ah—fine, Fine.
BARNETTE   Good. Good. I—I just had time to drop by for a minute.
MEG   Oh.
BARNETTE   So, ah, how's your granddad doing?

MEG   Well, not very, ah—ah, he's in this coma. (*She breaks up laughing*)

BARNETTE   I see . . . I see. (*To* BABE)   Actually, the primary reason I came by was to pick up that—envelope. I left it here last night in all the confusion. (*Pause*)   You, ah, still do have it?

(BABE *hands him the envelope*)

BARNETTE   Yes. (*Taking the envelope*)   That's the one. I'm sure it'll be much better off in my office safe. (*He puts the envelope into his coat pocket*)

MEG   I'm sure it will.

BARNETTE   Beg your pardon?

BABE   It's all right. I showed her the pictures.

BARNETTE   Ah; I see.

MEG   So what's going to happen now, Barnette? What are those pictures gonna mean?

BARNETTE (*After pacing a moment*)   Hmmm. May I speak frankly and openly?

BABE   Uh huh.

MEG   Please do—

BARNETTE   Well, I tell you now, at first glance, I admit those pictures had me considerably perturbed and upset. Perturbed to the point that I spent most of last night going over certain suspect papers and reports that had fallen into my hands—rather recklessly.

BABE   What papers do you mean?

BARNETTE   Papers that, pending word from three varied and unbiased experts, could prove graft, fraud, forgery, as well as a history of unethical behavior.

MEG   You mean about Zackery?

BARNETTE   Exactly. You see, I now intend to make this matter just as sticky and gritty for one Z. Botrelle as it is for us. Why, with the amount of scandal I'll dig up, Botrelle will be forced to settle this affair on our own terms!

MEG   Oh, Babe! Did you hear that?

BABE   Yes! Oh, yes! So you've won it! You've won your lifelong vendetta!

BARNETTE   Well . . . well, now of course it's problematic in that, well, in that we won't be able to expose him openly in the courts. That was the original game plan.

BABE   But why not? Why?

BARNETTE   Well, it's only that if, well, if a jury were to—to get say, a glance at these, ah, photographs, well . . . well, possibly . . .

BABE   We could be sunk.

BARNETTE   In a sense. But! On the other hand, if a newspaper were to get a hold of our little item, Mr. Zackery Botrelle could find himself boiling in some awfully hot water. So what I'm looking for, very simply, is—a deal.

BABE   A deal?

MEG   Thank you, Barnette. It's a sunny day, Babe. (*Realizing she is in the way*)   Ooh, where's that broken shoe? (*She grabs her boots and runs upstairs*)

BABE   So, you're having to give up your vendetta?

BARNETTE   Well, in a way. For the time. It, ah, seems to me you shouldn't always let your life be ruled by such things as, ah, personal vendettas. (*Looking at* BABE *with meaning*)   Other things can be important.

BABE   I don't know. I don't exactly know. How 'bout Willie Jay? Will he be all right?

BARNETTE   Yes, it's all been taken care of. He'll be leaving incognito on the midnight bus—heading north.

BABE   North.

BARNETTE   I'm sorry, it seemed the only . . . way.

(BARNETTE *moves to her; she moves away*)

BABE   Look, you'd better be getting on back to your work.

BARNETTE (*Awkwardly*)   Right—'cause I—I've got those important calls out. (*Full of hope for her*)   They'll be pouring in directly. (*He starts to leave, then says to her with love*)   We'll talk.

MEG (*Reappearing in her boots*)   Oh, Barnette—

BARNETTE   Yes?

MEG   Could you give me a ride just down to the corner? I need to stop at Helen's Bakery.

BARNETTE   Be glad to.

MEG   Thanks. Listen, Babe, I'll be right back with the cake. We're gonna have the best celebration! Now, ah, if Lenny asks where I've gone, just say I'm . . . Just say, I've gone out back to, ah, pick up some pawpaws! Okay?

BABE   Okay.

MEG   Fine; I'll be back in a bit. Goodbye.

BABE   'Bye.

BARNETTE   Goodbye, Becky.

BABE   Goodbye, Barnette. Take care.

(MEG *and* BARNETTE *exit.* BABE *sits staring ahead, in a state of deep despair*)

BABE   Goodbye, Becky. Goodbye, Barnette. Goodbye, Becky. (*She stops when* LENNY *comes down the stairs in a fluster.*

LENNY   Oh! Oh! Oh! I'm so ashamed! I'm such a coward! I'm such a yellow-bellied chicken! I'm so ashamed! Where's Meg?

BABE (*Suddenly bright*)   She's, ah—gone out back—to pick up some pawpaws.

LENNY   Oh. Well, at least I don't have to face her! I just couldn't do it! I couldn't make the call! My heart was pounding like a hammer. Pound! Pound! Pound! Why, I looked down and I could actually see my blouse moving back and forth! Oh, Babe, you look so disappointed. Are you?

BABE (*Despondently*)   Uh huh.

LENNY   Oh, no! I've disappointed Babe! I can't stand it! I've gone and disappointed my little sister, Babe! Oh, no! I feel like howling like a dog!

CHICK'S VOICE   Oooh, Lenny! (*She enters dramatically, dripping with sympathy*)   Well, I just don't know what to say! I'm so sorry! I am so sorry for you! And for little Babe here, too. I mean, to have such a sister as that!

LENNY   What do you mean?

CHICK   Oh, you don't need to pretend with me. I saw it all from over there in my own back yard; I saw Meg stumbling out of Doc Porters' pickup truck, not fifteen minutes ago. And her looking such a disgusting mess. You must be so ashamed! You must just want to die! Why, I always said that girl was nothing but cheap Christmas trash!

LENNY   Don't talk that way about Meg.

CHICK   Oh, come on now, Lenny, honey. I know exactly how you feel about Meg. Why, Meg's a low-class tramp and you need not have one more blessed thing to do with her and her disgusting behavior.

LENNY   I said, don't you ever talk that way about my sister Meg again.

CHICK   Well, my goodness gracious, Lenora, don't be such a noodle —it's the truth!

LENNY   I don't care if it's the Ten Commandments. I don't want to hear it in my home. Not ever again.

CHICK   In your home?! Why, I never in all my life— This is my grandfather's home! And you're just living here on his charity; so don't you get high-falutin' with me, Miss Lenora Josephine MaGrath!

LENNY   Get out of here—

CHICK   Don't you tell me to get out! What makes you think you can order me around? Why, I've had just about my fill of you trashy MaGraths and your trashy ways: hanging yourselves in cellars; carrying on with married men; shooting your own husbands!

LENNY   Get out!

CHICK (*To* BABE)   And don't you think she's not gonna end up at the state prison farm or in some—mental institution. Why, it's a clear-cut case of manslaughter with intent to kill!

LENNY   Out! Get out!

CHICK (*Running on*)   That's what everyone's saying, deliberate intent to kill! And you'll pay for that! Do you hear me? You'll pay!

LENNY (*Picking up a broom and threatening* CHICK *with it*)   And I'm telling you to get out!

CHICK   You—you put that down this minute—Are you a raving lunatic?

LENNY (*Beating* CHICK *with the broom*)   I said for you to get out! That means out! And never, never, never come back!

CHICK (*Overlapping, as she runs around the room*)   Oh! Oh! Oh! You're crazy! You're crazy!

LENNY (*Chasing* CHICK *out the door*)   Do you hear me, Chick the Stick! This is my home! This is my house! Get out! Out!

CHICK (*Overlapping*)   Oh! Oh! Police! Police! You're crazy! Help! Help!

(LENNY *chases* CHICK *out of the house. They are both screaming. The phone rings.* BABE *goes and picks it up.*

BABE   Hello! . . . Oh, hello, Zackery! . . . He showed them to me! . . . You're what! . . . What do you mean? . . . What! . . . You can't put me out to Whitfield . . . 'Cause I'm not crazy . . . I'm not! I'm not! . . . She wasn't crazy, either . . . Don't you call my mother crazy! . . . No, you're not! You're not gonna. You're not! (*She slams the phone down and stares wildly ahead*)   He's not. He's not. (*As she walks over to the ribbon drawer*)   I'll do it. I will. And he won't . . . (*She opens the drawer, pulls out the rope, becomes terrified, throws the rope back in the drawer, and slams it shut*)

(LENNY *enters from the back door swinging the broom and laughing*)

LENNY   Oh, my! Oh, my! You should have seen us! Why, I chased Chick the Stick right up the mimosa tree. I did! I left her right up there screaming in the tree!

BABE (*Laughing; she is insanely delighted*)   Oh, you did!

LENNY   Yes, I did! And I feel so good! I do! I feel good! I feel good!

BABE (*Overlapping*)   Good! Good, Lenny! Good for you!

(They dance around the kitchen)

LENNY *(Stopping)*   You know what—

BABE   What?

LENNY   I'm gonna call Charlie! I'm gonna call him up right now!

BABE   You are?

LENNY   Yeah, I feel like I can really do it!

BABE   You do?

LENNY   My courage is up; my heart's in it; the time is right! No more beating around the bush! Let's strike while the iron is hot!

BABE   Right! Right! No more beating around the bush! Strike while the iron is hot!

> *(LENNY goes to the phone. BABE rushes over to the ribbon drawer. She begins tearing through it)*

LENNY *(With the receiver in her hand)*   I'm calling him up, Babe— I'm really gonna do it!

BABE *(Still tearing through the drawer)*   Good! Do it! Good!

LENNY *(As she dials)*   Look. My hands aren't even shaking.

BABE *(Pulling out a red rope)*   Don't we have any stronger rope than this?

LENNY   I guess not. All the rope we've got's in that drawer. *(About her hands)*   Now they're shaking a little.

> *(BABE takes the rope and goes up the stairs. LENNY finishes dialing the number. She waits for an answer)*

LENNY   Hello? . . . Hello, Charlie. This is Lenny MaGrath . . . Well, I'm fine. I'm just fine. *(An awkward pause)*   I was, ah, just calling to see—how you're getting on . . . Well, good. Good . . .Yes, I know I said that. Now I wish I didn't say it . . . Well, the reason I said that before, about not seeing each other again, was 'cause of me, not you . . . Well, it's just I—I can't have any children. I—have this ovary problem . . . Why, Charlie, what a thing to say! . . . Well, they're not all little snot-nosed pigs! . . . You think they are! . . . Oh, Charlie, stop, stop! You're making me laugh . . . Yes, I guess I was. I can see now that I was . . . You are? . . . Well, I'm dying to see you, too . . . Well, I don't know when, Charlie . . . soon. How about, well, how about tonight? . . . You will? . . . Oh, you will! . . . All right, I'll be here. I'll be right here . . . Goodbye, then, Charlie. Goodbye for now. *(She hangs up the phone in a daze)*   Babe. Oh, Babe! He's coming. He's coming! Babe! Oh, Babe, where are you? Meg! Oh . . . out back—picking up pawpaws. *(As she exits through the back door)*   And those pawpaws are just ripe for picking up!

(*There is a moment of silence; then a loud, horrible thud is heard coming from upstairs. The telephone begins ringing immediately. It rings five times before* BABE *comes hurrying down the stairs with a broken piece of rope hanging round her neck. The phone continues to ring*)

BABE (*To the phone*)   Will you shut up? (*She is jerking the rope from around her neck. She grabs a knife to cut it off*)   Cheap! Miserable! I hate you! I hate you! (*She throws the rope violently across the room. The phone stops ringing*)   Thank God. (*She looks at the stove, goes over it, and turns the gas on. The sound of gas escaping is heard. She sniffs at it*)   Come on. Come on . . . Hurry up . . . I beg of you—hurry up! (*Finally, she feels the oven is ready; she takes a deep breath and opens the door to stick her head into it. She spots the rack and furiously jerks it out. Taking another breath, she sticks her head into the oven. She stands for several moments tapping her fingers furiously on top of the stove. She speaks from inside the oven*)   Oh, please. Please. (*After a few moments, she reaches for the box of matches with her head still in the oven. She tries to strike a match. It doesn't catch*)   Oh, Mama, please! (*She throws the match away and is getting a second one*)   Mama . . . Mama . . . so that's why you done it! (*In her excitement she starts to get up, bangs her head, and falls back in the oven*)

(MEG *enters from the back door, carrying a birthday cake in a pink box*)

MEG   Babe! (*She throws the box down and runs to pull* BABE'S *head out of the oven*)   Oh, my God! What are you doing? What the hell are you doing?

BABE (*Dizzily*)   Nothing. I don't know. Nothing.

(MEG *turns off the gas and moves* BABE *to a chair near the open door*)

MEG   Sit down. Sit down! Will you sit down?

BABE   I'm okay. I'm okay.

MEG   Put your head between your knees and breathe deep!

BABE   Meg—

MEG   Just do it! I'll get you some water. (*She gets some water for* BABE) Here.

BABE   Thanks.

MEG   Are you okay?

BABE   Uh huh.

MEG   Are you sure?

BABE   Yeah, I'm sure. I'm okay.

MEG   (*Getting a damp rag and putting it over her own face*)   Well, good. That's good.

BABE   Meg—

MEG   Yes?

BABE   I know why she did it.

MEG   What? Why who did what?

BABE   (*With joy*)   Mama. I know why she hung that cat along with her.

MEG   You do?

BABE   (*With enlightenment*)   It's 'cause she was afraid of dying all alone.

MEG   Was she?

BABE   She felt so unsure, you know, as to what was coming. It seems the best thing coming up would be a lot of angels and all of them singing. But I imagine they have high, scary voices and little gold pointed fingers that are as sharp as blades and you don't want to meet 'em all alone. You'd be afraid to meet 'em all alone. So it wasn't like what people were saying about her hating that cat. Fact is, she loved that cat. She needed him with her 'cause she felt so all alone.

MEG   Oh, Babe . . . Babe, Why, Babe? Why?

BABE   Why what?

MEG   Why did you stick your head into the oven?!

BABE   I don't know, Meg. I'm having a bad day. It's been a real bad day; those pictures, and Barnette giving up his vendetta; then Willie Jay heading north; and—and Zackery called me up. (*Trembling with terror*) He says he's gonna have me classified insane and then send me on out to the Whitfield asylum.

MEG   What! Why, he could never do that!

BABE   Why not?

MEG   'Cause you're not insane.

BABE   I'm not?

MEG   No! He's trying to bluff you. Don't you see? Barnette's got him running scared.

BABE   Really?

MEG   Sure. He's scared to death—calling you insane. Ha! Why, you're just as perfectly sane as anyone walking the streets of Hazlehurst, Mississippi.

BABE   I am?

MEG   More so! A lot more so!

BABE   Good!

MEG   But, Babe, we've just got to learn how to get through these real bad days here. I mean, it's getting to be a thing in our family. (*Slight pause as she looks at* BABE) Come on, now. Look, we've got Lenny's cake right here. I mean, don't you wanna be around to give her her cake, watch her blow out the candles?

BABE (*Realizing how much she wants to be there*) Yeah, I do, I do. 'Cause she always loves to make her birthday wishes on those candles.

MEG Well, then we'll give her her cake and maybe you won't be so miserable.

BABE Okay.

MEG Good. Go on and take it out of the box.

BABE Okay. (*She takes the cake out of the box. It is a magical moment*) Gosh, it's a pretty cake.

MEG (*Handing her some matches*) Here now. You can go on and light up the candles.

BABE All right. (*She starts to light the candles*) I love to light up candles. And there are so many here. Thirty pink ones in all, plus one green one to grow on.

MEG (*Watching her light the candles*) They're pretty.

BABE They are. (*She stops lighting the candles*) And I'm not like Mama. I'm not so all alone.

MEG You're not.

BABE (*As she goes back to lighting candles*) Well, you'd better keep an eye out for Lenny. She's supposed to be surprised.

MEG All right. Do you know where she's gone?

BABE Well, she's not here inside—so she must have gone on outside.

MEG Oh, well, then I'd better run and find her.

BABE Okay; 'cause these candles are gonna melt down.

(MEG *starts out the door*)

MEG Wait—there she is coming. Lenny! Oh, Lenny! Come on! Hurry up!

BABE (*Overlapping and improvising as she finishes lighting candles*) Oh, no! No! Well, yes—Yes! No, wait! Wait! Okay! Hurry up!

(LENNY *enters.* MEG *covers* LENNY'S *eyes with her hands*)

LENNY (*Terrified*) What? What is it? What?

MEG and BABE Surprise! Happy birthday! Happy birthday to Lenny!

LENNY Oh, no! Oh, me! What a surprise! I could just cry! Oh, look: *Happy Birthday, Lenny—A Day Late!* How cute! My! Will you look at all those candles—it's absolutely frightening.

BABE (*A spontaneous thought*) Oh, no, Lenny, it's good! 'Cause— 'cause the more candles you have on your cake, the stronger your wish is.

LENNY Really?

BABE Sure!

LENNY Mercy! (MEG *and* BABE *start to sing*)

LENNY (*Interrupting the song*) Oh, but wait! I—can't think of my wish! My body's gone all nervous inside.

MEG For God's sake, Lenny—Come on!

BABE The wax is all melting!

LENNY My mind is just a blank, a total blank!

MEG Will you please just—

BABE (*Overlapping*) Lenny, hurry! Come on!

LENNY Okay! Okay! Just go!

> (MEG *and* BABE *burst into the* "Happy Birthday" *song. As it ends,* LENNY *blows out all the candles on the cake.* MEG *and* BABE *applaud loudly*)

MEG Oh, you made it!

BABE Hurray!

LENNY Oh, me! Oh, me! I hope that wish comes true! I hope it does!

BABE Why? What did you wish for?

LENNY (*As she removes the candles from the cake*) Why, I can't tell you that.

BABE Oh, sure you can—

LENNY Oh, no! Then it won't come true.

BABE Why, that's just superstition! Of course it will, if you made it deep enough.

MEG Really? I didn't know that.

LENNY Well, Babe's the regular expert on birthday wishes.

BABE It's just I get these feelings. Now, come on and tell us. What was it you wished for?

MEG Yes, tell us. What was it?

LENNY Well, I guess it wasn't really a specific wish. This—this vision just sort of came into my mind.

BABE A vision? What was it of?

LENNY I don't know exactly. It was something about the three of us smiling and laughing together.

BABE Well, when was it? Was it far away or near?

LENNY I'm not sure; but it wasn't forever; it wasn't for every minute. Just this one moment and we were all laughing.

BABE Then, what were we laughing about?

LENNY I don't know. Just nothing, I guess.

MEG Well, that's a nice wish to make.

(LENNY *and* MEG *look at each other a moment*)

MEG   Here, now, I'll get a knife so we can go ahead and cut the cake
in celebration of Lenny being born!
BABE   Oh, yes! And give each one of us a rose. A whole rose apiece!
LENNY (*Cutting the cake nervously*)   Well, I'll try—I'll try!
MEG (*Licking the icing off a candle*)   Mmmm—this icing is delicious!
Here, try some!
BABE   Mmmm! It's wonderful! Here, Lenny!
LENNY (*Laughing joyously as she licks icing from her fingers and cuts
huge pieces of cake that her sisters bite into ravenously*)   Oh, how
I do love having birthday cake for breakfast! How I do!

(*The sisters freeze for a moment of laughing and catching cake. The
lights change and frame them in a magical, golden, sparkling glim-
mer; saxophone music is heard. The lights dim to blackout, and the
saxophone continues to play.*)

Miss Ida B. Wells

ENDESHA IDA MAE HOLLAND

CHARACTERS

MISS IDA B. WELLS
VOICE

SETTING

The play is set in Ida B. Wells' home in Chicago in 1928 with flashbacks to Ida's memories of the 1880s.

(*The scene is the study of* MISS IDA B. WELLS' *Chicago home. A big wooden desk sits just left of center angling towards up center. The desk is cluttered with papers, photos, books, and writing materials including an old typewriter. Behind the desk is a chair and a small book shelf on top of which sets a tea service. Just right off center is an arm chair and stool with a coat rack behind it. The time is early evening on an autumn day in the late 1920s)*
     WELLS *enters wearing a coat and hat and carrying a draw-string purse, a newspaper and a small package*)

WELLS (*To herself*)   . . . tell her what I did . . . why is it she heard my name so much. (*Still puzzling this, she sets her paper, package, and purse on the chair, removes her hat and coat, hangs them on the rack, picks up paper, package, and purse and crosses to sit at desk. Smiling to herself*)   Why is it she heard my name so much. (*She notices the audience for the first time*)   Oh! I didn't know you were here. (*Standing*)   I wasn't expecting anyone. Please, make yourself at home. (*She sits again*)   You know the funniest thing happened to me just now. I'd been to Sears and Roebuck and to pick up a copy of the paper and was on my way back here when I came upon these girls jumping rope. All of a sudden one of the girls dropped her end of the rope and came running over to me shouting: "Miss Wells? Miss Ida B. Wells?" I said, "Yes?" She said, "You are Miss Wells." "Yes, I am my dear," I told her. Then she said, "How come you're so famous?" (*Laughs*)   I said "What?" Then she explained that her teacher at the

---

*Dedicated to Mrs. Alfreda M. Barnett Duster (1904–1983), Ida B. Wells' daughter, for being an inspiration to me when I felt like I wanted to go way back and sit down.

YWCA's evening class asked all the students to name an important lady in history. She was the only Negro in the class, so she thought she sure better name a Negro lady. She named me. Only thing, when the teacher asked her what I'd done—she didn't know! But she thought it must have been something mighty great, cause she'd heard my name everywhere.

I told her it would take a long time to tell her all about what I'd done and she'd probably miss her supper. I said that I would go right home and start to write a book about my life so she could read about what I'd done. (*Laughs*) She was sure enough happy about that and ran back to her friends to tell them that Ida B. Wells was going to write a book for her. (*Laughs again*) Course I didn't tell her that I'd just been to Sears and Roebuck (*Opening package*) to pick up this ribbon for my typewriter. I've been planning to set my life down on paper for awhile now. She thought I was going to write a book just cause she asked me what I'd done. (*Finishes laughing and starts to work replacing the ribbon*) If Colored folks don't know what it is I've done I sure better put it down on paper. It shouldn't be too hard. I was a newspaper woman for a long time you know. Had a couple of papers of my own. Even wrote for Mr. T. Thomas Fortune's paper, *The New York Age*. (*Modestly*) So, I'm pretty adept with the pen as they say. (*As if someone in the audience spoke to her*) What's that you say? You don't know what it is I've done either? Well, I'm not surprised. (*She's been having trouble with the ribbon*) I suppose that you don't want to wait until my book comes out, especially if I have much more trouble with this. (*Giving up on the ribbon for the moment, she crosses right, past the desk*) Well . . . I don't want to keep you from your supper either, so how about if I just tell you about the important parts of my life? (*She senses a positive response from audience, there may be verbal exchange with audience*) Good. Now, let's see. The beginning's always a good place to start, don't you think?

My mother and father were slaves. I was born a slave on July 16, 1862, in Holly Springs, Mississippi. I'm the oldest of eight children. I attended Shaw University. My father was one of the founding board members of Shaw University. He and mother made sure I kept my head in some book or another. My father, Jim Wells, was the best carpenter in the county, if not the whole South. He even built our house. (*Crossing to desk and picking up a framed picture*) Here's a picture of them. Father was real civic-minded. He took part in just about everything that the Freedman's Bureau did in our town. Now, my mother, Elizabeth, was very religious. She was such a Christian that I was scared to 'think' bad thoughts around her. She was the best cook in town. My folks brought me up to know the importance of family. It's a good thing they did too, because when I was sixteen years old, the Yellow Fever Epidemic took their lives. It was left up to me to take care of the other children. Time was hard. The Thirty-Third Degree Masons came to our aid. They were some good people. I found work as a school teacher. So in '84, I was going to the country outside of Memphis to take this teaching job. That's when things started happening to me!

I had bought a first-class ticket on the C,O & S Railroad to get me there. When I tried to take my seat, a couple of the train's employees—and the 'conductor' tried to drag me back to the 'smokers car.' For a minute there, I didn't know what was happening: the conductor was dragging me by the arm: somebody else, with a lot of braids on his uniform had me in such a tight grip that my whole side went numb. Two of the women passengers grabbed hold of my legs and pulled me off my feet. It was rough going there for a minute or two. Then I started to participate . . . with feet and teeth. If I hada had pyreah gums really bad, there'd 've been a lot of dead first-class passengers. I can guarantee you that a lot of the ones I kicked—wish they'd been bit. My sense of justice was outraged. There was no way that I was going to let the 14th and 15th Amendments take low to Jim Crow! Not through me they weren't. I went back to Memphis, all bruised up, on the back seat of a dray wagon and filed suit against the railroad.

(*Sitting at desk again*) I hired a Colored lawyer to present my case. After months and months of delay—I found out that he'd been bought off by the railroad. I confronted him in his office.

(*As if in office*) I brought my case to you, sir, because you're the only Colored lawyer in town. And now you sit here and tell me that the railroad wants to pay me twenty dollars for taking away my rights?! Sir, it's not for me by myself that I'm trying to fight to keep our power. You and me both know that if we give up or give in to the railroad, we'll pass up the chance to help change things for our people. (*She listens to him for a moment, then rises in anger*) What do you mean you won't have time to work on my case no longer? Mr. Lawyer, sir, I bet you haven't had more than three cases in all the seven or eight years you been calling yourself a lawyer. Now all of a sudden you get a flood of cases so you can't afford to spend any more time on mine? Seems to me like you been bought off by the railroad, Mr. Honorable Attorney at Law.

(*To the audience*) I sure was mad. Well, since he was the only Colored lawyer in town, I had to hire an honest White one. Finally, there I was in the courtroom. Every seat was taken. All the White women were sitting there fanning themselves, while all the Colored women were hold- ing White women's babies. Judge Pierce was an ex-Union soldier from Minnesota. He rapped his gavel three times, then spoke in a voice that rung clear as a bell, so that even the babies stopped crying. (*Speaking like the judge*) I find on behalf of the plaintiff, Ida B. Wells, damages owed her of $500. I still have the headline from the *Memphis Appeal* here someplace. (*She searches through desk*) I keep it in case I ever need something to get my dander up. (*She finds it in a book*) Here it is. (*Holds it up and reads*) "Darkie Damsel Gets Damages." Well, the Supreme Court of Tennessee eventually overturned the decision. But what I couldn't understand was that none of my people seemed to feel it was a Race matter. Nobody would help and many people including friends were ashamed and quit talking to me. (*Putting the clipping back in the book*) So, I trod the winepress alone, determined, that if need be, I would be the sole sentinel for my Race. (*Picking up the typing ribbon and trying again to change it*) Now there's something about the South after the Civil War you've got to understand. She reached a peak around 1867 and '68 that had hardly been dreamed of before. There was military rule that protected Negro lives. Citizenship and the fran- chise had been conferred upon us. There were Negro office holders at state conventions. There were Negro men sitting in the lawmakers seats —in the heart of the Confederate states—abolishing the restrictions on voting and holding office, imprisonment for debt, and the legal ownership of human beings. When the votes were counted in Louisiana and Missis- sippi, there was roughly 97,000 White voters—and 224,000 Negro voters. Old man Lovejoy use to say, "The bottom rail is on the top!" It sure was something. But that didn't last long. Things began to change quickly. You see, White folks began to lose their control over us, so they organized themselves into secret societies, the best known is the Ku Klux Klan. Their purpose was to stop Negro participation in politics and to 'protect the virtue' of White women from the savage Black Beast. Their methods were death and destruction. Then with the Presidential election of 1876 the South chartered its own course. The Hayes Compromise gave the South freedom from federal intervention, which meant Home Rule and a mandate for White supremacy. The 14th and 15th Amendments became a joke—the bottom rail was back on the bottom.

(*She finishes with the typing ribbon, picks up the newspaper and crosses to chair at right and sits*) Well, it took some time, but I finally figured out what it was I wanted to be. (*She slaps newspaper against her hand*) A newspaper woman. My opportunity came when the men

who owned the *Free Speech and Headlight of Memphis* decided to sell
part ownership of their paper. So for $100 I started my journalistic career,
determined to print news that was crucial to the safety and progress
of the race, now that I had some say over things. I knew I could make
it work. Right away I started out complaining about the school where
I worked. It wasn't fit for dogs . . . I wrote about the rats, the leaking
roof, and the books that were so worn that they couldn't be read. I told
the people that something had to be done so that we could get on with
the business of teaching and learning. The School Board voted—to dis-
miss me! None of the parents came to my aid even though they knew
I was right. I think it's right to strike a blow against evil, but it bothered
me that a fight made in the interest of the Race didn't have the support
of the Race. Well Lord, since I no longer had a job, I had to make the
paper work. I traveled all over the South selling my paper and had sub-
scriptions in four states. It made me feel good, thinking that I was making
a difference in the way people thought. Everything was going in my
favor. Everybody in town was talking about me. (*In voice of southern
Negro woman*) "Honey chile, dere go Miss Ida B. Wells. She de one
dat gots de paper: Hit's her own dear paper too." (*To the audience*) I
tell you, I was walking real tall. My head was up mighty high on my
shoulders. Then one night, near bout dusk dark, something happened
that I will never forget. It changed the way I saw the whole world. Sometimes I hate to think about it. It makes my head hurt.

> (*She rises as if to brush away the memories. But they intrude any-
> way. She screams*) Oh my dear God! Somebody stop them! Some-
> body do something quick! (*Begs of audience*) Sheriff, Banker
> Matthews, Rev. Hale . . . Oh please somebody . . . Miss May . . .
> Mrs. Goldberg . . . don't let them burn him . . . Please, please
> somebody.

(*Sits at desk*) Three of our leading Colored businessmen died that day.
The White mob lynched them. Right then and there we Colored people
should've put a stop to those murders. I'd heard about lynchings taking
place in other parts of the South; but right there in Memphis, my friends
were killed. Nobody—not even me—lifted a hand to help them. Before
he died that day, Mr. Brown, he said—for us to go North. The Sunday
after the lynching everybody was in church. The preacher didn't say a
word about it; but they did some kinda praying. Everybody was scared
to talk about the lynchings. I decided right then and there to take a
stand. I beckoned for one of the ushers, and sent a note to Preacher
Perry, asking him to let me say a few words before the service was over.
Right after he opened the doors of the church—every sinner in town
joined church that Sunday—he said that the church would hear from

Miss Ida B. Wells. A hush fell over the people. It was quiet as a tomb.
I walked up near the pulpit, every eye in the room was on me.

There is no justice for us here. I can truthfully say that three of
us are missing from this service today. I can truthfully say that—
because I saw with my own eyes the hot fire eating into Mr.
Montgomery's body. I can truthfully say that—I heard Mr. James
begging for somebody to help him. I can truthfully say that—I saw
the very life leave Mr. Brown. Nobody went forward. Nobody. We
were scared. We were scared of the White people of Memphis; who
got together in a mob and went on a rampage in our section; all
on the word of a White storekeeper who don't want no Colored
competition. The only thing we can do is to save our money and
leave Memphis. Let's make Memphis a ghost-town. Memphis won't
protect our lives nor give us a fair trial in the court. What the city
of Memphis does—is allow us to be taken out and murdered—on
the word of any White person. I vow to you, right here and now
—and for those of you that want to tell the White people what I
say, hear me good! Me . . . Ida B. Wells, is this day taking up
the banner to put a stop to lynch-law. I'll use my newspaper and
whatever else I can—to indict the people of Memphis, or anywhere.
I'm going to do battle against lynchings!

After I finished speaking, nobody in the church would meet my eye.
They were all scared. A lot of them looked like they wished the floor
would open up under my feet. One man put his hands over his ears
trying to block out my words. (*Heatedly*) I didn't care if nobody liked
what I said. It was the truth. I wish I hada had Mr. Claude McKay's
poem about lynching to recite to the folks in the church. But wasn't
nobody doing much writing about lynch-law at that time; surely not us
Negroes. (*To the audience*) Have any of you ever read Mr. McKay's
poem? He sure put my feelings into words.

> His spirit in smoke ascended to high heaven
> his father by the cruelest way of pain
> Had bidden him to his bosom once again
> The awful sin still remained unforgiven
> all night a bright and solitary star
> Perchance the one that guided him
> Yet gave him up at last to fate's wild whim
> Hung pitifully over the swinging char
> Day dawned, and soon the mixed crowds came to view
> The ghastly body swaying in the sun:

The women thronged to look, but never a one
Showed sorrow in her eyes of steely blue;
And little lads, lynchers that were to be,
Danced round the dreadful thing in fiendish glee.

(*She returns to desk in somber mood. And continues rummaging*)   Lord, I wish that I could put so many feelings into so few words, like Mr. McKay and Mr. Dunbar and Mrs. Frances E.W. Harper. But I tell you one thing: I can sure nuff write a newspaper column. Now I know that a lot of you will think that I'm boasting and bragging on my writing . . . I am! I wrote an editorial in my paper . . . let me see can I find it, I'll read it to you. (*She continues rummaging in desk*)   I had to write it! They had just lynched eight Negro men. Five of these men, they said, 'looked' like they wanted White women. Those White people use to holler 'rape' so much, its a wonder that they didn't burn all the Negro men in the South! Sometimes they used the other excuses that our people were trying to take over and they had to stop race riots. (*Finds editorial*) Here it is! Course now, I'll just read a little of it and you'll get my point. I tell you—Ida B. Wells, hung em out to dry with this one.

> (*She reads*)   Nobody in this section believes the old 'threadbare' lies that all these Colored men assault White women. If southern White men aren't careful they'll over-reach themselves and a con-(*She re-cites from memory*)   clusion will be reached which will be very damaging to the moral reputation of their women.

(*Laughs and sits at desk*)   I can be honest with you now—I was a little scared after I low-rated White women's morals. They had done so bad, till somebody had to call them on it.

A few days later, I left town to drum up more business for the paper; it's a good thing that I did too, because while I was gone, a group of White 'businessmen' called on me. When they couldn't find me, they tore up my office and wrecked my Press. All the Colored people were told that *I* was the troublemaker; that they had to put a stop to *my* lies. The Colored people in Memphis was scared to death. Nobody supported me and some even condemned me. Years later, Preacher Perry told me that the whole church prayed for me; prayed that I didn't come back. I didn't go back! (*Standing*)   I headed to the North. (*With great force*)   I bought me two guns—and a razor. I knew I wouldn't be satisfied keeping quiet. The North needed to know what was happening to my people down South. I didn't know where to turn; I didn't know who to turn to. I did know that I couldn't give up. I rode the train on to the North.

I figured that maybe I could get a job with Mr. Fortune's paper, *The New York Age*; since it had already carried a couple of my columns from the South. (*She relives the experience retrospectively*)

I cleaned myself up in the restroom of the train station. Then I made my way to Mr. Fortune's office; and presented myself to his secretary. I could see in her face that I was looking bad. My suit was all wrinkled—my hair was a mess. I know I looked a sight. She didn't even want to announce me to Mr. Fortune. . . . She said that he had a visitor and that I should come back the next day. The fat was in the fire by this time. (*Takes a deep breath*) So I just took a deep breath and commenced to telling her off, in no quiet voice either. I must've scared the pore woman, because she ran pass me and went down the hall. When she came back there were two men with her. I knew right away which one was Mr. Fortune; I couldn't quite place the other gentleman, but he did look mighty familiar. (*To the audience*) The man with Mr. Fortune was real tall. He was about seventy or so years old. His gray hair hung to his shoulders. He was magnificent! He didn't say a word; he just wrapped his great arms around me and held me for the longest time. I was all musty and stanking—but he didn't seem to mind. Then Mr. Fortune said that we—me and Mr. Douglass should come back into his office. Mr. Douglass . . . Mr. Douglass . . . You don't mean to tell me that this is Mr. Frederick Douglass! I grabbed him then and held him so tight. I almost smothered him!

(*Moves to chair and rubs it gently*) You see this chair? I've had it near bout forty years. Mr. Douglass and his wife gave it to me when I set up housekeeping. Mr. Douglass and his wife were so kind to me. Many nights after I left work at the *Age*, Mr. Douglass and me would sit up way into the early morning—talking. (*Sits in chair*) Mr. Douglass had a troubled soul and I could feel that something was bothering him. Something was bothering me too. I didn't feel that I was doing enought for my people by just 'writing' about lynch-law. Mr. Douglass was no stranger to that sort of dilemma. (*Turns in chair and looks back across the years*)

When John Brown took his stand at Harper's Ferry, he asked Mr. Douglass to join him in the fight to free the slaves. Mr. Douglass preferred to fight with his pen, then with a gun. His friendship with John Brown was widely known. So when the law captured Brown they came looking for Mr. Douglass too. On the advice of his family and friends, Mr. Douglass took flight to England. He was lonely over there away from his family and friends and all the other people that loved him. Pretty soon, pore Mr. Douglass began to feel that he was no longer loved and began to question his actions in light of his refusal to help John Brown. He was tormented daily trying to find an answer. For thirty years he had kept all of this inside of him.

I can still see Mr. Douglas now, plain as day, with his head bowed and his soul torn in two parts, tormented about whether he had made the right decision. *(To the audience)* It was awhile before I spoke, but when I did I told the truth. I 'commanded' Mr. Douglass to raise his head up high. Because in my humble opinion, his newspaper, *The North Star*, had done more to move us along the way, than any single effort I knew of. My father, when he was alive, had gotten ahold of a copy of *The North Star*. Every Saturday night, we would all gather around and I would read the paper from front to back. It never bothered us that the paper was over a year old. My words helped ease Mr. Douglass' pain, and they also showed me that my writing was important. *(With great force)* Ida B. Wells may not be able to change the world—but I bet you a fat man I was set on helping make a difference. Right then and there I decided to start making speeches. Somebody would hear me; somebody had to hear me! Again, Mr. Douglass came to my aid. He gave me the chance to speak at the 1893 World Columbian Exposition, held here, in Chicago. *(With great pride)* I did some kinda speaking. Didn't know I had it in me. As mother use to say: A heap see but a few knows. *(She is apologetic)* I don't want you to think that I'm going to make a whole lotta speeches, that'll probably bore you to death; I'm not. I know that you want to get home to your supper—but I do want you to hear what I said at the Exposition.

(She rises and with great formality approaches the imaginary podium, takes a deep breath) I want to thank Mr. Douglass for allowing me the opportunity to bring the plight of Negro people in America, before you international visitors to Chicago. To those of you who traveled across America, to those of you who traveled from across the waters, I, Ida B. Wells, welcome you to this grand Columbian Exposition—this world showplace for the progress of man. All around you here, America is showing her industrial progress. Indeed, you visitors from other countries are seeing, for the first time: gadgets, all kinds of machinery and ideas—such as you've never seen before. Us Americans—including us Negro Americans, are seeing our own progress and feeling pride. For some Americans, this lifestyle is the very best. But behind this facade—there is problem on top of problem. Negro men are being dragged from their homes in the middle of the night. They're taken and hung from trees; they're burned to death. Crowds of people—I hope not none of you, stand around and say not one word to stop these lynchings. I have

a pamphlet here, that I wrote and financed. It is the record, that
I've collected on the Negro people that were lynched. I've also included a list of ways that you can help in my crusade to do battle
against lynch-law. Stop over near the table and pick up a pamphlet
or raise your hand and the gentleman over there, Mr. Paul Laurence
Dunbar will see that you get one. I thank you for listening.
My talk was received with such excitement. The people went wild with
applause. (*Moves toward desk*)   Later, I found out that the only people
that understood what I was saying were the few Negroes present; the
other White people were all foreigners who didn't understand but a few
words of English. The White Americans didn't even bother to come.
They'd accepted the South's 'threadbare lies'. A lot of the visitors to the
Exposition never went back home. Many of these immigrants just went
across town and moved in with their kin-folks or rented a room and
stayed. Around this same time, many Negroes migrated here too. They
thought that things would be different for them—once they got to the
North. Here in Chicago, they tabled our rights. Negroes could only do
housework or other kinds of unskilled labor.

(*Puts paper in typewriter*)   Yes mam, I did a lot of speaking in the
early nineties. Mr. William Lloyd Garrison came to hear me speak a
number of times. His father, Mr. Garrison, Senior, is the famous Aboli-
tionist; the one that worked so hard with Mr. Douglass. He takes after
his father too. He got so mad when I told him about the Memphis lynchings that he used his influence with some other businessmen, and they
turned down a loan that the city of Memphis was trying to get. I tell
you, I was just like an old ice-box: I wasn't going to keep nothing. I
was going to tell it all and to anybody. I wasn't going to let the South
'throw no brick and then hide their hand.' (*Sits at desk*)   Everybody
wanted me to speak to their club or organization. I had speaking engagements all over the northeast. I was forever on the go. (*Picks up small
jewelry box from the desk. She opens it with great care and takes out
a small pin*)   This is the pin the women gave me at my Testimonial in
New York. (*Pinning it to her bosom*)   I . . . o . . . l. . . a . . . Iola!
When I first started writing down South I took the name 'Iola'. I started
out writing for the Living Way, my church's newsletter. (*Laughs*)   I remember the time I wrote an article about the Mother's Board of my
church; where is it? (*She searches and then gives up*)   I can't find it
right now but I tell you—I ruffled a whole lotta feathers. The Mother's
Board got so mad about 'Iola's' article until they sent for Mother Moore
—who claimed to be some kin—a cousin or something to God. They
got pore old Mother Moore up off her sick bed to try and find the "hell
bound sinner, Iola." But I had Preacher Perry's word that he wouldn't

give me away. And he didn't. (*Pauses. Senses that she has gotten away from the subject*) Now where was I? Oh yes, I was telling you about my grand Testimonial. The old-timers said they had never in their lives seen anything like it. Mrs. Lyons and Mrs. Matthews of New York put it together to show their support for my crusade. (*She fondles pin*) They called together the leading Negro women of New York, Philadelphia, Delaware and Washington, DC. I had no idea that it was going to be such a grand affair.

(*Relives the experience*) When they brought me to the auditorium that evening about ten women escorted me down the aisle. As far as my eyes could see, people were sitting everywhere. Some were even standing. I was doing some kinda marching. (*Does so*) I looked up on the platform and there sat Molly Terrell; you probably know her by the name of Mary Church Terrell. But she'll always be 'Molly' to me because we grew up together in the South. And right next to Molly sat the world's foremost fighter for Women's Suffrage, Miss Susan B. Anthony. Right next to Miss Anthony sat Miss Jane Addams, the founder of Chicago's Hull House. To top it all off, there sat Mr. Douglass. (*To herself*) My Lord, "Ida B., you show nuff picking in high cotton." I kept pinching myself. Seems like my legs would give out any minute if I didn't hurry up and sit down. Molly Terrell got up and introduced me. She did some kinda speaking that night. Didn't know she had it in her. She called me a "torch bearer" and a woman whose voice was louder than any other in the struggle against lynch-law. The people gave me a standing ovation and a big lit-up sign started flashing the name 'Iola'. I lost control of myself; I couldn't stop crying. But I made my speech, with the tears rolling down my face. Molly came up behind me and without a word put her handkerchief in my hand. I wiped my eyes, kept right on crying—and never missed a word. I was kinda ashame after it was all over. Mr. Douglass told me that when I started crying —everybody in the audience could feel the depth of our suffering.

(*Moves to teapot and pours a cup of tea*) I been talking so long my throat's almost dry. (*She sips daintily with little finger crooked*) I started drinking tea in England. Right after my Testimonial, Miss Catherine Impey, Editor, of the *Anti-Caste*, a magazine that advocated equal rights for the native of India, invited me to visit England and lecture on anti-lynch struggles. Some Negro people said that I shouldn't go. But I felt that I was duty-bound to give the facts I had collected to the world. Some of our people thought that the trip to England would be self-serving. That I would have so much fun until I forgot about the struggle. When I finally got off that ship, I was sick as a dog. I just took a deep breath and waded right in with the big-shots. They got a lot of big-shots in England. Seems like everybody I met was royalty of some sort. I kinda hoped that they'ld give me a title. Can't you just hear it: 'Lady Ida B. Wells.' We'ld had to rope and tie Molly Terrell up tight; (*Relishes in the thought*) she'ld been so jealous. (*Sips daintily from the cup*)

(*Moves books and papers out of her way and sits on the edge of the desk*) There we sat: Rev. Asked, Mr. Axom, the Editor of the *Manchester Guardian*, Sir John Gorst, a member of Parliament, Miss Impey, and to my left sat—Lady Henry Somerset, the Countess of Aberdeen. The butler brought in the tea. Lady Somerset, herself, poured. Miss Impey picked up her cup and kinda crooked her little finger; Sir John picked up his cup and crooked his little finger more than Miss Impey's; now Lady Somerset, hers was 'really' crooked. But I was ready for them. They were all looking at my cup—even the butler. (*Relishes in the memory*) I tell you I was some ready for them. Mr. Douglass had got me ready, you know he'd been to England before. I picked up my cup, it felt like tissue paper in my hand. I picked it up—and crooked my little finger more then Lady Somerset could ever hope to crook hers. I could've told them . . . that Ida B. Wells, once I take a deep breath—you gone get some kinda action. (*Moves to armchair and sits*)

Yes mam, I tell you, that Lady Somerset was some grand. She had so much class. I think that I rubbed her the wrong way. If I remember right it was Rev. Asked that started the whole thing. He asked me about his good friend Rev. Dwight Moody. He wanted to know how had Rev. Moody helped in my crusade.

(*To the audience*) You all know that Rev. Moody was highly respected in this country and abroad. But he encouraged the drawing of the color line. He'd preach on separate days to the Negroes on his tours throughout the South. If he had said a few words in our favor, I believe that the other White folks would've listened to him. He never said a mumbling word. He gave the weight of his influence to the South.

Lady Somerset of all people took issue with what I said about Rev. Moody. She started talking about the use of expediency in order to conquer. Looked to me like she was getting a little hot under the collar. Then, she started telling me about 'her' good friend, Miss Frances Willard who was President of the Women's Christian Temperance Union, here, in America. I had to tell the truth—as tactful as I could.

I agreed that Miss Willard as President of the Temperance movement could exert a lot of influence. But she never, in all my knowledge, said a word against the South's 'threadbare lies'. In fact, Miss Willard had gone even further than Rev. Moody. At a meeting that the White folks was holding in the South, where they were defying the Constitution by suppressing the Negro vote, she went on record assuring them that when she returned to the North—all what they were doing in secret would remain a secret. She would remain loyal to them by pen and voice!

I could tell that Lady Somerset was upset with me—because her nose kinda flared out and her voice got real icy. I hated to say this because I knew that Lady Somerset had a deep respect for Miss Willard. But I couldn't for the life of me understand her compromising for the sake of stamping out whiskey and beer drinking—when people lives were at stake. Lady Somerset barely managed to hold on to her temper. She said that I was over-reacting. But, Miss Willard was slandering Negro people, left and right, in order to stay in the good graces with the very ones who were shooting, hanging and burning Negroes. I ask you now —was I over-reacting? Of course not! And I told her so too, in no uncertain words either! All in all, the day didn't go too bad. Mr. Axom said that I could write a column for his paper. I was glad of that because when the folks back home read my columns, they'd know that I was taking care of business and not, as a lot of them claimed, running around looking for a husband! It took Sir John Gorst to save the day. He proposed that a committee be formed to come to America and investigate what I charged. (*Laughs*) When the South heard about the committee, they rose with such indignation that the committee never came; But the idea that others were looking at them made them change a lot of their spots. When the next lynching occurred in Memphis, the White newspaper *condemned* it. Never before had the papers took a stand. On top of all this the southern papers even carried news about me returning to America.

I tell you, I was picking in high cotton. Negro women had started the Ida B. Wells Club, and they welcomed me home in a style fit for a queen. They laid out the Red Carpet! I felt so good. Lord, I felt so good. Even now I feel like cutting a step or two. (*She dances a couple of steps*)

It took ole 'slimey' Mr. Slayton to spoil my joy. (*To the audience*) Have you ever shook anybody's hand and knew right off that they were up to no-good? When I shook his hand I knew he was up to devilment. He wanted me to make speeches for his bureau. Speeches that he claimed the American people would *pay* to hear. He wanted me to talk on issues like temperance and suffrage—but not lynch-law! (*Takes a deep breath*)

I laid my finger longside his nose, and I told him, after I marched
him into the corner—that it would be sacrilegious for me to turn
aside in a money-making effort for myself. I positively refuse. Ida
B. Wells can't be bought—I'm not for sale!
When I finished glaring at Mr. Slayton he scurried off real quick. Lord,
I sure was something. (*Moves to bookshelf and picks up small vase*)
    Well I declare! Miss Anthony gave me this vase. (*Rubs it gently*)   It
sure is pretty. That Susan B. Anthony, she was some kinda woman. I
stayed with her for about four days in the '90s. (*Sits on edge of desk*)
    Those were great days for me as I sat at the feet of this great woman
    —this pioneer in the work of women rights. The day after I got
    there, she fired her stenographer—for refusing to take dictation from
    me. She had a lot of moxy about herself. She told me about the
    time she had to use expediency in order to conquer: Miss Anthony
    had asked Mr. Douglass not to attend their suffrage convention held
    in Atlanta, Georgia. Now Mr. Douglass was one of the few men that
    had supported her campaign; he went to most of the meetings and
    'always' sat on the platform as a honored guest. Pore Miss Anthony
    was scared that if she let Mr. Douglass attend; the southern White
    suffragettes wouldn't support the campaign—if they had to sit on
    the same platform with a Negro man—a former slave.
"Was I wrong to ask him not to attend, my dear?" Miss Anthony asked
me. (*Forceful but sensitive*)   "Yes, Miss Anthony I think you were wrong.
You may've made gains for suffrage; but you also confirmed White women
in their attitude on segregation." Miss Anthony didn't say nothing for
awhile—she just looked upside of my head. Don't get me wrong now
because I 'know' that Miss Anthony had high hopes that when White
women got the vote they would change things. My hopes weren't so
high. In my opinion, White women had set precedents of being power-
less; they had remained mute in determining social policies. If Miss Susan
B. Anthony could give in to racial pressure—Lord, we had a long way
to go. You know Miss Anthony took issue with my forthcoming marriage.
She told me that 'she' could never think of marriage and a family. That
she had to devote all her efforts to the cause. And that what my people
needed was 'someone' to carry the banner for them . . . 'someone' without
'other' obligations. (*Rises*)   I was going to carry the banner —I was also
going to marry Mr. Barnett too. Can you blame me?
    (*Glows with the following account*)   Me and Mr. Barnett did some
    kinda coteing. Everybody said we looked good together. You know
    Mr. Barnett was a lawyer and part-owner of Chicago's first Negro
    newspaper, *The Conservator*. He is a real Race man too. (*Admires
    wedding picture*)   My wedding day was the happiest day of my life.

My bridesmaids were so stunning. And the little flower girl threw the flowers all over the church. And there stood my love—Mr. Barnett. I tell you that 'everybody' was there. The Women's State Republican Committee had come and brought their husbands. Right after I married Mr. Barnett, I bought their paper. A lot of ole busybodies went around saying that I married him to get his paper and free legal advice. Mr. Barnett was a good catch; but Ida B. Wells-Barnett didn't have to use no tricks to get him. I guarantee you that.

Me and Mr. Barnett had four children: Charles, my oldest. I use to carry him with me on my lectures. Herman, my baby boy. Ida B., my namesake and Alfreda, my youngest. Mr. Barnett's first wife, Molly, passed on. They had two boys: Ferdinand, Junior, and Albert. A lot of the folks still call me *Miss* Wells. When they find out that I have children they start in asking, where is your husband. (*Laughs*)   Mr. Barnett don't mind when the folks call me Miss Wells. I think Miss Jane Addams was the first person to call me Mrs. Wells-Barnett. Wouldn't you know that it would take someone with her kind of class to do that. I consider Miss Addams the greatest woman in the United States.

Me and Miss Addams were different in a lot of ways. But we both tried to change America, in our own way. She tried to help the immigrants with her settlement—Hull House. Near the turn of the century, Miss Addams turned her attention to lynch-law. She wrote an article that offended me. Miss Addams' article that was widely printed called for a reform of the punishment! She had bought into the idea that Negro men were raping White women—she just didn't agree with the punishment used against them. Well, you *know* I had to say something—tactful, of course. I used the figures from the *Chicago Tribune* that they had compiled on lynchings over the years. I pointed out that the South was still using those old 'threadbare lies' to convince White folks in the North to understand even if they didn't condone their actions. Me and Miss Addams didn't have much to do with one another after our tiff in the papers. I guess I offended her. But I had to tell the truth!

Well anyway with the turn of the century, we Negroes were expecting a new day. We expected to be sweeping with a brand new broom! But this was not to be. In the South, state on top of state wrote Jim Crow laws on their books. In the North, as the Negro population grew discrimination ran rampant. The brand new broom wasn't sweeping clean atall. But by this time, Negro people from all walks of life were speaking out and demanding to be heard. I worked with the lot of them—trying to find solutions to our problems. You know Mr. Douglass was dead by now. But we did have Mr. Booker T. Washington who emphasized indus-

trial education. There was Mr. DuBois who was very astute. He knew
that color would be one of the major problems of the new century. Mrs.
St. Pierre Ruffin brought all the Negro women's clubs together under
a national banner. My old friend, Molly Terrell, she let selfish ambition
kill her influence. She tried to ignore my contributions to the struggle,
because she was afraid that I wanted to be President of the national
body of Colored women clubs. I did! Pore Molly—she was the best educated woman among us and she could've done so much. But people'll
find out about you. And when they do find out that you're for self—
it's hard to get elected dog catcher. (*She drops her head and ponders
for a moment*) I guess I can't be too hard on Molly, because I was
as aggressive as she is. I made a lot of mistakes too. If I could turn
back the hands of time—I would do a lot of things different. Over the
years, I discovered that I'm not the only one with a vision. Mrs. Mary
McCleod Bethune had a vision too. So did Molly Terrell . . . and a
lot of other folks—both Negro and White. At one time or another, Ida
B. Wells wore the mask that Mr. Dunbar writes so eloquently about.

> We wear the mask that grins and lies
> It hides our cheek and shades our eyes
> This debt we pay to human guile
> With torn and bleeding hearts we smile
> And mouth with myriad subtleties
> Why should the world be overwise
> In counting all our tears and sighs?
> Nay, let them see us, while
> We wear the mask
> We smile, but, O great Christ, our cries
> To thee from tortured souls arise
> We sing, but oh the clay is vile
> Beneath our feet, and long the mile
> But let the world dream otherwise
> We wear the mask.

Everytime I hear Mr. Dunbar's words, they shake me up inside. All
in all, when I look back over my life, Lord, I've worn so many hats.
I even started the Negro Fellowship League. I'd hoped that it would
be to the Negro what Hull House is to the immigrant. I organized the
Alpha Suffrage Club in order to mobilize Negro women of Illinois to
take part in voter registration. (*With great pride*) I was among the people that answered the call that led to the formation of the National Association for the Advancement of Colored People. I've established myself
as a woman to be reckoned with. But sometimes I feel like I want to

go way back and sit down. (*With renewed energy*)   I can't go way back and sit down because if I did things would not change for my people.

Well I guess I've talked enough today. So I just better let you go home and get your supper; and I'm going in here and get me and Mr. Barnett a bite to eat. I'm very happy you came. And if any of you should see on your way home, some girls jumping rope, you tell the one with the plaits on her head and the blue dress on that Ida B. Wells is feeling real good today, since I started writing about my life. Tell her that: I'm stating my position; leaving a record of my resistance; in the hope that it will inspire future generations. Good night.

FROM

Shango Diaspora:
An African-American Myth
of Womanhood and Love
(A Ritualdrama)

ANGELA JACKSON

CHARACTERS

GIRL/WATERGIRL/MS. WATERS A brownskinned Black woman, early to mid-twenties, warm, intelligent, and learning herself.

THE THREE WOMEN These three women are like musical energies. Woman No. 1 and Woman No. 2 are sopranos: Woman No. 3 is an alto, husky, a dreamer. They are three shades and styles of beauty —Afro, braids, and dreads, nothing extravagant or too unnatural. They are a trio of different expressions. Throughout the play they take the parts of The Women, the MammiWaters, The Voices, and The Sisters of Sympathy.

WOMAN NO. 1 Black woman from 30–45.

WOMAN NO. 2 Black woman a little younger and a shade less aggressive than Woman No. 1

WOMAN NO. 3 Black woman from 30–45. A dreamer. A kind woman.

WOMAN-ALONG-THE-WAY AND YEMOJA The first a Black woman of seniority—crazy, clipped, and harsh. Yemoja is a god. Full of jazz and magic. An ageless, lovely, self-acclaiming, absolutely autonomous, arrogant, and tender deity.

SHANGO A god. Blackman, virile, in his prime, late thirties to mid-forties, apparently. A Black, lean, god. Yoruba god of thunder, lightning, and fire. He is a scientist, magician, and ruler, thus has great intellect, stature and dignity. An African-Diaspora man of brilliance and masks.

THE FAN Black woman, same age as Ms. Waters. Simpering, manipulative, sharp, shallow, and a little sad.

THE CATS Three Black women, bitter and sad of any age. They are primarily dancers. They may have been playing scenery.

SENTRY/SOLDIER Shango's sentry, preferably male, with a forbidding voice.

SETTING

A Some Where in the Diaspora. A Black Space.

TIME

The Present. What John Wideman calls "African Great Time."

ACT 1

Scene 1

(*The setting is a city block. Girl on a porch seated sideways on a bannister, singing along with "Fire", Pointer Sister version. Three women on the street corner coming from work. In hats or scarves, carrying shoppingbag, briefcase, basket.*)

WOMAN NO. 1 (*Yells at girl aggressively*)   Hey, you! Hey, you there singin "Fire", what you know about it? What you know about Fire?

GIRL (*Turns to her. Defensive but firm*)   I know enough. I know about him.

WOMAN NO. 1   You know enough to call the Fire Department?

GIRL   I know enough. I learned *something* in school. Isis bathed Osiris in fire for immortality. To build a fire is to burn away the yellow eyes of wolves, to burn the howling out of the night. (*Pauses, voice softens*) In the kitchen where love is baked in loaves fire heats the stones.

WOMAN NO. 2   Girl, you talking about some kitchen fire. We talking about *Fire*.

WOMAN NO. 1 (*Interjects*)   Big Fire.

WOMAN NO. 3 (*Dreamily*)   Fire is the first and final fear. I saw Fire once. It was in a dream.

WOMAN NO. 2 (*Has taken out a Dream Book. Points to a section. Reads*)   To dream Fire is to dream prosperity, change, good luck, the sweet sex wish.

WOMAN NO. 3   He is a figure of force and fascination in an orange drama.

GIRL (*Saunters down steps. While the women remove hats and baskets, etc.*)   Legends I have heard tell of. Stoop front myths and sermons that made mature women sweat and stir the thick air. Young men shake their heads and touch hands in elaborate fives. Encounters I have watched him through. Flash fire flats housed his concubines. Beautiful and methodical in their wiles. Their kitchens all burned out. Their pots stone cold. I have heard of his hunger. His spirit unharnessed.

WOMAN NO. 1   Once, at a dry feast, drought, he ate three thousand trees.

WOMAN NO. 2   Once, he set a family outside into a freezing winter drift. Flames licked out through gutted windows like horrible children with their tongues stretched out. While a father stood in snow, barefoot, cursing Fire.

WOMAN NO. 3   When he walks he leaves premonitions. When women think of him they store their dreams like secrets poured in mason jars, persimmon, marmalade, Sunday morning, and harmonica. They remember the very first fig and the bent heat that swelled from Fire, from him, from them. Delicious!

WOMAN NO. 2   What do you know, girl? You think you an authority on Fire?

WOMAN NO. 3 (*Like a robot mother*)   Children should not play with fire.

WOMAN NO. 1 (*Bossy*)   Give me those matches, that cigarette lighter. Stand back from that stove. That fire'll fall on you.

WOMAN NO. 3 (*To imaginary children*)   If you are bad you will burn!

WOMAN NO. 2   Listen at what the mothers tell you. Be careful, girl.

WOMAN NO. 1, 2, AND 3   Hot! Hot! Hot!

GIRL (*Ignores them*)   I'll be alright.

WOMAN NO. 1   Oh, really? Just who do you think you are?

GIRL   It's too late. I already am who I am.

WOMAN NO. 2   Who are you?

WOMAN NO. 3 (*Looking into a hand mirror. Curious and crazy*)   I know who you are.

> (*The women get busy.* WOMAN NO. 3 *begins to braid* WOMAN NO. 2's *hair.* WOMAN NO. 1 *begins to wash and hang up clothes, she uses a scrub board. All fixtures are imaginary*)

GIRL (*Centerstage*)   I am the little girl who plays with the god of fire. He bites my lips, and scars my hands. "Little girl," he tells me, "Don't you know I'd run through you like a silver knife? Burn down all your trembling houses."

WOMAN NO. 1 (*An aside*)   That sound like a warning to me.

GIRL   "Yes," I tell him. "I have watched you a long, long time without winking. I know the cruelty of your ember. I have read your mark on women's eyes." (*Gestures*)   I touch him without squinting. He bites my lips and scars my hands. Full height he draws himself up. He is one flame that flares. Red and blue against the trees. Lightning. Over the sand. Over the houses.

"Listen, when I tell you, I am Fire, Little Girl. I am son and father of the sun. I will make you ash and curling smoke."

WOMAN NO. 2 (*An aside*)   That sound like warning no. 2.

GIRL   "I know," I whisper into the deep blue flame. My lips are red with him. "God of Fire who burns poison out of wounds. Son of Fire who bites the ice and makes it sweet. Father of Fire who watches the earth, you are a god of mercy. Have mercy on me. Be tender with my meat."

I look into his light and wink.

WOMAN NO. 1 (*An aside*)   You better been trying to wink.

GIRL   "Little Girl", he says, "Who owns you? Where is your home?"

WOMAN NO. 1 (*An aside*)   He say, "Where this fool come from?"

GIRL   "I am only a child. Water. Early to bed."

WOMAN NO. 2   Early to bed!

WOMAN NO. 1   She ready!

GIRL   River of invisible rises. The beautiful daughter of many people. I strike fire back at the sun and it is glass. Have you never seen the water that holds the fire? Cradles it and rocks it into weaving smoke? You must have something soft against you. You are more child than I. You are thirsty. And will burn yourself out.

WOMAN NO. 1 AND 2   You a bold little miss . . .

GIRL   "No," he snaps and hisses. He is full of caprice. He bites my lips and scars my hands. Curses me with thunder. I am too still, without a murmur. He is wary. A muscle of contempt. We watch each other. And we wait.

(GIRL *stops, pauses. Doesn't want to reveal the rest*)

WOMAN NO. 3 (*Kindly*)   Well, then what happened? You not just gone leave us hanging. What happened? Turn yo head around the other way so I can get this part. (*Addresses* GIRL, *then woman between her knees*)

GIRL (*Getting up enough nerve. Begins quickly, abruptly*)   Suddenly. He laughed. He held me up and opened his hand. Seven kinds of stone. Alight. I brushed the flame and fled. Wing-singed. Transformed into a trembling bird: a black wave flying from the sun. Breasts heaving and eyes broken open like lips. Now I know hunger and I am mouths. Who curved dizzy in his palm. I touched his flint and fled.

WOMAN NO. 1 (*Sticks clothes-pin under girl's nose*)   I coulda told you it woulda ended up that way.

WOMAN NO. 3 (*Chastises No. 1*) See there. That's not right. Be telling somebody I told you so. She don't want to hear that. (*To* GIRL) Go
on, honey, what was it like when he touched you?

GIRL Something struck me when he touched me. A deja vu over-
whelming. You were there . . . women ripping their corded hair, shouting my lost name.

WOMAN NO. 3 Did it hurt? His touch.

GIRL It was like a palmtree hard fell with the fist of its hand; while
the earth pit swallowed its own green seeds; all my futures were absorbed by a toothless mouth; everything moving with centrifugal force:
this body, a brownpaperbag doll, flattened against his wall. It was this
terrible, terrible deja vu I tore loose from, yet could not elude. So
here I go down the line of women wounded like a row of moons. And
we all look alike crying the same blues.

WOMAN NO. 1 (*Working with the clothes-pin again*) Did you think
you'd be any different? Did you think he'd treat you any different
than he treated them other women? Did you think you had gold between your legs? And that would make him want you?

GIRL I didn't think I had anything between my legs because he ain't
been between my legs.

WOMAN NO. 2 That's what's wrong with you.

GIRL He just touched me.

WOMAN NO. 3 Why did you run away?

GIRL I don't know. I don't remember. I just remember the flirtation
dance. The hesitation . . .

WOMAN NO. 3 You were afraid. Weren't you?

GIRL I guess. The feeling was picking me up. Carrying me away.

WOMAN NO. 3 Why didn't you go with it? You only wishing you
had gone. You look tired.

GIRL Every night sleep break me in two. Opens and spreads across
the cold. I loiter with my limbs askew and curve round a central heat.

WOMAN NO. 1 Still trying to get next to that heat, huh?

GIRL "Classic," my sister shakes her head when I tell her. "I did not
know such cases were still found." She is not sad for me but marvels
at the possibility: a woman so intense, so besieged. The heat a recurring
tropical disease.

  "Tell me who he is." Someone curious inquires. Even though they
don't know. They just assume it's got to be a man. How they know
it's a man? Got me sleepless. It might be *money*. It just might be
lack of money keeping me awake at night. *It might be inflation!*

WOMAN NO. 1 Inflated loneliness.

WOMAN NO. 2 Inflated lust.

WOMAN NO. 3   Love. There is somebody who's stricken you. You're in his aura. He wakes you in the middle of the night. He colors your forehead purple like a royal anointment or a bruise.

WOMAN NO. 2   Valerie Simpson say it's like a mark on you.

WOMAN NO. 1   Then she say, "Don't go, can it wait until tomorrow." Twenty four more hours before the misery stop or start.

WOMAN NO. 2   Misery stop or start. Miserable he there. You miserable when he gone.

GIRL (*To* WOMAN NO. 3)   What can I do?

WOMAN NO. 1   Take some valium and sleep it off.

WOMAN NO. 2   Do quickies and t.m.

WOMAN NO. 3   You have to go to him. Go to him with a sacrifice. You have to give something up. Go singing. Don't listen to them two filling you with fear. You have to dream with him. Or else you'll be left by yourself. Which wouldn't be bad to be a dreamer by yourself if you didn't want *him*. (*Sends her on her way*)   You have such a pretty voice. Go singing to him.

WOMAN NO. 2   Girl, he is really gonna get you this time.

WOMAN NO. 1   Girl, he is gonna kick your emotional ass.

(WOMAN NO. 3 *takes up imaginary broom. Sweeps, humming*)

WOMAN NO.1 (*To* WOMAN NO. 3)   Now, why you send that child on that wild goose chase so he can cook her goose for her?

WOMAN NO. 3   Wasn't no wild goose chase. Something she has to do.

WOMAN NO. 2   She need to be trying to avoid pain.

WOMAN NO. 3   How you avoid pain without avoiding feeling? It's all part of the ritual.

WOMAN NO. 1 AND 2   What ritual?

WOMAN NO. 3 (*Goes dreamy again*)   In autumns what I remember is my father and uncles gathering buckets and rakes doing the earth's duty with a calm and ritual therapy. They worked the wrinkled, sunset leaves into mountains like a sacrifice of lovely and faded women. The men gave leaves to fire. The smoke would rise black and full of husky, sexual smell. The men would lean on their rakes and watch. Their children would flutter and swirl around the smoke and bodies. My father would gather the ashes into buckets and discard them. Now his daughter is fallen, sunsets, and gathering her body for giving. It is a new time, for life, and fire must be fed.

(*Fade out on three women*)

ACT I

Scene 3

(*Setting: Smoke in the distance from a high place. That is Shango's lair/palace. The* GIRL *is journeying. Again, trees walk and stones move. Birds in flight. Bird signal songs. Flight from a big wind, a movement.*)

GIRL (*Watching the signs of animal flight. Worried. Muses*) When Fire struts/bewildered beasts scurry. From miles away birds set out a flurry of fear. (*A flurry among the trees. She cringes*) I smell the skin of smoke. I sense his presence near. His teeth that mark the barks of trees; his eyes peeling a path of leaves leaving the bones of slow bedazzled beasts settled beneath his feet. (*Hesitantly approaches a gate at the foot of a suggested stairwell. The stairwell has steps that are really landings. The steps curve. The steps are in darkness. She listens*) I hear his breathing. The soft rending of cloth. The soft tearing of the hair of air. (*She looks around her, warily*) A craziness of atmosphere, near his lair of brilliance and intrigue. (*Measures herself to meet the task*) My heart wide as a child's. A woman's aroma at my wrists, at my temples, behind my ears. (*Takes out perfume from her carrying basket. Carrying basket is full of goodies*) This craziness of atmosphere. I want to run. I want to stay. I'm wise enough to fear. Fool enough to linger here.

> (GIRL, *having decided to face Fire, prepares by dressing up. Adds a shirt of bright colored veils, jewelry. All this from her basket of goodies. A bowl is also in the basket*)

VOICE (*A warning voice, deep and stern, comes from nowhere and everywhere*) Who enters his electromagnetic field is polarized, pulled apart, limb from limb, shocked, wild in the head.

> (GIRL *pauses with hand outstretched toward the suggestion of a door/gate*)

VOICE OF WOMAN NO. 3 You must go to him with a sacrifice. Go singing. If you don't you'll never be free.
(GIRL *still hesitates*) You want a good night's sleep, don't you?

> (GIRL *opens door/gate.* GIRL *mounts the long, wide steps that are more like platforms. Lights go up on* SHANGO *on high. He is close*)

to a cloud. Clouds are stones. SHANGO *Fire Diaspora sits in a Huey P. Newton, big backed, bamboo chair. He reclines. Arrogantly. He remains in shadow, although all around him is illuminated. Perhaps he is flanked by drummers who are at a distance. He has one soldier, at least. He is being fanned by a woman. All in* SHANGO'S *palace wear African dress. Flamboyant fire colors. A great glaring light falls on the* GIRL'S *face. Blinds her)*

SOLDIER   Who comes?

GIRL   Only . . . a girl sleepless with praises. (*Shields her eyes*)

SOLDIER   Then praise.

   (*Light softens as* GIRL *kneels and bows deeply*)

GIRL   (*Begins tremulously. Gains confidence. It gets good to her. She is downright cocky by the end*)   Most Excellent Lord Shango. You were a god before music/fell and broke/into voices. Before the tribes were marked limb from limb, eye from eye, skin from skin, heart from heart, and brain before desire was formed out of hormone, mucus, and marrow. Before Osiris/you were a god. Before the market of salt, and spices and trade/beads before rice rose out of mud. Before bruteforce/you were a god before the deathhowl/before the Chain/before the Coffle . . .

THE FAN   (*Bored and jealous*)   My. My. My girl is so extravagant. Sweet child.

GIRL   (*Loud and determined*)   You were born before Hallelujah, as old as Hosanna! Before the plain and orangebreasted lizard made marriage patterns in the sand./Before the funeral of justice, before mercy, before '27, the flood, when the house was torn from its roots and twins were birthed on the roof./Before the river ran wild before the anger of water/before the beacon, and the lighthouse.

   (*Is so excited she rises in her speech.* SOLDIER *and* THE FAN *gesture her down. She ignores them*)

You were a being before the Hawk and the Holy Ghost danced as one on the corner of Celebration and Sanctuary, before the women of the creme sachet and toilet water lay with porcelain gods and works of art./You were there in the time of the North Star/in the Time of Moss that hugs the Tree of Memory. You are as old as the longing for Messiah. Your lifeline equatorial and your heart bleeds back from the long tunnel of the First God.

   You have accumulated more pain than I. I have heard of you. I know that I am young. Magician of two thousand smoke screens, griot of light years, people say that I am aglow, a star has set upon me. And I am patient as the moon.

SHANGO (*In shadow. Bored. Matter of factly*) You are a fool.

GIRL (*Before he can get his out of his mouth good*) Beyond a shadow . . . I am ready for giving. I have come singing. I know that I am young.

THE FAN Is that all, *little girl?*

GIRL (*Feisty*) I wasn't talking to you. (*To* FIRE) May we have privacy? I have brought an offering.

(SHANGO *snaps his fingers. All retreat to lower platforms. They watch and listen*)

(THE FAN *takes centerstage. She narrates the actions of the* GIRL *and* FIRE. FIRE *and the* GIRL *do dance actions in the shadows. A hot, hot, hot dance done in shadows with sparks shooting out*)

THE FAN (*Blase. Delighting in the* GIRL'S *fate*) She prepared a lamb for him. A sacrifice floating in herbs and blood and water seasoned with salt of camouflaged tears, onions, and three kinds of peppers, enough to kill a goat. (*She fans herself all the while*) Her mouth shaped half a plate of triumph. She held murder in her hands. He sat on his throne, a luxuriating storm. His neck was stiff as an eagle's. He watched the sway of her hips, heavy, widened as she walked with design. He took the dish and tasted it. He ground West African pepper with his teeth. He lulled his tongue inside the heat. Then he said, "This is not sweet enough. There is not enough salt." (*Gleefully*) He crushed her eyes for salt. He opened her veins for syrup and let her laughter over lamb. Devoured it. *His teeth cracked bone.* Devoured it. *He sucked the marrow.* Then, he roared for more. She gave him her mouth. He pulled her kisses till she was gaunt. Her joints grew thin as spider tapestries. Still. He said he was not satisfied. She fell behind her mask. Inscrutable. Wall of water, silent hieroglyphic of hurt. Reflecting, she watched his fine teeth glisten while he laughed.

(*A deep bass growl-laugh descends from the shadow and sparks. The two figures now tangled in erotic, and subtle violent embrace. A low fade on couple coupling. Then* GIRL *descends. Like a sleep-walker. She is off her center*)

GIRL (*More to self than to others. Disoriented*) Fire is absolute. You were absolutely right. I should have known. I had no ways. I had no means enough to know. I, who have always been water. More or less. Fire burns. Grates the eyes. Peels/flesh and sears. (*Gestures back toward* FIRE. *Turns to shout to Him)* Fire: you are absolute. There is no defense. A woman who loves Fire/who meddles with flame/ who flirts with tongues/will burn/will be/consumed.

(On a lower platform the village women appear. They are doing a Fire Dance. GIRL *descends toward them)*

In the village, on the street corners, the women raised their skirts and only fanned the flame. Fire rose around their thighs. Went through them and blossomed between their breasts.

Fire licked their ankles and they danced.

Fire: you are music/nobody has business listening to alone. *And when I touched you you were warm. I cupped the heat and laughed into the colored shadows you cast across my skin.* I was laughing, people say. Not like a little girl. They say, I raised my skirts delicately, like a lady, and danced. Til they only saw the smoke.

*(*GIRL *goes up in fire and smoke.* THE FAN *fans on like this happens everyday)*

(Blackout. Quick)

ACT II

Scene 2

(The GIRL's *house. Porch is illuminated. So is inside. There is only a bed. The* GIRL *is on it. Smoke rises from the bed suggesting smouldering ashes. The* THREE WOMEN *appear transformed into benevolent spirits all. They are the* SISTERS OF SYMPATHY. *All in dresses and headrags and/or gelees of royal blue, sky blue, and turquoise. There is little initial dialogue. Intense movement. They sweep into the* GIRL's *house. They make a semi-circle around her. Shaking their heads. One ministers to the* GIRL. *One goes to sweep the porch. Another builds a fire with a pot over it. They begin throwing things into the fire. Reciting)*

SISTER NO. 1 *(As she throws said item into pot)* Black cat bones. Mojo root. Essence of Van Van. Jasmine Perfume.

SISTER NO. 2 *(Accepts an invisible something from* SISTER NO. 3 *who ministers to the* GIRL. NO. 2 *gives the invisible thing to* NO. 1)* Pining from a young girl's heart. And bad news.

(SISTER NO. 1 *stirs the mixture. Then all move swiftly to* GIRL)

GIRL (*Sitting up in bed. Watching amazed and looking scared*)   Who are you?

(*The* SISTERS *speak almost simultaneously. One behind the other. They could be one person*)

SISTER NO. 1   Sisters of
SISTER NO. 2   Sympathy
SISTER NO. 3   But not too much.
ALL SISTERS   Too much sympathy not good for you.
SISTER NO. 1   We are interested in curing.
SISTER NO. 2   Self-sufficiency.
SISTER NO. 3   We have come to cure impurities. We've mixed water and magic over a tame fire. Anything can happen. We are in control.
SISTER NO. 2   You have been out of your element.
SISTER NO. 3   You have taken leave of your senses.
SISTER NO. 1   Let Fire get the best of you, huh?
SISTER NO. 3   He was a sweet child.
SISTER NO. 2   Known him since he was a boy.
SISTER NO. 1   But look at you random with assault. Disconcerted. Nearly anonymous with the fate's surprise, and such fabulous, fabulous misery.
SISTER NO. 3   Hair all over your head!
SISTER NO. 2   Eyes looking like hot peppers!
SISTER NO. 1   You are tone-deaf and stupid. While he has danced inside your inner mirror. Settled his sediment. You can't see.
SISTER NO. 3   You would see if you knew *your* eyes, your central equations, your orisha, your deity.
SISTER NO. 2   You must go to meet her.
GIRL (*Reluctantly*)   Is this another wild goose chase?
SISTER NO. 1   Do you want a good night's sleep?

(*Light begins to fade and* GIRL *rises and they help her prepare for her journey. Whispering all the while*)

ALL SISTERS   Believe her. Believe only her.

(*Light continues to fade*)

SISTER NO. 3   How you gone sing for him if you don't know your own song?
ALL SISTERS   Believe her.
GIRL   Who is she?

ALL SISTERS You'll know.

(Total fade as GIRL *stands on porch. Ready to go. Black stage. Except for one spot on* GIRL, *a blue spot, on* GIRL *at centerstage. She sing-speaks)*

GIRL *(Half singing. Half talking)*

He's a deep sea diver/c. c. rider.
He's a deep sea diver/c. c. rider.
Dipped his hand in water/turned to cider.

Heard of a woman/hoodoo in her hand.
Heard of a woman/hoodoo in her hand.
She live across forest/and burning sand.

I am the one with a burn/in my throat.
I am the woman/aburn in my throat.
Lightning scorched my music/couldn't save a note.

I simmered my gumbo/seasoned it hot.
I simmered my gumbo/seasoned it hot.
Dipped his hand in gumbo/stuck to the pot.

Heard of a woman/hoodoo in her hand.
Heard of a woman/hoodoo in her hand.
Her house past bamboo/and glistening sand.

(Slow fade on GIRL)

You Can't Judge a Book
by Looking at the Cover:
Sayings from the Life and
Writings of Junebug Jabbo Jones

JOHN O'NEAL AND BARBARA WATKINS

Prologue

The Po Tatum Hambone Blues

Po Tatum, Po Tatum, where you been?
"been to the city and I'm going again."
What you going to do when you get back?
"Take a little walk on the railroad track."

Po Tatum, Po Tatum have you heard?
Junebug's here and he's spreading the word.
Telling everybody you was his best friend.
Telling everybody how you's done in.
Telling how you had to leave away from home.
Telling how you had to hit the road alone.

When Po Tatum was just a little bitty baby
His mama was known to be a real fine lady.
His daddy was a man with a special skill
Could make people laugh and he knowed how to build.

' had a nice little farm and a real fine house
As Po growed up he learned to run his mouth.
They was doing pretty well till things got funny,
They run out of work and they run out of money.

Need money for the farm, need money for the house.
Money for the cat, and for the cat to catch the mouse.

You Can't Judge a Book by Looking at the Cover is volume two of a trilogy of plays.

Need money for clothes, need money for school.
Even need money to feed the old mule.

You run to the city trying to get you some money.
You run to the city trying to find your honey.
When you run out of money come to the end of your rope.
You run out of money you run out of hope.
Po Tatum!

That's the "Po Tatum Hambone Blues."
It was because of Po Tatum that I finally come to understand that I was supposed to be a storyteller. I'ma tell y'all how that come about.
That's for Po. (*Pouring a libation*)
That's for y'all. (*Raising a toast*)

A C T   I

Goin' to Chicago

Po was the youngest one of Miz Adeline and Mr. Jake Tatum's three boys. There's Ralph, Skinhead, and Po.

If you had seen him, you might have thought we called him Po cause he's so skinny. He's so skinny that he could get lost behind a telephone pole. But that ain't why we called him Po. We called him Po cause when he was seven years old, Miz Adeline, caught him eating a whole half-a-bushel of raw I'sh potatoes by himself. Miz Adeline, that's his mama, said, "Why you eat all them raw potatoes, son?"

He just grinned and said, "Cause I was hungry!"

Why he didn't gain no weight I don't know, as much as he would eat. That boy could eat some potatoes! That's why we called him "Po Tatum."

'Fore Po Tatum left home going to Chicago, he was one of the nicest fellows around. He'd go out of his way to try and help people. He'd always speak to people and everything.

I remember one time, Mr. Raggs got drunk and fell in old man Quinland's cesspool. Miz Maybelle, Mr. Raggs old lady, always beat him up real bad when he got drunk.

Mr. Raggs didn't always used to be like that, no! At one time he had one of the nicest little farms in Pike County. But then the City of McComb thought they could get a plant in there to make bullets for the war if they had Mr. Raggs' property. They told him he had to leave off his land and they took it over. Oh, they gave him a little bit of money for it, but they took away his pride. After that he was always getting drunk.

They never did get that ammunition plant in there neither.

Well, this particular time Mr. Raggs was trying to sneak in the back door, so to stay out of Miz Maybelle's way, and he misremembered and walked on them rotten boards over that cesspool and they give out from under him and he fell, kerplush, in all that stinky water! He made the biggest racket! Well, Po Tatum was the only one would help Mr. Raggs get out of that cesspool. Miz Maybelle wouldn't even beat him up till he went down to the Bogue Chitto River and got himself washed off.

Well, that's the kind of fellow Po was before he went off to Chicago. But he got to the city and his mind got turned around.

The Tatums come from this place out round the New Mt. Zion Community we called The Bottom. Mr. Jake was the Head Deacon at the New Mt. Zion Church and was the best carpenter around at the time. He had learned the carpenter trade from his daddy, Mr. Freeman Tatum, which they say he had been the main one to do most of the building on the Pike County Courthouse and most of the rich white people's homes around there. Mr. Freeman had built two homes for Col. Whitten.

The Tatums had scrimped and scrapped for years till they was able to build a real fine home down in The Bottom, as good or better than any they ever built for the white folk, in some ways. And they built it out of scraps of stuff they's able to save off whatever job they's working for the white people.

The Bottom was a special kind of place. It wasn't nothing but an old swampy piece of land didn't nobody want, but them that lived down there. But for years and years white folk just wouldn't go down there for nothing. It was said that in years past a bunch of runaway slaves and Red Indians had laid ambush and killed a bunch of white people there. For a long time after that the white folk wouldn't go down to the Bottom for nothing—not even the High Sheriff.

The first white man to go down there in modern times was old man Ebenezzer Winston, and he got there by accident. Eb was a sneaky, low-lifted sort of fellow, looked like an old mangy dog. All slumped over with his tail sucked up between his legs, he'd come sidling up to you and you couldn't tell, till he got right up on you, whether he's intent to lick you or bite you.

It was during the Depression—one day old Eb had been out looking for work and he fell asleep on his wagon. His mule, which it must have had something to do with the Tatums somewhere down the line, cause he wandered off up in The Bottom and stopped right in front of the Tatums' house. Eb woke up when the wagon stopped rocking from the walking of the mule. He figured out where he was and hightailed it back to town. He brought the High Sheriff out there to arrest Mr. Jake, "cause can't no uppity nigger afford a house that good no matter how hard him to work!"

But couldn't nobody 'round there figure out where Mr. Jake or his daddy had ever done anybody wrong. They'd nearly always finish whatever job they's working on on time, and often was able to save people's money on the project too. Since they couldn't find nobody to bring charges, they had to let him go. But after that, Mr. Jake wasn't able to get much carpenter work from the white folk. So, the way it turned out, he had to work harder to try to make something out that little swampy piece of land he had to call a farm.

It takes a heap of work *and* a heap of money to make do on a farm. Aw, you can pretty much stay in something to eat, but you pay hell trying to get ahead without no money.

The Tatums did some of everything trying to get ahead. They raised chickens, geese, hogs, some goats and a few cows, they had what was known to be the best bull thereabouts. People used to bring they cows from as far as Chrystal Springs to stud off that bull. And you know a good bull is half your herd.

Miz Adeline kept a good sized vegetable garden. They did they best trying to get ahead, but soon's they's able to get one step forward, something would come along and blow them two steps back.

Still and all Miz Adeline and Mr. Jake did as well or better than most. Things would probably have worked out all right cept for the fact that Mr. Jake got to bragging about how Phillip Anthony "Po" Tatum was going to be the first of they kin to go to college. Po wasn't even out of grade school yet but his daddy already seen him as the one who was going to put they family on a new footstand. "It's something about the boy. He look like a lawyer to me. Besides, he ain't never going to be fit for no real work, he too skinny!"

Po later told me that it many a night Mr. Jake would get that big dictionary book down and say, "Alright son, read me something. If you going to be a lawyer, you got to know all kinds of things." He'd make Po read three or four pages out of that dictionary book.

By the time Po was twelve years old, he'd worked his way up to the letter "M" in that dictionary. His mind got stuck on the word "Meterology." He wanted to know all about the weather. He told his daddy he needed a weather vane on top of the barn so's he could keep up with which way the wind was blowing. Mr. Jake didn't have enough money to buy one so he figured out how to make a weather vane out of scraps of stuff he had around the barnyard.

One Sunday afternoon after church, Mr. Jake set out to hitch that new weather vane to the hip of that tin roofed barn when this freakish little summer storm blowed up. A bolt of lightening, just as red as blood, hit and knocked him plumb off that roof. He had to've been dead before he hit the ground. The body almost landed on young Po.

Miz Adeline wan't nair bit of good after that. Seem like she just lost all interest in living. Miz Adeline was half Indian—long black hair down to here. It's a funny thing about them Indians—they get done living, they just ups and dies. She lingered on a good while, but she wasn't nair bit of good.

Like I said, Po was a nice young man, but with his Daddy dead and his Maw acting funny, Po got kind of lost. Guess he thought it was his fault what had happened.

Miz Caldonia Spencer, which everybody called her "Aunt Callie," had the farm next door to the Tatums. Being a retired school teacher she could see that neither Ralph, Skinhead nor Po's oldest sister, Miz Jeanine, was going to be able to do much with the young Po. Being an old friend of the family, she could see that there was little or no hope that Miz Adeline would ever get straight, so it didn't surprise nobody when she made it her business to try to keep Po from going sour.

Because of her arthritis she had to have help working the land so she would hire different people to help her do certain things—course she wouldn't pay them nothing more than good will but everybody considered her to be hiring right on.

At the time, Aunt Callie had three young calves which she hired Po to take care of. He got into it too. Took to wearing a cowboy hat and everything. I wasn't but a child at the time but I remember wondering how Po thought he could be a cowboy with neither six-shooter nor horse to ride.

Her idea was to make a school for Po out of them calves. She would teach him the different parts of the calf, that would be his biology lesson. She would have him to figure up how much corn or hay it would take to feed them and so forth so that would be his mathematics. For his english lesson she would have him make up little songs and things since he was so good with words. He had one song that went:

> I'm an old cowhand from Bogue Chitto land.
> My legs ain't bowed but my cheeks are tan.
> I'm a cowboy who knows all about a cow.
> I raise 'em real good cause I sure know how.

Get out of my way cause I'ma comming now,
Yippe-tie-yo-tie-yea!

Things were going on real good till one day Po come home from school
to find all three of Aunt Callie's calves sick. He said, "Aunt Callie, what's
wrong with my cows?"

"I don't know, son. Run over to Mr. Joe Whittie's and tell him to
come down here to look at them."

He run all the way to Mr. Whittie's and told him to come look at
his cows. Mr. Whittie come and he looked. He said, "Um-hum, yeah.
Um-hum, yeah. Um-hum, yeah. You got the red tick fever, son. That's
the red tick fever. Aunt Callie you got the red tick fever, that's what
it is, um-hum, the red tick fever. You got to go in town and tell Doc
Shultz that I said you got three calves with the red tick fever out here.
He'll give you a subscription and you take that to the drug store so you
can get the medicine it takes to fix the red tick fever. Um-hum!"

Po ran to Doc Shultz' office and Doc Shultz told him, "If Joe Wittie
said you got the red tick fever out there, you got the red tick fever all
right. Joe Whittie knows something bout cows . . . and horses . . . and
pigs and stuff like that. Here, you take this perscription to the drug
store. It's going to cost you about $75 for the treatment to cure all three
cows." Before either Po or Aunt Callie could come up with the $75,
all three of them cows died.

Po took and dug holes for them cows and buried them all by himself.
It wan't too long after that Po quit school and got a job at the Rainbow
Sign Casino. He swore he wasn't never going to be without money again.

Now up to this time I reckon I'd have followed Po to the gates of
hell. But when he start to get right wild, I begun to wonder. He took
to fancy dressing and hanging out on week-ends up in Macomb.

He did have the gift of gab! That boy coulda talked St. Peter into
letting the Devil pass through the Pearley Gates. He would make up
little rhymes and sayings quick as you could turn around. And don't
talk about no Dozens!

The dozens is a game we play, which the idea is to take advantage
of people. The way you supposed to take advantage of people is by making
them mad and upset. The way you make them mad and upset is by
talking bad about they mama. We call that game "the dozens."

Now if you like me, you wonder why they to call a game like that
"the dozens." What's a dozen got to do with your mama? So I did some
research on the subject. The best idea I been able to get on the subject
come from Miz Louise Anderson, a storyteller I know from Jacksonville,
North Carolina.

Miz Anderson traced the story back to slavery days. Course you understand, didn't nobody want to be no slave, but if you had to be a slave, you didn't want to be no cheap slave. Say they sell one person for five hundred or a thousand dollars. It come your turn to hit the block won't nobody bid more than fifty or sixty dollars for you. That makes you feel bad.

Well, it was some slaves they couldn't sell for doodley-squat. You say, "Hey boy, take this hoe go down there to chop that cotton." By the time you get down there to check on him he be sitting up on the fence row, waiting. You say, "Hey boy, I told you to chop that cotton!" He say, "I can't. The hoe's broke." You say "Alright then boy you go up to the barn and pitch that hay." So you take the hoe to get fixed but by the time you get to the barn, the barn's on fire! You tell him, "Boy, go down to the crick and send some water up here so we can put the fire out!" By the time you get that fire out, that slave's done run off.

Well, a slave like that you'd have to sell by the dozen and didn't nobody want to be in the dozen. If you get put in the dozen, that would mean your mama didn't raise you right, so that's a bad reflection on your mama. That's the best idea I've heard on how the game got its name.

So, while everybody else be struggling to remember one or two bad names to call your mother, Po be running off a string of bad names. And he'd put it in rhyme!

Say your mother's name might be "Mary." Po would say:

> Late last nite, snuck in to see Miz Mary.
> Mighta tried to kiss her but her face was too hairy.
> Your mama's got a face like a kitchen sink
> She's got to sneak up on a glass just to get herself a drink.

I hadn't never heard of Po being beat at playing the dozens or playing cards but one time. This fellow named Skipper Rowe come up from New Orleans. They called him "Tipper" cause he always walked around on his tiptoes like he's trying to sneak up on somebody. He always wore these little soft shoes that looked kinda like slippers. Said he had bad feet. He would always carry an umbrella rain or shine. Called everybody *little* something. "Hey, where you at, Li'l Bro? What's happening Li'l Mama?"

One time during "Spring Break," which always came during cotton chopping season, a bunch of us fellows had gathered up in the back room of Bugs' Underground Cafe to play tunk. Po was acting a fool that day. He was just sounding on folks and putting them in the dozens. But Tipper was hanging right in there with him just as quiet as could be. Finally, it come down to just the two of them. Po, running his mouth, and Tipper, just running them cards.

Before he knowed what had happened, Po was down to this last money. Po pulled the Queen of Spades and slapped it on the table. "Doggonit, I told your mama not to send me no more of her ugly pictures!"

Tipper pulled a card. Just as cool as could be, he said, "Hey, wait a minute, baby. You can say anything you want to about my mother or any one of her kin people. But if you just look like you going to say one bad word about *your* sweet momma, son, it's going to make *me* mad!" He'd laid down three aces and three deuces—ain't no way to beat that in tunk. "You country hip, Li'l Poppa, but your game is lame. Where I come from, we use chumps like you for batting practice."

"Now, Mr. Tatum, I'ma take your little chump change, go up front and buy everybody a nice cool RC Cola." After that, Po ain't had no more to do with Tipper and the dozens. Tipper be in a game of cards or somethin, Po go shoot some pool.

'For long, Po got his mind made up that he's going to the city. Every-time you seen him he be saying:

> Going to Chicago, Baby
> Heading for the city.
> Going to Chicago, Baby
> Heading for the city.
>
> Chica chica chica chica chica Chicago
> Chica chica chica chica chica Chicago
> Chica chica chica chica chica Chicago
> I'm gonna get the North bound train.

I musta been about thirteen or fourteen at the time. It was before I'd made up my mind to leave home myself. One day I asked him, "Why you got to go way to Chicago to get some money, they got plenty work right over here in New Orleans?"

"And they got the same old mean-ass white people they got here. Dan Skinner's got a first cousin down there's a big timer in the Waterfront Union. Dan's down there two or three times a year himself. He comes out to the Rainbow Sign Casino just bragging about the "mellow yellow creole gals" he finds down there. Col. Whitten's got a brother, four neph-ews and a son down there. They own the newspaper, a radio station and a bunch of other stuff. No, siree, Bob! It sounds too much like home to me. Besides, that's where old jive time Tipper Rowe comes from. What kind of rep you think I'm going to make with him around to get on my case?"

I'm going to the city
Where the women's really pretty
And they tell me that the money falls like rain.
I'm tired of picking cotton
Mississippi's gotten rotten,
Gonna pack my bag and jump the quickest train.

Going to Chicago, Baby
Heading for the city.
Going to Chicago, Baby
Heading for the city.

Chica chica chica chica chica Chicago
Chica chica chica chica chica Chicago
Chica chica chica chica chica Chicago
I'm gonna get the North bound train.

Po kept on like that every time you seen him, but after two or three months he just up and disappeared! It was a bunch of rumors as to why Po left town so quick like that.

It was a well known fact in a small circle that him and Becky Sawyers was making time. She was a waitress out there at the Rainbow Casino where Po was busting dishes. Becky Sawyers was good looking in a way but she on the thin side. She's so thin she could dodge raindrops in a good sized storm and not get wet. In that way her and Po made a good pair. She always wore these two long braids. Them braids was bigger than her legs. She was thin. But she was also white.

Some of y'all might be surprised that it was so much race mixing going on during the deep down Jim Crow days. But I'm here to tell you that there was plenty of it. See, old timey segregation had more to do with sitting down together. If you was standing up working or laying down working it was alright.

The Sawyers was what we used to call poor white trash. They wasn't nothing but sharecroppers just like the rest of us, but that's what we used to call them. When she was thirteen, Becky'd had a child for Dan Skinner, Col. Whitten's Overseer and Deputy Sheriff. Dan never made no move to marry her 'cause she had the reputation of being a "bad girl" —due to the child she'd had for him. 'Course Dan wasn't in no shape to get married no way, financial or otherwise. "Aw, I'll keep her for fooling around, but you want a wife, buddy, you got to get you a *good* girl."

So, when Po come along with his heavy line of rap, she must have figured, "If he's got the nerve to try me, then I sure got the nerve to try him." Plus, she knowed, if they ever got caught, she could always claim he's raping her.

Rumor had it that one night Dan Skinner had caught ol Po with Becky in the smoke house out back of the Casino, shot him dead and throwed his body in the Bogue Chitto River. For years after Po disappeared, every time a body washed up in the Bogue Chitto River, people would wonder, "Is that Po?"

A more likely story went that Po had found out where Antonio Dominuis "Stonewall" Whitten was keeping his money hid. Stonewall Whitten was Col. Whitten's younger brother. Col. Whitten and their older brother, Beaureguard Caesar Whitten, owned the bank in McComb and half the rest of everything around there. Stonewall didn't have a dime's worth of confidence in his brothers or their bank.

Stonewall claimed that when their daddy died, his brothers had cheated him out of his share of the family inheritance. Two or three times a year he would bring a legal action to try to get his money back. Every time he come down there his case would be thrown out of court. Every time they thrown him out of court, he would haul off and start preaching on the courthouse steps.

"Brethern and Sisteren of the righteous cause of the Confederation. Beware of the sins of sloth, greed and gluttony! Yeah, even also products of my father's seed, issue of my sainted mother's loin, have made league with the devil in hell in rapacious lust for your land and property. Through the devilish device of this Bank, aided and abetted by the officers of this Court, the Police Jury, the Sheriff, the Mayor, and the City Council they are bleeding you dry, dry, dry!

"I say we must rise up against this heathenistic oligarchy! Before the South can rise again, we must purge ourselves of these fiendish devils sporting the cloth and style of gentlemen!"

He made it plain and clear that he was calling for a rebellion amongst the white folks. The colored people knew the'd need a passport to get within a block of the Courthouse when Stonewall was down there preaching.

Stonewall would rather have died than put two pennies in that bank. Since it was the only bank around it was said that Stonewall had a way of stashing money in glass jars, strong boxes, anything, in places all over his plantation. Po had been heard to say that he knowed where Stonewall was keeping that money hid and that whenever Po needed some, he'd just sneak out there in the dead of night and take whatever he wanted.

You might can tell, Stonewall was somewhat peculiar. Where most folks would have used dogs for the purpose, Stonewall kept a pack of wild pigs to protect his property. Now that ain't necessarily as dumb as it first might seem. A hog is stronger, meaner and smarter than your average dog.

This particular story went that one night while Po was down there rooting for some of Stonewall's money, the biggest, baddest boar in the pack caught with Po fore he had the time to get out the hole with the money. Before Po was able to cut him bad enough to bleed it to death, that pig put a gash on the left side of Po's face from his ear to his lip.

Stonewall loved that wild hog more than he loved money. He's the first one I ever heard of to quit eating pork. He'd made his wife leave home cause she didn't want that thing sleeping in the bed with them when it was a baby.

After killing Stonewall's favorite wild boar and getting cut like that, Po knew it was time for him to grab his hat.

Po was feeling so low down that the belly of a rattlesnake would have looked like a bridge. He went that night and hopped an IC freight train going to Chicago.

> The old freight train's a rocking,
> My aching head's a popping
> Need me something just to ease the pain.
> Had to leave my home and family
> Cause this crazy cracker jammed me,
> I'm going and I won't be back again.

> Going to chicago, Baby, heading for the city.
> Going to chicago, Baby, heading for the city.
> Chica chica chica chica chica chicago,
> Chica chica chica chica chica chicago,
> Chica chica chica chica chica chicago,
> I done gone and caught the North bound train.

Home for the Funeral

It was five years more fore Po was seen again in Pike County. His mama Miz Adeline, had pined and pined till she couldn't pine no more. After Mr. Jake was killed like he was she didn't have much use for the world. Year by year, as their land would go a piece at a time, she just went more and more into herself. Whilst all her other children was gathered around her dying bed she kept calling for her baby one more time.

The problem of it was the family didn't know where in the world Po was. They used to get a money order from him once every month for three or four hundred dollars. But they hadn't heard a thing for over a year now. They's sitting there trying to figure out what to do and Skinhead said, "By God," let's go up to Mr. Jimmy Knowles store and call Junebug. Him and Po's tighter than the twine on Aunt Callie's corset. If anybody'd know where to find him Junebug would."

At the time, I was running this shoeshine stand at the Pontchartrain Hotel in New Orleans. They's kind of sometimy about me getting phone calls there. But when Long Distance called for me even the switchboard operator got excited.

"Pontchartrain Hotel, may I help you, please? . . . Long distance? . . . for Mr. J. J. Jones, one moment please. . . . I'm sorry, Operator, we don't have a Mr. Jones registered at this time. . . . What's that? . . . Junebug? Oh! You mean Junebug! Operator that's a Nee-ga-row! . . . Well! Excuse me please."

"What's this world coming to! Charles! Charles! Tell the shoeshine boy that he has a long distance telephone call!"

"Long distance? For Junebug? Boy-oh-boy! Boy-oh-boy! Boy-oh-boy! Long distance, for Junebug. Boy! Boy! You've got a Long Distance tele-phone call in here. Florine says you'll have to call em back on the pay phone if it takes more than three minutes. She can't have you tying up her lines."

"If it takes a week, a week'll do, turkey. And from now on it's *Mr. Boy* to you. You just mad cause you ain't never had no Long Distance telephone call. . . . Hello. This is *Mr.* Jones."

"HEY, LI'L DAVID, THIS IS SKINHEAD."

Right away I knowed who it was. Didn't but one person call me by my given name like that beside my mama. "You keep on like that you going to break the telephone, Skinhead. What's going on?"

"WE TRYING TO FIND PO. MAMA'S LOW DOWN SICK AND SHE BEEN CALLING FOR HIM."

"Miz Adeline's sick?"

"LOW DOWN SICK. TELL YOU THE TRUTH, I DON'T THINK SHE GOIN TO MAKE IT THIS TIME. WE AIN'T HEARD A WORD FROM PO IN OVER A YEAR."

"I ain't heard nothing from Po in the last little while myself, but I feel and believe that I can find him."

"ALL RIGHT, YOU GET TO HIM, THEN. TELL HIM HIS MAMA'S ON HER DIEING BED AND SHE CALLING FOR HIM."

"Alright, I'll do that, Skinhead. Tell all your brothers and people 'Hello.'"

"ALL RIGHT, LI'L DAVID. SO LONG, NOW."

It hurt me some bad to hear that. By me being so close to Po and all, Miz Adeline was next to my Mama in my mind. But finding Po was going to take more'n a notion.

The trouble was, Po didn't exactly live in no particular where. If he got in tight with some woman he'd stay with her for a while but mostly he'd live in his car. Every now and then, being as Po was none too swift in the writing department, he'd have this one particular lady friend of his to write me a letter. Whenever I wanted to get in touch with Po I had to write to this lady, which her name was Consuela LeBeaux. She's from Haiti. That's just South of Miami off in the Atlantic Ocean.

It took me a while but I's able to get her number from "Information." The operator put the call through for me.

"Miz Consuela, I'm trying to reach Po—, Well, I'll say, Phillip Anthony Tatum. I need to talk to him quick, fast, and in a hurry."

"You must be the one he calls, Junebug."

I was knocked out. Not only did she know who I was, she sounded like the original Honey-dripper!

"Philippe said you might call someday. Is there anything wrong?"

"Yes Mam, it is. I need to let Po know that Miz Adeline, His Mama, is on her dying bed and she's calling for him."

It got real quiet on the other end of the line. I thought we'd been cut off.

"Hello. Hello, Miz Consuela . . ."

"Yes. I'm here. I will get the message to him right away."

I couldn't tell what it was, but I knowed something was wrong by the way she said that. But when she said that one of them would call me back the next day, I went on back to work feeling like I had done something worthwhile. Early that next morning the porter came back to my shoeshine stand.

"Say *boy*. You're getting to be a regular business man around here. You got another one of them Long Distance telephone calls."

"Aw, hush up, man! . . . Hello."

"SHE GONE, LI'L DAVID. YOU FIND HIM?"

"Yes, I found him—leastwise I found somebody said they could get a message to him. I'll call em back right away. When's the funeral?"

"SATURDAY."

"Alright, I'll see you, Skinhead."

"I'LL SEE YOU, LI'L DAVID."

I called Miz Consuela back right away. She was mighty upset bout Po's dear mama but she was more upset cause she couldn't promise that Po was going to be able to make the funeral that coming Saturday. I didn't say nothing but I did wonder what it was that Po was so tied up in that he couldn't make it to his own mother's funeral. I later found out that Po had been in jail at the time and Miz Consuela didn't have no idea whether Po would be able to come up with some scheme to get out of jail in time to be to the funeral.

Me, I got to Four Corners late that Friday afternoon. Next morning at the funeral, they had the front four rows of the church on either side roped off for the family. Rev. Wright preached a powerful sermon. I reckon he was glad to have a funeral to preach that he didn't have to spend most of his time lying about the poor departed. Miz Adeline was one of the best and nicest people you ever going to meet.

Rev. Wright was done preaching and was about to open the casket so we could view the remains when it came a great racket outside of a car sliding to a halt. The door to the church popped open and there stood this lady, on high heeled shoes, which was more strap than shoe, she sorta pranced like a high bred filly, without touching the ground too hard. My eye followed her blue stockings up them long shapely legs till I almost embarrassed myself. Scared I was about to see something that I wasn't supposed to look at, my other eye jumped up to the woman's face which was covered by a little blue veil pinned to a little blue pancake hat tilted over her left eye. She licked her shiny red lips and dabbed her eye with this little blue handkerchief. She turned to hold the door open for Po Tatum!

He had on a white, double breasted seersucker suit, with a black silk shirt and a white polka-dot necktie and this wide brimmed white straw hat with a black and white polka-dot band. As he stepped in the church house, Po dabbed his forehead with his polka-dot handkerchief and sure enough, there was a long scar running from his ear to his lip on this side of his face that made him look like he's smiling all the time.

He walked up to the coffin, raised up the veil, bent down and kissed his mama. Then, slow like in slow motion, he slumped down on the floor and cried like a baby.

Up to that point it had not been such a sad funeral. But it's a sad thing to see a grown man cry. Everybody in the church busted out in tears. Skinhead, who ain't never been heard to whisper a day in his life, said, "Well I'll be a ring-tailed monkey."

It took Rev. Wright and Willie Gladstone a good while to get the service back under control. They finally got the casket loaded out onto the hearse. That being done, Po come back to the center of attention. All his brothers and sisters was hugging him and holding him trying to find out all that he'd done, and how he was and such.

Me, I turned my attention to the Blue Lady. Still feeling obliged not to look below the pearl looking necklace she wore, I said, "How do, M'am? I'm Junebug. You must be Miz Consuela."

"The name my Mama give me was Flora Belle. My Daddy's name was Washington. Do that sound like Consuela to you? Po, Daddy, Po! You ready to go?"

She walked as much as that tight fitting dress would let her to where Po was standing and he loaded her into that brand new 1951, powder blue Cadillac for the trip to the burying ground.

After a funeral, everybody meets at the house of the nearest of kin to talk and sip a little spirits to help out till the grief be kinda lifted. They had some food out there that day! Seemed like everyone ever owed Miz Adeline a favor tried to pay her back by bringing food that day. Everybody was talking about Po and how well he had to've been doing, what with them fancy clothes and that fancy car and that fine woman, he had to've been doing all right!

Aunt Callie leaned back in the rocking chair, scratched a match on the floor to light her pipe and said, "I have seen them come and I have seen them go. You can't judge a book by looking at the cover. I'm here to tell you!" Nobody said nothing back to Aunt Callie. Not so much because it's impolite to back talk old people, but because Aunt Callie's been known to put people in their place with little or no ceremony.

Knowing Aunt Callie, that got me to thinking.

Po still looked sad when the family got back from the graveyard, but the young boys crowding all around him would not let him have no peace. Out on the porch, all the young unmarried women fell in around Miz Flora Belle, which Po called her "Flukey."

Aunt Callie noticed how all of us youn'uns followed behind Po and Flukey with our minds. She rared back and blowed a big puff of smoke from her pipe and said, "Well, Phillip, it seems like you've gone off to the city and struck it rich, huh, son?"

"I wouldn't say that Aunt Callie, I'm doing all right, but I ain't found no cows to tend in the city."

"What have you found to tend in the city that will afford you a Cadillac car and that fancy, fast talking woman? Are you married to her? Or did you bring her here to make mock of your mother's funeral?"

"No'm, Aunt Callie, you know I wouldn't do nothing like that!"

"Then tell me just exactly what you have been doing, son. You happy enough to tell all these young boys, tell me."

Just then Ralph came in from the bedroom and said, "I'm sorry, Aunt Callie, Mam, but Po, we need to speak to you in the bedroom."

Po was glad to get out from that session with Aunt Callie. But what he didn't know was that he's going from the fat into the fire. I couldn't get in the room to see what they was saying, but with Skinhead in there I didn't have to.

"HOW COME YOU DIDN'T COME HOME WHEN WE GOT BURNED OUT? WHYN'T YOU LET SOMEBODY KNOW WERE YOU'S AT? YOU KNOW'D YOUR MAMA WAS SICK AND YOU'S HER FAVORITE! HOW CO—"

"I'm sorry, Skinhead," said Ralph, "but Po you know Daddy always did expect more out of you than he did any of the rest of us. We sure could use some extra help around here. If we don't give Whitten $500 by the end of the month, we stand to lose the 20-acre plot the family place used to stand on, the one with all the graves on it."

It must have been Po's oldest sister, Miz Jeanine, said, "How dare you bring that 'Floozy' woman to your own mother's funeral!"

"Her name ain't 'Floozy'! And if she's woman enough for me, she ought to be good enough for you."

The bedroom door popped open and everybody but Aunt Callie jumped to get at something like they hadn't been listening. Po, just as cool as a cucumber, walked over to where I was standing, "Junebug, my man, I've got some business in New Orleans. If you want a ride, you let the doorknob hit you where the good lord split you. Flukey, Baby, we got to rise and fly."

"You know me, daddy, I'm wake up in the morning ready to roll."

"Well, Junebug, you flying or crying?"

Everybody turned to see what I was going to do. Aunt Callie broke the silence by tapping the ashes of her pipe on the edge of the Prince Albert tobacco tin she was using as a spit can. She said to one of the young Tatum women standing nearby, "Help me up, darling. I believe I'm going back down to the kitchen, get some of that good yellow corn bread and some of that pot liquor off them collard greens." As she caned her way back toward the kitchen on her good foot, she sang:

> Oh, I done done
> Oh, I done done
> Oh, I done done
> I done done what you told me to do.

"All right, Mr. Po, I'm ready to go."

All the fellows followed us out to that new blue '51 Cadillac. Four or five of them fought to hold the door for Flukey, mainly so they could see her prance up to the car, bend in the middle, rotate those blue stocking knees into the plush upholstry of the new smelling car.

I cleared a space in the back seat for myself, but before Po could park hisself behind the steering wheel, they said, "Hey, Mr. Po, tell us where you going to go."

"That's for me to know and for you to find out."

"Aw, come on, Po. Lay one of them heavy rhymes on us, man."
Po thought abut it for a minute and said:

> My Mama just died,
> My Dad's a long time gone.
> I'm out here on the highway all a doggone lone.
> I'm digging like a dog for his very last bone
> Living for the city
> Trying to make a new home.
> I'm talking chica chica chica chica chica Chicago
> Chica chica chica chica chica Chicago
> Chica chica chica chica chica Chicago
> I'm out here on the road all alone.
> So long, y'all.
> So long, home.

Po slammed the door of that Cadillac, dropped it in gear and gunned it so it cut a dusty gash in Ralph's front yard.

We's half way to Franklinton fore I figured out what was going on. Miz Flukey had the map in her lap trying to tell him which way to go. I said, "Excuse me, m'am, but Po, you know Highway 51's the best, most direct route to New Orleans."

"We know that, darling. But we figure as long as we're out here in the country, we ought to take in the sights. Oh, Po, Daddy, look! There's a whole herd of bulls!"

"Ain't no such thing as a 'herd of bulls,' Flukey! Them's cows! To be so smart about the city, you sure are dumb about the country! You just lay back and let the groove do the moving, Junebug. See in these new Cadillac cars, you pay for your ride and get your rocking free."

I thought for a minute about why we's taking them back roads down to New Orleans and decided it wasn't none of my business and I was going to leave it alone.

That Cadillac rocked so steady that it wasn't long before I had dozed off to sleep. When I woke up Po was saying, "Wake up, Junebug, we in New Orleans!"

At the time, I's living in this little three room shotgun house down the street from the Dew Drop Inn in New Orleans. Flukey didn't like it 'nair bit. She went with Po that first night to play cards with Tipper Rowe and I ain't seen hide nor hair of her since.

Four days later, Po came driving up to the hotel, where I's working, in a different car—a maroon colored Lincoln Continental, fully loaded.

"Come on, Junebug, get you glad rags on. I'm gonna take you to Dookey Chase's restaurant for a high class dinner."

The next day I came home from work and all of Po's stuff was gone. It was a hundred dollar bill on the kitchen table with some printing in one corner. Said, "Keep this for good luck, Po."

It was a good while after that fore I caught up with Po again. But I later come to find that two days before Whitten was to foreclose the mortgage on the Tatum Family place which used to have that lovely house on it, Ralph and them got a money order from Chicago for $5,000 with a telegram from Po saying, "This is for my share of the funeral. I hope things work out fine."

A C T   I I

Letters From Jail

Chicken in the car and the car can't go
That's how you spell Chi-Ca-Go.

I be going around a lot telling stories and since I'm from the country, which most of us are in one way or the other, I tell a lot of country stories. Sometimes ci-ditty people try to hide from the light that shines through the tales I tell by just playing it off—they say, "Oh, that's just another old country boy talking." But I'm here to tell you I might look like a farmer but I ain't no fool!

You don't know what that word "ci-ditty" means do you?

Back home Miz May Ellen Gladstone, not that's Willie Gladstone's mama—she's a Jeter by birth, her people come from down in The Bottom too—they had the place on the other side of Aunt Callie's place from the Tatum's. She's the one that built up the funeral home that Willie runs now. Miz May Ellen is an A-number one good person. When the Freedom Riders first come to Macomb they stayed at her house. When the Sheriff set up road blocks to keep the director of this national Civil Rights Organization from comming to speak at the New Mt. Zion Church, Miz May Ellen sent a hearse to meet him at the airport in New Orleans, put him in a coffin, drove him through the road block straight to Rev. Wright's church. That's the kind of person Miz May Ellen was!

Right after Samella, Willie's little sister, was born their daddy Mr. Granville Gladstone had had a stroke. Miz May Ellen must have been too busy taking care of Mr. Granville, running the funeral home, and helping out with The Movement to take good care of those children. Willie's mean as a one-eyed cat, and Samella was alright before she got so "ci-ditty."

The summer before we started high school, Samella went to Chicago. She came back with all these fancy clothes 'n everything. She even took to sticking her nose up in the air and talking funny. I asked her why she be dressing strange and acting funny. She say, "You are just too, too country, sweetheart, that's how we do it in ci-ditty—I mean THE CITY!" Fore long it got to be a saying when anybody got their hips up on their shoulders—got things turned bassackwards and up-side-down —that they was "ci-ditty."

I don't know why Miz May Ellen couldn't see to do no better with her own kids cause she sure could see through everybody else.

When I came back from the Korean War, the Freedom Movement was in full swing in some places. My mind was made up and my heart was set. I went home and jumped right into it. Miz May Ellen was the only one of the so-called "big time" colored people would have something to do with me and The Movement.

She once took me to a meeting of the Better Business League of Greater Pike County in the Private Dining Room of the VF&W Rest and Lodge. I was trying to get them to come to a meeting to find out about the Supreme Court school desegregation issue.

Rev. Elmore Dooley, who ran Dooley's "One-Stop" Grocery Store and Grill—the reason they called it "One-Stop" is if you stopped there one time you wasn't likely to stop no more—he was the first one to his feet.

"Mr. President, Madam Secretary, and Members in good standing of the Better Business League of Greater Pike County. As a life long resident of this community, as a responsible business man, and minister of the Gospel, I feel it's my bounden duty to say before I go, y'all ought to leave this freedom mess alone! It ain't nothing but trouble and I ain't having nothing to do with it and if you was smart, you'd leave these shiftless Negroes alone too. These crazy white folks would just as soon's to kill any one of y'all as they would to shoot a wild dog."

There wasn't no way he could finish his march to the door without trying to get round Miz May Ellen. It wasn't no way she was going to let him get away clean.

"Rev. Elmore! I guess you ought to know a shiftless Negro when you see one. I don't know who or what you think you are. How much grocery do you sell to white folks? How many white foks thump your collection trays on Sunday morning? Hell! We're all just one step from the cotton patch anyway!"

That was the Spring of 1957. We never could get us a school case

in Pike County, but that fall they did get nine children to start the white
high school in Little Rock, Arkansas. After seeing the kind of stuff they
had in the paper about Korea, I knew you couldn't trust what was in
the newspaper so I figure I'd go over there to see for myself what was
going on.

It was October before I got this letter forwarded from home.

> July 20, 1957
> Consuela LeBeaux
> 4818 Drexel Blvd.
> Chicago, Ill.
>
> Dear Mr. Jones,
>
> Phillip wants to get in touch with you. Please let me know where
> you are so I can put you on his mail list. Write me at the above
> address or call me at CAlumet 2–4210.
>
> Sincerely yours,
>
> Consuela LeBeaux

It was two things seemed strange to me about this letter: number
1, this letter looked like it might have something to do with business
and I knew the only business Po's likely to be in at the time was monkey
business. Number 2, I couldn't figure out why I'd have to get on a "mail
list" to communicate with my friend.

I was staying at Mother Mason's Guest House on Elm St. Of course,
I could have stayed at the Hilton but I didn't want everyone to know
my business.

When my mail caught up with me it'd already been a good while
since Miz Consuela's letter had been sent. So I decided to call on the
phone and see what was going on.

It turned out that Po had got himself put back in jail. Miz Consuela,
the honey dripper, was just trying to help out by finding me since I
was the only one besides her he wanted to write to. If you wasn't on
their list, the jail house wouldn't let you communicate with him. They
had him at the State Penitentiary in Joliet, Illinois. He was doing time
for attempted manslaughter and about four other things.

It seems Po had won $1200 in a poker game from this white fellow
who had tried to duck out on him. Po had to run the man down to get
his money. But the game was in an all white neighborhood. When they
seen this colored man with a scar on his face and an eight-inch switch
blade chasing this white man, somebody called the police. Even so, Po

probably could have gotten away if he had just taken the money and gone on about his business, but no—he had to hang around giving the man a lecture about how honesty was the best policy and how it would put a bad light on his people if he didn't pay his debts in a timely way. So because of that he landed in Joliet with a 24-year sentence.

Now I don't want y'all to misunderstand what I'm about to say because I don't believe that it's right what's happening in the jails of this country. You got to understand that something's wrong when over 80% of the people in the jails of this country is either Black, Spanish, Indian, or some other denomination of poor people, when all took together, we don't make up 40% of the population. It just ain't right when a man who steals a $20 ham for his family might get three years in jail, while a man who steals $20,000,000 will get a warning and a little fine. And if they just have to give him some time, they send him to a camp with horseback riding, golf, tennis courts and private rooms in little bungalows they can stay in with their wives and girl friends or whatever.

No, I ain't in favor of jails and the way they are run, but I do think it was good for Po to get that little time when he did. The way he had been going, he might as well a tried to run through hell in a pair of gasoline drawers. If they hadn't put him in jail when they did, they'da had to put him in a pine box.

Po always did like to taste a little bit. But when he got to the city, somebody turned him on to dope. By the time he got busted he had begun to mess around with Heroin—snorting it and every now and then he pump a little bit. But when they put him in jail he got to reading and studying and practicing on his writing and all kinds of stuff.

You can see the difference in Po by the letters he would write:

June 16, 1957

Dear Brother Junebug,
How are you? Fine I hope. Here I sit behind these four walls of bars. Sad and lonely and all alone I write in this empty cell and dream about the times we was fishing on the Bogue Chitto River and wish that I had the wings of a dove and over these prison walls would I fly but since I am not no angel and will be here for a while I wish that you would send me news of the world outside and books that I can read. PLEASE don't tell my brothers and people where I am.

Your sad friend,
Philip A. Tatum

December 18, 1958

Dear Junebug,

I figured, "what the hell?" So I signed up to go to college. Bet you didn't know you could do that in jail? The worse they can do if I fail is kick me out of here. Don't I wish! Well, I had to do something to pass the time. So why not try college?

I figured I'd start off easy so I took this English composition course. It was not as easy as I thought but I came out OK.

I only made a "C", but that isn't too bad for a fellow dropped out of the ninth grade, is it?

I met this guy in the liberry named Robert Watson. You might as well say he volunteered to go to jail because he's in here for what he called a "sitting demonstration" at a private club in Springfield. He's a pre-law student. He went and made a sitting demonstration to test the law that says black folks can't go to places like that. He won't even take bail while his case is still in court.

It sounds dumb to me. I'm getting out of here as quick as I can. What's going on out there, have people gone crazy?

Your incarcerated friend,
Po

March 28, 1959

Dear Junebug,

I am into chess now. Are you hip to chess? There's this old dude in here that everybody thinks is crazy. Won't tell nobody his name or nothing. He has been here for 37 years and nobody knows his name. They call him "Old Dude".

The only thing Old Dude will do is play chess. He won't do that with just any and everybody either. But he did offer to teach me what he know about the game. Through that we got to talking.

It turns out that the Old Dude had first been sent up for 5 years for something they called "criminal syndicalism." I looked it up in the library here and near as I can understand, it's something like crime syndicate. The Old Dude had joined up with this syndicate they call a union they were trying to get at the Pullman Porter plant outside of Chicago. Thirteen of them got busted.

After a month or two at Joliet the warden sict one of his lap dogs on the Old Dude to make him rat on his partners. They got in a fight. The Old Dude hit the other guy with the handle of a wrench out the machine shop and called a guard. It took them so long to get that guy to the infirmary that he bled to death.

A month after that happened, they cut the other 12 guys loose but they convicted the Old Dude on a new charge of murder 1.

I'm glad you got me to let my family know what's happening. Ralph and Skinhead both came all the way up here twice to visit me. I told Consuela, "I feel more like a man now that I ain't got nothing to hide." She smiled and said, "You look more like a man to me too." I can't wait to get out of here!

Send me something about these people in Montgomery, Alabama. What do they think they are trying to do? I don't have too much to do with preachers ever since Deacon Johnny Green pulled the covers off Rev. Dr. A. B. C. Golightly. But this King fellow from Montgomery seems to be different. Maybe he's the one who can lead us out of the wilderness of North America.

Keep the books coming. After I get through with them, I put them in the prison library, so you helping at least a few more besides me . . . maybe.

Your studious friend,
P. A. Tatum

November 3, 1963

Dear Junebug,

I have to tell somebody! I'm still gloating about the fact that I did better in this course in "Modern Social Theory" than Babatunde did. Babatunde is just a thesis short of his Master's degree, and the professor said my final paper was "insightful, innovative, very interesting and that it deserves serious consideration." He gave Babatunde an "A" too but he wrote all over the brother's paper about how this point needed "further development" and so forth. I feel like I'm doing all right.

I wrote a critical review of the theoretical differences between W.E.B. DuBois and the White/Wilkins regime of the NAACP. It's really an interesting case study that reveals some of the basic problems that lie at the heart of the Afro-American struggle for freedom, justice, and equality in America. If you're interested, let me know. I'll send you a copy of the paper.

Thanks for your help hooking me up with that NAA lawyer for the Old Dude. After a year and a half of correspondence, I got a letter last week from the lawyer saying that he's willing to try for clemency for the Old Dude, considering the circumstances and some recent rulings on similar cases.

The only problem is, we buried the Old Dude last month.

Yours with undying hope for freedom,
P. Anthony Tatum

P.S. I'm up for parole next week. Wish me luck.

The Danger Zone is Everywhere

When I's in New Orleans, Mr. Ray Charles used to come to the Dew Drop Inn. He'd come out to the band stand after the band got everybody all warmed up and say, "I want y'all to meet the Raelettes. The Raelettes are International Stars. In case you didn't know what that word 'International' means, it means 'all over everywhere,' the Raelettes are International Stars. Help me sing the song girls. ' . . . the whole world is in an uproar, and the danger zone is everywhere . . . '"

The whole world was in an uproar and the danger zone was everywhere. That's what I's trying to tell Po when I went to visit him the last time 'fore he got out of jail, but he never heard a word I said. "No, Junebug, I'm a college graduate now. I'll get a good job when I get out of here and work my way through law school. I'm not fit for no real work anyway."

"How you think you going to get into somebody's law school, Po? You got a felony conviction record."

"Oh, Junebug, you don't understand. They have good lawyers meeting before the bar everyday with records worse than mine!"

I wondered what kind of "bar" he was thinking about.

They put Po in a halfway house on the Westside of Chicago till he could find a regular job. It was in a real crowded part of town. That part of town wasn't much different than the jail Po had come out of, except the jail was cleaner. Everybody had they little roosts to go to. It reminded me of how chickens used to be stacked in crates on a flatbed truck on the way to market. You go to your roost, you fasten three or four locks and a chain and there you be—them four walls is what you got to call home.

I was working with the Mississippi Freedom Democrats at the time. I had jumped at the chance when they needed somebody to do some organizing work in Chicago in 1964. Miz Consuela took to inviting us to her house over on Drexel Blvd. for Sunday dinner. The first time I went I made the mistake of asking Po how he was coming on his job hunt.

"I can't stand these jive time liberals, man! Things will be going on just fine till they find out I'm an ex-con, then the stuff gets funny. 'Mr. Tatum you're over qualified.' 'Mr. Tatum you're under qualified.' 'Mr. Tatum you're disqualified!' Give me a straight up, stomp down redneck any day!"

"You must learn not to be consumed by your own anger, Phillipe."

"If I am 'consumed' by anything, it is my 'legitimate discontent' as your Dr. King might say. I could go out of here this afternoon, after nine years out of circulation and get a stake for gambling or for selling drugs, for that matter, and have $500 or $1000 of my own to spend by tomorrow nite. Now, with a college degree, I can't even find a straight job that will pay $150 a week! Don't worry. I'm not going back into the life, but you have to understand that there's something wrong with the system that offers a man that kind of choice!"

He'd grab the Sunday paper and sit in the big easy chair by the window. He'd read a while, then he would stare out the window watching the children play while junkies went in and out of the empty brown brick building across Drexel Blvd. Po would cuss the newspaper. Miz Consuela would ask him, "If you find the newspaper so disturbing, why do you continue to read it?"

"Information is an essential requirement of modern life. Brother Malcolm is right! 'He who manipulates the media manipulates the minds of the masses.' I have to keep up with what the Devil is saying so I know what not to think!" He'd turn back to the newspaper in such a way that we knew not to say no more to him.

Finally, the brother got a job. They hired him to be a counselor at the Halfway House. When I pulled out of Chicago on the I.C. railroad, I felt like my friend Po was doing alright for himself. Me, I was tired of being where you couldn't see the sun go down for all the concrete and steel.

My work took me to a heap of different places. It was a lot of stuff for us Freedom Riders to do in the 60's. The next time I hit Chicago, he'd dug up Miz Consuela's whole back yard. Had some collard greens, I'sh potatoes, tomatoes, squashes, bell peppers, okra and some funny little plants he said was Miz Consuela's teas.

"Po, this garden looks near bout as good as back home."

"Yeah, Junebug, we've got to learn to get back to the land. As long as a people have a piece of land they've got something worth while. Junebug, my man, this is only the beginning. There's land all around

here. A vacant lot there, one there. And there's people all around who
can't hardly afford to eat. Now there's a likely combination: hungry people
and vacant land! All I have to do is put all this land to productive use
and I can feed the world!"

Sometime Po and me be talking and he'd jump track on me. I thought
we was talking about a little backyard garden and he's the new messiah
out to feed the whole world.

Still it made my heart feel good. He was almost like the old Po. Had
a look in his eye I hadn't seen since before Mr. Jake died. He even
started making up rhymes again.

> I got a garden in the city.
> My okra's really pretty
> Had no greens that taste so good since I was home.
> Had to put aside my shopping
> Grocery bill it got me rocking
> Had to leave that doggone grocery store alone.
>
> Living off my garden, baby
> Garden in the city
> Living off my garden, baby
> Garden in the city.
>
> Digga, digga, digga, digga, digga Chicago.
> Digga, digga, digga, digga, digga Chicago.
> Digga, digga, digga, digga, digga Chicago.
> Trying to find a way to make a new home!

Po was running up and down different streets all over the South Side
looking at vacant lots. He was still working at the Halfway House but
he had also organized something he called "Development of International
Gardens in Chicago."

"DIG in Chicago, you dig it?"

"What do you mean by that 'International' part?"

"All over everywhere! We got the potential to feed half the hungry
people in the world right here in Chicago!"

That was the first time I met Little Johnny Tadlow. He was a fine
looking fellow with a black leather jacket, a little crimp brim hat and
a gold tooth right here. Kept a big smile on his face so you could see
it.

"Brother Junebug, we figure there's an average of 3 lots in every block
where some house has been torn down, burned down or just about to
fall down, you dig? So if we just take this 6 block area from Drexel
to Woodlawn and from 43rd to 45th, that's approximately 4 acres. Now

if we convert that to productive land, it'll feed at least 10% of the people in this neighborhood. When we get this neighborhood organized, we're going to move on to the next one and the next one and so on and so forth. Besides affordable, fresh food for the people, this program will provide jobs for cats like us coming out of the joint, you dig? Now that's what you call reversing the cycle, Brother. Dig it!"

"And that's serious, real, productive, work! Not some jive-time make-work, dead-end gig for some dude downtown that don't care no more about us than Col. Whitten cared for his brother's pet pig."

Well, it worked! By spring of '66, "DIG in Chicago" had planted up a bunch of vacant lots on the South Side and a few out West. People come in droves from all over to buy those vegetables.

Those were the days! After they'd finish up the day's work they'd meet up somewhere, talk things over and have a nip. They was a fine bunch. Whenever I could, I'd be with them.

There was this one fellow they called "Deadeye"—had one eye—he lost the other one in Korea. He had the look of a blood hound.

Deadeye'd say, "Before I got to working in the garden project, things had got so hard, man, that I didn't have but a dollar forty-seven cents for lunch. I went to this little greasy spoon joint and this fine young sister come over. I said, 'Hey, Baby. What can I get good for a dollar forty-seven cents?' She say, 'I ain't your baby, Mister. The only thing you can get in here for a dollar forty-seven cents is hurt feelings. You need more than that to get a wish sandwich?' I said, 'A wish sandwich, what's that?' 'When you get two pieces of bread and a paper napkin and *wish* you had some meat.' Man, that woman offent my mantality! I got up and walked out of there so fast I tried to take the door off the hinges. Went down to the corner store and bought me half a pound of 'loney dog and saltine crackers! And that's what I had to eat off of for three days!"

Then there was this other old cat in the group called Hound. He looked kinda like a Basset hound. He said, "Oh Brother Deadeye. You're lucky you could afford that much. I was so broke when I became involved in the Dig in Chicago Project that I had to borrow eyewater to cry with!"

Those guys would carry on. When they weren't laughing and joking, they would be rapping on the problems of the world. When people get a sense of purpose in their lives, it seems like the whole world opens up to them.

Then, it come a day, that next fall, when it seem like the problems of the world blew in on them just as swift and mean as a cold wind off Lake Michigan.

The job fell to Po to try to explain to them what was happening. "Well, fellows, here's the situation. Fat Mack, the South Side Numbers Man, brought us a message from the mob. Said we have to start giving them half of what we make at our stores if we want to stay in business."

TADLOW   Forget that, Man! My granddaddy left Mississippi to get shed of sharecropping!

PO   That ain't all, Tadlow. As if that wasn't enough, the man downtown has issued building permits for four out of six of our sites on the South Side. They've got low income housing slated for these sites. Because of the money involved you can be sure that there's somebody big behind it. They plan to bring the bulldozers in tomorrow.

HOUND   They won't hold off long enough for us to get the harvest in?

TADLOW   They'll hold off as long as we make them hold off! Brother Hound. What we need is action, you dig, action! When y'all get done flapping you lips, meet me and my boys at the battle front.

DEADEYE   Cool it youngblood! Ain't no battlefront yet. We just got to make a plan for what we can all do together! And don't you forget, you still on parole.

TADLOW   And don't you forget that you got a good bunch of men depending on you for work and people counting on you for food, and all the guys counting on our organization for jobs. I ain't scared of the man or the mob. Besides, it's the principle of the thing. Ain't that what you been trying to rap to us about Po? Naw man. Meet me down at the battlefront.

PO   Let him go. He'll be back when he cools out.

The rest of them stayed there to make a plan. It was a good one too. They made leaflets, they got on the telephones, they knocked on doors, all night long they contacted people to get them to know what was going on so they would come out and stand with them. The next morning, before sun up, the whole block was full of people. They sang and bragged about how they wasn't "Goin to Let Nobody Turn Us Around," and "Going to Stay on the Battle Field," "Like a Tree Planted by the River" and lots more of those beautiful old songs. They had their arms locked and rocked back and forth. They was so many of them the trucks with the bulldozers on them couldn't even get in the neighborhood.

They were feeling real good as the early morning light got bright enough to see into the garden somebody screamed, "What's that out there?" Po hollered, "Don't y'all go trample down the product!" He fought his way through the crowd to the middle of the field and there was Little Johnny Tadlow. It didn't look like all that blood could have come from the one small round bullet hole in the middle of his forehead.

Po didn't even try to plant a garden the Spring of '67. He just went to sitting in the window at Miz Consuela's house staring out. Reminded me of how Miz Adeline was after Mr. Jake passed.

Miz Consuela would lite candles in the window and sit with him a while. She'd brew up these herb teas and get him to drink a little. Said it was his medicine. I wished I could have said something to make him laugh. A rhyme, a story. Everytime I'd go somewhere and come back Po look like he was worse off than the time before.

Sometimes Po be there. Sometimes Po be gone. Nobody know were to find him. He lost the job at the Halfway House. He come home hungry and tired. He sleep. He sit, looking out the window. Sometimes Po'd pop up and say something like he's talking to some people we couldn't see.

"A college degree offers little relief from the bondage of blackness in white America. A piece of paper is no passport from the prison of poverty! Brother Malcolm was right. If they won't let you win with the ballot, then you must lay claim to victory with the bullet . . . Somebody ought to do something about those buildings across the street."

When Po got to talking like that, I seen a kind of cold wildness in his eyes. Reminded me of old Stonewall Whitten back home preaching on the Courthouse Steps. I didn't have no recollection of Po being like that. His eyes used to sparkle and smile, even when he's talking bad about your mama.

Every summer was worse than the one before. Cities burning: Harlem, Watts, Newark, Detroit. Everytime somebody got killed it seemed like a little piece of Po would die too. He'd sit there looking at reports on TV rocking back and forth making something that sounded like an Indian Chant: "Burn, baby burn. Burn, baby burn. Burn, . . "

It rocked on and rocked on into 1968. That was the worse one of all. They killed Dr. King in Memphis, and the whole country went up in flames. They got young Bobby Kennedy in California. They brought the Democrats Convention to Chicago and the whole world was watching.

I was watching the Convention on television when up popped Po Tatum on the local news!

"Why are you trying to take over all these South Side Chicago buildings?"

"There's thousands of people with no place to stay and right now these empty buildings are nothing but shooting galleries for a bunch of junkies."

"But what you're doing is illegal, isn't it?"

"What is happening here now is immoral and destructive to the life of this community. We're trying to liberate these buildings."

"Mr. Tatum, isn't it true that you're blocking the rightful owners from acquiring permits for rehabilitation?"

"These buildings have been vacant for years. Why do you think these damn landlords just started this stuff when we started this action?"

"Who is this 'we' you refer to? Isn't it true that you represent no real constituency?"

"That's not true. I represent the people."

"Isn't that rather vague, sir? And isn't it true, Mr. Tatum, that you were recently released from Joliet State Prison on charges of attempted manslaughter, jail breaking, illegal gambling and a variety of other charges?"

"What the hell has that got to do with anything?"

"There you have it ladies and gentlemen. We taped this interview earlier today with Mr. Phillip A. Tatum at the site of a building on Drexel Boulevard that he's trying to 'liberate'. We have just learned that Mr. Tatum has occupied the building, he is believed to be armed and is considered extremely dangerous. We will update the story as the situation develops.

"Meanwhile, at the Democratic Convention—"

I hit the street flying.
It was a hell of a storm blowing in off the lake.
"Taxi! Taxi!"

Chica chica chica chica chica chica chic—
El'll take too long.

"Taxi!"

"Drexel and 47th. Quick!"

"Loop's blocked off."

Gotta go way out the way
Tanks in the streets of Chicago.
"Faster man, faster!"

Rolling South through a sea of blues
Rolling South through a sea of blues
Rolling South through a sea of blues
In the Windy City.
Who knows which way the wind blows?
Who knows which way the wind blows?

Who knows which way the wind blows?
In the Windy City.

"Faster man, Faster!
Right on Thirty-Seventh! Move it!"

Clap of thunder split the sky!
Cop cars scre-e-e-eaming around the corner!

"Flashing lights ahead."
"Uh-oh! Something's wrong."
"Cops got the street blocked at Fortieth and Drexel."
"Let me out here.
Keep the change."

Strange.
Police.
Blockades.
A sea of blues!

Police squat down behind they cars.
Guns pulled!

People milling around like it's a show going on.
"It's a crazy nigger holed up in that building."
"Yeah, they going to kill a coon today."
"Let me through."
"What's he trying to do?"
"I don't know."
"Let me through!"

I couldn't tell what come first—whether it was the gun shots, the thunder or some other kind of explosion.

The newspapers said it was Po that fired the first shot and that old building, which wasn't none too strong in the first place, just come tumbling down. With all that thunder and lightening it wasn't too many willing to swear as to what really did go on out there that day. 'Cept for one old man who swore, "I seen the face of a man in the clouds when a bolt of lightening just as red as blood hit and danced all around that building just when the police opened fire."

It taken them three days to clear away the rubble of that building and find the two bodies that was left up in there. One of them looked like it might be Po except for one thing. Miz Consuela swore Po left home that morning with a clean red shirt on. The body they found had on a green shirt.

Me and Miz Consuela, we taken what was thought to be Po's remains put them in the best coffin we could afford and took 'em down home. We buried it in a grave out there in The Bottom between Po's Ma and Pa.

EPILOGUE

You Can't Judge a Book by Looking at the Cover

I'ma tell you a story bout my old friend, Po.
Things he had to do, places he had to go.
Home boy going out to get some money,
If it hadn't been so sad it might have been funny.
Told all about the way that he was misunderstood,
His family and his friends thought that he was just a hood.
Told how the man misunderstood himself.
He went to get some knowledge, left the book up on the shelf.
He got the cover off the book, but didn't get what it had in it.
What should have took a week, he tried to get it in a minute.

You can't judge a book by looking at the cover.
You can read my letter but I bet you can't read my mind.
If you want to get down, down, down, you got to spend some time.
I want to talk with you,
I want to talk with you,
I wanna, wanna, wanna, wanna rap with you.
Hey!

When you grown up in the country, things are hard, times are tough.
Growing your own food but it never seems enough.
You too smart for the country, you got to get away.
Got to move to the city, got to be a better way.
So you move to the city, put the country stuff behind.
But when you hit the city, it starts to messin with your mind.
You struggle and you scramble just to do the best you can.
Think you working for a living? Hell, you working for The Man.
People stacked like chickens on the way to meet the slaughter.
Flopping all around the ground like fishes out of water.

Blind man on the corner, holding up a sign
It says, No more water, y'all, The fire next time!"

You can't judge a book by looking at the cover.
You can read my letter but I bet you can't read my mind.
If you want to get down, down, down, you got to spend some time.
I want to talk with you,
I want to talk with you,
I wanna, wanna, wanna, wanna rap with you.
Hey!

THE END

Two Kinds of People

LINDA PEAVY

CHARACTERS

GINNY MCCUBBINS
CARRIE MCCUBBINS
RYAN
MAURI
AUNT ETHEL
UNCLE WESLEY
B. J. MCCUBBINS

SETTING

The action takes place on the outskirts of Caledonia, Mississippi

Scene 1

(The stage is darkened. Church music can be heard in the background—a country church's congregational singing of favorite Southern Baptist hymns, i.e., "Love Lifted Me," "Shall We Gather at the River," "Amazing Grace," "There Shall be Showers of Blessing." Two low stools are at downstage left. In the background is a large platform (1' high, 30' long at the rear, 22' long at front) representing the interior of an elaborate home. Downstage right and center are two wicker chairs and several tropical plants, furnishings for the visible portion of a sunken living room. Six feet back from the front of the platform, brick steps lead up two feet to a second platform representing the kitchen, a BETTER HOMES AND GARDENS model whose stageright wall features a brick hearth and countertop burners, plus Jennaire grill and hood. A wall phone is to the right of the stove. The back wall is lined with customized cabinets and a refrigerator, and a door leads off to the hall. A 6' x 4' freestanding work/eat counter with high-backed bar stools is in the center of the kitchen floor space, and the suggestion of a wall is at stage left. This wall separates the kitchen from an elaborate bathroom that is part of the lower platform and accessed from the living

361

*room. The door in the center of the back wall of this bathroom
leads into the master bedroom. To the left of the door is a brass
towel rod hung with thick towels. To the right is a tall tropical plant.
A wicker chair is at stage right, and at stage left, downstage and
near the edge of the platform, is a round marble tub whose gold
fixtures feature a spout in the shape of a long-necked bird. Plants
surround the back edge of the tub.*

*As the play opens, the hymns fade out and an overhead spot
bathes the two stools in light.* GINNY *and* CARRIE *move from the
darkness of the platform at stage left into the edge of the spot.*
GINNY *is around 40, casually dressed in running shoes, dress jeans,
and a long-sleeved, oversized shirt she has tucked in to meet her
mother's expectations of appropriate dress for Wednesday night
prayer service at Mt. Salem Baptist Church.* CARRIE, *her mother,
around 70, is greying and walks with a very slight limp, the result
of a stroke several years back. She is proper, if not quite prim,
yet also soft and gentle, with a shy, infrequent smile. She wears
a casual shirtwaist dress or skirt and blouse and a lightweight nylon
jacket. Her shoes are laceup walking shoes, and she carries a handbag.*

*Waving and nodding to unseen churchgoers behind them, the two
women walk from the platform at stageleft over to the stools, with
GINNY leading the way. She goes around to the downstage stool,
opens the door for her mother, then circles the car to open her
own door and take her place on the upstage stool. As soon as GINNY
takes her place behind the wheel, CARRIE begins to watch the road
ahead, somewhat nervous about her daughter's driving. Within seconds, the two women freeze, but momentarily GINNY breaks her
freeze, rises from her stool, and moves downstage to meet the audience, leaving CARRIE frozen in her journey away from the church)*

GINNY   We're on our way home from prayer meeting. And we've been
there without my father, because he has gotten old enough and tired
enough that not even his long afternoon naps suffice to keep him awake
in the evenings. So we've been to church without him. It's the first
time I can remember going without him, but it's not the first time
for her. Since she doesn't drive, going without him usually means
catching a ride with her sister Ethel. But tonight I am the driver,
and my father is still very much along for the ride. (*Gestures toward
the stools in the spotlight*)   The blackness of this winding asphalt swal-
lows up my lights so completely I can hardly believe they are on bright.
My father would tell me to use my dimmer. But my father is at home,
resting.

We have not been resting. We have been praying. For rain. For sinners. For Hiram Beeson's kidney stone to pass. Those were a few of the evening's requests. There were others I can't remember. Now we're going home—after we stop by to see my cousin Mauri. She called this afternoon to invite us over for fig cake and iced tea, and on the way to church I managed to convince my mother we ought to go. After all, Dad's sleeping. He doesn't need us. And I'll be flying out tomorrow. When will I have another chance to talk to Mauri? (*Tosses her head back toward her mother*) I still can't believe she gave in so easily. Two miracles in one evening. Church and a visit, both without my father.

Mauri has not been to church. She gave up on Mt. Salem ten years ago, after the preacher, Brother Billy Sampson, repeated something she'd told him in confidence. She and Billy Sampson finished high school together. And college. Then he went to seminary and she went to visit an aunt in Tulsa and ended up staying there and marrying a Phillips Petroleum executive ten years her senior. She had Ryan, settled into the country club life, then moved back home about five years ago—after her husband was killed in a plane crash over Dallas. She moved back with money, she moved back in style, and she moved back to stay.

She's told me more than once that I ought to come back, too, but I always manage to evade the issue. I'll probably have to dodge it again tonight. She's easy enough to distract. All I have to do is mention how fantastic her house is looking, now that she's got the swimming pool finished and the patio bricked.

> (*As the next phrase is spoken, lights come up slowly on the house in the background and* GINNY *moves toward the house, adapting the mannerisms of a real estate salesperson*)

GINNY   The house *is* fantastic. Right out of *Better Homes and Gardens*. She's taken her time with it, finished out first one part and then another. It has been her life ever since she came back to Caledonia. She did the kitchen first, complete with a walk-in pantry and bins for whole-grain flours and dried fruits.

GINNY (*Moving to* CARRIE'S *side of the car, opening the door, and helping her mother out of her freeze and onto her feet*)   What's new this time?

CARRIE (*Arranging her handbag and picking her way across the driveway*)   The master bedroom's finished. (*Rising from her stool and accepting* GINNY'S *arm until she gets to her feet*)   And the bath. I haven't seen it yet, but it has a sunken tub.

(*As the two women rise, the spot on the stools fades and full lights come up on the living room and kitchen of the house they are about to enter. The sharp yapping of a poodle in a fenced run can be heard at stage left.* RYAN, *a sixteen-year-old in jeans, a t-shirt, and Nikes, enters the kitchen, then moves down to greet* GINNY *and* CARRIE *as they cross the yard toward the house*)

RYAN (*Shouting to the dog at stage left*) Hush up, ESPRIT! (*The dog continues yapping and he yells with more force*) Shut up, dog! (*He turns to face the two women, then stoops to receive a quick hug from* CARRIE *and a longer one from* GINNY) Hi, ya'll. Come on inside.

GINNY (*Backing off and sizing him up*) Don't tell me—let me guess. You've grown at least six inches since I last saw you.

RYAN (*Obviously pleased that she's noticed*) More like EIGHT inches, Aunt Ginny. You haven't been home since before I made varsity.

CARRIE (*Eager to share privileged information*) Ethel says he'll be all-state this year.

RYAN (*Properly modest*) If I'm lucky and get enough playing time. (*Eager to turn the subject away from himself*) Ya'll come on in. Mama's on the phone with Nana.

GINNY (*Looking around*) The house looks great. I hear you've done more to it.

RYAN (*Motioning them toward the bathroom to stage left*) Yeah. Mama's bedroom's done. And her bathroom, too. Come see the tub, Aunt Ginny. Mama'll be on the phone all night. You come, too, Aunt Carrie.

(*As the boy starts toward the bathroom,* CARRIE *follows close behind and* GINNY *moves after her. As they approach the tub,* RYAN *reaches out his hand and all three freeze, but* GINNY *breaks her freeze and turns to the audience*)

GINNY I am not his aunt, of course. I am his cousin. But here, second cousins of one's mother's age are always aunts. My mother is not his aunt, either. She is his great-aunt. It is hard for me to think of my mother as a great aunt, though I realize great-aunthood was inevitable. Just as she became a grandmother, so it was inevitable she would become a great aunt. And within a few years, when this sixteen-year-old boy marries and has children, she will become a great-great Aunt. And that will make her sound very old indeed.

She is not very old. She has just turned seventy. (*Steps back to get a better view of her mother, with the air of one who has come home to size up family matters in a few days' time*) But she is not very young, either. (*Continues her scrutiny by running her eyes along her mother's legs, as one might study the conformation of a piece of sculpture*) She moves well, despite a stroke that weakened her left leg some years ago. And she seems to be growing stronger as my father grows weaker. (*Moves back into place behind* RYAN *and* CARRIE *and resumes her freeze*)

RYAN (*Breaking freeze for all and speaking with pride*) See this swan? (*He pats the long-necked bird that serves as spout for the marble, sunken tub*) I had the basketball team over last week after the game in McComb, and one of the black guys told everybody at school that I was so rich I had this gold bird that didn't do nothing all day but spit out my bath water. (*He laughs, as do the two women, looks around as if deciding what to show them next, then motions toward the bedroom.*) Ya'll might want to look in there. Mama's finally got that kingsized brass bed she ordered out of that catalogue from Boston.

(*As* GINNY *and* CARRIE *move toward the door to the bedroom,* RYAN *starts back toward the living room*)

RYAN (*Over his shoulder*) I'll go get Mama.

(GINNY *and* CARRIE *move toward the open bedroom door and stop as if reluctant to enter a sacred space*)

GINNY (*Hands on hips*) Wow. He did mean kingsized.

CARRIE (*Shaking her head in wonder, looking to be sure* RYAN *is out of earshot, then giving* GINNY *a knowing look*) Wonder what a woman all alone wants with a bed that size?

GINNY (*Smiling—surprised, but pleased at her mother's hint of impropriety*) The same thing she wants with the tub.

(*As the two women stand looking in the bedroom,* MAURI *enters the bathroom. Thirty-eight, shapely, and attractive, she is dressed in the kind of casual jeans and shirt that cost a fortune without looking the least bit ostentatious. Her makeup is flawless, her long hair curled to perfection. She wears fashion with ease and exudes a substantiality that belies her careful attention to appearances. She is one of those women who has found herself in losing her husband, and it is evident she likes the person she has become and that any man who enters her life will do so on her terms. She does the right things for her parents and her son, yet she takes good care of herself as well*)

MAURI (*Catching them off guard and moving toward them for hugs*) Well, look who's finally come home!

GINNY (*Embracing* MAURI) About time, I guess.

MAURI (*Giving a cursory, but warm, hug to* CARRIE) Listen to her talk, Aunt Carrie. She knows she ought to come back down here and build that house across the lake.

GINNY I'd have to do some building to outshine this one. I can't believe that bedroom!

MAURI How'd ya'll like that brass bed?

CARRIE (*Risking a glance at* GINNY *while* MAURI'S *back is turned*) That's some bed, all right!

GINNY (*Moving toward the tub*) And this is no slouch of a tub, either. I'm amazed at what you've done with this place.

MAURI It's taken me long enough. And it's cost a fortune. But it's home and I like it.

CARRIE (*Unwilling to be left out*) Tell her about the solarium.

GINNY Solarium!

MAURI (*Laughing*) The about-to-be solarium. Ya'll come on in here and I'll show you.

> (MAURI *leads the way back into the living room, where she picks up a roll of architect's drawings from the coffee table and hands them to* GINNY. *As* GINNY *unrolls the plans and studies them,* CARRIE *moves in close, eager to see what no one has bothered to share with her before*)

MAURI I hate being closed in. When it's raining or too hot and sticky outside, I want to be able to sit here and look out—with nothing but clear glass between me and the pool. (*Moving to point out a section of the architect's drawing, then waving her arms in an expansive move that embraces all outdoors*) Those two walls are coming out.

CARRIE (*Alarmed*) How can you do that?

MAURI (*Smiling at her aunt's dismay and speaking with the hint of condescension that most persons using when addressing* CARRIE) Not all the way out, but when I'm done it will FEEL like they're gone. See (*Pointing to the plan*). There will be support beams here, and columns between these big windows. You'll be able to sit right here and see the patio and pool.

RYAN Clear out to the other side of the lake!

MAURI (*Giving* GINNY *a significant look*) Right over to where you ought to build that house. When you come home to stay.

RYAN Yeah, Aunt Ginny. Don't you want to come back down here where it's warm?

(GINNY *turns to answer, but the barking of Esprit the poodle off stage left spares her the effort*)

MAURI (*Moving down and out the door of the living room*) It's Mama. I told her you were here and she and Daddy decided to come over.

CARRIE (*To no one in particular and for no reason other than the fact that she should*) I wish your father were here.

(*As* GINNY *rolls up the architect's drawings,* ETHEL *and* WESLEY *enter from stage left.* ETHEL *is carrying the promised fig cake in a Tupperware carrier. Around 68, she has very little grey in her dark hair. A large woman, she moves with self-confidence that would imply that she is the older sister, though indeed she is two years younger than* CARRIE. *She wears dark pants, a bright blouse, tennis shoes and no jacket, despite the late hour. She is followed by* WESLEY, *her contemporary in age, but not in spirit. A tall, slight man,* WESLEY'S *every move is tentative, the actions of a man who is perpetually along for the ride but never in the driver's seat. His slacks show the sharp crease that only an iron can give. He wears a conservative sports shirt, a cotton jacket, brown dress shoes, and cataract glasses that cause him to turn his head to avoid or catch the proper light with which to observe his surroundings. As the couple arrives,* GINNY *moves to meet and embrace them in turn, and* CARRIE *gives* ETHEL *a hug and* WESLEY *a nod*)

ETHEL (*Depositing the covered cake on the counter*) Sorry, we're late, but I was at the funeral home.

WESLEY (*Depositing himself on the end stool at stage right*) She's always at the funeral home.

CARRIE Why, Wesley, you know better than that.

WESLEY (*Persisting in a familiar argument*) She's been to two funerals already this week and has another one tomorrow.

ETHEL (*Dropping herself down on a stool at the back of the counter*) Somebody has to do it.

(*The actors freeze as the voiceover begins, each one assuming an attitude that reflects their respective personalities.* MAURI *has her back to the group and the audience, ready to bring forth the items needed to serve the cake. She has been bustling in the kitchen ever since her mother and father entered the house.* CARRIE *is at the other end of the table, opposite* WESLEY. RYAN *is at the corner of the counter, between his grandparents.* GINNY *is seated between her* AUNT ETHEL *and her mother, and her freeze reflects a close scrutiny of her* AUNT ETHEL'S *face*)

GINNY (*Breaking her freeze and leaning toward* ETHEL *as if to confirm her initial observation*)   There is a bead of perspiration on Aunt Ethel's upper lip. It is a comforting sight, reminding me of trips to the garden with her when Mauri and I were small. Early in the morning when Aunt Ethel would come by for us, she'd be dry and cool, but after only a few minutes picking peas or pulling corn, there'd be a fine moustache of sweat. My mother never sweated. She worked just as hard as her sister did, but I never saw sweat on her upper lip. She sometimes had dark circles under her arms, but she never had sweat on her upper lip.

(*As* GINNY *resumes her freeze,* MAURI *breaks the freeze for all by setting a stack of plates on the countertop*)

ETHEL (*Rising to help her daughter*)   Why don't you let me get the tea?

MAURI (*Motioning to the refrigerator*)   It's ready to pour, but it's still warm. Ryan, would you put some ice in those glasses?

RYAN (*Moving to obey*)   Yes, ma'am.

ETHEL (*As she takes glasses from* RYAN, *pours in the tea, and sets glasses in place*)   Did you see the bedroom?

MAURI (*Cutting cake and passing out slices on dessert plates*)   They saw it, Mama. (*Turning to* GINNY)   Did you know that Mama's got a new bedroom, too?

RYAN (*Giving his grandfather a sly look*)   Yeah, one without Papa in it.

GINNY (*Risking her mother's raised eyebrows*)   Put him out to pasture, did you?

WESLEY (*Emphatically*)   I put HER out. Snores like a sawmill and keeps me awake all night. Hard enough for me to sleep as it is without that racket.

CARRIE (*Nodding*)   I know what you mean.

RYAN (*Laughing*)   But I bet you won't put Uncle B.J. out to pasture!

(CARRIE *lowers her eyes, embarrassed and knowing the boy is right.* ETHEL *gives* RYAN *a punch and a warning look, then moves to cover for her sister*)

ETHEL   Well, you know Wesley. He kept on complaining until I decided to move out and leave it to him. (*Proudly*)   I made that old storage closet into a room of my own. (CARRIE *is watching her intently*)   I even did the sheetrocking myself.

RYAN (*Reaching for another piece of cake*)   I helped her paint it. She was too chinchy to have it done right.

ETHEL (*Giving* RYAN *a punch in the ribs*) It IS done right!

RYAN (*Insistent*) But you don't have a gold bird to spit out your bath water.

ETHEL I don't even have a tub. Now leave me be and go do your homework.

RYAN (*Pinching at the cake*) Don't have any.

ETHEL Then go watch TV.

(*As* RYAN *exits,* WESLEY *picks up his favorite topic*)

WESLEY I sure am glad you and your mother came by, Ginny. If you hadn't, I'm sure this cake would have been left up at the funeral home. Do you know how long it's been since I had one of her cakes? She's made six or seven in the past month and carried every last one of them off to somebody else.

ETHEL (*Finishing the last of her cake*) He's exaggerating. But we HAVE had a run of funerals.

CARRIE (*Eager to be a part of the conversation*) Yes, indeed we have. (*Ticking the funerals off on her fingers*) First there was Mr. Corbin, and then Fannie Greer and Maudie Reynolds—both of them in the same week.

GINNY (*Startled*) Maudie Reynolds? She's too young to die.

WESLEY When'd you see her last?

GINNY (*Pausing to reflect*) I don't know. Yes, yes, I do. The summer Ryan was born. She was at the A&P with her granddaughter.

WESLEY (*Knowingly*) That was sixteen years back. Lot of us looked young sixteen years back.

ETHEL And a lot of us still look young.

CARRIE (*Taking up where she left off*) Anyway, after Maudie Reynolds there was Lonnie Butler and now Mr. Sweeney.

GINNY (*Aware that she has not been properly attentive to this litany of the dead*) Mr. Sweeney? Didn't he just have a birthday party last month?

CARRIE (*With the air of one who knows death takes special delight in striking down those who have parties*) Sure did. I wrote you about it, remember? Your Daddy and I went.

GINNY (*Nodding*) Yes, I remember. (*Turning to her* AUNT ETHEL) Did you go?

WESLEY Of course not. She waits 'til they're dead to go visit. Then carries them cakes they've got no use for while her own family goes begging.

ETHEL Hush your mouth.

WESLEY Funeralizing. That's what she's doing. Funeralizing. First this one and then that one dying. Black or white, it don't make any difference to her. If there's a funeral, she's got to be there. And with a cake.

MAURI (*Laughing*) It's true. First the undertaker comes to pick up the body, then Mama shows up with a cake.

GINNY Who died that's black?

ETHEL Minnie Mae's sister. The blind one that's lived with her for so long.

CARRIE (*Fishing for some proof that* GINNY *has not completely lost touch with what she once was and should be still*) You remember her, don't you?

(*The actors freeze with the question. Then* GINNY *breaks her freeze, stands as if to rise above the table talk, and confides to the audience*)

GINNY I do remember. Minnie Mae used to garden for my grandparents and Mauri and I used to play by the river behind her house while our mothers were picking pole beans or gathering okra. There were tall bushes of berries there, probably poisonous and definitely not edible. Once we painted our faces and arms with their deep purple juice and raced up and down the river, slapping our open hands against mouths spread wide in the "WAA, waa, waa, waa! WAA, waa, waa, waa!" of wild Indians. Never tame ones. It never occurred to us that Indians might be tame. We never went inside the house, but we knew that Minnie Mae's sister was lying somewhere in a darkened room, had been lying there for as long as we could remember. Diabetes, our mothers told us, as a warning against too much candy. That's what diabetes does to your eyes.

Now Minnie Mae's sister is dead, and now that I think about it, Minnie Mae herself must be close to 90. I don't see how she can possibly still be living there in that house by the river, with its purple berries growing undisturbed behind the garden she still raises for Aunt Ethel and Uncle Wesley. It is, after all, their land. (*Gestures toward her uncle and aunt as she drops onto her stool*) They just let her live there, as my grandparents did before them. As their parents did before that. (*Freezes*)

GINNY (*Breaking the group freeze*) Does Minnie Mae live out there all by herself now?

ETHEL Her daughter's been there since Christmas, but I don't know how long she plans to stay.

RYAN (*Returning for more cake and tea*) She better stay. If we lose Conrad, we don't have a prayer of taking state.

GINNY (*Savoring the idea*) So Minnie Mae's grandson's on your team?

RYAN (*Lifting cake onto his plate*)   Conrad's not ON our team. Conrad IS our team.

GINNY   That's great. (*Reaches to pour herself more tea*)

CARRIE (*Rising and reaching for* GINNY'S *glass*)   Here, let me get you some more ice, first.

RYAN (*Over his shoulder to his mother as he moves toward the hallway*) You tell Minnie Mae I said Conrad can come live with us if his mama moves back to Jackson.

> (*Still looking at his mother,* RYAN *runs directly into* CARRIE, *who is making her way slowly toward the refrigerator. The collision causes* CARRIE *to drop the glass, which shatters on the floor*)

MAURI   Now look what you've done!

CARRIE   He didn't do it. I did it. I've been so clumsy ever since . . .

RYAN   No, ma'am. I did it. I ran right into you.

MAURI   You sure did. And you can just get a broom and sweep up that glass.

CARRIE (*Stooping and trying to pick up pieces with her right hand, holding fast to the countertop with her left*)   You ought to make me use a plastic glass. I just can't seem to hold onto things the way I used to.

MAURI   You leave that be, Aunt Carrie. You'll cut yourself. Ryan can get it.

RYAN (*Returning with the broom and dustpan*)   I got it, Aunt Carrie, I got it.

GINNY (*Extending a hand to her mother*)   Let him do it, Mama. (*Setting* CARRIE *back in her chair*)   You're a good man with a broom, Ryan.

MAURI   He'd be better if he got more practice.

RYAN   I get plenty of practice! (*Turns to* CARRIE)   Just don't tell Uncle B.J. you saw me sweeping.

GINNY   Why not?

RYAN   Every time he sees me helping Mama with the dishes, he tells me I better go get my apron.

ETHEL (*Looking anxiously at* CARRIE)   He's just teasing.

CARRIE (*Rushing to defend B.J.*)   Sure he is. Why, your Uncle B.J. knows how to do dishes himself.

RYAN   No way!

CARRIE (*Pushing her luck*)   Sure he does. He helps me do dishes. Lots of times.

> (*All are shocked by this revelation, certain it cannot be true, and uncertain of the reasons for* CARRIE'S *fabrication*)

GINNY   When did Daddy ever wipe a dish?

CARRIE (*Defensively*)   I didn't say he dried them. I said he helps me sometimes. (*Groping for a way out*)   He hands me the dishes.

ETHEL (*To the rescue*)   Ryan, I thought you were watching TV . . .

RYAN   Ok. Ok. I'm going. (*Calling down from the hall*)   Aunt Carrie, you call me next time Uncle B.J. helps with the dishes. I want to come watch.

WESLEY (*To* GINNY)   How come your Daddy's not over here eating fig cake? (*Anticipating her answer and liking it before it is spoken*)

CARRIE (*Jumping in ahead of* GINNY)   He needs his rest.

WESLEY (*Pressing*)   How's he doing?

CARRIE (*Defensively*)   Fine. He just doesn't get out much at night anymore.

> (*As* UNCLE WESLEY *smiles and nods knowingly, the actors freeze, with* WESLEY'S *gloating smile as the primary focus*)

GINNY (*Breaking her freeze, rising, and moving stage right, behind* UNCLE WESLEY)   They have been in a contest, these two men. They have always been in a contest. "Wesley Haley's too good to get his hands dirty," my father used to say when we were small. "He calls himself the SUPERVISOR of the print shop, but you never see him get his hands dirty."

(*Moving downstage*)   My father's hands were always dirty. He ran a contracting business and kept watch over a fleet of heavy equipment the highway department would have been proud to own. He was always talking about what he'd done to fix a backhoe or dozer, and whenever we visited the yards with him on the weekends, he never failed to open a hood or at least kick a tire before we left. He spent most of his hours bending over this truck or that, pulling out engines, changing oil or plugs, or just checking to be sure everything looked good. And he came home smelling of oil and grease and sweat, came home with khakis that looked like the *before* part of the TIDE ads on the soap operas. I used to think all fathers went away clean and came home dirty until I was big enough to go to spend-the-nights with friends whose fathers wore suits and ties to work, went away smelling of aftershave, and came home smelling as good as when they'd left.

Uncle Wesley was like that. Except that he smelled of printer's ink. My father was right about his never getting dirty. I don't know whether he was right about his never doing a lick of hard work, but I never did see him dirty. It was always Aunt Ethel who went to the garden.

And it was Aunt Ethel who mowed the lawn and repainted the house and fixed the roof. Uncle Wesley was always at work. "AT work," my father was fond of reminding us, "not WORKING, but AT work. There's a difference."

"There's two kinds of people in this world," he always managed to say in front of Aunt Ethel and Uncle Wesley, "those who work hard," at this he'd turn to Aunt Ethel, "and those who hardly work," and at that he'd turn to Uncle Wesley. He never did more than that, but that was more than enough for my mother. She was caught between people she loved, and all she could do was cringe and bear it.

(*Looks upstage left, toward her mother*) She has often been in that position. And my father and I are the ones whose differences most often put her in the vise that threatens to squeeze the life from her. But not tonight. Tonight my father is resting, and Uncle Wesley's triumphant smile at the thought of being here, alive and well and strong enough to carry on with the women, cannot hurt my father and therefore cannot hurt my mother either. (*As she speaks this last line, she crosses in front of the counter and moves upstage toward her place, resting a protective hand on* CARRIE'S *shoulder before moving toward her own stool, resuming freeze, focused on her mother's face*)

WESLEY (*Breaking the group freeze*) Guess you heard there's not going to be a revival in July.

GINNY (*Taking the bait*) I thought Dr. Manly was coming back from Louisville to preach.

WESLEY He was. Already put it on his calendar, busy as he is, and promised to be here. With no guarantee of income except what we took up in offerings.

GINNY (*Going along with his line*) Then why isn't he coming?

WESLEY (*Triumphant*) Because Brother Billy says we don't need another revival. We had a good one in the spring, he says, and we ought to be satisfied.

GINNY (*Surprised*) Things sure have changed. I can't remember ever hearing a preacher say we didn't need another revival.

ETHEL (*Moving to head him off*) Well, we did have 32 baptisms in the spring.

WESLEY (*Too quick for her*) And not one of them's been back to church since. That Texas evangelist was some slick operator. Why, he talked money this and money that and insisted on being guaranteed $2000, plus a cut of the plate, before he'd come. I don't know why the deacons ever agreed to it, but they did.

ETHEL (*Firmly*) You could have voted against it.

WESLEY   I did, but they wouldn't listen to me.

CARRIE (*With conviction*)   They'd have listened to B.J.

GINNY (*Knowing her mother is right but uncomfortable in that knowledge and choosing to turn back to safer ground*)   Thirty-two baptisms in one week of revival? Mt. Salem only holds a few hundred people at a time. That must have been a record.

WESLEY   Thirty-two.

GINNY   Maybe they DON'T need another revival. Who's left to save?

CARRIE (*Flashing*)   Revivals aren't just for the lost.

WESLEY   Saved or lost, nobody'll be at summer revival. Brother Billy's called Dr. Manly and canceled the whole thing.

GINNY   I'm surprised he can get away with canceling a revival.

WESLEY   Looks to me like Billy Sampson can get away with just about anything he pleases. Why, if I live to be a hundred, he'll still be there in that church, preaching on Sundays and running that used car lot the rest of the week. He's got it made—income from two jobs and a rent-free parsonage. He'd be a fool to leave.

GINNY   If word gets out he's canceled Dr. Manly's revival, he's likely to be asked to leave.

WESLEY   Fat chance. He's got the deacons eating out of his hand. There's no way they're going to get rid of him. (*He settles back on his stool, then directs a question to* MAURI)   Got any more of that cake? Or did your mother make you freeze the other half in case somebody dies next week?

MAURI (*Reaching to cut another piece for him*)   Don't be silly, Daddy. Of course there's more. Who else wants more?

GINNY (*Extending her plate*)   I'll take another piece. Can't get cake like this in Colorado.

MAURI   Aunt Carrie?

CARRIE (*Hesitating, then joining in with unaccustomed abandon*) Why not? But make mine a little one.

WESLEY (*Forking in another bite of fig cake*)   I tell you what, in the old days a preacher wouldn't have gotten away with running things like Billy Sampson does.

GINNY   What do you mean?

WESLEY   I mean he'd get sent packing.

GINNY   You mean, they'd just tell him to leave?

WESLEY (*With conviction*)   Sure. I recall times when a preacher hardly got moved in before the deacons were telling him to move out. Just that quick. A preacher getting a full paycheck wouldn't have thought about holding two jobs, either. Not in those days.

(*The actors freeze for the voiceover, with* WESLEY *left in his pontificating stance*)

GINNY (*Breaking her freeze and turning to the audience*) I remember those days. Days when the children of various preachers were my playmates, when we spent hours climbing in the magnolia trees by the cemetery, sneaking into the baptistry to dunk one another under imaginary waters, peeking through a crack in the living room door to watch a shotgun wedding or listen to a sobbing mother's story of an alcoholic son. But I can't remember back quite far enough. The famous cases, the ones Uncle Wesley is talking about, all took place before I was born. Or when I was too little to understand much of what was going on. (*Turns back to* WESLEY *and resumes freeze*)

WESLEY (*Breaking group freeze*) You remember Brother Carter, don't you?

GINNY (*Risking a look at her mother*) I don't remember him, but it seems like there was some sort of scandal attached to his name.

(GINNY *watches her mother, afraid of her disapproval. However,* CARRIE *is smiling, a whimsical little smile from years long past.* ETHEL *is laughing out loud*)

ETHEL I remember Brother Carter. And it seems to me he did leave here in a hurry.

(ETHEL *and* CARRIE *and* WESLEY *nod among themselves.* GINNY *and* MAURI *exchange glances*)

MAURI (*Taking the lead*) What'd he do, anyway?

(GINNY *eyes her mother, but* CARRIE *remains smiling, unthreatened, since it is not her own daughter who has broached the forbidden question. When no one answers,* MAURI *persists*)

MAURI Something about a girl, wasn't it?

WESLEY It's always something about a girl where preachers are concerned. And Henry Carter was no different from the rest of them.

GINNY (*Growing bolder, yet avoiding her mother's eyes*) What was it?

(CARRIE *and* ETHEL *look at each other, equally awkward on this new ground*)

ETHEL Well, Effie Pennington SAID he made advances.

WESLEY (*Astounded by her euphemistic description*) Made advances? Why she said he put her up on the altar in the old church annex and pulled her pants down!

GINNY Did he?

WESLEY Don't know if he did or not, but I figure as big a heifer as she was he couldn't have lifted her up there all my himself. She had to have hopped up there, or else it was a lie. Whether or not it was true, the story ended his time at Mt. Salem. How much good do you think he'd have done after that?

ETHEL (*To* CARRIE) Wasn't Mother the one who finally asked him to leave?

CARRIE (*Surprised*) I never heard that.

　　(*The actors freeze with* CARRIE'S *reply*)

GINNY (*Breaking her freeze rising, and moving to stroke her mother's hair*) And maybe she didn't hear it. But then again, maybe she did. I have gradually come to realize that there are a good many things my mother chooses to forget she ever knew. And there are, conversely, a good many things she really never did know. My Aunt Ethel, though younger than she, was always trusted with more and has always chosen to forget less. I have still not figured out the reasons for these differences, but I have at least come to see that they exist.

　　Now, though my mother seems shocked to find out that her mother, my long-dead grandmother, helped convince an erring preacher to pack his bags and move on, she does not seem upset by this news. Miracle number three. We are here laughing about the foibles of former ministers, and my mother does not seem bothered. On the contrary, she is enjoying herself thoroughly, drinking iced tea and actually laughing out loud. (*Moving back to her stool*) But then, my father is not here. He is resting. (*Resuming freeze*)

RYAN (*Breaking the group freeze as he enters in response to the laughter of a few moments back*) What's so funny?

CARRIE (*Rising suddenly in alarm*) Goodness! Please excuse me. Too much iced tea! (*She rises and crosses slowly but deliberately toward the hallway door*)

RYAN (*Reaching for another piece of fig cake*) What's going on, anyhow?

MAURI Your grandpa's telling stories about Mt. Salem preachers. (*Moving the cake away from* RYAN) And you better not eat any more of that cake. Aunt Carrie might want to take some home to Uncle B.J.

CARRIE (*Over her shoulder as she disappears down the hallway*) He doesn't need it. He's supposed to leave off sweets.

MAURI (*Obviously surprised by her reaction*) Well, I never! Didn't you just tell me over the phone this morning that Aunt Carrie was baking up a batch of her pecan cookies? (GINNY *nods*)

ETHEL (*Defensively*)   She was probably baking them for Ginny.

WESLEY   Whoever she baked them for, I'll bet you five dollars B.J. ate half of them before dinnertime. I bet he's got his hand in that cookie jar right now.

RYAN (*Sneaking another pinch of cake*)   Then why can't he have some of Nana's cake?

GINNY (*Looking in the direction her mother has gone*)   I don't think this has anything to do with sweets.

MAURI (*Slapping* RYAN'S *hand as he reaches for still another pinch*)   Leave that cake be and go finish your movie.

RYAN   If you're telling preacher stories, I think I'll stay.

ETHEL   Don't you want to see the rest of the movie?

RYAN (*Not fooled by her gift*)   This is better than any movie. Besides, it was an old one.

GINNY   This is an old one, too. Older than your mother or me.

WESLEY   Older than your grandmother, too, if you want to go back that far.

CARRIE (*Back in record time and afraid she's missed something during her trip to the bathroom*)   What's that old?

WESLEY   Preacher stories. Take Brother Atwood, for instance.

ETHEL (*Chuckling*)   Somebody took him, took him off and nearly beat him to death.

(CARRIE *laughs out loud, and* GINNY *shows her surprise at seeing this unaccustomed side of her mother*)

CARRIE   That WAS a long time back. I heard those stories when I was a girl.

WESLEY   They were true, too. My father swore they were true.

RYAN   Tell us.

(GINNY *and* MAURI *exchange glances. It is obvious that* RYAN'S *question is about to yield information they have never been given.* ETHEL *and* CARRIE *exchange glances, knowing* RYAN *should probably not hear what they are about to reveal, but realizing that he is the one who has asked the question*)

ETHEL (*Making up her mind and forging ahead*)   Mrs. Harper got suspicious when her daughter Dora—you remember Dora? (*The question is directed to* GINNY *and* MAURI, *and both women nod*)   Well, Dora Harper must have been around fifteen or so when her mama noticed she was taking longer and longer to bring up the cows in the evening.

WESLEY   And that she always stood looking in the mirror, pinching her cheeks and biting her lips red before she set out to the pasture.

ETHEL   The Harper's back pasture ran down across the hollow behind the parsonage, and Mrs. Harper got so she'd watch and see how long it took Dora to get down there and back again.

RYAN (*Puzzled*)   What'd that have to do with the preacher?

MAURI (*Afraid his questions will end the story*)   Don't interrupt.

CARRIE (*Leaning forward with a giggle of the girlchild she must have been when she first heard this story*)   Mrs. Harper kept on watching and timing, and Dora kept on being later and later, until the day Mrs. Harper knew for sure.

RYAN (*Still puzzled*)   Knew what?

CARRIE (*Undaunted*)   Knew why she'd been so slow coming home.

RYAN   But WHY?

(GINNY *and* MAURI *exchange anxious glances, fearful that* RYAN *has spooked* CARRIE *into withdrawing once and for all and depriving them once again of hearing this story out. But* CARRIE *does not withdraw, but leans forward with a twinkle in her eye*)

CARRIE (*Sotto voce*)   Because Mrs. Harper saw her pull off her panties, wash them out, and hang them on the line to dry. (*She delivers the line triumphantly, letting the last few words fall one by one, like drops from the dripping panties on the line*)

RYAN (*Gleeful*)   Sure enough? (*He collapses in laughter*)   And she'd been in the cow pasture with the preacher?

(RYAN *slips from his stool and doubles over with laughter, finally dropping to the floor where he rolls and hoots in the contrived joviality of a teen let in on a grown-up's shady stories. Everyone dissolves into laughter, laughing at* RYAN'S *overreaction, laughing at the thought of Mrs. Harper's face when she saw Dora Harper hanging up those panties, laughing at the fact that they are all together, in this kitchen, laughing.*

The phone rings. The grown-ups ignore it, but RYAN *rolls over twice and lands on his knees, snatching up the receiver on the second ring. His face changes abruptly*)

MAURI   Who is it, Ryan?

(*The adults watch him rise to his feet, serious now, almost at attention*)

RYAN   Yes, sir, they're here.

(GINNY *looks at her mother.* CARRIE *is years older, having received the message before it is delivered*)

RYAN Yes sir, I'll tell 'em. (*He hangs up the receiver, almost as if he fears it will break in his hand, then turns to the others*)   It's Uncle B.J.

(*Already* CARRIE *is fumbling for her jacket and purse, withdrawing into the woman she was when this evening began. Though* GINNY *tries to be attentive to* WESLEY'S *attempts to revive the conversation, everyone knows the evening is finished*)

WESLEY Remember how Brother Benson had everybody fooled thinking he was staying in McComb every Saturday to preach live on the radio, when he was really taping the show early and spending the night with some woman?

(GINNY *gives* MAURI *and* ETHEL *hugs, keeping an anxious eye on her mother, who has gone straight to the door, where she stands, waiting*)

WESLEY (*Unwilling to give up*)   And do you recollect hearing how they found Brother Johnson lying out under the magnolias with that gospel singer from Wesson?

(*No one is listening.* GINNY *moves to the door beside her mother*)

WESLEY (*Persisting to the end*)   Ya'll don't have to rush off. It's early.

(*As* GINNY *and* CARRIE *move toward the two stools, lights go down on the house, the spot comes up on the stools, and the women walk into the circle of light*)

GINNY (*Helping her mother into the car*)   It is early. Early tomorrow. You've stayed out after midnight.

(CARRIE *is silent as* GINNY *takes her stool and grips the wheel. As the silence grows,* GINNY *watches her mother's face in the lights from the dash*)

CARRIE (*Breaking the silence*)   You know, your daddy was telling me just last week about how Martin Cole's wife fumes and fusses everytime he goes to town with your daddy. And I told your daddy Amanda Cole ought to know Martin needs to get away every once in a while. It does a man good to get away from his wife every once in a while.

(*The women freeze. Spot fades low, almost out, as lights come up on the area that served as bathroom for* MAURI'S *house as the spotlight over the stools goes down and out. The towel rack, plants, and wicker chair have been removed. A painting of a black man bowing his head over a loaf of bread adorns the back wall. The tub has been moved back toward the painting and transformed into a round kitchen table covered with a checkered and fringed plastic cloth. Three chairs are at the table. B.J. McCubbins, jaw dropped, impatience clear, stands staring out into the night, looking for his girls. A hibernating bear waked too soon from his sleep, he wears a pair of shorty pajamas with the top unbuttoned. His bay window hangs out over the drawstring top of the shorts. Seeing the approaching car, he draws himself up, ready to meet his wife and daughter.* GINNY *helps her mother from the car and the two women move into the kitchen as spot on car goes completely down)*

B. J. *(Demanding)* What was all that laughing I heard on the phone? You must have got ahold of some of that Al-key-hall, carrying on like that. *(He says the word so that each hated syllable stands out in naked relief)*

CARRIE *(Pulling his pajama bottoms up over his bay window so that his navel no longer yawns its disapproval)* You know better than that. We were just having fun, that's all. Aren't you sorry you didn't go?

B. J. *(Sneering)* Was Wesley there?

GINNY Yes. And Aunt Ethel and Ryan and Mauri.

B. J. *(Vindicated by her answer)* Then I'm glad I stayed home. *(He lowers himself into a chair, wide awake now, and ready)* Just like Wesley to put up with a hen party.

(Without so much as a glance over her shoulder, CARRIE *slips out of the room, savoring whatever she has left of the evening)*

B. J. It'd suit Wesley Haley just fine to sit around wasting time with a bunch of women.

(He pats the chair beside him, and GINNY *hesitates only a second before falling into place)*

B. J. *(Fully aware of his power)* You know, Ginny, I always did say there's two kinds of people in this world.

GINNY *(Resigned but pleased by her mother's escape)* I know, Daddy, I know.

For Lease or Sale

ELIZABETH SPENCER

Dedicated to David Hammond

CHARACTERS

EDWARD GLENN   a lawyer
PATSY   a girl of eighteen, his niece
MRS. GLENN   Edward's mother
LOLLIE PEEBLES   a friend of Mrs. Glenn's
CLAIRE YOUNGBLOOD   a visitor in town
PAUL WATERS   a friend of Patsy's
ALINE GLENN   Edward's ex-wife

SETTING

Large run-down old house on the outskirts of a small Mississippi town.

ACT 1

Scene 1

(Just after lunch on an early June day. The Glenn house, hall-living room where sitting area is centered around two sofas, one small, chairs, an ancient hand-winding victrola, an oil portrait of a gentleman of considerable worth and dignity, a cluttered desk, all backed by double doors with fanlights above and on either side. Glimpse of a porch outside, a portion of white columns. Stairs run up along one side of set. On the far right a door opens to the dining room and kitchen beyond. Architecture suggests a classic style of white Southern house, large and sprawling but not too grand. The furniture shows that it has not been too well kept up, has been much

lived in, with lots of empty space above stairs. There is an over-growth of green shrubbery at the windows and almost an intrusion of tree branches, suggesting that nothing has been pruned in an age; but afternoon light is coming through the doors and windows.

PATSY *is discovered, back to audience, staring out the windows, while the victrola plays "Bill Bailey.")*

EDWARD *(Calling offstage)* Patsy! Patsy! Patsy? Where is that survey?

PATSY What? *(Turns off the record)* I didn't hear you.

EDWARD *(Entering from the dining room and starting to search the desk)* I said what did Mother do with those surveying papers?

PATSY I never saw them.

EDWARD *(Remarking a large black umbrella lying across the end of the desk)* What's this doing here? *(He picks up the umbrella, looking at it cautiously)*

PATSY You got it out yourself. This morning. The paper said rain.

EDWARD *(Examining the umbrella)* None so far.

PATSY *(Searching the desk)* What's this?

EDWARD *(Looking at a folder of documents)* Under the umbrella, naturally. Where else?

(Crossing to put the umbrella in a china stand along with several walking sticks, etc. EDWARD *stops, turns it around and swings it meditatively like a golf club.* PATSY, *in a blue summer frock, picks up her stationery box and sitting in a chair much too large for her, resumes writing a letter)*

EDWARD Who would have thought she'd go away like that? Who'd have thought it?

PATSY *(Looking up)* Are you still on Claire?

EDWARD What do you mean, still?

PATSY Well, you met her Tuesday and we're all the way to Friday.

EDWARD You're sounding like Mama. Where is *she*, by the way?

PATSY *(Writing industriously)* It's her big day at the church—she told you. She's looking for programs, dressing . . .

EDWARD Oh, yes, on this historic day, she gives up the gavel of the Episcopal Missionary Society of exclusive ladies to Miss Edna Mae Sproggins.

PATSY I don't think Grandmama ever had a gavel exactly. But she thinks they might be making a thank you speech or giving her something. So she's got to be ready for anything.

EDWARD It's her graduation. *(He drops the umbrella in the stand, thumps at a crokinole set placed on a table in the corner near the stairs*) I wonder why she did it?

PATSY Who? What? Claire?

EDWARD Vanished. It wasn't like her.

PATSY Claire, Claire, Claire. Did you ever really care? I never noticed if you did. What was it got you so interested?

EDWARD Now that you mention it, I don't really know. I guess she wasn't that special. She had a nice way of laughing. Maybe that was it. A way of looking interested. She had intelligent manners.

PATSY (*Putting down her pen in exasperation*) Manners are not intelligent, they're just automatic. Like kneeling in church.

EDWARD She could probably do that intelligently, too.

PATSY (*Laying aside letter and stationery box to give her whole thought to the matter*) Well, Uncle Edward, if you feel like that why don't you go right straight and find her?

EDWARD I've got no time for trifling with romance. Not with a dozen appointments to keep about this house.

PATSY (*Picking up her letter again*) Then maybe she'll come find you.

EDWARD (*Glancing around, something ironic about his regret*) Soon nobody will be able to find us.

PATSY (*Alarmed*) You mean we're leaving that soon?

EDWARD (*Reflective*) It's possible. It's probable even. On the other hand, nothing's decided. What I mean is, God alone knows.

PATSY Weren't you going to let somebody buy it for a school?

EDWARD The Baptists have backed out on that deal. Funny, I can see any other of our abundant Southern religious sects here, but not the Baptists. Do you realize that after one set of hymns has been sung here and folding chairs brought into this very room and a black upright piano thumps along, this would never be the same again. One little hymn tune on a flat-sounding piano, played by some dedicated little country girl with curled-up blonde hair, and all we knew and know will fold right up and die.

PATSY (*Following where he points*) I guess there's no use getting so mournful about it.

EDWARD But just think, child: what are we going to know once it isn't here any more? It's easy to do things, go through the motions. But here—(*Telephone rings*)—here is our knowing. That's the hard part. (*A second ring. He makes no move to answer it*)

(PATSY *puts aside her letter and starts toward the telephone*)

EDWARD (*Catching her arm*) Just leave it.

(PATSY *succeeds in shaking him off with difficulty and almost picks up the receiver when he pulls her back*)

PATSY Why?

EDWARD (*Drawing her completely away from the telephone*) I know who it is, that's why. We're not answering.

PATSY (*Breaking away*) You can't be sure.

(EDWARD, *now half-teasing her, holds her away, while the ringing continues, then stops*)

PATSY (*Vexed and angry*) You can't do that! It might be for me! It's not fair . . . you're trying to ruin everything. Grandmama . . .

EDWARD (*Still firmly holding her, but speaking more persuasively*) No, now, you're not going to tell on me to her. Listen. That damn Piggie Waters with his real estate ideas has been calling me every day right about now. Sounding the same obnoxious way he used to in high school. A born operator. In his cradle, he thought up good bargains for teething rings. It upsets Mama—she came close enough to a heart attack over the Baptists. I won't have these people calling here. They know how to get me at the office. In fact . . . (HE *releases* PATSY, *and turns to examine the telephone*) If I knew how to do more than leave this thing temporarily off the hook, I'd be glad to do it. Somebody always puts it back again. (HE *begins unscrewing the receiver*)

PATSY Oh, no, Uncle Edward! Gosh, I'll be more cut off than ever. Please don't!

(PATSY *seizes his arm and they begin tussling over the telephone in a way that is part-affection, part-bullying. The small telephone table falls,* PATSY *trips over the cord, and the whole wiring pulls loose from the wall*)

MRS. GLENN (*Calling from above stairs*) Is that somebody at the door?

EDWARD Now we've done it. (*He jiggles the telephone*)

PATSY (*Aggrieved and close to tears*) It was all your fault. Now I'm like somebody on a desert island! Marooned!

EDWARD (*Righting the table, then going to sit beside her*) Now, it'll only be for a little while. (HE *holds her closer*) Besides, what's better than an island, just with Grandmama and me? Why, you're going to love it so, when the repair man comes, you'll run him out the front door.

PATSY (*Responding against her own will*) I still think it's awful.

EDWARD (*Moving to sit across from her*)   Listen, baby, this is serious.

MRS. GLENN (*From above*)   Edward! Patsy! I thought I heard the telephone.

EDWARD (*Calling*)   Nobody, Mother. (*To* PATSY)   If she asks who called, just say it was somebody wanting to buy the victrola. Something like that.

PATSY   Who'd want the victrola? It's five hundred years old.

EDWARD   Collector's item, silly goose.

PATSY (*Settling back in something like resignation*)   Worse luck for you. I can't see how Claire's going to call you.

EDWARD   She must have got tired of me anyway. Could that be possible?

(MRS. GLENN, *above, has begun to descend the stairs*)

PATSY   She didn't act like it.

EDWARD   That could have been her good manners.

PATSY   I guess you could still talk to her. Even if she's gone you could write.

EDWARD (*Amused*)   What would I say?

PATSY (*Clowning*)   I love you, I adore you, I can't endure this life without you!

EDWARD   One way to run her off permanently, with crap like that.

PATSY (*Noticing* MRS. GLENN'S *approach*)   Shhh!

EDWARD (*Springing to his feet as* MRS. GLENN *reaches the bottom of the stair*)   I've got your chair, haven't I?

MRS. GLENN   It's all right, Edward. I don't want to sew.

EDWARD   All dressed up for your big event.

MRS. GLENN   I thought you'd be gone to the office by now.

EDWARD   I'm leaving shortly. Where's your meeting?

MRS. GLENN   At the church. I've told you six times. You ought to listen.

EDWARD   What's the program this time? The poor Ugandans, benighted Brazil? The happy natives in Fiji-land?

MRS. GLENN   You wouldn't remember if I told you. I can't always remember myself. We try to keep track of the work.

EDWARD   Track away, Mother. Into darkest Africa.

MRS. GLENN   It's me they're honoring today. I hope my dress is all right.

PATSY   You look real pretty, Grandmama.

MRS. GLENN   And since it's so beneath you, Edward, you won't even have to drive me. Lollie Peebles is coming for me.

EDWARD   All dressed for the safari, too, I presume.

MRS. GLENN   Your elders may be your betters. I came down to ask what all this was I overheard about the victrola.

EDWARD   Just that I was thinking of selling it.

MRS. GLENN   Ridiculous! You can't sell the victrola, Edward. It's always been here. In the house.

EDWARD   But Mother, you call me all the way home from Mexico to help sell the house, and you say I can't sell the victrola. What do you want? To leave it in the house?

MRS. GLENN   I haven't quite thought it out. I just know what a comfort the victrola was to me when you were in the war.

EDWARD   What sort of comfort?

MRS. GLENN   Well, you were missing for a while, don't forget that. When I played it, I didn't worry quite so much. I can't say why. You remember, Patsy.

PATSY   I wasn't here then.

(*In the near distance, distinctly heard, a bulldozer starts up, soon followed by an earth-mover, then a full crescendo of other equipment. It is the familiar music of construction which garishly fills the scene. Silence among the three in the living-room. As the noise subsides a little, they can hear each other speak once more*)

EDWARD   They're tuning up a little late. (*The noise increases*)   Now we get the whole orchestra.

PATSY   I thought they'd gone on strike.

MRS. GLENN   I imagined they'd finished and gone home where they ought to be.

EDWARD   What? Finished a whole school building? They've got a few days to go, just for excavating. If we could afford to put in air conditioning, like civilized people, we could shut them out.

MRS. GLENN   *I* never thought air conditioning was especially civilized. It always gives me a cold. Much better to sleep with the windows open, upstairs, and the breeze so sweet.

EDWARD   But suppose you're not sleeping alone? Suppose the breeze isn't the sweetest thing around?

(PATSY, *who is reading a magazine, looks up and giggles*)

MRS. GLENN   Now, Edward . . .

EDWARD   Don't tell me you don't remember. Hot thoughts on a hot night, why you—

MRS. GLENN   Edward, stop it.

PATSY   Oh, I can leave. Just let me finish this paragraph.

EDWARD   Why bring her up so proper?

MRS. GLENN   I want her to be a lady, after all. A lady is—

EDWARD   A lady is just what?

MRS. GLENN   Oh . . . something just not common.

PATSY   But I don't want to be a lady or common either.

EDWARD   So what's your ambition, ma'am?

PATSY   Haven't I told you? I want to be an old maid. Then I won't
have to worry about either one.

EDWARD   Christ!

MRS. GLENN   Edward!

   (*Silence*)

EDWARD   At least we've still got a place to sit in, while we shock
each other. Maybe not for much longer.

MRS. GLENN   Didn't I write you that, or something like it, down
in Mexico? Didn't I tell you that?

EDWARD   Didn't I come home from Mexico, take up my seat at a
dusty desk, convince myself I had to take things over? Didn't I put
my mind to it? My shoulder to the wheel?

   (*As the noise swells temporarily,* EDWARD *goes to the door and
   looks out*)

God. Hundreds of new houses springing up all around us. You'd
think I'd be dying to meet the neighbors. I don't care who or what
lives in any of them. Something sure is wrong with Edward Glenn:
he just doesn't care.

MRS. GLENN   (*As the noise ebbs a little*)   I don't believe it's going
to happen, that we have to move. I lay in bed last night and thought
about it. Carefully, calmly, while you were up at the Townshends getting drunk . . . Oh, I've always known exactly where you were.

EDWARD   Nothing is the matter with the Townshends.

MRS. GLENN   Nothing at all, except nobody has ever seen them
sober.

EDWARD   Okay, so they drink.

MRS. GLENN   So I lay in bed and thought, All this nonsense, selling
this house, moving away. It isn't going to happen. We will always be
here. I'll be coming downstairs and hearing you children shush for
fear of my hearing something I shouldn't, as though nobody ever gave
birth to you at all, least of all me.

PATSY   You didn't give birth to me.

MRS. GLENN   To your mother, then. Same thing. And I'll always be
lying upstairs taking a nap in my slip on the first really hot day in
May and hear the side door slam and know it's the last day of school

and you—one of my children—is home with the report card. I know it's always going on.

PATSY   I'd just as soon it wasn't school you thought of. And report cards. That's for kids. I'm growing up.

MRS. GLENN   What's happened in a place goes on happening forever.

EDWARD (*As the construction noises modulate, swell and fade again*) Until they build a superhighway right through the living room. Then there might be a bit of difficulty when you come here to reminisce.

MRS. GLENN   It's true I might lose all my heartache if we moved. As well as my joy. I wouldn't think of your father in such a present way, perhaps. Do you know I often talk to him? Oh, just in my thoughts. Don't laugh.

PATSY   Honestly?

EDWARD (*Mocking to conceal his real interest*) Spiritualism . . . it's time we got you out of here.

MRS. GLENN   It is not like that. Don't be silly—both of you. I don't know anything about spirits. There's nothing scary about it. But especially since Nellie's too sick to cook any more, then poor old Sherman's died, and all we've got left is that cleaning girl twice a week . . . well, he *is* around more often.

EDWARD (*Mystified*) He didn't care for the servants?

MRS. GLENN   No, I mean he enjoys the space. To move around, you might say. To think things over. Oh, it's not that I ever see him. Just know he's here. I myself believe the experience is quite ordinary, people do not want to discuss it.

EDWARD   Do you argue? Do you fight?

MRS. GLENN   What's that got to do with you?

EDWARD   Well said.

PATSY   You think it wouldn't happen anywhere else?

MRS. GLENN (*Sighing impatiently*) Oh, it might, it might. But not so strongly perhaps. Just as if I asked myself, Now where did I leave my handkerchief? And then think, Well, I think it's upstairs. It's as if he said it.

EDWARD (*With interest*) And you say "Where?" and he says "on the bureau," and you say, "Yes, but in which room?" and he says . . .

MRS. GLENN   Something like that.

PATSY   I won't sleep a wink! I might see Granddaddy!

EDWARD   Go on, Mama.

PATSY   Tell some more.

MRS. GLENN (*Having gathered their attention to her in an archetypal way, suddenly shuts them off*) I don't think it's any of your business.

PATSY   So you're going to stop?

EDWARD   She's right. No, no, Patsy, she is right. We'd better behave.
Especially you.

PATSY   But I—

EDWARD   Stop this minute. Behave yourself.

MRS. GLENN   Don't you have to be uptown?

EDWARD   In a minute.

MRS. GLENN (*To* PATSY)   It's all right, honey. (*To* EDWARD)   She
doesn't like being talked to like that. You bully her.

EDWARD   She's got to learn.

MRS. GLENN   She's sensitive. Men are like that, honey. Look, she's
going to cry.

EDWARD   Well, don't notice her. Patsy, pay attention. Crying is *not*
sexually attractive. Make a note of it.

PATSY (*Crying harder*)   You're just the meanest thing!

MRS. GLENN   Poor little girl. Sister Annie was always sensitive like
that. I said to Papa once, how sensitive she was and he said, "I know,"
he said—he was saddling his horse—"I know," he said, "you might
as well shoot her."

(EDWARD *bursts out laughing*)

PATSY   Oh, you're awful, just awful! Both of you! And I'm an orphan,
too, on top of everything else! (*She throws down her magazine*)   Let's
sell the house today! (*She runs out of the room, crying*)   I hate you!
All I said was, Tell some more!

MRS. GLENN   She's right, Edward.

EDWARD   I know she's right, but she has to grow up. You have to
hurt them a little. (*He yawns*)

MRS. GLENN   She gets hurt because she worships you. She ought
to be out more, not cooped up here. The telephone, for instance. All
the way upstairs I thought I heard you arguing about it. Did you say
she couldn't use it?

EDWARD   Well, truth to tell, nobody can use it at the present moment.
There was a little accident with the cord.

MRS. GLENN   That does make a difference to her.

EDWARD   I'm going straight and report it. (*He picks up his hat and
is about to put on his coat*)

MRS. GLENN   Just spare me a minute, now. Did I tell you? That
girl was here.

EDWARD (*Dropping his coat*)   What girl? Where?

MRS. GLENN   Oh, she's not here now. She came last night. Running
over the lawn. Somebody stopped a car at the gate and she ran in.
She looked real pretty, I thought. It's funny, I hadn't thought that child

was pretty before. But out in the fresh air that way . . . and such a grand moon. Really, you know, that moon . . . Well, last night, just over the big old pecan tree, right through the wisteria vine. I never saw anything I admired so much . . . The dew so heavy she was carrying her shoes.

EDWARD   My God, she's killing me! Was it Claire you saw?

MRS. GLENN   The Youngblood girl. What's her name?

EDWARD   Claire. Of course.

MRS. GLENN   That's right. Claire. She came to say goodbye.

EDWARD   That's all? Just goodbye? Not even Write me . . . No promise to come back . . . Just Goodbye? Just like that?

MRS. GLENN   Edward, you do sound like the voice of doom. I think you just like to sound that way. What do you mean, Goodbye? You think she died? She's right over in Montgomery, Alabama. You could get in the car tomorrow morning and be over there by five o'clock even if you stopped to eat dinner.

EDWARD   You don't understand anything. Fools rush in. Having been a fool once too often, I've had it.

MRS. GLENN   Back to Aline. I know your feelings, but this girl did seem quite a different sort.

EDWARD   Do you have to go comparing any new woman I meet to Aline?

MRS. GLENN   *I* never forget Aline, no matter what you feel about her. Nor do you, I bet anything. It's just that you won't talk about it because of what happened to your children . . .

EDWARD (*Sharply*)   *My* children? They never got here.

MRS. GLENN   They were on the way. With the best care in the world, no one could have prevented those miscarriages. Nobody was to blame.

EDWARD (*Uncomfortably*)   So let's blame it on God . . . and forget it.

MRS. GLENN   But you're still angry, aren't you? It's what keeps you from looking at her letter . . . now where was it? (*She searches in a drawer, pulls a letter out from among others*)   I do think you ought to read it. It's been days ago she wrote it. She's concerned about the house.

EDWARD (*With considerable irony*)   How nice. (*He starts to reach for the letter, but changes his mind*)   Who wants to hear what his ex-wife has to say? Christ, he's heard it all already. Come on, now, Mama, what else did Claire say?

MRS. GLENN   Oh, Claire. All she said was Goodbye. I told you. I said she could see you if you were here, but you were not at home. You were up town, I said. She said you'd been so nice to her, and all.

EDWARD   " . . . and all . . . and all . . ."

MRS. GLENN   It makes me mad to be mocked. I'm not going to say another word.

EDWARD   Now, Mama. It's Patsy sounds like that. She takes after her father. Mother, I wouldn't for anything . . . You know I'm not sarcastic. You've always said, "Edward may be utterly worthless, but he's not sarcastic."

MRS. GLENN (*Laughing*)   Nobody ever thought you were worthless. All I said was, Edward is uptown at the drugstore.

EDWARD   The drugstore! Well, I guess it is something to say.

MRS. GLENN   You would prefer me to describe the Townshends?

EDWARD   Not really.

MRS. GLENN   She had to leave, she said, because her father was going to Florida and nobody was at home with her mother.

EDWARD   Hmmm . . . with that kind of talk she might even be rich.

MRS. GLENN (*Laughing but impatient*)   You just sit here and speculate, Edward. Why don't you go and find out? Ever since Aline there's been nothing but one of these girls after another. Don't tell me there wasn't somebody in Mexico . . . Edward, what were you doing in Mexico? I often ask myself, but no answer comes.

EDWARD   Nothing so much as thinking. It can take time, you know, if you do it right. Could be I never really tried it before.

MRS. GLENN   But you have to think *about* something, don't you? That's the part you never get to.

EDWARD   Maybe I get to it but I just don't talk about it.

MRS. GLENN   Exactly what I mean. Bottled up inside. It must be what's changed you so.

EDWARD (*Surprised*)   Changed me?

MRS. GLENN   Yes. Made you hard. Ugly to people. Even poor little Patsy's getting tired of it.

EDWARD   Could be you've just sat here in my absence and told yourself what a nice, polite, charming son you had.

MRS. GLENN   I know very well what you were like once. You simply are not the same.

EDWARD (*Negligent*)   O.K., so people change . . . maybe I have too.

MRS. GLENN   But talking about it? You just won't. Aline, for instance. Try as I might, you never would open up about her, not to me anyway.

EDWARD   Why blame anybody? Why make a bad thing worse?

MRS. GLENN (*Sighing*)   Well, the Glenns are loyal. They do say that.

EDWARD (*Prowling about restlessly*)   Who isn't loyal to their own mistakes? Ever think about it?

MRS. GLENN   Now you're twisting things again, saying that.

E D W A R D (*Back turned to her, shooting idly with crokinole*) There were things about Aline and me you never understood. I didn't want to have you understand, I guess. If she showed a different face to you, why, remember that. But with me—

M R S . G L E N N All those quarrels. Sometimes I thought the upstairs floor was falling in on me. What were they about? I never even wanted to hear.

E D W A R D High principles about eavesdropping certainly can leave people in the dark.

M R S . G L E N N What would I have heard?

E D W A R D You might not have approved of the language. That's a safe guess.

M R S . G L E N N Language about what?

E D W A R D Now, Mother, you weren't that innocent. Trying to run my business for me, for instance.

M R S . G L E N N That could be annoying.

E D W A R D (*Interrupting*) Money, for instance.

M R S . G L E N N It is true you've never cared very much for money, one way or the other. Maybe we just never think much about it. It's not our way to, is what your father used to say.

E D W A R D (*Ironic*) Well, it *was* her "way" to. And don't think she didn't have ways of getting what wasn't hers.

M R S . G L E N N (*Astonished*) You don't mean . . . ?

E D W A R D See what happens? You want to know, but then the shocks roll in. Earth shaking, volcanoes growling. Time to run indoors. No, she never exactly stole anything.

M R S . G L E N N You looked so fine together. What a good-looking pair! She was so crazy about you. I know you could have stopped whatever you didn't like.

E D W A R D Sure I could stop it. One time, a dozen times, fifty times. What next? You want to know what next? I'll tell you. Next came the fifty-first time.

M R S . G L E N N You could have asked me to help you.

E D W A R D (*Lightly, obviously tired of the subject*) The only way to stop Aline was to pick up a two-by-four and wham her over the head. You think you could have managed that?

M R S . G L E N N (*Softly*) It was my impression that you loved her.

E D W A R D Your impression, as usual, was correct. Now really, poking around in the past never dug up anything valuable. It's one old Southern custom too many. I've got to get along . . .

M R S . G L E N N You went away for that divorce decree, then you'd settled in fairly well except for that Crawford girl you kept running around with. What happened to her?

EDWARD (*Laughing*) Bunny Crawford! I'd almost forgotten. I think she must be floating around the Bahamas on somebody's yacht. Either that or she ran off with a motel owner from Houston. In other words, I don't know.

MRS. GLENN You're saying you don't care, I guess.

EDWARD I guess I did sound that way. No, Bunny wasn't in Mexico. Not that I know of. She may have checked in and out of Acapulco at some point, one place I never got to.

MRS. GLENN You must have known somebody there. Leaving suddenly the way you did, not a single word to anybody. Just a telephone call. Gone to Mexico!

EDWARD It is too much. See what I escaped? No wayward son to worry the life out of me. (*He prepares to leave*) I promise you, Mother. Our very next talk will be all about Mexico. The guided tour. But if it's girls you think you'll hear about—

(*The doorbell rings.* EDWARD, *startled, is obviously thinking it might be* CLAIRE. *He hurries to open it, but* LOLLIE PEEBLES *enters, carrying an enormous parcel*)

MRS. GLENN Lollie? What on earth? Why, you're way too early. We said two-thirty, I'm sure.

LOLLIE Now, Jeannie, you don't know what I'm here for! Now just you wait! (*She sets down a parcel, a large picture, wrapped in brown paper*) How are you, Edward. You both ought to know. Your telephone's out of order. Either that or somebody has monkeyed with the line for other reasons, I can't imagine what.

EDWARD Just that I like to talk business at the office, where I'm headed now, if you'll forgive me, Miss Lollie.

LOLLIE (*Catching his arm*) One minute more. You've got to have just one peek. We've all just been so proud. (*She sweeps the paper off in one grand gesture, revealing a garish painting of the Glenn house*)

EDWARD Oh, my God!

MRS. GLENN Why, Lollie! I'm overcome!

EDWARD As well you may be. Permanently.

LOLLIE (*Taking his comment for approval*) I just knew you'd be thrilled. And the biggest surprise of all—we all had a hand in painting it!

(PATSY *enters, coming in from the kitchen eating an apple*)

PATSY   What on earth is that?

EDWARD   Anyone might wonder. Now you'll have to excuse me, ladies. Business calls. Never mind, Patsy, Miss Lollie will be glad to explain everything. (*Hastens to leave*)

PATSY   Oh. It's the house.

LOLLIE   As I was saying, we all did our little bit . . . Look, here's a list of our signatures. The tree and drive by Mabel Gerner, the front porch by Esther Mae Reeves, pillars and roof by Georgia Whittaker, and the summer house by your old friend L. Peebles. In other words, ME!

MRS. GLENN   All signed and everything. How splendid!

LOLLIE   The minute we heard you were selling the house, we decided on doing it. This way you can take it with you, even though you're leaving it behind.

MRS. GLENN   Just imagine. I've been thinking that was impossible. Why, Lollie, you are just a genius—all of you. You're just plain geniuses.

PATSY   But nothing's that colour, is it?

MRS. GLENN   Patsy!

PATSY   I guess I hadn't noticed.

MRS. GLENN   You know, Lollie. You mustn't tell anybody, but I think my favorite part is the summer house.

LOLLIE   You aren't just saying that?

MRS. GLENN   Not a bit. I'm going to hang it here until we finally leave. (*With difficulty, she moves the painting to lean against the wall to the left of the double doors*)

LOLLIE   I think we can just go on now. We ought to be a little early anyway. (*She begins to shepherd* MRS. GLENN *toward the door*)

MRS. GLENN   Just a minute. I got so excited I forgot my hat. And the program notes. I haven't even looked.

LOLLIE   Then I'll just go on and wait for you in the car.

MRS. GLENN   I won't be a minute.

LOLLIE (*About to exit, but calling back*)   Better bring your umbrella, I just barely see the tip of a real ugly cloud. (*Exits*)

PATSY   What did you do that for, Grandmama?

MRS. GLENN   Do what, darlin?

PATSY   You know it's awful. You know what Uncle Edward is going to say, but you kept on ooh-ing and aah-ing.

MRS. GLENN (*Sighs*)   How could I hurt their feelings? You and Edward, you just have to learn—

PATSY (*Sulky*) Learn what?

MRS. GLENN How never to say exactly what you mean. It's part of having to be a lady.

PATSY So then if the person you're talking to is a lady too, nobody ever gets to say what they mean. Is that it?

MRS. GLENN You're getting too much like Edward. There is simply no need to be so smart.

PATSY In addition to everything else, I bet you hang it up.

MRS. GLENN Didn't you hear me promise?

PATSY (*Giggling good naturedly*) I thought maybe you didn't mean what you said that time either.

MRS. GLENN How you children do love to mix me up. *I* know what I mean, so there. I was telling Edward, without the telephone nobody can call you. (*She has begun to rummage in a closet below the stairs which shows every sign of being full of odds and ends*) No boys or anything, I mean. Now where have I put those papers from the program? And what did I do with my pills? (*She extracts, among other things, a long white feather boa, and stands for a moment, holding it out*) Will you look at that? Aline wore it, for that costume ball. How grand she did look! She won a prize if I'm not mistaken. (*She drops it over the arm of a chair and turning begins to mount the stairs slowly, while* PATSY *below, is busy closing up windows and curtains against the steadily increasing noise*) I'll just have to look upstairs. He's not fair to that child, not at all. Imagine a young girl without a telephone, in this day and age . . .

(*Horn sounds from the drive*)

MRS. GLENN In a minute, Lollie! (*Exits above*)

(PATSY *is industriously moving toward the kitchen when the doorbell rings, followed, at an interval, by a light knocking. She does not hear and exits toward the kitchen. The front door opens slowly and* CLAIRE YOUNGBLOOD *walks into the still scene*)

CLAIRE I was sure he was here. I saw his car. Why can't I ever find him? (*She looks around her as though probing a mystery. She is curious about the house, examines a large framed photograph from the table, hesitates before various antiquated articles of furniture*) Now, it seems, there's nobody. (*She sinks down in a deep armchair with an air of bewilderment*)

(PATSY *enters from the kitchen. The machines hum loudly*)

PATSY (*To herself*) It doesn't help to close things up. It's one more silly idea.

MRS. GLENN (*Coming downstairs with a sheaf of papers in one hand, her hat in the other*)   What's a silly idea?

PATSY   Oh, Grandmama, I didn't see you. It doesn't work to try to keep the noise out. (*She sees* CLAIRE)   Oh! I didn't see you either. (*She speeds off toward another part of the house, opening windows*)

MRS. GLENN (*Who has spotted* CLAIRE *immediately*)   You can't read in that corner. Turn on the light.

CLAIRE (*Rising politely*)   I wasn't reading. I just came back to—I think I'm making a nuisance of myself, always coming back.

MRS. GLENN   Child, I couldn't think for a minute who you were. I thought you might be one of mine, but then—how funny!—I couldn't think of your name, which with my own never happens, unlike some of my friends, no older than I am. No, I'm very good at the names of my own children. (*She sits down comfortably, near to* CLAIRE) But when it comes to Edward's various girl friends, I do sometimes get a little confused. Not recently! No, things have been rather quiet recently. Edward was in Mexico, you know. I don't know if he told you.

CLAIRE   Yes, I did know that. Where I'm visiting, they begged me to stay on for a day or so, but now that's about up, too. Edward— you see, Edward thinks I've gone, but when I tried to call—

MRS. GLENN   I know, he disconnects the phone. (*She smiles*) Because of business.

CLAIRE (*Mystified*)   Business?

(MRS. GLENN *nods, smiling*)

CLAIRE   At any rate, I did want to say goodbye, and maybe it might be better in person. It's been such a lovely time. It might never happen again, not just this way, and I—

MRS. GLENN (*After a silence during which she regards* CLAIRE, *meditatively*)   Yes, Edward is just about perfect when it comes to making up a lovely time.

CLAIRE   By "making up," you mean—?

MRS. GLENN   Oh, he really did like you, you know. Has mentioned you so much . . . well, I actually got tired of hearing about you. I've seen him that way before, but not for a while. Aline—the girl he divorced, or she divorced him—I'm not quite clear on it. Aline put a crimp in Edward for a time. He may be coming out of it. Who knows? My dear, you might get to be friends with me. They usually do. You should see my Christmas card list, the letters I get when they finally get married. "If only Edward and I," and so on. "What a wonderful mother-in-law," and so on. Such pretty girls, too. No more than you. But how I wish I had told them, one and all, from the very start: "Nobody knows about Edward . . . nobody knows." Maybe you can find out. When you do, tell me? Well, he should be here soon. I'm counting on him at present, more than on anyone else. You've heard of our problem?

CLAIRE   Just that you may be moving. Is that such a problem?

MRS. GLENN   The Glenns don't move, darlin'. Never! Have you seen the house before? The noise is terrible now, but that construction can't go on forever. We need someone who knows that, who can buy all of it, else we may have to move out and leave a sign up on the lawn. That would be awful, the house just standing here. No one to pay the up-keep. The property was redistricted, you see, and taxes went sky-high. In the old days, my husband would simply have prevented them! He would have taken the town map and just re-arranged it. So now you'll have an idea of how much I need Edward here, to attend to these things. And you—Promise me not to distract him too much.

PATSY (*Appearing from the rear*)   Can I bring her anything?

CLAIRE (*Rising to go*)   It's all right. I'll just go on now. Tell him I'll be here, for just a little while longer. (*She goes to the entrance door, turns*)   I've begun to wonder if Edward really exists.

PATSY (*As she exits off right once more*)   Sometimes I wonder that, too.

(*A car horn sounds persistently from outside*)

MRS. GLENN   Oh, my goodness, it's Lollie! I forgot all about her. (*A low rumble of thunder*)   Now it's going to rain, too. (*She takes up her umbrella—not the large black one Edward had noticed earlier —her papers and bag and settling her hat, turns to hold out her free hand to* CLAIRE'S)   Come and go often, my dear. When I mistook you for one of mine, perhaps I wasn't wrong. Edward . . . someday you'll run right into him.

PATSY (*From somewhere off stage*)   I wouldn't count on it.

CLAIRE   Just one more time to see him, that was all.

MRS. GLENN   But nothing is ever *quite* all, is it?

CLAIRE   I don't know . . .

(*The car horn sounds again, impatiently*)

MRS. GLENN   Coming, Lollie!

CLAIRE   Thank you . . . goodbye . . . (*As* MRS. GLENN *exits*)

Scene 2

(*An hour or two later. The livingroom is in semidarkness, rain is lashing at the windows. Thunder tumbles in the near distance. There is an occasional closer flash of lightning. Sound of persistent knocking. The door finally bursts open and* PAUL WATERS *comes into the room, hair plastered down with the rain, shedding water on the floor. The branches of shrubbery and trees wave at the windows. Simultaneously,* PATSY *appears from above, on the stairs, having heard the knocking.*)

PATSY   Who's there?

PAUL   It's me, Paul. Patsy? Excuse me for coming right in, but to tell the truth, I didn't see much of nothing else to do. (*He stands shaking off water, stamping his feet, etc.*)

PATSY (*Descending*)   Why, Paul Waters. Where did you come from?

PAUL (*Pointing behind*)   From out there. It got worse along the way. I had to push my bike. I started to turn around once or twice, but I kept on up the hill.

PATSY   Nobody's here but me. I got scared when it started. I hid my head under some pillows.

PAUL (*As another burst of thunder subsides*)   I'm real glad to see you, Patsy. Gosh, I wondered if you might even be in town. I haven't laid eyes on you since I graduated. I tried calling, but your phone went dead. I saw your uncle once and said I'd like to come by and he said something peculiar, like, if it was worth the risk I could try it.

PATSY   He's strange sometimes.

PAUL   Maybe he was right. It's like coming through a jungle in a hurricane to get up here. The gate sticks. I couldn't even find the sidewalk.

PATSY   But you made it.

PAUL (*Suddenly awkward, looking around him*)   Looks like I did.

PATSY (*Switching on lamps*)   Nobody's going to eat you. Come on in.

PAUL (*Approaching to the central area of the room*)   The last time I saw much of you was in that debate we had.

PATSY   We got on different sides about socialism. I forget which was which.

PAUL   You started out negative, but they switched you.

PATSY   Oh, that's right. I was really too young, just eleventh grade, but they asked me anyway. Glenda Ann Williford had to quit school.

PAUL   Everybody knew why . . .

PATSY   I knew what they said. Anyway . . . (*They both pause*) You could sit down.

PAUL (*Sitting far forward in an over-large chair*) What I came about, I heard you all might be selling this place. So I came thinking I might just say goodbye.

PATSY Are you going somewhere?

PAUL No, I'm not; you are.

PATSY When we sell the house, if we ever sell the house, I guess we'll have to go somewhere. But it's not sold yet.

PAUL I heard it almost was.

PATSY I guess they'd tell me last. Or next to last, right before Grandmama. Her heart's bad.

PAUL How do you feel about it? About leaving, I mean.

PATSY (*Sighs*) They say it's inevitable. (*She masters the long word with a grown-up air*) So I guess I have to resign myself. To fate, I guess you might say.

PAUL But maybe you'd be happy for a change.

PATSY I thought everybody liked this place.

PAUL Oh, I don't mean it's not pretty, up here on this big hill, historic, too, I guess. But Patsy, you're so cut off from everything else!

PATSY Anybody can find me that wants to. You did.

PAUL People get scared to. We were together at school all that time, and I was scared to. It's the set-up. Like you had a castle, some kind of drawbridge.

PATSY Oh, sure, I throw them in dungeons, I put poisoned mayonnaise on the sandwiches. It's just that people think . . .

PAUL What do they think?

PATSY Not what you said. I don't believe it's the house. I think it's me. They think I'm old-maidy, that I say mean things.

PAUL What gives you that idea?

PATSY Uncle Edward thinks things like that. Oh, I just love him and I think he's wonderful. I really do. But from what he tells me—well, I'm all the time getting my feelings hurt. I get worried.

PAUL About what?

PATSY Thinking I'm the way he says I am, somebody nobody could care about.

PAUL Well, you're not. Take it from me, Patsy. You might be just a little—well—prim.

PATSY Thanks. (*Silence*)

PAUL It might be just getting out would change all that kind of way you think. The lady now that used to be married to your uncle. You remember.

PATSY You mean Aline? Of course, I remember. She lived here. They both did.

PAUL Miss Aline, that's right. She changed a lot, once she got away.

PATSY How did she change?

PAUL She wears different kinds of clothes now. She looks more in line with just everybody else. I was thinking that might not be a bad thing.

PATSY I can't see why it's so good not to be special.

PAUL As long as you're not too special. I mean as long as you're somebody everybody can understand.

PATSY I never have seen Aline since she left. I just remember her from then, nothing later. (*She picks up the feather boa from the chair*) This was hers. She couldn't look better now. She was beautiful. (*She drapes the boa over her shoulders*) See what I mean?

PAUL Aw, take that off, Patsy. It doesn't suit you.

PATSY (*Puts the boa aside*) It's out of style anyway.

PAUL Gosh, it's getting darker and darker. You'd think it might be Judgment Day.

PATSY I'm not so scared since you're here with me.

PAUL (*As lightning flashes*) You needn't think I can do much about that.

PATSY Company is better than being alone. I'm going to wind up the victrola. We'll try to drown it out. Look, it's real old. I'll show you. You wind it up, like this, and put a record on.

PAUL (*Amid a heavy roll of thunder*) You better turn that up real loud.

(*The tune playing is "Dancing in the Dark."* EDWARD *enters from the front, drenched, and notices them, hears the music, stops. He closes the door with difficulty against the wind. The right of the stage is lighted differently from the left, where he stands observing as if from another room*)

EDWARD Out at the lake with that black water, clean and black at once. The radio on the pier with that song going in the night. Pines, how they stood in the dark, with Aline swimming out there alone, her hair all pinned up . . .

PATSY (*Still unconscious of* EDWARD) If we'd try to dance it might take our minds off being blown away.

PAUL (*Catching her, as they begin to sway together*) It's worth a try.

EDWARD Water black as sin, but clear and pure, spring water. I thought if I got her to take down her hair, pinned up like that . . . got her to let it loose, could I stand it? Probably not . . . Then I thought, I'd like it down anyway; there must be worse ways to die than sheer damned lust. So I dived in and she listened . . . she did it, she listened, she let it down. Her black hair, spreading out like a fan in that black pure water, swirling slow as a water moccasin . . . Jesus!

PATSY (*As thunder explodes*) Pretend we're on the Titanic!

PAUL   Going down? (*They hold closer, then kiss.* PATSY, *turning slowly, notices* EDWARD. *She pulls back from* PAUL)

PATSY   Oh, Uncle Edward. I didn't see you.

EDWARD (*Coming forward*)   I just was wondering as I fought my way home if you were safe, but I see you've found . . . protection.

(PAUL *and* PATSY *separate*)

PATSY (*Anxiously*)   It's all right, isn't it? If he's here—

EDWARD   Haven't you already decided that it is?

PAUL   I just came to say hello . . . I mean goodbye . . . well, I just came to see Patsy, sir. I'm Paul. I hope it's all right.

EDWARD   If it wasn't would you be somebody else?

PAUL   I just meant to say . . . Well, what did *you* mean? Paul Waters, I mean, is who . . .

EDWARD   Oh, and a Waters, too?

PAUL (*Laughs uneasily*)   Well, it's just who I am.

PATSY   I didn't get near so scared as I might have.

EDWARD   Obviously not.

PATSY   In fact, though it is a bad storm, I felt that I—

PAUL   I felt that I—

(*They both stop, exchange glances and laugh uneasily*)

EDWARD (*Turning to mount the stairs, having hung up his wet coat and, as an afterthought, turning Lollie's painting to face the wall*)   Any need you have of further protection, just call. (*He leans over the stair*) Patsy, can you play something different? That one takes me back to a hundred years ago, at the very least . . . to some pre-Waters age. (*Exits above; door slams*)

PAUL   What did I do?

PATSY (*Obediently cutting off the record*)   Nothing. I told you he was strange.

PAUL   Boy! You can say that again. (*He turns to* PATSY *with relief at being alone again*) Patsy, I—Well, I never enjoyed a storm so much . . .

PATSY   Me either.

(*They sit on the sofa together, holding hands*)

PATSY (*Happily*)   I wish we could go somewhere and get a coke. Listen, it's calming down. You remember that time the whole school went over to Gravelfield. We all went out for hamburgers. You know, I had this ambition. I was going to get one of those Wendy concessions out on the highway instead of starting right into college. Then I could ask you out to *my* place . . . Gosh, nothing *but* hamburgers.

PATSY   I could get you a coke and a sandwich. I was just kidding about the poison mayonnaise.

PAUL   I didn't exactly mean I was hungry. I mean, just to go with you to some place like anywhere else. Just to feel like everybody else. It's what I like best.

PATSY   You think we're different here. Well, we are. I'm living in a doomed house. We used to be the only sort of house you would even dream of wanting to come to, if you could. There was nothing to do but be glad you got invited. Now we're still different but we seem to be different on the down side, not on the top side. We just sit here and talk. We sit here and sit here. In a house about to be sold or fall down or get blown away or something. I don't really think we're ever going anywhere. So that must be how we want it.

PAUL   Well, I don't guess there's anything really wrong with it, come right down to it. There's nothing so bad about living here and being superior to the world and everybody in it.

PATSY   I don't think anybody cares whether we're superior or not. On top of that, I'm an orphan.

PAUL   I don't think that matters either. Except it's tragic.

PATSY   It's tragic, all right. Listen, I'd get you some whisky if I could find it. Uncle Edward keeps it, but he hides it. Grandmama throws it down the sink.

PAUL   I hardly touch the stuff. Daddy does. I stick to beer, but never mind. Patsy, don't misunderstand me. What I said about having a hamburger place, that's just an idea for making money. I'd start it off, then get somebody else to run it for me. I want to keep going in other ways, travelling, reading stuff. You've just got to get your money side set up. It's necessary.

PATSY   So they say. I don't guess I think enough about it.

PAUL   Have you got a lot of rooms upstairs?

PATSY   Too many.

PAUL   Come on, Patsy. How many?

PATSY   Dozens. All about the same.

PAUL   You're bound to know.

PATSY   I never counted.

PAUL   (*Laughing and moving closer to her*)   Patsy, you're really such a sweet girl. I really mean it. I don't care about how many rooms, what I came to say was what I just said—about you.

PATSY   I think you're nice to say it. Maybe it's true. I wonder about Uncle Edward though. He doesn't know how it is to have feelings, deep down, that don't show all the time. You can see that I do, though.

PAUL Of course I can.

PATSY You came to say goodbye, but I just hope you didn't mean goodbye forever. Leaving is not like dying.

PAUL Now that I'm actually here, leaving is about the last thing I want to do.

PATSY You mean you feel at home?

PAUL Where else could you play a victrola? Where else would you be glad to sit out a thunderstorm?

(The wind has sprung up again. A bolt of lightning strikes close by)

PATSY I don't know if you did sit it out yet. It's coming back, worse than ever. *(She is frightened)*

(EDWARD appears on the stairs above)

EDWARD Patsy, is Mother back? Don't tell me she's still at that church with all this going on.

(Another burst of thunder)

PATSY I didn't see her. I don't guess she's here. I forgot.

(Running footsteps outside. The door opens and CLAIRE runs in)

EDWARD *(Running downstairs to her)* Claire!

CLAIRE Edward! Oh, Edward! Thank heaven you're here. I was driving home when the cloud turned black. A tree blew across the road. All I could see was the drive to your house. I was so scared, I almost couldn't turn the car. Only to be here, only to be inside!

EDWARD Oh, Claire . . . *(Holds her)* Any wind that blows you here is magic. Let it blow. What a way to find you! *(He speaks over her head)* Patsy, it's Mother . . . we—

(MRS. GLENN and LOLLIE PEEBLES enter, dishevelled, hats knocked awry, umbrellas turned inside out, streaming with rain)

LOLLIE Alive . . . oh, at least, we're still alive. For a minute I doubted it.

MRS. GLENN We had to run out of the church. Oh, Edward, the lightning . . . It struck the steeple. Did you ever hear of such a thing? Your grandfather's window, Edward!

EDWARD What window?

MRS. GLENN The stained glass memorial window to the first Edward Glenn. It's all in pieces.

CLAIRE How terrible.

EDWARD   I think so far it's a swap worth having. (*He turns to* CLAIRE)   You're shaking like a rabbit. Hold on tight. There are worse fates than being blown away together.

PAUL   I'm Paul Waters, Mrs. Glenn. I just stopped in to see Patsy. I never expected . . . (*Thunder*)

MRS. GLENN   I'd ask you to sit down, but I doubt if you could hear me.

(PAUL *and* PATSY, EDWARD *and* CLAIRE *are clinging together as the thunder rolls*)

MRS. GLENN (*Turning to* LOLLIE)   Lollie, isn't there something wrong with the world when the church steeple gets struck by lightning?

LOLLIE   Somebody has turned our painting to the wall!

MRS. GLENN   It should not happen. Not to the church steeple. But what am I to think of it? These young people are all in love. Who's to answer me? Lollie! Concentrate!

(*Strong final flash of lightning. Amid general screams, the lights go out*)

ACT II

Scene 1

(*Next day, Saturday. Early afternoon. No sun at the window suggests a wet, overcast day following the storm of the day before. In the sitting room, a table and chair are overturned, a vase of spirea has spilled out on the floor, the furniture that was central to the room has been pulled back and rearranged.*)

(*Sound of laughter and talk from without.* PATSY *and* EDWARD *come onto the veranda before the entrance, each carrying a large sack of groceries*)

PATSY   So that's where it was exactly.

EDWARD   Found it at last, just where we read all summer on what —*Wind in the Willows*?

PATSY   No, I was older than that! *Treasure Island*! I wanted so to be a pirate!

EDWARD (*Chasing her through the door with a mock limp*) I'd be Long John Silver . . . out to get you. Raw head and bloody bones!

PATSY (*Running from him through the door*) Let's pull the weeds up. We can do it again. It's always shady there. And no mosquitoes.

EDWARD Just so I don't have to have another car wreck, break three ribs and fracture my wrist, all so as to convalesce and read to you —(*He notices the room for the first time and stops short*) What in hell is all this?

PATSY (*Also astonished*) I—I don't know. (*She takes the grocery sack from* EDWARD) Just let me put these down.

MRS. GLENN (*Calling from above*) Edward! Patsy! Are you home?

EDWARD We're here, but why are you? Your lunch can't be over yet. And what—?

MRS. GLENN (*Appearing on the stairway, obviously upset*) I decided not to go to any lunch. I simply did not feel well enough. Thank heaven that Providence prevented me! Edward, I am simply furious. Some awful man was here!

EDWARD What man?

MRS. GLENN How should I know what man? I'm sure he had no introduction to me, and furthermore no right whatsoever to be here at all. His card's there on the table. Oh, it was you who let him come. And not a word to me. None!

EDWARD (*Finding the card*) Oh, my God, Abe Jenkins. He was early.

MRS. GLENN He said he was an undertaker, working with old Mr. Slocum. Expanding . . . improving . . . I don't know what all. Down here without my knowledge. Daring to rearrange the furniture. Measuring the floor to his heart's content! I said to him: But no one here has died. What do you think you are about? So then he told me.

EDWARD Told you what?

MRS. GLENN Why that you were thinking of parting with this house to an undertaker! (*She has by now descended the stairs and is confronting* EDWARD) Thank heaven I decided against that lunch. By the time I got back, you might even have done it!

EDWARD (*Angry*) Mother, you cannot keep breaking up these business appointments. One after another—look what you did to the Baptists. Told them off for having a church that wasn't even a church, according to you.

MRS. GLENN They'd no idea about this place.

EDWARD So, out with them. Then, you wouldn't have old people around, smelling up the house . . . or children hanging from the chandeliers: no kindergarten. If you don't stop all this objecting, there's no way I can move.

(PATSY *enters from the kitchen*)

EDWARD (*To* PATSY)   Get her medicine. She's lost it again.

MRS. GLENN (*Still upset, but speaking more weakly*)   He was not even a gentleman. Not in the least. He dared to tell me he had very little time and would I move aside so he could size up the room. Do you mean to say, I asked him, I'm to get out of the way while you find a place for the coffin? I pushed over that table on him.

EDWARD   What's one broken table more or less?

PATSY (*Searching*)   It isn't anywhere.

MRS. GLENN   I left it in the dining room, I think. On the sideboard.

EDWARD (*Exasperated*)   You're just flying apart over nothing. Lie down. Rest.

MRS. GLENN (*Relenting*)   Oh, I know I did the wrong thing. But a funeral home? I couldn't bear it. I'd burn it first . . . to the ground.

PATSY (*From off-stage*)   If you won't let anybody have it, what will we ever do?

EDWARD   Sit here for the next century, considering various alternatives.

PATSY (*Poking her head through the door*)   Like what?

EDWARD (*Half to himself*)   Like whether to get drunk or go fishing. The only ones open to me at the moment.

(MRS. GLENN *lies on the couch.* EDWARD *goes to her*)

EDWARD   He's gone, Mother. Call it a bad dream. Edward's idea of fun. Wicked Edward. Drink something cold. Take your nap.

MRS. GLENN   We can simply walk out of this house and abandon it before we sink so low.

EDWARD   I never knew a funeral home was what you'd call low. Some of the finest houses wind up that way. If you try sticking it out here you know how you'll wind up, don't you? In what's known as "genteel poverty." Won't that be fun?

MRS. GLENN   Why not convert it into the Silver Slipper night club? Why not turn it into a house full of call girls? I intend to pray about it.

EDWARD   Mother, you know you don't believe in God.

MRS. GLENN   I don't believe in you for that matter. I believe, I believe! Furthermore, I don't mind being poor. The poor are often interesting. They haven't bored themselves to death making money.

EDWARD   We've been poor and interesting ever since I can remember. Would you really prefer this to turn into a new subdivision? There's room for twenty little houses here. Would you really like that?

MRS. GLENN   It does have a nice clean sound, a new subdivision. I think of rows of new bathroom fixtures, all different colours, like children's candy.

EDWARD   It may happen yet. God forbid, but it may. That boy of Patsy's—what's his name? Paul. I had some idea about him.

MRS. GLENN   What sort of idea?

EDWARD   Oh, that he might be in the subdivision business. Him or his family.

MRS. GLENN   He didn't say that.

EDWARD   A rabbit over my grave. That's all.

MRS. GLENN   And what did you do with yours? You know . . . that pretty child . . . Claire? She was here off and on. (*She sits up with an air of feeling better*)   I thought she ought to stay.

EDWARD   (*Negligent*)   She had to see something about her car. A tree fell on it. Something got smashed.

MRS. GLENN   I declare. Pretty soon you're going to go through the whole thing from love at first sight to infatuation, to disillusionment, quarrelling, parting—all in one afternoon. I do think you've rather perfected it. I even imagine I know why.

EDWARD   Here come the words of wisdom.

MRS. GLENN   Deny it if you like. I think their one purpose in your life is to keep your mind off Aline.

EDWARD   What proof have you got I even think about Aline?

MRS. GLENN   I just know you do, that's all. You wouldn't read her letter. That's proof.

EDWARD   Except I can't see what it proves.

MRS. GLENN   And another thing. The only thing you knew about that girl—what's her name? Claire?—the only thing you knew I told you.

EDWARD   I got news for you. That wasn't the only thing.

MRS. GLENN   "Running over the grass," I said. "Out in the moonlight . . ." I started you dwelling on her.

EDWARD   I was dwelling before that. Now she's borrowed my car till hers is ready.

MRS. GLENN   Then she'll be obliged to come back.

EDWARD   If she doesn't steal it.

MRS. GLENN   Tell Patsy never mind. I think the medicine was on that little table I overturned.

EDWARD   In that case . . . (*He searches on the floor, retrieves a small vial of pills*)   I think this must be it.

MRS. GLENN   You're sure that's what it is?

EDWARD   What else could it be? (*He turns a pill out into her palm*)

MRS. GLENN (*Taking medicine*)   Why, you simply never know what anything is. I'm told these pills are a sort of nitroglycerin, for instance.

EDWARD   So?

MRS. GLENN   It makes me think of exploding. First the storm, now the undertaker.

PATSY (*Entering from the right*)   Grandmama, don't you dare explode.

EDWARD   She already has. Patsy means, once a day is your limit.

MRS. GLENN   Do you remember your Uncle Thomas? He ran the family farm for us for years on top of years. One day he came in too hot, drank down a whole jar of ice water and got so sick we thought he'd die.

EDWARD   What was it? White lightning?

PATSY (*Venturing*)   Gin, maybe?

MRS. GLENN   No, it was ice water.

(*Silence*)

MRS. GLENN   I don't know what made him sick.

EDWARD   Something else to beware of—ice water.

PATSY   At least he didn't explode.

MRS. GLENN   Poor Thomas, he had other things go wrong. He courted Lila Saunders for years. He went through torments about her. Never came to anything.

PATSY   Not old Miss Saunders that teaches tenth grade?

EDWARD   Lord, is she still alive? Odd little glasses with wire rims?

MRS. GLENN   The same. He would come in from the country to see her, every Saturday night.

PATSY   Why wouldn't she marry him?

MRS. GLENN   She said she had some idea he was not the right religion. It was just an idea she had. Thomas didn't have enough religion of any kind that I know of. His mother may have baptized him Catholic but that was about as far as it went.

EDWARD   So they just went on and on, having dates? I never heard all of that.

MRS. GLENN   I think they enjoyed pining. Like Edward.

PATSY   She was born to be an old maid. Like me.

EDWARD (*Affectionately*)   Now, Patsy, honey, you've got to quit that kind of talk. I've teased you into thinking that way. What can I do with a pretty girl, especially one that's kin? You've got boys fighting through tornadoes, swimming through torrents. Just to find you.

PATSY (*Pleased*)   Now you're teasing the other way.

EDWARD   Hoping you'll like it better. Am I wrong?

PATSY   Well . . . maybe not.

MRS. GLENN   Just seeing you two children happy together . . . why it's better than any medicine. Maybe Thomas should never have left, he could have just gone on and on, courting Lila Saunders. When is being happy not being happy enough? I've always wondered. (*She starts to rise*) I won't be happy, for instance, until we can put all this back the way it's always been.

EDWARD   Sit down, Mother. You know we're not about to let you start lifting furniture. (PATSY *comes to help him, picking up small objects and straightening the rug where some flowers have overturned*) Patsy, what did you do with that boy?

PATSY   You mean Paul?

EDWARD   You've got so many? Who else? Yes, Paul.

PATSY   He's coming today. Pretty soon now. I promised to let him walk all around, see the garden, see the old arbor, and the summer house . . .

EDWARD   Patsy, watch your step.

PATSY   For snakes, you mean? Out in the garden?

EDWARD   In the garden, or wherever.

PATSY (*Giggling*)   You think he's so wicked?

EDWARD   What's his last name?

PATSY   Waters. Why?

EDWARD   Then his father has to be that fat-assed business type.

MRS. GLENN   Oh, Edward, there are any number of Waters. The county's full of them.

PATSY   He's not in business. It's me he likes.

EDWARD (*Truculent*)   I wouldn't trust it.

PATSY (*Giggling more*)   I can't wait to see him to tell about Miss Lila Saunders' boy friend. Furthermore, my uncle.

MRS. GLENN   Great uncle.

EDWARD   What happened to him, poor old Uncle Thomas? He didn't die of ice water, he didn't die of love.

MRS. GLENN   He died out West. I don't know what of. Your father went out to the funeral.

EDWARD   So he left us long before. I barely remember him.

MRS. GLENN   Well, he got tired. From lack of appreciation, I suppose. He married somebody very late on.

EDWARD   Anyone we knew?

MRS. GLENN   Oh, I never met her. Tell the truth, I can't even recall—

(EDWARD *is seated with legs outstretched, enjoying the reminis-*

cence. PATSY *is seated near* MRS. GLENN, *her back to the outer door. Only* EDWARD *can see the door)*

MRS. GLENN —her name. When your father returned, we asked him questions. You can imagine that. But he just never said very much.

(*The door opens familiarly but slowly. As though by not knocking she has reasserted her right to family membership,* ALINE *enters.* EDWARD *rises slowly while* MRS. GLENN *continues talking)*

MRS. GLENN You remember how he was. He disliked making harsh judgments as much as anybody I ever saw. His feeling was that if you had no favorable opinion, it was best not to comment—(*She breaks off, turns where* EDWARD *is looking, and falls utterly silent)*

EDWARD "Best not to comment"? Why, I'd say he was dead right, wasn't he? Sometimes it's best just to go on with whatever you were doing. I must take after Father. Now where was I? I was working on a fishing reel last week and repaired it. I must be admirable and clever still, even at age thirty-eight. I can still fix a reel. Feature that. I was also mending the playing arm of the victrola. It wobbles. I expect to finish that soon, although it hardly needs much work . . . Yet, the old machine's got some value and we might just have it appraised by a dealer for that month that's bound to come when we can't pay the gas bill. It's good for me! Life spins on and on, as it has to. Occasionally I drink the blood of pretty young ladies like Claire Youngblood, but we've all got our little weaknesses . . . Hello, Aline.

ALINE Hello, Edward.

EDWARD I'll just see if it works. (*He sets a record on the victrola, turns the crank)*

ALINE (*Reaching to turn the record off)* I think after all these years I'm worth a little more than that.

EDWARD Just three years.

ALINE That's long to me. (*To* MRS. GLENN) Hello, Mother.

MRS. GLENN Darlin', darlin'. My darlin' daughter. You've come home.

(*Out of real affection, the two women embrace.* ALINE *and* PATSY *hug each other)*

EDWARD (*Back at victrola repair, half to himself, but with increasing force)* Three years ago, that was the last time, wasn't it? No, come to think of it, it wasn't. I was at a picnic down on the Coast just last fall, and you charged out of nowhere, upsetting everything, drunk as a black witch on a broomstick right into the middle of that beach party.

You came like an apparition out of the dark, lightning striking a tree and the tree was me, myself, my body, ME! I took off for Mexico the next day. I'd be there yet, but Mama here, she had to have me. And now there you two women are, meeting, and greeting . . . How nice you are! How nice you are! (*He has bent to straighten a pile of records, but stands up suddenly and comes close, confronting her*) Hello, Aline. (*They exchange a quick, sudden, short, almost violent kiss*)

EDWARD (*Pulling back*) So that's over with . . .

ALINE I trust it is.

EDWARD (*Returning to anger*) You mean it's never so quick and easy? You mean one thing might lead to another? You mean in the past, once or twice, it has been known to lead . . . and lead . . .

MRS. GLENN (*Hastily, to* PATSY, *as though protecting her*) We put off what we had to do in the kitchen. Now, you come on, we'll just finish up . . .

(PAUL'S *voice is heard off-stage, from the porch, calling* PATSY)

PAUL Patsy!

(MRS. GLENN, *who does not hear* PAUL, *starts to shepherd* PATSY *toward the kitchen*)

MRS. GLENN It's just that I won't have you—

(PAUL *knocks and calls again*)

PAUL Hey, Patsy!

(PATSY, *torn but curious, looks to* EDWARD *for help and support, but absorbed with* ALINE, *he does not hear her*)

PATSY But it's him, it's Paul . . . I promised.

MRS. GLENN Oh . . . That one who came with the storm.

PAUL Is it okay if I come in? You did say just about this time, didn't you?

EDWARD You never can tell what will blow in here, one moment to the next. We just never know.

(*A movement in the shrubbery, at the window*)

PAUL Hey, Patsy!

EDWARD He needs another storm, to scare him through the door.

PATSY (*Stung*) He needs somebody nice enough to ask him in.

MRS. GLENN Go on, darlin'.

PATSY Wait! I'm coming! (*She flies through the door*)

MRS. GLENN (*In general, but largely to herself*) Aline and Edward
. . . when they start this way, there's just no stopping them. (*Moves
off toward the kitchen. Exits*)

PATSY It's all mixed up inside. Let's walk . . .

(ALINE *and* EDWARD *have composed themselves, though they both
seem only half-aware that dialogues among others have been exchanged. They know they are alone*)

ALINE (*Drawing herself together and standing apart from him*)
Edward, you must understand something. I didn't on my word of
honour, even know you were here.

EDWARD (*Catching her shoulder, in a softening mood. He brings her
closer, with regret and affection*) —leads to another. Leads and leads.

ALINE (*Softening*) That's better. It was the vicious sound you could
take on. You had it back again and for a minute, I—I couldn't bear
it.

EDWARD (*With rueful charm*) I was never vicious in my life before
you. (*Smiles at her*) Not know I was here? Impossible!

ALINE No, it's true. In fact . . . I had good reason to believe you
weren't here. I telephoned but no answer. I inquired. I even wrote.

EDWARD Then where's the letter? Cat ate it. (*Bullying, he advances
almost teasingly*) Come off it, Aline. (*She trembles with anger, but
controls herself*) You came for me. We both know it. Now come on.
Where to? The lake, the next town, the nearest motel? What did you
have in mind?

ALINE (*Drawing herself sternly upright*) No, Edward, I didn't come
to find you. No, it's true. Listen. I heard you were away, probably
in Mexico, that your mother was in trouble about the house. Mother
and Patsy, I thought. I *lived* here, you know. I *love* them. Can't you
imagine my feeling for them?

EDWARD I can well imagine it. But can't you, on the other hand,
imagine *my* feeling for them? Do you think I'd leave them unprotected?

ALINE I didn't know.

EDWARD You didn't *know*? (*Shocked, the words grind into him*) Oh,
Aline, you'll have my soul before you go. That or something like it.

ALINE You know I'm not lying about your mother. You *know* that.

EDWARD A knife can be smooth on one side and sharp as a razor
on the other. That's what I know.

ALINE Let's be practical. Our marriage—well, it's really over. We
know that.

EDWARD Yes, over. We know that.

ALINE Then tell me, please. What is all this? You're trying to sell
the house. There's the new research hospital out this way.

EDWARD Oh, you've heard all that. Everybody has. The racket of construction would be newspaper enough. All this "housing." They're at it every minute—except today, Saturday, thank God. They're leveling and grading a lot of terrain, moving in the "personnel." Land prices soaring, taxes gone sky high. Our shabby old town will be only a suburb of a suburb in a few years.

ALINE I guess it's progress, of a kind.

EDWARD More power to it. Here comes progress. I'm not for turning clocks back. Who's Edward Glenn to be worth a second thought? He comes and goes too much. Still has a place in the old law firm, can get his old twice-a-week teaching job back at the junior college school of business administration, legal branch. Does a little fishing, kills a duck or two in the winter, has a drink or two every time you see him, marriage broken up. And what's all this about Mexico?

ALINE I wondered that, too. What *is* all this about Mexico?

EDWARD Ah ha! Ah ha! Curiosity! I got to it finally. Why you came! It's clear at last. I knew I'd find out.

ALINE (*Trying once more not to show anger*) That's crazy of you. It's just perverse.

EDWARD (*Seriously*) There's nothing to tell about Mexico. I just went there. Lots of people do.

ALINE Did it change your life?

EDWARD Not that I've noticed. Do you think it did?

ALINE Not that *I* can tell.

EDWARD Then I guess it didn't. I felt too much for you, that was the whole trouble. I drowned like a rat in a barrel of home brew.

ALINE To put it politely.

EDWARD Always the lady.

ALINE It was what we did together . . . that's what you meant by feeling.

EDWARD I think I'm at complete liberty to doubt if anyone else could come within a country mile of "what we did together."

ALINE But your feelings for me, just for *me*? How often I wondered if you had any at all. Oh, I felt that, but I adored you so I couldn't admit it. But later, after I knew the truth about no more children, not ever any for us . . . My two babies. They came too soon to live.

EDWARD Why go back into it. It's over. It's done.

ALINE After the second? "Oh, you're safe, Mrs. Glenn." "Doctor, that's wonderful." "You're just fine, Mrs. Glenn. But one thing: You'll never have children, Mrs. Glenn. It's over."

EDWARD Are you into some cockeyed notion that I felt nothing? That none of it mattered to me?

A L I N E Oh, yes, I know, but I had to hear it every day, playing in my head like a broken record.

E D W A R D Great comparison.

(A L I N E *whirls on him*)

E D W A R D (*Before she can speak*) I know, I know. I'm low, vicious, loathsome. I lost back then whatever was supposed to keep me from being all that.

A L I N E (*Softly*) It was your way of getting back at life?

E D W A R D Maybe. (*Carelessly*) I just know I got in the habit.

A L I N E (*Flaring up again*) I've had to live my life out with what you said to me. If you pretend you don't remember—worse still if you really don't—then I can tell you, word for word. You said—

E D W A R D Stop! (*He stands, raising his hand. The room comes to a quivering stop and her emotion with it. She relaxes, watching him closely and slowly shakes her head*)

A L I N E (*Plaintively*) You rambled so, you stayed away for days at a time, you didn't like the sight of me.

E D W A R D I felt the future as something gone, snatched away. Finished. Gone!

A L I N E And then you said, when I tried to discuss it—

E D W A R D Don't.

A L I N E —that you'd found me in the ten cent store, why didn't I go back where I belonged.

E D W A R D (*After a pause, with exaggerated Southern courtesy*) Well, you know, Aline, it was in that charmin' house of business that I first had the honour of makin' yo' lovely acquaintance.

A L I N E It couldn't be anything but a joke to you. Maybe to you I was always a joke.

E D W A R D There've been times when I wished to God you were.

A L I N E I won't dwell on it. I just won't think about it. I won't.

E D W A R D There really isn't any other way. (*He turns back to work on the victrola*) Now, let me see—(A L I N E *moves with loving familiarity about the room, begins to draw some books she remembers from the shelves. Going further left, she adjusts the portrait, which is hanging somewhat crooked on the wall, and passes on to the painting of the house, now hanging between the foot of the stairs and the first entrance*)

A L I N E Where on earth did this come from?

E D W A R D Lollie Peebles' offering. She and the ladies of Mama's gang got together and painted it. (*He goes to join her before the painting*)

ALINE   How can she stand those women? Well, I suppose they meant well.

EDWARD   It's what we have to say, even if we choke on it. Remember the summer house, Aline? (*He draws her to him*)

ALINE   I can still smell the leaves.

EDWARD   Take down your hair. (*He unpins her hair and lets it fall around her face*)   That's better.

MRS. GLENN (*Descending the stair*)   I thought of it, I have it. She came to help us. This is what I saw, once I had time to think. Aline, did you notice how grown up Patsy is? Do you two want to get married again?

EDWARD   I think you may be on shaky ground, Mother.

MRS. GLENN   Who isn't on shaky ground? The ground we've always thought of as our own—Do you know we're having to leave, Aline? It's too much for us, but we have at least to try to make a good sale.

ALINE   But outside, you'll never be the same.

MRS. GLENN   I know that, I know. I wonder what it is we have? Why are we different? Nothing will hold us together if we leave.

(*With an air of having ventured far over the grounds,* PAUL *and* PATSY *enter from the front door*)

PATSY (*Eagerly*)   We just saw everything. (*To* ALINE)   Oh. Excuse me. This is Paul.

(*But simultaneously,* PAUL *and* ALINE *are greeting one another*)

PAUL   Hello, Miss Aline. Glad to see you.

ALINE   Hello there, Paul.

EDWARD   So you know each other.

ALINE   Why, of course. I've known Paul for ages.

EDWARD   The family circle. How it grows.

MRS. GLENN   I remember when Aline and Edward first met. I thought they'd never come in from the garden.

EDWARD (*Half to himself*)   Or the summer house.

MRS. GLENN   Here these children are . . . just the same. Aline's come to help us, Patsy.

(PAUL *and* PATSY *sit on a sofa together. He takes her hand, but his interest, as* ALINE *knows, is directed toward talk of the house*)

ALINE   Mother is right. I did come thinking I could help. My idea is—Well, it's a bit complicated, but I do want, so sincerely want, to explain.

EDWARD (*Rising impatiently*)   It's good of you, no doubt about it. Oh, it is good of you. You're turning into a good, honest, helpful woman. But for good, honest, helpful women, I don't have the feelings I have for you. Doesn't that matter?

ALINE (*Honestly*) I have feelings left over, too, even if damaged. But mostly, lately, it's come down to longing to see them, Mother and Patsy, I mean. There's nothing wrong with that.

EDWARD Nothing wrong with it. But you had a glow just now. It's gone.

ALINE Who can ever keep one?

MRS. GLENN She's like a daughter. A real one.

EDWARD I'm demoted. I shrink continually. Someday I'll be ten years old. (*To* ALINE) How to return to the summer house, ever, much less on a special dark night in fall. I remember the rustle of the leaves. And so do you. Now that will go, too, the little white pavilion. (*He bursts out*) Christ! Let's let it go all at once, clean and suddenly! What the storm tried to do but couldn't, let's do ourselves. Let's never change anything! To hell with Sunday schools, to hell with funeral homes, to hell with reformatories, town libraries, "retirement" homes, community housing projects, parks, kindergartens, and centers for the preservation of ante-bellum mansions! Let in the wrecking crew, let's get it over with, noble, fast and passionate. Let them bulldoze the trees, smash up the summer house, bite into the garden. Let's hear the nails shriek in the wood and see shining gently in the early morning light, the great steel orb of the wrecking ball just as it whams into the north wall where the windows are few and there's resistance for everything to crash and smash and tear—

MRS. GLENN (*Interested*) Should we be inside or outside, Edward?

EDWARD It will take some thought.

ALINE All this stalling he does. He thinks something will come to him.

MRS. GLENN There's not much time left to decide anything.

EDWARD I think it's run out already.

(*The victrola starts to play, having been jarred by* EDWARD'S *violent stirring about the room in his long speech above*)

VICTROLA Ramona, when the day is done I hear you call . . . Ramona, we'll meet beside the waterfall . . .

PAUL What a creepy song.

PATSY Once it went off in the attic in the middle of the night. Uncle Edward was coming in about two a.m. What it said was: "Ramona, I hear the mission bells above"! (*She laughs with delight, in the newness of love*)

EDWARD   Not quite the thing to hear when you're three-fourths plastered.

(CLAIRE *knocks and enters almost immediately afterward. She looks pale but pretty. She is noticeably younger than* ALINE)

CLAIRE (*As they all look up*)   I'm sorry, I didn't know you had company, Edward; the car—

MRS. GLENN   Oh, my goodness, she's here. Edward, you shouldn't have told her she could come. The thing about Edward, honey, is just that he won't stay here. Not for very long. Return from Mexico only means he might go back again, or somewhere else. Brazil maybe.

PAUL   The thing about Edward is, why make so much about it? He doesn't care if he's asked her here and she finds somebody else.

EDWARD (*Having overheard*)   Who for that matter, asked *you* here? People come, that's all. People come.

CLAIRE   You don't understand. I just came back to bring the car. I can pick it up now, Edward, if you'll take me. It was quite a hard job for the windshield, the glass being so shattered. The repair is temporary, but at least I can manage until they—(*She senses the atmosphere and trails off*)

EDWARD   It seems this is hardly the moment.

CLAIRE (*Recovering*)   Then I'll give you these. (*She holds out the keys*) I'll telephone someone. I'll . . . leave.

EDWARD (*Coming closer to her*)   But you're always leaving, honey. You just never quite make it.

CLAIRE   It has been hard to do.

MRS. GLENN   I made you more than welcome, child. Don't worry about Aline. They used to be married.

PAUL (*Manly and righteous*)   What everybody is saying is, Don't worry about anything. I wouldn't call it such good advice.

EDWARD   You've started proving it, haven't you, Mr. Waters? To her, of course. (*He indicates* PATSY)   That there's a lot of foolishness in the air. That Edward Glenn is no good because two women wind up in his livingroom at once. That will be your project from now on. Oh, yes, the eternal businessman! (*To* PATSY)   Poor baby! I raised you for better. Still, he's a man. Make the most of him.

PAUL (*Resentful*)   What we were talking about was you all. Not me.

EDWARD   What you were exposing was really yourself. Well, go on. Out with it.

PAUL   I just meant to say that I see for the first time that you're right to sell this house whether you have to or not. IT OUGHT TO GO. IT HAS TO GO. I see what it turns people into. It's not my business to say so. But I feel that way.

EDWARD You are righteous. You are upright. You are right. It has to go. But what you're really after is, Why do all these women turn to Edward Glenn?

MRS. GLENN Carrying on and quarreling. I've had enough of it. Aline, we've got to hear what you came for, what you had in mind in your letter. Edward, it is a major complaint against you, and in my opinion it is of some merit. You simply do not—

EDWARD There are hundreds of major complaints against me and every damn one of them has considerable merit.

MRS. GLENN But if we all keep talking at once . . . Oh, I was never made for all this business talk. How I wish I were.

PAUL I doubt if any ladies of your time was brought up that way, Mrs. Glenn.

MRS. GLENN Why, look at Lollie Peebles. She inherited that farm when Mr. Peebles died, and she runs it right along.

EDWARD Lollie Peebles will be the death of us all. Mama, have you had your nap? Claire (*He approaches her again*), if your magic is for borrowing, just for this little while, just for me, forget the car, go with Mother. You two—

MRS. GLENN Come along, child, we can look at old Kodak albums and find we're really second cousins twice removed—(*She mounts the stair slowly, with* CLAIRE *near her side*)

EDWARD (*Turning to the others*) So now, Aline, just what was it?

ALINE (*Debating inwardly, hesitant to go on*) I really think Paul here might be better at explaining—

EDWARD (*Wheeling around*) Paul!

PAUL Well, you see, Mr. Glenn . . . it's just that Miss Aline and Daddy, they got more or less what you might call in touch and they—

EDWARD And your daddy is more or less what they might call Waters, the real estate guy.

PAUL (*Proudly*) Yes sir, that's him all right.

EDWARD My God in heaven! Old Piggie Waters. Aline, you remember, I told you? Back in high school some of us named him that, for God's sake. It stuck.

PAUL Well, sir, he does know he used to be called that. I'm not right sure he appreciates it so much, but he can laugh about it.

EDWARD Not very loud, I imagine. Still if you've done that well up in Memphis real estate, it must help. (*To* ALINE) You've seen him? Recently?

ALINE Well, yes I have. I want to explain—

EDWARD So we all relate to Piggie. He's calling the shots, is that it?

PAUL   Mr. Edward, I think my daddy is just a real fine man. I guess you don't appreciate him because you haven't really got to see much of him in recent years.

ALINE   I'm firmly of that opinion, too. No, please be sensible. Paul, you and your father have both discussed all this. And I—

EDWARD   Well! Since Paul understands all this so well, he must be a chip off the old block. So why don't we just have a talk about it, me and this budding financial wizard.

PATSY   You're making fun of him! That's not fair!

EDWARD   You understand all this business, too, I guess, Patsy? Is that the message I'm getting?

PATSY (*Stung*)   I don't know anything about it, and I don't even care.

PAUL   Now, Patsy—

PATSY (*To* EDWARD)   So be mean to them for a change, instead of me! (*She marches out, toward the kitchen*)

EDWARD (*To* PAUL)   Have you ever had anybody tell you to be sensible?

PAUL   Yes, sir, I have, Mr. Edward.

EDWARD   So just how did it make you feel?

PAUL   Mad as hell, Mr. Edward.

EDWARD   Score one for you. This house deal is driving me up the wall. Next I'll hear that Claire up there talking to Mama is the confidential top secretary for the real estate firm of Waters, Waters, and Waters, with an electronic dictaphone machine running through her brain.

ALINE   Just learning to listen a little, you might—

EDWARD   How important learning is. Isn't it?

(EDWARD *kneels before a cabinet, pulls out a large silver tea pot and lifts out a bottle of bourbon. He sets it down decisively on a table near* PAUL, *pulling the table forward and between them and sitting down himself, with two glasses in hand, which he sets beside the bottle*)

EDWARD   Here you are, Mr. Waters. Now let's figure this all out man to man.

ALINE (*Hovering*)   Man to man?

EDWARD   It's what I said. Aren't you glad for me to talk to your business friend here, man to man? It seems to me like a particularly good idea. What's so wrong with it?

ALINE   Why nothing . . . nothing. Go right ahead.

EDWARD   Thank you kindly. (*He pours out bourbon in the glasses, turning his back to* ALINE) (*To* PAUL)   You do like bourbon, I suppose.

PAUL (*Hesitant and a little lost*)   Well, yes sir, sometimes I do.

EDWARD   Sometimes like right now. Drink up. It might put hair on your chest.

PAUL (*Defiant*)   I might have some already. (*He gulps down the whisky, coughs.* EDWARD *pours him another*)

ALINE   Edward—

EDWARD (*Ignoring her*)   Atta boy!

PAUL (*Sputtering*)   It's just that Piggie name that's so much a part of your thinking about Daddy. He must have been about my age when you give him that, and that might be the last time you thought much about him. There's just a heap of things can happen to change somebody, can't it?

EDWARD   I've never been so convinced of that. (*Half to himself*)   For Piggie Waters to come grunting and squealing into my life at this point, of all people. In the disguise of you and Aline, working for your father, too. What does he want with this place? Fodder for a bulldozer?

PAUL   No, sir, Mr. Edward, he wants it whole—preserved.

EDWARD   The motive is still obscure.

PAUL   Sir?

EDWARD   I said I still don't get it.

PAUL   Oh. I thought you said something else.

EDWARD   Well, I did say something else. But that's what it meant.

PAUL   It's just pure feeling that Daddy feels, Mr. Edward. Feeling for his old home town. Our house is still here, too, even if he does spend a lot of time in Memphis.

ALINE   Oh, he's very sincere.

PAUL (*Getting drunk and sentimental*)   Daddy said, "I jest can't imagine this place without the old Glenn house. I'd do just about anythang in this world to save it," was what he said. Why, he don't even want you all to *move*. He wants to keep you right on, but of course in some sort of apartment, or one of those outside buildings fixed up for you—and Patsy. But mainly for your mama, I guess. You—well, you're just not here very often, are you?

EDWARD   An apartment fixed up for Mother . . .

ALINE   Oh, it would just be grand!

EDWARD (*Ignoring her, but considering*)   So she'd never have to be anywhere else? Right here?

PAUL (*Proudly*)   That's part of the deal. Part and parcel. Daddy's dying to talk to you.

EDWARD   He did talk to me, early on. One reason I got to disconnecting the phone. I thought he was still after putting up a lot of different coloured boxes and calling it "housing."

PAUL He was at first, then he changed his mind. Now he says he can't get to first base with you.

EDWARD It's true. I was always stumped by Piggie. On the telephone he's turned into the lord of creation. I got to hand it to Memphis, Tennessee. They must have something going.

PAUL You can never judge what somebody is really like underneath it all. Why, when I first came up here—you know all that storm yesterday?—I just thought I'd maybe get to see Patsy again, but then too I felt like I might do something for Daddy. He had got scared to try. You all got this strange reputation—

EDWARD Your daddy knows we're no stranger than we ever were.

PAUL It just might be that everything has changed one way, but you all stayed the same. I was saying, that when I saw Patsy up here— well, I just plain felt different, that's all. If I can feel different, what I mean to say is, so can anybody.

EDWARD You might say that, like your Daddy before you, you just had some *pure* feelings.

ALINE Edward, for heaven's sake!

PAUL (*Bristling*) I know you'd laugh if I tried to tell you.

EDWARD Maybe I would.

PAUL Right now—the way I feel now—all I want to do is just everything I can. It does seem like you'd be more inclined to appreciate—

EDWARD Appreciate what?

PAUL Why, just what everybody feels, Mr. Edward.

(PATSY *enters from the kitchen, bearing a large coffee pot and cups on a tray*)

EDWARD I'm being sensible, Aline. (*He notices* PATSY) Patsy, our education is continuing. School is never over. We're having lessons now.

PATSY I do think Paul is sensible, Uncle Edward.

EDWARD I never wanted to dispute it, baby. What's all this?

PATSY Just some coffee. I thought it might calm everybody down.

EDWARD It's a thought. Let's go on a little. Lesson two. When we've got this apartment deal worked out, what happens to the rest of the house?

ALINE It's what Paul was beginning to explain. (*She helps herself to coffee, and so moves closer in*) There would naturally have to be some repair and renovation. You know that things have been running down for some time now. Why, the shutters fell off five years ago. We were always going to save to buy some new ones. Nobody makes such old things. They have to be customized.

EDWARD Customized. I see. So after the shutters, the new plumbing, the alterations here and there, and a brand new kitchen installed, and all the weeds yanked up in the yard, and the grape arbor chopped down to build a swimming pool . . . what then? Who comes to sport about and enjoy the fine old place?

ALINE (*Carefully*) It's just that on weekends only, for the most part, but perhaps sometimes during holidays as well, Piggie—I mean (*Laughs*) Alton T. Waters, as he's known now, would like to invite some very small groups of guests down for dinner or maybe to spend —oh, very occasionally—Saturday and Sunday. Never anyone Mother would disapprove of. She could always have the final say as to how many or even as to when. They would be—well, like guests.

EDWARD Ummm. I think I see. Yes, yes. (*Half to himself*) "They named me Piggie, but here I am now."

PAUL (*Getting all the way tight*) You haven't even got around to the figure Daddy is prepared to offer. It's what you might call—princely.

EDWARD Astonishing. Aline, while we're mulling all this over, why don't you call Mother and Claire down to have some coffee?

(ALINE *is at first about to move toward the stair, but stops*)

PATSY I can go. (*She starts forward, but sensitive to the suddenly freezing atmosphere, stops*)

ALINE What did you say her name was?

EDWARD Claire.

(*A silence falls.* EDWARD *is now seated at some distance from the others. Like old contestants, he and* ALINE *are watching each other narrowly, with clogged emotion.* MRS. GLENN *has started to descend the stairs with* CLAIRE *somewhat sleepily following behind*)

EDWARD (*Noticing* CLAIRE) It's getting late. It's nice here, when dark first begins to come down on us. Have you noticed? The slight mist, the soft air, the insects . . .

CLAIRE Yes, it's lovely. And lovely at night, too.

EDWARD (*Reaching out his arm*) Come here then and tell me about it. I was hoping for twilight, a fine sunset burning softly just off the edge of the hill, but you'll do just as well. No shoes again? Why, that's good.

CLAIRE (*Looking down*) Oh, dear, Mrs. Glenn dropped off to sleep and so did I. How careless!

EDWARD Never mind. I like it. It's very nice. We've had a little whisky, Paul here and I. I'll never be able to talk about this house without getting drunk. This failing, falling house is me . . .

ALINE (*To* PAUL) He gets in moods like this.

EDWARD (*Drawing* CLAIRE *farther to the left of the stage, while the others remain grouped around the table with sandwiches and coffee, on the right*) Let's you and me get rid of all this nightmare suburb together. Let's make a ghetto of it, right from the start. Let's scheme at it, and confound them. Let's go out every night and dig up their shrubs and tear up their flowers. Let's poison all their cats and dogs. Let's hire subversive and unsound teachers for their children, so they will withdraw them all from that brand new schoolhouse. You can think of good things, can't you? Aren't you inventive? Underneath your manners and your cool, cool looks, aren't you wild as a witch, a wild cat, a young hound bitch . . .?

PATSY (*To* PAUL) I expect he'll stop all that soon and start talking to you. I think he's just thinking it all over.

ALINE When *I* think how much trouble I was willing to go to out of the most sincere devotion. Edward, don't tell me even you can be so blind as not to see that. And why?

EDWARD Why indeed? A good question.

MRS. GLENN She wanted to help us. I told you that from the very first.

EDWARD Laden with good deeds, isn't she? But like all good deeds, the motive is concealed. Tell me, Aline, who did get Piggie Waters to change from "new development" to "preservation"? There's bound to have been a little mite of personal persuasion involved.

ALINE I never meant to take any credit for myself, but I did remember that we all used to know him, so I did go once to see him, up in Memphis.

EDWARD And how glad you both were to renew acquaintance, to talk over the old home town. You might be going into a little real estate business now, mightn't you? Come to think of it, you always did like this sort of dealing with first one angle, then another. You'd be splendid at it!

ALINE I think how I spend my time is not for you to comment on.

EDWARD Nobody had to tell you about our problem here, Aline. You raised your finely tuned hound nose to the breeze one morning and you smelled it.

ALINE I do have that property you gave me for a settlement. I'm bound to interest myself.

EDWARD Part of Father's old farm, miles away. No, it won't work. You determined to preside over us, property or not. But let's not mistake the name of it. One name for it is Helping Out. But turn the

log over and up comes the true name, all wriggling dark, with eyes
and feelers. It's called Walking over Edward. What does he matter,
what can he do, what is his opinion worth? Let's call it the coup de
grace, Aline, the final castrating act—

ALINE   Oh, God! How awful you are. I tried to get my message
through. I called, I wrote. Mother, you know I wrote to you.

MRS. GLENN   Edward, you should realize that. You know that letter
you never read.

EDWARD   Back to that again. So now, having delivered your message
in person, can't you, decently and quietly, leave?

ALINE   No thanks to me, of course. Not a word of thanks.

EDWARD   Was it thanks you wanted? I just didn't understand. Thanks,
why sure. Thanks, why certainly. I didn't get my signals straight. I
didn't know. I'm a little bit slow to catch on, now that my first youth
is spent. Thanks, thanks, thanks, Aline. A thousand thanks. Thanks
a million.

MRS. GLENN   Oh, why do they go on so? *I* was always fond of you,
Aline. It's only that you and Edward—you burnt each other up, some-
way. I do believe it's a purely personal matter, when people feel like
that.

ALINE   That "personal matter"—it was my life. (*She fixes on* EDWARD)

EDWARD   And mine.

(EDWARD *has picked up the black umbrella and raised it slightly.
He stands looking at it reflectively*)

EDWARD   Many a time I've thought how lovely it would be to brain
her with this. How splendid. (*He looks up*) You've done it now. It
didn't work so why linger? What's lacking? My love? Why, take that
too. Take it all. But go.

ALINE   (*Moving toward the door*) Goodbye, Mother. Goodbye,
Edward.

MRS. GLENN (*Rising, with arms outstretched to them both, tremulous*)
My children, always, both of you. Oh, to have something to say,
and no strength to make it clear. Important . . . how I see it now.
The church steeple, I mean . . .

(EDWARD, *moving to hold her up, as* ALINE *comes closer*)

ALINE   I don't understand.

EDWARD   Just that lightning struck the church. It worried her.

MRS. GLENN   It's bothered me so. Don't you see, Aline? With
Edward, life is like that . . . and so he is like that, too, like the lightning
is. He will strike down whatever it is you're trying to set up. He won't

give in to you, Aline. What are steeples for but striking down? I see that now. If only you—

ALINE   I can't make it out.

EDWARD   I know what she means. I doubt you ever will.

ALINE   She needs rest. I'm going.

MRS. GLENN   Steeples crashing, houses falling, tearing . . . what's that ever to what the two of you can do, tearing at my heart, when all I wanted was . . . you children safe here, together . . . happy . . . (*She sways, and grasps about blindly.* EDWARD *catches her*)

PATSY (*Running in*)   Grandmama, what is it? The medicine . . . where?

MRS. GLENN (*Weakly*)   Never mind it . . . I just want to be upstairs. In my own room . . . the window open, the breeze stirring, and the bees . . . how you can hear them in the clover on a quiet afternoon, all the way across the drive . . .

(ALINE *comes forward to help hold her up, but* EDWARD *gestures her away savagely, so that she starts back, stumbles and half falls*)

EDWARD (*Starting toward the stair with* MRS. GLENN)   Did you come for this, too, or does destruction just follow you around?

ALINE (*Gasping*)   I'll remember that forever.

PAUL (*From the stair*)   The idea of saying that to her, you bastard!

(CLAIRE *runs to the head of the stair and stands watching*)

PATSY   Here, Uncle Edward. Let me . . . .

(*They begin to mount the stairs slowly, as* CLAIRE *descends to help. . . .*)

Scene 2

(*Three days later. Evidence of the funeral having been held the day before is still to be noted by the arrangement of chairs in the room, and a few flowers fallen on the carpet.* LOLLIE PEEBLES *is turning from the front door with a sheet of paper in hand as* EDWARD *descends the stairs. From without there comes the sound of departing cars*)

LOLLIE   So they've gone now.

EDWARD   You mean that was the last of them?

LOLLIE   Except for me. I don't want to be thought of as intruding, but I do know from my own sad experience that when I lost Sam, certain things have to be done whether we feel like it or not. I was hoping to ease the burden on you and Patsy—

EDWARD I'm sure you have indeed, Miss Lollie.

LOLLIE —by making out this little list of all those kind souls, such long time friends, and their parents and grandparents, in many instances, before them. Now here we have it, all in a nut shell: There's Edna for the potato salad, and Mary Nell Satterfield for the ham, the Saunders family for that delicious jello whip with bananas, and Grace Eliot for the bread and pound cake both—I never know how she does it all! And then there was—

EDWARD Miss Lollie, if it is, as you say, and I'm certain I believe every word, all there in a nut shell, couldn't you just give me the nut shell itself, and run along now, too?

LOLLIE (*Reluctantly handing over the list as though passing over her authority*) Well, I suppose . . .

EDWARD (*Taking it*) We cherish the picture, we devour everything with gratitude, we'll return every last saucer with engraved thank-you notes, edged in black. So now . . .

LOLLIE If you only knew how I hate to close this door behind me.

EDWARD I understand that.

LOLLIE (*Opening the front door, but standing in it, lingering*) So many times I've stood here and bid my adieus.

EDWARD Yes, I know.

LOLLIE (*Tearfully*) I feel like saying, "Goodbye, Jeannie," for the last time.

EDWARD I know, Miss Lollie, But for the love of God, and Mother, and Father, and all the Glenns . . .

> (LOLLIE *is at last made to quit the doorway with one final wave. As* EDWARD *firmly closes the door and even turns the key on her, he looks up to see* ALINE *slowly descending the stair. She is in black, carrying a black overnight case*)

ALINE I do have to thank you, Edward, for letting me stay this one time more.

EDWARD I hadn't really thought about it until I saw you at the funeral. You looked—forlorn.

ALINE It was good of you.

EDWARD I suppose funerals must be for grieving. There's dignity in that.

ALINE For grieving but not for grievances? I'd like to hope you won't hold any of those.

(EDWARD *does not reply*)

ALINE   It's very strange, but that room I stayed in . . . I never remember seeing it before. It has bronze wallpaper and a small white bed. There's an oval mirror over the little dresser, blue, like looking into a pool. The window overlooks the back garden. I lived here for years but I never saw that room.

EDWARD   You dreamed it, maybe.

ALINE   You did understand, Edward?

EDWARD   Understand what?

ALINE   What I said about grievances. I really meant it.

EDWARD   Just what did you want me to understand?

ALINE   I'd like to leave knowing that everything's all right.

EDWARD   Why?

ALINE   It's only natural. I want to feel that the past is washed away, to know the slate is clean once more.

EDWARD   Like the blackboards at the schoolhouse?

ALINE (*Taking him more seriously than he intends*)   Exactly. If we could just have that agreement! Then I could go away in peace.

EDWARD   Peacefully thinking . . . that your soul was like a blackboard at the schoolhouse.

ALINE (*Stung and angry*)   I'm sure you find that very funny.

(EDWARD *does not reply*)

ALINE   Why won't you say it?

EDWARD   Say what?

ALINE   That we've each been wrong, done each other wrong. Coming here, I had such good intentions. Going away, I'd like to feel . . .

EDWARD   Feel what?

ALINE   Well . . . clean . . . free . . . forgiven . . .

EDWARD (*Ironically*)   Anything else?

ALINE   Yes, there's more. I've no plan at all anymore for the house. That was all for Mother anyway. But I'd just like to look back on this part of my life, the years here, to be able to take them out like something from an old chest, smelling so good and sweet. I could recall only the good things, then. I could feel alone with those thoughts from time to time, and I'd be happy.

EDWARD   It does sound nice.

ALINE (*Seriously*)   You, only you, could give me that. If you would.

EDWARD   You want me to do for you what I can't do for myself?

ALINE   You could try. I want to make a fresh start, you see. That's so important psychologically after all this. I think I deserve some tiny bit of help in doing that.

EDWARD   Where exactly do I, psychologically, get it from?

ALINE   Your trying at all would make it true. You know that. It would be . . . like a favour, a parting gift.

EDWARD   It's just that there aren't any gifts like that.

ALINE (*Softly and sadly, defeated*)   None?

EDWARD   None.

ALINE (*Smiling at him a little*)   A fake one, then, just for the moment?

EDWARD   They don't sell them. Not even at the ten cent store.

ALINE   Goodbye then. (*She still stands as though waiting*)   What was it we missed?

EDWARD (*Unlocking the door and opening it for her*)   Missed? We missed each other. (*He holds the door wide*)   Now for the love of God, and Mother, and Father, and Grandfather, and . . . Uncle Thomas. . .

(ALINE *goes slowly out and* EDWARD *closes the door on her softly and firmly.* PATSY *has entered from the rear during his last speech. She is wearing a light coat and has a bag slung over her shoulder*)

PATSY   . . . and Patsy . . .

EDWARD (*Wheeling around*)   Yes, by all means Patsy. You were there all the time? Where have you been these last few hours, with all those Lollies and Margies and Jessies and Edna Maes running me crazy? I'd rather be in a flock of Canadian geese at sunrise. (*He sits and puts his head in his hands, rubbing his brow with weariness*)   I was thankful to think you might still be asleep. Claire said she hadn't seen you.

PATSY   Claire?

EDWARD   I got her to stay on . . . to help. Then she hid upstairs. (*Laughs*)   Afraid of gossiping ladies. God knows, they terrify me, too. One Lollie Peebles alone could rout an army.

PATSY (*Absently*)   They brought all that food.

EDWARD   Inevitably.

PATSY   And Aline? She had to go?

EDWARD   She had to go.

PATSY   For good, you mean?

EDWARD   Afraid so.

PATSY   Then you didn't love her after all?

EDWARD   Sometimes, honey, love isn't all it's cracked up to be. (*He regards* PATSY *more closely*)   Patsy, where did you spring from: What the hell is going on?

PATSY   I didn't stay here last night, Uncle Edward. (*She pauses*) Uncle Edward, I went away with Paul.

EDWARD (*Sits down thoughtfully*) I think we're all a little bit crazy. How could we stand it if we weren't?

PATSY Stand to live, you mean?

EDWARD I mean you found some answer—the way you had to — on your own.

(*From abovestairs*, CLAIRE *appears and stands unobserved on the stairway*)

PATSY We don't need to talk about it, do we? I just wanted you to know. It was like he—well, like he was caring for me.

EDWARD (*Wearily*) But don't you see, baby? *He* was caring for you, but *I* wasn't.

PATSY (*Comes closer to him*) We can forgive each other then?

EDWARD Right. (*A silence*) Something you've got to understand. Time runs out, the moments go. Haven't you noticed? You know how I thought Mother was showing her age, getting a little bit off her rocker, not letting me get to first base about selling this place, undertakers thrown out, church people, old people, nothing to suit her for one minute?

PATSY It really did get kind of weird, didn't it?

EDWARD There's another way of seeing all that. It finally got through to me. A little thick-headed these days, that's all. But finally even I catch on. That we were together all along, Mother and I, else why did I let her get away with it? She wanted me here, and the funny thing is, I wanted that too. I think she knew it, felt it. I never had the slightest notion of selling this house. Where would I go? This is home.

PATSY You didn't know it?

EDWARD Hiding it from myself, I guess. Not letting myself think. It was a trick I got into, after Aline. No, you don't understand it now. (*Kisses her forehead*) File it away . . . where you can get at it later, some day maybe. A bargain?

PATSY I promise.

EDWARD I never did get to tell Mother very much about Mexico.

CLAIRE Tell me sometime. (*They both look up*) I was thinking I might be needed with all those mourners here and all that food. But I didn't have the courage to come out. What would they think? You with a strange girl here and your mother hardly buried? I was scared all night. The floor boards creaked and shifted.

EDWARD Did you imagine you had died, and didn't know it? Have you thought you might be mad?

CLAIRE (*Sitting down to think*)   All I imagine is I wouldn't really like
   to live here, Edward. It's too huge, it's too unsettling. It broods. If
   one must have old things, there must be a small old house somewhere.
EDWARD (*Absently*)   In a wood, by a stream. (*He turns suddenly to*
   PATSY, *who starts in fright. He holds her*)   Was he good to you, baby?
   Are you okay? Nothing to it, really, is there? All a lot of foolishness?
   Don't feel bad? Why feel anything? Except for joy . . .

   (PATSY, *who has been uncertain and anxious, now throws her arms
   around him in relief*)

PATSY   Oh, you understand, you understand! Why did I ever think
   you wouldn't?
PAUL (*Calling from without*)   Patsy! Patsy!
EDWARD (*Ironic*)   You can see what it meant to him. He can't let you
   go anywhere, can't leave you alone.
PATSY   But Grandmama—it was her funeral yesterday. You have to
   be respectful, don't you?
EDWARD   I'm not the one to ask, honey. She was on the side of life,
   that's all I know.
PATSY   But just the same, how could I? I loved her. How could I?
EDWARD   She understands. Her spirit, any minute now, will say so.
PATSY   I don't want any spirits! Just real people! Oh! (*She tries not
   to cry, but finally sits down wiping her eyes in distress*)   I'm sorry,
   but who can I say it to?
EDWARD   There's an Olmec god in Mexico, but he's a long way off.
PAUL (*Entering through the back without knocking*)   I thought it over,
   Patsy. 'Scuse me, but I'm just not going to sit out there on the street,
   waiting for you to come tell me when it's okay. I decided to drive
   right up and come right in. It's the way I feel! (*He moves to center
   stage, a man confronting* EDWARD, *who is standing between him and*
   PATSY. CLAIRE *is still standing on the stair, looking down*)   I'm taking her away, Mr. Glenn. I don't think it's good for her here.
EDWARD   It's high time I lost everything.
PATSY (*Rising to go to* PAUL)   Uncle Edward means we don't give
   him anything. That we're all for ourselves, not him. (*Involuntarily,
   she clasps* PAUL'S *hand, and womanly, turns to* EDWARD *though
   still speaking to* PAUL)   Why aren't we better to him? Can't we
   do something just for him—give him something?
EDWARD (*Almost alarmed*)   Give me something?
PATSY   But I want to. (*She is puzzled at herself*)   So much.
EDWARD   We deal in might-have-beens.
PAUL   Mr. Glenn, even if you don't take Daddy's offer, which was certainly far and away the best you'll ever find, I still think you have

to do something here along those lines or some other. You're a victim here of the population explosion, that's how I see all of you. It's part of a world problem, that's all. They've ruined your part of town, all the hills and woods you remembered, torn up the farms, built the new school, re-routed the creek, dispossessed everybody else, then closed in on you. I see you now in a different light. Not the Glenns and this town any more, but people like you in any town, part of the general picture. There's nothing personal about it. I just think you had bad luck—that's all.

EDWARD   As to location, or as to mortality?

PAUL   Oh, I wasn't so much thinking about your mother dying. Except that I was real sorry.

EDWARD   I'm sorry, too.

PATSY (*Earnestly*)   We're all sorry. But I'm back now, Uncle Edward. I'm back home. I'm here with you. We're all here, here with you.

(EDWARD *debates silently, rises, prowls the room. He rearranges some of the chairs at right, so that the room in that part begins to resemble the way it was in former times.* CLAIRE *comes down and silently begins to help, and when he stops to speak, she continues to bring things to order*)

EDWARD (*Speaking deliberately but not specifically addressing any one person*)   When Patsy's mother and father died, it was because of this house. They had come home for a weekend visit and as it was a terribly hot spell we were having they decided to sleep in the turret. We used to have a sort of turret, a sort of lookout on the back, as well as a screened balcony because it was high up and the windows drew a draft. Her father just didn't know how weak the supports were, having been an amateur carpenter and built a good part of it himself. So they were up there in the cool of the night, the two of them, and along about two in the morning, there came a creaking and groaning like a demolition squad had moved in to get an early pre-dawn start and that whole little section of the house disengaged itself and stood alone and aslant for a time, like the tower of Pisa for several seconds instead of several hundred years—and then it crashed. They were killed. Instantly.

(*A silence follows*)

PAUL   Where was Patsy?

EDWARD   Patsy had been put to sleep in a small cupboard room just beneath a window. Lots of windows up there. She sailed out on the air and landed unharmed in a rose bush. I remember it well.

PATSY (*Vexed to tears*) It didn't happen! You shouldn't joke about things like that! My father was killed in the war. He was a hero. He was decorated posthumously. And my mother—

EDWARD My sister Mary George—

PATSY My mother just isn't with us, that's the truth. She grieved so, and—and—

PAUL I know about it, Patsy. (*Gently*) Don't worry. All I know is what people say.

PATSY I don't know what they say.

PAUL Nothing so bad. Just that she got to drinking. Anybody could do that.

EDWARD Do they say she's down in Jackson, in the state asylum? With her daughter up here giving herself airs, making out she's an "orphan"?

PATSY I was going to tell him but now you've spoiled it. He'll hate me, now. But maybe you want that, maybe you want him to! (*She jumps to her feet*) You're trying to run him away! Oh, I can see that. It was you I loved. It's you I always loved. You must know that. I'll hate you now.

EDWARD You couldn't.

PATSY How hard I'll try!

PAUL I won't be happy till I get her past that gate out there, out into the sun—yes, the sunlight, the good old awful plain everyday sunshine. I wanted to see the inside of this place just about all my life. Now I have—

PATSY (*Imploring* EDWARD) Uncle Edward, after Grandmama, you were all I had. All I knew . . . was you . . .

(*As if avoiding both her words and confronting her,* EDWARD *has risen and advanced to center stage, his back to the three of them*)

EDWARD But you know still. You'll always know. You just know more, that's all. You can see the bad with the good. Is that too much for you?

PATSY (*Rising to pursue and stand behind him, hands clenched*) There doesn't have to be any bad. Didn't have to be. You've turned it loose on us now. I've wanted so to see Paul here with us—with you and me—coming and going, to show him everything, but always with you near. To be near you, both of us—always near you.

EDWARD (*Turning, pulls her to him, holding her*) Don't want any of that plain old sunshine he's jawing about? Want to stay around shadowy Uncle Edward?

PATSY I never thought of leaving you. I just never thought of it.

EDWARD (*To* PAUL) Wherever you take her, you'll never take me away from her. (*He kisses her tenderly, but with control, on the side of her face*) That's my triumph. (*He shoves her away, as though returning her to* PAUL) (*To* PAUL) I had to show you that. But you'd see it anyway. You'd have to.

PAUL Sometimes I'd like to knock the living hell out of you.

EDWARD Now you're talking. Go right ahead.

PAUL (*Gathering* PATSY *to him, under his arm*) We're going now. This is it.

(CLAIRE *has left off what she has been doing and unable not to speak, comes forward*)

CLAIRE (*To* EDWARD) Please comfort her . . . how could you hurt her that way?

(PATSY *at the last moment of going, looks back, runs to* EDWARD'S *arms and out again*)

PAUL We mean to stay good friends and all.

PATSY It will be different then.

PAUL You can visit. Maybe he'll change.

PATSY It won't be the same.

(EDWARD, *moved but silent, waits while the car starts, clutches gravel, speeds away. Then there is silence filling the room with the sound of insect grinding*)

EDWARD Thank God they finished excavating. I'll have no more bulldozers for company. Just hammers and nails for a while. Then back to locusts and tree frogs. And the slither of lizards on the garden walks. It isn't true we've got no sun here. He wanted it to sound so noble, taking her off, that he threw that in for the ring of it. There's sun everywhere, out in the yard, the garden. Did you like that boy? Paul?

CLAIRE Edward, what are you? I thought perhaps I knew you, even loved you, or might. Now I see what I never saw before, never dreamed of. How could you run that girl away like that? Love is need, for one thing.

EDWARD Did you want me to hold on to her forever?

CLAIRE A little decency, a gently breaking away . . .

EDWARD The time for that had passed.

CLAIRE It seems to me she's still here, and crying . . .

EDWARD You don't think I feel that, too?

CLAIRE Then who are you? Monster? Man? Lover? Husband? Death? Life?

EDWARD A good assortment. Why not all of them? Or would you like to pick and choose?

CLAIRE (*Breaks off and laughs girlishly at him, without hysteria, though with the ring of someone able to enter a new phase*) House selling is not really a subject anymore, I guess.

EDWARD Over and done with.

CLAIRE Are you planning to stay here till they break down the doors and find you? Or will you tear it down around you, pull it down like Samson?

EDWARD Not after I've gone and laden it this way with other people's blood and tears. Not to say wrath. Aline . . . she could have bit a nail in two. Gone, and admitting it now, never could before. It's me in charge. Mama's will will be in probate. Who knows better than a country lawyer how to hold these things up? I can make a stab at delaying tactics, for something like the next fifty years.

CLAIRE You may even have to reconnect the telephone.

EDWARD (*Smiling as he notices* CLAIRE *as a person, woman, instead of someone he is talking to*) What about you and me? Let's smoke a cigarette, have a drink, start a family.

CLAIRE (*Laughing at him*) I came to say goodbye, Edward. Remember?

EDWARD Some weeks ago.

CLAIRE I thought I was needed. Or imagined it maybe. Maybe I wanted to imagine it. But your mother did welcome me. So did you. (*She turns to ascend the stairs*) I'll get my things.

EDWARD They needed me, too. Or so they said. They called me back from Mexico. It's dangerous—to bring a man home.

CLAIRE (*Looking around*) Where are they now?

EDWARD All gone. Even the ghosts are silent.

CLAIRE Time for me to go, too. (*She exits up the stairs*)

EDWARD (*Alone and restless, talking as he wanders about, taking down the painting* LOLLIE PEEBLES *brought and closing it with some difficulty in a closet beneath the stairs*) Anybody might think I schemed it all. (*Softly*) Mother? (*Louder*) Mother? Peace is a calm wind at twilight, a swelling of white curtains. Patsy? (*Silence*) But everything as always hangs on a thread, is strung by a thread together. I have a moth on a thread, a large white moth. (*He flips on the victrola. Music fills the quiet room—"Dancing in the Dark."*) Claire?

(CLAIRE *emerges from above, small overnight case in hand, wearing her short white jacket and white chiffon scarf*)

EDWARD   A visiting angel spreads her wings to fly away. It's a rule.

CLAIRE   What did you say?

EDWARD   I said you looked so pretty, running through the moonlight. (*He drags some of the chairs aside, making space for them*)

CLAIRE   How could you know?

EDWARD   I was told. I can visualize. (*He takes her face in his hands, bends to kiss her. She responds or wishes to, but pulls away*)

CLAIRE   Think of them all . . . your mother, Patsy, Aline. I'm all that's left, and so you're just with me, but the message is, There's such a risk in it. Oh . . . too much! (*She hastens toward the door in something like fright. She pushes, but finds it latched, not the glass inner door, but the screen. The music rises compelling. She sets down her bag and tries to work the latch, and failing throws her arms up against the screen, almost in terror, and so hangs there for a moment undecided, like a large white moth, hanging on to the screen*)   In some ways you frighten me so.

EDWARD   I know.

CLAIRE   Why can't I reason?

EDWARD   At some point or other, we leave all that.

CLAIRE (*Still holding to the screen*)   Then what can I do?

EDWARD (*Hand reaching toward her*)   You can dance with me, Claire. Dance with me . . .

(*She turns and slowly reaches out her hand to his. They begin to sway together to the music*)

EDWARD   . . . then we'll decide . . .

CURTAIN

The Glass Menagerie

TENNESSEE WILLIAMS

CHARACTERS

AMANDA WINGFIELD *the mother. A little woman of great but confused vitality clinging frantically to another time and place. Her characterization must be carefully created, not copied from type. She is not paranoiac, but her life is paranoia. There is much to admire in Amanda, and as much to love and pity as there is to laugh at. Certainly she has endurance and a kind of heroism, and though her foolishness makes her unwittingly cruel at times, there is tenderness in her slight person.*

LAURA WINGFIELD *her daughter. Amanda, having failed to establish contact with reality, continues to live vitally in her illusions, but Laura's situation is even graver. A childhood illness has left her crippled, one leg slightly shorter than the other, and held in a brace. This defect need not be more than suggested on the stage. Stemming from this, Laura's separation increases till she is like a piece of her own glass collection, too exquisitely fragile to move from the shelf.*

TOM WINGFIELD *her son. And the narrator of the play. A poet with a job in a warehouse. His nature is not remorseless, but to escape from a trap he has to act without pity.*

JIM O'CONNOR *the gentleman caller. A nice, ordinary, young man.*

SETTING

SCENE   *An Alley in St. Louis.*
PART I   *Preparation for a Gentleman Caller*
PART II   *The Gentleman Calls*
TIME   *Now [c. 1944] and the Past.*

THE AUTHOR'S PRODUCTION NOTES

Being a "memory play," *The Glass Menagerie* can be presented with unusual freedom of convention. Because of its considerably delicate or tenuous material, atmospheric touches and subtleties of direction play a particularly important part. Expressionism and all other unconventional techniques in drama have only one valid aim, and that is a closer approach to truth. When a play employs unconventional techniques, it is not, or certainly shouldn't be, trying to escape its responsibility of dealing with reality, or interpreting experience, but is actually or should be attempting to find a closer approach, a more penetrating and vivid expression of things as they are. The straight realistic play with its genuine frigidaire and authentic ice-cubes, its characters that speak exactly as its audience speaks, corresponds to the academic landscape and has the same virtue of a photographic likeness. Everyone should know nowadays the unimportance of the photographic in art: that truth, life, or reality is an organic thing which the poetic imagination can represent or suggest, in essence, only through transformation, through changing into other forms than those which were merely present in appearance.

These remarks are not meant as a preface only to this particular play. They have to do with a conception of a new, plastic theatre which must take the place of the exhausted theatre of realistic conventions if the theatre is to resume vitality as a part of our culture.

The Screen Device   There is *only one important difference between the original and acting version of the play* and that is the *omission* in the latter of the device which I tentatively included in my *original* script. This device was the use of a screen on which were projected magic-lantern slides bearing images or titles. I do not regret the omission of this device from the present Broadway production. The extraordinary power of Miss Taylor's performance made it suitable to have the utmost simplicity in the physical production. But I think it may be interesting to some readers to see how this device was conceived. So I am putting it into the published manuscript. These images and legends, projected from behind, were cast on a section of wall between the front-room and dining-room areas, which should be indistinguishable from the rest when not in use.

The purpose of this will probably be apparent. It is to give accent to certain values in each scene. Each scene contains a particular point (or several) which is structurally the most important. In an episodic play, such as this, the basic structure or narrative line may be obscured from the audience; the effect may seem fragmentary rather than architectural. This may not be the fault of the play so much as a lack of attention in the audience. The legend or image upon the screen will strengthen the effect of what is merely allusion in the writing and allow the primary point to be made more simply and lightly than if the entire responsibility were on the spoken lines. Aside from this structural value, I think the screen will have a definite emotional appeal, less definable but just as important. An imaginative producer or director may invent many other uses for this device than those indicated in the present script. In fact the possibilities of the device seem much larger to me than the instance of this play can possibly utilize.

The Music   Another extra-literary accent in this play is provided by the use of music. A single recurring tune, "The Glass Menagerie," is used to give emotional emphasis to suitable passages. This tune is like circus music, not when you are on the grounds or in the immediate vicinity of the parade, but when you are at some distance and very likely thinking of something else. It seems under those circumstances to continue almost interminably and it weaves in and out of your preoccupied consciousness; then it is the lightest, most delicate music in the world and perhaps the saddest. It expresses the surface vivacity of life with the underlying strain of immutable and inexpressible sorrow. When you look at a piece of delicately spun glass you think of two things: how beautiful it is and how easily it can be broken. Both of those ideas should be woven into the recurring tune, which dips in and out of the play as if it were carried on a wind that changes. It serves as a thread of connection and allusion between the narrator with his separate point in time and space and the subject of his story. Between each episode it returns as reference to the emotion, nostalgia, which is the first condition of the play. It is primarily Laura's music and therefore comes out most clearly when the play focuses upon her and the lovely fragility of glass which is her image.

The Lighting   The lighting in the play is not realistic. In keeping with the atmosphere of memory, the stage is dim. Shafts of light are focused on selected areas or actors, sometimes in contradistinction to what is the apparent center. For instance, in the quarrel scene between Tom and Amanda, in which Laura has no active part, the clearest pool of light is on her figure. This is also true of the supper scene, when her silent figure on the sofa should remain the visual center. The light upon Laura should be distinct from the others, having a peculiar pristine clarity such as light used in early religious portraits of female saints or madonnas. A certain correspondence to light in religious paintings, such as El Greco's, where the figures are radiant in atmosphere that is relatively dusky, could be effectively used throughout the play. (It will also permit a more effective use of the screen.) A free, imaginative use of light can be of enormous value in giving a mobile, plastic quality to plays of a more or less static nature.

Scene 1

(The Wingfield apartment is in the rear of the building, one of those vast hive-like conglomerations of cellular living-units that flower as warty growths in overcrowded urban centers of lower middle-class populations and are symptomatic of the impulse of this largest and fundamentally enslaved section of American society to avoid fluidity and differentiation and to exist and function as one interfused mass of automatism.

The apartment faces an alley and is entered by a fire escape, a structure whose name is a touch of accidental poetic truth, for all of these huge buildings are always burning with the slow and implacable fires of human desperation. The fire escape is included in the set—that is, the landing of it and steps descending from it.

The scene is memory and is therefore nonrealistic. Memory takes a lot of poetic license. It omits some details; others are exaggerated, according to the emotional value of the articles it touches, for memory is seated predominantly in the heart. The interior is therefore rather dim and poetic.

At the rise of the curtain, the audience is faced with the dark, grim rear wall of the Wingfield tenement. This building, which runs parallel to the footlights, is flanked on both sides by dark, narrow alleys which run into murky canyons of tangled clotheslines, garbage cans, and the sinister latticework of neighboring fire escapes. It is up and down these side alleys that exterior entrances and exits are made, during the play. At the end of TOM'S *opening commentary, the dark tenement wall slowly reveals (by the means of a transparency) the interior of the ground floor Wingfield apartment.*

Downstage is the living room, which also serves as a sleeping room for LAURA, *the sofa unfolding to make her bed. Upstage, center, and divided by a wide arch or second proscenium with transparent faded portieres (or second curtain), is the dining room. In an old-fashioned what-not in the living room are seen scores of transparent glass animals. A blow-up photograph of the father hangs on the wall of the living room, facing the audience, to the left of the archway. It is the face of a very handsome young man in a doughboy's[1] First World War cap. He is gallantly smiling, ineluctably smiling, as if to say, "I will be smiling forever."*

The audience hears and sees the opening scene in the dining room

---

[1] American infantryman.

*through both the transparent fourth wall of the building and the
transparent gauze portieres of the dining-room arch. It is during
this revealing scene that the fourth wall slowly ascends, out of sight.
This transparent exterior wall is not brought down again until the
very end of the play, during* TOM'S *speech.*

   *The narrator is an undisguised convention of the play. He takes
whatever license with dramatic convention is convenient to his pur-
poses.*

   TOM *enters dressed as a merchant sailor from alley, stage left,
and strolls across the front of the stage to the fire escape. There
he stops and lights a cigarette. He addresses the audience.*)

TOM   Yes, I have tricks in my pocket, I have things up my sleeve. But
I am the opposite of a stage magician. He gives you illusion that has
the appearance of truth. I give you truth in the pleasant disguise of
illusion.

   To begin with, I turn back time. I reverse it to that quaint period,
the thirties, when the huge middle class of America was matriculating
in a school for the blind. Their eyes had failed them, or they had failed
their eyes, and so they were having their fingers pressed forcibly down
on the fiery Braille alphabet of a dissolving economy.

   In Spain there was revolution. Here there was only shouting and
confusion.

   In Spain there was Guernica.[2] Here there were disturbances of
labor, sometimes pretty violent, in otherwise peaceful cities such as
Chicago, Cleveland, Saint Louis . . .

   This is the social background of the play.

(MUSIC)

   The play is memory.

   Being a memory play, it is dimly lighted, it is sentimental, it is
not realistic.

   In memory everything seems to happen to music. That explains
the fiddle in the wings.

   I am the narrator of the play, and also a character in it.

   The other characters are my mother, Amanda, my sister, Laura,
and a gentleman caller who appears in the final scenes.

   He is the most realistic character in the play, being an emissary
from a world of reality that we were somehow set apart from.

---

[2]During the Spanish Civil War the city of Guernica was heavily bombarded by Franco's
forces.

But since I have a poet's weakness for symbols, I am using this character also as a symbol; he is the long delayed but always expected something that we live for.

There is a fifth character in the play who doesn't appear except in this larger-than-life-size photograph over the mantel.

This is our father who left us a long time ago.

He was a telephone man who fell in love with long distances; he gave up his job with the telephone company and skipped the light fantastic out of town . . .

The last we heard of him was a picture post-card from Mazatlan, on the Pacific coast of Mexico, containing a message of two words— "Hello—Good-bye!" and no address.

I think the rest of the play will explain itself. . . .

(AMANDA'S *voice becomes audible through the portieres*)

(LEGEND ON SCREEN: "OÙ SONT LES NEIGES"[3])

(*He divides the portieres and enters the upstage area*)

(AMANDA *and* LAURA *are seated at a drop-leaf table. Eating is indicated by gestures without food or utensils.* AMANDA *faces the audience,* TOM *and* LAURA *are seated in profile. The interior has lit up softly and through the scrim we see* AMANDA *and* LAURA *seated at the table in the upstage area*)

AMANDA (*Calling*) Tom?

TOM Yes, Mother.

AMANDA We can't say grace until you come to the table!

TOM Coming, Mother. (*He bows slightly and withdraws, reappearing a few moments later in his place at the table*)

AMANDA (*To her son*) Honey, don't *push* with your *fingers*. If you have to push with something, the thing to push with is a crust of bread. And chew—chew! Animals have sections in their stomachs which enable them to digest food without mastication, but human beings are supposed to chew their food before they swallow it down. Eat food leisurely, son, and really enjoy it. A well-cooked meal has lots of delicate flavors that have to be held in the mouth for appreciation. So chew your food and give your salivary glands a chance to function!

(TOM *deliberately lays his imaginary fork down and pushes his chair back from the table*)

[3]"Where are the snows [of yesteryear]?" From François Villon's "Ballade of Dead Ladies."

T O M   I haven't enjoyed one bite of this dinner because of your constant directions on how to eat it. It's you that make me rush through meals with your hawk-like attention to every bite I take. Sickening—spoils my appetite—all this discussion of—animals' secretion—salivary glands—mastication!

A M A N D A   (*Lightly*)   Temperament like a Metropolitan star! (*He rises and crosses downstage*)   You're not excused from the table.

T O M   I'm getting a cigarette.

A M A N D A   You smoke too much.

(L A U R A *rises*)

L A U R A   I'll bring in the blanc mange.

(*He remains standing with his cigarette by the portieres during the following*)

A M A N D A   (*Rising*)   No, sister, no, sister—you be the lady this time and I'll be the darky.

L A U R A   I'm already up.

A M A N D A   Resume your seat, little sister—I want you to stay fresh and pretty—for gentlemen callers!

L A U R A   I'm not expecting any gentlemen callers.

A M A N D A   (*Crossing out to kitchenette. Airily*)   Sometimes they come when they are least expected! Why, I remember one Sunday afternoon in Blue Mountain—(*Enters kitchenette*)

T O M   I know what's coming!

L A U R A   Yes. But let her tell it.

T O M   Again?

L A U R A   She loves to tell it.

(A M A N D A *returns with bowl of dessert*)

A M A N D A   One Sunday afternoon in Blue Mountain—your mother received—*seventeen!*—gentlemen callers! Why, sometimes there weren't chairs enough to accommodate them all. We had to send the nigger over to bring in folding chairs from the parish house.

T O M (*Remaining at portieres*)   How did you entertain those gentlemen callers?

A M A N D A   I understood the art of conversation!

T O M   I bet you could talk.

A M A N D A   Girls in those days *knew* how to talk, I can tell you.

T O M   Yes?

(I M A G E : A M A N D A A S A G I R L O N A P O R C H , G R E E T I N G C A L L E R S)

AMANDA They knew how to entertain their gentlemen callers. It wasn't enough for a girl to be possessed of a pretty face and a graceful figure—although I wasn't slighted in either respect. She also needed to have a nimble wit and a tongue to meet all occasions.

TOM What did you talk about?

AMANDA Things of importance going on in the world! Never anything coarse or common or vulgar. (*She addresses* TOM *as though he were seated in the vacant chair at the table though he remains by portieres. He plays this scene as though he held the book*) My callers were gentlemen—all! Among my callers were some of the most prominent young planters of the Mississippi Delta—planters and sons of planters!

(TOM *motions for music and a spot of light on* AMANDA)

(*Her eyes lift, her face glows, her voice becomes rich and elegiac*)

(SCREEN LEGEND: "OU SONT LES NEIGES")

There was young Champ Laughlin who later became vice-president of the Delta Planters Bank.

Hadley Stevenson who was drowned in Moon Lake and left his widow one hundred and fifty thousand in Government bonds.

There were the Cutrere brothers, Wesley and Bates. Bates was one of my bright particular beaux! He got in a quarrel with that wild Wainwright boy. They shot it out on the floor of Moon Lake Casino. Bates was shot through the stomach. Died in the ambulance on his way to Memphis. His widow was also well-provided for, came into eight or ten thousand acres, that's all. She married him on the rebound—never loved her—carried my picture on him the night he died!

And there was that boy that every girl in the Delta had set her cap for! That beautiful, brilliant young Fitzhugh boy from Greene County!

TOM What did he leave his widow?

AMANDA He never married! Gracious, you talk as though all of my old admirers had turned up their toes to the daisies!

TOM Isn't this the first you've mentioned that still survives?

AMANDA That Fitzhugh boy went North and made a fortune—came to be known as the Wolf of Wall Street! He had the Midas touch, whatever he touched turned to gold!

And I could have been Mrs. Duncan J. Fitzhugh, mind you! But —I picked your *father*!

LAURA (*Rising*) Mother, let me clear the table.

AMANDA No, dear, you go in front and study your typewriter chart. Or practice your shorthand a little. Stay fresh and pretty!—It's almost time for our gentlemen callers to start arriving. (*She flounces girlishly toward the kitchenette*) How many do you suppose we're going to entertain this afternoon?

(TOM *throws down the paper and jumps up with a groan*)

LAURA (*Alone in the dining room*) I don't believe we're going to receive any, Mother.

AMANDA (*Reappearing, airily*) What? No one—not one? You must be joking! (LAURA *nervously echoes her laugh. She slips in a fugitive manner through the half-open portieres and draws them gently behind her. A shaft of very clear light is thrown on her face against the faded tapestry of the curtains.* MUSIC: "THE GLASS MENAGERIE" UNDER FAINTLY. *Lightly*) Not one gentlemen caller? It can't be true! There must be a flood, there must have been a tornado!

LAURA It isn't a flood, it's not a tornado, Mother. I'm just not popular like you were in Blue Mountain. . . . (TOM *utters another groan,* LAURA *glances at him with a faint, apologetic smile. Her voice catching a little*) Mother's afraid I'm going to be an old maid.

(*The Scene Dims Out with "Glass Menagerie" Music*)

Scene 2

"Laura, Haven't You Ever Liked Some Boy?"

(*On the dark stage the screen is lighted with the image of blue roses.*

Gradually LAURA'S *figure becomes apparent and the screen goes out.*

The music subsides.

LAURA *is seated in the delicate ivory chair at the small clawfoot table.*

She wears a dress of soft violet material for a kimono—her hair tied back from her forehead with a ribbon.

She is washing and polishing her collection of glass.

AMANDA *appears on the fire-escape steps. At the sound of her ascent,* LAURA *catches her breath, thrusts the bowl of ornaments away and seats herself stiffly before the diagram of the typewriter keyboard as though it held her spellbound.*

Something has happened to AMANDA. *It is written in her face as she climbs to the landing: a look that is grim and hopeless and a little absurd.*

She has on one of those cheap or imitation velvety-looking cloth coats with imitation fur collar. Her hat is five or six years old, one of those dreadful cloche hats that were worn in the late twenties and she is clasping an enormous black patent-leather pocketbook with nickel clasps and initials. This is her full-dress outfit, the one she usually wears to the D.A.R.[4]

Before entering she looks through the door.

She purses her lips, opens her eyes very wide, rolls them upward and shakes her head.

Then she slowly lets herself in the door. Seeing her mother's expression, LAURA *touches her lips with a nervous gesture)*

LAURA   Hello, Mother, I was—(*She makes a nervous gesture toward the chart on the wall.* AMANDA *leans against the shut door and stares at* LAURA *with a martyred look)*

AMANDA   Deception? Deception? (*She slowly removes her hat and gloves, continuing the sweet suffering stare. She lets the hat and gloves fall on the floor—a bit of acting)*

LAURA   (*Shakily*)   How was the D.A.R. meeting? (AMANDA *slowly opens her purse and removes a dainty white handkerchief which she shakes out delicately and delicately touches to her lips and nostrils)* Didn't you go to the D.A.R. meeting, Mother?

AMANDA   (*Faintly, almost inaudibly*)   —No—No. (*Then more forcibly*)   I did not have the strength—to go to the D.A.R. In fact, I did not have the courage! I wanted to find a hole in the ground and hide myself in it forever! (*She crosses slowly to the wall and removes the diagram of the typewriter keyboard. She holds it in front of her for a second, staring at it sweetly and sorrowfully—then bites her lips and tears it in two pieces)*

LAURA   (*Faintly*)   Why did you do that, Mother? (AMANDA *repeats the same procedure with the chart of the Gregg Alphabet)*   Why are you—

AMANDA   Why? Why? How old are you, Laura?

LAURA   Mother, you know my age.

AMANDA   I thought you were an adult; it seems that I was mistaken. (*She crosses slowly to the sofa and sinks down and stares at* LAURA)

LAURA   Please don't stare at me, Mother. (AMANDA *closes her eyes and lowers her head. Count ten)*

AMANDA   What are we going to do, what is going to become of us, what is the future? (*Count ten*)

[4]Daughters of the American Revolution.

LAURA Has something happened, Mother? (AMANDA *draws a long breath and takes out the handkerchief again. Dabbing process*) Mother, has—something happened?

AMANDA I'll be all right in a minute, I'm just bewildered—(*Count five*)—by life. . . .

LAURA Mother, I wish that you would tell me what's happened!

AMANDA As you know, I was supposed to be inducted into my office at the D.A.R. this afternoon. (IMAGE: A SWARM OF TYPEWRITERS) But I stopped off at Rubicam's Business College to speak to your teachers about your having a cold and ask them what progress they thought you were making down there.

LAURA Oh. . . .

AMANDA I went to the typing instructor and introduced myself as your mother. She didn't know who you were. Wingfield, she said. We don't have any such student enrolled at the school!

I assured her she did, that you had been going to classes since early in January.

"I wonder," she said, "if you could be talking about that terribly shy little girl who dropped out of school after only a few days' attendance?"

"No," I said, "Laura, my daughter, has been going to school every day for the past six weeks!"

"Excuse me," she said. She took the attendance book out and there was your name, unmistakably printed, and all the dates you were absent until they decided that you had dropped out of school.

I still said, "No, there must have been some mistake! There must have been some mix-up in the records!"

And she said. "No—I remember her perfectly now. Her hands shook so that she couldn't hit the right keys! The first time we gave a speed-test, she broke down completely—was sick at the stomach and almost had to be carried into the wash-room! After that morning she never showed up any more. We phoned the house but never got any answer"—while I was working at Famous and Barr, I suppose, demonstrating those—Oh!

I felt so weak I could barely keep on my feet!

I had to sit down while they got me a glass of water!

Fifty dollars' tuition, all of our plans—my hopes and ambitions for you—just gone up the spout, just gone up the spout like that.

(LAURA *draws a long breath and gets awkwardly to her feet. She crosses to the victrola and winds it up*)

What are you doing?

LAURA   Oh! (*She releases the handle and returns to her seat*)

AMANDA   Laura, where have you been going when you've gone out pretending that you were going to business college?

LAURA   I've just been going out walking.

AMANDA   That's not true.

LAURA   It is. I just went walking.

AMANDA   Walking? Walking? In winter? Deliberately courting pneumonia in that light coat? Where did you walk to, Laura?

LAURA   All sorts of places—mostly in the park.

AMANDA   Even after you'd started catching that cold?

LAURA   It was the lesser of two evils, Mother. (IMAGE: WINTER SCENE IN PARK)   I couldn't go back up. I—threw up—on the floor!

AMANDA   From half past seven till after five every day you mean to tell me you walked around in the park, because you wanted to make me think that you were still going to Rubicam's Business College?

LAURA   It wasn't as bad as it sounds. I went inside places to get warmed up.

AMANDA   Inside where?

LAURA   I went in the art museum and the bird-houses at the Zoo. I visited the penguins every day! Sometimes I did without lunch and went to the movies. Lately I've been spending most of my afternoons in the Jewel-box, that big glass house where they raise the tropical flowers.

AMANDA   You did all this to deceive me, just for deception? (LAURA *looks down*)   Why?

LAURA   Mother, when you're disappointed, you get that awful suffering look on your face, like the picture of Jesus' mother in the museum!

AMANDA   Hush!

LAURA   I couldn't face it.

(*Pause. A whisper of strings*)

(LEGEND: "THE CRUST OF HUMILITY")

AMANDA (*Hopelessly fingering the huge pocketbook*)   So what are we going to do the rest of our lives? Stay home and watch the parades go by? Amuse ourselves with the glass menagerie, darling? Eternally play those worn-out phonograph records your father left as a painful reminder of him?

We won't have a business career—we've given that up because it gave us nervous indigestion! (*Laughs wearily*)   What is there left but dependency all our lives? I know so well what becomes of unmarried women who aren't prepared to occupy a position. I've seen such pitiful cases in the South—barely tolerated spinsters living upon the grudging patronage of sister's husband or brother's wife!—stuck away in some little mouse-trap of a room—encouraged by one in-law to visit another —little birdlike women without any nest—eating the crust of humility all their life!

Is that the future that we've mapped out for ourselves?

I swear it's the only alternative I can think of!

It isn't a very pleasant alternative, is it?

Of course—some girls do *marry*.

(LAURA *twists her hands nervously*)

Haven't you ever liked some boy?

LAURA Yes, I liked one once. (*Rises*) I came across his picture a while ago.

AMANDA (*With some interest*) He gave you his picture?

LAURA No, it's in the year-book.

AMANDA (*Disappointed*) Oh—a high-school boy.

(SCREEN IMAGE: JIM AS HIGH-SCHOOL HERO BEARING A SILVER CUP)

LAURA Yes. His name was Jim. (LAURA *lifts the heavy annual from the claw-foot table*) Here he is in *The Pirates of Penzance*.

AMANDA (*Absently*) The what?

LAURA The operetta the senior class put on. He had a wonderful voice and we sat across the aisle from each other Mondays, Wednesdays, and Fridays in the Aud. Here he is with the silver cup for debating! See his grin?

AMANDA (*Absently*) He must have had a jolly disposition.

LAURA He used to call me—Blue Roses.

(SCREEN IMAGE: BLUE ROSES)

AMANDA Why did he call you such a name as that?

LAURA When I had that attack of pleurosis—he asked me what was the matter when I came back. I said pleurosis—he thought that I said Blue Roses! So that's what he always called me after that. Whenever he saw me, he'd holler, "Hello, Blue Roses!" I didn't care for the girl that he went out with. Emily Meisenbach. Emily was the best-dressed girl at Soldan. She never struck me, though, as being sincere. . . . It says in the Personal Section—they're engaged. That's—six years ago! They must be married by now.

AMANDA Girls that aren't cut out for business careers usually wind up married to some nice man. (*Gets up with a spark of revival*) Sister, that's what you'll do!

(LAURA *utters a startled, doubtful laugh. She reaches quickly for a piece of glass*)

LAURA But, Mother—
AMANDA Yes? (*Crossing to photograph*)
LAURA (*In a tone of frightened apology*) I'm—crippled!

(IMAGE: SCREEN)

AMANDA Nonsense! Laura, I've told you never, never to use that word. Why, you're not crippled, you just have a little defect—hardly noticeable, even! When people have some slight disadvantage like that, they cultivate other things to make up for it—develop charm—and vivacity—and—*charm*! That's all you have to do! (*She turns again to the photograph*)
One thing your father had *plenty of*—was *charm*!

(TOM *motions to the fiddle in the wings*)

(*The Scene Fades Out with Music*)

Scene 3

LEGEND ON SCREEN: "AFTER THE FIASCO—"

(TOM *speaks from the fire-escape landing*)

TOM After the fiasco at Rubicam's Business College, the idea of getting a gentleman caller for Laura began to play a more and more important part in Mother's calculations.
It became an obsession. Like some archetype of the universal unconscious, the image of the gentleman caller haunted our small apartment. . . .

(IMAGE: YOUNG MAN AT DOOR WITH FLOWERS)

An evening at home rarely passed without some allusion to this image, this specter, this hope. . . .
Even when he wasn't mentioned, his presence hung in Mother's preoccupied look and in my sister's frightened, apologetic manner—hung like a sentence passed upon the Wingfields!
Mother was a woman of action as well as words.

She began to take logical steps in the planned direction.

Late that winter and in the early spring—realizing that extra money would be needed to properly feather the nest and plume the bird—she conducted a vigorous campaign on the telephone, roping in subscribers to one of those magazines for matrons called *The Homemaker's Companion*, the type of journal that features the serialized sublimations of ladies of letters who think in terms of delicate cuplike breasts, slim, tapering waists, rich, creamy thighs, eyes like wood-smoke in autumn, fingers that soothe and caress like strains of music, bodies as powerful as Etruscan sculpture.

(SCREEN IMAGE: GLAMOR MAGAZINE COVER)

(AMANDA *enters with phone on long extension cord. She is spotted in the dim stage*)

AMANDA   Ida Scott? This is Amanda Wingfield!

We *missed* you at the D.A.R. last Monday!

I said to myself: She's probably suffering with that sinus condition! How is that sinus condition?

Horrors! Heaven have mercy!

—You're a Christian martyr, yes, that's what you are, a Christian martyr!

Well, I just now happened to notice that your subscription to the *Companion's* about to expire! Yes, it expires with the next issue, honey! —just when that wonderful new serial by Bessie Mae Hopper is getting off to such an exciting start. Oh, honey, it's something that you can't miss! You remember how *Gone With the Wind* took everybody by storm? You simply couldn't go out if you hadn't read it. All everybody *talked* about was Scarlett O'Hara. Well, this is a book that critics already compare to *Gone With the Wind*. It's the *Gone With the Wind* of the post-World War generation!—What?—Burning?—Oh, honey, don't let them burn, go take a look in the oven and I'll hold the wire! Heavens —I think she's hung up!

DIM OUT

(LEGEND ON SCREEN: "YOU THINK I'M IN LOVE WITH CONTINENTAL SHOEMAKERS?")

(*Before the stage is lighted, the violent voices of* TOM *and* AMANDA *are heard*)

(*They are quarreling behind the portieres. In front of them stands* LAURA *with clenched hands and panicky expression*)

(*A clear pool of light on her figure throughout this scene*)

TOM   What in Christ's name am I—

AMANDA (*Shrilly*)   Don't you use that—

TOM   Supposed to do!

AMANDA   Expression! Not in my—

TOM   Ohhh!

AMANDA   Presence! Have you gone out of your senses?

TOM   I have, that's true, *driven* out!

AMANDA   What is the matter with you, you—big—big—*idiot!*

TOM   Look!—I've got no *thing*, no single thing—

AMANDA   Lower your voice!

TOM   In my life here that I can call my *own!* Everything is—

AMANDA   Stop that shouting!

TOM   Yesterday you confiscated my books! You had the nerve to—

AMANDA   I took that horrible novel back to the library—yes! That hideous book by that insane Mr. Lawrence.[5] (TOM *laughs wildly*) I cannot control the output of diseased minds or people who cater to them—(TOM *laughs still more wildly*) BUT I WON'T ALLOW SUCH FILTH BROUGHT INTO MY HOUSE! No, no, no, no, no!

TOM   House, house! Who pays rent on it, who makes a slave of himself to—

AMANDA (*Fairly screeching*)   Don't you DARE to—

TOM   No, no I mustn't say things! *I've* got to just—

AMANDA   Let me tell you—

TOM   I don't want to hear any more! (*He tears the portieres open. The upstage area is lit with a turgid smoky red glow*)

(AMANDA'S *hair is in metal curlers and she wears a very old bathrobe, much too large for her slight figure, a relic of the faithless Mr. Wingfield. An upright typewriter and a wild disarray of manuscripts is on the drop-leaf table. The quarrel was probably precipitated by* AMANDA'S *interruption of his creative labor. A chair lying overthrown on the floor. Their gesticulating shadows are cast on the ceiling by the fiery glow*)

AMANDA   You *will* hear more, you—

TOM   No, I won't hear more, I'm going out!

AMANDA   You come right back in—

TOM   Out, out, out! Because I'm—

[5]D.H. Lawrence (1885–1930), English novelist, author of *Lady Chatterley's Lover*, and other novels.

AMANDA   Come back here, Tom Wingfield! I'm not through talking to you!

TOM   Oh, go—

LAURA (*Desperately*)   —Tom!

AMANDA   You're going to listen, and no more insolence from you! I'm at the end of my patience!

(*He comes back toward her*)

TOM   What do you think I'm at? Aren't I supposed to have any patience to reach the end of, Mother? I know, I know. It seems unimportant to you, what I'm *doing*—what I *want* to do—having a little *difference* between them! You don't think that—

AMANDA   I think you've been doing things that you're ashamed of. That's why you act like this. I don't believe that you go every night to the movies. Nobody goes to the movies night after night. Nobody in their right minds goes to the movies as often as you pretend to. People don't go to the movies at nearly midnight, and movies don't let out at two A.M. Coming in stumbling. Muttering to yourself like a maniac! You get three hours' sleep and then go to work. Oh, I can picture the way you're doing down there. Moping, doping, because you're in no condition!

TOM (*Wildly*)   No, I'm in no condition!

AMANDA   What right have you got to jeopardize your job? Jeopardize the security of us all? How do you think we'd manage if you were —

TOM   Listen! You think I'm crazy *about the warehouse*? (*He bends fiercely toward her slight figure*)   You think I'm in love with the Continental Shoemakers? You think I want to spend fifty-five *years* down there in that—*celotex interior!* with—*fluorescent—tubes!* Look! I'd rather somebody picked up a crowbar and battered out my brains— than go back mornings! I *go!* Every time you come in yelling that God damn "*Rise and Shine!*" "*Rise and Shine!*" I say to myself, "How *lucky dead* people are!" But I get up. I *go!* For sixty-five dollars a month I give up all that I dream of doing and being *ever!* And you say self—*self's* all I ever think of. Why, listen, if self is what I thought of, Mother, I'd be where he is—GONE! (*Pointing to father's picture*) As far as the system of transportation reaches! (*He starts past her. She grabs his arm*)   Don't grab at me, Mother!

AMANDA   Where are you going?

TOM   I'm going to the *movies!*

AMANDA   I don't believe that lie!

TOM (*Crouching toward her, overtowering her tiny figure. She backs away, gasping*) I'm going to opium dens! Yes, opium dens, dens of vice and criminals' hang-outs, Mother. I've joined the Hogan gang. I'm a hired assassin, I carry a tommy-gun in a violin case! I run a string of cat-houses in the Valley! They call me Killer, Killer Wingfield, I'm leading a double-life, a simple, honest warehouse worker by day, by night a dynamic *czar* of the *underworld, Mother.* I go to gambling casinos, I spin away fortunes on the roulette table! I wear a patch over one eye and a false mustache, sometimes I put on green whiskers. On those occasions they call me—*El Diablo!* Oh, I could tell you things to make you sleepless! My enemies plan to dynamite this place. They're going to blow us all sky-high some night! I'll be glad, very happy, and so will you! You'll go up, up on a broom-stick, over Blue Mountain with seventeen gentlemen callers! You ugly —babbling old—*witch.* . . . (*He goes through a series of violent, clumsy movements, seizing his overcoat, lunging to the door, pulling it fiercely open. The women watch him, aghast. His arm catches in the sleeve of the coat as he struggles to pull it on. For a moment he is pinioned by the bulky garment. With an outraged groan he tears the coat off again, splitting the shoulder of it, and hurls it across the room. It strikes against the shelf of* LAURA'S *glass collection, there is a tinkle of shattering glass.* LAURA *cries out as if wounded*)

(MUSIC. LEGEND: "THE GLASS MENAGERIE")

LAURA (*Shrilly*) My glass!—menagerie. . . . (*She covers her face and turns away*)

(*But* AMANDA *is still stunned and stupefied by the "ugly witch" so that she barely notices this occurrence. Now she recovers her speech*)

AMANDA (*In an awful voice*) I won't speak to you—until you apolo-gize! (*She crosses through portieres and draws them together behind her.* TOM *is left with* LAURA. LAURA *clings weakly to the mantel with her face averted.* TOM *stares at her stupidly for a moment. Then he crosses to shelf. Drops awkwardly on his knees to collect the fallen glass, glancing at* LAURA *as if he would speak but couldn't*)

("*The Glass Menagerie" Steals in as the Scene Dims Out*)

Scene 4

(The interior is dark. Faint light in the alley.

A deep-voiced bell in a church is tolling the hour of five as the scene commences.

TOM *appears at the top of the alley. After each solemn boom of the bell in the tower, he shakes a little noise-maker or rattle as if to express the tiny spasm of man in contrast to the sustained power and dignity of the Almighty. This and the unsteadiness of his advance make it evident that he has been drinking.*

As he climbs the few steps to the fire-escape landing light steals up inside. LAURA *appears in nightdress, observing* TOM'S *empty bed in the front room.*

TOM *fishes in his pockets for door key, removing a motley assortment of articles in the search, including a perfect shower of movie-ticket stubs and an empty bottle. At last he finds the key, but just as he is about to insert it, it slips from his fingers. He strikes a match and crouches below the door)*

TOM *(Bitterly)*   One crack—and it falls through!

(LAURA *opens the door)*

LAURA   Tom, Tom, what are you doing?

TOM   Looking for a door key.

LAURA   Where have you been all this time?

TOM   I have been to the movies.

LAURA   All this time at the movies?

TOM   There was a very long program. There was a Garbo picture and a Mickey Mouse and a travelogue and a newsreel and a preview of coming attractions. And there was an organ solo and a collection for the milk-fund—simultaneously—which ended up in a terrible fight between a fat lady and an usher!

LAURA *(Innocently)*   Did you have to stay through everything?

TOM   Of course! And, oh, I forgot! There was a big stage show! The headliner on this stage show was Malvolio the Magician. He performed wonderful tricks, many of them, such as pouring water back and forth between pitchers. First it turned to wine and then it turned to beer and then it turned to whiskey. I know it was whiskey it finally turned into because he needed somebody to come up out of the audience to help him, and I came up—both shows! It was Kentucky Straight Bourbon. A very generous fellow, he gave souvenirs. (*He pulls from his back pocket a shimmering rainbow-colored scarf*) He gave me this. This is his magic scarf. You can have it, Laura. You wave it over a canary cage and you get a bowl of gold-fish. You wave it over the gold-fish bowl and they fly away canaries. . . . But the wonderfullest trick of all was the coffin trick. We nailed him into a coffin and he got out of the coffin without removing one nail. (*He has come inside*) There is a trick that would come in handy for me—get me out of this 2 by 4 situation! (*Flops onto bed and starts removing shoes*)

L A U R A   Tom—Shhh!

T O M   What're you shushing me for?

L A U R A   You'll wake up Mother.

T O M   Goody, goody! Pay 'er back for all those "Rise an' Shines." (*Lies down, groaning*)   You know it don't take much intelligence to get yourself into a nailed-up coffin, Laura. But who in hell ever got himself out of one without removing one nail?

(*As if in answer, the father's grinning photograph lights up*)

SCENE DIMS OUT

(*Immediately following: The church bell is heard striking six. At the sixth stroke the alarm clock goes off in* A M A N D A ' S *room, and after a few moments we hear her calling: "Rise and Shine! Rise and Shine! Laura, go tell your brother to rise and shine!"*)

T O M (*Sitting up slowly*)   I'll rise—but I won't shine.

(*The light increases*)

A M A N D A   Laura, tell your brother his coffee is ready.

(L A U R A *slips into front room*)

L A U R A   Tom!—It's nearly seven. Don't make Mother nervous. (*He stares at her stupidly. Beseechingly*)   Tom, speak to Mother this morning. Make up with her, apologize, speak to her!

T O M   She won't to me. It's her that started not speaking.

L A U R A   If you just say you're sorry she'll start speaking.

T O M   Her not speaking—is that such a tragedy?

L A U R A   Please—please!

A M A N D A (*Calling from kitchenette*)   Laura, are you going to do what I asked you to do, or do I have to get dressed and go out myself?

L A U R A   Going, going—soon as I get on my coat! (*She pulls on a shapeless felt hat with nervous, jerky movement, pleadingly glancing at* T O M.

Rushes awkwardly for coat. The coat is one of AMANDA'S, *inaccurately made-over, the sleeves too short for* LAURA) Butter and what else?

AMANDA (*Entering upstage*) Just butter. Tell them to charge it.

LAURA Mother, they make such faces when I do that.

AMANDA Sticks and stones can break our bones, but the expression on Mr. Garfinkel's face won't harm us! Tell your brother his coffee is getting cold.

LAURA (*At door*) Do what I asked you, will you, will you, Tom?

(*He looks sullenly away*)

AMANDA Laura, go now or just don't go at all!

LAURA (*Rushing out*) Going—going! (*A second later she cries out.* TOM *springs up and crosses to door.* AMANDA *rushes anxiously in.* TOM *opens the door*)

TOM Laura?

LAURA I'm all right. I slipped, but I'm all right.

AMANDA (*Peering anxiously after her*) If anyone breaks a leg on those fire-escape steps, the landlord ought to be sued for every cent he possesses! (*She shuts door. Remembers she isn't speaking and returns to other room*)

(*As* TOM *enters listlessly for his coffee, she turns her back to him and stands rigidly facing the window on the gloomy gray vault of the areaway. Its light on her face with its aged but childish features is cruelly sharp, satirical as a Daumier print[6]*)

(MUSIC UNDER: "AVE MARIE")

(TOM *glances sheepishly but sullenly at her averted figure and slumps at the table. The coffee is scalding hot; he sips it and gasps and spits it back in the cup. At his gasp,* AMANDA *catches her breath and half turns. Then catches herself and turns back to window*)

(TOM *blows on his coffee, glancing sidewise at his mother. She clears her throat.* TOM *clears his. He starts to rise. Sinks back down again, scratches his head, clears his throat again.* AMANDA *coughs.* TOM *raises his cup in both hands to blow on it, his eyes staring over the rim of it at his mother for several moments. Then he slowly sets the cup down and awkwardly and hesitantly rises from the chair*)

TOM (*Hoarsely*) Mother. I—I apologize, Mother. (AMANDA *draws a*

---

[6]Honoré Daumier (1808–1879), French painter and caricaturist.

quick, shuddering breath. Her face works grotesquely. She breaks into childlike tears) I'm sorry for what I said, for everything that I said, I didn't mean it.

AMANDA *(Sobbingly)* My devotion has made me a witch and so I make myself hateful to my children!

TOM No, you *don't.*

AMANDA I worry so much, don't sleep, it makes me nervous!

TOM *(Gently)* I understand that.

AMANDA I've had to put up a solitary battle all these years. But you're my right-hand bower! Don't fall down, don't fail!

TOM *(Gently)* I try, Mother.

AMANDA *(With great enthusiasm)* Try and you will SUCCEED! *(The notion makes her breathless)* Why, you—you're just *full* of natural endowments! Both my children—they're *unusual* children! Don't you think I know it? I'm so—*proud!* Happy and—feel I've—so much to be thankful for but—Promise me one thing, Son!

TOM What, Mother?

AMANDA Promise, Son, you'll—never be a drunkard!

TOM *(Turns to her grinning)* I will never be a drunkard, Mother.

AMANDA That's what frightened me so, that you'd be drinking! Eat a bowl of Purina!

TOM Just coffee, Mother.

AMANDA Shredded wheat biscuit?

TOM No. No, Mother, just coffee.

AMANDA You can't put in a day's work on an empty stomach. You've got ten minutes—don't gulp! Drinking too-hot liquids makes cancer of the stomach. . . . Put cream in.

TOM No, thank you.

AMANDA To cool it.

TOM No! No, thank you, I want it black.

AMANDA I know, but it's not good for you. We have to do all that we can to build ourselves up. In these trying times we live in, all that we have to cling to is—each other. . . . That's why it's so important to—Tom, I—I sent out your sister so I could discuss something with you. If you hadn't spoken I would have spoken to you. *(Sits down)*

TOM *(Gently)* What is it, Mother, that you want to discuss?

AMANDA *Laura!*

(TOM *puts his cup down slowly)*

(LEGEND ON SCREEN: "LAURA")

(MUSIC: "THE GLASS MENAGERIE")

TOM —Oh—Laura . . .

AMANDA (*Touching his sleeve*)   You know how Laura is. So quiet but —still water runs deep! She notices things and I think she—broods about them. (TOM *looks up*)   A few days ago I came in and she was crying.

TOM   What about?

AMANDA   You.

TOM   Me?

AMANDA   She has an idea that you're not happy here.

TOM   What gave her that idea?

AMANDA   What gives her any idea? However, you do act strangely. I—I'm not criticizing, understand *that!* I know your ambitions do not lie in the warehouse, that like everybody in the whole wide world —you've had to—make sacrifices, but—Tom—Tom—life's not easy, it calls for—Spartan endurance! There's so many things in my heart that I cannot describe to you! I've never told you but I—*loved* your father. . . .

TOM (*Gently*)   I know that, Mother.

AMANDA   And you—when I see you taking after his ways! Staying out late—and—well, you *had* been drinking the night you were in that —terrifying condition! Laura says that you hate the apartment and that you go out nights to get away from it! Is that true, Tom?

TOM   No. You say there's so much in your heart that you can't describe to me. That's true of me, too. There's so much in my heart that I can't describe to *you!* So let's respect each other's—

AMANDA   But, why—*why*, Tom—are you always so *restless?* Where do you *go* to, nights?

TOM   I—go to the movies.

AMANDA   Why do you go to the movies so much, Tom?

TOM   I go to the movies because—I like adventure. Adventure is something I don't have much of at work, so I go to the movies.

AMANDA   But, Tom, you go the movies *entirely* too *much!*

TOM   I like a lot of adventure.

(AMANDA *looks baffled, then hurt. As the familiar inquisition resumes he becomes hard and impatient again.* AMANDA *slips back into her querulous attitude toward him*)

(IMAGE ON SCREEN: SAILING VESSEL WITH JOLLY ROGER)

AMANDA   Most young men find adventure in their careers.

TOM   Then most young men are not employed in a warehouse.

AMANDA   The world is full of young men employed in warehouses and offices and factories.

TOM   Do all of them find adventure in their careers?

AMANDA   They do or they do without it! Not everybody has a craze for adventure.

TOM   Man is by instinct a lover, a hunter, a fighter, and none of those instincts are given much play at the warehouse!

AMANDA   Man is by instinct! Don't quote instinct to me! Instinct is something that people have got away from! It belongs to animals! Christian adults don't want it!

TOM   What do Christian adults want, then, Mother?

AMANDA   Superior things! Things of the mind and the spirit! Only animals have to satisfy instincts! Surely your aims are somewhat higher than theirs! Than monkeys—pigs—

TOM   I reckon they're not.

AMANDA   You're joking! However, that isn't what I wanted to discuss.

TOM (*Rising*)   I haven't much time.

AMANDA (*Pushing his shoulders*)   Sit down.

TOM   You want me to punch in red at the warehouse, Mother?

AMANDA   You have five minutes. I want to talk about Laura.

(LEGEND: "PLANS AND PROVISIONS")

TOM   All right! What about Laura?

AMANDA   We have to be making some plans and provisions for her. She's older than you, two years, and nothing has happened. She just drifts along doing nothing. It frightens me terribly how she just drifts along.

TOM   I guess she's the type that people call home girls.

AMANDA   There's no such type, and if there is, it's a pity! That is, unless the home is hers, with a husband!

TOM   What?

AMANDA   Oh, I can see the handwriting on the wall as plain as I see the nose in front of my face! It's terrifying!

More and more you remind me of your father! He was out all hours without explanation!—Then *left! Good-bye!*

And me with the bag to hold. I saw that letter you got from the Merchant Marine. I know what you're dreaming of. I'm not standing here blindfolded.

Very well, then. Then *do* it!

But not till there's somebody to take your place.

TOM   What do you mean?

AMANDA   I mean that as soon as Laura has got somebody to take care of her, married, a home of her own, independent—why, then you'll be free to go wherever you please, on land, on sea, whichever way the wind blows you!

But until that time you've got to look out for your sister. I don't say me because I'm old and don't matter! I say for your sister because she's young and dependent.

I put her in business college—a dismal failure! Frightened her so it made her sick at the stomach.

I took her over to the Young People's League at the church. Another fiasco. She spoke to nobody, nobody spoke to her. Now all she does is fool with those pieces of glass and play those worn-out records. What kind of a life is that for a girl to lead?

T O M   What can I do about it?

A M A N D A   Overcome selfishness!

Self, self, self is all that you ever think of!

(T O M *springs up and crosses to get his coat. It is ugly and bulky. He pulls on a cap with earmuffs*)

Where is your muffler? Put your wool muffler on!

(*He snatches it angrily from the closet and tosses it around his neck and pulls both ends tight*)

Tom! I haven't said what I had in mind to ask you.

T O M   I'm too late to—

A M A N D A (*Catching his arm—very importunately. Then shyly*)   Down at the warehouse, aren't there some—nice young men?

T O M   No!

A M A N D A   There *must* be—*some* . . .

T O M   Mother—(*Gesture*)

A M A N D A   Find out one that's clean-living—doesn't drink and—ask him out for sister!

T O M   What?

A M A N D A   For *sister!* To *meet!* Get *acquainted!*

T O M (*Stamping to door*)   Oh, my *go-osh!*

A M A N D A   Will you? (*He opens door. Imploringly*)   Will you? (*He starts down*)   Will you? *Will* you, dear?

T O M (*Calling back*)   YES!

(A M A N D A *closes the door hesitantly and with a troubled but faintly hopeful expression*)

(SCREEN IMAGE: GLAMOR MAGAZINE COVER)

(*Spot* A M A N D A *at phone*)

A M A N D A   Ella Cartwright? This is Amanda Wingfield! How are you, honey?

How is that kidney condition? (*Pause*)

Horrors! (*Pause*)

You're a Christian martyr, yes, honey, that's what you are, a Christian martyr!

Well, I just now happened to notice in my little red book that your subscription to the *Companion* has just run out! I knew that you wouldn't want to miss out on the wonderful serial starting in this new issue. It's by Bessie Mae Hopper, the first thing she's written since *Honeymoon for Three*.

Wasn't that a strange and interesting story? Well, this one is even lovelier, I believe. It has a sophisticated, society background. It's all about the horsey set on Long Island!

Scene 5

(LEGEND ON SCREEN: "ANNUNCIATION." *Fade with music.*

It is early dusk of a spring evening. Supper has just been finished in the Wingfield apartment. AMANDA *and* LAURA *in light-colored dresses are removing dishes from the table, in the upstage area, which is shadowy, their movements formalized almost as a dance or ritual, their moving forms as pale and silent as moths.*

TOM, *in white shirt and trousers, rises from the table and crosses toward the fire-escape.*)

AMANDA (*As he passes her*)   Son, will you do me a favor?

TOM   What?

AMANDA   Comb your hair! You look so pretty when your hair is combed! (TOM *slouches on sofa with evening paper. Enormous caption "Franco Triumphs"*)   There is only one respect in which I would like you to emulate your father.

TOM   What respect is that?

AMANDA   The care he always took of his appearance. He never allowed himself to look untidy. (*He throws down the paper and crosses to fire-escape*)   Where are you going?

TOM   I'm going out to smoke.

AMANDA   You smoke too much. A pack a day at fifteen cents a pack. How much would that amount to in a month? Thirty times fifteen is how much, Tom? Figure it out and you will be astounded at what you could save. Enough to give you a night-school course in accounting at Washington U! Just think what a wonderful thing that would be for you, Son!

(TOM *is unmoved by the thought*)

TOM   I'd rather smoke. (*He steps out on landing, letting the screen door slam*)

AMANDA (*Sharply*)   I know! That's the tragedy of it. . . . (*Alone, she turns to look at her husband's picture*)

(DANCE MUSIC: "ALL THE WORLD IS WAITING FOR THE SUN-RISE!")

TOM (*To the audience*)   Across the alley from us was the Paradise Dance Hall. On evenings in spring the windows and doors were open and the music came outdoors. Sometimes the lights were turned out except for a large glass sphere that hung from the ceiling. It would turn slowly about and filter the dusk with delicate rainbow colors. Then the orchestra played a waltz or a tango, something that had a slow and sensuous rhythm. Couples would come outside, to the relative privacy of the alley. You could see them kissing behind ash-pits and telephone poles.

This was the compensation for lives that passed like mine, without any change or adventure.

Adventure and change were imminent in this year. They were waiting around the corner for all these kids.

Suspended in the mist over Berchtesgaden,[7] caught in the folds of Chamberlain's umbrella—[8]

In Spain there was Guernica!

But here there was only hot swing music and liquor, dance halls, bars, and movies, and sex that hung in the gloom like a chandelier and flooded the world with brief, deceptive rainbows. . . .

All the world was waiting for bombardments!

(AMANDA *turns from the picture and comes outside*)

AMANDA (*Sighing*)   A fire escape landing's a poor excuse for a porch. (*She spreads a newspaper on a step and sits down, gracefully and demurely as if she were settling into a swing on a Mississippi veranda*) What are you looking at?

TOM   The moon.

---

[7]Adolf Hitler's retreat in the Bavarian Mountains.
[8]Neville Chamberlain, England's Prime Minister before World War II, made several efforts to appease Hitler—an appeasement that came to be symbolized by the umbrella he always carried with him.

AMANDA   Is there a moon this evening?

TOM   It's rising over Garfinkel's Delicatessen.

AMANDA   So it is! A little silver slipper of a moon. Have you made a wish on it yet?

TOM   Um-hum.

AMANDA   What did you wish for?

TOM   That's a secret.

AMANDA   A secret, huh? Well, I won't tell mine either. I will be just as mysterious as you.

TOM   I bet I can guess what yours is.

AMANDA   Is my head so transparent?

TOM   You're not a sphinx.

AMANDA   No, I don't have secrets. I'll tell you what I wished for on the moon. Success and happiness for my precious children! I wish for that whenever there's a moon, and when there isn't a moon, I wish for it, too.

TOM   I thought perhaps you wished for a gentleman caller.

AMANDA   Why do you say that?

TOM   Don't you remember asking me to fetch one?

AMANDA   I remember suggesting that it would be nice for your sister if you brought home some nice young man from the warehouse. I think that I've made that suggestion more than once.

TOM   Yes, you have made it repeatedly.

AMANDA   Well?

TOM   We are going to have one.

AMANDA   *What?*

TOM   A gentleman caller!

(THE ANNUNCIATION IS CELEBRATED WITH MUSIC)

(AMANDA *rises*)

(IMAGE ON SCREEN: CALLER WITH BOUQUET)

AMANDA   You mean you have asked some nice young man to come over?

TOM   Yep, I've asked him to dinner.

AMANDA   You really did?

TOM   I did!

AMANDA   You did, and did he—*accept?*

TOM   He did!

AMANDA   Well, well—well, well! That's—lovely!

TOM   I thought that you would be pleased.

AMANDA   It's definite, then?

TOM   Very definite.

AMANDA   Soon?

TOM   Very soon.

AMANDA   For heaven's sake, stop putting on and tell me some things, will you?

TOM   What things do you want me to tell you?

AMANDA   *Naturally* I would like to know when he's *coming!*

TOM   He's coming tomorrow.

AMANDA   *Tomorrow?*

TOM   Yep. Tomorrow.

AMANDA   But, Tom!

TOM   Yes, Mother?

AMANDA   Tomorrow gives me no time!

TOM   Time for what?

AMANDA   Preparations! Why didn't you phone me at once, as soon as you asked him, the minute that he accepted? Then, don't you see, I could have been getting ready!

TOM   You don't have to make any fuss.

AMANDA   Oh, Tom, Tom, Tom, of course I have to make a fuss! I want things nice, not sloppy! Not thrown together. I'll certainly have to do some fast thinking, won't I?

TOM   I don't see why you have to think at all.

AMANDA   You just don't know. We can't have a gentleman caller in a pig-sty! All my wedding silver has to be polished, the monogrammed table linen ought to be laundered! The windows have to be washed and fresh curtains put up. And how about clothes? We have to *wear* something, don't we?

TOM   Mother, this boy is no one to make a fuss over!

AMANDA   Do you realize he's the first young man we've introduced to your sister?

It's terrible, dreadful, disgraceful that poor little sister has never received a single gentleman caller! Tom, come inside! (*She opens the screen door*)

TOM   What for?

AMANDA   I want to ask you some things.

TOM   If you're going to make such a fuss, I'll call it off, I'll tell him not to come!

AMANDA   You certainly won't do anything of the kind. Nothing offends people worse than broken engagements. It simply means I'll have to work like a Turk! We won't be brilliant, but we will pass inspection. Come on inside. (TOM *follows, groaning*) Sit down.

TOM   Any particular place you would like me to sit?

AMANDA   Thank heavens I've got that new sofa! I'm also making payments on a floor lamp I'll have sent out! And put the chintz covers on, they'll brighten things up! Of course I'd hoped to have these walls repapered. . . . What is the young man's name?

TOM   His name is O'Connor.

AMANDA   That, of course, means fish—tomorrow is Friday! I'll have that salmon loaf—with Durkee's dressing! What does he do? He works at the warehouse?

TOM   Of course! How else would I—

AMANDA   Tom, he—doesn't drink?

TOM   Why do you ask me that?

AMANDA   Your father *did!*

TOM   Don't get started on that!

AMANDA   He *does* drink, then?

TOM   Not that I know of!

AMANDA   Make sure, be certain! The last thing I want for my daughter's a boy who drinks!

TOM   Aren't you being a little bit premature? Mr. O'Connor has not yet appeared on the scene!

AMANDA   But will tomorrow. To meet your sister, and what do I know about his character? Nothing! Old maids are better off than wives of drunkards!

TOM   Oh, my God!

AMANDA   Be still!

TOM   (*Leaning forward to whisper*) Lots of fellows meet girls whom they don't marry!

AMANDA   Oh, talk sensibly, Tom—and don't be sarcastic! (*She has gotten a hairbrush*)

TOM   What are you doing?

AMANDA   I'm brushing that cow-lick down!
　　　What is this young man's position at the warehouse?

TOM   (*Submitting grimly to the brush and the interrogation*) This young man's position is that of a shipping clerk, Mother.

AMANDA   Sounds to me like a fairly responsible job, the sort of job *you* would be in if you just had more *get-up.*
　　　What is his salary? Have you any idea?

TOM   I would judge it to be approximately eighty-five dollars a month.

AMANDA   Well—not princely, but—

TOM   Twenty more than I make.

AMANDA   Yes, how well I know! But for a family man, eighty-five dollars a month is not much more than you can just get by on. . . .

TOM   Yes, but Mr. O'Connor is not a family man.

AMANDA He might be, mightn't he? Some time in the future?

TOM I see. Plans and provisions.

AMANDA You are the only young man that I know of who ignores the fact that the future becomes the present, the present the past, and the past turns into everlasting regret if you don't plan for it!

TOM I will think that over and see what I can make of it.

AMANDA Don't be supercilious with your mother! Tell me some more about this—what do you call him?

TOM James D. O'Connor. The D. is for Delaney.

AMANDA Irish on *both* sides! *Gracious!* And doesn't drink?

TOM Shall I call him up and ask him right this minute?

AMANDA The only way to find out about those things is to make discreet inquiries at the proper moment. When I was a girl in Blue Mountain and it was suspected that a young man drank, the girl whose attentions he had been receiving, if any girl *was*, would sometimes speak to the minister of his church, or rather her father would if her father was living, and sort of feel him out on the young man's character. That is the way such things are discreetly handled to keep a young woman from making a tragic mistake!

TOM Then how did you happen to make a tragic mistake?

AMANDA That innocent look of your father's had everyone fooled!

He *smiled*—the world was *enchanted!*

No girl can do worse than put herself at the mercy of a handsome appearance!

I hope that Mr. O'Connor is not too good-looking.

TOM No, he's not too good-looking. He's covered with freckles and hasn't too much of a nose.

AMANDA He's not right-down homely, though?

TOM Not right-down homely. Just medium homely, I'd say.

AMANDA Character's what to look for in a man.

TOM That's what I've always said, Mother.

AMANDA You've never said anything of the kind and I suspect you would never give it a thought.

TOM Don't be so suspicious of me.

AMANDA At least I hope he's the type that's up and coming.

TOM I think he really goes in for self-improvement.

AMANDA What reason have you to think so?

TOM He goes to night school.

AMANDA (*Beaming*) Splendid! What does he do, I mean study?

TOM Radio engineering and public speaking!

AMANDA Then he has visions of being advanced in the world!

Any young man who studies public speaking is aiming to have an executive job some day!

And radio engineering? A thing for the future!

Both of these facts are very illuminating. Those are the sort of things that a mother should know concerning any young man who comes to call on her daughter. Seriously or—not.

TOM One little warning. He doesn't know about Laura. I didn't let on that we had dark ulterior motives. I just said, why don't you come and have dinner with us? He said okay and that was the whole conversation.

AMANDA I bet it was! You're eloquent as an oyster.

However, he'll know about Laura when he gets here. When he sees how lovely and sweet and pretty she is, he'll thank his lucky stars he was asked to dinner.

TOM Mother, you mustn't expect too much of Laura.

AMANDA What do you mean?

TOM Laura seems all those things to you and me because she's ours and we love her. We don't even notice she's crippled any more.

AMANDA Don't say crippled! You know that I never allow that word to be used!

TOM But face facts, Mother. She is and—that's not all—

AMANDA What do you mean "not all"?

TOM Laura is very different from other girls.

AMANDA I think the difference is all to her advantage.

TOM Not quite all—in the eyes of others—strangers—she's terribly shy and lives in a world of her own and those things make her seem a little peculiar to people outside the house.

AMANDA Don't say peculiar.

TOM Face the facts. She is.

(THE DANCE-HALL MUSIC CHANGES TO A TANGO THAT HAS A MINOR AND SOMEWHAT OMINOUS TONE)

AMANDA In what way is she peculiar—may I ask?

TOM (*Gently*) She lives in a world of her own—a world of—little glass ornaments, Mother. . . . (*Gets up.* AMANDA *remains holding brush, looking at him, troubled*) She plays old phonograph records and—that's about all—(*He glances at himself in the mirror and crosses to door*)

AMANDA (*Sharply*) Where are you going?

TOM I'm going to the movies. (*Out screen door*)

AMANDA Not to the movies, every night to the movies! (*Follows quickly to screen door*) I don't believe you always go to the movies! (*He is gone.* AMANDA *looks worriedly after him for a moment. Then vitality and optimism return and she turns from the door. Crossing to portieres)* Laura! Laura! (LAURA *answers from kitchenette)*

LAURA Yes, Mother.

AMANDA Let those dishes go and come in front! (LAURA *appears with dish towel. Gaily)* Laura, come here and make a wish on the moon!

(SCREEN IMAGE: MOON)

LAURA (*Entering*) Moon—moon?

AMANDA A little silver slipper of a moon.
Look over your left shoulder, Laura, and make a wish!

(LAURA *looks faintly puzzled as if called out of sleep.* AMANDA *seizes her shoulders and turns her at an angle by the door)*

Now,!
Now, darling, *wish!*

LAURA What shall I wish for, Mother?

AMANDA (*Her voice trembling and her eyes suddenly filling with tears)*
Happiness! Good fortune!

(*The violin rises and the stage dims out)*

(*The Curtain Falls)*

Scene 6

(IMAGE: HIGH SCHOOL HERO)

TOM And so the following evening I brought Jim home to dinner. I had known Jim slightly in high school. In high school Jim was a hero. He had tremendous Irish good nature and vitality with the scrubbed and polished look of white chinaware. He seemed to move in a continual spotlight. He was a star in basketball, captain of the debating club, president of the senior class and the glee club, and he sang the male lead in the annual light operas. He was always running or bounding, never just walking. He seemed always at the point of defeating the law of gravity. He was shooting with such velocity through his adolescence that you would logically expect him to arrive at nothing short of the White House by the time he was thirty. But Jim apparently ran into more interference after his graduation from Soldan. His speed had definitely slowed. Six years after he left high school he was holding a job that wasn't much better than mine.

(IMAGE: CLERK)

He was the only one at the warehouse with whom I was on friendly terms. I was valuable to him as someone who could remember his former glory, who had seen him win basketball games and the silver cup in debating. He knew of my secret practice of retiring to a cabinet of the wash-room to work on poems when business was slack in the warehouse. He called me Shakespeare. And while the other boys in the warehouse regarded me with suspicious hostility, Jim took a humorous attitude toward me. Gradually his attitude affected the others, their hostility wore off and they also began to smile at me as people smile at an oddly fashioned dog who trots across their path at some distance.

I knew that Jim and Laura had known each other at Soldan, and I had heard Laura speak admiringly of his voice. I didn't know if Jim remembered her or not. In high school Laura had been as unobtrusive as Jim had been astonishing. If he did remember Laura, it was not as my sister, for when I asked him to dinner, he grinned and said, "You know, Shakespeare, I never thought of you as having folks!"

He was about to discover that I did. . . .

(LIGHT UP STAGE)

(LEGEND ON SCREEN: "THE ACCENT OF A COMING FOOT")

(*Friday evening. It is about five o'clock of a late spring evening which comes "scattering poems in the sky"*)

(*A delicate lemony light is in the Wingfield apartment*)

(AMANDA *has worked like a Turk in preparation for the gentleman caller. The results are astonishing. The new floor lamp with its rose-silk shade is in place, a colored paper lantern conceals the broken light fixture in the ceiling, new billowing white curtains are at the windows, chintz covers are on chairs and sofa, a pair of new sofa pillows make their initial appearance*)

(*Open boxes and tissue paper are scattered on the floor*)

(LAURA *stands in the middle with lifted arms while* AMANDA *crouches before her, adjusting the hem of the new dress, devout and ritualistic. The dress is colored and designed by memory. The arrangement of* LAURA's *hair is changed; it is softer and more becoming. A fragile, unearthly prettiness has come out in* LAURA:

she is like a piece of translucent glass touched by light, given a momentary radiance, not actual, not lasting)

AMANDA (*Impatiently*) Why are you trembling?

LAURA Mother, you've made me so nervous!

AMANDA How have I made you nervous?

LAURA By all this fuss! You make it seem so important!

AMANDA I don't understand you, Laura. You couldn't be satisfied with just sitting home, and yet whenever I try to arrange something for you, you seem to resist it.

(*She gets up*)

Now take a look at yourself.

No, wait! Wait just a moment—I have an idea!

LAURA What is it now?

(AMANDA *produces two powder puffs which she wraps in handkerchiefs and stuffs in* LAURA'S *bosom*)

LAURA Mother, what are you doing?

AMANDA They call them "Gay Deceivers"!

LAURA I won't wear them!

AMANDA You will!

LAURA Why should I?

AMANDA Because, to be painfully honest, your chest is flat.

LAURA You make it seem like we were setting a trap.

AMANDA All pretty girls are a trap, a pretty trap, and men expect them to be.

(LEGEND: "A PRETTY TRAP")

Now look at yourself, young lady. This is the prettiest you will ever be!

I've got to fix myself now! You're going to be surprised by your mother's appearance! (*She crosses through portieres, humming gaily*)

(LAURA *moves slowly to the long mirror and stares solemnly at herself*)

(*A wind blows the white curtains inward in a slow, graceful motion and with a faint, sorrowful sighing*)

AMANDA (*Off stage*) It isn't dark enough yet. (*She turns slowly before the mirror with a troubled look*)

(LEGEND ON SCREEN: "THIS IS MY SISTER: CELEBRATE HER WITH STRINGS!" MUSIC)

AMANDA (*Laughing, off*) I'm going to show you something. I'm going to make a spectacular appearance!

LAURA What is it, Mother?

AMANDA Possess your soul in patience—you will see! Something I've resurrected from that old trunk! Styles haven't changed so terribly much after all. . . .

(*She parts the portieres*)

Now just look at your mother!

(*She wears a girlish frock of yellowed voile with a blue silk sash. She carries a bunch of jonquils—the legend of her youth is nearly revived. Feverishly*)

This is the dress in which I led the cotillion. Won the cakewalk twice at Sunset Hill, wore one spring to the Governor's ball in Jackson!
See how I sashayed around the ballroom, Laura?

(*She raises her skirt and does a mincing step around the room*)

I wore it on Sundays for my gentlemen callers! I had it on the day I met your father—
I had malaria fever all that spring. The change of climate from East Tennessee to the Delta—weakened resistance—I had a little temperature all the time—not enough to be serious—just enough to make me restless and giddy!—Invitations poured in—parties all over the Delta!—"Stay in bed," said Mother, "you have fever!"—but I just wouldn't—I took quinine but kept on going, going!—Evenings, dances! —Afternoons, long, long rides! Picnics—lovely!—So lovely, that country in May—All lacy with dogwood, literally flooded with jonquils! —That was the spring I had the craze for jonquils. Jonquils became an absolute obsession. Mother said, "Honey, there's no more room for jonquils." And still I kept on bringing in more jonquils. Whenever, wherever I saw them, I'd say, "Stop! Stop! I see jonquils!" I made the young men help me gather the jonquils! It was a joke, Amanda and her jonquils! Finally there were no more vases to hold them, every available space was filled with jonquils. No vases to hold them? All right, I'll hold them myself! And then I—(*She stops in front of the picture.* MUSIC) met your father!
Malaria fever and jonquils and then—this—boy. . . .

(*She switches on the rose-colored lamp*)

I hope they get here before it starts to rain.

(*She crosses upstage and places the jonquils in bowl on table*)

I gave your brother a little extra change so he and Mr. O'Connor could take the service car home.

LAURA (*With altered look*)   What did you say his name was?

AMANDA   O'Connor.

LAURA   What is his first name?

AMANDA   I don't remember. Oh, yes, I do. It was—Jim!

(LAURA *sways slightly and catches hold of a chair*)

(LEGEND ON SCREEN: "NOT JIM!")

LAURA (*Faintly*)   Not—Jim.

AMANDA   Yes, that was it, it was Jim! I've never known a Jim that wasn't nice!

(MUSIC: OMINOUS)

LAURA   Are you sure his name is Jim O'Connor?

AMANDA   Yes. Why?

LAURA   Is he the one that Tom used to know in high school?

AMANDA   He didn't say so. I think he just got to know him at the warehouse.

LAURA   There was a Jim O'Connor we both knew in high school— (*Then, with effort*)   If that is the one that Tom is bringing to dinner —you'll have to excuse me, I won't come to the table.

AMANDA   What sort of nonsense is this?

LAURA   You asked me once if I'd ever liked a boy. Don't you remember I showed you this boy's picture?

AMANDA   You mean the boy you showed me in the year book?

LAURA   Yes, that boy.

AMANDA   Laura, Laura, were you in love with that boy?

LAURA   I don't know. Mother. All I know is I couldn't sit at the table if it was him!

AMANDA   It won't be him! It isn't the least bit likely. But whether it is or not, you will come to the table. You will not be excused.

LAURA   I'll have to be, Mother.

AMANDA   I don't intend to humor your silliness, Laura. I've had too much from you and your brother, both!

So just sit down and compose yourself till they come. Tom has forgotten his key so you'll have to let them in, when they arrive.

LAURA (*Panicky*)   Oh, Mother—*you* answer the door!

AMANDA (*Lightly*) I'll be in the kitchen—busy!

LAURA Oh, Mother, please answer the door, don't make me do it!

AMANDA (*Crossing into kitchenette*) I've got to fix the dressing for the salmon. Fuss, fuss—silliness!—over a gentleman caller!

(*Door swings shut. LAURA is left alone*)

(LEGEND: "TERROR")

(*She utters a low moan and turns off the lamp—sits stiffly on the edge of the sofa, knotting her fingers together*)

(LEGEND ON SCREEN: "THE OPENING OF A DOOR!")

(TOM *and* JIM *appear on the fire-escape steps and climb to landing. Hearing their approach, LAURA rises with a panicky gesture. She retreats to the portieres*)

(*The doorbell. LAURA catches her breath and touches her throat. Low drums*)

AMANDA (*Calling*) Laura, sweetheart! The door!

(LAURA *stares at it without moving*)

JIM I think we just beat the rain.

TOM Uh-huh. (*He rings again, nervously.* JIM *whistles and fishes for a cigarette*)

AMANDA (*Very, very gaily*) Laura, that is your brother and Mr. O'Connor! Will you let them in, darling?

(LAURA *crosses toward kitchenette door*)

LAURA (*Breathlessly*) Mother—you go to the door!

(AMANDA *steps out of kitchenette and stares furiously at* LAURA. *She points imperiously at the door*)

LAURA Please, please!

AMANDA (*In a fierce whisper*) What is the matter with you, you silly thing?

LAURA (*Desperately*) Please, you answer it, *please!*

AMANDA I told you I wasn't going to humor you, Laura. Why have you chosen this moment to lose your mind?

LAURA Please, please, please, you go!

AMANDA You'll have to go to the door because I can't!

LAURA (*Despairingly*) I can't either!

AMANDA Why?

LAURA I'm *sick*!

AMANDA I'm sick, too—of your nonsense! Why can't you and your brother be normal people? Fantastic whims and behavior!

(TOM *gives a long ring*)

Preposterous goings on! Can you give me one reason—(*Calls out lyrically*) COMING! JUST ONE SECOND!—why you should be afraid to open a door? Now you answer it, Laura!

LAURA Oh, oh, oh . . . (*She returns through the portieres. Darts to the victrola and winds it frantically and turns it on*)

AMANDA Laura Wingfield, you march right to that door!

LAURA Yes—yes, Mother!

(*A faraway, scratchy rendition of "Dardanalla" softens the air and gives her strength to move through it. She slips to the door and draws it cautiously open*)
(TOM *enters with the caller,* JIM O'CONNOR)

TOM Laura, this is Jim. Jim, this is my sister, Laura.

JIM (*Stepping inside*) I didn't know that Shakespeare had a sister!

LAURA (*Retreating stiff and trembling from the door*) How—how do you do?

JIM (*Heartily extending his hand*) Okay!

(LAURA *touches it hesitantly with hers*)

JIM Your hand's *cold*, Laura!

LAURA Yes, well—I've been playing the victrola. . . .

JIM Must have been playing classical music on it! You ought to play a little hot swing music to warm you up!

LAURA Excuse me—I haven't finished playing the victrola. . . .

(*She turns awkwardly and hurries into the front room. She pauses a second by the victrola. Then catches her breath and darts through the portieres like a frightened deer*)

JIM (*Grinning*) What was the matter?

TOM Oh—with Laura? Laura is—terribly shy.

JIM Shy, huh? It's unusual to meet a shy girl nowadays. I don't believe you ever mentioned you had a sister.

TOM Well, now you know. I have one. Here is the *Post Dispatch*. You want a piece of it?

JIM Uh-huh.

TOM What piece? The comics?

JIM Sports! (*Glances at it*) Ole Dizzy Dean[9] is on his bad behavior.

---

[9]Baseball pitcher for the St. Louis Cardinals.

TOM (*Disinterest*) Yeah? (*Lights cigarette and crosses back to fire-escape door*)

JIM Where are *you* going?

TOM I'm going out on the terrace.

JIM (*Goes after him*) You know, Shakespeare—I'm going to sell you a bill of goods!

TOM What goods?

JIM A course I'm taking.

TOM Huh?

JIM In public speaking! You and me, we're not the warehouse type.

TOM Thanks—that's good news.
    But what has public speaking got to do with it?

JIM It fits you for—executive positions!

TOM Awww.

JIM I tell you it's done a helluva lot for me.

(IMAGE: EXECUTIVE AT DESK)

TOM In what respect?

JIM In every! Ask yourself what is the difference between you an' me and men in the office down front? Brains?—No!—Ability?—No! Then what? Just one little thing—

TOM What is that one little thing?

JIM Primarily it amounts to—social poise! Being able to square up to people and hold your own on any social level!

AMANDA (*Off stage*) Tom?

TOM Yes, Mother?

AMANDA Is that you and Mr. O'Connor?

TOM Yes, Mother.

AMANDA Well, you just make yourselves comfortable in there.

TOM Yes, Mother.

AMANDA Ask Mr. O'Connor if he would like to wash his hands.

JIM Aw, no—no—thank you—I took care of that at the warehouse. Tom—

TOM Yes?

JIM Mr. Mendoza was speaking to me about you.

TOM Favorably?

JIM What do you think?

TOM Well—

JIM You're going to be out of a job if you don't wake up.

TOM I am waking up—

JIM You show no signs.

TOM The signs are interior.

(IMAGE ON SCREEN: THE SAILING VESSEL WITH JOLLY ROGER AGAIN)

TOM   I'm planning to change. (*He leans over the rail speaking with quiet exhilaration. The incandescent marquees and signs of the first-run movie houses light his face from across the alley. He looks like a voyager*)   I'm right at the point of committing myself to a future that doesn't include the warehouse and Mr. Mendoza or even a night-school course in public speaking.

JIM   What are you gassing about?

TOM   I'm tired of the movies.

JIM   Movies!

TOM   Yes, movies! Look at them—(*A wave toward the marvels of Grand Avenue*)   All of those glamorous people—having adventures—hogging it all, gobbling the whole thing up! You know what happens? People go to the *movies* instead of *moving!* Hollywood characters are supposed to have all the adventures for everybody in America, while everybody in America sits in a dark room and watches them have them! Yes, until there's a war. That's when adventure becomes available to the masses! *Everyone's* dish, not only Gable's![10] Then the people in the dark room come out of the dark room to have some adventures them-selves—Goody, goody!—It's our turn now, to go to the South Sea Island —to make a safari—to be exotic, far-off!—But I'm not patient. I don't want to wait till then. I'm tired of the *movies* and I am *about to move!*

JIM (*Incredulously*)   Move?

TOM   Yes.

JIM   When?

TOM   Soon!

JIM   Where? Where?

(THEME THREE MUSIC SEEMS TO ANSWER THE QUESTION, WHILE TOM THINKS IT OVER. HE SEARCHES AMONG HIS POCKETS)

TOM   I'm starting to boil inside. I know I sound dreamy, but inside —well, I'm boiling!—Whenever I pick up a shoe, I shudder a little thinking how short life is and what I am doing!—Whatever that means, I know it doesn't mean shoes—except as something to wear on a traveler's feet! (*Finds paper*)   Look—

JIM   What?

TOM   I'm a member.

JIM (*Reading*)   The Union of Merchant Seamen.

[10]Clark Gable, popular movie star.

TOM   I paid my dues this month, instead of the light bill.

JIM   You will regret it when they turn the lights off.

TOM   I won't be here.

JIM   How about your mother?

TOM   I'm like my father. The bastard son of a bastard! See how he grins? And he's been absent going on sixteen years!

JIM   You're just talking, you drip. How does your mother feel about it?

TOM   Shhh!—Here comes Mother! Mother is not acquainted with my plans!

AMANDA (*Enters portieres*)   Where are you all?

TOM   On the terrace, Mother.

(They start inside. She advances to them. TOM is distinctly shocked at her appearance. Even JIM blinks a little. He is making his first contact with girlish Southern vivacity and in spite of the night-school course in public speaking is somewhat thrown off the beam by the unexpected outlay of social charm)

(Certain responses are attempted by JIM but are swept aside by AMANDA's gay laughter and chatter. TOM is embarrassed but after the first shock JIM reacts very warmly, grins and chuckles, is altogether won over)

(IMAGE: AMANDA AS A GIRL)

AMANDA (*Coyly smiling, shaking her girlish ringlets*)   Well, well, well, so this is Mr. O'Connor. Introductions entirely unnecessary. I've heard so much about you from my boy. I finally said to him, Tom—good gracious!—why don't you bring this paragon to supper? I'd like to meet this nice young man at the warehouse!—Instead of just hearing him sing your praises so much!

I don't know why my son is so stand-offish—that's not Southern behavior!

Let's sit down and—I think we could stand a little more air in here! Tom, leave the door open. I felt a nice fresh breeze a moment ago. Where has it gone to?

Mmmm, so warm already! And not quite summer, even. We're going to burn up when summer really gets started.

However, we're having—we're having a very light supper. I think light things are better fo' this time of year. The same as light clothes are. Light clothes an' light food are what warm weather calls fo'. You know our blood gets so thick during the winter—it takes a while fo' us to *adjust* ou'selves!—when the season changes . . .

It's come so quick this year. I wasn't prepared. All of a sudden —heavens! Already summer!—I ran to the trunk an' pulled out this light dress—Terribly old! Historical almost! But feels so good—so good an' co-ol, y' know. . . .

TOM Mother—

AMANDA Yes, honey?

TOM How about—supper?

AMANDA Honey, you go ask Sister if supper is ready! You know that Sister is in full charge of supper!

Tell her you hungry boys are waiting for it.

(*To* JIM)

Have you met Laura?

JIM She—

AMANDA Let you in? Oh, good, you've met already! It's rare for a girl as sweet an' pretty as Laura to be domestic! But Laura is, thank heavens, not only pretty but also very domestic. I'm not at all. I never was a bit. I never could make a thing but angel-food cake. Well, in the South we had so many servants. Gone, gone, gone. All vestige of gracious living! Gone completely! I wasn't prepared for what the future brought me. All of my gentlemen callers were sons of planters and so of course I assumed that I would be married to one and raise my family on a large piece of land with plenty of servants. But man proposes—and woman accepts the proposal!—To vary that old, old saying a little bit—I married no planter! I married a man who worked for the telephone company!—That gallantly smiling gentleman over there! (*Points to the picture*) A telephone man who—fell in love with long-distance!—Now he travels and I don't even know where!—But what am I going on for about my—tribulations?

Tell me yours—I hope you don't have any!

Tom?

TOM (*Returning*) Yes, Mother?

AMANDA Is supper nearly ready?

TOM It looks to me like supper is on the table.

AMANDA Let me look—(*She rises prettily and looks through portieres*) Oh, lovely!—But where is Sister?

TOM Laura is not feeling well and she says that she thinks she'd better not come to the table.

AMANDA What?—Nonsense!—Laura? Oh, Laura!

LAURA (*Off stage, faintly*) Yes, Mother.

AMANDA You really must come to the table. We won't be seated until you come to the table!

Come in, Mr. O'Connor. You sit over there, and I'll—
Laura? Laura Wingfield!
You're keeping us waiting, honey! We can't say grace until you come
to the table!

(*The back door is pushed weakly open and* LAURA *comes in. She
is obviously quite faint, her lips trembling, her eyes wide and staring. She moves unsteadily toward the table*)

(LEGEND: "TERROR!")

(*Outside a summer storm is coming abruptly. The white curtains
billow inward at the windows and there is a sorrowful murmur and
deep blue dusk*) (LAURA *suddenly stumbles—she catches at a chair
with a faint moan*)

TOM Laura!
AMANDA Laura!

(*There is a clap of thunder*)

(LEGEND: "AH!")

(*Despairingly*)

Why, Laura, you *are* sick, darling! Tom, help your sister into the living
room, dear!
Sit in the living room, Laura—rest on the sofa.
Well!

(*To the gentleman caller*)

Standing over the hot stove made her ill!—I told her that it was just
too warm this evening, but—

(TOM *comes back in.* LAURA *is on the sofa*)

Is Laura all right now?
TOM Yes.
AMANDA What *is* that? Rain? A nice cool rain has come up!

(*She gives the gentleman caller a frightened look*)

I think we may—have grace—now. . . .

(TOM *looks at her stupidly*)

Tom, honey—you say grace!
TOM Oh . . .
"For these and all thy mercies—"

(They bow their heads, AMANDA *stealing a nervous glance at* JIM. *In the living room,* LAURA, *stretched on the sofa, clenches her hand to her lips, to hold back a shuddering sob)*

God's Holy Name be praised—

(The Scene Dims Out)

Scene 7

(A Souvenir.

Half an hour later. Dinner is just being finished in the upstage area which is concealed by the drawn portieres.

As the curtain rises LAURA *is still huddled upon the sofa, her feet drawn under her, her head resting on a pale blue pillow, her eyes wide and mysteriously watchful. The new floor lamp with its shade of rose-colored silk gives a soft, becoming light to her face, bringing out the fragile, unearthly prettiness which usually escapes attention. There is a steady murmur of rain, but it is slackening and stops soon after the scene begins; the air outside becomes pale and luminous as the moon breaks out.*

A moment after the curtain rises, the lights in both rooms flicker and go out)

JIM   Hey, there, Mr. Light Bulb!

(AMANDA *laughs nervously)*

(LEGEND: "SUSPENSION OF A PUBLIC SERVICE")

AMANDA   Where was Moses when the lights went out? Ha-ha. Do you know the answer to that one, Mr. O'Connor?

JIM   No, Ma'am, what's the answer?

AMANDA   In the dark!

(JIM *laughs appreciatively)*

Everybody sit still. I'll light the candles. Isn't it lucky we have them on the table? Where's a match? Which of you gentlemen can provide a match?

JIM   Here.

AMANDA   Thank you, sir.

JIM   Not at all, Ma'am!

AMANDA   I guess the fuse has burnt out. Mr. O'Connor, can you tell a burnt-out fuse? I know I can't and Tom is a total loss when it comes to mechanics.

(SOUND: GETTING UP: VOICES RECEDE A LITTLE TO KITCH-ENETTE)

Oh, be careful you don't bump into something. We don't want our gentleman caller to break his neck. Now wouldn't that be a fine howdy-do?

JIM   Ha-ha!

Where is the fuse-box?

AMANDA   Right here next to the stove. Can you see anything?

JIM   Just a minute.

AMANDA   Isn't electricity a mysterious thing?

Wasn't it Benjamin Franklin who tied a key to a kite?

We live in such a mysterious universe, don't we? Some people say that science clears up all the mysteries for us. In my opinion it only creates more!

Have you found it yet?

JIM   No, Ma'am. All these fuses look okay to me.

AMANDA   Tom!

TOM   Yes, Mother?

AMANDA   That light bill I gave you several days ago. The one I told you we got the notices about?

(LEGEND: "HA!")

TOM   Oh—Yeah.

AMANDA   You didn't neglect to pay it by any chance?

TOM   Why, I—

AMANDA   Didn't! I might have known it!

JIM   Shakespeare probably wrote a poem on that light bill, Mrs. Wingfield.

AMANDA   I might have known better than to trust him with it! There's such a high price for negligence in this world!

JIM   Maybe the poem will win a ten-dollar prize.

AMANDA   We'll just have to spend the remainder of the evening in the nineteenth century, before Mr. Edison made the Mazda lamp!

JIM   Candlelight is my favorite kind of light.

AMANDA   That shows you're romantic! But that's no excuse for Tom. Well, we got through dinner. Very considerate of them to let us get through dinner before they plunged us into everlasting darkness, wasn't it, Mr. O'Connor?

JIM   Ha-ha!

AMANDA   Tom, as a penalty for your carelessness you can help me with the dishes.

JIM   Let me give you a hand.

AMANDA   Indeed you will not!

JIM   I ought to be good for something.

AMANDA   Good for something? (*Her tone is rhapsodic*)   *You?* Why, Mr. O'Connor, nobody, *nobody's* given me this much entertainment in years—as you have!

JIM   Aw, now, Mrs. Wingfield!

AMANDA   I'm not exaggerating, not one bit! But Sister is all by her lonesome. You go keep her company in the parlor!
  I'll give you this lovely old candelabrum that used to be on the altar at the Church of the Heavenly Rest. It was melted a little out of shape when the church burnt down. Lightning struck it one spring. Gypsy Jones was holding a revival at the time and he intimated that the church was destroyed because the Episcopalians gave card parties.

JIM   Ha-ha!

AMANDA   And how about you coaxing Sister to drink a little wine? I think it would be good for her! Can you carry both at once?

JIM   Sure, I'm Superman!

AMANDA   Now, Thomas, get into this apron!

(*The door of kitchenette swings closed on* AMANDA's *gay laughter; the flickering light approaches the portieres*)

(LAURA *sits up nervously as he enters. Her speech at first is low and breathless from the almost intolerable strain of being alone with a stranger*)

(THE LEGEND: "I DON'T SUPPOSE YOU REMEMBER ME AT ALL!")

(*In her first speeches in this scene, before Jim's warmth overcomes her paralyzing shyness,* LAURA's *voice is thin and breathless as though she has just run up a steep flight of stairs*)

(JIM'S *attitude is gently humorous. In playing this scene it should be stressed that while the incident is apparently unimportant, it is to* LAURA *the climax of her secret life*)

JIM   Hello, there, Laura.

LAURA (*Faintly*)   Hello. (*She clears her throat*)

JIM   How are you feeling now? Better?

LAURA   Yes. Yes, thank you.

JIM   This is for you. A little dandelion wine. (*He extends it toward her with extravagant gallantry*)

LAURA   Thank you.

JIM   Drink it—but don't get drunk!

(*He laughs heartily.* LAURA *takes the glass uncertainly; laughs shyly*)

Where shall I set the candles?

LAURA   Oh—oh, anywhere . . .

JIM   How about here on the floor? Any objections?

LAURA   No.

JIM   I'll spread a newspaper under to catch the drippings. I like to sit on the floor. Mind if I do?

LAURA   Oh, no.

JIM   Give me a pillow?

LAURA   What?

JIM   A pillow!

LAURA   Oh . . . (*Hands him one quickly*)

JIM   How about you? Don't you like to sit on the floor?

LAURA   Oh—yes.

JIM   Why don't you, then?

LAURA   I—will.

JIM   Take a pillow! (LAURA *does. Sits on the other side of the candelabrum.* JIM *crosses his legs and smiles engagingly at her*)   I can't hardly see you sitting way over there.

LAURA   I can—see you.

JIM   I know, but that's not fair, I'm in the limelight. (LAURA *moves her pillow closer*)   Good! Now I can see you! Comfortable?

LAURA   Yes.

JIM   So am I. Comfortable as a cow! Will you have some gum?

LAURA   No, thank you.

JIM   I think that I will indulge, with your permission. (*Musingly unwraps it and holds it up*)   Think of the fortune made by the guy that invented the first piece of chewing gum. Amazing, huh? The Wrigley Building is one of the sights of Chicago—I saw it summer before last when I went up to the Century of Progress.[11] Did you take in the Century of Progress?

LAURA   No, I didn't.

JIM   Well, it was quite a wonderful exposition. What impressed me most was the Hall of Science. Gives you an idea of what the future

[11]Chicago World's Fair, 1933–1934.

will be in America, even more wonderful than the present time is! (*Pause. Smiling at her*) Your brother tells me you're shy. Is that right, Laura?

LAURA   I—don't know.

JIM   I judge you to be an old-fashioned type of girl. Well, I think that's a pretty good type to be. Hope you don't think I'm being too personal —do you?

LAURA (*Hastily, out of embarrassment*) I believe I *will* take a piece of gum, if you—don't mind. (*Clearing her throat*) Mr. O'Connor, have you—kept up with your singing?

JIM   Singing? Me?

LAURA   Yes. I remember what a beautiful voice you had.

JIM   When did you hear me sing?

(VOICE OFF STAGE IN THE PAUSE)

VOICE (*Off stage*)

> Oh blow, ye winds, heigh-ho,
> A-roving I will go!
> I'm off to my love
> With a boxing glove—
> Ten thousand miles away!

JIM   You say you've heard me sing?

LAURA   Oh, yes! Yes, very often. . . . I—don't suppose—you re-member me—at all?

JIM (*Smiling doubtfully*) You know I had an idea I've seen you before. I had that idea soon as you opened the door. It seemed almost like I was about to remember your name. But the name that I started to call you—wasn't a name! And so I stopped myself before I said it.

LAURA   Wasn't it—Blue Roses?

JIM (*Springs up. Grinning*) Blue Roses!—My gosh, yes—Blue Roses!

That's what I had on my tongue when you opened the door!

Isn't it funny what tricks your memory plays? I didn't connect you with high school somehow or other.

But that's where it was; it was high school. I didn't even know you were Shakespeare's sister!

Gosh, I'm sorry.

LAURA   I didn't expect you to. You—barely knew me!

JIM   But we did have a speaking acquaintance, huh?

LAURA   Yes, we—spoke to each other.

JIM   When did you recognize me?

LAURA   Oh, right away!

JIM   Soon as I came in the door?

LAURA   When I heard your name I thought it was probably you. I knew that Tom used to know you a little in high school. So when you came in the door—Well, then I was—sure.

JIM   Why didn't you *say* something, then?

LAURA   (*Breathlessly*) I didn't know what to say, I was—too surprised!

JIM   For goodness' sakes! You know, this sure is funny!

LAURA   Yes! Yes, isn't it, though . . .

JIM   Didn't we have a class in something together?

LAURA   Yes, we did.

JIM   What class was that?

LAURA   It was—singing—Chorus!

JIM   Aw!

LAURA   I sat across the aisle from you in the Aud.

JIM   Aw.

LAURA   Mondays, Wednesdays, and Fridays.

JIM   Now I remember—you always came in late.

LAURA   Yes, it was so hard for me, getting upstairs. I had that brace on my leg—it clumped so loud!

JIM   I never heard any clumping.

LAURA   (*Wincing at the recollection*) To me it sounded like— thunder!

JIM   Well, well, well, I never even noticed.

LAURA   And everybody was seated before I came in. I had to walk in front of all those people. My seat was in the back row. I had to go clumping all the way up the aisle with everyone watching!

JIM   You shouldn't have been self-conscious.

LAURA   I know, but I was. It was always such a relief when the singing started.

JIM   Aw, yes, I've placed you now! I used to call you Blue Roses. How was it that I got started calling you that?

LAURA   I was out of school a little while with pleurosis. When I came back you asked me what was the matter, I said I had pleurosis—you thought I said Blue Roses. That's what you always called me after that!

JIM   I hope you didn't mind.

LAURA   Oh, no—I liked it. You see, I wasn't acquainted with many —people. . . .

JIM   As I remember you sort of stuck by yourself.

LAURA   I—I—never have had much luck at—making friends.

JIM   I don't see why you wouldn't.

LAURA   Well, I—started out badly.

JIM   You mean being—

LAURA   Yes, it sort of—stood between me—

JIM   You shouldn't have let it!

LAURA   I know, but it did, and—

JIM   You were shy with people!

LAURA   I tried not to be but never could—

JIM   Overcome it?

LAURA   No, I—I never could!

JIM   I guess being shy is something you have to work out of kind of gradually.

LAURA (*Sorrowfully*)   Yes—I guess it—

JIM   Takes time!

LAURA   Yes.

JIM   People are not so dreadful when you know them. That's what you have to remember! And everybody has problems, not just you, but practically everybody has got some problems.

You think of yourself as having the only problems, as being the only one who is disappointed. But just look around you and you will see lots of people as disappointed as you are. For instance, I hoped when I was going to high school that I would be further along at this time, six years later, than I am now—You remember that wonderful write-up I had in *The Torch?*

LAURA   Yes! (*She rises and crosses to table*)

JIM   It said I was bound to succeed in anything I went into! (LAURA *returns with the annual*) Holy Jeez! *The Torch!* (*He accepts it reverently. They smile across it with mutual wonder.* LAURA *crouches beside him and they begin to turn through it.* LAURA'S *shyness is dissolving in his warmth*)

LAURA   Here you are in *The Pirates of Penzance!*

JIM (*Wistfully*)   I sang the baritone lead in that operetta.

LAURA (*Raptly*)   So—beautifully!

JIM (*Protesting*)   Aw—

LAURA   Yes, yes—beautifully—beautifully!

JIM   You heard me?

LAURA   All three times!

JIM   No!

LAURA   Yes!

JIM   All three performances?

LAURA (*Looking down*) Yes.

JIM Why?

LAURA I—wanted to ask you to—autograph my program.

JIM Why didn't you ask me to?

LAURA You were always surrounded by your own friends so much that I never had a chance to.

JIM You should have just—

LAURA Well, I—thought you might think I was—

JIM Thought I might think you was—what?

LAURA Oh—

JIM (*With reflective relish*) I was beleaguered by females in those days.

LAURA You were terribly popular!

JIM Yeah—

LAURA You had such a—friendly way—

JIM I was spoiled in high school.

LAURA Everybody—liked you!

JIM Including you?

LAURA I—yes, I—I did, too—(*She gently closes the book in her lap*)

JIM Well, well, well!—Give me that program, Laura. (*She hands it to him. He signs it with a flourish*) There you are—better late than never!

LAURA Oh, I—what a—surprise!

JIM My signature isn't worth very much right now.

But some day—maybe—it will increase in value!

Being disappointed is one thing and being discouraged is something else. I am disappointed but I am not discouraged.

I'm twenty-three years old.

How old are you?

LAURA I'll be twenty-four in June.

JIM That's not old age!

LAURA No, but—

JIM You finished high school?

LAURA (*With difficulty*) I didn't go back.

JIM You mean you dropped out?

LAURA I made bad grades in my final examinations. (*She rises and replaces the book and the program. Her voice strained*) How is—Emily Meisenbach getting along?

JIM Oh, that kraut-head!

LAURA Why do you call her that?

JIM That's what she was.

LAURA You're not still—going with her?

JIM I never see her.

LAURA It said in the Personal Section that you were—engaged!

JIM I know, but I wasn't impressed by that—propaganda!

LAURA It wasn't—the truth?

JIM Only in Emily's optimistic opinion!

LAURA Oh—

(LEGEND: "WHAT HAVE YOU DONE SINCE HIGH SCHOOL?")

(JIM *lights a cigarette and leans indolently back on his elbows, smiling at* LAURA *with a warmth and charm which lights her inwardly with altar candles. She remains by the table and turns in her hands a piece of glass to cover her tumult*)

JIM (*After several reflective puffs on a cigarette*) What have you done since high school? (*She seems not to hear him*) Huh? (LAURA *looks up*) I said what have you done since high school, Laura?

LAURA Nothing much.

JIM You must have been doing something these six long years.

LAURA Yes.

JIM Well, then, such as what?

LAURA I took a business course at business college—

JIM How did that work out?

LAURA Well, not very—well—I had to drop out, it gave me—indigestion—

(JIM *laughs gently*)

JIM What are you doing now?

LAURA I don't do anything—much. Oh, please don't think I sit around doing nothing! My glass collection takes up a good deal of time. Glass is something you have to take good care of.

JIM What did you say—about glass?

LAURA Collection I said—I have one—(*She clears her throat and turns away again, acutely shy*)

JIM (*Abruptly*) You know what I judge to be the trouble with you? Inferiority complex! Know what that is? That's what they call it when someone low-rates himself!

I understand it because I had it, too. Although my case was not so aggravated as yours seems to be. I had it until I took up public speaking, developed my voice, and learned that I had an aptitude for science. Before that time I never thought of myself as being outstanding in any way whatsoever!

Now I've never made a regular study of it, but I have a friend who says I can analyze people better than doctors that make a profession of it. I don't claim that to be necessarily true, but I can sure guess a person's psychology. Laura! (*Takes out his gum*) Excuse me, Laura. I always take it out when the flavor is gone. I'll use this scrap of paper to wrap it in. I know how it is to get it stuck on a shoe.

Yep—that's what I judge to be your principal trouble. A lack of confidence in yourself as a person. You don't have the proper amount of faith in yourself. I'm basing that fact on a number of your remarks and also on certain observations I've made. For instance that clumping you thought was so awful in high school. You say that you even dreaded to walk into class. You see what you did? You dropped out of school, you gave up an education because of a clump, which as far as I know was practically nonexistent! A little physical defect is what you have. Hardly noticeable even! Magnified thousands of times by imagination!

You know what my strong advice to you is? Think of yourself as *superior* in some way!

LAURA In what way would I think?

JIM Why, man alive, Laura! Just look about you a little. What do you see? A world full of common people! All of 'em born and all of 'em going to die!

Which of them has one-tenth of your good points! Or mine! Or anyone else's, as far as that goes—Gosh!

Everybody excels in some one thing. Some in many!

(*Unconsciously glances at himself in the mirror*)

All you've got to do is discover in *what*!
Take me, for instance.

(*He adjusts his tie at the mirror*)

My interest happens to lie in electro-dynamics. I'm taking a course in radio engineering at night school, Laura, on top of a fairly responsible job at the warehouse. I'm taking that course and studying public speaking.

LAURA Ohhhh.

JIM Because I believe in the future of television.

(*Turning back to her*)

I wish to be ready to go up right along with it. Therefore I'm planning to get in on the ground floor. In fact I've already made the right connections and all that remains is for the industry itself to get under way! Full steam—

(His eyes are starry)

Knowledge—Zzzzzp! Money—Zzzzzzp!—Power!
That's the cycle democracy is built on!

(His attitude is convincingly dynamic. LAURA *stares at him, even her shyness eclipsed in her absolute wonder. He suddenly grins)*

I guess you think I think a lot of myself!
LAURA   No—o-o-o, I—
JIM   Now how about you? Isn't there something you take more interest in that anything else?
LAURA   Well, I do—as I said—have my—glass collection—

(A peal of girlish laughter from the kitchen)

JIM   I'm not right sure I know what you're talking about.
What kind of glass is it?
LAURA   Little articles of it, they're ornaments mostly!
Most of them are little animals made out of glass, the tiniest little animals in the world. Mother calls them a glass menagerie!
Here's an example of one, if you'd like to see it!
This one is one of the oldest. It's nearly thirteen.

(MUSIC: "THE GLASS MENAGERIE")
(He stretches out his hand)

Oh, be careful—if you breathe, it breaks!
JIM   I'd better not take it. I'm pretty clumsy with things.
LAURA   Go on, I trust you with him!

(Places it in his palm)

There now—you're holding him gently!
Hold him over the light, he loves the light! You see how the light shines through him?
JIM   It sure does shine!
LAURA   I shouldn't be partial, but he is my favorite one.
JIM   What kind of a thing is this one supposed to be?
LAURA   Haven't you noticed the single horn on his forehead?
JIM   A unicorn, huh?
LAURA   Mmmm-hmmm!
JIM   Unicorns, aren't they extinct in the modern world?
LAURA   I know!
JIM   Poor little fellow, he must feel sort of lonesome.
LAURA   *(Smiling)* Well, if he does he doesn't complain about it. He

stays on a shelf with some horses that don't have horns and all of them seem to get along nicely together.

JIM   How do you know?

LAURA (*Lightly*)   I haven't heard any arguments among them!

JIM (*Grinning*)   No arguments, huh? Well, that's a pretty good sign! Where shall I set him?

LAURA   Put him on the table. They all like a change of scenery once in a while!

JIM (*Stretching*)   Well, well, well, well—
    Look how big my shadow is when I stretch!

LAURA   Oh, oh, yes—it stretches across the ceiling!

JIM (*Crossing to door*)   I think it's stopped raining. (*Opens fire-escape door*)   Where does the music come from?

LAURA   From the Paradise Dance Hall across the alley.

JIM   How about cutting the rug a little, Miss Wingfield?

LAURA   Oh, I—

JIM   Or is your program filled up? Let me have a look at it. (*Grasps imaginary card*)   Why every dance is taken! I'll just have to scratch some out. (WALTZ MUSIC: "LA GOLONDRINA")   Ahhh, a waltz! (*He executes some sweeping turns by himself then holds his arms toward* LAURA)

LAURA (*Breathlessly*)   I—can't dance!

JIM   There you go, that inferiority stuff!

LAURA   I've never danced in my life!

JIM   Come on, try!

LAURA   Oh, but I'd step on you!

JIM   I'm not made out of glass.

LAURA   How—how—how do we start?

JIM   Just leave it to me. You hold your arms out a little.

LAURA   Like this?

JIM   A little bit higher. Right. Now don't tighten up, that's the main thing about it—relax.

LAURA (*Laughing breathlessly*)   It's hard not to.

JIM   Okay.

LAURA   I'm afraid you can't budge me.

JIM   What do you bet I can't. (*He swings her into motion*)

LAURA   Goodness, yes, you can!

JIM   Let yourself go, now, Laura, just let yourself go.

LAURA   I'm—

JIM   Come on!

LAURA   Trying!

JIM   Not so stiff—Easy does it!

LAURA   I know but I'm—

JIM   Loosen th' backbone! There now, that's a lot better.

LAURA   Am I?

JIM   Lots, lots better! (*He moves her about the room in a clumsy waltz*)

LAURA   Oh, my!

JIM   Ha-ha!

LAURA   Oh, my goodness!

JIM   Ha-ha-ha! (*They suddenly bump into the table,* JIM *stops*)   What did we hit on?

LAURA   Table.

JIM   Did something fall off it? I think—

LAURA   Yes.

JIM   I hope it wasn't the little glass horse with the horn!

LAURA   Yes.

JIM   Aw, aw, aw. Is it broken?

LAURA   Now it is just like all the other horses.

JIM   It's lost its—

LAURA   Horn!
It doesn't matter. Maybe it's a blessing in disguise.

JIM   You'll never forgive me. I bet that that was your favorite piece of glass.

LAURA   I don't have favorites much. It's no tragedy, Freckles. Glass breaks so easily. No matter how careful you are. The traffic jars the shelves and things fall off them.

JIM   Still I'm awfully sorry that I was the cause.

LAURA   (*Smiling*)   I'll just imagine he had an operation. The horn was removed to make him feel less—freakish!

(*They both laugh*)

Now he will feel more at home with the other horses, the ones that don't have horns. . . .

JIM   Ha-ha, that's very funny!

(*Suddenly serious*)

I'm glad to see that you have a sense of humor.
You know—you're—well—very different!
Surprisingly different from anyone else I know!

(*His voice becomes soft and hesitant with a genuine feeling*)

Do you mind me telling you that?

(LAURA *is abashed beyond speech*)

I mean it in a nice way. . . .

(LAURA *nods shyly, looking away*)

You make me feel sort of—I don't know how to put it!
I'm usually pretty good at expressing things, but—
This is something that I don't know how to say!

(LAURA *touches her throat and clears it—turns the broken unicorn in her hands*)

(*Even softer*)

Has anyone ever told you that you were pretty?

(PAUSE: MUSIC)

(LAURA *looks up slowly, with wonder, and shakes her head*)

Well, you are! In a very different way from anyone else.
And all the nicer because of the difference, too.

(*His voice becomes low and husky.* LAURA *turns away, nearly faint with the novelty of her emotions*)

I wish that you were my sister. I'd teach you to have some confidence in yourself. The different people are not like other people, but being different is nothing to be ashamed of. Because other people are not such wonderful people. They're one hundred times one thousand. You're one times one! They walk all over the earth. You just stay here. They're common as—weeds, but—you—well, you're—*Blue Roses!*

(IMAGE ON SCREEN: BLUE ROSES)

(MUSIC CHANGES)

LAURA   But blue is wrong for—roses. . . .
JIM   It's right for you!—You're—pretty!
LAURA   In what respect am I pretty?
JIM   In all respects—believe me! Your eyes—your hair—are pretty!
Your hands are pretty!

(*He catches hold of her hand*)

You think I'm making this up because I'm invited to dinner and have to be nice. Oh, I could do that! I could put on an act for you, Laura, and say lots of things without being very sincere. But this time I am. I'm talking to you sincerely. I happened to notice you had this inferiority complex that keeps you from feeling comfortable with people.

Somebody needs to build your confidence up and make you proud instead of shy and turning away and—blushing—
Somebody—ought to—
Ought to—*kiss* you, Laura!

(*His hand slips slowly up her arm to her shoulder*)

(MUSIC SWELLS TUMULTUOUSLY)

(*He suddenly turns her about and kisses her on the lips*)

(*When he releases her,* LAURA *sinks on the sofa with a bright, dazed look*)

(JIM *backs away and fishes in his pocket for a cigarette*)

(LEGEND ON SCREEN: "SOUVENIR")

Stumble-john!

(*He lights the cigarette, avoiding her look*)

(*There is a peal of girlish laughter from* AMANDA *in the kitchen*)

(LAURA *slowly raises and opens her hand. It still contains the little broken glass animal. She looks at it with a tender, bewildered expression*)

Stumble-john!
I shouldn't have done that—That was way off the beam. You don't smoke, do you?

(*She looks, up, smiling, not hearing the question*)

(*He sits beside her a little gingerly. She looks at him speechlessly —waiting*)

(*He coughs decorously and moves a little farther aside as he considers the situation and senses her feelings, dimly, with perturbation*)

(*Gently*)

Would you—care for a—mint?

(*She doesn't seem to hear him but her look grows brighter even*)

Peppermint—Life Saver?
My pocket's a regular drug store—wherever I go . . .

(*He pops a mint in his mouth. Then gulps and decides to make a clean breast of it. He speaks slowly and gingerly*)

Laura, you know, if I had a sister like you, I'd do the same thing as Tom. I'd bring out fellows and—introduce her to them. The right type of boys of a type to—appreciate her.

Only—well—he made a mistake about me.

Maybe I've got no call to be saying this. That may not have been the idea in having me over. But what if it was?

There's nothing wrong about that. The only trouble is that in my case —I'm not in a situation to—do the right thing.

I can't take down your number and say I'll phone.

I can't call up next week and—ask for a date.

I thought I had better explain the situation in case you—misunderstood it and—hurt your feelings. . . .

(*Pause*)

(*Slowly, very slowly,* LAURA'S *look changes, her eyes returning slowly from his to the ornament in her palm*)

(AMANDA *utters another gay laugh in the kitchen*)

LAURA (*Faintly*) You—won't—call again?

JIM   No, Laura, I can't.

(*He rises from the sofa*)

As I was just explaining, I've—got strings on me.

Laura, I've—been going steady!

I go out all of the time with a girl named Betty.

She's a home-girl like you, and Catholic, and Irish, and in a great many ways we—get along fine.

I met her last summer on a moonlight boat trip up the river to Alton, on the *Majestic*.

Well—right away from the start it was—love!

(LEGEND: LOVE!)

(LAURA *sways slightly forward and grips the arm of the sofa. He fails to notice, now enrapt in his own comfortable being*)

Being in love has made a new man of me!

(*Leaning stiffly forward, clutching the arm of the sofa,* LAURA *struggles visibly with her storm. But* JIM *is oblivious, she is a long way off*)

The power of love is really pretty tremendous!

Love is something that—changes the whole world, Laura!

(The storm abates a little and LAURA *leans back. He notices her again)*

It happened that Betty's aunt took sick, she got a wire and had to go to Centralia. So Tom—when he asked me to dinner—I naturally just accepted the invitation, not knowing that you—that he—that I—

(He stops awkwardly)

Huh—I'm a stumble-john!

(He flops back on the sofa)

(The holy candles in the altar of LAURA'S *face have been snuffed out. There is a look of almost infinite desolation)*

*(*JIM *glances at her uneasily)*

I wish that you would—say something.

(She bites her lip which was trembling and then bravely smiles. She opens her hand again on the broken glass ornament. Then she gently takes his hand and raises it level with her own. She carefully places the unicorn in the palm of his hand, then pushes his fingers closed upon it)

What are you—doing that for? You want me to have him?—Laura?

(She nods)

What for?

LAURA   A—souvenir . . .

(She rises unsteadily and crouches beside the victrola to wind it up)

(LEGEND ON SCREEN: "THINGS HAVE A WAY OF TURNING OUT SO BADLY!")

(OR IMAGE: "GENTLEMAN CALLER WAVING GOOD-BYE!— GAILY")

(At this moment AMANDA *rushes brightly back in the front room. She bears a pitcher of fruit punch in an old-fashioned cut-glass pitcher and a plate of macaroons. The plate has a gold border and poppies painted on it)*

AMANDA   Well, well, well! Isn't the air delightful after the shower? I've made you children a little liquid refreshment.

(Turns gaily to the gentleman caller)

Jim, do you know that song about lemonade?

"Lemonade, lemonade
Made in the shade and stirred with a spade—
Good enough for any old maid!"

JIM *(Uneasily)*   Ha-ha! No—I never heard it.

AMANDA   Why, Laura! You look so serious!

JIM   We were having a serious conversation.

AMANDA   Good! Now you're better acquainted!

JIM *(Uncertainly)*   Ha-ha! Yes.

AMANDA   You modern young people are much more serious-minded than my generation. I was so gay as a girl!

JIM   You haven't changed, Mrs. Wingfield.

AMANDA   Tonight I'm rejuvenated! The gaiety of the occasion, Mr. O'Connor!

(She tosses her head with a peal of laughter. Spills lemonade)

Oooo! I'm baptizing myself!

JIM   Here—let me—

AMANDA *(Setting the pitcher down)*   There now. I discovered we had some maraschino cherries. I dumped them in, juice and all!

JIM   You shouldn't have gone to that trouble, Mrs. Wingfield.

AMANDA   Trouble, trouble? Why, it was loads of fun!

Didn't you hear me cutting up in the kitchen? I bet your ears were burning! I told Tom how outdone with him I was for keeping you to himself so long a time! He should have brought you over much, much sooner! Well, now that you've found your way, I want you to be a very frequent caller! Not just occasional but all the time.

Oh, we're going to have a lot of gay times together! I see them coming!

Mmm, just breathe that air! So fresh, and the moon's so pretty!

I'll skip back out—I know where my place is when young folks are having a—serious conversation!

JIM   Oh, don't go out, Mrs. Wingfield. The fact of the matter is I've got to be going.

AMANDA   Going, now? You're joking! Why, it's only the shank of the evening, Mr. O'Connor!

JIM   Well, you know how it is.

AMANDA   You mean you're a young workingman and have to keep workingmen's hours. We'll let you off early tonight. But only on the condition that next time you stay later.

What's the best night for you? Isn't Saturday night the best night for you workingmen?

JIM   I have a couple of time-clocks to punch, Mrs. Wingfield. One at morning, another one at night!

AMANDA   My, but you *are* ambitious! You work at night, too?

JIM   No, Ma'am, not work but—Betty! (*He crosses deliberately to pick up his hat. The band at the Paradise Dance Hall goes into a tender waltz*)

AMANDA   Betty? Betty? Who's—Betty!

(*There is an ominous cracking sound in the sky*)

JIM   Oh, just a girl. The girl I go steady with! (*He smiles charmingly. The sky falls*)

(LEGEND: "THE SKY FALLS")

AMANDA (*A long-drawn exhalation*)   Ohhhh . . . Is it a serious romance, Mr. O'Connor?

JIM   We're going to be married the second Sunday in June.

AMANDA   Ohhhh—how nice!

Tom didn't mention that you were engaged to be married.

JIM   The cat's not out of the bag at the warehouse yet.

You know how they are. They call you Romeo and stuff like that.

(*He stops at the oval mirror to put on his hat. He carefully shapes the brim and the crown to give a discreetly dashing effect*)

It's been a wonderful evening, Mrs. Wingfield. I guess this is what they mean by Southern hospitality.

AMANDA   It really wasn't anything at all.

JIM   I hope it don't seem like I'm rushing off. But I promised Betty I'd pick her up at the Wabash depot, an' by the time I get my jalopy down there her train'll be in. Some women are pretty upset if you keep 'em waiting.

AMANDA   Yes, I know—The tyranny of women!

(*Extends her hand*)

Good-bye, Mr. O'Connor.

I wish you luck—and happiness—and success! All three of them, and so does Laura!—Don't you, Laura?

LAURA   Yes!

JIM (*Taking her hand*)   Good-bye, Laura. I'm certainly going to treasure that souvenir. And don't you forget the good advice I gave you.

(Raises his voice to a cheery shout)

So long, Shakespeare!
Thanks again, ladies—Good night!

(He grins and ducks jauntily out)

(Still bravely grimacing, AMANDA *closes the door on the gentleman caller. Then she turns back to the room with a puzzled expression. She and* LAURA *don't dare to face each other.* LAURA *crouches beside the victrola to wind it)*

AMANDA *(Faintly)* Things have a way of turning out so badly.
I don't believe that I would play the victrola.
Well, well—well—
Our gentleman caller was engaged to be married!
Tom!

TOM *(From back)* Yes, Mother?

AMANDA Come in here a minute. I want to tell you something awfully funny.

TOM *(Enters with macaroon and a glass of the lemonade)* Has the gentleman caller gotten away already?

AMANDA The gentleman caller has made an early departure.
What a wonderful joke you played on us!

TOM How do you mean?

AMANDA You didn't mention that he was engaged to be married.

TOM Jim? Engaged?

AMANDA That's what he just informed us.

TOM I'll be jiggered! I didn't know about that.

AMANDA That seems very peculiar.

TOM What's peculiar about it?

AMANDA Didn't you call him your best friend down at the warehouse?

TOM He is, but how did I know?

AMANDA It seems extremely peculiar that you wouldn't know your best friend was going to be married!

TOM The warehouse is where I work, not where I know things about people!

AMANDA You don't know things anywhere! You live in a dream, you manufacture illusions!

(He crosses to door)

Where are you going?

TOM I'm going to the movies.

AMANDA That's right, now that you've had us make such fools of ourselves. The effort, the preparations, all the expense! The new floor
lamp, the rug, the clothes for Laura! All for what? To entertain some
other girl's fiancé!

Go to the movies, go! Don't think about us, a mother deserted,
an unmarried sister who's crippled and has no job! Don't let anything
interfere with your selfish pleasure!

Just go, go, go—to the movies!

TOM All right, I will! The more you shout about my selfishness to me
the quicker I'll go, and I won't go to the movies!

AMANDA Go, then! Then go to the moon—you selfish dreamer!

(TOM *smashes his glass on the floor. He plunges out on the fire
escape, slamming the door.* LAURA *screams—cut by door*)

(*Dance-hall music up.* TOM *goes to the rail and grips it desperately,
lifting his face in the chill white moonlight penetrating the narrow
abyss of the alley*)

(LEGEND ON SCREEN: "AND SO GOOD-BYE . . .")

(TOM's *closing speech is timed with the interior pantomime. The
interior scene is played as though viewed through sound-proof glass.*
AMANDA *appears to be making a comforting speech to* LAURA *who
is huddled upon the sofa. Now that we cannot hear the mother's
speech, her silliness is gone and she has dignity and tragic beauty.*
LAURA's *dark hair hides her face until at the end of the speech
she lifts it to smile at her mother.* AMANDA's *gestures are slow
and graceful, almost dancelike, as she comforts the daughter. At
the end of her speech she glances a moment at the father's picture—
then withdraws through the portieres. At close of* TOM's *speech,*
LAURA *blows out the candles, ending the play*)

TOM I didn't go to the moon, I went much further—for time is the
longest distance between two places—

Not long after that I was fired for writing a poem on the lid of
a shoe-box.

I left Saint Louis. I descended the steps of this fire escape for a
last time and followed, from then on, in my father's footsteps, attempting to find in motion what was lost in space—

I traveled around a great deal. The cities swept about me like dead
leaves, leaves that were brightly colored but torn away from the
branches.

I would have stopped, but I was pursued by something.

It always came upon me unawares, taking me altogether by surprise. Perhaps it was a familiar bit of music. Perhaps it was only a piece of transparent glass—

Perhaps I am walking along a street at night, in some strange city, before I have found companions. I pass the lighted window of a shop where perfume is sold. The window is filled with pieces of colored glass, tiny transparent bottles in delicate colors, like bits of a shattered rainbow.

Then all at once my sister touches my shoulder. I turn around and look into her eyes . . .

Oh, Laura, Laura, I tried to leave you behind me, but I am more faithful than I intended to be!

I reach for a cigarette. I cross the street, I run into the movies or a bar, I buy a drink, I speak to the nearest stranger—anything that can blow your candles out!

(LAURA *bends over the candles*)

—for nowadays the world is lit by lightning! Blow out your candles, Laura —and so good-bye. . . .

(*She blows the candles out*)

(THE SCENE DISSOLVES)

Native Son

RICHARD WRIGHT AND PAUL GREEN

CHARACTERS

BIGGER THOMAS   *A Negro youth twenty or twenty-one years old.*
HANNAH THOMAS   *His mother, fifty-five.*
VERA THOMAS   *His sister, sixteen.*
BUDDY THOMAS   *His brother, twelve.*
CLARA MEARS   *His sweetheart, twenty.*
JACK HENSON
"G. H." RANKIN
GUS MITCHELL   *Cronies of Bigger and about his age.*
ERNIE JONES   *A cafe and night club owner.*
HENRY G. DALTON   *A capitalist, about fifty-five.*
ELLEN DALTON   *His wife, about fifty.*
MARY DALTON   *Their daughter, twenty-two or three.*
PEGGY MACAULIFE   *The Dalton cook and maid, forty.*
JAN ERLONE   *A labor leader, twenty-eight.*
JEFF BRITTEN   *A private detective and local politician, forty-five.*
DAVID A. BUCKLEY   *State's attorney, forty.*
EDWARD MAX   *An elderly lawyer.*
MISS EMMET   *A social worker.*
A NEWSPAPERMAN
Other newspapermen, neighbors, guards, a Judge, and others

TIME

The present.

PLACE

The Black Belt of Chicago.

From the novel by Richard Wright

Scene 9

(The sound of the mob dies away and the curtain goes up on the court room, two weeks later.

Behind the desk, on an imposing dais at the rear, sits the Judge, draped in a long black gown, and with a gray and heavy juridical face. Hanging directly above him, and behind, is the picture of an eighteenth century statesman resembling the likeness of Thomas Jefferson and surmounted by the graceful folds of the Stars and Stripes. Down in front of the Judge's desk is an oblong table. Between the desk and the table sit the Sheriff, the Clerk and the Court stenographer. To the right and left rear, somewhat framing the scene, stand two Militiamen at stiff attention, their bayoneted rifles held straight by their sides. At the right front sit HANNAH THOMAS, VERA and BUDDY. BUDDY is holding tightly to his mother's hand. In the same position at the left sit the DALTONS and PEGGY. The two women wear veils and are in deep mourning. BUCKLEY, the Prosecuting Attorney, is sitting to the right of DALTON. At the table, with his back to the audience is BIGGER. He seems to pay no attention to what is going on around him. The scene is in darkness as the curtain rises, and out of this darkness comes the deep tumult of many voices, and then other voices raised in argument. As if in rhythm to the banging of the Judge's gavel the light comes swiftly up on the scene, showing EDWARD MAX and BUCKLEY, both on their feet, in front of the Judge's stand.

MAX, now that we see him in the light, is a big, flabby, kindly-faced man, with something sad and tragic in the pallid whiteness of his skin and the melancholy depths of his eyes. His hair is silvery white. There is a general air of poverty and yet of deep abiding peace about him. BUCKLEY is a suave, well-built man of about 40, with the florid, commanding face of the American business executive. He wears a carnation in the lapel of his morning coat)

BUCKLEY *(Shouting)*   Your Honor!

MAX *(Quietly)*   I am not out of order, your Honor.

BUCKLEY   The counsel for the defense cannot plead this boy both guilty and insane!

MAX   I have made no such plea.

BUCKLEY   If you plead him insane, the State will demand a jury trial.

JUDGE   Go on, Mr. Max.

MAX   Your Honor, I am trying to make the Court understand the true

nature of this case—I want the mind of the Court to be free and clear
—And then if the Court says death, let it mean death. And if the
Court says life, let it mean that too. But whatever the Court says, let
it know upon what ground its verdict is being rendered.

(*Glancing at his notes*)

Night after night I have lain without sleep trying to think of a way to
picture to you, and to the world, the causes, the reasons, why this
Negro boy sits here today—a self-confessed murderer—and why this
great city is boiling with a fever of excitement and hate. And yet how
can I, I ask myself, make the picture of what has happened to this
boy show plain and powerful upon a screen of sober reason, when
a thousand newspaper and magazine artists have already drawn it in
lurid ink upon a million sheets of public print? I have pled the cause
of other criminal youths in this court as his Honor well knows. And
when I took this case I thought at first it was the same old story of
a boy run afoul of the law. But it is more terrible than that—with
meaning more far-reaching. Where is the responsibility? Where is the
guilt? For there is guilt in the rage that demands that this man's life
be stamped out! There is guilt and responsibility in the hate that
inflames that mob gathered in the streets below these windows! What
is the atmosphere that surrounds this trial? Are the citizens intent
upon seeing that the majesty of the Law is upheld? That retribution
be dealt out in measure with the facts? That the guilty, and only the
guilty, be caught and punished? No!

BUCKLEY   I object, your Honor!

MAX (*Continuing*)   The hunt for Bigger Thomas has served as a political
excuse, not only to terrorize the entire Negro population of this city,
but also to arrest hundreds of members of suspect organizations, to
raid labor union headquarters and workers' gatherings!

BUCKLEY   Objection!

JUDGE   Objection sustained! Strike all that from the record. You will
confine your remarks to the evidence in the case.

MAX   Your Honor, for the sake of this boy, I wish I could bring to you
evidence of a morally worthier nature. I wish I could say that love,
or ambition, or jealousy, or the quest for adventure, or any of the more
romantic emotions were back of this case. But I cannot. I have no
choice in the matter. Life has cut this cloth, not I. Fear and hate
and guilt are the keynotes of this drama. You see, your Honor, I am
not afraid to assign the blame, for thus I can the more honestly plead
for mercy! I say that this boy is the victim of a wrong that has grown,
like a cancer, into the very blood and bone of our social structure.
Bigger Thomas sits here today as a symbol of that wrong. And the
judgment that you will deliver upon him is a judgment delivered upon

ourselves, and upon our whole civilization. The Court can pronounce the sentence of death and that will end the defendant's life—but it will not end this wrong!

BUCKLEY   Your Honor, I object—

JUDGE   The Court is still waiting for you to produce mitigating evidence, Mr. Max!

MAX   Very well. Let us look back into this boy's childhood. On a certain day, he stood and saw his own father shot down by a Southern mob —while trying to protect one of his own kind from violence and hate —the very violence and hate represented in the mob gathered around this court-house today. With his mother and sister and little brother, Bigger Thomas fled North to this great city, hoping to find here a freer life for himself and those he loved. And what did he find here? Poverty, idleness, economic injustice, race discrimination and all the squeezing and oppression of a ruthless world—our world, your Honor —yours and mine! Here again he found the violence and the degradation from which he had fled. Here again he found the same frustrated way of life intensified by the cruelty of a blind and enslaving industrial mechanism. It is that way of life that stands on trial today, your Honor, in the person of Bigger Thomas! Like his forefathers, he is a slave. But unlike his forefathers, there is something in him that refuses to accept this slavery. And why does he refuse to accept it? Because through the very teachings of our schools and educational system he was led to believe that in this land of liberty men are free. With one part of his mind, he believed what we had taught him— that he was a free man! With the other he found himself denied the right to accept that truth. In theory he was stimulated by every token around him to aspire to be a free individual. And in practice by every method of our social system, he was frustrated in that aspiration. Out of this confusion, fear was born. And fear breeds hate, and hate breeds guilt, and guilt in turn breeds the urge to destroy—to kill.

(The Judge is now listening intently to MAX)

BUCKLEY   (*Shouting out*)   I object! All this is merely an attempt to prove the prisoner insane—

JUDGE   (*Rapping with his gavel*)   Objection over-ruled.

MAX   (*Turning toward* MR. AND MRS. DALTON)   Consider these witnesses for the State, Mr. and Mrs. Dalton. I have only sympathy for these poor grieving parents. You have heard their testimony and you have heard them plead for leniency toward this boy.

(Pause)

Well may they plead for leniency for perhaps they are as guilty of this crime as he is!

BUCKLEY   Your Honor—

MAX   Unconsciously, and against their will, they are partners in this drama of guilt and blood. They intended no evil—yet they produced evil.

BUCKLEY (*Furiously*)   I object. He is impugning the character of my witnesses.

MAX (*Quietly*)   I am not. I have only sympathy for them. But I am trying to state the facts, and these are the facts. This man rents his vast real estate holdings to many thousands of Negroes, and among these thousands is the family of this boy, Bigger Thomas. The rents in those tenements are proportionately the highest, and the living conditions the worst of any in this city. Yet this man is held in high esteem. Why? Because out of the profits he makes from those rents, he turns around and gives back to the Negroes a small part as charity. For this he is lauded in the press and held up as an example of fine citizenship. But where do the Negroes come in? Nowhere. What do they have to say about how they live? Nothing. Around the whole vicious circle they move and act at this man's behest, and must accept the crumbs of their own charity as Mr. Dalton wills, or wills not. It is a form of futile bribery that continues, and will continue, until we see the truth and stop it. For corpses cannot be bribed—And such living corpses as Bigger Thomas here, are warnings to us to stop it, and stop it now before it is too late—

BUCKLEY   Your Honor! (*The Judge waves him down, and* MAX *goes on*)

MAX   One more word, your Honor, and I am done.

(*Pointing towards the portrait on the wall at the rear*)

There, under that flag, is the likeness of one of our forefathers—one of the men who came to these strange shores hundreds of years ago in search of freedom. Those men, and we who followed them, built here a nation mighty and powerful, the most powerful nation on earth! Yet to those who, as much as any others, helped us build this nation, we have said, and we continue to say, "This is a white man's country!" Night and day, millions of souls, the souls of our black people, are crying out, "This is our country too. We helped build it—helped defend it. Give us a part in it, a part free and hopeful and wide as the everlasting horizon." And in this fear-crazed, guilt-ridden body of Bigger Thomas that vast multitude cries out to you now in a mighty voice, saying, "Give us our freedom, our chance, and our hope to be men." Can we ignore this cry? Can we continue to boast through every medium of public utterance—through literature, newspapers, radio, the pulpit—that this is a land of freedom and opportunity, of liberty and justice for all—and in our behavior deny all these precepts of charity and enlightenment? Bigger Thomas is a symbol of that double-dealing, an organism which our political and economic hypocrisy has bred. Kill him, burn the life out of him, and still the symbol of his living death remains. And you cannot kill Bigger Thomas, for he is already dead. He was born dead—born dead among the wild forests of our cities, amid the rank and choking vegetation of our slums —in the Jim Crow corners of our busses and trains—in the dark closets and corridors and rest rooms marked off by the finger of a blind and prejudiced law as Black against White. And who created that law? We did. And while it lasts we stand condemned before mankind— Your Honor, I beg you, not in the name of Bigger Thomas but in the name of ourselves, spare this boy's life!

(*He turns to his seat at the table beside* BIGGER. *Immediately the roar of the crowd outside swells in upon the scene. The Judge bangs with his gavel again and the lights dim down. For a moment the noise continues and then dies away as the lights come up again.* BUCKLEY *is now addressing the Judge. His manner is earnest, kindly and confident*)

BUCKLEY   The counsel for the defense may criticize the American nation and its methods of government. But that government is not on trial today. Only one person, the defendant, Bigger Thomas, is on trial. He pleads guilty to the charges of the indictment. The rest is simple and brief. Punishment must follow—punishment laid down by the sacred laws of this Commonwealth—laws created to protect that society and that social system of which we are a part! A criminal is one who goes against those laws. He attacks the laws. Therefore the laws must destroy him. If thine eye offend thee, pluck it out; and if the branch of a tree withers and dies, it must be cut off lest it contaminate the rest of the tree. Such a tree is the State through whose flourishing and good health we ourselves exist and carry on our lives. The ruined, the rotten and degraded must be cut out, cleansed away so that the body politic itself may keep its health. I sympathize with the counsel for the defense. I understand his point of view, his persuasive argument. But the simple truth is, your Honor, he is deluded. His thinking, his arguments, run contrary to the true course of man and man's sound development. Yes, if the Defense wishes, let us speak not in terms of crime, but in terms of disease. I pity this diseased and ruined defendant. But as a true surgeon, looking to the welfare of the organic body of our people, I repeat that it is necessary this diseased member be cut off—cut out and obliterated —lest it infect us all unto death. Your Honor, I regret that the Defense has raised the viperous issue of race and class hatred in this trial. Justice should, and must be, dispensed fairly and equally, in accordance with the facts, and not with theories—and justice is all I ask. And what are the facts? That this Bigger Thomas is sane and is responsible for his crimes—And all the eloquent tongues of angels or men cannot convince this honorable court that it and I and others gathered here are the guilty ones. Bigger Thomas is guilty and in his soul he knows it.

Your Honor, in the name of the people of this city, in the name of truth and Almighty God, I demand that this Bigger Thomas justly die for the brutal murder of Mary Dalton!

(*Through the whole scene, the spectators have remained motionless, and even* BUDDY *has sat like a little black statue, his eyes fastened straight on the bowed figure of his brother. As* BUCKLEY *takes his seat, the lights begin to dim on the scene, and once again the sound of the great mob outside permeates the room in a heavy, undulating drone. The scene seems to recede from us, and now, out of the thickening gloom, comes the voice of the Judge*)

JUDGE'S VOICE   Bigger Thomas, stand up.

(*The murmur of the mob continues*)

BLACKOUT

Scene 10

(*The sound of the mob dies away and the curtain goes up on the death cell. It is a few weeks later.*

Directly across and separated by only a few feet of corridor is the death chamber, its heavy iron door closed. There is a barred door in the left wall of the cell, and on the wall at the right a porcelain wash basin is fastened, sticking out like a frozen lip. Along the wall at the right rear is an iron cot covered with a white morgue-like sheet. The atmosphere is one of scientific anesthesia and deathly cleanliness.

Seen through the slanting bars at the left rear are two uniformed guards seated at a little table playing rummy. One is an elderly man, the other much younger. The cell is lighted by a single electric bulb on the ceiling, and the streaking shadows of the bars cut across the figures of the two guards behind.

When the curtain rises, BIGGER *is standing against the wall by the door, looking out to the front, with his body half turned towards the rear. He is dressed in a white short-sleeved shirt open at the throat, and dark gray flannel trousers, one leg of which is slit open from the knee down. His head is shaved, and he is staring out after the retreating forms of his mother, sister and brother. Sobbing, the mother tries to go back to* BIGGER, *but is restrained by the younger guard who rises to meet her)*

HANNAH   My boy, my poor boy—
BUDDY   Ma, don't do that! Ma—

(HANNAH *is led away and her sobs die out.* BIGGER *continues to stare after her without a sound)*

FIRST GUARD (*In a quiet voice laying down a card*)   That old woman takes it hard.
SECOND GUARD (*Coming back*)   It's her son.
FIRST GUARD (*Jerking his head toward* BIGGER)   He don't seem to care though.
SECOND GUARD   Since that time he cried all night long, he don't say much.
FIRST GUARD   And how he cried—But reckon that old water hose stopped him—

(*There is a rush at the left and* BUDDY *runs up to the cell bars and grips them in an agony of grief)*

BUDDY   Ma says don't you worry—we gonna take care of you—later.
SECOND GUARD   Go on, sonny.
BUDDY   And it gonna be at Reverend Hammond's church, Bigger. And plenty of flowers—and folks, Bigger.

(*At a gesture from the* FIRST GUARD, *the* SECOND GUARD *leads* BUDDY *off.* BIGGER *has stood motionless.* BUDDY *goes away, straining his eyes on* BIGGER *to the last)*

BIGGER (*Calling quietly*)   Tell Vera good-by.
BUDDY'S VOICE (*Brokenly*)   Yeh, yeh. Good-by—ee—
(*His voice dies away*)
FIRST GUARD (*With meaningless comfort calling toward* BIGGER)   I know—Time passes slow. Ten more minutes, boy, that's all.

SECOND GUARD (*Returning*)   Then eight seconds after that you won't worry. Just take a deep breath—eight seconds! Go ahead and talk, son. Make it easier, maybe.

(*But* BIGGER *remains silent*)

FIRST GUARD   Your lawyer's here—

(BIGGER *shakes his head*)

SECOND GUARD   He'll wanta walk with you in case—

BIGGER   Don't need nobody—

SECOND GUARD (*Admiringly*)   Got iron in his blood, all right, I'll say that.
(*He seats himself at the table again*)
Damn, he's tough!

(*They resume their card playing. A third guard comes up to the door out of the darkness, followed by* MAX. *He goes back the way he came. The* SECOND GUARD *lets* MAX *into the cell and then reseats himself, his face still caught in its look of hurt and nauseous pain.* MAX *stands mopping his brow, his face flabby and old*)

MAX   No word yet, son. I'm sorry.

BIGGER (*In a muffled voice*)   That's okay, Mr. Max.

MAX   We're doing all we can. Mrs. Dalton's with the Governor now. There's maybe still a chance—

BIGGER (*With an odd touch of shame as he suddenly indicates his shaved head*)   They changed my looks.

MAX   Mr. Dalton too. He's got power. I'm still hoping—

BIGGER   I'm all right, Mr. Max. You ain't to blame for what's happened to me. (*His voice drops to a low, resigned and melancholy note*)   I reckon—uh—I—uh—I just reckon I had it coming. (*He stands with his lips moving, shaking his head, but no words come*)

MAX (*Leaning forward*)   What is it, Bigger?

BIGGER (*In a heavy expiring breath*)   Naw.

MAX   Talk to me, Bigger. You can trust me, you know that.

BIGGER   Trust or don't trust, all the same. Ain't nobody can help me now. (*He sits down, his lips moving inaudibly again*)

MAX (*Quietly*)   What are you trying to say, Bigger?

BIGGER (*After a moment, shouting*)   I—I just want to say maybe I'm glad I got to know you before I go!

MAX   I—I'm glad I got to know you too, Bigger. I'll soon be going, son. I'm old. But others will carry on our fight—

BIGGER   What I got to do with it?

MAX   And because of you—whether you live or die, Bigger, we will be nearer the victory—justice and freedom for men. I want you to know that.

BIGGER (*His voice dropping down*) Ain't nobody ever talked to me like you before. (*He breaks off and turns distractedly about him*) How come you do it—and you being a white man? (*With wild impulsiveness*) You oughta left me alone. How come you want to help me in the first place, and me black and a murderer maybe ten times over?

MAX (*Placing his hand on* BIGGER'S *shoulder as he pulls away*) Bigger, in my work—and the work the world has ahead—there are no whites and blacks—only men. And you make me feel, Bigger, and others feel it—how badly men want to live in this world—to say here is where I once was. This was me, big and strong . . . till the years quit falling down. You feel like that, don't you, Bigger? You felt like that?

BIGGER Sometimes I wish you wouldn't ask me all them questions, Mr. Max. Goddamit, I wish you wouldn't. (*He chokes on his words, in regret and impotent despair, and then regains his voice*) I was all set to die maybe. I was all right. Then you come and start talking, digging into me, opening up my guts.

MAX I want to understand you, get near to you, Bigger.

BIGGER (*Almost whispering*) Understand me. She said that—understand me—(*His voice dies out. The guards now sit muffled and motionless in the gloom*)

MAX And she was trying to help you, wasn't she? (*Pause*) Don't you know she was trying to help you?

BIGGER She made me feel like a dog! Yeah, that's the way all of 'em made me feel. In their big house I was all trembling and afraid. (*His voice trails off again*)

MAX (*Suddenly*) Didn't you ever love anybody, Bigger?

BIGGER Maybe I loved my daddy. Long time ago. They killed him. (*Suddenly shouting as he springs up and begins to pace the cell*) Goddamn it, there you start again. You mix me all up! (*With a wild moan*) You make me feel something could happen—something good maybe—(*Frenziedly*) You creep in on me, crowd me to the wall, smother me and I want my breath, right up till that lightning hits me. Go away, Mr. Max.

MAX That day I said we had made you what you were, a killer—maybe I was wrong—I want to know I was wrong—(*He gazes at* BIGGER *with white pained face*)

BIGGER (*Softly, half to himself*) His po' face like the face of Jesus hanging on that wall—like her face too.

MAX You killed Clara. Why? She loved you, she was good. You say you killed her.

BIGGER (*Stopping his pacing*) Yeh, I killed her—

MAX   You're not crazy, and there's not that kind of crazy logic in this world. I ask you and all the time you say, "I just did." That's not it, not it.

BIGGER   Then I didn't kill her. They said I shot her. I didn't. Wasn't no use talking 'bout it. She didn't count. I just let 'em say it.

MAX (*An uncertain joy in his voice*)   You didn't shoot her?

BIGGER   One their bullets went clean through her. I had her in my arms, I let her fall down—

MAX (*With a shout*)   We could have proved it. It might have—Thank God. (*He sinks down on the cot, staring at* BIGGER)

BIGGER   But I killed her just the same. All the time I'd been killing her the way I'd been killing myself. She'd suffered for me, followed me, and I didn't want it—wanted to be free to walk wild and free with steps a mile long—over the houses, over the rivers, and straddling the mountains and on—something in me—

MAX   And you didn't want to be hindered—you'd kill anything that got in your way—

BIGGER   Reckon so. But I wasn't thinking of that then.

MAX (*Watching him*)   And would you kill again, Bigger, if you could?

BIGGER (*Quieting down*)   I   dunno—Naw—Yessuh,   I   dunno. Sometimes I feel like it. Maybe you're wrong now and I am bad and rotten the way you thought at the trial—made bad, and like that other man said. I dunno what I am—got no way to prove it. (*Wetting his lips*)   All the time I lie here thinking, beating my head against a wall, trying to see through, over it, but can't. Maybe 'cause I'm gonna die makes me want to see—know what I am maybe. How can I die like that, Mr. Max?

MAX   If we knew how to live, Bigger, we'd know how to die.

BIGGER   Yeh, people can live together but a man got to die by himself. That don't make sense—He needs something to die by more than to live by. (*As* MAX *is silent*)   I ain't trying to dodge what's coming. But, Mr. Max, maybe I ain't never wanted to hurt nobody—for real I ain't, maybe. (*His eyes are wide as he stares ahead, straining to feel and think his way through the darkness*)

MAX   Go on, Bigger.

BIGGER   Seem like with you here try to help me—you so good and kind—I begin to think better. (*Shaking his head again*)   Uh, but why the folks who sent me here hate me so? That mob—I can hear 'em still—'Cause I'm black?

MAX (*With gentle, yearning comfort*)   No, that's not it, Bigger. Your being black just makes it easier to be singled out in a white man's world. That's all. What they wanted to do to you they do to each other every day. They don't hate you and they don't hate each other. They are men like you, like me, and they feel like you. They want the things of life just as you do, their own chance. But as long as these are denied them—just so long will those millions keep groping around frightened and lost—angry and full of hate—the way you were, Bigger. (*He pauses*) Bigger, the day these millions—these millions of poor men —workers, make up their minds—begin to believe in themselves—

BIGGER   Yeh, reckon the workers believe in themselves all right. Try to get into one them labor unions. Naw, Mr. Max. Everywhere you turn they shut the door in your face, keep you homeless as a dog. Never no chance to be your own man. That's what I always wanted to be—my own man—(*Staring at* MAX) Honest to God, Mr. Max, I never felt like my own man till right after that happened—till after I killed her.

MAX (*Fiercely*)   No, Bigger.

BIGGER   Yeh—and all the peoples and all the killings and the hangings and the burnings inside me, kept me pushing me on—up and on to do something big—have money like that kidnap note—power— something great—to keep my head up—to put my name on the hot wires of the world—big—And, yeh, and all the bad I done, it seemed was right—and after they caught me I kept saying it was right and I was gonna stand on it, hold it—walk that long road down to that old chair—look at it, say, "Do your worst! Burn me. Shoot your juice, and I can take it. You can kill me but can't hurt me—can't hurt me" —It's the truth, Mr. Max, after I killed that white girl, I wasn't scared no more—for a little while. (*His voice rises with feverish intensity*)   I was my own man then, I was free. Maybe it was 'cause they was after my life then. They made me wake up. That made me feel high and powerful—free! (*With growing vehemence*)   That day and night after I done killed her—when all of them was looking for me—hunting me—that day and night for the first time I felt like a man. (*Shouting*)   I was a man!

MAX (*Loudly*)   You don't believe that, Bigger.

BIGGER   Yeah, yeah, I felt like a man—when I was doing what I never thought I'd do—something I never wanted to do. And it was crazy —wrong and crazy. (*With a piteous childlike cry*)   Why, Mr. Max? Why!

MAX   That's the answer men must find, Bigger.

BIGGER (*Lowering his head*)   I'm all right now, Mr. Max—I'm all right. Don't be scared of me. I'm all right. You go on. I don't feel that way now. It didn't last.

MAX   It never lasts, Bigger.

(*The dynamo in the death chamber at the left begins to hum, and the light in the ceiling of* BIGGER'S *cell dims down and then regains its brilliance. The humming dies away*)

BIGGER They 'bout ready now. (*Whispering queerly*) And that midnight mail is flying late.

MAX Hold onto yourself, son. There's still a chance—

BIGGER They ready but I can't see it clear yet. (*Licking his lips*) But I be all right, Mr. Max. Just go and tell Ma I was all right and not to worry none—see? Tell her I was all right and not crying none.

MAX (*His words almost inaudible now*) Yes, Bigger.

BIGGER Yeh, I'm going now and ain't done it, ain't done it yet.

MAX What, Bigger?

BIGGER (*Panting and beating his fists together*) Nothing really right yet—like what I wanted to do. Living or dead, they don't give me no chance—I didn't give myself no chance.

(*The two guards rise from the table. They look off and up at the left rear*)

FIRST GUARD Well—

SECOND GUARD Yeah.

(*A low mournful harmony, hardly heard at first, begins among the prisoners in the cells stretching away to the rear. The* THIRD GUARD *comes swiftly up out of the darkness. He hands a telegram to* MAX *who seizes it.* BIGGER *begins gazing up at the ceiling of his cell, as if listening for a sound afar off*)

MAX (*In a low voice*) Bigger. (*He opens the telegram—For an instant he looks at it and then his shoulders sag slowly down. He murmurs*) Want to read it, son— (*But* BIGGER *does not answer.* MAX *sticks out his hand in farewell, his face old and broken, then lets it fall*)

FIRST GUARD One minute past midnight.

SECOND GUARD All right, son.

(*They start moving toward the cell.* BIGGER *still stands with his face lifted and set in its tense concentration*)

BIGGER (*In a fierce convulsive whisper*) There she comes—Yeh, I hear you. (*Far above in the night the murmuring throb of an airplane motor is audible.* BIGGER'S *voice bursts from him in a wild frenzied call*) Fly them planes, boys—fly 'em!—Riding through—riding through. I'll be with you! I'll—

FIRST GUARD   Come on, he's going nuts! (*He quickly unlocks the cell and they enter*)

BIGGER (*Yelling, his head wagging in desperation*)   Keep on driving! —To the end of the world—smack into the face of the sun! (*Gasping*)   Fly 'em for me—for Bigger—

> (*The sound of the airplane fades away and now the death chant of the prisoners comes more loudly into the scene. In the dim corridor at the rear the white surplice of a priest is discerned*)

SECOND GUARD (*Touching* BIGGER *on the arm*)   This way, son.

> (*They start leading him from the cell. As if of its own volition the door to the little death house opens and a flood of light pours out.* BIGGER, *with his eyes set and his shoulders straight, moves toward its sunny radiance like a man walking into a deep current of water. The guards quietly follow him, their heads bent down*)

MAX (*Staring after him, his big white face wet with tears*)   Good-by, Bigger. (BIGGER *enters the door*)

PRIEST'S VOICE (*Intoning from the shadows*)   I am the resurrection and the life.

> (*The death chant of the prisoners grows louder. The door to the death house closes, cutting off the light*)

THE END

Fannie Lou Hamer:
This Little Light of Mine. . .

BILLIE JEAN YOUNG

ACT I

FANNIE LOU HAMER "Pee-pi, pee-pi, where you little lamb? Way down in the valley. Birds and the butterflies picking at his eyes and the po' lil' thing it cry, mama. Mama gone, papa gone, they shall bring some horses, white and black, purple and gray, all them pretty little horses. When you wake, you'll eat a hoe cake and ride the pretty little pony. Go to sleep, go to sleep, go to sleepy little baby. Mama run away, papa couldn't stay, there's nobody but the baby. Go to sleep, with your by you ba, go the sleepy little baby."

I AIN'T NO STRANGER TO STRUGGLE. My mama taught me that song; her mama taught it to her. My granmama was a slave. I used to sing that song to my babies, too. See, we had to leave the babies on the end of the row while we was picking cotton, and you would just have to hope and pray that the antses and flies and mosquitos and things didn't get on your baby. Every year, we get through picking cotton, sheer-cropping for the white man, my mama still wouldn't have no money to feed us, so she would ask the people for the little cotton they had done left in the field, and didn't want to be bothered with trying to gather, if we could scrap it. We would just walk for miles and miles, sometimes it would be cold and the ground would be frozen over and we wouldn't have no shoes, and my mama would take paper and rags and tie our feet up. And we would just walk from field to field picking cotton, my mama and her chillun, scrapping cotton.

"Pee-pi, pee-pi, where you little lamb? Way down in the valley. Birds and the butterflies picking at his eyes and the po' lil' thing it cry, mama. Mama gone, papa gone, they shall bring some horses, white and black, purple and gray, all them pretty little horses."

ISSAQUENA That was Mrs. Fannie Lou Hamer, or at least that's how

I saw her one day talking to a bunch of small children over in Edwards, Mississippi. "Every once in a now and then somebody moves in such a way that makes us jerk up and take notice. Mrs. Hamer made some decisions during the 1960s that made some of us stand up and follow; feeling a little stronger and going a little further because of the chances she took—Mississippi will never be the same!" Bernice Reagon said that about Mrs. Fannie Lou Hamer. Miss Hamer made me jerk up and take notice. I'm Issaquena Hopewell and I'm still hopeful that something good can come of me. I'm still hopeful that something good can come of you, too. That's why I wanna tell you about this woman, name of Fannie Lou . . . Hamer was her name. I love my Southland, I like the soil and yes, I like the dirt, and yes, I picked a little cotton, too. "Jump down turn around, pick a bale of cotton, jump down turn around, pick a bale a day . . ." When she was six years ole, Miss Hamer got tricked into picking cotton. Before that she was a little child playing on the end of the row. See, children during those days didn't get hold of fruit and junk food like they do now everytime somebody comes from the store. My mama says at Christmas time, (and she right along the same age with Miss Hamer) they would get an apple and an orange and maybe a little stick of peppermint candy if they were lucky. And the rest of the time, you didn't see no treats. You remember how loud apples and oranges used to smell at Christmas time? That's cause it was an unfamiliar smell to you. Those smells didn't enter the house too often. Anyway, the man told Fannie Lou that if she picked 30 pounds of cotton that day, she could have anything she wanted from the commissary. That was his store, on the plantation. Fannie Lou was just a baby girl, and you know she wanted those treats out of the store. So she picked cotton hard, this little crippled girl trying to pick 30 lbs. of cotton (you know she had polio when she was a child). Course, the plantation owner was delighted when she did. He just rared back and laughed and gave her a cookie and some gum that she picked out at the store. And the next day, you see, he *required* her to pick 60 pounds. That's how Fannie Lou started on her cotton picking career at age 6. When she quit picking cotton 39 years later, she was 45 years old and she was picking 2–300 pounds of cotton a day.

This sharecropping thing was a evil system that replaced slavery. Some people called it working on halves, all about the same—slavery, sharecropping, or on halves—you do the work, white man get the money. Didn't make no difference what you called it. Come to think of it, Miss Hamer was good about looking at things with a straight eye, and calling it what it was. She was a direct person, wasn't after no foolishness and beating around the bush—and she would tell you how she felt about things, not just tell you something to make you think she agrees with you like some people do. I saw her at one of those women's conventions that was so popular many years ago in the East one time, Miss Hamer had been invited to speak. Well, you know, the woman who spoke before Miss Hamer really let the hammer down. Women had just started to talking out loud about how low down some men could be. So, this woman went on and on, and on about how bad all the men were. Miss Hamer was the next speaker.

FANNIE LOU "I don't know 'bout-y'all's mens, but my man is a tall man, and we both know how to stand up!" She was through with that. Mrs. Hamer had a way of getting right to the point of things.

ISSAQUENA Now, Miss Hamer was talking about her husband, Perry Hamer. People call him Pap. Good man. Miss Hamer was a good woman. She and Pap was good for each other. Miss Hamer and Pap would come in from the field some time and when they was through with supper and everything, they would sit out on the porch and talk, try to cool off before they went to bed. "Come on, give mama some sugar fore you to go bed; that's it, give Pap some sugar, too. Now say your prayers. God gon' know if you don't say your prayers. Now, git, git to bed. Good nite. You know school done started. Pity and a shame ain't nothing up there at that raggedy school but the teachers and them walls and the chillun. Chillun is apt, too. You know them chillun what come in here from up north, them is apt chillun, too. You know they tell me that Negroes can vote in other places; that we is got a right to vote. Naw, like in the 'lections. You know, like they have in Sunflower County, like to vote for school board, sheriffs and things. You hear 'em talking 'bout it all the time, who winning and everything, but you don't hear 'em say nothing 'bout us voting. Well, if the colored peoples is voting in other places, then we oughta be 'lowed to vote heah. What 'cha think? Make any kinda sense to you? Pap, I wanna go to Indianola to try to register to vote. Well, yes, I know we got to eat and sleep, but that's all we ever been working for, Pap, eating and sleeping. We ain't got nothing but ourself and these chillun, and a new debt every yeah. I know we could do better than this. Pap, don't you see? This 1962; I'm 45 years old. We not getting no younger. We running this place. I'm the timekeeper here. I know what this place make; you do, too, 'cause you managing it. Ah, they ain't gon' never call you the manager but you doing it just the same. But it ain't gon' never do nothing for us. I'm thinking 'bout the chirren and you and me, too. Ah, Pap, I done already signed my name to the list to go to Indianola to register next Friday. Don't you think one of us should go? Nothing fail but a try and we sho ain't got nothing to lose. Pap? Pap?

Come By Here/Cum Bah Yeah

"Cum bah yeah, my Lawd, cum bah yeah;
Cum bah yeah, my Lawd, cum bah yeah;
Cum bah yeah, my Lawd, cum bah yeah,
O' Lawd, cum bah yeah."

FANNIE LOU Our Heavenly Father, I come before your throne of under-served kindness with bowed head and humbled heart, asking you to show me the way, Lord. We lost chillun crying in the wilderness on these plantations in Mississippi, and we need you to guide us and protect us, and teach us what is right. Jesus, it was you who said that out of the mouths of babies the truth could come. If these chillun is telling us the right thing Lord, if there is a way to change Mississippi to make things better for colored people, show us now. If this is what you set before me, Lord, then I don't want nothing else. If it's your will for me to be a slave, show me, Lord. But if this not your will, show me what to do. Lord, you said if we take one step, you'll take two; I want you to hear me now. I come before you in the name of Jesus, Lord. Show us what to do. Help us, teach us, guide us, go with these young folks, go with all of us, the old folks and the young folks, help us to see the truth. And Lord if its not in you will, I don't want no parts of it, but if it's your will, Lord, if you want us to make a move, Jesus, I beg you, just show me some kind of sign. If you help us, Lord, I promise to obey you and do your will, I promise to go in your name, Lord, show us the shining star, lead us out of the darkness in Mississippi, we want you to go with us, stand by us. We know that we are your chillun, that you is a powerful God. And I know, Father; that with you all things is possible. You can deliver us from the hand of iniquity and from the jaw of the lion just like you delivered Jonah from the belly of the whale, just like you was with the Hebrew boys in the fiery furnace, went down with Moses to Egypt and told old Pharoh to let your people go, I know, Lord, that you can deliver us. This is you humble servant, Lord, Fannie Lou, asking you, Jesus, to innercede for the dark chillun of Mississippi. We your chillun, Lord, you said so, we know, Lord that you don't make no difference in respect of color. You said, "suffer little children come unto me" and you didn't name no color. Well, your chillun is suffering Lord, in Mississippi, and I'm coming to you in the only way I know how, on my knees, begging you Jesus, to have mercy, have mercy on us, O Lord. Have mercy upon you lost chillun. And when all is said and done, done all we can do on this earth, and the old flesh is dead and rotton, I ask for a home in your kingdom, Father. Yes! Yes! In Jesus name we pray, Amen.

Song

"Ask the savior to help you,
Comfort, strengthen and keep you,

Jesus is willing to help you,
He will carry you through."

FANNIE LOU   Well, you know, today's the day, Pap, for me to go to Indianola to put my name on the voters registration list. Now, Pap, what kinda answer is that. "If I got to go, I got to go?" I would have a fit if I turn over one morning and I didn't find you in the bed. But I got to go. I got to. OK? OK.

That's what he meant. "If I got to go, I got to go." Pap understand; Pap a mess. Know what he told me bout going down here to register? "Fannie Lou, ya picking in the right cotton to get your hundred." Huh! "Good Morning, my name is Fannie Lou Hamer and I'm here to regis-ter to vote." (*She practices saying it*)   "My name is Fannie Lou Hamer and I'm here to register to vote. Yes'm Fannie Lou, that's my name, yes'm register to vote. Probably be more like that!

Song

"Ain't gonna let nobody turn me 'round,
Turn me round, turn me round;
Ain't gonna let nobody turn me 'round,
Gonna keep on a walking, keep on a talking,
Marching up the freedom land.
Ain't gonna let no police turn me 'round,
Turn me 'round, turn me 'round,
Ain't gonna let no police turn me 'round,
I'm gonna keep on walking, keep on a talking,
Marching up the freedom lane."

ISSAQUENA   Now, the white people was mad about these 18 colored people going to Indianola on a bus to try to register to vote. They even called Fannie Lou's boss man, old man Cropper. Now Cropper was really mad! Here was Fannie Lou right up under his nose, pulling something like that. So when the courthouse people called him to let him know that one of the colored people off his place was in Indianola trying to register to vote, he went straight to Pap. Thought Pap didn't know nothing bout it. "Well, Pap, do you know what Fannie Lou is doing?" Pulling his hands in and out of his khaki pants pocket, and he was already sweating that early, so his shirt and his hair was plastered to his head. He was hot? "Pap, do you know what that woman is doing, your wife?" Pap stood back and looked at him: "Yes, sir, my wife told me where she was going when she left home." Well, that was kind of a surprise to old man Cropper, got really red in the face when Pap said that. "Well, you tell Fannie Lou I wanna see her soon as she get home." And he went on back across the road to his own house. Well, soon as Miss Hamer come home, Cropper was back out in the yard wanting to talk to her. "Fannie Lou, I like you and Pap, y'all hard working people, earnest people, like to keep y'all 'round. But I can't have you down at that courthouse stirring up trouble. You gon' have to go down there and take your name off that vote list, or get offa my place one." Miss Hamer was ready for that: "Well, no sir, I was registering for myself; I didn't register for you." Well, the upshot of that was Cropper put Miss Hamer out that night. Her and the children, Virgie Ree and Dorothy went and stayed with the deacon's wife that night. Pap took 'em and he come on back home. Next morning, here come Cropper again. "Well, Pap, what did Fannie Lou say?" You know a white person can ask you a impossible question, "What you thing my wife say when you put her out of her house, white man?" Pap was saying to hisself.

Pap looked at 'em: "Well you know she gone cause you told her she couldn't stay here. I'm gon' finish my crop and I'm gon' be gone." Cropper knowed he was beat then. He jumped back: Had finally hit that white man in his hip pocket where it hurt! "You tell Fannie Lou to come on back home, then, things'll be just like they always was." This time, Pap put his hands in his overall bib, pulled on the straps and popped the strap: "Well, no sir, she say that's just the trouble, she don't want things to be like they always was!" Pap took Miss Hamer and the children to a little house in the woods and they stayed there till he finished the crop and got them a house in Ruleville off the plantation.

Now, Miss Hamer 'nem name was mud. People say they was running like rats! Put out their house. You know how people do. Look around Miss Hamer would be gone all the time. People say she was with the civil rights workers. Something was going on all the time. Sometime Miss Hamer would take other people to meetings with her. It was mostly SNCC students and workers here (this is SNCC country); SCLC mostly had a lot of workshops and training in other states. Miss

Hamer was coming from a workshop with some more people when she was put in jail in Winona, Mississippi. See, they were "sitting in" at the lunch counters in those little high priced coffee shops they have in the bus stations. Well, that worked for a while but when they got to Winona, Mississippi, they were arrested. You ever see somebody get a whipping? See it was mostly ladies/women. Miss Hamer, June Johnson, Euvester Simpson, Miss Annelle Ponder and James West. They carted those people off to jail. Now I didn't see it, but they tell me those people took a beating. Say the white people beat them to within a inch of their lives. Had prisoners whipping Miss Hamer. Black people. Don't that make you mad? Wa-show! Wa-show!

FANNIE LOU   Well, Pap, I was PICKING IN THE RIGHT COTTON TO GET MY HUNDRED. Hell, Baby, I picked a whole bale. No, its all right. I want to sit up, I can sit up, I need to talk to you, Pap, and tell you how I feel. Naw, not this, these just old fleshy wounds, they'll heal. I need to tell you what happened to me inside, being in jail, getting beat up, listening to them innocent chillun crying and screaming. It done something to me, Pap. I ain't scared. Oh, I can't say I wasn't scared while it was happening. We was all scared. I was so scared for them chillun I had wit me, scared one of em might get killed and it would be on my conscience that I led em to they death. I didn't want to have to face they parents about that. But God is good, and He let us all live.

They tried to kill us, Pap. When they come at me, they had a big colored man. A prisoner, and he beat me for them while they stood around and looked, drinking; and they give him whiskey and he beat me until my skin was hard, baby; and all the time they was callin me a communist or something, making out like I done some thing to hurt somebody, asking me questions about other people. And when that prisoner got tired, they brought out another colored prisoner and he beat me some more. They beat us until they couldn't have no fun out of it nomore. And I kept hearing them talking. They was lower than dogs, Pap. They tried to fool us out the jail one nite so they could shoot us down and say we was trying to escape. I won't scared no more, and I told them you just gone haveta kill me in my cell; I ain't going nowhere. Euvester Simpson was in the cell with me. They didn't know what to do with us, Pap. I could hear em talking about putting us in the river and you know, its a funny thing, Pap, the more scared they got about what they had done, the braver I felt. I wasn't scared no more. It didn't make no difference whether they beat me any more or not. I wasn't scared. Thought maybe I was going crazy for not being scared. Shh, don't say it. I can't hate nobody. I feel sorry for them jailers and sheriffs; I feel sorry for anybody that could let hate wrap them up, ain't no such a thing as I can hate anybody and hope to see God's face, no matter how evil they is. Shh, shh. Pap. I know. Don't say it. You know I'm gon' be right back out there. For us. We can make it, just don't let nothing separate us. It's you and me, Pap, forever.

Song

"Gonna lay down my burdens down by the riverside,
Down by the riverside, down by the riverside,
Gonna lay down my burdens down by the riverside,
To study war no more. I ain't gon' study war no more,
I ain't gon' study war no more, I ain't gon' study war no more."

ACT II

FANNIE LOU (*Mass meeting speech*) From the 4th chapter of St. Luke, beginning at the 18th verse: "The spirit of the Lord is upon me, because he has *annointed* me to *preach* the *gospel* to the poor . . . He have sent me to bind up the brokenhearted, *preach deliverance* to the captives, and *recovery of sight* to the blind, to set at *liberty them that are bound*, to preach *the acceptable year of our Lord*." Now, the time has come that was Christ's purpose on earth. And we've only been getting by by paying our way to hell. But the time is out. While Simon of Serene was helping Christ to bear his cross up the hill, he said: "Must Jesus bear this cross alone and all the world go free?" He said: "No, there's a cross for everyone, and there's a cross for me. This consecrated cross I'll bear 'til death shall set me free. And then go home a crown to wear, for there's a crown for me."

And there's no easy way out; we've just got to wake up and face it, folks. And if I can face the issue, you can, too. You see, things what's so pitiful about it, the men been wanting to be the boss all these years, and the ones that ain't up under the house is under the bed. But you see, that's poison, it's poison for us not to speak for what we know is right. As Christ said from the 17th chapter of Acts and the 26 verse: "Hadth made of one blood all nations for to dwell on the face of the earth." Then, it's no difference to have different colors. And, brother, you can believe this or not; I've been sick of this system for as long as I can remember.

I heard some people speak of depression in the '30s. In the '20s it was 'pression with me. De'pression'! I have been as hungry, it's a funny thing, since I started working for Christ. It's kinda like in the 23rd Psalm when he said: "Thou prepareth a table before me in the presence of mine enemy. Thou annointed my head with oil and my cup runneth over." And I have walked through the valley of the shadow of death, because it was on the 10th of September in 1962 when they shot 16 times in a house. And there it wont a foot over the bed where my head was, but that night I wont there. Don't you see what God can do? Quit running around trying to dodge them, because this Book say: "He that seeketh to save his life shall lose it anyhow." So, as long as you know you're going for something, you put up the life. Then we can be like Paul and say: "I have fought a good fight, and I have kept the faith." You know, it's been a long time. People, I have worked, I have worked hard as anybody. I have been picking cotton and would be so hungry, and one of the poison things about it, would be wondering what I was gon' cook that nite. But, you see, all of then things was wrong, see. And I have asked God, and I've said: "My Lawd . . . (and you have, too, and there ain't no need in you lying and saying you ain't!) My Lawd, please to open the way for us, to please make a way for us where I can stand up and speak for my race and speak for these hungry children." And he opened the way and all of them opened a bank account. You, see, he made it so plain for us: He sent a man to Mississippi, was the same man Moses had with him to go to Egypt; tole him to go down in Misipi and tell Ross Barnett to let my people go!

"This Little Light of Mine"

"This little light of mine, I'm gon' let it shine,
This little light of mine, I'm gon' let it shine.
This little light of mine. I'm gon' let it shine,
Let it shine, let it shine, let it shine.
Everywhere I go, Lord, I'm gon' let it shine,
Everywhere I go, Lord, I'm gon' let it shine,
Everywhere I go, Lord, I'm gon' let it shine,
Let it shine, let it shine, let it shine."

"This little light of mine, I'm gon' let it shine,
This little light of mine. I'm gon' let it shine.
This little light of mine, I'm gon' let it shine,
Let shine, let it shine, let it shine."

ISSAQUENA   Well, rocked on, rocked on. It was a lot of people getting registered to vote in the state of Mississippi. Black people, poor people, Black and white, but they ran up against a problem. The regular democratic party in Mississippi wouldn't let the people participate as Democrats with them. In 1964, coming upon the presidential elections, the people decided to organize a party of their own, a political party of their own. Miss Hamer, 'nem organized the Mississippi Freedom Democrats, held an election statewide in Mississippi and took 68 delegates to the Democratic National Convention in Atlantic City, New Jersey, and asked the national Democrats to seat them instead of the all-white regular Democratic party delegation. Miss Hamer 'nem got dressed up; they even had a chance to sit in smoke filled rooms.

FANNIE LOU Senator Humphrey, I ain't no stranger to struggle. You know, lots of things happen to you in this Movement work. But I been in a struggle all my life, Senator Humphrey. It was a struggle to get 68 of us here as delegates from the cotton fields of Mississippi to Atlantic City, New Jersey, to the National Democrat convention, but we kept a struggling and we made it here. And we is asking you to help. Now, we organized this Mississippi Freedom Democratic Party because of a struggle. I'm the Vice President and I'm representing the Freedom Democrats here today because the President of the MFDP is in jail this minute in Missippi because of a struggle for freedom. We are struggling in Missippi as colored people who is being denied the right to vote. We knows that. I don't wanna know about the Democratic Party and the Vice Presidential nomination. It's the reg'lar Democrats that's fighting us in Missippi. Senator Humphrey, you can help us in this struggle if you want to; you just got to get up your nerve and go in there and do it!

Mr. Wilkins, I know that you is a good spokesperson for the Negro peoples, and for the NAACP: I'm is not a sophisticated a politician is you. And I know that you can speak clearer than me . . . sometimes. But, you know, Mr. Wilkins, I ain't never seed you in my community in Missippi, and them is the people I represents, them is the people I speaks for. And they done already told me that we didn't come all this 'a way for no two seats, since all a' us is tired!

Senator Humphrey, I know lots of people in Mississippi who have lost they jobs for trying to register to vote. I had to leave the plantation where I lived and worked in Sunflower County. Now, if you lose this job of vice president because you help the MFDP, everything will be all right, God will take care of you. But if you take this vice president nomination like this, why, you will never be able to do any good for civil rights, poor people, for peace, or any of them things you talk about. Senator Humphrey, I'm gon' pray to Jesus for you.

Mr. Chairman, and the Credentials Committee, my name is Mrs.

Fannie Lou Hamer and I live at 626 East Lafayette Street, Ruleville, Sunflower County, Mississippi. It was the 31st of August, 1962 that 18 of us traveled to Indianola to try to become first class citizens. We was met by Mississippi mens, highway patrolmens, and they only allow two of us to take the literacy test at a time. We were not allowed to register to vote in the state of Mississippi. And I was run away from my home the same day because I refused to take my name off the application. And we have been fighting for our lives ever since. In 1963, six of us was taken off a bus in Winona, Mississippi and carried to jail and beat to within a inch of our lives. I was placed in a cell with a young woman called Miss Euvester Simpson. I begin soon to hear sounds of licks and horrible screams. "Can you say, Yes sir, Nigger!" Can you say yes sir?! And I could hear Annelle Ponder screaming, then I hear her praying; and it wasn't too long before three white mens come to my cell for me.

ISSAQUENA Now when Miss Hamer started to telling bout the beating, President Johnson called a press conference, some of 'em say it was because they spotted an iceberg over in East Siberia. Some say it was to get Miss Hamer off the TV. Now, you see the president got Miss Hamer off the TV then, but Miss Hamer was the kind of woman you couldn't shut her mouth. She continued over the years as the Movement grew, Miss Hamer did, too. She gave interviews to people sometimes in the years to follow. And after that, she just spoke for herself!

FANNIE LOU I thank you; I thank you. To the president of Morehouse College, faculty and student body, brothers and sisters: I want to thank you for inviting me here. I have just left Tougaloo College where this morning I received a honorary Doctorate of Humane Letters; and I am on my way to Howard University where I expect to receive another honorary Doctorate of Humane Letters. And I wants to thank you, Morehouse, for this Plaque.

FANNIE LOU Sunflower County, I think is worse than Rhodesia, South Africa because it is Smith with a power structure over there, and its one man here, the Senator, and these landowners is the worst in the world. They are beginning to tell the people that they shouldn't get registered, and telling 'em to leave the freedom schools alone. And they using these poverty programs for one of the biggest political frauds in the history of our time and they are using our kids like political football. And we are fighting this because its so unjust. The director of the CAP agency admitted to me that the chairman of the poverty program in Sunflower County is a member of the White Citizens Council. Still, the government grant people like that money to enslave us

more. We need federal registrars to get the people registered in Sunflower County, and some political education so that they will understand this white man's trick because as long as this white man control
the money, he's gon' control the Negro. We need us some land so
we don't have to be dependent on this man; got to get us a freedom
farm. Now we have proof that they going to people that's been on
welfare and telling em if they didn't get their children away from those
freedom schools where we been set up, you know, some people teaching a year, some 9 months out of the year, that they wasn't gon' get
any welfare 'til they would pull 'em out the freedom schools and put
them in the white. It's the biggest, it's the biggedest, crookedest stuff
that ever was handed out through Washington, D.C., and 'tis nothing
but political tricks.

Sunflower County is still one of the most poverty stricken places
in the whole country. People for the past, I say 300 years, been eating
poke and grits—poking they feet under the table and gritting they
teeth. And we just about tired of that, too.

You see, the thing about these bills, its OK to pass a bill; but what
are you gon' do about enforcing the laws already on the books. If the
Constitution means something to me, enforce it. Lot of people think
because we had a Voting Rights Bill, everything is all right. But it
not. They do a lot of things undercover, but they do the same thing.
If they get a chance, they'll lynch a man just as quick as they did
in 1925. They is working to preserve segregation and one way they
can do it is to use this poverty money to get a whole lot of work done
on these plantations so they can keep they money and use it to keep
things more segregated than they was. You, see, this white man know
how to faneuver; we got to learn how to faneuver, too. You know,
this here poverty money is just like manna. We can stand here and
catch it when they drop it outta Washington, D.C., but if we don't
never learn how to make us none, we ain't gon' never have none.
That's economic power. It disturbs me very much that for 400 years,
whites identified with white power, and one innocent man said, Black
power, and look like its gon' turn the world upside down. You know,
you have Jewish Holidays, the Italians have a holiday, white people
have their day, Puerto Ricans, St. Patrick Day, but Black people can't
say a thing. This is a tactic. We just got to understand that ever nation
on earth got to identify with its people, wherever they are. It's nothing
wrong with being Black and if we get any power whatsoever, what
would you call it? You couldn't say pink power, it's Black power, but
the press is treating us like criminals. They even tried to brand me
a communist and I know much about communism as a horse do about

Christmas. Do communism mean the same thing as the things we fighting for? I've never seen a communist to know one in my life. Communism? We fighting hungryism, the right to eat, have a decent job, a home. A lot of people can't understand what I mean when I say I'm not fighting for equal rights. If you raise questions about all the things we've been faced with in this country and we have been the only people in this country that've been nonviolent and could stand up for dignity and human respect, you can understand what I mean when I say I'm not fighting for equal rights. You think about the background of a white man what they have done to the Indians and what they have done to every generation after generation of human beings you can understand why I don't want equal rights. I'm fighting for something they never knowed too much about, human rights. See, whether you Jewish, Chinese, Mexican, Indian, Italian, Japanese, Puerto Rican, whatever race you are, I'm concerned about you if you a human being. And they don't know too much about human respect 'cause if they did, we'da been treated better.

I question *America*! I used to say when I was working hard in the cotton fields, if I can just go to Washington—to the Justice Department —to the FBI—get close enough to let them know what was going on in Mississippi, I was sure that things would change in a week. Now that I have traveled across America, been to the Congress, to the Justice Department, to the FBI, I am faced with the things I'm not sure I wanted to find out. The sickness in Mississippi is not a Mississippi sickness. This is America's sickness.

What's gon' help Black people? What I really feel is necessary is that the Black people in this country will have to upset this applecart. We can no longer ignore the fact that America is not the land of the free and the home of the brave . . . there is so much hypocrisy in America. The land of the free and the home of the brave is all on paper. It don't mean anything to us. The only way we can make this thing work is bring this thing out to the light that have been under the cover all these years. The scriptures have said, the things that have been done in the dark will be known on the housetops.

FANNIE LOU (*From selected speeches*) Now that we have forced this man to give us welfare, our share of the taxes, where is we going to take it to? The question for Black people is not when is the white man going to give us our rights, or when is he going to give us good education for our children, or when is he going to give us a job. If the white man gives you anything, just remember when he gets ready he will take it right back. We got to take it for ourselfs.

I don't believe in separationism, a house divided against itself cannot stand, and neither can a nation. This country produces separatists. America is sick, and man is on the critical list.

They assassinated Dr. King, then passed a law telling us how good they is; in 1972, we can buy a home on their side of town, now how in hell can we do that when we can't pay the rent where we are now? But that law did have something in it for me; if I get three people there and tell em the truth, they'll put me in jail for conspiracy and inciting to riot. They didn't get Martin Luther King long as he was middle class, but when he said he would organize the poor folks, white and Indians as well as Black, they said, 'we gotta kill this nigger.' And it ain't Memphis. It is the same kind of conspiracy killed King that killed Kennedy and killed Malcolm X. Now, they got the concentration camps ready and all I can say is, we better be ready; we better be ready.

I'm never sure anymore when I leave home whether I'll get back or not. It seem like to tell the truth today is to run the risk of getting killed. But if I fall, I'll fall five feet four inches FORWARD in the fight for freedom. I'm not backing off of that, and nobody don't need to cover the ground I walk on as far as freedom is concerned!

Let's face it, what's hurting the Black folk that's without is hurting the white folk that's without! If the white folks fight for theyself, and the Black folk fight for theyself we gon' crumble apart. These are things we gon' have to fight together. We got to fight in America for all the people, and I'm perfectly willing to help make my country what it have to be.

Christianity is being concerned about your fellow man, not building a million dollar church wile people are starving right around the corner. Christ was a revolutionary person, out there in the streets where it was happening. That's what God is all about, and that's where I get my strength. We have to realize just how grave the problem is in the United States today and I think the 6th chapter of Ephesians, the eleventh and twelfth verses helps us to know . . . what it is we are up against. It says: "Put on the whole armor of God, that ye may be able to stand against the wiles of the devil. For we wrestle not against flesh and blood but against principalities, against powers, against the rulers of the darkness of this world, against spiritual wickedness in high places." This is what I think about when I think of my own work in the fight for freedom.

And there was delivered unto him the book of the prophet Isaiah. And when he had open the book he found the place where it is written, the spirit of the Lord is upon me, because he hath annointed me to preach the gospel to the poor; he hath sent me to heal the brokenhearted, to preach deliverance to the captives and recovery of sight to the blind, to set at liberty them that are bound; to preach the acceptable year of our Lord.

Precious Lord

"Precious Lord, take my hand,
Lead me on, let me stand.
I am tired, I am weak, I am
  worn.
Through the storm, through
  the night,
Lead me on to the light.
Take my hand, precious Lord,
  lead me on."

THE END

FROM
The Colonnade

STARK YOUNG

CHARACTERS

MAJOR DANDRIDGE

JOHN DANDRIDGE

MISS ELLEN DANDRIDGE

MISS MARY DANDRIDGE

EVELYN DANDRIDGE

COUSIN TOM

MR. BOBO

MR. STEDMAN

OSCAR

ACT 1

(*The drawing-room of the old Dandridge place, which they call Flower House, is a big, white room panelled in wood. Beginning near the west corner and running a little more than half way across the back of the room and looking out south over a flat terrace and the garden, run very high French windows with sashes sliding up higher than a man's head. Not far from the front in the west wall is another window. They have curtains of an old purplish-rose chintz. A long table with a lamp and books runs parallel to the west wall, down toward the front. Against it sits a davenport. Not far from the long windows and just off the center of the stage is a Louis XVI armchair. On the east side of the room is a small sofa of the same style. Behind it an old square piano of rosewood, with a guitar lying on it. The arrangement of the sofa and the chairs shows that the fireplace, if it could be seen, would be where the footlights are and would face the windows to the terrace.*

The davenport and the chairs are upholstered in a soft cream color and the sofa in the same color, but with a pattern of flowers.

The carpet over the floor is of silk Brussels, a kind found in old Southern houses, black with faded wreaths of flowers. The whole room has a sort of glowing, faded elegance about it.

531

The door on the east leads into the hall, and another door opens into a study back of the drawing-room.

It is ten o'clock in the morning and the sun pours down over the flagstones of the narrow terrace which lies on the ground level, and the garden beyond.

MAJOR DANDRIDGE *is a man of seventy years, in appearance very like General Lee. He finishes putting some papers lying on the table and takes them across to* MR. STEDMAN, *who sits on the sofa)*

MAJOR DANDRIDGE   I wanted to do this yesterday, Mr. Stedman, but I was too late to catch you. Your lawyers are busy men.

MR. STEDMAN   Sorry, Sir. I hope I didn't put you to extra trouble, you look tired, Major Dandridge.

MAJOR DANDRIDGE (*Giving him the papers*)   Tired? I am rather. I thought this business finished and done years ago. However—I very much wish to get it done now before my son returns.

MR. STEDMAN   When do you expect him, is there much to it? What?

MAJOR DANDRIDGE   Almost any minute. The papers are sound, I feel sure, but I'd rather have a lawyer go over them again.

MR. STEDMAN   I see. Well, where do we start? Ah, here we are. What?

MAJOR DANDRIDGE   By the way, if you won't mention this to my son, you'll oblige me, Sir. I judge it better that he should not know anything about this affair, since it does not concern him. (*A noise of blows comes from somewhere outside*)   What's that knocking? (*Goes over to the terrace and listens*)   I've heard it before, can't make out what 'tis. However—

(*The negro servant in a white jacket enters from the windows*)

OSCAR   Major, what time's Mr. John comin', please, Sir? We been wantin' to know.

MAJOR DANDRIDGE   I don't know, Oscar, but almost any time now he's due.

OSCAR   Sho' is hard to tell zactly, when you don't know. Thank you, Sir. (OSCAR *goes out into the hall*)

MAJOR DANDRIDGE   Oscar's in the seventh heaven, he dotes on John.

MR. STEDMAN   So? (*Turning through the papers*)   Not much here, these papers, Major, matter of half an hour, I reckon.

MAJOR DANDRIDGE (*Standing near the armchair*)   That's good, Sir. The fact is I'm not sure that John would see this matter as I do, Mr.

Stedman. I'm never quite sure what he'll think. My son has never given me a moment's worry in his life, Sir, but naturally we don't always agree.

MR. STEDMAN   You'd hardly expect it always, at twenty-four.

MAJOR DANDRIDGE   And I'll tell you, I'm anxious to spare him for another reason, after this strain of course that he's undergone lately. He went to Kentucky, you may or may not know, to see his mother when she was dying, my wife when she was dying.

MR. STEDMAN   His mother dying? No, I didn't know—I'm very sorry, Major. (MR. STEDMAN *moves as if to offer* MAJOR DAN-DRIDGE *his hand, but stops half way and resumes his seat*)

MAJOR DANDRIDGE   Thank you. Thank you. I appreciate your sympathy, but there's no occasion to discuss it, if you'll excuse me. I thought it my son's duty to go and see his mother at such a time.

MR. STEDMAN   I think you were entirely right, Sir.

(MAJOR DANDRIDGE *goes over to the table and turns the pages of a book.* MR. STEDMAN *proceeds with the examination of the papers. Voices raised and in some sort of altercation are heard approaching from the garden.* MAJOR DANDRIDGE *turns his head to listen a moment, and then smiles*)

MISS ELLEN   Sis Mollie, I will not. You *shall* take it.

MISS MARY   No, you.

MISS ELLEN   I won't. You can't stand the sun.

MISS MARY   I can, madam. Why are you so stubborn?

MISS ELLEN   Well, leave it there, Missy.

(*The* MAJOR'S *two sisters enter.* MISS ELLEN, *the taller of the two, is also the older. There is something about her, about her manner, her slender body, her hair, her voice and what she says. She is somewhat deaf, but would hear better if she paid as anxious attention as* MISS MARY *would if she heard badly.* MISS MARY *is a little woman with an honest, combative, kind and affectionate face, and quaint awkward little movements*)

MISS MARY   Oh, I beg your pardon, we beg your pardon. (*Goes to* SISTER) Now, Sis Tellie, you see what you've done, they'll think we are crazy.

MISS ELLEN (*Coolly*)   They'll think right, I'm afraid. How d'ye do, Mr. Stedman.

MR. STEDMAN   Good morning, ladies. How are you, Miss Mary? (*Shaking hands*)   How are you, Miss Ellen?

MISS ELLEN   Very well. It's a pleasure to see you.

MAJOR DANDRIDGE Why, what's the matter with you girls?

MISS ELLEN Oh, it's this sister of mine, you may know. She was bound and determined I should have the parasol.

MISS MARY And, of course, Sister Ellen'd rather die than take it.

MISS ELLEN I don't mind the sun. I like it. Mary knows she can't stand the sun.

MAJOR DANDRIDGE It shows how much she loves you, Sister.

MISS ELLEN Oh, there's no doubt about Mollie's loving those she loves. She'd die for you. Mollie would give you her head. She'd not only give it to you, but she'd knock you down to make you take it.

MISS MARY Lay on, Macduff! Poor dear—

MISS ELLEN That's all right, Mary, that's enough about us. Just remember other people are not interested because we are. We've been down having the colonnade swept out, Brother Al.

MISS MARY So many leaves! I said to my sister, 'Sis Tellie, it's like babes in the wood.

MISS ELLEN Nobody else ever goes there but my nephew, the place is neglected.

MAJOR DANDRIDGE No, I for one never go there. I'd have pulled it down if it weren't for John.

MISS MARY I always think of Father as walking there, after he finally got it built to suit him.

MAJOR DANDRIDGE My wife—my wife used to sit with him, she liked it too.

MISS MARY I remember as a little girl meeting Father there one morning. He said to me, "Well, little roseleaf."

MAJOR DANDRIDGE To me the thing is entirely unattractive. To begin with it has no relation to the rest of the place here, of course. I dislike that fantastic sort of thing. But John's worse about it than his—than my father was. I've come to think of that colonnade as representing a particular streak in the Dandridge family.

MISS ELLEN It's beautiful this month with all those old roses and the jasmine, too. The loveliest corner of the garden.

MISS MARY Well, do let's have things as pretty as possible for him. I declare it makes me sick to think of the child's having to go through all this with his mother. I know what it is to see anybody die. And you know how he is, Brother Al.

MAJOR DANDRIDGE I know, Sis Mollie.

MISS MARY It's because he's a poet, bless his heart!

MISS ELLEN I hope John goes on writing.

MAJOR DANDRIDGE Many a young man takes to poetry, it's a phase they pass through.

MISS MARY Well, I don't know much about poetry, but I know our nephew could be one of the greatest poets of the South if he tried.

MISS ELLEN This place is dusted every morning, but it needs it again.

MISS MARY And just think, he'd been home only six weeks. Lord knows I hope nothing else will happen.

MISS ELLEN What's happened now, Mollie? You're a perpetual raincrow. Mollie ought to have gone on the stage.

MISS MARY That's all right, Mollie told you things wouldn't be ready in time for them, and neither would they if John had come two days earlier as we were expecting him. These two days for the wedding were a blessed thing for us.

MR. STEDMAN The wedding? Whose wedding, not John's?

MAJOR DANDRIDGE I must ask your pardon. I don't seem to remember anything this morning. Mr. Stedman, John's married, on the way home, to a young lady in Memphis.

MISS MARY Evelyn Oliver.

MAJOR DANDRIDGE It all sounds unusual, so soon after his mother's death; but there are details about it we've not heard yet. I've had a telegram. He's known the young lady before, of course. Colonel Oliver's daughter, you know of the family, of course, everybody knows who the Olivers are.

MISS ELLEN Of course.

MISS MARY I know one thing at least, you may be sure she's a lovely young woman if our boy loves her.

MISS ELLEN At least we'll have a garden of flowers for the young lovers. I never saw the garden more flourishing.

MISS MARY Oh, Sister mine, romantic as usual.

MISS ELLEN You hear that, Mr. Stedman. I'd like to know who had all the beaux and every man she met falling in love with her, Mollie knows she did. Nobody was ever in love with me, and if they were, I didn't know it. I liked men well enough till they began to look foolish. Cousin Dolly used to say I kicked a man before he ever proposed. It was a long time ago. Mollie, I'm afraid Mr. Stedman will think us very silly.

MISS MARY (*Taking* MAJOR'S *arm*) We must go. Come on, Brother Al. Hurry up, Tellie.

MISS ELLEN I'm coming, Mollie.

MISS MARY You'll excuse us, Mr. Stedman? We'll take a last peep at their room.

MISS ELLEN And I've got to get the flowers around. Somebody ought to take a stick to me.

(They go out into the hall with MAJOR DANDRIDGE. MR.
STEDMAN *looks at the papers.* MR. BOBO *enters. He is a gentleman
of sixty, hearty and plump, bold in front, with a goatee and mustache
in the style of the Third Empire, and numerous fobs and seals hanging from his watch chain)*

MR. BOBO   Good morning again, Mr. Stedman, where have they gone?

MR. STEDMAN   Upstairs, I believe, to the bridal suite.

MR. BOBO   Married! What a pace they go, young people these days.
So you're at those papers. Alex's shown them to me. Told me about
the letters. Do you know, I'd like to see Ned's boy. Ned was a fine
fellow, wild as an Indian, I grant you, but a fine man, great friend
of mine. But that's a long time ago! Al's anxious to get the thing settled
before John comes.

MR. STEDMAN   So far as I've been able to see it's— (OSCAR *comes
in)*   Well, Oscar.

OSCAR   Mr. Baron, where's de Major and Miss Ellen?

MR. BOBO   They're upstairs, Oscar.

OSCAR   Dey's comin' up de drive.

MR. BOBO   Who?

OSCAR   Mr. John and his wife, das who—

MR. BOBO   Run up and tell them. (OSCAR *goes out)*   I hope John's
father is going to make him some kind of settlement now that he's
married.

MR. STEDMAN   He will undoubtedly. The Major's a rich man, you
know. But I think he's more cut up by his wife's death than he shows,
Mr. Bobo.

MR. BOBO   Rest assured. He'll just tighten up the girth and dig his
knees in. (COUSIN TOM *enters from the study, a slender, gentle old
man, tall, with a mustache and short square beard and old-fashioned,
thick hair, now gray, but very carefully brushed)*   Here's Thomas.
Mr. Stedman, you know Colonel Wallace.

COUSIN TOM   Good morning, Mr. Stedman, glad to see you, Sir.

MR. STEDMAN   Colonel Wallace, how are you, Sir? I'm very glad
to see you, Sir. I was seeing that pamphlet of yours. What is it you
call it? The one where you prove—

COUSIN TOM   The Vision of Daniel.

MR. STEDMAN   That's it, where you prove that the Book of Daniel
prophesies the Revolutionary War, Sir. You make quite a case, I must
say, Sir. What?

COUSIN TOM   Yes, the power of prophecy in the Scripture is beyond
our comprehension. Take, for example, the dragonic character of the

Book of Revelation, Twelfth Chapter, the red dragon with his seven heads and ten horns. The only government that fits this prophecy is that of the United States for reasons I shall show in my next pamphlet. And I prove that Monroe in his second term is horn No. 1 of the red dragon; Adams from 1825 to 1829 is horn No. 2; et cetera, et cetera.

MR. STEDMAN Absolutely. Have they come? What's that, don't I hear 'em?

(COUSIN TOM *sits down on the davenport and reads a pamphlet*)

MR. BOBO They're a long time comin'. Ah, here they are.

(MR. BOBO *goes out on the terrace, and you can hear the greetings being exchanged*)

MR. STEDMAN I'll go in the study here.

(*He goes out.* JOHN *walking between his* AUNTS, *his arms linked through theirs, enters.* EVELYN *follows not far behind, walking with the* MAJOR. *Both* EVELYN *and* JOHN *are in summer traveling clothes.* MR. BOBO *comes in last*)

MISS MARY We've given them a peep through the garden coming this way.

JOHN Why, Sir, Cousin Tom, how are you, Cousin Tom?

(COUSIN TOM *rises, pushes his spectacles down to the end of his nose deliberately and holds out his hand*)

COUSIN TOM Delighted to see you back, Sir! And this is—?

MISS ELLEN This is your new cousin Evelyn, Cousin Tom. And this is Cousin Tom, dear.

EVELYN (*Kissing him*) Cousin Tom!

COUSIN TOM My dear, I'm delighted to see you. Welcome to Mississippi!

MISS ELLEN Cousin Tom's making us a little visit. (JOHN *walks slowly about the room as if more or less looking it over*)

EVELYN I'm so glad, Cousin Tom.

COUSIN TOM They kindly make me very much at home here. What's that? (*He goes over and pokes his stick into the plant outside nearest the window*) Thought I heard that infernal cricket.

EVELYN Our train was a little late. I said to John "Will we ever get there?"

OSCAR (*Comes in and stands in front of the door at the back*) 'Scuse me, Mr. John, I put de grips in de room.

JOHN   Thank you, Awse.

MISS MARY   And here's some more of the family on the walls. There's John's grandmother, our dear mother, and here's our father, and father's father—

EVELYN   He's a duck, he looks like Cousin Tom. Look at Cousin Tom, don't you love the dear old thing, so tall and slender. He's got an elegance, hasn't he? And Mr. Bobo with his seals and things! Cousin Tom, John told me about your writing.

COUSIN TOM   My dear, alas, I'm a very poor scholar. You've married the man who can talk a bird off a limb.

EVELYN   And this one, who's he? I like him.

MISS ELLEN (*to* JOHN)   Well, dear, she's beautiful and has style. You'd hardly know whether to say her hair was red or say it was gold.

MISS MARY   It's well you do, my dear, in this family! For that's our Uncle Leonidas, my father's brother.

JOHN (*To* OSCAR, *who still stands at the back grinning, with his eyes on* JOHN)   I'm glad to see you again, Awse.

OSCAR   Yas, Sir, it's ten days you been gone, Mr. John.

EVELYN (*Looking at the picture*)   Leonidas!

MAJOR DANDRIDGE   Judge Leonidas Dandridge, the lion of the family. I remember on my wedding journey, two days after we'd left, my mother sent me a message, "Come home at once, your Uncle Leonidas is here."

EVELYN   And did you go?

MAJOR DANDRIDGE   We had to.

EVELYN   Imagine!

MR. BOBO   Worth it, he was a character. On one occasion—

EVELYN   But where's the colonnade? John's colonnade?

MISS ELLEN   Here, over here, dear, from the terrace, now look.

EVELYN   Oh, it's lovely! And so many roses! But it's so solemn, isn't it?

MISS ELLEN   And the fountain?

JOHN   How clear the light is today!

EVELYN   Aye, aye, Auntie, John's always talking about light. All along on the train he kept saying "Look!" But what I can't get over is there's light here everywhere, but still it's all so solemn. We laugh and talk, but it's so solemn.

MISS MARY   You're just a little tired, I reckon, from that long trip on the train. Tellie, we mustn't keep the child. She'll want to go to her room.

EVELYN   We had a fountain when I was a child, but it was always choking up.

MISS MARY   Come on, I'll rescue you, darling.

EVELYN   Perhaps I better, I'm draggled. We'll be down again soon, won't we?

MISS MARY   Before you can say Jack Robinson. Good-bye everybody. Isn't it lovely having a niece?

(MR. BOBO *goes and opens the door and stands bowing them out. He follows them into the hall and closes the door after him*)

MISS ELLEN   You'll excuse me, dear, I'll run and see after some of the housekeeping. You know how slow I am and lazy. You stay here with your father. And, Cousin Tom, will you help me a moment?

(JOHN *gives her a little hug around her thin shoulders. She goes out, following* COUSIN TOM *along the terrace*)

MAJOR DANDRIDGE   Well, my boy—

JOHN (*Laughingly*)   So Cousin Tom is making us a little visit, is he, Father?

MAJOR DANDRIDGE   Yes.

JOHN   How long is it he's been here now?

MAJOR DANDRIDGE   Three years, I believe.

JOHN   And Mr. Bobo?

MAJOR DANDRIDGE   Only a month or so, he'll stay till New Year, I reckon. I'd have sold the horse if it hadn't been for him. The automobile's enough. And you'll have one now too. But Baron wants the horse, he lives in horses.

JOHN   That you'd know by all those horse phrases of his. And is Cousin Tom as busy as ever with the prophecy?

MAJOR DANDRIDGE   He's half way through the Book of Revelation. He's found some sort of black angel for abolition, I believe.

JOHN   Father, how can you stand it, so much company like this? And the same stories forever?

MAJOR DANDRIDGE   But, Son, what would you have me do, they are gentlemen? And old friends as well.

JOHN   I suppose so.

MAJOR DANDRIDGE   I'm sorry they trouble you.

JOHN   Oh, no, it's not that, not that, necessarily. It's largely my state of mind.

MAJOR DANDRIDGE (*Going to windows*)   What's that knocking? I keep hearing it.

JOHN   I heard it. Strange.

MAJOR DANDRIDGE   However—what's your state of mind, my boy? Sit down. I know this has been a trying experience.

(JOHN *walks around the room slowly, looking about, as if to study it*)

JOHN   It seems hardly the same.

MAJOR DANDRIDGE   What?

JOHN   The place. This room.

MAJOR DANDRIDGE   Nothing has been changed, Sir.

JOHN (*Shaking his head*)   I know, I know it.

MAJOR DANDRIDGE   It's only you are tired, almost anybody would find it hard to bear the sight of suffering of—some one near death, like that.

JOHN   That part of it was not so bad, Father. I realize now I've scarcely thought of it.

MAJOR DANDRIDGE   No?

JOHN   I want to try and tell you.

MAJOR DANDRIDGE   You're sure you wouldn't rather wait and not talk now.

JOHN   I feel as if I were going to be talking world without end. You'll think me gone off my head, I know.

MAJOR DANDRIDGE   No, Son, no. You must remember I've known you a long time. Sit down, you'd better sit down.

JOHN   Thank you, Father. (*He sits in the corner of the davenport, near the front of the stage*)

MAJOR DANDRIDGE   Well?

JOHN   Well, Father, I'm going to try to tell you, I want to. You know, Father, on the way up to Kentucky I said to myself, "It's a strange thing to be going to see my mother, and she dying, and I wouldn't even recognize her now if she came down the aisle of this coach." It seemed odd.

MAJOR DANDRIDGE   Yes, naturally.

JOHN   I had always seemed to know about her. I mean I had felt that she was not to be loved or remembered.

MAJOR DANDRIDGE   Nothing had been said to make you think so, I remind you of that.

JOHN   Oh, no, Father, I don't mean to reflect on you at all. You have never said anything to me against my mother. Not a word.

MAJOR DANDRIDGE   I'd have been a cad, Son.

JOHN   But you never were, Sir. You told me that she had gone away when I was a little boy.

MAJOR DANDRIDGE   You were three when your mother went away.

JOHN   And so naturally I thought she must have been the wrong sort of woman to leave me like that and to leave you. My aunts never told me anything. Naturally a child would ask where its own mother was. I asked and I was told that she had gone away. Somehow I soon learned not to ask about her.

MAJOR DANDRIDGE Your aunts scarcely knew your mother. They were away at school in Canada when your mother was living here. I asked them not to talk of her to you. And nobody else knows anything about the matter, outside the bare fact that she went away.

JOHN They never did. And so I put her down as—as—I thought that my mother must have been—

MAJOR DANDRIDGE I understand, John.

JOHN I thought of that when I went up to her room. It was in a little house.

MAJOR DANDRIDGE She would never take any money from me. She had a little money of her own.

JOHN I was thinking it was not easy to be there, but that you were right in having me go, when they showed me up to her room. And then when the girl opened the door I saw her—Oh, Father—!

MAJOR DANDRIDGE Son—

(MAJOR DANDRIDGE *gets up and goes over and stands by* JOHN. JOHN *puts his hands over his eyes and springs up, and walks across the room. His father says no more, but takes the place* JOHN *has left on the davenport*)

JOHN Oh, it's terrible.

MAJOR DANDRIDGE What?

JOHN Oh, I mean—You see I had always thought of her as bad, wrong, I naturally would—. But when I saw her—She was so beautiful.

(MAJOR DANDRIDGE *presses his hands together.* JOHN *walks up and down the room*)

I ran across the room to her and fell on my knees. She was holding up her arms to me. She kept saying "This is my son, Nurse, this is my son. He has come to see me." Then she asked, Father, if you were well.

MAJOR DANDRIDGE (*Abruptly*) Did she have a good nurse?

JOHN Yes, I think, very. I sat down on the edge of her bed and talked; she asked me to tell her about myself. It was in the evening then and I couldn't stay long because she was weak. I was to go again next morning. But when I went next morning the nurse told me that my mother had died in the night.

(MAJOR DANDRIDGE *sits for a long while without moving, silent.* JOHN *leans on the piano. He runs a finger across the strings of the guitar on the piano and then suddenly mutes it with his palm. His father rises and goes to the window looking out on the terrace, and stands with his back to the room*)

JOHN   But it's not my mother's death I'm thinking of. That seems an incident when she was—when she was what she was. And I'm thinking of myself. (*He sits in the armchair to the left of the windows*) You see, there were two shocks when I saw my mother. First, that life could be so beautiful in any one, so fine! I never knew the human soul could look like that. (*He stops to look at his father, who sits motionless, looking at the floor ahead of him*) Never knew it could look like that!

MAJOR DANDRIDGE (*Without moving*)   Yes.

JOHN (*After a pause*)   And then I thought of how I had thought of her, had misjudged her, the ridiculous irony of it, so horrible and thin! And then I thought of how we may be doing this same thing about everybody, everything, all the time like fools—Oh, God, like fools!

MAJOR DANDRIDGE (*Comes and stands by the chair*)   Oh, no, my boy, you're all upset. I know how a man feels about his mother, it's only natural.

JOHN   No, Father! Not about his mother. It was not because she was my mother. My generation's not so strong on mothers as such, you know. Though, of course, I remembered what she had gone through for me. It was what she was. What she was herself, I tell you!

MAJOR DANDRIDGE   Well—? (*He takes his place again on the davenport*)

JOHN   And I don't miss my mother now as if—as I would some one I had memories of, associations. It's more terrible than that because it's wider, because it's less personal—it concerns—it's about all life. (*Pause*)   And what this has done to me I want to tell you—to try. (*He rises and begins to walk about*)   For the first time in my life I feel free. I don't care what happens. I know that the one thing worth anything is this reality.

MAJOR DANDRIDGE   What reality?

JOHN   I know I'll talk like a fool if I try to say, but that's no matter. I've seen so many people who were not fools and amounted to nothing.

MAJOR DANDRIDGE   Go on; we're all fools.

JOHN   I'm afraid it's not like a Southern gentleman; he's manly, he is allowed to be passionate, oratorical. But this I feel is so obscure, isn't it? Unhumorous, low-class—. I know I ought to be talking about trees or politics and let what I am in here (*He strikes his breast*) be implied in it, as the muscles of the body may be inferred through a well-cut suit of clothes. You can see my training has not been wasted, I at least know what a gentleman would be expected to do.

MAJOR DANDRIDGE I don't understand you.

JOHN Forgive me, Father—I was trying to insult myself and hurt you, I think. I'm sorry, one gets so stupid. I'll try to tell you. Because I don't see the reason for any relationships any more unless people know each other; all the rest is only clutter and waste of life. My God, don't we know that's what most people do all the time, that's why they bore themselves and everybody else to death. I'm through with it. I'm hard. I want life to hit me, to simplify me, that is, and make me throw out everything that won't mean fiercely something to me, that's mine, that feeds me, and destroys me, if you like. I can see Michelangelo's picture—how God reaches across the void and touches life first into Adam? It's like that for me now! It's all through me. And I never understood before how life in us can never go back or stay fixed, but must always go on. I mean, go on, do you see? Oh, how I talk!

MAJOR DANDRIDGE I don't mean to be unkind, my boy, or too unintelligent. I've been building my life around yours and I know we shall go on together.

JOHN Father, I hope so.

MAJOR DANDRIDGE But this sounds to me like some modern doctrine of egotism—I'm not sure just what.

JOHN It may be. I don't see that naming it means anything.

MAJOR DANDRIDGE No? Perhaps you're right. My generation had too many names for things. (*Without a sense of certainty*) Well, Son, in my position there's not a great deal I can say, you see that. You act like a man who has seen a vision. It seemed right that you should go and see your mother. but looking at what you were just saying, may I ask how all this you feel affects your actions in the future?

JOHN Only in this way I think—I hope to bring my actions closer to what I am.

MAJOR DANDRIDGE (*Anxiously*) To stay here with us?

JOHN Yes. Of course, a part of this is that I'll want to write more. I've been leading a secret life, as it were, you see, writing, thinking, telling almost nobody. I've been trying it a long time, off and on. But I never could make it go, somehow. But now I think I can, I'm sure—

MAJOR DANDRIDGE You can write here with us.

JOHN Yes, Father.

MAJOR DANDRIDGE   Writing will be a good diversion for you. We'll give you your grandfather's study. And, Son?

JOHN   Yes, Sir!

MAJOR DANDRIDGE (*Rising and going over toward the west corner of the room*)   I know you'd like me to tell you what the trouble was, why your mother went away as she did. You've a perfect right to expect it.

JOHN   Well, naturally, Father, I've been wondering since I saw her. I don't know what to think. I've thought and thought.

MAJOR DANDRIDGE   That's only natural. I suppose now you blame me for most of it?

JOHN   I don't feel any more that there's any use in blaming any one, Father. Things happen too deep down in us for that. In our own selves we must kneel down, I suppose.

MAJOR DANDRIDGE (*Looking a long time at* JOHN *before speaking*)   I'll tell you sometime soon, not now, if you will excuse me. I mean I prefer to wait, so soon after—

JOHN   Certainly, Father, I understand how it is, some day a little later.

MAJOR DANDRIDGE   Did she look very—pale?

JOHN   Pale, but her eyes were blue.

MAJOR DANDRIDGE (*Moving toward the terrace*)   Here's your Aunt Mollie. (JOHN *goes to meet* MISS MARY, *who comes in from the hall*)

MISS MARY   We're in a great stir upstairs, it's too funny! Lawsy, Brother Al!

MAJOR DANDRIDGE (*Turning to her*)   What is it, Sis Mollie? You've been having a lark, I see by your eyes.

MISS MARY   Give me the other keys to the store-rooms, dear, please. Sis Tellie started her by showing her some of the relics and now the child's got to see everything. She's wild over the things. Oh, dear, when we are young.

JOHN   What things, Auntie?

MAJOR DANDRIDGE   Sis Mollie, you know, some of the things up there—but no matter—

MISS MARY   The dresses and hats, you know, and those old trunks of Ma's.

(MAJOR DANDRIDGE *takes the key off his ring and gives it to her*)

MISS MARY   Thank you. (*On the way out she stops by the piano and pats* JOHN *on the arm*)   Isn't it nice to have our boy back again. All last year far away in New York and Europe worse still! We'll never let you out of our sight any more.

(JOHN *puts his arm around her shoulder and kisses her brow.* MISS MARY *hurries out. The two men remain standing and there is a pause*)

MAJOR DANDRIDGE (Presently) Well, John—Sis Mollie's coming in reminds me—how in this state of mind—after so much—did it happen that you should marry? I mean, of course, just at this juncture? Not that I intend any criticism of you. I'm sure there was some good reason. (*The* MAJOR *sits down on the sofa at the left*)

JOHN I was going to tell you, Father. It will seem odd, quixotic, but it's part of what I felt. I knew Evelyn three years ago, the summer before I went to New York, when I was visiting Cousin Julian in Memphis. We were in love with each other, not wholly, I knew that, but at any rate there was something—

MAJOR DANDRIDGE I understand. She's a beautiful woman, John.

JOHN Well, in the end—I suppose I must tell you—we went further than we had intended, we lost our heads.

MAJOR DANDRIDGE You—?

JOHN Yes, Father. And after that we began to fall out constantly. I left. I knew it was a rotten thing to do, but then men do it. Well, when I saw my mother I got the notion I'd go to Evelyn. I had heard that she was on a dangerous path, going the pace harder and harder—

MAJOR DANDRIDGE You don't mean to say she had become— ! My god A'mighty!

JOHN No, not yet, but wild, reckless with men. I heard it on all sides. It seemed clear at once what I would do. I had laid violent hands on her life, I thought, and I wanted to see it through. So I went by and persuaded her to marry me.

MAJOR DANDRIDGE Honorable thing to do, of course—

JOHN What was?

MAJOR DANDRIDGE If things could have been different, it would have been—fortunate.

JOHN It was obviously fantastic, I know that perfectly.

MAJOR DANDRIDGE If you care nothing for her at all, perhaps.

JOHN No, no, that's just it, when I saw her again I felt the old attraction, felt it stronger. We felt an attraction, both of us. I felt happy over it. I tried to tell myself it was masculine pride over my noble action. I knew better. Or that I was merely in an exalted mood. But it wasn't so. The minute we saw each other we knew it was the same. Knew we felt as we had felt before about each other. Luckily. If it hadn't been like that, I mean if we hadn't attracted each other, and

I'd asked her to marry me, it might have been foolish—before we got through with it.

MAJOR DANDRIDGE   I hope it will all turn out for the best, my boy. I hope she can be happy here. Your aunts will weave the whole thing into a romance.

JOHN   Aunt Mollie will, I know, bless her heart!

MAJOR DANDRIDGE   Your Aunt Ellen's just as bad; she wasn't suckled on novels for nothing. Finest women in the world those two, none like 'em.

JOHN (*Impulsively*)   Father, I do want to say I appreciate the way you've taken all this. I know it's not easy for you. I know how you feel about the family.

MAJOR DANDRIDGE   Don't give a thought to it. No, no, what's an old father for?

(JOHN *goes up and puts his hand on his father's shoulder for a second. The* MAJOR *does not move, and* JOHN *lets his hand fall and at the sound of footsteps outside goes over toward the terrace a foot or two.* MR. STEDMAN *comes in from the hall*)

MR. STEDMAN (*Opening the door*)   Well, Sir, are you free now?

MAJOR DANDRIDGE (*Discomfited, turning*)   Yes, yes, Mr. Stedman, in a moment. Here's John; have you shaken hands with him?

MR. STEDMAN   How are you, John? Didn't see you, Sir, I beg your pardon.

JOHN   How are you; I'm glad to see you, Sir.

MR. STEDMAN   So you're to be congratulated, I hear. What?

JOHN   Thank you. Thank you, Mr. Stedman. Am I in the way? Is there something you want to talk over?

MAJOR DANDRIDGE   No, not at all. Just a little legal business with Mr. Stedman. We'll spare you the bother of it. Nothing really.

MR. STEDMAN   Absolutely.

JOHN   Spare me? But why shouldn't I be bothered? If I'd prefer to be?

MAJOR DANDRIDGE   Why? Why should both of us be bothered? Run along to Evelyn. And here's Sister with the flowers.

(MISS ELLEN *enters with a bowl of roses followed by* OSCAR, *who carries a great vase of larkspurs. She puts the roses on the far end of the table*)

JOHN   See what we have here!

MISS ELLEN   Oscar, you can put them on the piano. No, not there, further over. Move the guitar a little. Now will you bring the others, please?

OSCAR Yas'm. Sho will.

(COUSIN TOM *comes in.* COUSIN TOM *has an open Bible on his palms. He pushes his spectacles down on his nose and stands watching* MISS ELLEN *and waits.* OSCAR *enters with a jar of syringas and poppies*)

MAJOR DANDRIDGE But Sister, you're our good fairy, aren't you?

MISS ELLEN It's just like me. I got up at six to do the flowers and then didn't get them ready in time. Here, Oscar, we'll put the big bowl of those roses and lilies on this end of the table, if you'll get them. Why, Cousin Tom, can I do something for you?

COUSIN TOM Yes, if you will. Tell me, this word's in fine print here on the margin. Is it *born?* Or is it *horn?* You girls' eyes are better'n mine. I can't see.

MISS ELLEN It's horn, Cousin Tom.

COUSIN TOM Ah, ah—good. I might have known. The first horn—. Then that proves it. I've got the capture of Fort Sumter unmistakably foreseen.

MR. STEDMAN (*As he goes out into the hall*) Really, Sir? I'm only sorry I must rush away, but I promised my wife not to be late. Good morning, Sir. (*To the others*) Good morning!

(*Every one bows to* MR. STEDMAN *and returns his good morning. Meantime* OSCAR *has brought the bowl and puts it on the table*)

MISS ELLEN And now, Oscar, go up and tell Miss Evelyn and Miss Mary that dinner will be ready in a very few minutes.

OSCAR (*Going out*) Yes'm.

(MISS ELLEN *stands arranging the flowers*)

COUSIN TOM Shame, Ellen Dandridge wasn't a man.

JOHN Nobody can do that like you, Aunt Ellen.

MISS ELLEN Yes, but this is Flower House, we must live up to the name.

JOHN Father, you're sure we hadn't better clear up this law business or whatever it is, talk it out now?

MAJOR DANDRIDGE Oh, no, no, or at least some other time.

MISS ELLEN Is there something private your father wants to say to you, dear?

MAJOR DANDRIDGE No, Sister, don't go.

JOHN No, Aunt Ellen, not now, later.

(JOHN *goes over and links his arm through* MISS ELLEN'S *as she is putting the last touches to the flowers*)

MISS ELLEN Do you know who really gave this place the name Flower House? Of all people, your Uncle Leonidas!

CURTAIN

ACT II

(*After a moment's wait the curtain rises again. It is toward two o'clock in the afternoon. The blinds to the windows are closed, the light filters through the green shutters. Every one has just come in from the dining-room.* MISS ELLEN *is seated in the armchair.* EVELYN, *having changed her travelling suit for a light frock, sits on the davenport with* MR. BOBO *on her left.* COUSIN TOM *has taken a chair near* MISS ELLEN. MISS MARY, *with her guitar in her hands, sits on the sofa, behind which the piano is, and* JOHN *leans against the end of it that is farthest from every one.*

MAJOR DANDRIDGE *is adjusting one of the shutters to divert the blinding glare outside*)

COUSIN TOM Well, ladies, if I had had the ordering of that dinner I would not have changed it by a single item.

MISS MARY I'm afraid you are partial to us, Cousin Tom.

MAJOR DANDRIDGE (*Securing the blind*) That's better. The afternoon light's overpowering.

EVELYN Oh, it's much better. No use trying to live up to this day, it's too bright for mortal eyes. Father, you're a dear. And everything's wonderful. The trunks have come, the phonograph has come, safe and sound. And— (*She pats the place beside her to the right and the* MAJOR *sits down*)

MISS MARY Sit down, Sonny Man. (*Her fingers wander softly over the strings of the guitar.* JOHN *takes the seat at her right on the sofa without speaking and sits there looking off into space*) It's fine to have our boy again!

JOHN I missed you, Auntie.

MISS MARY Bless my nephew's heart for saying so!

(*She pats his hand and then goes back to the guitar. She begins an old air, so softly that only a few notes of it can be heard.* JOHN *remains silent, looking down at the floor and off into space, with his hands in his pockets)*

COUSIN TOM   And you've never heard about Leonidas Dandridge, Cousin Evelyn? None of the stories?

MISS MARY *(To* JOHN*)*   Poor old dear, he tells them over every day.

JOHN   For the last three years, hasn't he? *(She nods)* It seems incredible. And Father has no sense of humor.

COUSIN TOM   Well, you must know that Leonidas was a wag.

MAJOR DANDRIDGE   Proverbial.

COUSIN TOM   And he was always up to practical jokes, Leonidas was. Nothing stopped him. He'd usually been drinking, of course, every one drank those days. Well, on one occasion Brother Bates was staying with him—

EVELYN   Who was Brother Bates?

COUSIN TOM   Bates was a traveling preacher.

MAJOR DANDRIDGE   Circuit rider.

COUSIN TOM   Yes. And powerful religious! And a character. He was the only preacher Leonidas Dandridge could put up with. Where was I? Oh, yes, on one occasion, Brother Bates stopped to spend the night at the house. There was other company that night and Bates had to sleep in the office. You know the offices those days were rooms out in the yard, away from the big house. Well, Leonidas' father had been a doctor and had left behind him a skeleton. So he hung the skeleton over the door some way r'other in the office and that night when Bates retired to his quarters and opened the door, the skeleton fell down on him and clapped its arms around old Bates. And Bates let out a yell— *(He laughs heartily.* MAJOR DANDRIDGE *and* EVELYN *laugh and* MR. BOBO *nods and smiles)*

EVELYN   I don't believe it. How awful, Cousin Tom!

COUSIN TOM   And, Baron, you tell about the creek, Baron.

MR. BOBO   No, go on, Thomas, tell it.

EVELYN   Do, please, Mr. Bobo.

*(*MISS MARY *stops playing and puts her hand through* JOHN'S *arm and kisses his shoulder)*

MISS MARY   Never mind, dearest! I know it's hard for our Sonny man, these old stories and all.

MR. BOBO   Well, on one occasion Leonidas was taking a walk down by Wallace Creek, just west of his place. He had just crossed the stream when he saw a man on horseback stopping at the edge. "Will you tell me, Sir, if I can get across without swimming?" the man asked. There'd been rains and the Creek was widened out and it was so muddy you couldn't tell anything about the depth. Leonidas himself had just crossed on a log footbridge to one side, but it was hidden from the man by the willows; at least he didn't see it. "I'll tell you, my friend," said 'e, "it's deep but you can get across all right if you'll take off your clothes and tie them around your neck and stand up in the saddle." The man thanked him and began to undress and Leonidas went on his way. But a little piece down the road he hid in some willows and watched to see what would happen. (COUSIN TOM *bursts into a fit of laughter*) Pretty soon he saw the man standing up naked on his saddle with his clothes round his neck and starting across. The water came about up to the horse's knees. (*Great laughter*)

EVELYN Oh, Mr. Bobo, Mr. Bobo! I don't believe it. How terrible!

MR. BOBO Well, Sir, they said you could hear that man swearing in the next county.

EVELYN It's the funniest thing I ever heard in my life. I love stories.

MR. BOBO (*Rising and beginning to walk about the room, much puffed up*) On another occasion Leonidas was in New York at the old Fifth Avenue Hotel. He couldn't find the butterknife on the table, so he reached over and cut off a piece of butter with his knife. At this a dude sitting next to him called out to the waiter, "Waitah, Waitah, bring another plate of butter, this man's stuck his knife in it." Leonidas didn't say a word, he just picked up the plate of butter and slapped it on the dude's face, so. S 'e "Waitah, Waitah, bring another plate of butter, this man's stuck his nose in it." (*Laughter*)

(MR. BOBO'S *cuff drops off and falls on the floor. He replaces it quickly.* EVELYN *makes a gesture of helping him adjust the clasp. He holds out his arm to her*)

EVELYN (*Fastening the cuff*) What a terrible man, Mr. Bobo!

MR. BOBO But the best story of all was on one occasion when he had been drinking again; it was Christmas week; and he sent his man Solomon to call all the darky women on the place into the back-yard—

MISS ELLEN (*Cooly*) Has Mr. Bobo been telling the story of the time Uncle Leonidas made the darky women sit on the brickbats in the backyard?

MISS MARY (*Puts down the guitar and goes over to her*) Oh, Tellie, he was just telling it—

MISS ELLEN Oh, I'm so sorry, please excuse me, Mary. I keep telling you I ought to stay in my own room; I'm not fit to be in company.

MAJOR DANDRIDGE No, no, Sister, Sis Tellie doesn't mean that. It's all right. Go on, Baron. (MISS MARY *kisses her sister on the brow*)

EVELYN   Yes, go on, Mr. Bobo.

MR. BOBO   Oh, that's all there was, you've heard the point.

MISS MARY   Please excuse my sister, Mr. Bobo. The poor darling didn't hear you.

MR. BOBO   Perfectly all right, ladies, I assure you. Some other time. Just as well.

(JOHN *goes over and pats* MISS ELLEN *on the shoulder and leans down to her ear*)

JOHN   It's nothing, Aunt Ellen, Mr. Bobo doesn't mind. Besides I didn't hear you. Mr. Bobo, please go on, I didn't hear Aunt Ellen, what she said.

MR. BOBO (*Who has sat down again in a chair*)   Oh, it's nothing except that Leonidas made them all sit in cotton baskets on the brickbats and cackle like hens. (*Every one laughs*)

COUSIN TOM   And Leonidas stood on the back and split his sides laughing.

MISS MARY   And poor Cousin Dolly, she was upstairs crying her eyes out.

EVELYN   Who's Cousin Dolly?

MISS MARY   His wife, my dear. You might know some woman would have to bear the burden of it.

COUSIN TOM (*Rising*)   Well, I must get to my work.

MR. BOBO   Won't you play something, Miss Molly? How about the Harp on the Shore?

MISS MARY   No, Mr. Bobo, thank you, I'll play tonight after supper. Cousin Tom's right, we'll all get to work. That is we ought to take our naps.

MR. BOBO   Thomas actually has discovered positive proof of the Civil War. (*He laughs*)

COUSIN TOM   Laugh, if you like, Baron, at the prophecy in Scripture.

MR. BOBO   Oh, that's all right, Thomas. I know you're doing a great work for religion. Only you'll have to let me take it easy; you see, an old horse has to have a loose harness.

(*All rise, the party breaks up.* MISS MARY *goes over to* JOHN, *who is standing, leaning on the back of the sofa*)

MISS MARY   Poor sweetness, go take a siesta, these old people wear you out. Lord knows you've heard 'em often enough.

JOHN   And yet it's a sweet, gentle way of living.

MISS MARY   Living? Of course. But you're just—

JOHN   And human, has a sort of fragrance about it. But I'm out of it, out of it. My social charm is plainly all used up, Auntie.

MISS MARY Oh, no, dear, you'll feel all right soon, you're just worn out. It was terrible for you in Kentucky, Auntie knows.

MISS ELLEN (*Rising*) Come, Mary, you need a nap if anybody does. You're a perfect cricket.

MISS MARY That's just like Sister, Evelyn, whenever she's sleepy she begins to talk about my needing to take a nap. Shall we go?

(COUSIN TOM *and* MISS MARY *and* EVELYN *start out*)

MISS ELLEN John, are you coming too?

JOHN No, Aunt Ellen— (MR. BOBO *opens one of the shutters on to the terrace and lets into the room a blinding glare. He disappears, closing the shutters after him*) I'll stay down a while with Father.

(MAJOR DANDRIDGE *stands somewhere near the far end of the table.* JOHN *goes back to his seat on the sofa. For some minutes nothing is said*)

MAJOR DANDRIDGE John, you don't seem to feel in a very social mood today, Son.

JOHN No, Father, I don't. I'm sorry, Father.

MAJOR DANDRIDGE That's all right, Son. Give yourself time to recuperate. We can't always be gay, though doubtless we owe it to social life to try. However—

JOHN How well I remember that, Father, your telling me, "We must make a brave front, keep our backs up." In the copybook style, or the grand manner in morals; but then I was a little boy.

MAJOR DANDRIDGE It's all right.

JOHN Father?

MAJOR DANDRIDGE Yes, yes?

JOHN (*Rising and coming over nearer* MAJOR DANDRIDGE) I may as well tell you; I somehow can't get this business of Mr. Stedman's, though it may sound absurd, out of my mind. That I was not to know, I mean that I was not to be bothered with. Perhaps because, as Auntie says, I'm a little tired.

MAJOR DANDRIDGE Oh, so you're still on that. It's nothing. Son, I don't want to be bothering you with these affairs just yet. Time enough, time enough.

JOHN No, Father, I'd prefer being told, Sir. If I'm to be here on the estate I ought to share the—the whole situation with you.

MAJOR DANDRIDGE You will in time.

JOHN Of course. What bores me with myself is that I kept thinking of this during dinner—shows it's in my mind the wrong way. Perhaps it's because just now especially I'm in no mood to feel myself wrapped in wool, wafted along in a balm of illusion. I'd like straight blows if any.

MAJOR DANDRIDGE No blows at all. You don't think I'd deceive you about a thing of this sort, do you, John?

JOHN Why, deceive me, no. No, Father, I don't. Why should I? I just feel that I don't want anything coming between us, Sir.

MAJOR DANDRIDGE No, assuredly not.

JOHN I mean with me feeling the way I do. I was telling you this morning, since—since—

MAJOR DANDRIDGE I understand. But—You won't take my advice, you won't trust my judgment when I say that I consider it useless to burden you with such an affair?

JOHN Father, I'd rather not, I'd rather have everything open between us. I'd appreciate your telling me.

MAJOR DANDRIDGE Very well, I'll tell you. Sit down, there's nothing very alarming about the whole thing. (MAJOR DANDRIDGE *sits down on the davenport and* JOHN *draws up* MISS ELLEN'S *chair opposite him*) It's an old disagreeable subject almost forgotten in the family. Very distasteful to me. However, lately it's come up again.

JOHN When?

MAJOR DANDRIDGE While you were away on this trip to Kentucky. You knew I had a brother. Ever heard of your Uncle Ned?

JOHN A little.

MAJOR DANDRIDGE Well, the less you heard the better. Who told you? Your mother, did your mother tell you? Did she?

JOHN No, Father, I told you this morning I saw my mother only a little while. Aunt Ellen told me.

MAJOR DANDRIDGE What did she tell you?

JOHN That he was wild and that later he went to Texas and never came back.

MAJOR DANDRIDGE Well, so he didn't. But his son, your cousin, Ned, has been heard from.

JOHN Him I never heard of.

MAJOR DANDRIDGE I suppose not. Well my brother was a wild boy and by the time he was of age he was a hard gambler and he drank too much. His share of the estate, the part your grandfather had decided to give Ned, was along the river bottom, fine lands. In fact, Father was about to settle a piece of land on each of us when Ned's rumpus with Old Bill Edwards came to his ears. Bill Edwards lived beyond the Creek, his business was largely the lending of money at exorbitant rates. Well, Ned, it seems, had borrowed time and again from Bill Edwards; he needed money to pay his gambling debts and his sprees. He paid the money back, sometimes at once, sometimes longer, two or three months. But he was reckless about getting his receipts for the payments, et cetera. In those days gentlemen gave their word of honor, paper was not necessary. Well, at any rate one fine day Bill Edwards rode up and demanded payment on a certain loan. Ned was certain the load had been paid. Bill Edwards said no. There was no receipt to be found, Ned was at sea in such things, which was exactly what old Bill Edwards had been counting on. Words passed between them, and the upshot was my brother knocked him down. But when Father heard of it, heard of the fight, the gambling, the debts, and, most of all, the acquaintance with old Bill Edwards, he said nothing to anybody, but went to his lawyer and cut Ned off without a copper, he did that. Your grandfather, Son, was an upright man, but very strict in matters of business and conduct and especially about the company we kept. Your grandmother died when I was born. Well, that's all there was to it. Ned hung around a few days, but he never asked any favors, he was too proud. Then he suddenly disappeared and later I heard he was in Texas. Never saw Brother Ned until Father's death, he came back then for a short time. (JOHN *starts to protest*)

MAJOR DANDRIDGE   Wait. Now turns up his son, he's written me a letter, claiming the land back. His father, he writes, died this spring. Some shyster lawyer fellow has put that in his head. That Ned should have contested the will. So I've had Stedman going over the papers.

JOHN   Mr. Stedman.

MAJOR DANDRIDGE   He said they were quite straight, all the deeds, no doubt about the legality of the thing. (*A long silence*)   Well?

JOHN (*With a little laugh*)   These lawyers are great chaps.

MAJOR DANDRIDGE   Why, what do you mean, Son?

JOHN   I mean that Mr. Stedman thinks because those papers are straight, there's nothing else to be said. The universe begins and ends in law.

MAJOR DANDRIDGE   Well, naturally the legality of the deeds is what concerns a lawyer.

JOHN   Naturally.

MAJOR DANDRIDGE   But you seem to imply something else.

JOHN   It's only that we're not all lawyers; of course, there's no reason we need see it that way. But that's obvious.

MAJOR DANDRIDGE   I understand you. You mean we should have a superior code? You mean the position the law takes is insufficient?

JOHN   But, Father, of course it is not mere legality, I know the legality is perfect enough. That's easy enough to dispose of. If we take that tack, the thing is legal and very fine. But—what's legality when we know better? I'm talking about this, that there's no reason why this man should pay so for his father's being wild. You know what I mean. Why should we take this in our hands, this judgment, when it's been made wrong already?

MAJOR DANDRIDGE You mean that whatever side I take you will take the contrary, that we begin by disagreeing. No, no, you are right to shake your head, I apologize, I don't mean that.

JOHN That's all right, I know, Father, how you feel. But we can give my cousin what he ought to have, of course.

MAJOR DANDRIDGE Eh? The property? It happens to be mine just now, if I may remind you.

JOHN That's not worthy of you, Father.

MAJOR DANDRIDGE You're right, Son. I ask your pardon. I don't want any division between us of any sort, you know that. But about this land—

JOHN It's the kind of thing we just don't do, that's all. It's not worth what it costs.

MAJOR DANDRIDGE (*Scornfully, rising and walking about*) Oh! And what will we do, then, may I ask?

JOHN If it came to a choice between two things? Go back to New York if that means me.

MAJOR DANDRIDGE (*Moved, changing his tone*) Son, you know how much it is my wish that you stay here.

JOHN It's mine, too, Father; I want to stay.

MAJOR DANDRIDGE (*Showing excitement again*) But, however, if you went to New York, what would you do?

JOHN Try to write. I could manage somehow, I think.

MAJOR DANDRIDGE And how would that help your cousin, Mr. Ned Dandridge?

JOHN I'd try to pay him.

MAJOR DANDRIDGE $30,000? You'd soon write that much, do you think?

JOHN I could pay something perhaps. I'd be out of it at least.

MAJOR DANDRIDGE Wash your hands of it, eh?

JOHN And when you've thought it over, I feel sure, Father—when you come to think it over—

MAJOR DANDRIDGE Think it over, my God, I thought of nothing else night and day for three months once, when you were a baby, Sir!

JOHN Oh, it was then?

MAJOR DANDRIDGE   Yes. Then! I settled this question long ago, Son, long ago. I know you don't intend it that way, but I feel obliged to tell you that the attitude you are taking now reflects on me and my conduct. On the family, I must ask you to think of that!

JOHN   I don't see why you need take it that way, I certainly don't mean to reflect on your conduct, Father. But when you come right down to it, Father, I think that's hardly the question. The question at this point involves only the restoration of the land.

MAJOR DANDRIDGE   Then, since you prefer to leave me out of account—

JOHN   No, Father—

MAJOR DANDRIDGE   No question exists on earth that can be cut down to one single consideration like that. If age and experience have taught me anything, they've taught me that.

JOHN   It's not leaving you out of account, Sir; there may have been abundant circumstances to exonerate your action.

MAJOR DANDRIDGE   See here, John, I'm not asking you to excuse my behavior, or anybody else.

JOHN   I'm thinking of myself, I suppose. The moment I see myself submitting to the settlement, I see my mother—

MAJOR DANDRIDGE (*Violently*)   Let's leave your mother out of the question, please. You'll oblige me.

JOHN   You said it's only thirty thousand. That would leave us enough still, surely.

MAJOR DANDRIDGE   With your aunts' share of the estate we have two thousand acres to Flower House; this is only a few hundred, you know that, three hundred at best.

JOHN   And you're not the man to set much store by money. Then in this business you must have some other, better reason.

MAJOR DANDRIDGE   It hardly matters what reason I might have from the way you take my opinion, Sir.

JOHN   Why, not at all, Father! No, really, don't think that.

MAJOR DANDRIDGE   I'll hardly solicit your approval on every step I've ever taken!

(*They stand without anything to say to each other.* EVELYN *comes in, in a lace negligee*)

EVELYN   You people have been talking like trumpets. But it's no matter. We're not asleep anyway. I'll never go to sleep! I never saw such lovely things! The silk is so marvelous, you couldn't find the like of it these days for love or money. I never dreamed we'd own a museum. But it is hot up there! Under the roof. John, have you seen the dresses and things? There's one old mantle—and your old finery, Father, you were a dandy in your time, weren't you?

MAJOR DANDRIDGE So, you're at that, are you? Then you might as well have these things now. (*He goes to drawers on the right wall and takes out a box as he talks*) They were my mother's, she loved jewels. What do you think of them? (*He opens a case,* EVELYN *gives a cry of joy*)

EVELYN Pearls! Oh, Father! Look, John! Old pearls, on ribbons. And the cameo! And this ring! You just can't believe it. (*She puts the things on and shows herself to them*) Now. (*She strikes a pose and then another.* JOHN *is silent as he looks at her*) Why, John, what's the matter! You are a death's head. What is it? What is it, Father?

JOHN Tell Evelyn, please, Father.

MAJOR DANDRIDGE You mean—?

JOHN Yes. Please tell her, Father.

MAJOR DANDRIDGE Very well. I will! Because of my brother's way of living my father cut him off and left everything to me. The transaction was perfectly legal, all the papers and so on. That was years ago. The son has stirred the matter up, he claims a share of the estate. Now John wants me to give it back to the son, my brother's part of the estate.

EVELYN Why, John, why do you, if it is all legal and perfectly all right?

JOHN It's not perfectly all right, Evelyn. Because this man's father was wild and my grandfather cut him off is no reason we should have everything and the other man nothing.

EVELYN But he deeded it to Father, he's told you that! Wasn't it his to do as he liked with? Father, John's just sick and on a highhorse today, that's all. We'll see, come on, John, and go up with me.

(MISS MARY *comes to the hall door*)

MISS MARY But, gracious me, you all are kicking up! And what on earth's that pounding out at the stable, Brother Al?

MAJOR DANDRIDGE Oscar must go and see to it.

MISS MARY You must come and go to sleep, everybody. It's a rule in this house, in summertime. You're naughty, all of you. (*She notices the jewels*) Oh, look, the Queen of Sheba! Solomon in all his glory!

EVELYN Aren't they wonderful. Look, Auntie. And you're a sweet old dear to play with me.

MISS MARY The idea! We don't have a lovely new niece every day.

EVELYN But I've a secret too.

MISS MARY What?

EVELYN You wait and see later. Wait till you see me! Oh, boy! (MR. BOBO *comes in from the terrace*)

MAJOR DANDRIDGE Baron, do you know what that noise is?

MR. BOBO It's only old Fancy. He's always had the collie in the stall with him, you see. And now the collie's chained up, Fancy won't stay in there without him. He's trying to kick the place down.

MAJOR DANDRIDGE Fancy's getting to be an old fool. I'll sell him on a farm.

MR. BOBO Oh, no, fine piece of horseflesh. I'd hang on to 'im, Alex.

MAJOR DANDRIDGE Course you would, Baron.

MR. BOBO Can't expect to teach an old horse new tricks, not right off the bat.

MAJOR DANDRIDGE My son was just saying you couldn't teach a new horse old tricks.

MR. BOBO (*Laughing*) Eh? John's a wag! He'll stick his fingers under your ribs. Your husband's a wag, Miss Evelyn.

EVELYN (*Cooly*) Oh, yes, John's quite a wag, a perfect Uncle Leonidas.

JOHN Am I?

EVELYN (*Unfastening the necklace and banging it down on the table. In a cutting tone*) Aren't you?

JOHN I seem to be more of a bore than anything else.

EVELYN (*Putting her arm through* MISS MARY'S) Well, we're going up, will you come?

JOHN (*Glancing at his father*) In just a second.

MISS MARY What's the matter with all of you, you need some sleep.

(EVELYN *and* MISS MARY *go out by way of the hall.* MR. BOBO *opens the window to the terrace.* JOHN *sits down at the far end of the davenport,* MAJOR DANDRIDGE *takes the armchair*)

MR. BOBO I'll see, Al, what can be done about Fancy.

(*He disappears, leaving the door open. The blinding light strikes* JOHN *in the face. He first tries holding his hand up to screen his eyes, then he changes his seat to a chair near his father*)

JOHN Father, I don't know why I seemed to annoy you so, Sir. I'm sorry, I was just awkward about it, I suppose. I didn't mean to criticise you, what I meant was merely to express what I think would be the right thing to do about this estate business.

(MAJOR DANDRIDGE *makes no reply, and the two men sit for a moment without speaking. Suddenly from upstairs breaks in the sound of a phonograph playing a piece of jazz music. It joins the blare of light from the terrace)*

MAJOR DANDRIDGE (*Starting slightly and then recomposing himself in his chair*)   What's that? Ah, yes.

JOHN   Evelyn's phonograph.

(*They sit silent a few moments while the music goes on*)

JOHN   And, Father, I was thinking that perhaps we could settle this matter with a payment in money, the value of my uncle's share, instead of breaking up the estate. That would be fair and square enough.

(MAJOR DANDRIDGE *instead of replying glances over toward the direction from which the sound of the phonograph comes.* JOHN *rises and goes over and shuts the hall door. On his way back to his seat he closes the terrace window. The quiet light returns to the room.* JOHN *sits down again near his father. A silence for a moment, save for the phonograph*)

JOHN   To do it that way, Father?

MAJOR DANDRIDGE   I'm sorry if I seem unreasonable, John, but that wouldn't change matters one iota. I'm very sorry.

JOHN   Then, Father, I'm sorry too.

(JOHN *and* MAJOR DANDRIDGE *say no more, but sit each of them looking down at the floor. The sound of the phonograph continues*)

CURTAIN

ACT III

(*Three-fourths across the stage, from the right, south, runs a colonnade of five pairs of columns without bases and with simple capitals, on which rests the flat roof. The whole rests on a platform of flagstones, above two steps leading up on the front and north sides. The colonnade is the fine dull golden yellow seen in Roman palaces and gardens.*

Through the columns the last blue before darkness is seen in the east, above the floor one or two dark pointed cedars appear.

You can hear a fountain plashing, off somewhere, and now and then a bird.

EVELYN *comes in from the left and goes up the west steps into the colonnade. She wears an old dress of figured muslin, with a skirt flounced up to the waist, above which is a white satin bodice, low-cut on the shoulders and a rose between her breasts. She has done her hair in the same period and put some roses in it. She walks the length of the colonnade, and half way back again, stands looking off toward the east for a while, and then descends the steps on that side and disappears into the garden.*

In a moment, MAJOR DANDRIDGE *and* MISS MARY *enter from the left. They come along the front of the colonnade, but do not mount the steps. In the playing of this act the light, the music, the beauty surrounding and flooding the scene must be used to dilate, and to make possible the pitch and intensity of, the emotions of the characters, the words used, the poetry given expression to)*

MAJOR DANDRIDGE (*Pointing south*)   There she goes now, down the rose walk.

MISS MARY   I don't know, Brother Al, whether it's quite safe for the child to be down here this time o' night. It's so near the negro cabins down here, don't you think so? So many things could happen. You know what I mean. Tellie says I'm just nervous, but then you never can tell, I say. Of course, a moon's coming up, but still—

MAJOR DANDRIDGE   You may be right, Sis Mollie, I'll stay till John comes out, he'll be coming down directly.

MISS MARY   How sweet the roses smell!

MAJOR DANDRIDGE   But what on earth, Sis Mollie, do you and Tellie mean by letting Evelyn put on that dress?

MISS MARY   I don't know, Brother Al, now don't lay it on us. Tellie showed her a few of the things and she would see them all. We had no idea she was going to do it.

MAJOR DANDRIDGE   I know, but—my wife's dress—it's not very considerate of me.

MISS MARY   Dressing up was the surprise she had for us today. She didn't know—you remember she was talking of her secret after dinner. That was a dress she had made for a lawn party, I remember when she wore it, we copied it from a picture. (*Taking his arm and leaning over to kiss his sleeve*)   The child just didn't think, like most young people, and she still doesn't know whose dress 'tis. But there's no use mentioning it now, and spoiling the child's pleasure; we can tell her later sometime. There're lots of other clothes if she wants to dress up. And after all, she hasn't had much of a honeymoon coming straight here. You don't know young people.

MAJOR DANDRIDGE   That may be. Well, at least—at any rate I'd hardly have thought you or Tellie could have been so—so inconsiderate.

MISS MARY   Of course not, I should say not.

MAJOR DANDRIDGE   I'm very sorry it happened, so soon after— of course, you see what I mean.

MISS MARY   Yes, dear, I understand. And I'm sure the child would feel dreadfully about it if she knew. But I must leave you and go find Tellie. You want me to tell Evelyn on the way.

MAJOR DANDRIDGE   Please, if you will. I'll wait here.

(*She disappears on the right into the garden and her brother begins to walk slowly up and down the colonnade.* EVELYN *comes along between the columns from the right*)

EVELYN   Why, Father! Auntie has me quite scared, telling me it's not safe down here by myself.

MAJOR DANDRIDGE   No, daughter, I hardly think's it's safe. Not of late. You read the papers and know how it is. I'm waiting for you. We'll sit here a while till John comes out.

EVELYN   That's lovely, Father. How do you like me in this dress?

MAJOR DANDRIDGE   You look very pretty, my dear.

EVELYN   But you don't look at me! Scarcely at all. I don't believe you do like it. Look at me.

MAJOR DANDRIDGE   Perhaps the trouble is you look as pretty in one thing as another to my old eyes.

EVELYN   Oh, if you say that, of course—

MAJOR DANDRIDGE   So there. Sit down here.

(*He shows her to the bench by the last pillar on the west, and sits down beside her*)

MAJOR DANDRIDGE   There's something I want to talk to you about, daughter.

EVELYN   Yes, Sir.

MAJOR DANDRIDGE   It's this business about the land. John'll be here any moment. The point simply is that you've got to help me. I know John. Men like him seem to talk things off; they look manageable, but they have a hard line right through them. John won't budge in this. I can see he's already set, just like—

EVELYN   Like—like what, Father?

MAJOR DANDRIDGE   Like his mother. But no matter, he's a fine boy, and we must get all this settled. But you're no fool, Evelyn, and you'll see the point.

EVELYN   The trouble is, Father, I don't like to meddle in John's affairs.

Besides, if it's only a matter of money, there's enough without this man's part, isn't there? And you don't care about money anyway. So what's the difference. If it's not something besides the money, I can't see the difference.

MAJOR DANDRIDGE There's not time now to thrash the whole business out again.

EVELYN And then, Father, besides, you see we haven't been married long.

MAJOR DANDRIDGE So much the better. He'll pay more attention to you.

EVELYN Do you think so?

MAJOR DANDRIDGE I know what a woman's influence over a man can be.

EVELYN John and I seem almost strangers sometimes. Lately especially, I mean since we came here to Flower House. I don't understand what John's driving at, it seems to me, half the time. I'm not artistic and John is. But sometimes, too, nobody's got more just horse sense than John has—when he's not off on some streak.

MAJOR DANDRIDGE Well, he's in love with you. You have an attraction for him now at first—Oh, you know what I mean. You young people know everything nowadays. At any rate you don't want John to be a pauper on you.

EVELYN For goodness' sake, I should say I don't.

MAJOR DANDRIDGE Yes, where would you be? Then make him give it up. I can see already none of the rest of us are going to be able to do it. I've tried to say as little as I could so as not to oppose him any more than I could help. John shows he's been under a strain. But that doesn't mean I'm going to give up to him, as he's counting on now. You must bring him round, Evelyn. And tonight. Will you?

EVELYN (*Looking at the* MAJOR *a moment before she answers*) I'll try.

MAJOR DANDRIDGE Well, then—but he's coming now. Look, the moon is rising, there, just over the pine trees. What a thing life is! I'll go. Remember, daughter.

(*He goes out to the left.* EVELYN *does not rise but sits there tightening her lips. The moonlight falls on the columns and down across the floor of the colonnade.* JOHN *comes in from the west end of the colonnade and hurries to her*)

JOHN Oh, Evelyn, you alone here? I stopped a moment on the terrace, Auntie was playing her guitar. She was playing the fandango for Cousin Tom. How beautiful you look, how beautiful you look against the column in that dress. Oh, my dear! All during supper—

(He sits for a moment beside her and raises her hand to his lips. She smiles but remains quiet)

JOHN But look at this night. *(He rises and leans against the column on the other side of the colonnade and stands looking about him)* What a night, my God, what a night! It's incredible. I always forget how beautiful it can be down here. I always know when it's like this that I love my own country best after all, my own South. Look at the moonlight over everything. You could read by it, couldn't you! Over the columns and the stones of the pavement. And out over the garden, Evelyn. It's like a heart beating.

EVELYN You can smell the roses, do you smell them?

JOHN Yes. And the jasmine smell is everywhere. And the sound of the fountain, the water—water and the moon are the most beautiful things in the world. I dreamed once that I was dead and was buried by the light of the moon, and that water was falling from somewhere on my heart and made a sound like the strings of a harp. A foolish dream, but the kind you remember, I suppose, though you pretend you don't. Listen—

(From off to the southeast come the notes of a guitar and a man's voice singing. The music seems to spread through the garden. They remain silent a moment listening)

EVELYN What, you mean the music?

JOHN Yes, they're beginning to sing, at the quarters, And you'll hear a mocking-bird start up after them in a second. They've got an old drum they play sometimes that sounds as if it had dropped out of Africa, perhaps we'll hear it.

(They are silent a moment. A bird begins)

JOHN There he is, I told you. I know him. Is there any place in the world where it's like this on a summer night. The air is warm, glowing. Like a faun it is. Look at the columns, how they gleam against the garden around, look how clear and straight the line of them is.

(A long silence, in which EVELYN moves once or twice a little restlessly. JOHN walks up and down for a moment, then disappears behind one of the columns. The guitars go on playing and the man's voice in the song. The bird breaks in now and then. You hear at intervals the fountain plashing)

EVELYN *(Sharply)* John! John, where are you?

(He comes quickly to her)

JOHN Here I am. Why, Evelyn, are you frightened, forgive me. *(He sits at her side and puts his arm about her)* I'm sorry.

EVELYN No, but you disappeared. It's too lonesome here by myself. Don't disappear, John, like that.

JOHN Darling, I won't. Of course, I won't. But I was thinking—

EVELYN What were you thinking?

JOHN There was a little wind passed over the garden down there. Did you hear it?

EVELYN I didn't notice it, John—well?

JOHN It was like a sigh. Like a sigh, in this night here. I was thinking of the nostalgia of all this beauty. Of the nostalgia of a night like this.

EVELYN What's nostalgia, John?

JOHN Homesickness.

EVELYN Oh!

JOHN I was thinking of the homesickness of all this, homesickness for something, I don't know what. I don't know what it is. *(He rises and leans his hand against the pillar opposite her, the second pillar from the end of the colonnade, and looks out over the garden)* Always about what's beautiful there's a sense of things ending. How I felt that as a child when I heard music far off down the street! Hearing it die down to less and less. And here tonight! In this place my mother loved. This place sick with the unexpressed in people's lives—a magnificent splendor of desire in us and the necessity to express ourselves, and after that an end! And two people tied together by something that makes them almost hate each other. Look at the moonlight on the fountain there!

EVELYN Well, I must say I like that!

JOHN What, Evelyn?

EVELYN Your wanting to be alone like this. I mean your saying so to my face.

(He drops down to the seat beside her again)

JOHN Why, my dearest, my dear, you don't know what you say. I need you more than ever; without you to turn to I'd be lost now. It's through you I lose myself, in all this beauty—here! It's through your body I get the sense of another soul. It's through my passion for you that I feel so the passion of this night. And otherwise—

EVELYN Otherwise what? My Lord, John, you talk like a book!

JOHN Well, to quote a book, then—otherwise, as Plato said, I'd only trace obscurely the footsteps of my obscure desire.

(He throws his arms about her and draws her to him. A drum begins to beat, and joins the music the negroes are making)

EVELYN *(Presently)* You hurt me. *(She half frees herself from his arms)* John, you say you love me. I want to ask you something.

JOHN *(Startled by her tone)* Why, Evelyn, what? What do you want to ask me?

EVELYN Will you do it?

JOHN If I can. Ask me, my dear; you never ask me to do anything for you.

EVELYN Well, I ask you now.

JOHN What? Tell me.

EVELYN I want you to drop this quarrel with your father about the money, the land.

(His arms fall down loosely to one side)

About this cousin of yours who's kicking up a row to get the land back. Now. *(He is silent)* Well, I've asked you. *(He nods his head)* Will you do it John?

JOHN Evelyn—

EVELYN Yes?

JOHN You don't know what you're asking!

EVELYN Oh, I do too. I'm not a child. Legally the land belongs to your father. And he's got his head dead set on not giving it up. Besides, that Ned Dandridge—isn't that his name?—is a rotter anyhow. He'd just throw the whole business away like his father. So what's the use? At any rate your father's not going to give in, I can tell you that. And what's more, do you know something?

JOHN What?

EVELYN It's not just this honor and family stuff that's holding Father so tight, there's something else.

JOHN Think so? What?

EVELYN I know it. There's something sure's you're born. But I can't make it out. Something makes him so absolutely set. But I can't make it out.

JOHN Then we're none the wiser.

EVELYN Then all the more I say what's the use of getting yourself disinherited about something that's none of your business and wouldn't help the other man either? You'll have Father blowing up the way your grandfather did, cutting off everybody like an old fool. So there's no need to argue.

JOHN You don't understand. I'm not arguing.

EVELYN   Stop saying I don't understand. Besides where'd I be if you get cut off from every red cent Father has? We'd be in a nice mess. You might think of me as well as yourself.

JOHN   Sweetheart—

EVELYN   Don't call me sweet names if you won't do anything I ask you.

JOHN   But you see—I've told you about the change in my life, in me. I can't take this land when it's my cousin's. You can see that. What I am, and whatever I may write, depends on this.

EVELYN   But the writing is still in the air.

JOHN   No, if you and I went away and tried our fortune, I don't believe we'd fail, Evelyn.

EVELYN   We can discuss all that later.

JOHN   And since I saw my mother—

EVELYN   I know about your mother, John, and all that. But you won't need to write if you come into this estate.

JOHN   I won't need to write—

EVELYN   No.

JOHN   But you see—

EVELYN   You wouldn't need to.

(*He looks at her a moment but makes no answer. The drum has stopped, and the singing, but you can hear the guitars still playing.* EVELYN *moves her shoulders from side to side, a little restlessly*)

JOHN   The columns make a line and yet they are all single; and between the lines of them the moon makes a path of light.

EVELYN   Scott, you're literary tonight, aren't you! I swear there's always a world of something whirling around you. But what I mean is I want you to promise me to let this business drop.

JOHN   I'm not so much concerned about the land, the money end of it; what I want is not to seem to set myself up against him, hurt him by seeming to judge him. That's what I want to work out.

EVELYN   But if he won't give in, you'll promise me, you'll drop it?

JOHN   I can't. I can't do it.

(*She goes and stands beside him, leaning toward him*)

EVELYN   You won't do that for me, John?

JOHN   I can't, Evelyn, I can't. I couldn't love you as I do tonight and do it.

EVELYN   Oh, I know all that, I reckon. I could not love thee, dear, so much, loved I not honor more, and so on. You think you love me, then? (*He tries to take her in his arms, but she pushes him gently away*)   No, no, let's think straight about this. You don't love me, John.

JOHN Don't you see? You're like the picture of my mother when you stand there in this old dress you've found, my mother when she was a girl. Don't you see how it is with me?

EVELYN I see. I ask you something, something that can't help anybody anyway, since your father's not going to give in, and I ask you and you won't do it for me.

(She moves away from him. He steps down one step and stands turned away from her, looking into space. The singing at the cabins comes a little louder, and now a woman's voice has joined the man's)

JOHN Tonight I love you, you know that.

EVELYN Tonight you—but I don't call that love. Will you do it, will you promise? You can tell your father in the morning. Will you, John? *(He makes no answer)* Will you?

JOHN *(In a low voice)* Wait.

(There is a long pause, while the music plays, now louder, now softer. EVELYN stands in the colonnade, not knowing exactly what move to make. The music pours out over the garden)

JOHN This moonlight, and the garden and these flowers and the music, and you looking like my mother—all of it breaks me down. What shall we say of a man's character who lets this beauty here make him give up what he thinks is right? But on the other hand what shall we say of a man's character who can be made blind and deaf to such beauty as this?

EVELYN That's right, go on and philosophize! It's you ought to have been the bishop.

JOHN It's strange, it's strange to be so betrayed!

EVELYN John—

JOHN That all this beauty that fills the soul should betray it too!

EVELYN If you love me, if you want me, you'd do it.

JOHN Everything that's beautiful—life is like that, who can understand it? Evelyn—

(She walks away and stands with her back to him, looking out over the garden)

EVELYN Yes.

JOHN Look at the moonlight on the steps.

EVELYN I see it.

(She comes and stands behind him, a step above)

JOHN   Did you hear that little wind just then coming into the garden in the leaves? The singing goes in with it; but the strings of the guitars kept strumming against it.

EVELYN (*She turns gently facing him and draws his head down to her*) I'm glad they keep it up, I love their music, John!

JOHN   What?

EVELYN   Will you? Will you do what I ask you? (*The stream of the music pours in. He suddenly puts up his hands on her arms and buries his face against her bosom*)   Well, will you.

JOHN   Evelyn!

EVELYN   Will you?

JOHN   Yes.

CURTAIN

ACT IV

(*The next night. The windows of the drawing-room are open and the terrace and garden outside are flooded with moonlight. You can hear voices now and then from the dining-room across the hall, and* MR. BOBO's *laugh.*

JOHN *comes in from the terrace. He is bareheaded, and his face pale. He walks around the room, looking long at the portraits, the objects there. Once he looks out of the window a moment, then again at the various things in the room, then he leans absently against the piano. He plucks one of the strings of the guitar with his forefinger, but almost as soon silences it. After a while he goes back to the window and disappears along the terrace.*

Presently MAJOR DANDRIDGE, *in a white suit, enters from the hall, and almost immediately* EVELYN *opens the doors of his study and joins him. She wears a pale green dress of some thin silk, rather extreme in fashion*)

MAJOR DANDRIDGE   Well, Evelyn! Daughter.

EVELYN (*Going up and kissing him on the cheek*)   Good evening, Father. You're too late for supper.

MAJOR DANDRIDGE   I'll have something later, plenty of time. Why, what's the matter, my dear, you look white? Where's everybody, where are the others?

EVELYN   They're still at supper. I was not hungry. And it was so warm in there; I've been sitting by the window in the study. I was waiting for you, Father.

MAJOR DANDRIDGE   Were you, that's good. What is it? Sit down.

EVELYN   No, I'll stand, Father, thank you, for a minute at least. You sit down, I know you're tired. You've been out since early this morning. I know you're tired. I know how tired I get in Memphis, there are so many people you must see and so many things to do. The whole truth is, you're either in or out. If you're in you've got to go, go. If you don't you drop out absolutely. And after all, having men buzzing around you is exciting, though you get sick of their being all alike. I'll say that for John, he's different enough. Goodness knows you never know what—I feel lazy, and tired, I've paced the house today. It's every bit as bad as standing at parties or dancing. Why don't you sit down, Father?

MAJOR DANDRIDGE   (*Sitting on the sofa*)   I am tired, too many things on hand this time of the year. Property is a burden, my dear; uneasy lies the head that wears a crown, eh? Especially nowadays in Mississippi. You can't get labor and you can't do the work yourself. I'd like a glass of water. No, sit still, I'll ring for Oscar, he'll no doubt get here in his own sweet time. (*He rings the bell near the mantelpiece and returns to the sofa*)   I'm worried too about John. Where is he? Is he at supper now?

EVELYN   No, Father, John has been keeping to himself all day. I've had the day to myself I can tell you. I haven't seen him. That's what I want to talk to you about.

MAJOR DANDRIDGE   Isn't that business settled yet?

EVELYN   Father, I'm not sure I can do what you asked me to. I mean make John give up that point about the land.

MAJOR DANDRIDGE   Why, my God A'mighty, how? I thought that was done for. Couldn't you manage him last night?

EVELYN   Oh, yes, that. I could do that. He gave in at last.

MAJOR DANDRIDGE   Of course he would, any man would.

EVELYN   But I don't know now whether I have a right to make him give up like this. To use what I am to him to break his will. You know what I mean, it's as if he were a child. There's one thing I try to comfort myself with. It may excuse what I did last night a little. I don't believe now that I was just trying to make him do what you wanted him to do and give up that point about the land. What kept me after him was partly that, oh, yes, of course. But maybe some of it was because I'm in love with him and I'm jealous of his not doing what I want. I know some of it's that, I'd rather think it about myself anyway. It's not so low.

MAJOR DANDRIDGE That's your private affair, Daughter; that's between you and John. It might be more delicate to leave out all that.

EVELYN Well, if it comes to that it might have been a little more
delicate to leave me out entirely. But I don't care whether it's delicate
or not, it's true. I'm not delicate. At any rate then about this business
proposition of the land, I don't know whether I have a right to influence
John because he loves me enough to let me. I don't know! I feel as
if I had my own soul to save. I mean I feel as if I had killed a man.
(*She sits down on the davenport and bursts into sobs*)

MAJOR DANDRIDGE Oh, come, come, come, come, dear! Come
now! I don't mean to be hard, but this thing has to be managed somehow or other. We stoop to anything if we have to perhaps. That is
to say, with honor! You did it for John's own good, of course you did.
It's for his own good absolutely. I'll soon be in my grave, what can
it matter to me?

EVELYN I know. Perhaps it is. But you see last night when we went
to our room, I mean after an hour, last night after a while, I could
hear him, I knew he was awake. The room was as dark as pitch. I
knew he was awake, though. I couldn't sleep. I spoke to him but he
wouldn't answer me. And early this morning, soon after day, he got
up and slipped out of the room. But I saw his face. (*She sobs*) I could
see his face! I tell you I saw how he looked.

MAJOR DANDRIDGE (*Patting her hand*) Now, now!

EVELYN I feel as if I had killed him!

MAJOR DANDRIDGE Oh, no, no, John is like this, he was always
like this. His mother was exactly the same. All tense in spirit.

EVELYN I feel as if I had killed him!

MAJOR DANDRIDGE Oh, there, there! You'll see—it's hard on all
of us, his aunts will be worried sick about it. Do you think I enjoy
this struggle with my own son? My only boy? And if you think I enjoy
asking my son's wife to help me against him, you're mighty mistaken.
I can tell you that!

EVELYN I can't keep my promise to you, Father. I can't ask him to
do it, I just can't now, and I won't.

MAJOR DANDRIDGE Well, you will! Be sure of that! You're hysteri-
cal, and I don't blame you. But it's your affair as much as the rest
of us. This is not a play or a romance or something like that, it's a
family crisis. You don't want to live in a garret, do you?

EVELYN Of course not. But I've been thinking why should this one
piece of land put us in the garret? And the more I think of it the
more it seems impossible that this should be the real reason for all
our row, not just this keeping a piece of land. There must be something
else. What is it, I ask myself over and over, what is it?

MAJOR DANDRIDGE We won't go into a discussion of that, there's never an issue without its complications. But the main item is this, as you must see, I don't intend to give up my own decision because of a lot of highjinks. We've had that before in this family.

EVELYN Before?

MAJOR DANDRIDGE Yes, and quite enough. And when we had it before I didn't give up. But then what's that got to do with it? We've talked so much about it now that there's no turning for me. I've got to keep to my decision. And I reckon you're thinking what a stubborn old man I am. Well, we are a stubborn family. You've got yourself into a stubborn lot, my daughter, and you might as well put that in your pipe and smoke it. But then there's your side of it. Property's property. And more so than ever these latter days. It's a money age. If it's not I don't know what it is, aye God! Certainly it's something different from what the world was when I grew up.

EVELYN This room is suffocating.

MAJOR DANDRIDGE And you want your children to have the best chance possible. (*He goes over and opens wider the glass door to the terrace, and begins to walk about as he speaks*) I'll open the window there wider. Now.

EVELYN I'm not going to have any children.

MAJOR DANDRIDGE What?

EVELYN Not for a while at least. Plenty of time for that when—

MAJOR DANDRIDGE When what, may I ask?

EVELYN Later.

MAJOR DANDRIDGE I see.

EVELYN I never heard John talk as he's been talking lately.

MAJOR DANDRIDGE Oh, no, no, John is like this. I tell you he's always been like this—so was his mother—you never saw this side of him, that's all.

EVELYN I hate this side of him.

MAJOR DANDRIDGE Well, you'll have to learn to take it. It's a part of him and I'm afraid a large part.

(*There is a pause*)

MAJOR DANDRIDGE Well, at least this thing about the land is settled in my mind. And, Evelyn, you'll be sensible enough to help me, I hope. Who's that out there? John ought to be coming in by now. I'll call him. Will let you talk with him a little.

(*He goes out on the terrace and calls.* EVELYN *arranges herself and sits down at the end of the davenport nearest the front of the stage.* JOHN *enters, from the terrace, leaving his father outside)*

JOHN   Evelyn! (*seeing her*)   Oh, Evelyn—

EVELYN   John, where have you been? I've missed you all day.

(*He comes and sits down impulsively by her side and clasps her hand in both his own*)

EVELYN   Why, John, what's the matter?

JOHN   Evelyn, I've been walking about all day. I've been thinking, but—Evelyn, I must tell you, I can't keep the promise I made you last night. I know it seems rotten after I gave you my word and all that. But I can't keep it.

EVELYN   Why, John, you needn't get so excited about it. You see I was already sorry I insisted like that. I don't ask you to keep your word, if you think not.

JOHN   You release me? You mean it's all right?

EVELYN   But you know it was for your good, after all, I did it; it's for your good, John, not to insist on going against your father's wishes about this money.

JOHN   Was it for that, are you sure? Oh, my dear, I've been worrying about that, thinking—you see I was afraid to ask myself the question straight out—it seemed too horrible that you'd use my love, use your beauty last night, to make me give up my—what I believe. It would have been like betraying me, now, wouldn't it? And, of course, if you thought it was for my good, it was different so far as we are concerned, you and I. Of course, I want to believe that. But it *is* different, isn't it?

EVELYN   Of course it is, don't look so tragic.

JOHN   Even if I don't keep my word?

EVELYN   Of course. Besides, I don't ask you to keep it. I couldn't let you do anything just for love of me that you didn't believe you ought to do. And I just told Father I couldn't hold you to your promise. So you see how I feel.

(*He looks at her a moment and drops his head on her breast for a long time. Then you can hear footsteps*)

EVELYN   Some one is coming in, John.

(*He sits up.* OSCAR *enters from the hall*)

JOHN   It's Awse.

EVELYN   Father rang for him. Oscar, you can find Major Dandridge on the terrace or somewhere out there.

OSCAR Yes'm. (*He goes out to the terrace*)

(JOHN *claps his hands between his knees and sits there looking at the floor. Presently he speaks without turning his head*)

JOHN Evelyn, what do you think of it here?

EVELYN Here at Flower House? Suits me if it suits you, John. It's damn quiet of course, but I'll get used to that.

JOHN (*Getting up and walking about*) But I wonder sometimes if I can stand it—the place, the days and nights passing, the smell of the flowers and the sound of the wind in the garden, and all this gentleness and fineness and this affection and good breeding. And not through education and intelligence, not that, but through love and simplicity of heart, so much understanding and such endless patience, no matter how far off the question is! It bears in on you, it leaves you exposed to life; you are at the mercy of life in this place. You are laid open to everything, oh, God! If it were more sordid, more brutal, more violent, like the commonplace tragic that people talk about, I could stand it better. But it's more terrible because it *is* so beautiful. It's more tragic. It breaks you down more, I tell you. (*He comes and sits by her on the davenport*)

EVELYN Oh, John, John, you're just stirred up. Come and sit down by me.

JOHN And these old people, every one of them right in his own way! And all of them gradually getting older and going to pieces! And loving me and wanting me to have my own life! And everyone keeping up his standard of living, trying to converse whether he feels like it or not, everyone holding himself to the idea he has of how things ought to be, and meanwhile underneath in them the course of life goes on just the same, all its force and depth and violence! I tell you I know, as I must have always known if I had any sense—great artists say nothing else—the beautiful is the terrible. And the tragic is life working its will on you. Isn't it?

EVELYN My God, John! I wish you'd try to control yourself. There! (*She leans over and kisses his hair*) Yes, life goes on all the same you can better bet. Besides I can't see it's all so beautiful. Father's holding on about this property. What's really the reason for that?

JOHN I don't know, I don't know. But it's something very close to him. I know that much. It doesn't do any good to talk about it, does it, do you think? Here's Awse.

(OSCAR *comes in with a tray and glasses*)

EVELYN It's the water Father wanted. You'd better call him, Oscar.

OSCAR   Yes'm. (*He goes out on the terrace.*)

EVELYN (*Straightening* JOHN'S *cravat*)   Your tie!

> (MAJOR DANDRIDGE *enters.* JOHN *rises and stands until his father is seated*)

Father, Oscar's brought the water for you.

MAJOR DANDRIDGE   Thank you. (*He sits down in the armchair without doing anything about the water*)   Well, Son, it's a fine night, isn't it? Do you know, I was just thinking out there of a guest we had years ago, Fernandez, a preacher, Methodist preacher, stopped here over night, a night like this, full moon shining. You were about three years old, no, two, that's right. We showed him over the place, the fountain had just been rebuilt, I remember. Well, he liked it all but the Colonnade. He wanted to leave it. And do you know why? There was something heathen about it, he said. Heathen. Funny how men will take things! I was thinking of old Fernandez just now.

JOHN   It's funny: I've been thinking several times today of a little chap I knew in New York; name was Manuel. He was a Portuguese, I think, something like that. He was a simple little fellow, with an open, natural face, gay and lively; had a temper hot enough to cut your throat, but without any malice, without a touch. I was thinking today, his soul sat in him like a flower on a child's breast. And he seemed to understand everything you felt. He loved things. He was a painter. His family in Lisbon were very rich and wanted him to be a diplomat. He worshipped his father and all his family. You know how a Latin family especially can be. But he had left it all, because he knew he couldn't make any life of his own if he stayed. And nothing was anything to him any more but what belonged to his own life. He loved things, but he knew what he had to do, if he was to come to anything. I was thinking today how he laughed and seemed so gay and light, but how he had it all straight in his head and never swerved from it. Little old Manuel! Under his waistcoat he used to wear a red scarf that he had worn at home.

> (*Evelyn crosses her knees, and sits with her lips pressed together*)

EVELYN   I don't know, he sounds tiresome to me.

MAJOR DANDRIDGE   Well, he may have been a very interesting fellow, I've no doubt he was, Son. But still I don't understand why a man of your culture should get anything out of him.

JOHN (*Rising and walking about, speaking warmly*)   You see we're stuck, we're dead. We want some wild blood pouring through. We're such dull eggs that these wild birds like Manuel attract us. They are reckless. Yes. They are drawn toward death. But meantime life is free in them. They are pure in their way as saints in theirs are pure, because life *is* free in them, unattached, and tied to nothing. It drives, it burns itself out in flame, it ends.

MAJOR DANDRIDGE Ah, Son, what sort of talk is this?

JOHN *(Bitterly)* Well, I don't belabor anybody with it any too often.

MAJOR DANDRIDGE No, that's true, I don't mean to be harsh, Son.

JOHN *(More gently)* That's all right, Father, all right, I know you don't.

MAJOR DANDRIDGE But I can't see how there can be any connection of such ideas with a man's character!

JOHN And I can't see how there can be any separation of them from a man's character.

MAJOR DANDRIGE Well, what in the name of God do you think then?

JOHN *(Speaking with great excitement, the argument of his soul with the world around him)* It's no great matter what I think, I suppose. But then we're all openly egoists and dead set on our own thoughts these days, my generation is. The only way I can tell you is that I think of life as one stream of vitality, forces moving through us like wind through trees, carrying us into forms, decisions, crises. Under its power our individuality that seems so much is just a scratch on the surface.

MAJOR DANDRIDGE You mean to tell me you've resigned yourself to drifting any way the wind blows?

JOHN *(Speaking more calmly and laughing a little)* I mean that the difference is that I don't think that I know what I'm going to do.

MAJOR DANDRIDGE Well, I'm no artist of course, but the question occurs to me how can you write if you have no more conviction than this?

JOHN But it's just this sense of freedom that I'm building my hopes on. I'd like to be free, without any obstruction to whatever works in me, whatever reflection of life, whatever flies off from things. If I don't have that I'm lost, I know, for the writing I might do would be a certain kind of realism—

MAJOR DANDRIDGE I haven't read authors like Zola and the rest, but I know the sort of taste they cater to.

JOHN Oh, no, Father, it's not that, not by a long sight!

MAJOR DANDRIDGE That's fortunate. Then tell me—naturally I'm interested, though I'm a layman.

JOHN You see we've had already the dumb gray of abandoned farms, city sweat shops, back alleys, ashbarrels and disease. That's no more real than everything else. I don't want to decide that one thing is the reality in life and another isn't. I'd like to find a medium that was not afraid of warmth, beauty, that let all this have its chance as well as the drab and dismal, that is comic or tragic as you please, but glows, sings, darkens, dulls, as life does. I mean a realism that is so real and so precisely true and close that it becomes poetic, gives back their dream to things. What I mean is that the great point in art is to keep the life going in it, no matter what theory you follow. Everything moving in the stream of all life, but seen too with its own particular life on it. But I'm chattering everybody's head off, I don't know, I'm shaken up today, I suppose, but you see I've had my head full of these thoughts all day.

EVELYN So that's what you've been thinking of all day! John, do sit down and not pace up and down so.

JOHN Excuse me. (*He sits beside her on the davenport*)

MAJOR DANDRIDGE Son, I don't mean to be arguing. But from what you seem to imply, I should judge that all of us here must seem to you very wrong, on the wrong track.

JOHN (*Quietly*) No, no, Father, life goes on here in its own way. It's fine enough. I've got no substitute to offer. Everybody must find his own event and his own art of living. But then I have to find mine of course.

EVELYN *I* understand what John means, Father.

MAJOR DANDRIDGE Am I to understand that you plan not to stay here with us?

JOHN Stay here? I don't see necessarily that it should be impossible.

MAJOR DANDRIDGE Impossible! There you sound like your mother.

JOHN (*He speaks quietly and almost absently*) Well, and if I do?

MAJOR DANDRIDGE I can see she poisoned your mind against me. That's it, that's what it is, or you wouldn't be so set. She gave you a full account of her side of the case, I haven't a doubt. And you could see the justice of her position. Naturally. You were her son. Why don't you just say you've got your head set and there's no use in anybody saying anything?

JOHN Father, I told you my mother didn't even mention your name, except to ask how you were; she couldn't, there was not time. I told you that, Sir.

MAJOR DANDRIDGE You were always like her. I'd rather a son of mine had never been born—

JOHN Father, that's too much—

MAJOR DANDRIDGE I don't ask you to criticize what I say, Sir.

JOHN Then why bring my mother in? What's she got to do with it? I won't keep harping on my poor mother, I tell you.

MAJOR DANDRIDGE Very well, leave her out then.

JOHN And at any rate there's something in this whole business I can't make out.

EVELYN John!

(JOHN *gets up and walks toward the window, and stands there looking out. Then having mastered his excitement he turns and moves a little toward his father, and stands there beside the armchair while his father speaks*)

JOHN Father, what was this that made my mother go away? You said I ought to know, can you tell me now?

MAJOR DANDRIDGE I will, and I hope you'll draw certain conclusions from it. When my father died, your grandfather Dandridge, Ned came back to see him; when he heard that Father was sick. Nothing was said about the land. After Father's funeral nothing was said. He was too proud, Ned, much too proud to speak of it. Your mother proposed that we ask him to remain for a visit. He was looking rather broken up. Well, he did. In fact, he remained a good deal longer than I had expected him to. Then one night—he was too proud to mention the affair to me one way or another—one night I saw him, twilight it was, walking in the colonnade with my wife, your mother. And pretty soon she came to me here in this very room. "Alexander," she said. God! I remember how she said Alexander, not Al—"I think you ought to give the land back to Ned now." "Why? Has he been asking you to get it back for him?" I said. It seemed, according to her, that Ned had said nothing to her about it except to answer her questions. He had some pride even about that. (*The* MAJOR *rises and walks about*) "Then, my dear," I said, "you'd better let men's affairs alone, much better." She said nothing more then and left the room. But next day she started again. And that night, too. I began to see that it wasn't only principle with her. I saw that she was in love with my brother. And I told her so flatly. She denied it. But she wouldn't give up her point. (*Silence*)

JOHN And then? What, Father?

MAJOR DANDRIDGE I lost control of myself. She was so much to me, your mother, you see.

JOHN (*Gently*) Yes, Father.

MAJOR DANDRIDGE And the life we had together got worse and worse. You were just three years old that month. It got so bad we saw that living together was out of the question. Neither of us would give in. She said she couldn't bear it any longer. "It's impossible!"

she said. "And wrong too," she said. She said that it would not be right to let you come up in such a home as ours had got to be. I said I'd fight for you in the courts, for after all you bore our name, you were a Dandridge. She went away. She said she would come back to me when I wanted her.

JOHN   But you did want her.

MAJOR DANDRIDGE   Wait. If I'd given up about the land and if I believed that she—that she—

JOHN   Oh, God!

MAJOR DANDRIDGE   But she little knew me. I never gave in.

(JOHN *and* EVELYN *go to him*)

EVELYN   Well, it can't do any good thinking about it all now, can it, Father! It can't do any good. And I'm sure she understands now how it all was. Come and sit by me, Father.

MAJOR DANDRIDGE   And all that time of course I knew she was off there by herself!

(JOHN *turns away and stands near the terrace window*)

EVELYN   Come on, Father, won't you, please?

MAJOR DANDRIDGE   Did she mention the land to you—tell you about it?

JOHN (*Without turning his head*)   No, Father, not a word, I told you that, Father.

MAJOR DANDRIDGE   It's strange then that you should—should— agree with her like this! So identically. I mean I seem to have to meet the whole affair all over again.

(EVELYN *takes hold of his hand and draws him over to a seat beside her on the davenport*)

MAJOR DANDRIDGE   That's all right, Daughter, thank you. (*There is a pause*)

JOHN (*Losing control of himself*)   So it's my mother you're fighting still! That's it! It's not money, not family, not principles! Oh, no! It's this damned feeling against my mother! That you won't give in on even now.

MAJOR DANDRIDGE (EVELYN *keeps a strong hold on his hand*)   I must request you to remember to whom you are speaking, Sir, in my house.

EVELYN   John, you ought to be ashamed to talk to Father like that!

(MISS MARY *comes in*)

MISS MARY   What is it, Brother Al? John, what is it? I could hear your voices clear in the dining-room.

(JOHN *breaks into a laugh*)

EVELYN   John!

MISS MARY   What is it? What is it all about? Oh, my Lord! What is it, Brother Al?

(*Goes to* JOHN, *who turns and becomes one of the group*)

MAJOR DANDRIDGE   Oh, it's what I was telling you about, last night, Mollie.

JOHN   Oh, no! No, it's not that for me, Auntie, not that, it's something else.

MISS MARY (*Wiping her eyes before she speaks*)   I don't understand it very well, but I know your father will do what's right, dear. He has his own honor to think of. (*She goes and stands beside her brother*) Here they come!

EVELYN (*Trying to pat the* MAJOR'S *hand*)   Of course he will.

MISS MARY   We missed you at supper, dear.

JOHN   I wasn't hungry.

MISS MARY   I told Jane to put you up something. You can have it later.

JOHN   That's good of you, thank you, Auntie.

(MISS ELLEN *and* MR. BOBO *and* COUSIN TOM *come in from the hall.* MAJOR DANDRIDGE *rises and draws* MISS ELLEN'S *armchair back an inch or two for her. She wears a gray silk dress, with lace at the throat and wrists.* MR. BOBO *draws up a chair to* MISS MARY'S *right.* COUSIN TOM *sits on the sofa to the left, takes out a pamphlet and begins to read.* JOHN *remains standing at the end of the table, near the terrace*)

MISS MARY   Sit down, dear, you're restless. You'll wear yourself out.

(JOHN *shakes his head and smiles*)

JOHN   Auntie and her first aid!

MISS ELLEN   What is it the child says, he's going to paint the colonnade?

MISS MARY   Now how on earth did the poor thing get that idea? (*She goes over and leans down to* MISS ELLEN'S *ear*)   Hush, honey, I'll tell you later.

MISS ELLEN (*Pushing her away*)   Go away, Mary, I don't want you to explain.

MISS MARY (*Going back to her seat*) You see, that's the way it is. She'll kill me some day, she'll break my back.

MISS ELLEN I often think that I'm Newton's law. Or is it Keller, or is Keller in astronomy? At any rate there are three laws. The first is that a body at rest continues in that state unless acted upon by some outside force. Well, I'm this body and Mollie is the outside force. The second law is that a body in motion continues to be in motion unless acted upon by some outside force. I'm the outside force and Mollie is this body in motion.

MISS MARY That's the way she goes on, analyzing everything to pieces, the dear old thing!

(JOHN *kisses* MISS ELLEN'S *forehead*)

MISS ELLEN What color, dearest, will you paint it?

JOHN Red, I'm afraid.

MISS ELLEN You're a rascal, John Dandridge!

(*All except* EVELYN *and* COUSIN TOM *laugh*)

EVELYN Don't be silly, John

JOHN Am I silly?

EVELYN And don't be funny. That's not funny.

MISS ELLEN (*Reaching for his hand*) John, darling, you're just tired out. You're our sweet sonny boy. You've always been and always will be.

MR. BOBO I think we may consider it certain (*Shouting*) I say I think I may consider it certain, Miss Ellen, that times have changed—I remember on one occasion Colonel—

MISS ELLEN Dearest, what did you see in New York that was as lovely as these nights?

MISS MARY (*Jumping up and going over to her*) Poor child, she doesn't know she's interrupting.

MISS ELLEN That's all right, Mary.

MISS MARY Mr. Bobo was talking.

MISS ELLEN (*Pushing her away*) I understand, Mary.

(MISS MARY *sits down*, JOHN *pats* MISS ELLEN *on the shoulder*)

MISS ELLEN That's all right, dear. Your Auntie is right, I'm always intruding. I ought to die.

JOHN No, no. (*Pats her shoulder*) Now Auntie, look what you've done. Let her alone, please. Nobody ever knows how sweet Aunt Tellie is.

EVELYN Of course she is. Of course we do. But people have to live.

MISS MARY Well, Sister Ellen's mighty sweet, but you just have to control her. You see yourself how the poor darling interrupts people. She tells me to tell her things and then when I do you see how she acts. She's just upset because she sees that John is tired.

MISS ELLEN (*Patting* JOHN'S *hand and then studying it a moment as she holds it by the fingertips*) How like your mother's your hands are! I don't remember her very well of course but I remember her hands.

(MISS MARY *shakes her head*)

MISS ELLEN There, that's all right, run on dear. I'm a good-for-nothing old thing, that's what I am. Don't spoil me. Dear, you've always been very good to me.

JOHN Think who you are! Almost a bishop.

MISS MARY Now look, you dear children, at the moonlight. (*The sound of strings and of singing comes from the quarters*) And listen, the darkies are singin' again. They sing every night now, these nights. What is it in their music?

(*The singing, far-off, faint, continues through the act. The woman's voice now rises higher, the man's follows*)

JOHN (*At the window*) How clear it is! Even the edges of the leaves are clear.

MISS MARY But don't talk in that tone, Son. It's worse than Hamlet.

MAJOR DANDRIDGE It's just that our generation doesn't understand these matters, Mollie. Don't you see? We're out of it.

JOHN Not Hamlet, Auntie. On the contrary.

MISS MARY (*Wiping her eyes*) What do you mean, darling?

JOHN I mean one doesn't wish to escape; one asks for life only as a painter asks for colors.

MISS MARY I know I'm not literary, but I hate these old modern books!

EVELYN Well, they don't all have to be like the stuff John reads.

(*The music has grown fainter, there are strings but no voices*)

JOHN Look at the moonlight out here. The life in the garden moves in it like music.

EVELYN Oh, for God's sake! I beg your pardon, Auntie, but John will drive us all crazy.

(JOHN *turns off the lights, all but the lamp on the table, which shines on* EVELYN'S *magazine. The moonlight streams in*)

JOHN Don't you think so, Mr. Bobo?

MR. BOBO.　Eh. I don't follow you, my boy.

JOHN　That the moon covers us all as if we moved in music?

MR. BOBO　Oh, come, you jester, don't try to put a joke under my old ribs!

(MR. BOBO *goes over to* COUSIN TOM)

MISS MARY　Dear, I wish you'd tell us about the play. I saw a manuscript, I mean a note for a play on your table.

JOHN　I've been making notes. (*He turns to the window again*)

MISS ELLEN　It seemed to me a delightful idea, darling, the play.

MISS MARY　Well, now isn't it the funniest thing the way the poor darling seems to hear sometimes? (*Going to* MISS ELLEN)　You didn't hear, did you, what the child is saying? About a play.

MISS ELLEN　Mollie, I did. I say I think the idea of the play is delightful. And I hear in New York they are doing plays with masks. I'd like that. Will you do that? (JOHN *smiles and shakes his head*)　I like it because I've seen so much of people's faces. And of course it's classical. I'm sick of actresses' faces in the magazines. And besides, the ability to substitute is what distinguishes man from the beasts.

MISS MARY　Well, that's an idea for you! Uncle Leonidas used to say Ellen Dandridge has brains enough for a bishop.

MISS ELLEN　Uncle Leonidas liked brandy.

JOHN　My play is a mere flash in the pan, just sketching about. I'll never finish it.

MISS ELLEN　Why, dear? I hope you will.

JOHN　No. My kind of thing if I ever do it will be done because life comes close to us. It will come out of the passion of ourselves.

(*There falls a silence. The singing has begun again. You hear the wild music coming up from the quarters. Then* MAJOR DANDRIDGE, *who has sat withdrawn into himself ever since he last spoke, turns to* JOHN *coldly*)

MAJOR DANDRIDGE　I should have to approve of myself very highly before I tried that.

EVELYN　Gracious, Father, I declare you sound positively jealous.

(MAJOR DANDRIDGE *turns quickly*)

MAJOR DANDRIDGE　Jealous?

COUSIN TOM (*Rising and coming over to the others*)　I've got it. These infernal prophecies are hard to track down. But I've got it. The South became a seven-stated confederacy at Montgomery, Alabama, in 1861. This seven-stated confederacy is called a seven-horned lamb by St. John.

MISS MARY It was not much like a lamb, Cousin Tom.

COUSIN TOM When Lincoln attempted to recruit Fort Sumter the seven-horned lamb opened the first seal in the book in the right hand of him who sat on the throne! Ah!

EVELYN It's perfectly wonderful, Cousin Tom!

(COUSIN TOM *goes to the terrace, turning his head sidewise to listen*)

MISS MARY He's not there, Cousin Tom. Oscar drove them all away today. The dry leaves, that's what you hear; they sound like crickets.

EVELYN Why doesn't Cousin Tom like crickets? Why don't you, Cousin Tom?

COUSIN TOM I've always detested them, my mother never could abide 'em either. Oscar did a good deed, Cousin Mary. The seven plagues of Egypt were mostly crickets.

MISS MARY Locusts, Cousin Tom. One of them.

COUSIN TOM Same thing, Mollie Dandridge.

MISS ELLEN Sit down, dear.

EVELYN Yes, John, for heaven's sake sit down!

(JOHN *sits down to* MISS MARY'S *right, smiling at* MISS ELLEN)

MISS ELLEN I remember when John was a little fellow, he couldn't have been more than three, I took him out to see the stars one night. I had just come back from studying astronomy under Dr. Adams, it amused me to take that up those days. Well, I showed the little man the constellations, and he listened as I pointed them out to him. I said, There's Orion and there's the Big Dipper, and there are the Pleiades and so on. And when I had done, John looked at me and said, "Don't you think you're fooling me, I know you're just trying to see if you remember them yourself." Fancy! And the worst of it was he was right. I was. But think of his saying that!

MISS MARY Just like him. I remember too—

MISS ELLEN Well, Evelyn, what pretty fashions are there for our niece this summer?

(EVELYN *smiles gaily but does not get up. She holds open the magazine for* MISS ELLEN *to see a picture there and makes a little face at the style as if to say how silly she thought it*)

MISS ELLEN Well, they're not the first foolish fashions, I can assure you. But to go back, do you notice how bright Jupiter is these evenings? It's remarkable. Until the moon comes up, that is. Then of course we have another glory. What a beautiful poem that is about the glory of the moon and another glory of the stars.

MISS MARY (*Going over to her*)   That's Ecclesiastes, Tellie, in the Bible.

MISS ELLEN (*Pushing her away*)   Mary, we've all heard of the Bible, dear.

MR. BOBO   Astronomy is a great subject. My father used to read us a passage out of Lucretius about the heavenly bodies, and there was a very excellent quotation he had, also from the Latin, about the car of night. Or rather the horses:

"Currite, currite, O noctis equi," it said, and they used to tease me by saying I'd like Latin more if it had all been about horses. I can hear my father laugh now.

MISS ELLEN   Strange how we remember things. I remember when I was a child during the war how bright Jupiter was. We used to talk about it as we sat on the South porch. That was when Cousin Mary Bullock was staying with us and Cousin Obedience and Nellie Davis and Charles. Charles was just a boy then. They used to come for long visits those days. Cousin Obedience stayed all during the war. But it wasn't any trouble. You see mother had her maid and I had mine, my two nurses, and—oh, pardon me, Mary, I didn't know you were talking. Go right on, Mary.

MISS MARY (*who began to talk when* MISS ELLEN *was saying "It wasn't any trouble." She speaks faster than her sister, it is often impossible to distinguish what either one of them says.* JOHN *sits looking from one to the other of them quietly*)   I was reading today that in Arkansas they've discovered an emerald mine. I wonder if they're the real, genuine emeralds. A dreadful state Arkansas is of course, but I've always thought emeralds the most beautiful stones of all. That's all right, Tellie— (*She goes over and taps* MISS ELLEN *on the arm*)

MISS ELLEN   What is it, Mary?

MISS MARY   Didn't you ask me to remind you if you began to pick threads off your lap? It's not very elegant.

MISS ELLEN   No, Mary, I'd never ask you to remind me of anything. I'm too smart for that. You'd carry it out to the death. Evelyn, dear, your Auntie is a second Atlas! She'd hold the world up on her shoulders if she could and make it revolve too.

MISS MARY   Well, I'm sure I think Atlas a very noble character. I remember Uncle Leonidas used to say the day would come—

(EVELYN *gets half way up and sits down again.* JOHN *sits still, looking rather absently now and then at whoever happens to be speaking*)

MISS MARY   Why, what is it, dear? Can I get you something?

EVELYN   Nothing, Auntie, I'm just jerky, that's all. Please pardon me.
I'm not used to so much quiet in the evenings, not yet. And the doves
have been moaning around here all day, aren't they doleful? But I
love these old places down here in our South. Of course, though, in
Memphis every night there was something. But that was tiresome.
Listen at those voices, aren't they lovely! It's wonderful to sing!

JOHN   Father? Will you excuse me? Auntie? I'm going for a turn in
the garden, if I may?

MAJOR DANDRIDGE   Certainly, Son, the air will refresh you.

(JOHN *goes to the window, then looks round and comes back and
snatches up* MISS ELLEN'S *hand between his own and presses it
to his lips, and goes quickly out*)

MISS ELLEN   Mollie?

(MISS MARY *goes over to her*)

MISS ELLEN   Is anyone talking?

MISS MARY   Wait a minute, Tellie.

MR. BOBO (*To* COUSIN TOM)   I'm going to look after him, Tom. The
boy needs some friend to talk with him.

(*He goes out by way of the hall*)

EVELYN   For goodness' sake let's have a little light on the subject!

(*She rises, switches on light and resumes her seat.* COUSIN TOM
opens his pamphlet and busies himself again. MISS MARY *goes over
and switches the light off again, and returns to her seat. The moonlight comes back into the room. The music has at last stopped entirely*)

MISS MARY   If you don't mind, honey, let the child have it just moonlight if he wants it.

EVELYN   Oh, very well, I don't really mind of course.

MISS MARY   Your lamp's all right, isn't it, dear?

EVELYN   Certainly. (*She begins to turn the pages of the magazine*)

EVELYN   Gracious! Everything's upside down these days. Look at
these high collars and short skirts. And I've got such terrible legs,
like piano posts; I say they're my family skeleton! But the skirts are
getting longer, so my legs are saved.

(COUSIN TOM *looks up from his pamphlet at last across at her*)

COUSIN TOM   What?

MISS MARY   No, no, no, dear! My mother used to tell me that ladies' feet were pinned to their skirts.

EVELYN   Excuse me, Auntie. John's got me nearly out of my wits. I declare, when people begin a certain kind of talking, I just—!

MAJOR DANDRIDGE   Evelyn, we all know we can't agree with John. But the boy is worn out. We can at least have some sympathy for him. He comes honestly by a very high-strung temperament.

EVELYN   Well, Father, I like that, after you yourself made me—

MAJOR DANDRIDGE   I only meant to remind you of his trouble. Don't be offended, my dear. John was never like other boys. He is more—we who love him can make allowances.

EVELYN   What's the matter with John is you've all spoiled him to death!

(The various people present may look up after such a remark but they make no comment. MR. BOBO *comes in from the hall door to the left)*

MR. BOBO   Well, it's a fine night, it's hard to get oneself indoors. (*He sits down on the sofa by* COUSIN TOM)

EVELYN (*Dropping her magazine on the floor*)   All the magazines are rotten!

MR. BOBO (*In a low voice to* COUSIN TOM)   Entertain these people while I think of some way to tell them. John's gone.

COUSIN TOM   My God, gone?

MR. BOBO   Yes, to the train, north. I saw him; we're to send his things.

COUSIN TOM   It will kill his father.

MR. BOBO   Go on, say something.

(COUSIN TOM rises and goes over to the davenport)

COUSIN TOM   Have I shown you this likeness of my nephew, ladies?

EVELYN   No, Cousin Tom, do!

(COUSIN TOM takes the guitar from the piano and puts it into MISS MARY'S *hands)*

COUSIN TOM   Come, play something, Cousin Mollie, won't you?

(She bows and begins to finger the strings, smiling. COUSIN TOM *draws up a chair at* EVELYN'S *elbow)*

This is the oldest boy, Harry.

(The MAJOR *and* EVELYN *look at the photograph.* MISS ELLEN *stands in the window)*

MISS ELLEN   Mollie, where's John?

MISS MARY   In the garden, honey, he's in the colonnade, I reckon.

MISS ELLEN   Do you? I'm afraid it would be lonely there. (*She holds her old, white hand to the moonlight*)

EVELYN   But this one! Why, Cousin Tom, he's the image of you!

(MR. BOBO *makes a motion to rise but sits down again and covers his face with his hands as* MISS MARY *begins playing softly an old air on her guitar. For a moment there is silence*)

MISS ELLEN (*Looking at her hand*)   Though you couldn't be lonely with such moonlight. Not very lonely.

(*The others sit listening to the guitar*)

MISS ELLEN (*Without turning her head or being heeded by the company*)   Mr. Bobo, why don't you tell them?

CURTAIN

PATRICIA BOATNER (1936) was born in Pascagoula, Mississippi, but spent most of her "growing up" years in Long Beach, Mississippi, graduating from the same school building where she entered third grade. As a child, she was a voracious reader who rewrote every exciting story for role-playing. As an adult, she says writing "preserved my sanity when my children were small, and enhanced my personal identity as they grew up."

During a nine year residency in East Tennessee, Boatner was writer and editor for *Lenoir City News* and *Loudon County Herald*, where she received Tennessee Press Association honors. Her freelance work included articles in *An Encyclopedia of East Tennessee* and *An Appalachian Teachers' Studies Guide*, both published by the Children's Museum of Oak Ridge through a National Endowment for the Humanities grant. In 1986, after returning to the Gulf Coast, she completed her novel, *All Our Tomorrows*, which was published in 1988.

Her play *So Tender a Bond* was named one of the winners in the 1987 Festival of Southern Theatre at the University of Mississippi, the first winner by a resident of Mississippi. After excellent critiques by prominent critics, the play underwent rewrite before other productions, including a home-town run at Gulfport Little Theatre. Boatner has also had several one-acts produced and has won numerous playwriting competitions.

Her one-act play *Allie's Mark* premiered at Gulfport Little Theatre in January 1988. This play was inspired by her beloved grandmothers, who greatly influenced her childhood and who lived their last years in nursing homes. "Allie's momentary victories are actually great ones," she says, "for they give her strength, dignity, and that necessary sense of making a mark in life, right to the end."

Although her work continues to be diverse, she says stage scripts "seem to strike the heart of it all—getting maximum effect through minimum words." Of growing up on the Mississippi coast, Boatner says, "I didn't realize then that life here was any different than in other parts of Mississippi. Now I know I had the best of many worlds. There were the unlimited horizons of the sea and sky, yet the comforting confines of a small town and a warm, loving family. Wherever I am, whatever I'm doing, the core of me is anchored to the land where I grew up, and to its people. That anchor gives me both stability of soul and freedom of spirit, so that as I write I might lose myself completely for a while without the fear that the condition will be permanent."

CHARLIE R. BRAXTON (1961) was born in McComb, Mississippi, and received most of his education through the public school system there. He received a degree from Jackson State University and has spent his entire life in Mississippi. Of this Braxton says, "When I look back on my life in the Magnolia state, thus far, I feel a strong sense of being. By that I mean, I feel that my soul is deeply rooted in the soil of this state. Like the bittersweet gutbucket blues of Robert Johnson, I belong here."

Braxton is the author of a volume of poems, *Obsidian from the Ashes*, published in 1990.

LARRY BROWN (1951) was born in Oxford, Mississippi, and has lived in Lafayette County for most of his life. For the last fifteen years he has lived at Yocona with his wife, Mary Annie, and their three children. He was a firefighter for sixteen years for the Oxford Fire Department, from late 1973 until early January 1990, but retired early to pursue a career full-time as a writer.

His short stories have appeared in various literary magazines such as *Greensboro Review, Fiction International, Mississippi Review, Carolina Quarterly, St. Andrews Review,* and *Chattahoochee Review.* His short fiction has appeared in several anthologies, most notably *The Best American Short Stories 1989. Facing the Music,* his first collection of stories, won the literature award from the Mississippi Institute of Arts & Letters in 1989. His first novel, *Dirty Work,* appeared in fall of 1989, and his new collection of stories, *Big Bad Love,* will appear in 1990. His publisher is Algonquin Books of Chapel Hill, North Carolina.

Brown has adapted *Dirty Work* to the stage for American Playhouse who filmed a version of the play for PBS. When not writing, Brown travels to various universities and literary gatherings throughout the South to read from his work.

ROBERT CANZONERI (1925) was born in San Marcos, Texas, and grew up in Clinton, Mississippi, the son of a Sicilian–turned–Baptist minister. In 1943 he joined the United States Navy and upon discharge, attended Mississippi College, receiving a B.A. in 1948. An M.A. from the University of Mississippi followed in 1951. After teaching at several universities and colleges, Canzoneri received a Ph.D. from Stanford University. Since 1965 he has been at Ohio State University. His books include

"*I Do So Politely*": *A Voice from the South* (1965), *Watch Us Pass* (1968), *Men with Little Hammers* (1969), *Barbed Wire and Other Stories* (1970), *A Highly Ramified Tree* (1976), which won the Ohioana award for the best book of the year in the field of autobiography, and *Potboiler: An Amateur's Affair with La Cuisine*, a book of essays about cooking, with recipes, was published in 1989 by North Point Press.

Canzoneri writes: "My interest in theater—as audience—goes back to one-act plays at Clinton High School directed by Miss Nellie Magee, and powerful productions of *Bury the Dead* and *Ceiling Zero* directed by Cokey Held at Mississippi College. In college I had the privilege of being in several plays under Miss Nellie's direction, and in 1948 was named best leading actor in the state MEA contest (though only four colleges competed, as I recall, and two of those were all-girl schools). At the University of Mississippi I played a hillbilly religious fanatic in *Hell Bent for Heaven*, and while teaching at Georgetown College, in Kentucky, had the pleasure of doing Prospero in a production of *The Tempest* designed by Irene Corey and directed by Orlin Corey. Back at Mississippi College, on the faculty, I got to play Macbeth, and at the Jackson Little Theatre the dual lead of Terrence Rattigan's *Separate Tables* opposite Jane Reid-Petty. It was at Mississippi College that I began to write for the stage. Three of my one-acts were produced there; one was bought for a book of comedies; another had subsequent productions as far north as Michigan; the third I mercifully destroyed. Another one-act I directed for a summer workshop at the Jackson Little Theatre. At Mississippi College, Charles Knox wrote the music and I did the book and lyrics of a musical satire called *The Peace Gimmick*, which had a nice run in 1962 at the Marjorie Lyons Playhouse in Shreveport, Louisiana, under Orlin Corey's direction and with designs by Irene Corey. For years afterward I concentrated on fiction, poetry, and nonfiction, but was commissioned in the early 1970s by the State of Mississippi to write a play about the siege of Vicksburg, a subject that had interested me since boyhood visits to the battlefield park. The project went forward through the completion of the script and the choice of land for an amphitheater before it got into some kind of political hassle and was abandoned; it pleases me that the play will see the light of day in this volume. My most recent play, *Knots*, involves Sicilian-Americans—inspired by some of my relatives—in California."

WILLIAM FAULKNER (25 September 1897–6 July 1962) was born in New Albany, Mississippi. When he was five years old his family moved to Oxford, Mississippi, where he lived most of his life except for brief periods spent in Hollywood and Charlottesville, Virginia. Faulkner's education was sporadic. Dropping out of high school in his senior year, he attended the University of Mississippi as a special student for only one year (1919–20). He was a voracious reader and, through his friend and earliest critic, Phil Stone, was introduced to modern writers, including the French Symbolist poets. Their influence, along with the influence of Thomas Hardy and William Butler Yeats, can be seen in Faulkner's first book, *The Marble Faun*.

Influenced by Sherwood Anderson, Faulkner wrote his novel, *Soldier's Pay*, which appeared in 1926. Its publication began an extraordinary prolific career. The next decade produced eight novels, including many of the finest he would write: *The Sound and the Fury* (1929), *As I Lay Dying* (1930), *Light in August* (1932), and *Absalom, Absalom!* (1936). However, his creative output was not matched by financial returns, so, in 1932, Faulkner went to Hollywood as a screen writer, a position he kept, under financial duress, until 1948, when the commercial success of *Intruder in the Dust* and its subsequent sale to the movies enabled him to return to Mississippi. With the exception of tours for the State Department and time spent as a writer-in-residence at the University of Virginia, he remained in Oxford the rest of his life. Faulkner won numerous awards for his fiction, including the 1949 Nobel Prize and two Pulitzer Prizes, one for *A Fable* (1954) and another for *The Reivers* (1962). His accomplished short fiction appears in *Collected Stories* (1950) and *Uncollected Stories* (1979).

Robert Penn Warren said, "The study of Faulkner's writing is one of the most challenging tasks in our literature. It is also one of the most rewarding." Faulkner, who admitted that he had learned to write "from other writers," advised hopeful poets and novelists to "read all you can."

Faulkner's manuscripts and papers are at the University of Virginia, the University of Texas at Austin, Yale University Library, the New York Public Library, and the University of Mississippi.

SHELBY FOOTE (1916) was born in Greenville, Mississippi, where he was educated in the public schools. He attended the University of North Carolina from 1935–37 and served in Europe as a captain of field artillery during World War II. According to Foote, his parents were not literary. He writes, "My principal connection with a literary home was through my friendship with the Percys (William Alexander Percy, author of *Lanterns on the Levee*, and his three nephews, among them Walker Percy). There were literally thousands of books in the Percy house. It's probable that if those Percy boys hadn't moved to Greenville, I might never have become interested in literary things.

"I wrote five novels in five years in Greenville," Foote said, "I wrote all of them on Washington Avenue. But that was the beginning of my writing life and sort of the first chapter of it." Twenty years elapsed after his first five novels, but in 1974 publication of his massive three-volume history, *The Civil War: A Narrative* was completed. According to Polk and Scafidel (*An Anthology of Mississippi Writers*, 1979 University Press of Mississippi), Foote "brought to the writing of his heavily researched history not just the historian's reservoir of facts and dates but also the novelist's eye for meaningful detail and capacity for understanding and depicting character. In addition, his history reflects the novelist's natural way with story-telling and a superb, clear, prose style." It was a unique achievement and won him a nomination for the Pulitzer Prize.

His first five novels were *Tournament* (1949), *Follow Me Down* (1950), *Love in a Dry Season* (1951), *Shiloh* (1952), and *Jordan County* (1954). Foote's sixth novel, *September, September,* was published in 1977. He now lives in Memphis, Tennessee, and is working on a seventh novel.

RUTH FORD (1920) was born in Hazlehurst, Mississippi. She attended Mississippi State College for Women (now Mississippi University for Women) and received a B.A. and M.A. from the University of Mississippi. Like her brother Charles Henri Ford, she began an early artistic career. Ford first appeared on stage in 1937 at the Ivoryton (Connecticut) Playhouse as Nanny in *Ways and Means*. Her New York debut was a year later at Mercury Theatre as Jane in *The Shoemaker's Holiday*. Since then Ford has had many theatre and film roles and has toured nationally and internationally. She lives in New York City.

Ruth Ford adapted, with the assistance of William Faulkner, the novel *Requiem for a Nun* to the stage. It was first produced at the John Golden Theatre in New York on January 28, 1959, and starred Ruth Ford as Temple Drake and her husband Zachary Scott as Gavin Stevens.

William Faulkner wrote: "This play was written not to be a play, but as what seemed to me the best way to tell the story in a novel. It became a play, to me, only after Ruth Ford saw it as a play and believed that only she could do it right. When in English, it is her play. What she adds to it, to make it a better play, is Ruth Ford."

PAUL GREEN (1894–1981) was born on a farm in Harnett County, near Lillington, North Carolina. Upon graduation from the University of North Carolina in 1921, he received a fellowship to study philosophy at Cornell University. Returning to the University of North Carolina in 1921 Green began teaching philosophy and later became professor of dramatic art. Green's most popular plays were *In Abraham's Bosom*, for which he was awarded a Pulitzer Prize in 1927; *The Field of God* (1927); *The House of Connelly* (1931); and *Roll Sweet Chariot* (1934). Richard Wright especially liked Green's one-act *Hymn to the Rising Sun* (1935) and suggested it for production to the Chicago unit of the Federal Negro Theater. The stage collaboration between Richard Wright and Paul Green of Wright's novel *Native Son* is documented in *The Unfinished Quest of Richard Wright* (1973) by Michel Fabre and *Richard Wright: Daemonic Genius* (1988) by Margaret Walker. The play was presented on Broadway in 1941 in ten scenes with Canada Lee in the leading role as Bigger Thomas. *Native Son* was directed by John Houseman and produced by Orson Welles as a Mercury Theater production.

EVANS HARRINGTON (1925) was born in Birmingham, Alabama. When he was three his family moved to Clinton, Mississippi, where his father, a Baptist minister, attended Mississippi College. After serving twenty-eight months in the United States Naval Air Corps, Harrington attended Mississippi College where he received a B.A. degree. His M.A. and Ph.D. are from the University of Mississippi. The author of four novels and thirteen short stories, Harrington has been widely published in magazines including *Saturday Evening Post* and *Southern Review*.

Harrington has lived most of his life in Mississippi, and he feels that connection when he begins to write: "Most of my fiction has stemmed from my uncle Scott Harrington's farm in the southeastern corner of Simpson County, where I spent many day-dreaming boyhood summers. But by the time I wrote *The Battle of Harrykin Creek* (1975) I had lived in Faulkner's Oxford and steeped myself in his work so long that Granny Millard, Bayard, Ringo and all the other characters were as alive to me as people from my own region,"

Now Emeritus Professor of English at the University of Mississippi, Harrington lives and writes in Oxford.

BETH HENLEY (1952) was born in Jackson, Mississippi, where she graduated from Murrah High School. She wrote her first play, *Am I Blue*, while taking a playwriting course at Southern Methodist University. It was performed her senior year in college.

In 1981 Henley won the Pulitzer Prize for *Crimes of the Heart*. Henley says, "I wrote it in Los Angeles, where I was trying to act. It was so hard trying to get a job out there. I had an acting agent, but she never called and I'd sit at home all day long. I was working with a group of actors and I thought I'd just write a play with parts for people our age. I thought I might as well do something while I was sitting around. I wrote *Crimes of the Heart* in 1978 and it was performed in Louisville in 1979. It took me three months to write the first draft. I had to do a lot of rewrites on it, a rewrite every production. I had to do one rewrite before it went to Louisville, and then one during rehearsals at Louisville, and then for all the other productions I worked on it."

Henley says two different ideas gave her inspiration for *Crimes of the Heart*. One was based on her paternal grandfather who had gotten lost in the woods in Hazlehurst. Henley says, "For three days he was lost in the woods. They had picnic tables, helicopters, and paratroopers out there. The Copiah County newspaper wrote, 'Thirty foot snake found in search for W.S. Henley!' The governor came down. It was just a huge deal. People were out on horseback and on foot. The Coca-Cola people came in their trucks and advertised free cokes. Anyway, my grandfather was just walking through the woods, and according to him was never lost. He knew where he was—Copiah County. He found this little shack and the people there brought him into town. At the town gas station some people were saying, 'They're gonna find that old man, but he'll be dead.' And he said, 'No they are not! Here I am alive!' So he returned alive after three days. I thought that would be a good idea for a play—a family crisis bringing everybody back home. It was too close: I couldn't get a lead on writing a play about my grandfather getting lost in the woods, but I had the idea—a family and everybody gets back home. Secondly, I heard this story about Walter Cronkite sitting on the front porch of a rich person's house in the South. In the story a little black kid comes up to the house and says he wants some ice cream. The owner of the house socked the child in the face and said, 'Don't you ever come around to this front door again.' I thought, 'I'd like to kill somebody for just being cruel like that to some innocent person,' So that gave me the idea of Zackery beating up on Willie Jay. I thought it would be interesting to write about a character who tries to kill somebody, but you'd be in their corner rather than against them. So I combined the two ideas."

Henley's other plays include *The Miss Firecracker Contest* and *The Wake of Jamie Foster*. She has also written several screenplays.

ENDESHA IDA MAE HOLLAND was born in Greenwood, Mississippi, and transformed herself from a poor teenage prostitute to an award-winning playwright with a Ph.D. In 1965, at the age of twenty-one, she left Mississippi on a train to attend the University of Minnesota. On the train Holland remembers, "I promised myself a lot of things, but most of all I promised my mama that I would make something out of myself like she always wanted." She pledged also that she would no longer steal or prostitute. The promise to her mother was an unspoken one. Her mother had been murdered when the Ku Klux Klan burned their family home in Greenwood.

Of her growing up Holland writes: "I never knew of any accomplishments by black people. I had never heard of a black person writing a book. As a teenager the most famous black woman I knew was Miss Candy Quick, who danced at the fair. Her picture was on the tents, in color and bigger than life, and the men would chant her name. To me, she was go great."

The civil rights movement changed her life. In the early 1960s, civil rights workers from the North moved into Greenwood to distribute food to the poor black community and to help them register to vote. By age nineteen Holland had been jailed thirteen times for activities connected with the civil rights movement. In the summer of 1963 Holland was sent along with other activists to Parchman, the state penitentiary. During the next thirty-three days in Parchman the black prisoners were abused so severely that the Justice Department arranged for their release and flew them to New York to receive medical care. This was Holland's first time to leave Mississippi. In New York Holland impressed activists with her ability to tell a story. She became part of a fund-raising tour to northern cities, one of which was Minneapolis. While there Holland jokingly said she would return someday to attend the university. She did after some of the people she met sent her train fare to return.

Twenty years later Holland had also obtained a Ph.D. in American Studies from the University of Minnesota. Presently she is a visiting assistant professor and coordinator of the Third World Women's Component in the department of American Studies/Women's Studies at the University of Buffalo.

Her one-woman drama *Miss Ida B. Wells* was written in 1983. It depicts the life of the Mississippi-born slave Ida B. Wells, who became a civil rights activist and led a campaign against the lynching of black men in the late 1880s. Wells was a newspaperwoman and her impassioned editorials in the *Memphis Free Speech* created such a furor that she was forced to flee to the North in 1892. The play is set in Wells's home in Chicago in 1928 with flashbacks to her memories of the 1880s and her battles with racism. In writing the play, Holland drew on biographical sources and also on the friendship she enjoyed with Wells's daughter Alfreda M. Barnett Duster.

Of her writing Holland says, "I write because it hasn't been written. I'm very interested in preserving the past, the stories of the bold women, the brave women, the frustrated women. I'm collecting history and putting it together in playscript form."

ANGELA JACKSON (1951) was born in Greenville, Mississippi, the fifth of nine children and the last in her family born in Mississippi. Of those early years Jackson says, "The place where I was born, that section of town was called Brown's Addition, and I like that a lot. In my mother and father's children you can see two different personalities, and it comes from the sense of place. There's a difference between those of us who were born in Mississippi, and those of us who were born in Chicago, so I think that just being there did seem to make a big difference in that I wasn't an absolute product of the city. Which is not to say that the city that I knew as a child was that much different than Greenville, in Brown's Addition."

Jackson is considered to be one of the most talented writers to emerge from Chicago's Organization of Black American Culture (OBAC) Writers Workshop which celebrated its twentieth year by publishing *NOMMO: A Literary Legacy of Black Chicago (1967–1987)*. She has published her work in a wide number of magazines, anthologies, and periodicals. Her four books of poetry are *Voo Doo/Love Magic* (1974), *The Greenville Club* (1977), *Solo in the Boxcar Third Floor E* (1985), *The Man with the White Liver* (1985), and *And All These Roads Be Luminous: Selected Poems* (1991). Her writing has appeared in *Story Quarterly, Black Scholar, Chicago Review, Callaloo, Open Places*, and *TriQuarterly*, among others. Jackson is the winner of the Conrad Kent Rivers Memorial Award from *Black World* magazine, the Academy of American Poets Award, the Edwin Schulman Fiction Prize, and a Before Columbus Foundation American Book Award. In 1977 Jackson was selected to represent the United States at the Second World Festival of Black and African Arts and Culture (FESTAC) in Lagos, Nigeria. That same year she received one of the two premier Illinois State Arts Council Creative Writing Fellowships. In 1978 she received a creative writing fellowship from the National Endowment for the Arts. *Ebony* magazine, in its August 1982 issue, included her among "Women to Watch in the 1980s." Jackson received the second Hoyt W. Fuller Award for Literary Excellence in 1983 and that same year was writer-in-residence at Stephens College (Columbia, Missouri). In 1986 Jackson returned to Chicago to teach and to complete revisions on her novel *Treemont Stone*.

JOHN O'NEAL was born in Cairo, Illinois, a town he says was "about fifty-fifty black and white and located in one of two southernmost counties in the state." O'Neal says, "This gave it a culture very similar to many parts of the South." O'Neal received a B.A. in English and philosophy from Southern Illinois University, where he also studied playwriting. Active in the civil rights movement, O'Neal became field secretary for the Student Nonviolent Coordinating Committee (SNCC). In the winter of 1963 SNCC student directors O'Neal, Doris Derby, and Gilbert Moses, met on the campus of Tougaloo College, near Jackson, Mississippi, a center for activist groups in the South. There they formed Free Southern Theater (FST), conceived as a unique method to connect art and politics and to foster social changes by developing a black rural and urban audience to support the civil rights movement. The founders later wrote, "Black people must have their own theater. Broadway and regional theater are irrelevant to black lives. There must be a form in which the theatricality of the black church, the black freedom movement, black music, black militancy—black power in its widest and deepest sense— can be made into myth, allegory, public performance." In the summer of 1964 pilot plans focused on a ten-week session. Five plays were scheduled: *Purlie Victorious, Do You Want to Be Free, Lower Than the Angels, Day of Absence,* and *Great Gettin' up Mornin'.* Later that year *In White America* opened with an integrated cast drawn from the Mississippi Summer Project. FST moved permanently to New Orleans in 1966 where O'Neal served as director until it closed in 1980.

O'Neal's writing for theater has been recognized by numerous awards and fellowships, including the Louisiana Artist's Fellowship, the National Endowment for the Arts, and the Rockefeller Foundation. He has also written under commission for the Play Group of Knoxville, Tennessee, and for the world renowned San Francisco Mime Troupe. In addition to his years as artistic director of the Free Southern Theater, O'Neal has worked as a guest director for the Play Group, the Kuumba Theater of Chicago, and Southern Illinois University. He also has numerous credits as an actor and has toured widely with the FST and in the role of Junebug Jabbo Jones. His residencies as touring artist often include educational programs for students in formal and informal settings ranging from the elementary to post-graduate levels. Currently he is serving as visiting professor at Cornell University in Ithaca, New York.

O'Neal's trilogy of plays that form "Sayings from the Life and Writings of Junebug Jabbo Jones" are collections of tales drawn from the rich oral heritage of African-Americans. Volume I, *Don't Start Me to Talking or I'll Tell you Everything I Know,* takes place from slavery times to the 1930s. Volume II, *You Can't Judge a Book by Looking at the Cover,* moves forward from rural issues to urban lifestyles into the height of the civil rights movement. Volume III, *Ain't No Use in Goin' Home, Jodie's Got Your Gal and Gone,* will chronicle the experiences of African-Americans in the United States military. The fictional Junebug Jabbo Jones is a Mississippian. When asked why, O'Neal explained it this way: "Mainly because of the role Mississippi played in the movement. The state was historically the greatest symbol of oppression and exploitation of black people. It was a big plantation state where cotton was king and was—correspondingly—the state with the biggest black population. As I look at the map of black distribution, it is still one of the most heavily populated states percentage–wise for blacks. For that reason, it became the center of the movement's activities."

LINDA PEAVY (1943) was born in Hattiesburg, Mississippi. She received a B.A. from Mississippi College in 1964 and an M.A. in English from the University of North Carolina at Chapel Hill in 1970. After teaching English from 1964 to 1966 at Central High in Jackson, Mississippi, and from 1966 to 1969 at Glen Oaks Senior High in Baton Rouge, Louisiana, she became an instructor in English at Oklahoma Baptist University. Since 1974 Peavy has lived with her family in Bozeman, Montana, working as a writer, editor, and lecturer. Her fiction, poetry, and essays have appeared in numerous periodicals, including *Southern Exposure, South Dakota Review, Texas Review, Cottonwood, Plainswoman, Crab Creek Review,* and *Memphis* magazine. In partnership with Ursula Smith, Peavy has co-authored *Women Who Changed Things* (1983), a collective biography of nine turn-of-the-century women of achievement, and *Dreams into Deeds: Nine Women Who Dared* (1985), a collective biography featuring women from the National Women's Hall of Fame.

In 1984, Missoula Children's Theatre commissioned and produced Peavy's first musical, *Family: A Portrait of Today.* In 1985–86, Peavy and Smith composed the libretto for Eric Funk's *Pamelia,* a work the two authors based on letters exchanged between Montana pioneers Pamelia and James Fergus. A choral suite from *Pamelia* was premiered in Carnegie Hall in May 1989 and the full opera was performed in Billings later that same year. *Pamelia* has been the subject of a television documentary by Doris Loeser. The Fergus letters also served as the basis for another Peavy-Smith work, *The Goldrush Widows of Little Falls* (1990). The two authors are currently completing *Women in Waiting: The Home Frontier in the Westward Movement.*

Of her drama Peavy says, "As one of five cousins who lived within a mile of each other, I was constantly involved in livingroom plays of all sorts—from puppet shows to operas. All our productions were enthusiastically supported by parents, grandparents, and aunts and uncles, whose patience I took for granted until my own children grew old enough to begin a neighborhood troupe, the Peavy Basement Players. *Two Kinds of People* is dedicated to those who endured and encouraged my earliest dramatic efforts and to those who are carrying on the family tradition."

ELIZABETH SPENCER (1921) was born in Carrollton, Mississippi, to a family that had lived in Carroll County since the 1830s. In 1942 she received a B.A. in English from Belhaven College in Jackson, Mississippi. Upon graduation, she attended Vanderbilt University where she received an M.A. degree. Afterwards Spencer taught at Northwest Mississippi Junior College, Ward-Belmont School, and University of Mississippi, where she published her first novel, *Fire in the Morning*. Since 1953 she has worked full time as a writer and teacher, and her publications include eight novels and more than forty short stories.

In addition to *Fire in the Morning* (1948), Spencer's books include *This Crooked Way* (1952), *The Voice at the Back Door* (1956), *The Light in the Piazza* (1960), *Knights and Dragons* (1965), *No Place for an Angel* (1967), *Ship Island and Other Stories* (1968), *The Snare* (1972), *The Stories of Elizabeth Spencer* (1981), *Marilee* (1981), *The Salt Line* (1984), and *Jack of Diamonds and Other Stories* (1988). Her two-act play, *For Lease or Sale*, was produced by Playmakers Repertory Company, Chapel Hill, North Carolina, in 1989. Her short stories—which have appeared regularly for four decades in *The New Yorker, Atlantic, Southern Review*, and *McCall's*—have received many awards and have been included in *O. Henry Prize Stories* and *The Pushcart Prize: Best of the Small Presses*.

Since the late 1950s Spencer's fiction has increasingly reflected the international settings she has come to know from living in Italy and Canada. Her intelligent and imaginative responses to these places have defined her concerns as a writer of fiction, placing her in the tradition of Henry James and other literary travelers who can accurately be described as citizens of our civilization.

Spencer continues to be inspired by the South. Of her native state she writes: "Mississippi gave me a wonderful cross-current to writing— when I was growing up the old had been set in its ways since the Civil War, but the new was making itself felt. Writers respond especially to this sort of tension. Then, too, there was such a wide variety of individuals, so many wildly different characters, everyone with their own story, all to be met with daily. The challenge was not where to find material, but how best to use it in a modern fiction which would engage intelligence and feeling. All my early books came out of Mississippi and many still do. Memory keeps so many things, and rather than lose them, it may even make them richer."

Spencer has received many awards for her writing including a Guggenheim Fellowship (1953), the Rosenthal Foundation Award of the American Academy of Arts and Letters (1957), the Kenyon Review Fellowship in Fiction (1957), the McGraw-Hill Fiction Award (1960), the Henry Bellamann Award for creative writing (1968), the Award of Merit Medal for the Short Story by the American Academy of Arts and Letters (1983), election to the American Institute of Arts and Letters (1985), and, most recently, a Senior Award Grant in Literature from the National Endowment for the Arts (1988).

Spencer lived for many years in Montreal, but now lives in Chapel Hill, where she teaches at the University of North Carolina. Her manuscripts and papers are located at the University of Kentucky Library in Lexington.

Of *For Lease or Sale* Spencer says, "I first wrote this play script when living in Montreal, long before moving to Chapel Hill. It started on impulse: I had long wanted to write a play. One day it occurred to me that most of the novelists and/or story writers I knew had said that they wanted to write a play. I thought: If I simply go on saying this and never doing it, how do I know whether I can do it or not? So I sat down without much idea of how to begin. What does one do first? I didn't know, so I sat and tried to visualize something.

"What came to me first was a stage, the old-fashioned proscenium kind, with curtains drawn back. Two people were on it, talking. Furniture, set comfortably about, was worn, Victorian, likeable. The two people were a man, neither young nor old, in his late thirties perhaps, and a young girl. The girl was writing a letter, box of letter paper held on her knees. I listened to what they were saying. Only then did I know, from hearing them, what their talk—and therefore the play—was about. I could tell by their accents they were from no where near Montreal. They were Mississippi to the core, and were kin, uncle and niece. They had lots of feeling for one another. . . . "The script as I first wrote it was shaggy. Like a big yard in spring, it needed a lot of pruning and weeding. When I got to Chapel Hill in 1986 I was approached by Playmakers Repertory Company executive producer Milly S. Barranger, asking if I had a playscript. I let her see it, expecting a firm and gentle 'No thanks.' However, a script reading was held, and artistic director David Hammond came: this was a turning point. He liked the language, and the characters, and the plot. He wanted to work with me on shaping the script.

"For one intense month in the summer of 1987, we went at it, working like crazy. By late summer it was done. A few changes since, but substantially done. Now with a new title (at first I had simply called it "Edward"), it was produced in the Paul Green Theatre from 25 January to 12 February 1989."

NAYO BARBARA MALCOLM WATKINS (1940) was born in Atlanta, Georgia. She attended the University of Pittsburgh, Jackson State University, and the University of Mississippi. Watkins is past director of the Mississippi Cultural Arts Coalition and a founder of the Jackson Writers/Actors Workshop. Her poetry has been anthologized in *New Black Voices* (1970), *Black Culture* (1972), *Mississippi Earthworks* (1982), and will appear in *Black Southern Voices*, edited by John O. Killens. In addition to writing poetry Watkins co-wrote, with John O'Neal, the play *You Can't Judge a Book By Looking at the Cover: Sayings from the Life and Writings of Junebug Jabbo Jones.* The play premiered and ran for six weeks at Wisdom Bridge Theatre in Chicago and is included in touring presentations of Junebug Productions. Watkins also worked on Junebug III: *Aint No Use in Going Home, Jodie's Got Your Gal and Gone*, a play about militarism and the Black experience, developed in conjunction with the Cornell University Department of Theater. It opened in 1989 at the Oakland Ensemble Company.

Watkins toured extensively with BlackArt South, the writing workshop of Free Southern Theatre of New Orleans. From 1970 to 1987 she read and performed at numerous community, academic, and social events in Mississippi. In July 1987 Watkins moved to Minneapolis, Minnesota, to become the executive director of At the Foot of the Mountain Theater, the oldest women's professional theater in the United States. She was a 1990 Mentor for Inroads Program of the Loft: A Literary Place. Watkins received a 1990 Jerome Foundation Travel and Study Fellowship to study organizational implementation of cultural, cross-cultural and multi-cultural programming in United States theater.

TENNESSEE WILLIAMS (1911–1983) was born Thomas Lanier Williams in Columbus, Mississippi, After living his early years in various Mississippi towns, his family moved to St. Louis. This environment and its effect on the young Williams is described in his play *The Glass Menagerie* and his short story "Portrait of a Girl in Glass." Williams attended the University of Missouri from 1929 to 1931, when he was withdrawn by his father because of his failure to pass ROTC (Reserve Officers' Training Corps). He then worked for three years (1931–34) at the International Shoe Company in St. Louis and, as a way of escaping tedium, began to write more and more. Quitting his job, he attended Washington University before receiving a degree from the University of Iowa in 1938.

Williams revised an earlier script called "The Gentleman Caller" into *The Glass Menagerie.* It opened in Chicago on December 26, 1944 and was his first professional success. In 1945 it moved to Broadway. With this impressive start, Williams began his career as one of the world's most popular playwrights. He won two Pulitzer Prizes, one for *A Streetcar Named Desire* and another for *Cat on a Hot Tin Roof*, and four New York Drama Circle Critics Awards for these two plays, as well as for *The Glass Menagerie* and *The Night of the Iguana*. Many of Williams's plays have been made into films.

After he changed his name to "Tennessee," the first work to bear his new name was "The Field of Blue Children," printed in *Story* in September 1939. About his name change Williams writes, "I was christened Thomas Lanier Williams. It is a nice enough name, perhaps a little too nice. It sounds like it might belong to the son of a writer who turns out sonnet sequences to Spring. As a matter of fact, my first literary award was $25.00 from a Woman's Club for doing exactly that, three sonnets dedicated to Spring. I hasten to add that I was still pretty young. Under that name I published a good deal of lyric poetry which was a bad imitation of Edna Millay. When I grew up I realized this poetry wasn't much good and I felt the name had been compromised so I changed it to Tennessee Williams."

Williams divided much of his time between New Orleans, his home in Key West, and the Hotel Elysee on East 54th Street in New York where he died.

RICHARD WRIGHT (1908–1960) was born in Adams County, Mississippi, "too far back in the woods to hear the train whistle," to a country schoolteacher mother and an illiterate sharecropper father. Because of his mother's illness and his father's eventual abandonment, his childhood was one of poverty, frequent moves from relative to relative, and interrupted schooling. His first published story, "The Voodoo of Hell's Half Acre," was printed in September 1924 in the *Southern Register*, the local black newspaper in Jackson, Mississippi. In 1925 he graduated from Jackson's Smith-Robertson Public School. It was the last year he spent in school.

Wright was a voracious reader. While working in Memphis, he discovered the work of H.L. Mencken and began to read some of the works mentioned in Mencken's *Prefaces*, along with a wide variety of other works. In 1927 he moved to Chicago, where he would remain for ten years. In 1932 Wright joined the American Communist Party, believing that he had finally found a group interested in the plight of the American black. He had begun writing poetry and short stories earlier, and now, on behalf of the Party, his work began to appear in such publications as *New Masses*, *Left Front*, and *Partisan Review*.

In 1937 Wright moved to New York, where he was Harlem editor of the *Daily Worker*. His first book, *Uncle Tom's Children*, was published in 1938. This was followed by his two most famous works. *Native Son*, published in 1940, is the tragic tale of a Mississippi-born black in Chicago. Its success was phenomenal, and assured Wright a place in American literature. In 1945 *Black Boy*, an autobiographical work based on his traumatic childhood in Mississippi, was released.

By 1944 Wright had left the Communist Party and in 1946, unreconciled to the continuing racism in the United States, he and his family moved to Paris, France. There he was to remain until his death. After moving to France he was active in establishing such organizations as the Society of African Culture and working with such African leaders as Leopold Senghor, later president of Senegal, and Aime Cesaire from Martinique. Among Wright's nonfiction works of this time are *Black Power* (1954) and *Pagan Spain* (1957).

Wright's fiction includes *The Outsider* (1953) and *Savage Holiday* (1954). In addition, three works were published posthumously—*Eight Men* (1961), *Lawd Today* (1963), and *American Hunger* (1977).

Margaret Walker, who knew Richard Wright in the late 1930s when they worked together on the Chicago Writers' Project of the Works Progress Administration, writes in her 1988 book *Richard Wright Daemonic Genius*: "My first impression of Richard Wright has been a lasting impression. He was a daemonic genius, an intellectual giant of his times, a writer of strong sensibility, and the most highly sensitized person I have ever known. He was a writer of great power and passion but, nevertheless, a human being with the same weaknesses and flaws of all human beings. . . . Wright belongs in four great literary traditions: southern Gothicism, American naturalism, Afro-American humanism, and World realism. He is clearly southern and Gothic and belongs to the strange, if not bizarre, school that incorporates violence, the supernatural, the macabre, the grotesque, the abnormal, and the fantastic. . . . Nearly every piece of fiction he wrote ended tragically and almost always involved grisly murders. His imagination was Gothic, and his vision was tragic."

Wright's manuscripts and papers are located at the Beinecke Library at Yale University. The Schomburg Collection in the New York Public Library contains letters from Wright's family in Mississippi. The Princeton University Library contains approximately five hundred letters Wright exchanged with his agent Paul R. Reynolds, Jr. and editors between 1938 and 1957.

BILLIE JEAN YOUNG was born in Selma, Alabama. She began directing community theater in her native state in 1969 where she cofounded and directed the Black-Belt Arts and Cultural Center for four years. Young studied theater at Judson College for Women (Marion, Alabama) where she was graduated Magna Cum Laude in 1974, becoming the first African-American woman to receive a degree from Judson. With $100 that the theater had given her, Young drove to Samford University, Cumberland School of Law, in Birmingham. "I had absolutely nothing," she says, "but I talked to the dean and he gave me a scholarship; he told me he knew how far it was from my hometown to the law school there and he knew it was far more than the 150 miles I had traveled." While earning a Juris Doctorate from Samford University, Young directed the Black Fire Dance Company and Theatre and upon graduation she cofounded (with Julia Winn) the Branch Heights Dance Company and Theatre in Eutaw, Alabama. In 1979 Young was named an Outstanding Woman of America for her work in developing community theater and artists. Young is currently director of the Southern Rural Women's Network which she founded in 1981 in Jackson, Mississippi. On the Board of Directors of the Repertory Theatre of Mississippi and Eco-Theater of West Virginia, Young is adjunct faculty in Jackson State University's Department of Speech and Dramatic Art. Her book of poems, *The Child of Too*, was published in 1982.

In 1983 Young wrote directed her nationally-known one-woman show *"Fannie Lou Hamer: This Little Light . . . "* which is based on the life of Mississippi Delta freedom fighter Fannie Lou Hamer (1917–1977). Young has performed this show in twenty-seven states, Central America, and the Caribbean. In recognition of her work in preserving the history of African-American women through this performance and for her community organizing work, Young was named a 1984 MacArthur Fellow by the John D. and Catherine T. MacArthur Foundation. From 1985–1987 Young lived and worked in the Central American country of Belize where she taught drama and produced theater with high school students. She is currently writing about that experience. In 1986 *"Fannie Lou Hamer: This Little Light . . . "* received further distinction when Young's performance was taped and placed in the archives of the Smithsonian's National Museum of American History.

In *Wild Women in the Whirlwind: Afro-American Culture and the Contemporary Literary Renaissance* (1990), a collection edited by Joanne M. Braxton and Andree Nicola McLaughlin, Young states in her essay, "This Little Light of Mine: Dramatizing the Life of Fannie Lou Hamer," that the idea to do *"Fannie Lou Hamer: This Little Light . . . "* arose on a day in early December 1982, on a Delta Airlines flight out of Washington, D.C. She writes, "Because books and progressive magazines were hard to come by in Mississippi, I'd gone to a bookstore and bought several copies of *Sojourner Magazine* which had run a series of articles about Fannie Lou Hamer. I planned to give them to Mississippians for Christmas presents. On the plane headed home, I finally got a chance to settle down and read a copy myself. I was again brought face to face with her—

Mrs. Hamer. It was prophetic. In the months and now years to come, I was to be reminded continually that she exerted the control and provided the impetus for my work. Fannie Lou Hamer continues to speak to people today through *"Fannie Lou Hamer: This Little Light. . ."* through her life, by her example."

If Young is to be remembered, she says she wants it to be for her one-woman performance of Hamer. "I want people to understand her for what she did for us," says Young. "My daddy was a sharecropper and I know what that means. I picked the cotton, I grew up like Fannie Lou Hamer did, and I was fortunate that people like her had gone before me."

The Southern Rural Women's Network has established a Fannie Lou Hamer memorial Scholarship Fund to assist needy Mississippi women who show a marked potential for leadership in their communities.

STARK YOUNG (1881–1963) was born in Como, Mississippi, and moved to Oxford, Mississippi, in 1895. He attended the University of Mississippi and received a B.A. with honors in 1901. In 1902 he earned an M.A. in English from Columbia University. Returning to Mississippi, he taught at Water Valley, then at the University of Mississippi. From 1907 to 1915, he taught at the University of Texas and from 1915 to 1921 at Amherst College, Amherst, Massachusetts. In 1921 Young resigned from academic life and began writing and reviewing on a full-time basis in New York. He became drama critic for the *New Republic* and an editor of *Theatre Arts Magazine.*

In the next forty years, Young distinguished himself as a critic, poet, translator of Chekhov, novelist, essayist, editor, painter, and playwright. He wrote thirty plays, many of which he directed. He is best remembered for his novel, *So Red the Rose* (1934), a story of the Civil War that preceded *Gone with the Wind*, but never attained its popularity or commercial success. He died in New York on January 6, 1963.